Hong Kong, August '95.

CHINA REVIEW 1995

Related titles already published

China Review (1991)
Edited by Kuan Hsin-chi
and Maurice Brosseau

China Review 1992
Edited by Kuan Hsin-chi
and Maurice Brosseau

China Review 1993
Edited by Joseph Cheng Yu-shek
and Maurice Brosseau

China Review 1994
Edited by Maurice Brosseau
and Lo Chi Kin

China Review
1995

EDITED BY
Lo Chi Kin,
Suzanne Pepper,
AND
Tsui Kai Yuen

The Chinese University Press

© **The Chinese University of Hong Kong** 1995

All Rights Reserved. No part of this publication may
be reproduced or transmitted in any form or by any
means, electronic or mechanical, including photocopying,
recording, or any information storage and retrieval
system, without permission in writing from
The Chinese University of Hong Kong.

ISBN 962–201–677–4

THE CHINESE UNIVERSITY PRESS
The Chinese University of Hong Kong
SHA TIN, N.T., HONG KONG

Printed in Hong Kong by Regal Printing Co., Ltd.

Steering Committee

Maurice Brosseau
Hsi-sheng Ch'i
Kuan Hsin-chi
Y. Y. Kueh
Paul Chun-kuen Kwong
Lo Chi Kin
Yun-wing Sung
T. L. Tsim

Contents

Preface	ix
Contributors	xi
Abbreviations	xvii
Major Statistics of the PRC, 1994	xxi
Chronology	xxiii
Willy Wo-lap Lam	

1. The Year of the Dog: In the Shadow of the Ailing Patriarch
   Jean Philippe Béja
2. The Civil Service System: Policy Formulation and Implementation
   Tao-chiu Lam and Hon S. Chan
3. Central-Provincial Relations
   Jae Ho Chung
4. From Confrontation to Compromise: A Historical-Structural Account of the Rapid Deterioration of Cross-Straits Relations in 1994
   Timothy Wong
5. Calling the Tune without Paying the Piper: The Reassertion of Media Controls in China
   Joseph Man Chan
6. The Legal Reform
   Edward J. Epstein and Chong Tin Cho
7. China and International Organizations
   Gerald Chan
8. China's Foreign Relations in the Asia-Pacific Region: Modernization, Nationalism and Regionalism
   Quansheng Zhao
9. China Defence Budgeting: Structure and Dynamics
   Ka Po Ng
10. China-Hong Kong Relations
    T. L. Tsim

11. Inequality and Stratification in the Nineties
    Deborah S. Davis
12. The Family Status of Chinese Women in the 1990s
    Jean K. M. Hung
13. Reforms in the Social Security System
    Chack Kie Wong
14. China's New Labour Law: Forging Collective Bargaining from the Rusting Iron Rice Bowl
    David Peetz
15. Production Politics and Labour Identities: Migrant Workers in South China
    Ching-kwan Lee
16. Community Festivals in Post-Mao South China: Economic Transformation and Cultural Improvisation
    Helen F. Siu
17. Bringing Religion into the Socialist Fold
    Chan Kim-kwong
18. Regaining the Initiative for Education Reform and Development
    Suzanne Pepper
19. Economic Development and Institutional Change: Vascillating at the Crossroads
    Carsten Herrmann-Pillath
20. Fiscal Reform in 1994
    Christine Wong
21. Financial Restructuring
    Tsang Shu-ki
22. The Rural Economy of China
    Yunhua Liu
23. Foreign Trade and China's Growing International Presence
    Ho Yin-ping
24. The Evolution of China's Stock Markets
    Henry M. K. Mok
25. The Individual and Entrepreneurship in the Chinese Economic Reforms
    Maurice Brosseau

Index

Preface

In the years since 1978 when the reform and open-door policies were launched, China has been changing rapidly. Like past editions, *China Review 1995* attempts to capture the important changes during the year preceding. The difficulty of the job lies less in identifying topics and events worth reporting than in controlling the length of the volume.

In 1994, major developments in China included macroeconomic adjustments, attempts to restructure the financial system, the continuing rush toward commercialization and a market economy, and historical meetings concerning mainland-Taiwan and Sino-US relations. In addition to the above, *China Review 1995* also covers a wide range of political, economic, and social issue facing China today.

We wish to thank our contributors for giving of their time to produce so extensive a selection of essays. We appreciate their indulgence in adhering to the schedules that publication of an annual volume on current events entails. We also thank The Chinese University Press for sponsoring in early January 1995, a workshop where draft chapters were discussed before further polishing, thereby providing valuable assistance to our contributors. We also acknowledge with gratitude the professionalism of the staff of the Press who have again endeavoured to assure the highest quality possible in the preparation of this volume, the fifth in the series.

The Editors
May 1995

Contributors

JEAN PHILIPPE BÉJA is a graduate from the Institut d'Etudes Politiques, Paris, in political science. He holds a MA in Chinese from the Sorbonne and a Ph.D. in Far Eastern Studies from the Paris VII University. He has been a senior research officer at the French National Centre for Scientific Research, Paris, and is presently scientific director of the French Centre for Contemporary China (Hong Kong), as well as chief editor of the bimonthly *Perspectives Chinoises* and *Chinese Perspectives*. He is involved in research on Chinese intellectuals and the state, the opposition forces in China, sociopolitical change in the People's Republic, and Hong Kong politics.

MAURICE BROSSEAU is Research Officer at the Hong Kong Institute of Asia-Pacific Studies, The Chinese University of Hong Kong. He co-edited the first four volumes of *China Review*.

CARSTEN HERRMANN-PILLATH is the Professor of Chinese Economic Studies at Duisburg University in Germany. After completing his majors in Economics and Sociology and a Ph.D. in Economics, he has published about sixty research reports and articles as well as five books on China's economic development. Most recent contributions are in 1994 (in German): "Economic Integration by Networks: The Relations Between Taiwan and the PRC," and in 1995, "Market Economy in China: History, Structure, Transportation," and *Economic Development in China's Provinces and Regions: A Statistical Handbook*.

GERALD CHAN is Lecturer in International Relations, Department of Politics, Victoria University, Wellington, New Zealand. In 1995, he is also an exchange scholar in the Department of International Politics, Peking University, and Visiting Professor in the Faculty of Law, Kobe-Gakuin University. He is an advisory board member of the *New Zealand Journal of East Asian Studies*.

HON S. CHAN teaches at the Department of Public and Social Administration, City University of Hong Kong. He has published widely on public administration in China and Hong Kong and on environmental management in China.

JOSEPH MAN CHAN is Chair and Senior Lecturer in Journalism and Communications at The Chinese University of Hong Kong. Research interests include international communication, communications development, political communication, impact of information technology, and popular culture. He has published in various international journals and co-authored *Mass Media and Political Transition: The Hong Kong Press in China's Orbit* (NY: Guilford Press, 1991).

CHAN KIM-KWONG, Chaplain of Chung Chi College, The Chinese University of Hong Kong, and Honorary Research Fellow of the Department of East Asian Studies, University of Leeds, UK. He received a Ph.D. from the University of Ottawa and a D.Th. from the Pontifical St. Paul University. Some of his recent publications are: *Towards A Contextual Ecclesiology: The Catholic Church in the PRC 1979–1983*; *Struggle for Survival: The Catholic Church in China from 1949–1970*, and, as co-author, *Prayers and Thoughts of Chinese Christians and Protestanism in Contemporary China*.

CHONG TIN CHO graduated in politics from The Chinese University of Hong Kong and in Chinese and Hong Kong law from Peking University and the University of Hong Kong. He is currently a trainee solicitor with Fred Kan & Co.

JAE HO CHUNG is Assistant Professor in Chinese Politics at the Hong Kong University of Science and Technology. He holds a Ph.D. in political science from the University of Michigan. As a specialist in central-local relations and policy dynamics in China, he has contributed to leading journals including *The China Quarterly*, *Studies in Comparative Communism* and *Pacific Affairs*. He is currently writing a book on the provincial implementation of decollectivization.

DEBORAH S. DAVIS, Professor and Chair of the Department of Sociology, Yale University. Author of *Long Lives: Chinese Elderly and the Communist Revolution* and co-editor of *Chinese Society on the Eve of Tiananmen*, *Chinese Families in the Post-Mao Era*, and *Urban Spaces in Contemporary China* is currently working on a study of the middle classes in urban China since 1945.

EDWARD J. EPSTEIN is a Solicitor and Manager of the China Practice Group in London, of international lawyers, Clifford Chance. He studied Chinese law at the Chinese People's University in Beijing and at the Centre for Chinese Legal Studies, Columbia University. From 1986 to 1995, he was Senior Lecturer in Law at the University of Hong Kong where he taught Chinese law.

YIN-PING HO is Lecturer in the Department of Economics at The Chinese University of Hong Kong. An earlier article he wrote on China's foreign trade appeared in *China Review 1993*.

JEAN K. M. HUNG is the Assistant Director of the Universities Service Centre at CUHK. She received her M.Phil. in anthropology from The Chinese University of Hong Kong. She has published articles on women's dual roles in Hong Kong and mainland China journals.

Contributors

TAO-CHIU LAM teaches at the Department of Management, Hong Kong Polytechnic University and is concurrently a doctoral student at the Contemporary China Centre, Australian National University.

WILLY WO-LAP LAM is the China Editor of the *South China Morning Post*. A graduate of the University of Hong Kong and the University of Minnesota. He is the author of three books on China. *China After Deng Xiaoping: The Power Struggle in Beijing since Tiananmen* was published in early 1995 by John Wiley & Sons.

CHING-KWAN LEE is a Lecturer in the Sociology Department, The Chinese University of Hong Kong. She holds a Ph.D. in sociology from the University of California, Berkeley. She has published articles on the subjects of gender and production politics in Hong Kong and south China. Her current research interests include gender and the professions, the impacts of economic restructuring on Hong Kong's working class families and feminist discourses in Hong Kong.

YUNHUA LIU, Lecturer in economics at Nanyang Technological University, Singapore, received his Ph.D. in economics from Ohio State University in 1993. His research interests include economic development in rural China, international trade of Southeast Asia as well as urban economics. His recent articles about China's rural economy are published in: *Economic Development and Cultural Change*, *Quarterly Review of Economics and Finance*, and *China Economic Review*.

LO CHI KIN is Managing Director of C. K. Lo & S. Lam Limited, a public affairs lobbying and counselling firm. He is also a freelance commentator on current affairs in Hong Kong and China.

HENRY M. K. MOK graduated with distinction from Hong Kong Baptist College. He earned his MA in Economics from the University of Toronto, Canada, and the degrees of Master of Urban and Regional Planning, Master of Social Work and Ph.D. in Economics from the University of Hawaii at Manoa. He joined The Chinese University of Hong Kong in January 1988 and is now Lecturer in the Department of Decision Sciences and Managerial Economics. He is currently Director of the Center for Financial Research on China (CFRC) and Director of Research Development at the Asia-Pacific Institute of Business of The Chinese University of Hong Kong.

KA PO NG, formerly assistant editor at *China News Analysis*, is project coordinator at the Universities Service Centre in The Chinese University of Hong Kong. He has published on China's political affairs and particularly the armed forces.

DAVID PEETZ is Assistant Secretary in the Australian Department of Industrial Relations, Canberra. He has taught at the Universities of Sydney and New South

Wales and worked in the office of the Minister for Employment and Industrial Relations. He has published articles on union membership, collective bargaining, industry policy, fiscal policy, payment systems, international affairs, and is co-editor of *Wealth, Poverty and Survival: Australia in the World* and *Workplace Bargaining in the International Context*.

SUZANNE PEPPER holds a Ph.D. in political science from the University of California, Berkeley. She has written several articles and monographs on Chinese education policy. Her most recent study, *Radicalism and Education Reform in 20th Century China*, will be published this year by Cambridge University Press.

HELEN F. SIU is Professor of Anthropology and Chair of the Council on East Asian Studies at Yale University. A native of Hong Kong, she received her Ph.D. at Stanford University in 1981. Her research interests are the history and culture of south China, and contemporary Chinese literature. Her publications include *Agents and Victims in South China: Accomplices in Rural Revolution* (Yale 1989); *Furrows: Peasants, Intellectuals and the State* (ed. Stanford 1990).

TSANG SHU-KI is Senior Lecturer in the Department of Economics, Hong Kong Baptist University. He obtained a BA in philosophy and political science from the University of Hong Kong and a Ph.D. in economics from the University of Manchester. His current research efforts cover Chinese economic reforms in finance and agriculture, as well as the country's long-term development strategy.

T. L. TSIM is a fellow of Shaw College and director of T. L. Tsim & Associates, Limited.

KAI YUEN TSUI is currently Lecturer in Economics at The Chinese University of Hong Kong. His areas of research include interregional disparities in China, economic development of less developed countries and social choice theory with special emphasis on the design of multidimensional indices of well-being.

CHACK KIE WONG is a Lecturer in the Social Work Department, The Chinese University of Hong Kong. Before he joined the university, he worked as a social worker for more than 13 years. He received his Ph.D. from the University of Sheffield, UK. He is the author of a book on social action in Hong Kong and has published several articles on social work and social change, social development, and social policy. His current research project is concerned with China's economic reform and the transformation of its welfare system.

CHRISTINE WONG is Professor of Economics at the University of California, Santa Cruz. During 1995 and 1996 she is Resident Scholar at the Asian Development Bank, Manila, Philippines. She has written frequently about economic reform, problems of decentralization and rural industrialization in China. Her recent publications include *Fiscal Management and Economic Reform in the People's*

Republic of China (co-authored), Hong Kong, Oxford University Press, 1995; *and Economic Reform in the People's Republic of China*, in P. Rana, Editor, *Economic Liberalization in Asian Centrally Planned Economies*, Volume II (of three volumes), Hong Kong, Oxford University Press, forthcoming 1995.

TIMOTHY WONG received his Ph.D. in Sociology at the University of Manitoba, Canada in 1992. Since then he has worked as a Research Officer in the Hong Kong Institute of Asia-Pacific Studies at The Chinese University of Hong Kong. A frequent contributor to local newspapers and magazines, Dr Wong's major research interests include social and political development in both Taiwan and Hong Kong.

QUANSHENG ZHAO (Ph.D., University of California, Berkeley) is a tenured Associate Professor of political science at Old Dominion University in Norfolk, Virginia; and Associate-in-Research at the Fairbank Center, Harvard University. His books include *Interpreting Chinese Foreign Policy* (Oxford University Press, 1995), *Japanese Policymaking* (Praeger, 1993, selected as "Outstanding Academic Book" by *Choice*), and *Politics of Divided Nations* (coeditor), (University of Maryland Law School, 1991).

Abbreviations

ACFTU	All China Federation of Trade Unions
ADB	Asian Development Bank
APEC	Asia-Pacific Economic Co-operation
ARATS	Association for Relations Across the Taiwan Strait (PRC)
ASEAN	Association of Southeast Asian Nations
ATM	Automatic teller machine
BBC	British Broadcasting Corporation
CADB	China Agricultural Development Bank
CBCM	Chinese Bishops' Conference in the Mainland
CC	Central Committee
CCC	Chinese Christian Council
CCP	Chinese Communist Party
CCPIT	China Council for the Promotion of International Trade
CEC	Central economic city
CFETS	China Foreign Exchange Trade System
CICT	Consolidated Industrial and Commercial Tax
CIETAC	China International and Economic Arbitration Commission
CMC	Central Military Commission
COC	Coastal open city
COCOM	Coordinating Committee for Multilateral Export Controls
COEC	Central Organization and Establishment Commission
COSTIND	Commission in charge of Science and Technology and Industry of National Defence
CPPCC	Chinese People's Political Consultative Conference
CSRC	China Securities Regulatory Commission
CSSG	Central Small Study Group
DPP	Democratic Progressive Party (Taiwan)
EBF	Extra-budgetary funds
EDZ	Economic development zone
EEF	Extra-establishment funds
ETDZ	Economic and Technological Development Zone

EU	European Union
FABC	Federation of Asian Bishops' Conference
FDI	Foreign direct investment
FEC	Foreign exchange certificate
FEER	*Far Eastern Economic Review*
FETC	Foreign Exchange Trading Centre
FFE	Foreign-funded enterprise
FIE	Foreign-invested enterprise
GATT	General Agreement on Tariffs and Trade
GDP	Gross domestic product
GNP	Gross national product
GSP	Generalized System of Preferences
GVIO	Gross value of industrial output
IAEA	International Atomic Energy Agency
IBRD	International Bank of Reconstruction and Development
IEB	China Import and Export Bank
IGO	Intergovernmental organization
ILO	International Labour Organization
IMF	International Monetary Fund
INGO	International non-governmental organization
IO	International organization
IPS	Institute of Population Studies
JLG	Joint Liaison Group
KMT	Kuomintang (Nationalist Party, Taiwan)
MAC	Mainland Affairs Council (Taiwan)
MFA	Multifibre Arrangement
MFN	Most-favoured-nation (trade status)
MOFERT	Ministry of Foreign Economic Relations and Trade
MOFT	Ministry of Foreign Trade
MOFTEC	Ministry of Foreign Trade and Economic Cooperation
NBFI	Non-bank financial institutions
NCNA	New China News Agency
NIC	Newly industrialized country
NIE	Newly industrializing Economies
NPC	National People's Congress
NTB	Nontariff barrier
NTS	National tax system
OCA	Olympic Council of Asia
OECD	Organization for Economic Cooperation and Development

Abbreviations

OTC	Over-the-counter
PAP	People's Armed Police
PBOC	People's Bank of China
PLA	People's Liberation Army
PPP	Purchasing-power parity
PRC	People's Republic of China
PSB	Security forces (Public Security Bureau)
PWC	Preliminary Working Committee
R&D	Research and development
RAB	Religious Affairs Bureau
RMB	*Renminbi* (Chinese dollar)
RMRB	*Renmin ribao* (People's Daily)
ROC	Republic of China (Taiwan)
SAEC	State Administration of Exchange Control
SAIC	State Administration for Industry and Commerce
SAR	Special Administrative Region (Hong Kong)
SCMP	*South China Morning Post*
SDB	China State Development Bank
SEC	State Education Commission
SEF	Straits Exchange Foundation (Taiwan)
SEZ	Special economic zone
SHSE	Shanghai Securities Exchange
SIPRI	Stockholm International Peace Research Institute
SOE	State-owned enterprise
SSTC	State Science and Technology Commission
SWB	*Summary of World Broadcast*
SZSE	Shenzhen Stock Exchange
TRA	Taiwan Relations Act
TSPM	Three Self Patriotic Movement
TSS	Tax sharing system
TVE	Township and village enterprises
UFWD	United Front Work Department
UIA	Union of International Association
VAT	Value-added tax
WF	Women's Federation
WTO	World Trade Organization
ZGSHTJNJ	*Zhongguo shehui tongji ziliao* (Chinese Social Statistics)
ZGTJNJ	*Zhongguo tongji nianjian* (Chinese Statistical Yearbook)

Major Statistics of the PRC, 1994

	Unit	1994	Growth rate (%)
(1) Year-end total population	million persons	1198.5	1.1
(2) Gross domestic product (GDP)	billion RMB	4380	11.8*
GDP — primary sector	billion RMB	823.1	3.5*
GDP — secondary sector	billion RMB	2125.9	17.4*
GDP — tertiary sector	billion RMB	1431	8.7*
(3) Grain production	million tons	444.5	−2.5
(4) Cotton production	million tons	4.25	13.6
(5) Industrial value added	billion RMB	1835.9	18*
(6) Total investment in fixed assets	billion RMB	1592.6	15.8*
State sector		1135.4	34.2**
Collective sector		275.8	23.6**
Urban and rural residents		181.4	22.9**
(7) Growth of money supply (M2)	% change		34.4
(8) Consumer price index (CPI)	% change		24.1
Urban CPI			25.0
Rural CPI			23.4
(9) Total value of exports	billion US dollars	121	31.9
(10) Total value of imports		115.7	11.2
(11) Foreign capital actually utilized	billion US dollars	45.8	17.6
(12) Primary school net enrolment rate	%	98.4	
(13) Drop-out rate of primary school students	%	1.85	
(14) Hospital beds	thousand beds	2832	1.3
(15) Per-capita expenditure of residents in cities and towns	RMB	3179	8.8*
(16) Per-capita net income of peasants	RMB	1220	5*
(17) Unemployment rate in cities and towns	%	2.9	

Notes: * the growth rate is in real terms.
** the growth rate is in nominal terms.

Sources: "1994 nian guomin jingji he shehui fazhan de tongji gongbu" (1994 Statistical Communiqué of Economic and Social Development of the PRC), *Renmin ribao* (People's Daily), overseas edition, 2 March 1995.

Chronology of 1994

Willy Wo-lap Lam

JANUARY

Beijing took a big step toward currency reform on the **1st**, when the central government scrapped its official exchange rate and floated the *Renminbi*. The Chinese unit was devalued by 33% to trade at 8.7 to the American dollar. The exchange rate remained largely stable throughout the year. The success in currency reform was a reason behind the surge of the country's foreign reserves to US$51.6 billion.

The grain crisis was highlighted on the **5th**, when central authorities admitted they had rushed 700,000 tonnes of emergency grain supplies to city centres along the southeast coast. The State Planning Commission also announced price ceilings for staples such as rice, wheat and oils. In the summer, Beijing re-imposed control over the procurement and distribution of grain and cotton. Partly because of floods in grain producing areas, yield for the year was 444.5 million tonnes, 2.5% less than the historical high of 1993.

The People's Liberation Army (PLA) completed an important reshuffle in the **first week** of the month by changing the commanders and commissars of different military regions. The personnel changes, which were decided at a Central Military Commission meeting in December 1993, was in the interest of rejuvenation and the further purge of officers close to disgraced former chief political commissar Yang Baibing. Commander of the Beijing Military Region Wang Chengbin retired in favour of one of his deputies, General Li Laizhu. In the Chengdu Military Region, Yang ally Zhang Gong stepped down and was succeeded by another vice-commander of the Beijing region General Zhang Zhijian. Reshuffles at the district level went on throughout the year.

Vice-Premier Zhu Rongji announced at a national meeting on banking held from the **12th** to the **15th**, that the tight-money policy would be continued because the "inflationary pressure can go up at any time." Banks were asked to refrain from the unlawful raising of funds and interest rates, as well as engaging in non-core businesses such as investments in the stock and property markets. Zhu, who is also Governor of the People's Bank of China, said that all funding for major infrastructure projects would have to be co-ordinated by the new State Development Bank.

FEBRUARY

President Jiang Zemin signalled a conservative turn in economic policy by vowing support for the ailing state enterprise system during a trip to Shanxi that ended on the **3rd**. Jiang told cadres that Beijing was "sympathetic" with the difficulties of government firms, adding that the leadership "will give them necessary assistance and it will stay in the same boat with the broad masses of workers."

The President saluted the quasi-Maoist goal that the country must go down the "road of common prosperity." On the same trip, he praised the book *Di sanji yanjing kan Zhongguo* (Viewing China with a Third Eye) by hardline theorist Wang Shan, which was regarded as a manifesto of "neo-authoritarianism."

Taiwan President Lee Teng-hui significantly boosted the image of the island through unofficial visits to tourist spots in the Philippines, Indonesia and Thailand from the **6th** to the **16th**. While putatively on vacation, Lee met with senior government officials including Presidents Fidel Ramos and Suharto. The apparent success of Lee's "holiday diplomacy" was partly based on Taipei's "look south" strategy of boosting investment in Southeast Asian countries. Beijing lodged protests with these countries, which included the cancellation of a National People's Congress (NPC) delegation to Manila.

The State Council announced regulations on the **6th** forbidding foreigners from converting Chinese or setting up religious schools and organizations. The 13-article stipulation said foreigners could not set up places of worship or related offices. The regulations were seen as an attempt to control the fast growth of christianity which had apparently been exacerbated by the influx of foreign missionaries.

The nation was alarmed by the frailty of Deng Xiaoping as a brief footage of his Lunar New Year appearance in Shanghai was aired on national television on the **9th**. The patriarch had to be supported on both sides by his daughters, and he had difficulty focusing his gaze. Official news agencies quoted Deng as saying that "I think Shanghai has good conditions to be developed faster." By contrast, conservative party elder and Deng foe Chen Yun, who was shown on TV the same day, seemed to look healthier. Chen's conditions had also deteriorated markedly, leading the Politburo to circulate an emergency notice on his health in May.

MARCH

The leadership laid down a cautious development plan at the second session of the Eighth National People's Congress from the **10th** to the **22nd**. The target growth rate was 8 to 9%, and inflation would be kept down to 10%. The austerity programme, which started in mid-1993, would be continued. The ceiling for fixed-assets investments, including those by coastal provinces, was 1,300 billion yuan. Bonds of 100 billion yuan were floated to cover a projected budget deficit of 66.9 billion yuan, as well as domestic and foreign debts totalling 129.2 billion yuan. Pride of place was given to agriculture, with a generous package of aid for 500 major grain producing counties and 150 cotton production bases.

Premier Li Peng stressed the correct handling of the "relationship between growth, reform and stability" as well as the need to ensure "sustained, fast and healthy" development. Li emphasised tough political discipline and beefing up the security apparatus. The army got a budget allocation of 52.04 billion yuan, up to 20% from 1993.

Reporter Xi Yang of Hong Kong's *Ming Pao* newspaper was sentenced on the **28th** to 12 years in jail for allegedly leaking state secrets concerning financial matters. This triggered large protests organized by Hong Kong journalists and pro-democracy groups. On the 15th of November dissident journalist Gao Yu was sentenced to a six-year jail term for leaking "important, confidential state secrets" to Hong Kong publications. Gao was first detained in October 1994. Throughout the year, Chinese authorities halted a number of Sino-Hong Kong joint-venture projects in the media.

National People's Congress Chairman Qiao Shi lobbied for bigger powers for the legislature in a speech on the **23rd** calling for "strengthening legislation with the spirit of reform." Qiao also underscored the fact that the NPC had "supervisory functions over the government, the court and the procuratorate." He added that supervision work did not mean "interference" in these departments. The year saw the passage of a record 16 laws. Arguments broke out between the NPC and different government departments over the contents and wording of legislation in the area of education, banking, bankruptcy, and statutes governing judges and procurators.

Beijing's relations with Taiwan — and its tourist industry — suffered a devastating blow on the **31st** when 24 Taiwan tourists and eight Chinese staff perished on a boat in Qiandao Lake, Zhejiang province. Three local ruffians were subsequently arrested — and executed — for robbing the passengers and later setting the vessel on fire. Anti-mainland feelings were rampant in Taiwan because of Beijing's initial refusal to lift the news blackout on the incident. China's tourist industry, as well as regional airlines including Hong Kong's Cathay Pacific, incurred considerable losses.

APRIL

In a joint statement in the *People's Daily* on the 6th, President Jiang Zemin and Premier Li Peng urged leaderships of all levels to find work for the estimated half a million soldiers who had been demobilized in late 1993. Describing them as "treasures of the state," the two leaders pointed out that finding them employment would contribute to social stability. Guangdong, apparently anxious to secure the support of the PLA, placed the largest number of officers

Chronology of 1994

and soldiers. Friction between PLA units and local authorities continued in the year over issues such as land use and other business disputes.

The Chinese government revealed the extent of the crisis hitting state enterprises when it announced on the **22nd** that 370,000 industrial units above the village level had piled up losses of 17.6 billion yuan in the first two months of the year, up 5% from 1993. Forty-seven per cent of all government-owned units were in the red. "Triangular debts" had reached an all-time high of 300 billion yuan. Strikes, mainly by workers who had been owed months of salaries, were reported in cities including Xian, Wuhan, Harbin and Shenyang. In early 1995, Beijing claimed that the percentage of money-losing enterprises had dropped to 35% by late 1994.

"Black hand" dissident Wang Juntao was given medical bail and put on an America-bound plane on the **23rd** in an apparent effort by Beijing to conciliate international opinion. Wang, accused of being a mastermind behind the 1989 pro-democracy movement, was sentenced to 13 years in prison in 1991. He later set up a China Institute in New York in a bid to continue his fight for democracy in China. Other dissidents allowed to leave the country later in the year included legal scholar Yu Haocheng, who took up a fellowship at Columbia University.

Beijing lodged a strong protest on the **29th** against the meeting in the White House the day earlier between exiled Tibetan leader the Dalai Lama and American President Bill Clinton. The Chinese Foreign Ministry said it was a "serious interference" in China's domestic affairs. Washington indicated that it hoped high-level talks between the Dalai Lama and Beijing would continue. On the **28th**, Beijing revealed that while it had engaged in talks with delegations from the exiled Tibetan government, they had bogged down because of the latter's alleged refusal to concede Chinese sovereignty over Tibet.

MAY

Beijing marked the 75th anniversary of the May Fourth "Enlightenment" movement by asking the nation's youths to shoulder the "historic mission" of bringing China into the 21st century. The *People's Daily* called upon students to abide by the "main theme of the times," meaning socialism, patriotism and collectivism. On the same day, however, veteran Professor Xu Liangying, sometimes known as the "conscience of China," was put under house arrest for trying to sponsor a signature campaign urging the release of dissidents and the observance of the ideals of science and democracy.

The veteran Minister of Radio, Film and Television Ai Zhisheng was relieved of his post on the **12th** in an apparent bid by the leadership to improve public perception of its handling of the media. Ai was associated with hardline measures such as banning satellite dishes and Sino-foreign film productions. He was replaced by the vice party secretary of Jiangsu Sun Jiazheng, who was described by the official news agencies as "familiar with ideological work." Ai, however, continued to exercise influence over ideology and the media in his new role as vice-head of the party's Leading Group for Ideology and Propaganda.

Factional strife within the Communist Party broke into the open on the **23rd** as a commentary in the *People's Daily* made an oblique but strong criticism of Deng Xiaoping's reforms. The article by theorist Ren Zhongping, entitled "Correctly handling the contradictions among the people under new circumstances," hinted that negative phenomena such as money worship, "illegal business operations," corruption and bureaucratism could be traced to misguided reform measures. In an apparent reference to Tiananmen Square, Ren warned against using "rough and violent" methods to defuse political crises.

American President Bill Clinton indicated on the **27th** that the decision to grant most-favoured-nation (MFN) status to China would be de-linked from the human-rights conditions in the country. Announcing that he would renew MFN to Beijing for another year, Clinton said advances in human rights would be better achieved by "engaging the Chinese." At the same time, Washington slapped a ban on the imports of Chinese arms and ammunitions worth US$200 million a year. Existing sanctions related to the 4 June 1989 crackdown, including those on technology transfer, would be maintained.

JUNE

Air safety in China was cast into doubt when a Soviet-made Tu-154 aircraft belonging to China Northwest Airlines crashed in Xian on the **6th**. All 166 passengers, including three Hong Kong residents, were killed. Chinese civil aviation authorities later put a moratorium on the purchase of Soviet-era aircraft.

Nineteen senior officers, including the commanders of the seven military regions, were promoted full generals on the **9th**, putting the total number of top brass with such a senior ranking to 42. The move was seen as an effort by President Jiang Zemin, also Chairman of the Central Military Commission (CMC) to bolster his position. Among those promoted were the Vice Chief Political Commissar Wang Ruilin, who was also Head of the Deng Xiaoping Office. Jiang's efforts to promote General Wang as CMC Secretary General, however, were reportedly frustrated by opposition from senior generals.

Appalling workplace safety standards were highlighted when an estimated 50

Chronology of 1994

workers perished in a fire that gutted a textile factory in the Zhuhai Special Economic Zone on the **16th**. The building collapsed the next day, killing another eight workers who had been ordered by the Hong Kong partner of the joint venture to retrieve cotton in the premises. On the **4th**, 11 workers were killed when a Shenzhen factory collapsed. The All-China Federation of Trade Unions later issued orders to clamp down on malpractices in joint-venture factories. The latter included employers locking windows and doors to prevent theft.

Beijing gave the special economic zones (SEZs) a shot in the arm when President Jiang Zemin toured Guangdong province from the **15th** to the **21st**. Jiang, who is believed to favour Shanghai over Guangdong as the pace-setter for reform, affirmed the "correctness" of Deng Xiaoping's policies on the zones. He denied reports that since most open cities had been given preferential policies akin to the SEZs, the latter had lost their uniqueness. The President warned cadres in Shenzhen, however, that it must remain a "socialist SEZ" and not become "an expanded part or a continuation of Hong Kong."

JULY

China adopted its first-ever *Labour Law* on the **5th** in an attempt to strengthen protection for its 560 million workers and to improve workplace safety. The 13-chapter statute contained stipulations on labour contracts, minimum-wage levels, safety regulations, protection of women and children, vocational training, resolution of labour disputes, and legal responsibilities. However, no provisions were made for workers' rights to organize strikes although these were enshrined in the constitution. There was also no mention of the formation of unofficial trade unions.

Beijing announced on the **12th** the *Detailed Regulations on the Implementation of the State Security Law* in an apparent bid to tighten control over dissidents and infiltration by "hostile foreign forces." The rules defined as an "enemy" organization any unit that "regards with hostility the administration of the people's democratic dictatorship as well as the socialist system." Police organs were empowered to tackle hostile activities including the "fabrication and distortion of facts; the publication and dissemination of words and opinion; and the production and broadcast of audio-visual material which endangers state security."

Chinese authorities in the northwestern region of Ningxia passed a law on the **17th** barring religious bodies "from interfering in administrative affairs that should be dealt with by the government." Local officials accused unnamed Muslim clergies of "using the cloak of religion to meddle unduly in education, marriage and family planning." The remote area had in recent years witnessed violent gang warfare among rival factions and sects. In February, 20 people including four Muslim clerics were given stiff sentences for gang fights that resulted in 49 deaths.

The development of the inchoate "shareholding economy" was cast into doubt when China halted new stock issues on the **29th**. China Securities Regulatory Commission Chairman Liu Hongru suspended all share issues scheduled for 1994 as well as those already delayed from 1993. The Shanghai index for the Chinese-held "A" shares had plunged nearly 80% from the all time high of February 1993. To lure more capital to the markets, Beijing said it would increase the number of investment mutual funds and institutional investors. Joint-venture fund-managing firms would also be asked to attract certain categories of overseas funds into the A-share market.

AUGUST

The Chinese Communist Party indicated on the **12th** that it was drafting detailed anti-corruption regulations for party members for the first time in its 73-year history. The Central Commission for Disciplinary Inspection (CCDI) said it was putting together the *Regulations on Supervision within the Party* and the *Regulations on Disciplinary and Inspection Work in the Party*. At a just-finished national meeting on laws and supervision, CCDI cadres pointed out that the worsening problem of corruption could not be cracked "unless there are well-defined laws, and unless the laws are enforced."

The Ministry of Labour released on the **16th** projections that there would be 268 million unemployed Chinese by the end of the century. The ministry pointed out that by the year 2000, "there will be 68 million people in cities and over 200 million in rural areas waiting to be placed." Beijing indicated at the same time that steps would be taken to stop mass lay-offs by state enterprises. Factories about to dismiss large numbers of workers had to pay the government "placement fees" to handle the unemployed. Enterprises would also be discouraged from firing "aged employees" or hiring labourers from the countryside.

The Chinese leadership reiterated after a four-day meeting on the economy that ended on the **16th** that controlling inflation was the national priority. Senior cadres converging on the Beidaihe summer resort indicated that the government would take measures including raising the interest rate and curtailing capital projects that had won approval but not yet started. Presiding over the conference, Executive Vice-Premier Zhu Rongji criticized the view among some liberal economists that "inflation is harmless" or that fighting unemployment was more important than containing soaring prices.

The Communist Party Central Committee promulgated on the **23rd** an *Outline for the Implementation of Patriotism*. The 7,500-character document urged schools and other mass organizations to take as their priority the propagation of patriotism and socialism. It said that the goal of patriotic education was to "energise the spirit of the people, boost their cohesiveness, and establish the self-respect and pride of the people." At the same time, other Communist party departments issued orders that patriotic films and songs be featured on national television as well as in karaoke bars.

SEPTEMBER

President Jiang Zemin began a historic five-day tour of Russia on the **2nd**. He and counterpart Boris Yeltsin agreed that both countries would not target strategic nuclear missiles at each other. An agreement covering the western section of the joint border was also signed. Moscow raised the issue of the large number of Chinese illegal immigrants and overstayers in Russia, with more than 60,000 in Moscow alone.

Premier Li Peng announced a comprehensive strategy to combat inflation at a State Council meeting on the **5th**. The plans effectively rolled back price reform and reinstated centralized administration of the economy. The prices of more than 20 kinds of foodstuffs and services came under government control. The state kept a tight rein over the wholesale and retail activities of grain, cotton and other staples. Fixed-asset investments were frozen. Later in the year, Beijing introduced legislation against profiteering and sent price inspection teams to the provinces and cities. Grain coupons were restored in several regions. Inflation in 1994 rose to 21.7%, the highest level since 1949.

American President Bill Clinton announced a new deal for Taiwan on the **8th**, which amounted to the first major shift in US policy on Taiwan in 15 years. Taiwan would be allowed to change the name of its American office from the Co-ordination Council for North American Affairs to the Taipei Economic and Cultural Representative Office. Certain American cabinet officials would be allowed to visit Taiwan. Senior Taiwan officials including the president would be permitted to transit through the US. Beijing slammed the move, saying that it would "seriously affect the development of Sino-US relations."

President Jiang Zemin toured France from the **8th** to the **12th**, marking a restoration of relations which soured when Paris decided to sell 60 Mirage fighters to Taiwan in 1992. French firms landed 12.2 billion francs of business. Jiang put forward four principles for ties between China and Western Europe, which were anchored on economic symbiosis. They included "seeking mutual benefits and making up for each other's shortfall" and "seeking common ground despite differences." Five months earlier, Paris re-opened its consulate in Guangzhou.

Security in the Chinese capital was called into question at the Mid-Autumn Festival on the **20th** when lieutenant Tian Mingjian of the local garrison ran amok and fired his automotic weapon at crowds in the heart of Beijing. Among the more than 30 killed were an Iranian diplomat and his son. President Jiang Zemin ordered an immediate tightening of discipline among army and security personnel.

The rise of the so-called Shanghai Faction in Chinese politics was confirmed at the fourth plenum of the 14th Central Committee, which was held in the capital from the **25th** to the **28th**. Shanghai party secretary Wu Bangguo and Shandong party secretary Jiang Chunyun were inducted into the expanded Central Committee Secretariat. Shanghai Mayor Huang Ju, who succeeded Wu as Shanghai party boss, was made a member of the Politburo. The leadership also decided that Wu and Jiang would in March 1995 be promoted vice-premiers in charge of industry and agriculture respectively. The plenum passed a resolution on "party construction," principally the resuscitation of the Chinese Communist Party's 800,000 cells in the countryside.

OCTOBER

Patriarch Deng Xiaoping watched the fireworks that celebrated the 45th founding of the People's Republic of China on the **1st**. The occasion was a quiet family party at the Ying Pavilion in the Zhongnanhai party headquarters. The patriarch's health deteriorated markedly in the winter, setting off a frenzy of speculation over his impending death. The second editions of the first two volumes of the *Deng Xiaoping wenxuan* (Selected Works of Deng Xiaoping) were published on the 2nd of November.

Beijing flexed its muscles as a nuclear power on the **7th** by detonating its second test blast in four months. The Chinese Foreign Ministry reiterated that China had exercised "great restraint" in testing procedures. It reaffirmed support for international efforts to ban nuclear weapons. Western seismologists said they had recorded data consistent with a medium to large nuclear explosion in an underground facility at Lop Nor in Xinjiang. Throughout the year, Washington was unsuccessful in engaging the Chinese in discussion on non-proliferation issues.

China and the United States re-established high-level military contacts with a visit by Defence Secretary William Perry from the **16th** to the **19th**. Talks centred on nuclear non-proliferation, converting defence plants to civil production, and openness in military matters. However, Washington had yet to lift sanctions on

Chronology of 1994 xxxiii

the transfer of military technology imposed after the Tiananmen Square massacre.

Premier Li Peng began a historic five-day visit to South Korea on the **31st** at the invitation of President Kim Young-sam. Both sides signed agreements on civil aviation, nuclear energy for peaceful purposes, in addition to investment and trade. Li, the highest-level Chinese official to visit Seoul, also discussed with his host peace in the Korean Peninsula follwing the death of North Korean leader Kim Il-sung in July.

NOVEMBER

Cross-Straits dialogue on direct communications and transport was given added urgency on the **14th**, when President of Soochow University Winston Chang suffered a stroke and fell into a coma while attending an academic conference in Beijing. Taipei decided later in the month that Dr Chang, an illegitimate son of the late president Chiang Ching-kuo, had to follow standard regulations and transit through Hong Kong on his way back to Taipei.

The profile of China — and President Jiang Zemin — was raised when he attended an informal summit of the heads of state of the Asia-Pacific Economic Co-operation (APEC) countries in Bogor, Indonesia on the **15th**, Jiang took the occasion to lobby for improvements in China's trading position, including early assession to the General Agreement on Tariffs and Trade. He also sought assurance from countries including the United States and Japan on the "one China policy." The Chinese president said he would never meet Taiwan President Lee Teng-hui on an international occasion. Jiang extended an invitation for this American counterpart Bill Clinton to visit China at the convenient time.

Sino-Vietnamese relations took a leap forward with a five-day visit to Vietnam by President Jiang Zemin which began on the **19th**. During this first-ever Vietnam tour by a Chinese President, Jiang signed a joint communiqué with his hosts on the avoidance of force in settling territorial disputes in the South China Seas. Earlier in the year, disputes arose over oil-drilling rights west of the Spratly islands. The communiqué also made reference to bilateral trade and Vietnam's non-governmental relations with Taiwan.

Beijing issued a call for non-inflationary growth and central control at a four-day national work meeting on the economy beginning the **28th**. Inflation would be kept at around 13 to 15% in 1995. The leadership also endorsed a cautious plan for the reform of state factories that would be based on "building up a modern enterprise system." Unemployment and pension benefits were introduced to avoid de-stabilizing social effects. Beijing urged local leaders to "treat well the relationship between reform, development and stability." The seven major tasks for the next year were: curbing inflation; boosting agriculture; reforming state enterprises; ensuring efficient growth; cutting consumption; expanding the open-door policy; and strengthening government control.

DECEMBER

History was made in the democractic development of Taiwan when elections were held on the **3rd** for the positions of provincial governor and the mayors of Taipei and Kaohsiung. Kuomintang-backed James Soong was elected provincial governor by 56% of the 8.4 million voters. However, in the symbolically important capital city of Taipei, Democratic Progressive Party candidate Chen Shui-bian romped home with 44% of the 1.8 million ballots. The New Party, which was founded by right-wing politicians among the KMT, gained seats in the municipal and provincial assemblies. Taipei later announced that direct presidential elections would be held in March 1996.

A total of 320 primary school students perished in a fire at a theatre hall in the oil city of Karamay in the Xinjiang Autonomous Region on the **8th**. All but one of the exits of the facility were locked up or blocked. Nineteen senior officials of the region were penalized. On the 27th of November, 233 disco-goers were killed in a fire in Fuxin, Liaoning. More than 2,200 people lost their lives in 30,000-odd fires in the year. In the same month, Beijing rushed through emergency regulations on safety regulations of entertainment and other public facilities.

The Beijing Intermediate People's Court meted out sentences of three to 20 years to nine dissidents on the **16th**. The nine were among the "Beijing 15" activists who were detained in mid-1992 for alleged counter-revolutionary crimes. The heaviest jail term went to Beijing Languages Institute lecturer Hu Shigen for heading a counter-revolutionary group. Washington severely criticized the sentencing a day later.

Negotiations on China's re-entry into the GATT failed to be concluded at the 19th session of the GATT working party on China, which closed in Geneva on the **20th**. Beijing decried the "boycott by a few signatory parties," principally the United States. The Chinese government said it would not accept "excessive demands" that it adopt standards of a developed country. Beijing also plotted elaborate strategies for being a founder member of the World Trade Organization.

President Jiang Zemin re-hoisted the flag of "scientific and democratic decision-making" when he spoke at a national meeting on the soft sciences on the **24th**. Jiang called upon specialists in the field — a mixture of information sciences, cybertechnics, statistics and public administration — to provide the party and government with "scientific proof and evidence" for their decision making.

1

The Year of the Dog: In the Shadow of the Ailing Patriarch

Jean Philippe Béja

The 3rd plenum of the 14th Party Central Committee in Autumn 1993 had announced that 1994 would be a crucial year for the enforcement of the new reform agenda which planned to transform loss-making state enterprises into profit-making market oriented firms. Such an ambitious programme required a strong and united leadership. However, this was not really the case as 1994 was pervaded by rumours about the deterioration of paramount leader Deng Xiaoping's health, and the impending struggles which might follow his death. The Year of the Dog started with images of an ailing Deng Xiaoping on television and closed on persisting rumours about the deterioration of his health. These facts reminded Chinese and foreign observers alike that the question of succession remains the principal problem in China today.

From the standpoint of political science, an unresolved succession poses two sets of questions. One concerns the legitimacy of the regime: if a political system has no agreed upon mechanisms for succession, every time a leader disappears, the very roots of the regime can be put into question. The second set of problems has more to do with conjuncture: how do various factions jockey for power before and after the death of the leader?

These two sets of questions are present in the Chinese situation.

Can the Present Leadership Create a New Legitimacy Or Renew the Old One?

In revolutionary regimes, there is constant difficulty when the time comes for the founding fathers to transfer power to their successors. After Mao's death, the founders' generation still had many representatives, and Deng Xiaoping could take over in part thanks to the role he had played during the conquest of power phase. The failure of Hua Guofeng to remain at the top can also be partly explained by his absence of credentials in this regard.

Naturally, the situation is quite different now, because the founders of the regime are all very old and cannot seriously pretend to continue to lead the country. China, therefore, will be governed by a new generation. But, as there are no institutionalized mechanisms of succession, the persons presently in power are facing a serious legitimacy problem. Whatever the number of official positions held by Jiang Zemin, his legitimacy comes mainly from his appointment by Deng Xiaoping. Therefore, many in the ruling circles of the Communist Party think that he will have trouble surviving his mentor. And, since the early 1990s, people close to Deng Xiaoping, whether his close relatives or his office, have managed to let it be known that the paramount leader was not always satisfied with his designated successor.

Given these circumstances, Jiang's task has consisted in trying to reinforce his legitimacy. But, obviously, he has been confronted with many challenges, as faith in the superiority of socialism and in the sagacity of the "core leader" of the third generation has been put into doubt. Is it possible to give a new lease of life to the wavering attraction of Marxism-Leninism?

Neo-Maoism as a New Legitimacy?

The centennial ceremonies of Mao's birthday, which culminated at the end of 1993, gave a certain impetus to an attempt at reviving a modernized form of Maoism. Whereas the population was more interested in collecting memorabilia, some people in theoretical circles started to think that, after all these years of disaffection with ideology, it would be possible to resort to Neo-Maoism to tackle the increasing inequalities of development and the deterioration of moral and social norms. These forces have capitalized on the new vogue for the person of Mao as a symbol of clean cadres, and tried to use this nostalgia to come up with a new political agenda. Of course, it is very difficult to name the exponents of that search for a new legitimacy, but people around the think tank of the *Beijing Qingnian bao* like Pan Yue, Liu Huaqing's son-in-law, have shown a certain interest in these ideas and have supported the thesis contained in a book which had significant repercussions in 1994, *Looking at China through the Third Eye*.[1] The author, who pretends to be the German sinologist Luoyininger, denounces the excesses of the reform, especially the development of inequalities and the increasing corruption of communist cadres. He considers that farmers now constitute a threat for the regime and proposes to re-establish a system similar to the people's communes, in order to keep them from rushing toward the cities. He is terrified by the weakening of the central government and the stratification of society. Wang Shan acknowledged having written this book. But he denies it could be considered to a certain extent emblematic of this Neo-Maoist revival.[2] In the face of a growing moral crisis, of increasing corruption at all levels in the party, and of disaffection for old ideological norms, a strongman could capitalize on the sympathy for Mao which, as the centennial showed, is still quite widespread in society. Such a strongman could also capitalize on the discontent which the reforms have provoked in terms of developing inequality and the relative fall in living standards for farmers and state enterprises employees. Re-establishment of strong residency controls, use of political movements to educate people, and serious struggle against corruption and inequalities, constitute some of the recipes the book proposes. It has aroused interest in intellectual circles because of the frankness of its criticism of Deng Xiaoping's reforms. But the remedies it proposes have been largely dismissed by liberal social scientists and intellectuals.[3] It is still too early to judge the real impact of these theories, but they did have an appeal on certain members of the Chinese élite. Jiang Zemin himself recommended the book to leading cadres, saying that the opinions expressed therein were worth studying. It was only later that he condemned it and that it was prohibited.[4]

Nationalism, the Magic Formula?

Like one of his predecessors Hua Guofeng, Jiang Zemin owes his position to designation by the ailing strong man. If Hua's legitimacy was represented by Mao's famous sentence "With you in charge, I feel at ease" (*ni banshi, wo fangxin*), Jiang's is due to his description by Deng as the "core" (*hexin*) of the new leadership. This surely explains why, as Lin Biao and Hua before him, he has been eager to develop a cult of the leader and of the leader's thought. The year 1994 has seen an amazing deployment of personality cult, from study sessions of Deng's thought, to its elevation as "contemporary China's version of Marxism."[5] On 29 August 1994, Jiang Zemin, talking to democratic party representatives, declared: "Judging from the overall situation of party building, ideology building should be given top priority to push ahead and continuously deepen the study of Comrade Deng Xiaoping's theory on building socialism with Chinese characteristics."[6]

But some forces deny Jiang Zemin the monopoly of the cult of the leader. On the vigil of the 45th anniversary of the foundation of the People's Republic, a large exhibition of pictures of Deng was staged at the Museum of History on Tiananmen Square. It had been set up by Guangdong province, which also prepared a large-scale dance "epic" entitled *The Sun of the New Epoch*.[7] So even the celebration of the New Helmsman's thought is at the centre of a power struggle between Jiang and his foes. Will these plaudits be enough to enhance Jiang's legitimacy after

Deng's death? Perhaps not and that might be why the legitimacy Jiang Zemin and his supporters have been proposing lately is a revised version of nationalism: aware that old style socialist values have been terribly devalued since 1989 for both domestic and international reasons, they have revived the old objective of a "strong country and a prosperous nation" which has haunted Chinese thinkers and leaders since the 1840s.

In order to achieve it, Jiang and his associates do not hesitate to turn to Confucius, whose 2545th birthday was celebrated in great pomp in October 1994. An international symposium, addressed by Singapore's patriarch Lee Kuan Yew, was held to commemorate the event.[8]

A new tolerance of Confucianism could help the party unite all the overseas Chinese whose help has been crucial to China's development. In the late 1980s, the fascination for the Four Dragons' economic success had already prompted a renewed interest in traditional philosophy, which was instrumental in the vogue of "neo-authoritarianism." Present day neo-conservatives, who are obsessed with the need for unification of thought, are also resorting to the Great Sage in order to instill respect for the elders.

If the official inheritors of the May 4th Movement whose slogan was "Down with Confucius shop" (*dadao Kong jiadian*) do not hesitate to rehabilitate the Sage in order to reinforce their right to rule, they have nonetheless not abandoned their traditional (communist) way of acting. Pushed by its structural constraints, the party under Jiang has used old action models such as study sessions in patriotism and large scale "education campaigns" directed to the youth in order to popularize the new patriotic ideas, albeit with very little success. The case of the new model character, a woman named Han Suyun who took care of her husband's family in Shanxi, despite its terrible poverty, to allow him to work in the army, is especially interesting: her virtues are "love of the motherland, love of the party, love of her family," a mixture of Confucian and patriotic values.[9] This filial character has replaced the early Deng period martyr Zhang Zhixin, who was executed in 1969 because she refused to bow to the torturers who tried to make her renounce her faith. At that time, the party needed to go against the tide of Maoism, and the model characters were persons of conviction. Deng was trying to establish a new social contract and needed the collaboration of the most daring members of society.

Today, Jiang Zemin and the leaders who support him need obedient subjects, therefore they have created the character of Han Suyun, whom we could call a Confucian Lei Feng of our times. The question is: will Chinese youth really try to emulate such a character?

In September 1994, the 4th plenum of the 14th Central Committee emphasized the necessity to reinforce democratic centralism, showing that old habits die hard and that Jiang is unable to find new solutions to the problems faced by China. That call is not likely to settle the question of official corruption which keeps developing and affects the image of the cadres in the population. When the leaders avail themselves of every opportunity to get rich, the led are not eager to sacrifice their personal interests on the altar of patriotism.

Jiang does not hesitate to use the more traditional aspects of nationalism, the first of which is to complete the unification of China. During the celebrations of the Chinese New Year, he tried to appear as the benevolent leader replacing the imperial figure of Deng Xiaoping. His keynote speech, which was the main subject of the evening news TV broadcast on Chinese New Year's eve[10] was directed to Taiwan: though the contents of the speech did not represent anything new,[11] by making it, and by extending an invitation to meet Lee Teng-hui, either in Taiwan or in Peking, he tried to appear as the hero who will enter Chinese history as the ultimate unifier of the nation. A summit meeting between the two presidents would undoubtedly reinforce Jiang's hand in the post-succession struggle. By making these proposals, Jiang Zemin tries to complete the task started by Deng Xiaoping with the return of Hong Kong to Chinese sovereignty. A success in cross-straits relations would obviously enhance his patriotic legitimacy, and he will undoubtedly continue to emphasize this aspect of his action in the years to come.

A Democratic Legitimacy?

Besides these two attempts to capture legitimacy, one should mention the people who argue in favour of a democratic legitimacy as the only realistic alternative. Their voice is not very strong and they have been silenced by the crackdown on dissent in March–April 1994,[12] but they still exist, not only outside but also inside the party. In June 1994, the *Hong Kong Economic Journal* published a speech that former secretary-general Zhao Ziyang pronounced at the 4th plenum of the 13th Central Committee, where he defended his handling of the Tiananmen protests.[13] The fact that just five years after the upheaval, sources in China made public a speech delivered by a disgraced party leader to a very secret conclave, shows that some people have not abandoned the idea of obtaining his rehabilitation.

Then, in December, a Hong Kong monthly, *Cheng Ming*, published the minutes of the meeting of January 1987 where party secretary-general Hu Yaobang resigned.[14] These two episodes show that the exponents of democratization, or at least, those who are ready to allow a certain amount of freedom of organization to society, still constitute a real strength inside the party. In June 1994, many articles appeared in *Dangxiao luntan* (Party School Forum) complaining of the lack of popular participation in politics. Similarly, political scientist Wu Dacheng cited, in an academic journal article, Zhao Ziyang's report at the 13th Party Congress about the necessity of separating party and government.[15]

The exponents of democratization have some public outlets, journals such as *Dushu*, *Dongfang* and more academic periodicals such as *Zhongguo shehui kexue jikan*, published in Hong Kong by a non-official (*minban*) research centre based in Peking and run by a lively young intellectual named Deng Zhenglai. Another of these journals is the Canton-based *Xiandai yu chuantong* (Modernity vs Tradition), which publishes articles on socio-economic and political change. These journals do not hesitate to advocate democratization, which they see as the equivalent of modernization in the political realm. They openly criticize some practices of the present leadership. "In the leading organs, the one man one vote, equal vote system has not yet become a permanent feature of the system," wrote Gao Fang in *Xiandai yu chuantong*. "Some leaders, before they step down, advise everybody to choose a successor they have designated, or even nominate him. It is not possible yet to have leaders nominated by the voters in an election with more candidates than position."[16] Challenging the official position on the excellence of the Chinese multi-party system, the author declares: "The democratic parties should be real parties, ruling parties sharing power with the Communist Party, and the Chinese People's Political Consultative Conference (CPPCC) should be a sort of senate."[17] And some criticisms which violate the sacrosanct "four cardinal principles"[18] are also printed in the columns of the journal: "If one is unable to develop socialist democracy from one's own initiative and consciously, one can eventually be constrained to enforce capitalist democracy. If one persists in maintaining a sclerotic centralized old system, it will be difficult to avoid finding oneself in a dead-end. Only if China correctly draws the lessons of the changes in the Soviet Union and Eastern Europe, and develops socialist democracy with all its strength, will it be able to build socialism with Chinese characteristics, and will the cause of reform reap its fruits."[19]

The exponents of this thesis think that after the death of Deng, the era of strongmen will be over, and that it will be necessary to have the rule of the party legitimized by a willing population. They recognize the necessity of allowing social forces to create autonomous organizations. Some party cadres and intellectuals are already taking part in discussion sessions with the leading lights of these semi-official journals. It is difficult to assess precisely the strength of the people who are faithful to Hu Yaobang and Zhao Ziyang in the apparatus, but it is important to note that after 1989, there have not been any large-scale purges. Apart from some symbolic figures in the intelligentsia, most functionaries of the party at the middle and upper levels have retained their positions. It will be interesting to observe the attitude they will adopt when the moment of succession comes.

It is still too early to know which one of these three conceptions of legitimacy will win the day when the 90-year-old leader has disappeared.

An Endless Succession Struggle

All along the Year of the Dog, the official press has kept emphasizing that the leadership which "has come after" Deng Xiaoping was united with Jiang Zemin as its core. The truth is that, as long as the patriarch is alive, internal struggle will remain under cover, and appearances will be kept. But, as in most communist systems, and as has been the case since the foundation of the People's Republic, the Chinese Communist Party has been ridden with factional struggle. However, these factions are less and less structured around a political line, and therefore alliances tend to vary more rapidly than was the case during the 1970s.

Many clues have shown that the succession struggle was becoming quite fierce. The contradictions which have appeared in the official media about Deng Xiaoping's movements and health are the most significant. In June, the Hong Kong *Wen Wei Po*, quoting authorized sources, said that Deng Xiaoping had recently spent time in Qingdao,[20] to review the situation in Shandong. The day after, the spokesman for the Ministry of Foreign Affairs denied that information, but refused to state where he was. As a matter of fact, the *Wen Wei Po*, which is tightly under Peking's control had undoubtedly received this information from the higher echelons of the leadership.

Another set of contradictions about Deng Xiaoping's health has been even more striking. In an interview published in the *New York Times* in January 1995, Deng's favourite daughter, Deng Rong, stated that her father's health was "declining day by day," a formula which differed from most of her previous declarations. Moreover, she declared that the June 4th episode "[had been] a tragedy," and that the question of reconciliation with the victims "[was] something which [would] be up to those who [came] afterward."[21] Even though many observers agree in considering Deng Rong to be impulsive, nobody seriously believes that she could have given an interview to a journalist of the *New York Times* without having consulted the Politburo. It is all the more surprising that she talked about such sensitive questions in what can appear almost a direct attack against the present leadership. Indeed, if the verdict on the June 4th massacre was to be reversed, an important constituting factor of the present leadership's legitimacy would disappear, and the reappraisal of Zhao Ziyang's dismissal would become a possibility.

In fact, the day after, the Ministry of Foreign Affairs, contradicted Deng Rong's declaration. Even more surprising, she herself said that her declarations had been misinterpreted, and that she had not said that the patriarch's health was declining day by day.[22]

Then she declared that, after her father's death, "the most important [would be] that the leadership group remain united and, secondly, that its policies be an effective continuation of the policies implemented in the past decade." During her trip to France and the United States, she reiterated her declarations about her father's good health and insisted that the question of succession had been solved.[23] Later, Wu Jieping, a doctor and a vice-president of the National People's Congress, declared to *Der Spiegel* — and then denied it — that since Deng was a man of 90 years, his health could deteriorate suddenly.[24]

These episodes show that some people at the highest echelons try to weaken Jiang Zemin's position by emphasizing the importance of Deng's health. The fact that every time the persons who declared that he was not faring well deny it almost immediately, shows that the pressure is very strong. The Deng Rong episode shows that some of the candidates to the succession, who have the ear of Deng's family, are ready to put the question of June 4th back on the agenda. It could even be interpreted as a change of opinion by Deng himself, which could explain why the present leadership spent so much energy to have Deng Rong correct her declarations.[25]

Still in the beginning of 1995, another episode indicated that struggles at the top echelons of power were intensifying. On 13 February 1995, Zhou Beifang, chairman of one of the most famous Hong Kong listed Chinese companies, Shougang International, was arrested for "economic crimes." His father, Zhou Guanwu, the party secretary of the Capital Steel Mill (Shougang) announced his retirement at the age of 77. The elder Zhou is very close to Deng Xiaoping who delivered a speech at the factory in 1992. It is the first time since the campaign against corruption was launched at the end of 1993, that so influential a person has been arrested. But it is even more interesting to note that Deng Zhifang, Deng Xiaoping's youngest son, was a manager in Shougang International. The arrest of Zhou Beifang could therefore be interpreted as an attack on the Deng family, in the wake of Deng Rong's declarations. What really happened might never be known, but it is worth noticing that lately, there has been a score of anomalous events, signalling an intensification of factional strife.

These fierce though veiled battles have prevented the leadership from making any significant breakthrough in policies. During the 45th year of life of the People's Republic, despite a Central Committee (CC) plenum and sessions of the NPC, the "collective leadership with Jiang Zemin as its core" has not advanced any new idea or new policy. Differing from the situation at the time of the 35th anniversary in 1984, when the decision had been taken (with mitigated success) to extend reform to state enterprises, no initiative was taken last year. Whereas a genuine enthusiasm for Deng Xiaoping had manifested itself on 1 October 1984,[26] there had been nothing of the sort in 1994, and the celebrations were masked with speculation about the health of the paramount leader. Far from being the triumphant coronation of Jiang Zemin, the huge parade left very few memories in the minds of Peking residents.

The Fourth Plenum (25–28 September 1994) of the Central Committee

Feeling that his mentor was about to disappear from the scene, Jiang Zemin has taken steps to reinforce his position in the leading apparatus: the clearest manifestations of this attempt at control have been the promotion of 19 new senior generals in May, and the promotion of two of his Shanghai associates to the Politburo and the Secretariat in the wake of the 4th plenum of the 14th Central Committee which lasted from 25 to 28 September. Huang Ju, the first secretary of the Shanghai municipal party committee, was promoted to full Politburo membership while

Politburo members Wu Bangguo from Shanghai and Jiang Chunyun from Shandong were made members of the Secretariat. This is not necessarily a sign of self-confidence from Jiang Zemin as it is not good, in the context of succession, when the central leadership does not represent the whole country. All the more so that Shanghai representatives were already quite numerous at the centre. Besides the four former or present Shanghai mayors or party secretaries, in the last five years, many cadres of the Eastern metropolis have been promoted: Ba Zhongtan, Chief of the People's Armed Police (former chief of police of the Puqu in Shanghai), Gong Xinhan, now vice-head of the Central Propaganda Department and a former vice-secretary of the Shanghai party committee, Zhou Ruijin, now a vice-editor of the *People's Daily*, who was vice-editor in chief of Shanghai *Jiefang ribao* (Liberation Daily), and the former vice-secretary of the Shanghai party committee Zeng Qinghong, now the chief of the General Office of the Central Committee (*Zhongyang bangongting*). This massive promotion of Shanghai cadres gives observers a sense of *déjà vu*, and, even if the situation is completely different, the importance given to the metropolis of east China, a feature that has been prominent only since 1989, reminds one of the impressive presence of Shanghai cadres in the 1975 Politburo Standing Committee.[27] However, those who have been promoted at the plenum are not only Shanghai leaders — Huang Ju and Wu Bangguo are also alumni of Qinghua, like Zhu Rongji. Wu has been made vice-chief of the small group on the economy and finance, on a par with Zhu Rongji, the chairman of the group being Jiang Zemin.[28]

If it has resulted in the promotion of Jiang's associates, the 4th plenum has, however, failed to provide answers to the pressing challenges that China has been facing since early 1994 (such as inflation, corruption, social unrest, etc.). The plenum did not ensure that the succession might proceed without tensions, nor did it elaborate any new policy. Instead of tackling the economic situation, the plenum only reinforced Jiang's faction, and stated that "it is necessary to continue to place the party's ideological construction in first place, as planned."[29] And the fact that the decision adopted by the plenum insists on the reinforcement of "democratic centralism" and the reconstruction of the party at the grassroots levels shows that the leadership does not feel secure.

However, the triumvirate constituted by Jiang, Zhu Rongji and Li Peng, does not seem to be ridden with quarrels. Although Zhu has often been presented as a rival to Jiang Zemin, it appears that both men could work hand in hand at the central level as they had at the local level in

Shanghai. Since he took over the direction of the People's Bank of China and launched his policy of reinforcement of the centre through the establishment of so-called macro-economic controls, Zhu has come to positions much closer to those of Jiang Zemin's: the modernizing technocrat is as convinced as the neo-conservative ideologue that stability is the first and foremost condition of success (*wending yadao yiqie*). Consequently, he has put his expertise at the service of the Secretary-General, while Li Peng has concentrated on relations with foreign powers. The old opposition between reformers and conservatives has been losing ground, and the triumvirate which constitutes the present leadership agrees on the fact that economic development must not provoke imbalances which could threaten social stability. They agree that, if necessary, reforms can be suspended in order to avoid social conflicts. This is the reason why, after the summer meeting of Beidaihe, the leadership has agreed to make the struggle against inflation its first priority. The only trouble is that this endeavour has not been successful, and 1994 has turned out to be the worst year since 1949 with a rate of inflation officially running at 24.2%.[30]

Zhu and Li did not oppose Jiang's promotion of nineteen senior PLA officers as full generals, a move which was widely viewed as an attempt to reinforce his support in the military. This promotion was actually the largest since the 1960s, and it has been reported that Jiang had not consulted Deng Xiaoping before making his decision on such a sensitive subject. His move has, however, apparently succeeded as Zhang Zhen, vice-chairman of the Central Military Commission, wrote that "Jiang Zemin as the core of our third generation of collective leadership has paid much attention to the inheritance and glorification of the fine tradition of the army,"[31] showing his support on the symbolic occasion of the anniversary of the creation of the PLA.

All through the year, Jiang Zemin has tried to reinforce his position by moving proxies to the top of the PLA, and of the Central Committee, and apparently, he has been relatively successful. However, this power structure might well be challenged when the patriarch disappears. Already, some signs, besides the contradictions in official versions about the patriarch's health, have appeared. At the beginning of January 1994[32] and once again at the beginning of 1995,[33] Yang Shangkun, the former strong man who was expelled from power in 1992 and who still enjoys prestige in part of the army, went for a glamorous tour of Guangdong, showing the province support that the central government has been denying it lately. Some analysts in the capital believe that Yang has not completely lost hopes of making a come back to the highest positions, and that he might well join forces with Zhao Ziyang in the post-Deng period.[34]

The Sessions of NPC and CPPCC (March 1994)

The year had also been marked by the second session of the 8th NPC and the session of CPPCC, which have not been particularly significant in 1994. There is a saying: "*Zhongyang huishou, renda jushou, zhengxie paishou*" (The centre waives its hand, the NPC raises its hands, and the CPPCC claps its hands).[35] Even though in the NPC Qiao Shi and Tian Jiyun, two associates of former secretaries-general Hu and Zhao, and in the CPPCC Li Ruihuan and Wang Zhaoguo, two leaders close to Zhao in the 1980s, and Ye Xuanping, the artisan of the Guangdong miracle, occupied leading positions, they were not especially active in 1994.

The history of other communist regimes shows that upon the death of the Great Helmsman, when a leader wants to push for democratization, he advocates the reinforcement of the Supreme Congress and of the organs of the United Front. With their history as belonging to the liberal faction, these cadres might make these organizations a power basis in the struggle which will undoubtedly follow Deng Xiaoping's death. The fact that during the year, Qiao Shi and Li Ruihuan have made trips abroad and have received many leaders of foreign parliaments, shows that they have not abandoned their hope to play a major role in the post-Deng era.

The low profile they conspicuously adopted *vis-à-vis* the initiatives of Jiang, Zhu and Li, suggests that Qiao Shi and Li Ruihuan are trying to distance themselves from the present leadership and may be making a bid for power in the not too distant future. Despite this, the session of the NPC has not seen any breakthrough.

On 15 March, the NPC adopted an electoral law for the by-election of two members of its standing committee. This law provided that there would be only two candidates for two positions to be filled. Some representatives criticized this measure as a setback from what had become a new custom in 1987, with more candidates than posts to be filled.[36]

The session of the NPC closed on 22 March. Among the nine decisions which had been adopted, the one which provoked the most heated debate had been the discussion on the budget. It was also the one which collected the smallest number of positive votes, 2,110 while 337 either voted against, 225 abstained and 49 refused to vote. Most opponents did not agree with the refusal to tolerate a budget deficit.[37] Indeed, the new budget banned deficits at all levels of government. During the discussion, contradictions between backward and advanced regions came to light: "There's an imbalance of development, so the current budget may be beneficial to the eastern areas but the western regions will be affected adversely," said Liu Ronghui, a deputy form Shaanxi.[38]

Whereas in his report, Li Peng had forecast a 9% growth rate, many deputies from the provinces sang a different tune. For example, Wang Yang, vice-governor of Anhui, announced that his province had registered a 22% growth rate in 1993, and that it should be allowed to continue: "If (we) don't allow provinces like Anhui to have faster growth in the coming years, then China will have difficulty reaching a new (economic) level in the coming 10 or 15 years."[39] Under pressure from the provinces, it is very difficult for the centre to enforce its austerity programme. In his speech to the NPC on 11 March, Finance Minister Liu Zhongli announced a budget deficit of 66.9 billion yuan compared to 20.5 billion the year before (30 billion if the same method of accounting is adopted). In a bid to contain it and to prevent cadres from liberally spending public money, he declared: "Any firm or institution that owes their workers wages shall not buy cars or other high-grade consumer goods." Whereas in 1992, a total of 29.6 billion yuan had been spent on subsidizing prices, he announced that 37.3 billion would be spent for the same purpose in 1994.[40]

Tian Jiyun, vice-chairman of the NPC, called for cadres to respect the law and said it was important to develop legislation in order to facilitate and to protect reform. He declared that people should feel that it is shameful to violate the law.[41] The NPC and CPPCC failed to achieve agreement on the pace of reform. Despite the decisions made at the 3rd plenum of the 14th Central Committee in November 1993 to accelerate the reform of state firms, He Guanghui, vice-chairman of the Commission for the Restructuring of the Economy indicated that it was "impossible and unnecessary" for all state units to become joint-stock concerns.[42] As the *Wen Wei Po* wrote in a commentary, "in the interest of maintaining stability, the party centre has decided temporarily to slow down the introduction of some reforms."[43]

The NPC set the goal of maintaining inflation within 10% during the year. "Our goal is, of course, not just stability, but growth.... The series of measures being adopted to promote stability will contribute to growth." Li Peng declared in the amendments he made to his *Government Work Report*.[44] This report was adopted by 2,655 votes for, 23 against, 25 abstentions and 18 not taking part in the vote.

The Preoccupations of the Populace and Its Perception of Political Problems in 1994

As there is no press freedom in China, it is very difficult to have an idea of the way ordinary citizens react to political developments. But, worried by the state of public opinion, the leaders often resort to opinion polls in order to know what citizens consider the most pressing issues. Although the results of these polls are sometimes amended to please the officials who read them, we can take them as a reference.

When asked what were the main problems in 1994, 79.8% of the 20,000 persons surveyed by the State Statistical Bureau in October 1994 put price rises in the first position. And when asked what measures the government should take to maintain social order, 83.4% answered that it should control price rises.[45]

A survey of 174 experts in all fields showed that they thought that the main problems which had not been tackled in 1994, were the following: reducing the differences between regions (46.9%); controlling inflation (44.9%), revitalizing state firms (48.1%); punishing officials guilty of corruption (35.7%). These were quite representative of the general public's preoccupations.[46]

Although the government had put the struggle against inflation at the top of its agenda, promising that prices would not rise more than 10%, the effort had been far from successful. The official figure for 1994 was 24.2%, the highest increase since 1949. An even more serious fact was that price rises were especially high for daily necessities. In the cities, the prices of cereals rose by 47%, of meat by 36%, and of vegetables by 37%.[47] According to official statistics, inflation caused deteriorating living standards for 20% of the urban population and as much as 50% in some cities.

An opinion poll showed that 25.01% of workers felt that their standard of living had decreased in 1994, and 11.01% felt that it had decreased a lot, a higher percentage than for any other social stratum.[48]

Among those who suffer most are the workers employed in loss-making state enterprises. Official figures attest that 5 millions are unemployed (a rate of 3%) and that 20 millions can be considered as victims of disguised unemployment and do not receive their whole salary (their monthly income is less than 103 yuan per capita),[49] whereas only 1.3 million workers receive unemployment benefits. Inflation hits them very seriously and they have seen their standard of living deteriorate last year.[50]

According to statistics provided by the State Statistical Bureau, from January to September 1994, 44.5% of state firms had been losing money, a 8.1% rise over 1993. A survey done in 12 cities and districts of Shanxi showed that 56.7% of the workers could not receive their whole salaries.[51] Under these circumstances, it is not surprising that workers are more worried than other social strata by price rises: an opinion poll shows that 83.71% of them consider inflation as the main problem they are facing against 79.8% for the whole population and only 72.7% for peasants.[52]

Perhaps for the same reason, workers are less supportive of the statement that "the social situation is basically stable," with 53.19% in support against 58.33% for society as a whole.[53] Of the workers, 64% say that improvement of accommodation is their principal hope.[54] However, they are far from convinced that privatization of housing is a good solution for them. An opinion poll in Shenyang showed that 30% of the workers surveyed were against it.[55]

Polls indicate that people attach great importance to the struggle against corruption. But any interview shows that they usually do not believe in the commitment of the leadership to fight it because some of the most corrupt officials are often the offspring of more senior officials who are the real power-holders. *Xinhua*, the official news agency, reported in March that corruption was so widespread in the province of Anhui that 300,000 cadres, one out of five, accepted bribes.[56] In the countryside, clashes between peasants and officials are ever more frequent, often because of expropriation by cadres who want to develop land, or sell it to developers. These conflicts have been very numerous in Guangdong in the past year, and the government has failed to prevent the eruption of violent fights. In March and April 1994, incidents occurred involving conflict between peasants and the Public Security at Dansui, Zengcheng, in southeastern Guangdong.[57] The authorities had tried to prevent farmers from creating organizations to defend their interests, provoking serious discontent among them. But for the time being, farmers' agitation does not threaten the power of the Communist Party. Such rural unrest has remained limited to villages or at most prefectures (*diqu*), and has never extended to provinces or to the whole country.

The problem is nevertheless quite serious. According to official statistics, in 1994, 6 million mu of agricultural land had been lost, as local cadres were selling big chunks of land for industrial development or real estate speculation.[58] These might be the reasons why a large proportion of the farmers — 24.89% according to a survey done by the Institute of

Sociology of Chinese Academy of Social Sciences and the State Statistical Bureau — thought that "the situation in agriculture is not stable." According to that survey, 69.1% thought that their standard of living had neither deteriorated nor improved during 1994.[59]

Inflation and the deepening of reforms have led to an increase in inequalities. According to official statistics, the average urban income was 3 times higher than the average rural income in 1994, while the ratio was only 1.8 in 1978, and 2.9 in 1993. If one takes into account the free services that are at the disposal of urban dwellers, the ratio is closer to 4. In 1994, the income of the 20% wealthiest urban dwellers was 13 times superior to that of the 20% poorest rural inhabitants.[60] And in the process of reforms, the richer and the poorer are more and more numerous. Besides, whatever the improvement of their lot, the income of the peasants who continue to till the land is much lower than that of those who go to the cities to do the hardest jobs. According to a survey done in Anhui, in 1994, the average yearly income of a peasant tilling the land was 678.32 yuan against 2,220.80 for a person who worked 220 days in town.[61]

The situation cannot be termed dramatic, but citizens often feel that they are victims of official abuse, and that the centre does not help them to fight injustice. As the popular rhymed sentence goes, "The tenth and lowest category of citizens are the people: they are the ones who should make revolution and study Lei Feng," which means that the ordinary citizen, the so-called "masters of the country" must sacrifice themselves while others strike it rich.[62] As a matter of fact, workers think that they belong to the lower middle and lower class in terms of income, and have the worst image of themselves among the urban dwellers.[63]

If officials are usually omnipotent in the political sphere, a few members of the new class of entrepreneurs have been trying recently to have a say in political affairs. In a district situated in a coastal province, one private entrepreneur spent 300,000 yuan to obtain the help of a vice-mayor, and, through offering gifts and banquets, succeeded in being elected a member of the standing committee of the district People's Congress. In Hainan, the manager of a chemical factory offered soap and other products to voters in order to be elected to the district People's Congress.[64] There are numerous similar cases, and this suggests that the new emerging classes are trying to gain a measure of political power.[65] This trend could be important for the future of the Chinese political system.

If people do not talk about the necessity for democratization, they do not believe that a renewed emphasis on "democratic centralism" will be able to solve the most pressing problems they are confronted with in their daily life. If in most conversation, Peking's people like to vent their discontent (*faxie buman*), intellectuals are interested in talking about the struggles at the summit between "conservatives" and "reformers." Although official media keep saying that there are no such things as factions at the top of the Communist Party, everyone among middle cadres and intellectuals tries to interpret the *Renmin ribao* editorials through this lens. In November 1994, a survey of 4,650 cadres, most of them Communist Party members although some were members of the minor democratic parties, was done at the request of the State Council. The goal of that survey was to know what those responsible people thought would happen after Deng's demise. The vast majority answered that there would be some kind of trouble. As to the reasons for that pessimism, 2,695 persons — 58% of those surveyed explained it by the lack of legal guarantees and of an efficient system of control; 1,583 persons, 34%, thought policies changed too much and too often, and that it was difficult to be sure of what would happen next.

This opinion was particularly widespread among the 725 persons belonging to the democratic parties or higher professionals as 96% of them believed that the absence of legal guarantees was the most serious danger. Absence of faith in the future comes from the perception that there is default of institutionalization in the regime. So far as the main objects of discontent in political life were concerned, first came corruption, the abuse of privileges by government and party cadres; second, the continuing inflation; third, the constant deterioration of public values and morals; and fourth, the deterioration of public order.

Presenting the results of this poll on 3 January 1995, the head of the Propaganda Department of the Central Committee, Ding Guan'gen, declared: "the existence of these problems influences directly the forces of the party and the masses, influences the speed with which the people of the whole country will build socialism with Chinese characteristics. But the main problem is that the middle and higher cadres have lost confidence in their ambitions and in the party."[66]

So far as the lower ranking officials are concerned, they are less and less interested in the slogans launched by the party centre.

In the wake of the 4th plenum of the Central Committee, the national press published many articles blaming local and provincial cadres for localism and greed. In the countryside, many meetings were held to remind officials of their duty and to take action to give new life to party cells,[67] as local cadres seemed often more interested in the development of religious activities than in the studying of Marxism-Leninism. In Henan, between 1992 and 1994, 186 temples had been built without the authorization of the Bureau of Religious Affairs. Temple festivals have been multiplying, often encouraged by local cadres who either believe in religion or think that it offers good opportunities to make money for the village.[68]

Despite the appeals by the Central Committee urging local and leading cadres to pay attention to party work styles, party cadres at the local level tend to be more concerned with traditional behaviour or with the "modernization of their personal standards of living" than with the enforcement of democratic centralism, whereas at the higher levels, many official are pessimistic about the near future.

Stability, the Keyword

With such a crisis of confidence lagging, and the impending change of generation at the top, the leadership is confronted with the problem of ensuring succession in a stable environment. But what does stability mean?

Since the beginning of the 1980s, all Chinese leaders have agreed that it should mean engineering economic development and retaining political control by the party. But this leaves room for very different policies.

In 1992, during his trip to the south, Deng answered that "only fast development passes the test of reason." This conclusion was the result of the analysis he had made of the collapse of the Soviet Union. In the fall of 1993, the 3rd plenum of the 14th Central Committee continued in this direction and decided that the transformation of loss-making state enterprises in profit-making market oriented firms was a priority. Nothing had to be feared from fast growth rates.

But fast development is risky as it develops imbalances in the economic and social spheres. Therefore, some leaders think that stability means low inflation, and balanced growth rates, while others think that a measure of inflation should be tolerated so that living standards improve and *laobaixing* stay calm.

During the second session of the 8th National People's Congress in March 1994, Li Peng announced his intention to keep growth rates within 9%, and inflation below 10%. As we have seen earlier, the actual figures were quite different with a growth rate of 11.8% and a 24.2% rate of inflation. This might explain why, during the fall of 1994, the media criticized the "unconditional admirers of market economy."

In fact, given this obsession with stability, coupled with the insecurity created by the impending death of Deng Xiaoping, most far-reaching and much needed political and economic reforms had been postponed. A divided leadership whose legitimacy is not secure can hardly take bold measures, and the obsession with stability has led to immobilism in many a field. And as in any period when instability is looming, there have been attempts at reinforcing the powers of the central government.

A New Deal between the Centre and the Regions

The leadership — whether so-called modernizing technocrats such as Zhu Rongji or "conservative" as Zou Jiahua — considers that stability means establishing a new deal between the centre and the regions, reinforcing the centre through macro-economic controls put into practice by the banks, and safeguarding the state economy. Naturally, developed areas resent this limitation to their autonomy and try to strike back, creating yet another source of tension. The financial reform which gave back the privilege of raising taxes to the central government came into practice at the beginning of 1994. It was the fruit of a compromise as the centre promised the richer regions that they would not lose revenue. But, as it was rolling back the bold decision of the 3rd plenum, postponing the transformation of state enterprises into market oriented firms for fear of social unrest, the centre tried to re-establish its grip on the regions. The State Council announced in mid-May that it had taken back the power to sell state firms to foreigners, which till then belonged to provinces and municipalities.

Just a few months after the NPC meeting, in May 1994, Zhu Rongji went to Wuhan and Zhengzhou and had a meeting with the leaders of seven provinces. He told the provincial leaders that before launching all out reform, it would be necessary to bring inflation under control, and to adjust and control the financial markets. He also announced that it was necessary to help ailing state enterprises.[69]

Then, he ordered Zhejiang and Guangdong to grow more grain and asked Guizhou to grow less tobacco.[70]

In August, the State Council urged richer provinces and municipalities to help poorer regions. If Jiangsu and Shandong agreed to do so, Guangdong was less enthusiastic and argued that it had suffered floods and had to provide for the needs of the poorer inhabitants in the northern part of the province.[71] Despite these natural catastrophes, the gross domestic product of the province had grown by 18.9% in 1994, faster than the 18.5% of 1993.[72] According to a recent report by Hu Angang, who seems to have become the Cassandra forecasting that the fate of Yugoslavia threatens China, disparity between the richer and poorer provinces has kept growing since 1990, despite policy changes which allow the provinces of the interior to attract foreign investment. According to his figures, the GDP of Shanghai has risen from 7.4 times that of Guizhou in 1991, to 8.4 times in 1992.[73]

Even though the central government has dwelled on the necessity for richer provinces to help poorer ones, the latter find fault with its general policy. Some of the leaders of the poorer areas think that the centre does not give enough help and enough freedom to develop their regions. The centre has reacted, and in April 1994 Zhu Rongji went on a tour and sacked the long time Secretary of the provincial party Committee of Heilongjiang, Sun Weiben, for having failed to improve the situation in that northern province. At that time, it had been widely interpreted as a move to deepen reform. But in fact, in his report to the provincial People's Congress, Sun had emphasised that Heilongjiang was full of problems posed by the huge numbers of state industrial enterprises which had no money to pay wages. Already in 1992, he had advocated the transformation to a market economy. But he complained that the centre had asked him to solve the crisis without giving enough funds for reconversion or leaving enough leeway to enforce a really liberal policy. On the other hand, Sun dwelled on the fact that his province contributed enormous amounts of grain to the national economy, grain which was paid at ridiculous prices. His replacement by Yue Qifeng, a Liaoning Secretary,[74] will not be able to solve the problems, and this appears more as an episode in the Peking political struggle rather than an effort at solving the huge problems which weigh on the province.[75]

In July 1994, Zhu Rongji went to Qinghua University to explain that he could not sleep and had lost five pounds because of the problems of the central and local taxes. He said that originally the centre intended to leave 20% of the product of taxes to the local echelon, but they refused; he then proposed 40%, and they still refused. Therefore, despite the fiscal reform, "the growth rate of the fiscal revenue pocketed by the centre was inferior to the growth rate of the revenue pocketed by the localities."[76]

Social Unrest ...

The leaders realize that in order to maintain stability it is necessary to spare state enterprises from trouble, because the Communist Party does not want to alienate the "working class," and fears the challenge workers could pose to socio-political stability. In 1994, the number of arbitrated industrial disputes rose by 50% compared to the year before, and reached the number of 12,538. As most disputes are usually not declared, the real number was much higher. Strikes and industrial action have also occurred in joint-ventures in Guangdong and Fujian. For example, in Zhuhai, at the Wei-Wang Data Communication Company in May 1994, more than 1,000 workers went on strike to protest attempts by the management to lower wages, and to ask for the implementation of labour regulations. Other protest movements happened in Japanese joint-ventures[77] in Dalian, in Taiwanese joint-ventures in Shenzhen, etc.[78]

Officials have admitted that demonstrations, strikes and sit-ins in front of government buildings had multiplied because of the problematic financial situation of 44.5% of industrial state enterprises.[79] Very often, these workers protest because they have not been paid for months. In Harbin in 1994, some workers demonstrated in front of the provincial government office because they had not received their salaries for six months. In some factories of Heilongjiang, workers have been given food coupons worth 40 yuan instead of their salaries. In some factories and mines in Sichuan, guns and truncheons have been distributed to factory leaders, so that they can protect themselves against angry workers.

In Handan, Hebei, in July 1994, after two workers of a bicycle factory committed suicide because they had not been paid for several months, thousands of workers organized a protest in front of the city hall. This was only one of the demonstrations which involved tens of thousands of workers in this town.[80]

Statistics provided by provincial Federations of Trade Unions show that the number of industrial conflicts rose by 155% for the first half of 1994 in Shandong. More than half of these conflicts were caused by the deterioration of living conditions. In Hubei, the number of conflicts also rose and two of them involved more than 5,000 workers. The same could be said of Hebei and Peking.[81]

The government's strategy has been two-fold: well aware that the deepening of reforms constitutes a real threat to the job security of workers in state enterprises, it often tries to mollify the demonstrating workers by giving in to some of their requests. Although the transformation of loss-making firms was supposed to be the central task for 1994, this strategy was suspended and, after March, subsidies were discretely re-established.

In order to quell the workers' anger, a new labour law was adopted in July 1994, setting the maximum work time at 44 hours per week, and stipulating an equal treatment for women. The law also envisaged the need for social protection, but it was silent on the right to strike.[82] As it has been implemented only since 1 January 1995, it is too early to judge if it has improved the situation of the Chinese workers.

But apart from this attempt to give more rights and benefits to angry workers, the government has not hesitated to crack down seriously on the people who try to organize free trade unions. In many state firms, some autonomous unions have been created, especially in the south of the country. They usually appear in one factory, and have no links to the others. They seem to function as mutual help organizations. For instance, when a factory cannot pay its workers their wages, the unofficial body helps with the search for alternative employment. Some of these organizations have also been in touch with the local NPC deputies.

After trying in vain to integrate such factory branch unions into the official organization, authorities have launched crackdowns. In April 1994, 16 persons were arrested — among them four workers, three unemployed workers, and five intellectuals — for trying to organize a preparatory Chinese Trade Unions committee.[83]

In March 1994, Zhou Guoqiang, a lawyer who had acted as counsel to exiled labour leader Han Dongfang in August 1993, and Yuan Hongbing, a professor of law at Peking University, sent a letter signed by 200 persons to the NPC to denounce the persecutions inflicted upon factory workers. In the same month, they applied to the authorities for the registration of a league for the Protection of Workers' Rights. In its charter, the league asked for recognition of the right to strike, for the right to form farmers' unions, and for the protection of independent workers' (*mingong*) rights.[84] Not only did the government refuse to register the new league, but Zhou and Yuan were arrested and have not been heard of since. A few weeks later, Wei Jingsheng, who had been freed just on the eve of the vote on China's candidature for the Olympic Games in September 1993, disappeared once more. The fact that he was in a good position to act as a bridge between intellectual and workers' dissent might be a reason for his arrest.[85] On 16 December 1994, it was learned that Liu Jingsheng, a veteran labour organizer, was given a 15-year sentence for "having organized counter-revolutionary groups."

This crackdown shows that the party is still obsessed with the danger of the birth of a Chinese "Solidarity," which has been lingering since 1981. This fear has naturally increased with the deterioration of the material and symbolic situation of the working class who is less and less presented as the "master of the country."[86]

... and Crackdown on Dissent

Besides worker agitators, the party has reinforced its surveillance of dissidents. In a very Soviet-like manner, used in Shanghai in previous years, dissidents have been subjected to police harassment. Every time a foreign head of government visited Peking and Shanghai, or at the approach of sensitive anniversaries, most famous dissidents were either taken for trips in the provinces or prevented from leaving their homes. This strategy reminds one of that adopted by the Czech police in the 1980s: every time a foreign leader would visit Prague, the most famous dissidents would be rounded up and sent to jail.

In Peking, people like 1989 student movement leader Wang Dan have been harassed and are not allowed to leave home without an impressive escort of plainclothes policemen. Similarly, Chen Ziming cannot receive friends. Chen is one of the famous dissidents who, together with Wang Juntao, was sentenced to 13 years in jail in 1990 and then freed on parole during the vigil for the American decision on most-favoured-nation status (MFN) in May 1994. Every time Chen tries to leave his apartment, he is followed by five plainclothes policemen, and has been virtually under house arrest since his "liberation."

Among the Shanghai dissidents who have suffered this sort of treatment are Yang Zhou from the Society for Human Rights and Bao Ge who organized the movement for reparations from Japan. This type of police harrassment, used against Wang Ruowang or other dissidents during the 1980s as well, is now used also in Peking.

Workers unrest worries party leaders. Therefore, in order to ensure "stability," they have changed their more lenient attitude of 1993, when they seemed eager to improve their international image, and have launched a series of crackdown against dissent since the start of 1994. Party leaders fear that dissidents who, in a period of calm do not represent a challenge to the regime, will capitalize on workers' discontent and take advantage of the eventual death of the old leader to give a political colour to this anger. All factions agree on this attitude.

The crackdown on dissent also allows the Communist Party to make a show of force in front of Western countries. During the first half of the year, the Central Committee has scored numerous victories on that front, culminating with Bill Clinton's decision to de-link MFN from human rights. This way, they have showed pro-democracy activists that they should not expect any help from Western countries who are only interested in investing in China to take advantage of its extraordinary rate of growth, its potential market and its cheap labour.

The fear of unrest became another reason to postpone most of the far-reaching reforms which were supposed to take place during the crucial (*guanjian*) year of 1994. During the summer, Zhu Rongji summed up the new attitude of the leadership: "Reform does not mean lifting all controls on the economy, because that would inevitably lead to a big swing in prices, a chaotic market and severe economic setbacks." In this line of thought, the state procurement prices of cereals, cotton and oil-making plants were raised by 40%, and the government decided to grant farmers 6.5 billion yuan of low-interest loans. In order to fight galloping inflation, some measures of administrative price control were taken in large cities. Faced with a shortage of cotton (production in 1993 had fallen to 3.76 million tons, compared to the record of 6.25 million in 1984) due both to the shrinking land dedicated to it and to speculation, the central government, in a first move, decided to raise the purchase price to 500 yuan per 50 kgs, compared to 370 at the beginning of the year. It also prohibited the sale of raw cotton to private traders and tried to re-establish the monopoly of procurement.[87]

A Weak Attempt against Corruption

If inflation, price hikes and failure to get their wages were at the roots of workers' unrest, another factor, which had played a very important role in the explosion of 1989,[88] was official corruption. Although the campaign launched in 1993 failed to hit the so-called tigers (the higher-ups who are involved in corruption), it continued during 1994. During the NPC meeting of March 1994, Ren Jianxin, President of the Supreme People's Court, declared that since 1993, 22,016 persons had been sentenced for economic crimes, of which 6,863 were sent to jail for five years or more. Although he announced that 69 were division-rank and seven were ministerial level cadres, he agreed that much remained to be done.[89] From January to November 1994, the People's Procuratorate opened 24,990 cases of economic criminality in the whole country, 35.4% more than for the same period in 1993.[90] From 1993 to the end of the first half of 1994, 143,000 cadres and party members were sanctioned, among which more than 10,000 were sentenced by the courts.[91] Things did not improve according to official statistics, as for the first eleven months of 1994, 32,800 persons were charged with economic crimes, up 65% from the same period in 1993.[92]

The 3rd plenum resolution in 1993 had reiterated that "it is necessary to continue to do well in improving the party's work style and deepen the anti-corruption struggle in a deep-going and sustained manner."[93] Few people believe in the efficiency of these measures, because few sentences were imposed on cadres above the district level. During the first six months of 1994, 44,105 persons received sanctions for breach of party discipline or of state laws, among whom only 7 were province-level officials, with 99 at the bureau (*ting*) or prefectural level, and 1,141 at district level. These affairs are mainly serious economic crimes.[94]

The numerous meetings dedicated to the eradication of corruption inside the party show that the leadership is aware of the seriousness of the threat. Since the end of 1993, the State Council has held three meetings on this theme. In early 1995, Li Peng reiterated the importance of the necessity to fight bad trends inside the party, and declared that "the victories achieved in the struggle against corruption are still far from the expectations of the masses." He specifically referred to the excesses in real estate speculation. He declared that the fight to prevent corruption, which represents a vital challenge to Party rule, "must be enforced under the supervision of the National People's Congress, the CPPCC, and the organs of public opinion."[95]

In February 1995, the arrest of Zhou Beifang, chairman of the Hong Kong listed companies Shougang Concord and Shougang International was presented as a breakthrough in the struggle against corruption. Although details are not yet available, and because the case might involve political struggle at the centre, this case suggests that the government has decided to strike a few tigers in order to quench the people's thirst for justice.[96]

However, despite the number and solemnity of the meetings and speeches dedicated to the eradication of corruption, it keeps rising, and ordinary citizens do not believe in the dedication of the leaders, all the more so as their offspring are very often at the centre of financial scandals.

Renewed Control of Public Opinion

Stability also means cracking down on publishing houses, to ensure that propaganda is in the leaderships' hands. At the end of January 1994, the biggest gathering of propaganda workers since 1957 took place in Peking, during which the head of the Propaganda Department, Ding Guan'gen, gave a very orthodox speech: "Give help, do not add confusion; sing the leitmotif of socialism, patriotism, collectivism, avoid cacophony; pay attention to social benefits and not the profit motive...."[97] This gathering set the pace for the leadership's policy in that field. But, times have changed, and publishers have been catering to the needs of the general public by providing "small newspapers" (*xiao bao*) which present both information about delinquency, soft porn stories and articles about life of actors and pop stars. There is also room for more theoretical journals such as *Xiandai yu chuantong, Zhongguo shehui kexue jikan, Dongfang, Dushu* etc. which can escape the bulk of pressure from the Propaganda Department.

However, the authorities have cracked down on journalists and publishers: in April 1994, Hong Kong daily *Ming Pao* journalist Xi Yang was sentenced to 12 years for "selling state secrets," while in December, Gao Yu, a regular contributor of the pro-Peking *Jingbao* (The Mirror in Hong Kong), was given a sentence of 6 years. A few publishers in Shaanxi, Xinjiang and elsewhere were also dismissed or forced to write self-criticisms. Despite these strong signals from the central government, publishers have continued to issue books that the Propaganda Department does not like either because they make money or out of conviction. One such example is a bandit novel about a triad war which ends in a massacre ordered by characters with names like Li Pang, Yang Xiakun, etc.[98]

Thanks to the development of the market economy, quasi-private publishing houses have appeared in the last two years. In 1994, the Propaganda Department increased seizures of books and even arrested some people. The publishers of the above-mentioned bandit novel found themselves in trouble, and six persons were sacked while another is still being held in detention.

It is easier to crackdown on periodicals than on books. On 27 December 1994, one of the most famous liberal weeklies, the *Xiandai ren bao* was closed, officially because it had no more *guakao danwei* (sponsoring organization). The process through which the weekly was closed is most revealing of the variety of problems which plague contemporary China. That weekly distinguished itself in the mid-eighties by publishing articles by Wang Ruowang, Yan Jiaqi, Jin Guantao, Wang Ruoshui, most of the major "bourgeois liberal" thinkers of the time. Twice it was almost closed by the government, once after the anti-bourgeois liberal campaign of early 1987 and once after the June 4 massacre. But, after Deng Xiaoping's trip to the south, *Xiandai ren bao* seized the opportunity to establish a joint-venture with the company that publishes *Ming Pao* in Hong Kong, which owned more than 70% of the shares. The joint venture company Guandong Xiandai ren baoye jingying youxian gongsi was created in August 1993 with the agreement of the Guangdong publication bureau and the provincial propaganda department. The periodical was such a success that in June 1994 it became a daily. However, in October 1993, as part of its crackdown on the media, the Press and Publication Bureau of the central government issued an order prohibiting the establishment of joint ventures in the publishing business.[99] This affair is quite revealing. First of all, it was a case of contradiction between the centre and the provinces. "Approved personally by a Politburo member, the order was issued by the State Press and Publications Administration on 21 November," an informed source said.[100] But it took more than one month for the Guangdong authorities to order the closure of the paper which took place only on 31 December.

The second problem is in the joint-venture area. Since the Xi Yang affair, the Communist Party has borne a grudge against the then director of *Ming Pao*, Yu Pun-hoi. The closure of the newspaper might be part of a larger plan to expel him from the Chinese editorial scene. Denials by Zhou Shengying, director of the Guangdong Press and Publication Bureau cannot be taken at face value: "It's not because it's too outspoken. There have not been many deviations. Nor is it because of its Hong Kong partner. The only reason basically is it does not have a sponsoring unit."[101]

This episode illustrates the ambiguity of the emergence of civil society in China: just as liberal intellectuals have used the *guakao danwei* (umbrella unit) to escape state control,[102] the latter still retains the power of intervention. When it was created in September 1985, the paper was registered under the Guangdong branch of the China Council for the Promotion of International Trade. In July 1994, after almost ten years of operation, the council suddenly realized it had no experience in this field and had to sever the relationship. The operators looked for new sponsors and members of the Guangdong People's Congress were at first very enthusiastic.[103] But later, they all backed down. This shows that the legal figure of *guakao danwei*, used by most outspoken intellectuals in the 1980s and still common in the 1990s, can also be used by the party to restrict freedom of expression. This very subtle tactical move, invented in the early 1980s, is not the equivalent of legal guarantees and underscores the limitations that the party's capacity to intervene can impose on society in today's People's Republic.

Conclusion

With factional struggles mounting in preparation for the moment of succession, Chinese leaders showed little initiative on the domestic front during 1994. Backing away from the most controversial item on the reform agenda, they showed a remarkable immobility which allowed them to escape major crisis. Evidently consensus was strong within the government, however, when it was deemed necessary to crack down on dissent, and opposition forces seemed very weak at the start of 1995. Nevertheless, the volatility of the social situation and apparent instability of the current political line-up do not allow the observer to rule out the possibility of a major crisis when the time for succession arrives. The legitimacy of the present leadership team is very weak indeed, and the political configuration could easily change. This might explain why leaders react so rigidly and are so little inclined to make concessions either in domestic or in foreign policy.

With so fragile an internal situation, it is remarkable that Chinese leaders have been able to play out their hand so skillfully in foreign relations during the first half of 1994.

With Westerners on human rights, with England on Hong Kong, and with her Asian neighbours in the South China Sea, the People's Republic has adopted a hard line. The whole leadership appears united in its attitude toward Western countries but, except in the case of Vietnam, it is much more flexible in its relations toward Southeast Asian countries. China, which is increasingly becoming a regional power which exerts a great attraction on its neighbours because of the growth rate of its economy, appears more and more as a candidate to regional leadership. But if China is to continue its growth, it cannot afford to treat foreign partners too harshly and during the second half of the year had to back down on a number of subjects. China had to compromise with Taiwan on the Qiandao Lake and Hiroshima affairs.[104] And Peking suffered a great humiliation by having to accept rejection as a founding member of the World Trade Organization (WTO). In mid-November, 31 banks, 24 of them Japanese, wrote to Zhu Rongji asking him to pay back a debt of US$600 million, some of which was a decade old. At the same time, the Lehman Brothers Bank of New York denounced two Chinese state companies for not honouring debts amounting to around 100 million dollars. Having used the argument of its fast growth to the utmost, China must realize that there are limits to the capacity of capitalist tolerance. *The Economist*, which was instrumental in the 1992 China craze recently downgraded China from B to C for secure investments. The Chinese leadership, which thought that the honeymoon between multinationals and the Middle Empire was a structural element of the world situation has had to come to terms with reality: propaganda can be efficient only if it falls on ready ears. When the tide turns, even the most solid evidence of healthy development cannot convince investors to return. And Jiang Zemin's triumph on MFN has soon been followed by a large movement of disaffection toward his country in economics, sports, and politics. The present leadership, while successfully ridding itself of pressure on human rights by adopting a hard line, has had to back down on a number of issues and has ended the year in considerable retreat.

Notes

1. Luoyininger (trans. by Wang Shan), *Disan zhi yanjing kan Zhongguo*, (Taiyuan: Shanxi renmin chubanshe, 1994).
2. About this book, see the in-depth analysis by Michel Bonnin, "Le retour du vieil oeil," *Perspectives chinoises*, No. 24 (Juillet-aôut 1994), pp. 56–65.
3. For a typical reaction of "liberal bourgeois" intellectuals, see "Luoyininger yu tade yanjing" (Luoyininger and His Eye) by Wang Meng, the writer who has been Minister of Culture until 1989, *Dushu*, No. 9 (1994); pp. 25–31, which launched the attack on the book.
4. See *South China Morning Post* (Hong Kong), 17 February 1995 and *Eastern Express* (Hong Kong), 7 January 1995.
5. See Quotation by Hu Jintao in *Qiushi* (Seeking Truth), No. 16 (August 1994), p. 4, quoted in Maurice Brosseau, "Political Transition: a Test of Deng Xiaoping's Reforms," *China News Analysis*, No. 1526 (1 January 1995), p. 7.

6. See "Jiang Zemin Plenum Briefing," *Xinhua*, 29 September 1994, in FBIS-CHI-94-189, p. 26.
7. See *South China Morning Post*, 20 September 1994.
8. See Willy Wo-lap Lam's analysis, "Rattled Jiang Seeks a Confucian Lifeline," *South China Morning Post*, 28 September 1994.
9. See *Renmin ribao*, 5 January 1995.
10. See *CCTV*, 7 o'clock news broadcast, and *Renmin ribao*, 31 January 1995.
11. See Jiang Zemin's speech in *Xinhua*, 31 January 1995.
12. Cf. *infra* pp. 26–28.
13. *Hong Kong Economic Journal*, 4 June 1995, translated into English in *Eastern Express*, 6 June 1994.
14. Luo Bing, "Qun 'zuo' dao Hu milu" (Secret Notes on the Toppling of Hu by a Group of Leftists), *Cheng Ming*, No. 206 (December 1994), pp. 11–15.
15. See Willy Wo-lap Lam's article, "Jiang Woos the Army to Stem Peking's Division of Power," *South China Morning Post*, 6 July 1994.
16. Gao Fang, "Zhongguo de zhengzhi tizhi gaige," (The Reform of China's Political System), *Xiandai yu chuantong* (Modern vs Tradition), No. 5 (1994), pp. 45–46.
17. Ibid. p. 47.
18. Socialism, Marxism-Leninism-Mao Zedong thought, People's Democratic Dictatorship and leadership of the Communist Party.
19. Gao Fang, "Zhongguo de zhengzhi tizhi gaige" (Note 16), p. 47.
20. *Wen Wei Po* (Hong Kong), 23 June 1994.
21. *The New York Times*, 13 January 1995.
22. *Sunday Morning Post*, 29 January 1995: In a declaration to the *Weekend*, an Australian Newspaper, Deng Rong said: "What I was trying to say is that he was getting older and older, but I didn't use the expression day by day."
23. See her declarations on French Television, *Le 20 heures*, France 2, 4 February 1995.
24. *Ming Pao* (Hong Kong), 12 February 1995 and 15 February 1995.
25. Interview with a leading cadre close to Zhao Ziyang.
26. It is during the parade on Changan jie and Tiananmen that Peking University students had deployed their sign with "Xiaoping, nin hao" (Xiaoping, How are you?) which showed a new familiarity between the leader and the led.
27. At that time, Wang Hongwen, who had worked in a Shanghai factory, and Zhang Chunqiao, who had led the "January storm" in Shanghai were both members of the Standing Committee, while Jiang Qing emphasized the role of the metropolis in the Cultural Revolution.
28. *Ming Pao*, 7 November 1994.
29. *Xinhua*, 28 September 1994, "Plenum Issues Communiqué," FBIS-CHI-94-189, p. 23.

30. *South China Morning Post*, 11 January 1995.
31. *Qiushi*, No. 15 (1994).
32. Luo Bing, Li Zijing, "Yang Shangkun nanxun mudu weixiang" (The Dangerous Phenomena Seen by Yang Shangkun during His Trip to the South), *Cheng Ming*, No. 199 (May 1994), pp. 8–10.
33. Yang made a trip to Shenzhen in the first half of January 1995, *Ming Pao*, 26 January 1995.
34. Conversations in Peking with liberal intellectuals and cadres in 1993–1994.
35. Quoted in *Ming Pao*, 7 March 1994.
36. *Ming Pao*, 16 March 1994.
37. *Ming Pao*, 23 March 1994.
38. Quoted in *South China Morning Post*, 23 March 1994.
39. *South China Morning Post*, 10 March 1994.
40. Quoted in *South Morning China Post*, 12 March 1994.
41. *South China Morning Post,* 16 March 1994.
42. See *South China Morning Post*, 22 March 1994.
43. *Wen Wei Po*, 22 March 1994.
44. Xinhua, 22 March 1994.
45. Zhu Qingfang, "1994–1995 nian renmin shenghuo zhuangkuang" (The Situation of the People's Standard of Living in 1994–1995), in *Shehui lanpi shu: 1994–1995 nian Zhongguo shehui xingshi fenxi yu yuce* (Blue Book on Society: Analysis and Forecast of the Social Situation in China in 1994–1995), (Peking: Zhongguo shehui kexue chubanshe, 1995), p. 196. The question of public order, which is also quite present in people's minds, is raised only by 33.05%. Lu Jianhua, "1994 nian shehui ge jieceng dui shehui xingshi de jiben kanfa" (The Opinions of Various Social Strata toward the Social Situation in 1994), ibid., p. 31.
46. Lu Jianhua, Yang Guodong, Shen Tong, "1994–1995 shehui xingshe: zhuanjia wenjuan diaocha zonghe fenxi" (Social Situation in 1994–1995: Analysis of Views from Experts), in *Shehui lanpi shu* (Note 45), p. 45.
47. Zhu Qingfang (Note 45), p. 195.
48. Lu Jianhua (Note 45), p. 36.
49. Feng Tongqing "1994–1995 nian: Zhongguo zhigong zhuangkuang qi dongxiang" (1994–1995: General Situation of Workers and Employees, and Perspectives), in *Shehui lanpi shu* (Note 45).
50. Ibid. p. 199.
51. Feng Tongqing (Note 50), p. 296. Their average salary was 138 yuan per capita against an average of 270 yuan for the province.
52. Lu Jianhua (Note 45), p. 35.
53. Ibid., p. 35.
54. Feng Tongqing (Note 50), p. 295.
55. Ibid., p. 297.

56. *South China Morning Post*, 30 April 1994.
57. See Lucien Bianco, "Campagnes: le retour des vendettas," *Perspectives chinoises*, No. 24 (July–August 1994), pp. 6–9.
58. Declaration by the Director of the State Land Administration Bureau, Zou Yuchuan in *South China Morning Post*, 21 February 1995.
59. Lu Jianhua (Note 45), p. 37.
60. Ibid., pp. 197–98.
61. Fan Ping, "1994 nian nongmin zhuangkuang" (The General Situation of Farmers in 1994), in *Shehui lanpi shu* (Note 45), p. 312.
62. "Shideng gongmin, laobaixing, xuexi Lei Feng, gan geming," *Cheng Ming*, No. 192 (October 1993), p. 94.
63. Feng Tongqing (Note 50), p. 304.
64. *Ming Pao*, 11 September 1994.
65. See also *Ming Pao*, 11 September 1994.
66. The results of this poll were kept secret. It was conducted by the press bureau of the government through the propaganda departments of most provinces and directly administered cities. *Cheng Ming*, No. 208 (February 1995), pp. 13–14.
67. *South China Morning Post*, 31 October 1994.
68. Feng Jinyuan, Hu An, "1994 nian de zongjiao zhuangkuang" (The Situation of Religion in 1994), in *Shehui lanpi shu* (Note 45), pp. 257–58.
69. Ruan Ming, "Lun dashu zhongyang quanwei" (Emphasizing the Prestige of the Centre), *Cheng Ming*, No. 208 (February 1995), p. 79.
70. *South China Morning Post*, 18 May 1994.
71. See *South China Morning Post*, 21 July 1994 and 18 August 1994.
72. See *South China Morning Post*, 16 February 1995.
73. Ibid.
74. See Jacques de Golfiem, "Changements de cadres provinciaux," *Perspectives chinoises*, No. 24 (July–August 1994), p. 35.
75. Interview with a deputy to the CCPPC of Heilongjiang, February 1995.
76. Chen Hui, "1994–1995 nian Zhongguo zhengzhi xingshi" (The Political Situation in China in 1994–1995), in *Shehui lanpi shu* (Note 45), p. 265.
77. *China Labour Bulletin*, No. 4 (July 1994), p. 5.
78. See *China Labour Bulletin*, No. 3 (1994), p. 10.
79. See the declarations of Chen Qingtai, Vice-minister of the State Economic and Trade Commission published in *Ming Pao*, 29 October 1994.
80. *Ming Pao*, 17 August 1994.
81. Feng Tongqing (Note 50), p. 297.
82. *Renmin ribao*, 6 July 1994. For an analysis of the *Labour Law*, see *China Labour Movement*, No. 6 (August 1994), p. 7.
83. See *Dangdai* (Contemporary), April 1994, pp. 20–21.
84. For the full text of the charter; see *China Labour Bulletin*, No. 2, pp. 14–16.

85. See Jean Philippe Béja, "La nébuleuse démocratique," *Perspectives chinoises*, No. 23 (mai–juin 1994), p. 11.
86. See *La lettre d'information*, Paris, No. 25 (1 January 1995).
87. See Jean Philippe Béja, "Quarante cinq ans et toujours courtisée," *Perspectives chinoises*, No. 24 (juillet/août 1994), p. 5.
88. On this subject see, J. P. Béja, M. Bonnin, A. Peyraube, *Le tremblement de terre de Pékin* (Paris: Gallimard, 1991).
89. *South China Morning Post*, 16 March 1994.
90. Wen Shengtang, "1994 nian fan fubai douzheng xingshi" (The Struggle Against Corruption in 1994), in *Shehui lanpi shu*: (Note 45), pp. 137–38.
91. *Renmin ribao*, 29 October 1994.
92. *South China Morning Post*, 15 February 1995.
93. "Plenum Issues Communique," *Xinhua*, in FBIS-CHI-94, 29 September 1994, p. 23.
94. Chen Hui (Note 76), p. 264.
95. China Central Television News, *Evening News*, 15 February 1995.
96. *South China Morning Post*, 18 and 19 February 1995. *Ming Pao*, 18 and 19 February 1995.
97. Willy Wo-lap Lam, "Party Plans to Keep All News Good News," *South China Morning Post*, 2 February 1994.
98. *Luan she yuanyang meng* (Dreams of Eternal Love in a World of Chaos), (Harbin: Beifang wenyi chubanshe, 1993).
99. *Dangdai*, January 1995, p. 33.
100. See Chan Wai-fong's article in *South China Morning Post*, 26 January 1995, and Yan Zhenzi's in *Dangdai*, January 1995, pp. 32–35.
101. Ibid.
102. On the way the emerging civil society looked for ways to express itself, see Jean Philippe Béja, "Regards sur les salons chinois," *Revue française de sciences politiques*, Vol. 42, No. 1(February 1992), pp. 56–82.
103. Ibid. There are obviously no official sources on such an argument, but the survey by Chan Wai-fong is very thorough and its contents have been confirmed by many interviews conducted in the milieu of Chinese media.
104. In April 1994, all the 24 members of a tourist group were killed during an excursion on the Lake Qiandao, Zhejiang. At first, the PRC declared it was an accident but then, under pressure from Taiwan, had to confess that it was a murder. In September 1994, the Asian Olympic Committee Chairman had invited Lee Teng-hui to Japan to attend the Asian Games which were to take place in Hiroshima in October. The Chinese government protested and threatened to boycott the games if a Taiwanese official went to Japan. But, even though Lee declined the invitation, a Taiwanese Vice-Prime Minister went to Hiroshima, and the Chinese did not boycott the games.

2

The Civil Service System: Policy Formulation and Implementation

Tao-chiu Lam and Hon S. Chan

The Chinese government promulgated the Provisional Regulations on State Civil Servants (hereafter "Provisional Regulations") in August 1993.[1] This was followed by a national conference on the implementation of the new civil service system and the accompanying reform of the wage system in September 1993.[2] Beginning in October 1993, China has formally entered into the phase of transition to a civil service system. The transitional phase will take about three years or a bit longer. Chinese officials suggest that this new framework of personnel management marks a major departure from the established structure of cadre management maintained since the 1950s.

This chapter provides an overview of the civil service system by examining the policy making process and the main issues in the first year of implementation. It is the argument of this chapter that while the effort to establish a civil service represents a novel approach to state personnel management and even to state administration, the substance of the civil service system has changed substantially between what was initially proposed in 1987 and what is being implemented now. These changes should be understood by reference to the politics surrounding the civil service system. The politics of the civil service system has been rooted in the fact that, first, there were continuing differences within the highest echelon of the party over the civil service system, despite the party's 13th Congress having decided in late 1987 to establish a state civil service; second, the structure of power and institutional arrangement after the 13th Congress created barriers for enforcing the policy endorsed by the Congress; and most important of all, the relatively favourable political environment for the civil service system has completely changed in the aftermath of the Tiananmen crackdown.

Both these changes and the basic continuity in China's civil service system are examined in this chapter. The first section looks at the continuity: the emphasis that the concept of cadre is too broad and general, and the need for developing a more differentiated system of personnel management based on the principle of management by categories. Regardless of the political fluctuations in the past decade, this idea has consistently

---

We would like to thank Hsin-chi Kuan for helping us improve an earlier draft of this chapter. Thanks are also due to Keith Forster for editing and comment. City University of Hong Kong's financial support to this project is also gratefully acknowledged.

informed the effort to introduce a civil service system. A related terminological confusion in the existing literature is also noted.

Sections two and three are concerned with the political dynamic and its impact on the substance of the civil service system. Section two details the political processes shaping policy formulation. The main changes are examined schematically in section three by comparing, along several important dimensions, what were proposed (or implied) in the 13th Congress proposal and what later went into the "Provisional Regulations." This comparison helps illustrate the main points of contention in the development of China's civil service system. It also sheds some light on how far the proposed framework has departed from the old system of cadre management, and how this framework differs from the civil service systems in other countries.

The implementation problems are briefly sketched in section four. The implementation strategy and the accompanying problems are first examined, followed by a discussion of how perceptions among the rank and file cadres, and the simultaneous implementation of administrative reorganization, have tended to give rise to the problem of "implementation bias."

I. Civil Service System as a Measure of Reform

The analyses of China's civil service system are filled with a common terminological confusion. Many analysts have labelled the attempt to introduce a civil service system in China "civil service reform."[3] This reflects the failure to maintain a clear conceptual distinction. Scholars of Chinese politics have often used the term civil service to refer to the segment of the polity which is variously called state organs (*guojia jiguan*), administrative organs (*xingzheng jiguan*), or simply administration (*xingzheng*) in China.[4] As a result, reform that affects personnel management in state organizations has been called civil service reform.

For the purpose of studying the problems and the implications of the current reform, the label of civil service reform is misleading. The issue is not merely a matter of terminology, because this label tends to obscure rather than illuminate key aspects of the current reform. It is perhaps no coincidence that analysts from outside China focus either on the implication of the proposed reform for the *nomenklatura* of the Communist Party, or on the extent to which it approximates the Western standard of meritocracy.[5] Much of the literature examines specific rules and practices in various standard personnel areas, such as recruitment, performance appraisal and discipline, etc. Overall, these analyses view the current reform effort primarily as a measure to reform various aspects of personnel management. Most of these analyses, however, fail to attribute sufficient importance to the fact that the current reform effort is not so much a reform of a civil service already in place as it is an attempt to bring a new system into existence. Chinese officials and scholars, not coincidentally, do not call the current reform civil service reform. They have consistently used the expression "implementing and establishing a state civil service system" (*tuixing he jianli guojia gongwuyuan zhidu*).[6] The point, however, is not whether our discussion should conform to the usage within China. What is important is that, we believe, terminology does shape our analytical focus. At present, many important issues in the effort to establish a civil service system have been largely ignored.

To put the matter in proper perspective, we begin with the fact that China has neither had a distinct civil service nor made much effort to set apart a distinct civil service from the extremely large pool of state cadres,[7] both conceptually and in terms of the institutions of management. This is not to say that no distinction at all has ever been drawn among different types of institutions and, to a lesser extent, different types of cadres in China. A long standing and sometimes meaningful distinction has been drawn between state organs, service units (*shiye danwei*) and economic enterprises (*qiye*). However, on the whole, such distinctions have been overshadowed, at the conceptual level, by the concept of cadre; and at the institutional level, first by unifying all important cadre management power in the hands of the party committees and their organization departments, and second by unifying the administration of personnel issues in one single ministry in the State Council. Before the Ministry of Personnel was created in 1988, the Ministry of Labour and Personnel unified personnel management of all three sections. Even after the latter was broken into two separate ministries, i.e., the Ministry of Labour and the Ministry of Personnel, and a division of labour was made between the two, it is still apparent that management of cadres in the State Council is still concentrated in the Ministry of Personnel. Of course, the Ministry of Personnel is dwarfed by the Central Organization Department in important matters of cadre control and management.[8]

What comes with the attempt to establish the civil service system is a novel, and potentially fundamental, approach to reforming China's deeply rooted cadre management system. It is built on the understanding that the very concept of state cadre itself and the accompanying unified system of management are great barriers to better personnel management. As a result, in the first place the concept of cadre should be reconsidered to pave the ground for greater reform.[9] In place of the unified system of management associated with the concept of cadre, it has been proposed that a system of management by categories (*fenlei guanli*) should be developed. "That the concept of the 'state cadre' is too general and lacks a scientific classification" tops the list of defects of the cadre management system identified in Zhao Ziyang's Work Report to the 13th Party Congress.[10] Although many other features originally outlined in this document have been repudiated (see discussion below), the idea of management by categories has consistently remained a guiding force.[11]

In this light, the establishment of the civil service bears as much on the relationship among different components of the polity as it does on various aspects of personnel management. First and foremost, it is concerned with such complicated and politically divisive issues as what should be the scope of the civil service (and by implication, the scope of the state), how distinctive the state civil service should be in relation to other types of cadres, and how such distinctiveness should be maintained. Some of these have been prominent issues in the process of formulating the "Provisional Regulations," and have affected policy design in many significant ways. Many related issues have also become main concerns in the implementation stage. In particular, the issue of the distinctiveness of the state civil service will continue to be a highly contentious issue in the making of China's civil service system, particularly at the local level where the scope of the state civil service will be defined by many forces other than regulations issued by the central government.

II. From the 13th Party Congress to Promulgation: The Politics of Policy Formulation

It should not come as a surprise that policy making for the civil service system has been a highly political process. The concept of a civil service system, particularly when it was conceived in the mid-1980s, cannot be easily reconciled with the established structure of cadre management tightly controlled by the party. It is no wonder, therefore, that the civil service system was part and parcel of a more comprehensive political structure reform programme, which sought to introduce significant changes to party-state relations. The politics of policy formulation with regard to the civil service system has centred on the different understanding of the roles and the jurisdictions of the party in controlling state cadres. Although the 13th Congress's endorsement of the comprehensive reform programme seemed to mark a victory of Deng Xiaoping and Zhao Ziyang, important differences over the role of the party and related issues persisted. According to Susan Shirk, even before the Party Congress, the conservatives were able to gain important concessions from Deng and Zhao, for instance, over the pace of abolishing party core groups in government organs.[12] As typical of policy making in China, the Party Congress also only gave approval to the principles, "with nettlesome details left for future resolution."[13] In addition, the institutional arrangement at the apex of the party-state structure following the 13th Party Congress proved to be barriers for enforcing the reforms already approved. However, on the whole the political climate prior to the pro-democracy movement in May-June 1989 was still quite favourable to political structure reform. This favourable political climate evaporated completely after the suppression of the pro-democracy movement.

Proposing the Political Structure Reform Programme and the Civil Service System

The political structure reform programme was formulated under the direct leadership of Zhao Ziyang. Zhao was the leader of a high-level task force appointed by the Party Central in September 1986 to study the problems of the political system, and to make recommendations for reform to the 13th Party Congress.[14] This high-level group was established after China's paramount leader, Deng Xiaoping, was convinced of the urgency of more comprehensive and radical political structure reform. From mid-1986, Deng urged faster political structure reform on several occasions.[15] In July 1987, the Central Small Study Group (hereafter CSSG) drafted a paper entitled "An Overall Conceptual Scheme on Political Structure Reform" (*zhengzhi tizhi gaige de zhongti shexiang*) which was approved by the 7th plenum of the 12th Central Committee, and later formally endorsed by the 13th Party Congress.[16]

The overall tone of the political structure reform during this period centred on the important yet sensitive question of the relationship between the party and the state. In fact, Deng Xiaoping set the theme of the reform on this all-important issue. He attributed many defects of the political system to the failure to separate the functions of the party from those of the state.[17] This main theme is fully reflected in the recommendations of the CSSG. Separation of the party and the state is not only the first of the seven areas of political structure reform recommended by the group, it is also viewed as a pre-condition for reforms in other areas to succeed.[18]

The civil service system proposed during this period was directly influenced by the decision to make a greater separation of the party and the state.[19] Both the guiding idea and the specific measures proposed by the CSSG concerning the civil service system carried profound implications for the sensitively guarded *nomenklatura system*.[20] The overall conceptual scheme approved by the 7th plenum of the 12th Central Committee explicitly suggests that the proposed Ministry of Personnel should directly manage civil servants up to a certain level.[21] And this document also divided the civil servants into two categories: political affairs and administrative affairs, with the implication that the party shall be responsible for managing the former category while the latter should be given to the Ministry of Personnel. This logic of thinking was also evident in the resolution of the 13th Congress. The Work Report endorsed by the Congress stated that the political affairs civil servants should continue to be managed by party committees, while the administrative affairs civil servants would be managed according to state civil servant regulations.[22] By implication, this meant that some changes to the existing system of vesting all cadre management power in the party committees and organization departments were to be made. Although there were painstaking efforts to distance this proposal from the division of politicians and career bureaucrats, and from the constitutional separation of politics and administration in Western democracies, the underlying rationale behind the civil service system bears considerable resemblance to these constitutional principles. We will return to this point when discussing the differences in the overall objectives to be achieved by the civil service system developed in 1987 and at present.

However, the 7th plenum failed to make specific recommendations about which levels of cadres should be handed to the Ministry of Personnel. Nor did the resolution of the 13th Congress make clear what was suggested by the statement that "the administrative affairs civil servants would be managed according to state civil servant regulation." Much of the details was left to be worked out through considerable bargaining. As we shall see below, this situation allowed the Central Organization

Department and the conservatives within the leadership to hinder the reform effort.

It is pertinent to note that although the Central Organization Department was nominally responsible for making specific recommendations for reforming the cadre and personnel management, its role was overshadowed, from September 1986 to the 13th Congress, by Zhao's CSSG. As a matter of fact, the crucial decision of establishing a civil service system was determined by the CSSG in opposition to the Central Organization Department's suggestion. The specialist research and discussion group led by Cao Zhi, in its first report, did not recommend the introduction of a civil service system.[23] This recommendation was vetoed by Zhao's aides serving the CSSG. Cao Zhi's specialist group was even disbanded temporarily, probably because its recommendations did not accord with the established views of Zhao and his aides. The decision was made first by Zhao's aides, and the specialist group was asked to find justification for it.

Political Manoeuvre and Drafting the Civil Service Regulations

As alluded to above, the Party Congress only endorsed the principles, leaving important details of the civil service system to be worked out later. The post-Congress structure of power and institutional arrangements were crucial to how the principles approved by the Party Congress were enforced. Several developments in these respects both before and after the 13th Congress need to be noted.

Following the forced resignation of Hu Yaobang from the position of general secretary in early 1987, the political tide in China had in fact gradually turned against Deng Xiaoping and his protégé Zhao Ziyang. Although they succeeded in getting the 13th Congress to endorse the programme of political structure reform, their powers had been circumscribed in many ways. Most important of all, despite his intention to continue to hold the premiership, Zhao Ziyang was forced to vacate it for Li Peng and take up the position of general secretary of the party. According to Chen Yizi, Zhao had only nominal power: he neither had power over economic policy making as he used to have when he was premier, nor did he have power over the selection of leaders that theoretically belonged to the party leader. All important personnel decisions, Chen Yizi said, were made by a small group of veteran leaders.[24]

This structure of power had tremendous implication for carrying out the decisions arrived at by the 13th Party Congress. After the CSSG was disbanded, Zhao Ziyang was deprived of an institutional instrument with adequate political authority to push the reform forward. Although Zhao Ziyang attempted to exert some influence over the direction of the 13th Congress programme from the position of general secretary,[25] it appears that he was restricted in many ways. Chen Yizi even suggests that, due to resistance from the conservatives, the programme of political structure reform was basically not implemented at all.[26]

As far as the civil service system was concerned, the locus of power shifted decisively to the State Council under Li Peng. A new Ministry of Personnel was established in March 1988, and it was charged with the responsibility of drafting the civil service regulations. Compared to other measures of the political structure reform which, according to Chen Yizi, were rarely implemented, the civil service system appeared to be an exception. However, such apparent continuity should not be allowed to obscure the important disagreement and conflict within the highest leadership, and the political manoeuvre among Zhao Ziyang, Li Peng and the Ministry of Personnel.

The Ministry of Personnel had a strong interest in the proposed civil service system, and naturally, pushed earnestly for faster implementation. However, Zhao Ziyang and Li Peng's respective positions on the civil service system did not seem to be consistent with their institutional interests. "Where you stand depends on where you sit" does not seem to be applicable here. Although the civil service system endorsed by the 13th Party Congress proposes to give more power to the State Council, Li Peng did not support it in the late 1980s when he became premier. On the other hand, it also appeared to be not in Zhao's organizational interest to hand some power over the control of cadres to the State Council. This apparent paradox has been vividly noted by Shirk:

> ... the declared positions of the CCP general secretary and the government premier were reversed: Zhao Ziyang, who had just been transferred from premier to party general secretary after Hu Yaobang's purge in January 1987, spoke for the principle of delegation from party to government.... From the government side, the newly appointed Premier Li Peng spoke out against the diminution of party authority.[27]

It seems that differences between Zhao Ziyang and Li Peng were mainly ideological, rather than organizational or institutional. This observation should be qualified by the fact that at least after the 13th Congress,

Zhao Ziyang did not seem to control the Central Organization Department, the interest of which would be most affected by the civil service system proposed by the 13th Congress. Song Ping, widely considered a staunch conservative, was made head of the Central Organization Department in May 1987 and was elected a Politburo member later.

Both the substance of the civil service system and the question of how fast it should be introduced were subjects of controversy. Integral to the substance of the civil service system was the issue of whether state cadres at the level of vice-minister or equivalent in the central government should be managed by the newly formed Ministry of Personnel or continued to be managed by the party through the Central Organization Department. According to the logic of the proposal of the 13th Congress, officials at this level fall into the administrative category and, thus, should be managed by the Ministry of Personnel.[28] However, as noted before, no clear resolution on this was reached at the Party Congress. And there was strong resistance to this proposed change, particularly from the Central Organization Department under Song Ping. Despite such resistance, Zhao Ziyang tried to win power in cadre management for the new Ministry of Personnel, but was only partially successful. In the second half of 1988, the management of two batches of officials was transferred from the Central Organization Department to the State Council and the Ministry of Personnel.[29] At the same time, at the National Organizational Work Conference held in June 1988, it was still determined that cadres at the vice-ministerial level should continue to be managed by the Central Organization Department.[30]

The Ministry of Personnel was asked to draft the civil service regulations, and to arrange and administer pilot schemes. However, its effort had been severely affected by Li Peng's opposition to, or lack of interest in, the civil service system. In his Work Report to the first meeting of the 7th National People's Congress (NPC) held in March–April 1988, Li Peng only made a short reference to the civil service system. Despite the strong enthusiasm from the Ministry of Personnel, he decided to postpone further the pilot scheme and veto other ideas suggested by the Ministry of Personnel in a high-level State Council meeting in October 1988. In the Work Report to the second meeting of the 7th NPC held in March 1989, he did not even mention the civil service system, casting widespread doubt on its future.[31]

Because of the lack of support from the State Council, officials in the Ministry of Personnel turned to Zhao Ziyang for support. After the State Council meeting which decided to postpone the work on the civil service system, the Personnel Minister, Zhao Dongwan, "reported" personally to Zhao Ziyang to obtain his support concerning the pace of reform. As testimony to the disagreement between Zhao Ziyang and the State Council, the ministry sent two separate reports on establishing and implementing the civil service system to the State Council in late 1988 and the Standing Committee of the Politburo in early 1989.

Obviously with some support from Zhao Ziyang, the Ministry of Personnel was able to ignore and even resist Li Peng's reservations in the year between its formation in May 1988 and the Tiananmen crackdown. It was not unusual that the position of the Ministry of Personnel differed noticeably from those of Li Peng and the State Council. For example, although Li Peng, against the desire of the Ministry of Personnel, decided in October 1988 that the pilot scheme should be postponed to 1990, the ministry still continued actively to arrange it. Zhao Dongwan reportedly said that while 1988 was a year for paper work, 1989 should be a year for action. Zhao Ziyang personally arranged for the state organs to participate in the pilot scheme because the State Council controlled by Li Peng was least enthusiastic.[32] Not all of these organs picked up by Zhao Ziyang joined the pilot scheme with the same degree of enthusiasm, however. The Ministries of Foreign Relations and Supervision first joined the pilot scheme reluctantly, did not follow through with concrete action, and finally withdrew. The Ministry of Personnel managed to start the pilot scheme on the eve of the political turmoil in May-June 1989, only to find that it was impeded in one way or another because of the lack of determined support from the State Council.

Apart from endeavouring to implement the pilot scheme quickly, the Ministry of Personnel also pushed for the early promulgation of the "Provisional Regulations." In a meeting with personnel department officials from some localities, Zhao Dongwan optimistically indicated that the draft of "Provisional Regulations" would shortly be released publicly to society to seek comments.[33] This was vetoed by Li Peng in October 1988. Li Peng, probably fearing that this would make the civil service a *fait accompli*, instead suggested that the draft should be released only within the party-state bureaucracy. In May 1989, the Ministry of Personnel issued the 16th draft of the "Provisional Regulations" within the personnel system.

In light of the precarious political foundation of the programme of political structure reform in 1988 and early 1989, it is remarkable that the 16th draft of the "Provisional Regulations" was basically in line with the main spirit of the 13th Congress. But the politics of drafting the civil service regulations and arranging the pilot scheme clearly reflects the complexity and difficulty of a reform that carried (and was perceived to carry) important implications for one of the most guarded spheres of the party's power: control of cadres. At the same time, this process also underlines a common feature of policy making: enforcing a decision reached by an authoritative policy making body is by no means simple and easy. Finally, this story suggests that Zhao Ziyang's programme of political structure reform had already encountered tremendous obstacles even before the Tiananmen crackdown.

Stalemate after the Tiananmen Crackdown

With the demise of Zhao Ziyang in June 1989, the most crucial support for the civil service system (and other measures of political structure reform) disappeared. However, probably because of Deng Xiaoping's insistence on preserving the *status quo* and on adhering to the lines of the 13th Party Congress,[34] no authoritative decision has ever been made to terminate the civil service system altogether, therefore giving room for the Ministry of Personnel to manoeuvre. The progress of the pilot scheme, of course, was even more severely affected and frustrated by a total lack of support from the highest leadership. Meanwhile, in light of the decision of the Party Central to tighten party control and officially to give up the objective of separating the party and the state,[35] the Ministry of Personnel's officials also quickly realized that the 16th draft released in May 1989 needed to be substantially revised to reflect the new party line.

The intention to reflect the new party line aside, they found that clear and specific instructions on how to go about the revisions were not forthcoming. The Personnel Minister managed to make a report on the civil service system to the new party general secretary, Jiang Zemin, and Song Ping, who in June 1989 became member of the Standing Committee of the Politburo, and, reportedly, succeeded in gaining their support for the programme. But the minister failed to gain a meeting with Premier Li Peng to discuss the future of the civil service system. This implied that Li Peng did not support it, at least for the moment. Li Peng's support proved to be decisive because, in the division of labour among the Standing Committee members, he seemed to be responsible for personnel and organizational work.[36] What is more important, although Jiang and Song both expressed their support for the programme to continue, no official decision was made by any authoritative policy making body in 1989 and for the entire year 1990. In early 1991, Deputy Personnel Minister Cheng Lianchang was finally able to gain a meeting with State Council Secretary-general Luo Gan and the deputy secretary-general, and Li Peng's personal secretary, Li Shizhong. Although they did not express opposition to the civil service system in principle, they made it clear that the earlier version of the regulations required substantial revision. Luo Gan also refused Cheng Lianchang's request to make a formal report to the State Council after the meeting.

As a result of the lack of a clear and determined position by the leadership (as opposed to individual leaders) on the issue, the term civil service system neither was mentioned at all in central policy papers and official documents, nor did it appear in the mouthpieces of the party such as the New China News Agency or the *People's Daily*. The latter reportedly refused to publish any article about the civil service system. Although the 7th plenum of the 13th Party Committee held in December 1990 called for strengthening the reform of the personnel system, it did not specifically mention the civil service system.

Li Peng's reservations concerning the civil service system was clearly passed on to the supporters of the programme during the national meeting of heads of personnel departments (of provinces and central ministries) in March 1991. At the meeting, Li Peng reportedly made very negative remarks about the work of the Ministry of Personnel on the civil service system,[37] causing the already slowly moving work on the pilot scheme to come to a near grinding halt. Key officials responsible for monitoring the pilot scheme, obviously frustrated, recommended the pilot scheme be suspended to wait for clear central instructions. On the other hand, Li Peng did not entirely reject the civil service system; he only demanded that the civil service system should be aligned with China's national situation, or *guoqing*. What Li Peng meant by China's national situation seemed to refer to the following: the party and the state cannot be separated; there should be circulation of cadres; cadres should be chosen from the rank of the workers and peasants and from those who have practical experience, etc.[38]

It was only in October 1991 that Li Peng openly recognized the legitimacy of the civil service system in a meeting of the Central Organization and Establishment Commission (hereafter COEC), therefore dispelling the atmosphere of ambivalence and uncertainty that had been in existence even before June 1989. It is not clear to us why there was such a sudden change in Li Peng's position. It might be due to the fact that, in light of his scathing criticism at the March meeting, the Ministry of Personnel had revised the earlier draft of the civil service regulations to meet his requirements. It might also be due to the fact that since the decision of introducing a state civil service system went into the report endorsed by the 13th Party Congress, it was difficult to reverse it entirely. Li did acknowledge in the COEC meeting that because the decision was made by the 13th Party Congress, it had to be enforced. On separate occassions, officials of the Personnel Ministry also emphasized this factor. However, before there is further information, these accounts should remain speculative.

Finally, in December 1991 Li Peng agreed to meet the Personnel Minister, Zhao Dongwan, and to listen to his report on the civil service system. This indicated that he had agreed to continue with the civil service system. However, both in this meeting and the COEC meeting earlier, Li Peng gave a number of specific instructions on the civil service system which, as we will show later, had shaped the substance of the civil service system as reflected in the "Provisional Regulations." For the first time since the Tiananmen crackdown, in late 1991, such central mass media as CCTV, *People's Daily* and *Guangming ribao* began to carry reports on the civil service system.

With Li Peng's consent, what remained to be decided were only matters of technicality, pace and timing of the formal promulgation of the "Provisional Regulations." The Work Report to the 14th Party Congress, presented by Jiang Zemin in October 1992, for the first time since early 1988, explicitly gave endorsement to the civil service system in a central official document.[39] However, the substance of the civil service system had changed greatly from what was originally envisioned in Zhao Ziyang's programme of political structure reform. We turn to these changes in the following section.

III. The 13th Party Congress Proposal and the "Provisional Regulations": A Comparison

The "Provisional Regulations" cover practically every area of personnel management, from the basic right and obligation of the civil servants, to performance appraisal and dismissal. It has a total of 18 chapters and 88 articles. Not everything in it is new. In fact, many articles merely codify practices already in existence.[40] A major characteristic of the civil service system is that it seeks to develop a coherent, systematic, and legal framework for personnel management. The "Provisional Regulations" have been issued as an administrative order of the State Council, but it is planned that in a couple of years, it will be passed into law by the National People's Congress. It will be supplemented by a set of subordinate regulations on specific areas of personnel management, some of which have already been released, others will probably be released soon.

Substantial revisions were made in the "Provisional Regulations" to the 13th Party Congress proposals and the 16th draft issued by the Ministry of Personnel for comments in May 1989. These revisions on the whole make the current civil service system completely different from the one conceived earlier. In this section, we compare these two conceptions along with several important dimensions. Table 1 summarizes the main differences in a schematic way.

Table 1. A Schematic Comparison of the 13th Party Congress Proposal and the "Provisional Regulations"

	13th Party Congress proposal	Provisional regulations
Overall objectives	Efficiency, clean administration, stability and policy continuity	Efficiency, clean administration, liveliness and vitality of state organs
Concept of cadre	To be abandoned gradually	Continue to be used
Impact on party-state relationship	Yes but not clear	No
Impact on *nomenklatura* system	Yes but not clear	No
Formal recognition and protection of career security	Yes	No
Scope of recruitment through examination	Both non-leading and leading positions	Only non-leading positions at or below the level of Head of Branch
Transfer from outside the civil service	Subject to examination	Not subject to examination
Boundary between the state civil service and other sectors	To be maintained through control from the civil service	Blurred
Wage system	Grade system	Position and grade system

Objectives

The first dimension concerns the overall objectives to be achieved by the civil service system. Despite continuity in such objectives as enhancing efficiency, and having a lean and clean administration, there are striking differences. The greatest contrast lies in the earlier emphasis on the stability of state administration and policy continuity, and the later shift to the emphasis on the "liveliness and vitality" (*shengji he huoli*) of the state bureaucracy. Although policy continuity was not explicitly set as an objective either in the 13th Party Congress Work Report or the 16th draft, it was in fact one of the guiding principles behind many specific features manifested in the 16th draft. Stability of state administration was more openly embraced, both in the 13th Party Congress Work Report and in the 16th draft.[41] In a significant sense, the arguments raised there are not much different from the justification for bureaucratic competence, career security and political neutrality in Western democratic countries.[42]

The post-Tiananmen leadership, in particular Li Peng, has a very different understanding of the main problems of state administration, and therefore sets different objectives to be achieved by establishing the civil service system.[43] Li Peng decisively twisted the basic thrust of the civil service system when he met the Personnel Minister, Zhao Dongwan, in December 1991. He stressed that China's civil service system should focus on developing a mechanism of elimination (*taotai jizhi*), and a mechanism enabling the new to supersede the old (*xinchen daixie jizhi*).[44] Here Li Peng focused on the problems associated with the "iron rice bowl," the *de facto* existence of lifelong employment, and the need for a mechanism to allow government to kick those unwanted, unsuited or the redundant out of the state bureaucracy. This orientation was probably also influenced by the overall political atmosphere and the needs of the new leadership. If nothing else, the mechanism of elimination fits perfectly well with the needs for housecleaning after the Tiananmen crackdown. As a result, the opening article of the "Provisional Regulations" no longer contains the term stability as it did in the 16th draft. An official responsible for drafting the document has admitted that this reflects an important change in its basic orientation.[45] The mechanism enabling the new to supersede the old has become one of the three main pillars of China's civil service system nowadays, the other two being the mechanism promoting competition and motivation, and the mechanism ensuring good and clean government.[46]

It is interesting to note that Zhao Ziyang and Li Peng each picked different problems of the cadre management system as objects of reform. This might be rooted in the difference in their ideological stances. However, it is worth noting that Zhao Ziyang and his aides viewed the reform of the cadre management system largely as a constitutional concern, while to Li Peng the reform was just a technical matter. "[P]olicy makers do not face a given problem," states Charles Lindblom. Instead, different people often derive different problems from the same phenomenon.[47] What is examined here surely supports this argument.

Career Security

These different views of the problems to be solved by the civil service system have shaped many aspects of personnel management. Most directly affected by the change of objectives is the issue of career security. In the 13th Congress proposal, it is clearly stated that administrative affairs civil servants are to have permanent tenure in office.[48] It is not hard to see why a permanent tenure system is needed for promoting such objectives as administrative stability and policy continuity. Providing career security was also viewed as instrumental in helping craft a relatively autonomous realm of administration. This line of thinking has been severely criticized in the aftermath of the Tiananmen crackdown. The so-called mechanism of elimination means that the government should be given the flexibility to expel people from the civil service. Our interviewees suggested that this was one of Li Peng's major concerns in his meeting with Zhao Dongwan in December 1991 when he gave specific instructions to the Ministry of Personnel on drafting the "Provisional Regulations." Li Peng even explicitly rejected the system of permanent tenure and proposed a "contract system" (*pingren zhi*). In response to Li Peng's instructions, in 1992, officials from the Ministry of Personnel began to stress "keeping the exit unimpeded."[49]

It is important to note that the "Provisional Regulations" do not entirely follow Li Peng's views. Article 45 on the "Contract System" of Chapter 9 of the "Provisional Regulations" reads, "An appointment system shall apply to state civil servants, but some positions shall come under a contract system."[50] While at face value an "appointment system" is not equivalent to permanent tenure, it comes close to it, especially when it is placed alongside the "contract system."[51] This is because in Chinese usage nowadays only in a "contract system" is a fixed period of employment clearly set out. In this context, the main real difference between an "appointment system" and a "contract system" seems to be that the former does not set a fixed period of employment while the latter does. However, even with the continuing prevalence of the "appointment system,"[52] compared with the 16th draft, on the whole the "Provisional Regulations" make it easier for the government to punish and even expel officials from the civil service. Unlike the 16th draft where articles on reward and punishment form a chapter, articles on punishment in the "Provisional Regulations" have formed a separate chapter and have become more elaborate, indicating that punishment has been given heavier weight.

Implications for Existing Political Institutions and Rules

Another major difference concerns the implications of the proposed civil service system for existing political institutions and rules. As shown earlier, the 13th Party Congress proposal carried considerable implications for the party-state relationship, the established *nomenklatura* system, as well as the very concept of cadre itself. These three aspects are closely related. The concept of cadre is central to the existing *nomenklatura* system because the whole structure of the latter is built on it. If the concept is scraped, the *nomenklatura* system has to be reconstructed accordingly. Similarly, the *nomenklatura* system is a core element in the question of the party-state relationship. Although before and after the 13th Party Congress, there were heated controversies about how far the reform should touch on these areas, our analysis shows that in the earlier version, the civil service system did affect them in certain significant ways. For example, it was proposed that the importance of the concept of cadre should gradually diminish as the system of management of categories is fully developed. The Ministry of Personnel was to share some of the power of the Central Organization Department, which literally meant some degree of separation of the party and the state. Although the extent of actual impact seemed to have been quite limited because of obstacles to reform in 1988 and the first half of 1989, the 16th draft released on the eve of the eruption of the pro-democratic movement did not depart much from the spirit of the 13th Party Congress.

In contrast, the present framework has minimal impact on these three fronts. There is no longer any suggestion that the concept of cadre shall vanish, although, as emphasized in section one, the principle of management by categories is still maintained. The main theme in the post-Tiananmen political scene has been that the party and the state cannot, and should not, be separated. In recent years, China has not even bothered to pay lip service to the nominal separation of the party from the state, as reflected, for example, in the phenomenon of more and more officials holding party and government positions concurrently. The *nomenklatura* system will be preserved (see discussion below on the scope of recruitment for illustration). In this direction, the Central Organization Department issued a revised *nomenklatura* in May 1990 to take back some of the power delegated to the State Council in 1988. The same document also recentralized some of the power decentralized to the provincial-level party committees in 1984.[53]

Scope of Recruitment, and the Distinctiveness of the State Civil Service

If we are to find one persistent theme running through the development from the mid-1980s to the present, this is recruitment through competitive examination. No obvious disagreement seems to exist on the importance of open competition and examination. Although Li Peng refused to support the civil service system in 1988 and 1989, he was very enthusiastic about recruitment through examination.[54] Therefore, in early 1989, the Ministry of Personnel and the Central Organization Department were allowed to issue a formal notice requiring state administrative organs to use examinations to recruit employees.[55] Open recruitment examinations have widely been held at both central and local levels since then.

Nonetheless, careful analysis reveals that, even on this quesiton, there is also an important difference between the earlier draft and the "Provisional Regulations." This is related to the scope to which recruitment examination is to apply. In the 16th draft, both junior and senior civil servants, and both leading and non-leading positions, fall within the scope of recruitment. This means that all those who enter the civil service from outside are considered new recruits, and therefore should be subject to some forms of recruitment examination. Accordingly, the 16th draft and its subsidiary rules on recruitment and examination provide three types of examination; one for those applying for junior and non-leading positions, one for those possessing recognized professional qualification, and one for those assuming leading positions from outside the civil service.

The scope of recruitment is reduced and limited to the non-leading positions below the level of branch head (*kezhang*) in the "Provisional Regulations." The greatest change is that those entering the civil service from outside no longer fall into the category of recruitment, and are not subject to any form of control from the civil service. These people now fall into the category of "transfer" (*diaoren*), which is now considered a form of circulation (*jiaoliu*). "Transfer" refers to circulation of personnel between the civil service and other institutions, such as party organs, service units and enterprises, while other forms of circulation, such as change of positions at the same level (*zhuanren*), or rotation (*lunhuan*), are circulation within the civil service.[56] This change seems to be a deliberate measure to minimize the impact of the civil service system on the existing *nomenklatura* system, because the new provision rules out any control other than the *nomenklatura* system over lateral entry into the civil service. This also means that the Ministry of Personnel has lost its position in instituting some control over the transfer of personnel from outside the civil service. The issue of transfer was raised in the ministry in as early as 1988. Unrestricted transfer was then rejected in favour for some control over lateral entry due to the insistence of the Personnel Minister, Zhao Dongwan.

The restriction of the scope of recruitment, therefore, will make the civil service less distinctive than it was initially intended to be. Movement of personnel among different types of institutions regulated by the unitary *nomenklatura* system will blur the boundary between the civil service and those institutions. This will also reduce their differences and uniqueness as well. As a corollary to this, contrary to the early proposal that the party organs, mass organizations and social associations should develop different systems of personnel management, now these organizations will adopt the same framework designed for state administrative organs. In September 1993, the Party Central issued a notice requiring party organs to implement a system of personnel management modelled on the "Provisional Regulations."[57] Even the Song Qingling Foundation has adopted a personnel system modelled on the "Provisional Regulations."[58]

Wage System

The final important difference is in the area of the wage system. On this issue, the 16th draft and the "Provisional Regulations" have manifested aspects of both continuity and change. Points of continuity include: (1) a regular mechanism of wage increases for civil servants; (2) increasing the range of wages for junior civil servants; and (3) raising the overall wage level for civil servants (and employees in service units) to keep up with recent increases in income in economic enterprises and the non-state sector.

Although a regular mechanism of wage increases seems a common phenomenon in every rational personnel system, such a mechanism has never been institutionalized in China. A regular mechanism means two things: first, it refers to rules governing the upward movement of employees on the salary scale apart from promotion; second, it refers to regular adjustment of the entire salary scale according to a price index. Both of these were lacking in China's old wage system, although the principle of regular increase in wage increment was laid down long ago in 1956 and was reiterated in 1985.[59]

Many defects and tensions in China's wage system can be traced to the absence of a regular mechanism of wage increases. For example, because there has been no regular way for the wage system to adjust to inflation in the past decade or so, state organs have been forced to resort to improvisation and *ad hoc* methods to cope with inflation. This has resulted in the situation wherein an increasingly large proportion of the actual benefits received by employees comes from such items as bonuses and subsidies of various sorts. This not only has had an adverse effect on the systematic and proper management of remuneration, but has also discouraged state agencies from properly performing their functions. In order to help their employees cope with inflation, many state agencies have been forced to resort to "creative revenue earning" (*chuangshou*) activities, many of which, indirectly or even directly, impede them in properly performing their functions.

Another problem of the old wage system was that the range of salaries for junior level cadres was too narrow, making promotion the only way to obtain a wage increase. This has put tremendous pressure on the expansion of the number of leading positions in the bureaucracy. It has also led to widespread frustration on the part of many junior cadres because of the problem of a "wage plateau." "Wage plateau" means that one's salary reaches the top of the corresponding scale early in one's career because the range is too small. Third, it is generally felt that the income of employees in state administrative organs has declined compared with the income of those employed in economic enterprises and the non-state sector. An increase of the overall wage levels is deemed necessary to make a career in the state civil service attractive.

Both the 16th draft and the "Provisional Regulations" address these three issues, but in different ways. The wage system proposed by the 16th draft is called a "grade system" (*zhideng gongzizhi*), while the new wage system is called a "position and grade wage system (*zhiwu jibie gongzizhi*)."[60] The "grade system" moved further from the old wage system which was based almost entirely on administrative positions (Table 2). Under the grade system, an administrative position itself does not carry a salary, only the grade to which it corresponds does. Each administrative position corresponds to a number of grades. For example, it was proposed that a division head fall into grades 11 to 13 in a scale of 18 grades. Each grade will be further broken into 6 to 12 sub-grades. Under this system, a salary increase (besides promotion) can be achieved in one of the following three ways: (1) moving to a higher grade that corresponds to a given position; (2) moving upward a sub-grade within a given grade; and (3) adjusting the wage level according to the price index.[61] The salary of civil servants will come in four parts: grade salary, seniority salary, basic salary and bonus. Because reform of the wage system was still in an exploratory stage in early 1989, there was no detailed plan on the structure of grades and the overall level of salary increases.

The present "position and grade system" differs from the previous proposal in that now both position and grade carry a salary (Tables 3 and 4). In late 1991, Premier Li Peng gave specific instructions to Personnel Ministry officials to adopt this new system, which is modelled on the wage system used in the military.[62] A comparison of Table 2 and Table 3 suggests that this new wage system and the wage system adopted in 1985 both contain the element of position salary. Moreover, instead of creating sub-grades within each grade, under the new system the sub-grades are attached to administrative positions. Therefore, as shown in Table 3, while there will be only one level of salary for each grade (ranging from 55 yuan for grade 15 to 470 yuan for grade 1), each administrative position has 3 to 8 salary points (for example, the premier has 3 points, and junior officers have 8). On the whole, these changes attempt to limit the impact of the new system on the established cadre structure. They help preserve the importance of administrative positions.

Chinese leaders are likely to find that the new wage system will not help much in achieving their expressed objective — using it to alleviate the pressure on the expansion of leading positions in the bureaucracy. Under the new system, because remuneration is still linked directly to administrative positions, the pressure is unlikely to disappear easily. More importantly, a great deal of the benefits a higher position carries has little to do with salary.

Table 2. Basic and Position Salary Standard Table of Administrative Employees in Central and Provincial State Organs (1985)

(Unit: yuan)

Position	Basic salary	Position salary standard						Total of basic and position salary					
		1	2	3	4	5	6	1	2	3	4	5	6
State President/Vice President Premier	40	490	410	340				530	450	380			
Vice Premier/State Councillor	40	340	300	270				380	340	310			
Minister/Provisional Governor	40	270	240	215	190	165		310	280	255	230	205	
Vice Minister/Vice Provisional Governor	40	215	190	165	150	140		255	230	205	190	180	
Director of Department/Bureau (si/ju/ting zhang)	40	165	150	140	130	120		205	190	180	170	160	
Vice Director of Department/Bureau (fu si/ju/ting zhang)	40	140	130	120	110	100		180	170	160	150	140	
Head of Division (chuzhang)	40	130	120	110	100	91	82	170	160	150	140	131	122
Vice Head of Division (fu chuzhang)	40	110	100	91	82	73	65	150	140	131	122	113	105
Head of Branch (ke zhang)	40	91	82	73	65	57	49	131	122	113	105	97	89
Officer at the rank of Head of Branch (zhuren keyuan)													
Vice Head of Branch (fu kezhang)	40	73	65	57	49	42	36	113	105	97	89	82	76
Officer at the rank of Vice Head of Branch (fu zhuren keyuan)													
Officer (keyuan)	40	57	49	42	36	30	24	97	89	82	76	70	64
Junior Officer (banshiyuan)	40	42	36	30	24	18	12	82	76	70	64	58	52

Source: "Zhonggong zhongyang guowuyuan guanyu guojia jiguan he shiqi danwei gongzuo renyuan gongzi zhidu gaige wenti de tongzhi" reprinted in *Renshi gongzuo wenjian xuanbian* (Selection of Documents on Personnel Works), Vol. 8 (Zhongguo renshi chubanshe, 1986), p. 367.

Table 3. Salary Standard Table of Position and Grade Salary System (zhiwu jibie gongzizhi gongzi biaozhun biao)

(Unit: yuan/month)

Position	Position salary 1	2	3	4	5	6	7	8		Grade salary Grade	Salary standard	Basic salary	Seniority salary
Premier	480	555	630							1	470	90	
Vice Premier/State Councillor	400	460	520	580						2	425	90	
Minister/Provincial Governor	330	380	430	480	530					3	382	90	
Vice Minister Vice Provincial Governor	270	315	360	405	450					4	340	90	
										5	298	90	
										6	263	90	
Director of Department/Bureau	215	255	295	335	375	415				7	228	90	
Vice Director of Department/Bureau	175	210	245	280	315	350				8	193	90	
										9	164	90	
Head of Division/County Head	144	174	204	234	264	294				10	135	90	One yuan for each year of service
Vice Head of Division/Vice County Head	118	143	168	193	218	243				11	111	90	
Head of Branch Officer at the rank of Head of Branch	96	116	136	156	176	192	216			12	92	90	
Vice Head of Branch Officer at the rank of Vice Head of Branch	79	94	109	124	139	154	169			13	77	90	
Officer	63	75	87	99	111	123	135	147		14	65	90	
Junior Officer	50	60	70	80	90	100	110	120		15	55	90	

Source: Department of Wage, Security and Welfare, Ministry of Personnel (ed.), *Yijiujiusan nian jiguan shiye danwei gongzi zhidu gaige gongzuo shouce* (1993 Manual of Reform of the Wage System of State Organs and Service Units), p. 70.

Table 4. Table of the Relationship between Grade and Position

Grade	Position
1	Premier
2	Vice Premier
3	State Councillor; Minister / Provincial Governor
4	Minister / Provincial Governor; Vice Minister
5	Vice Minister; Vice Provincial Governor; Director of Department/Bureau
6	Director of Department/Bureau; Vice Director of Department/Bureau
7	Vice Director of Department/Bureau; Head of Division / County Head
8	Head of Division / County Head; Vice Head of Division / Vice County Head
9	Vice Head of Division / Vice County Head; Head of Branch / Officer at the rank of Head of Branch
10	Head of Branch / Officer at the rank of Head of Branch; Vice Head of Branch / Officer at the rank of Vice Head of Branch
11	Vice Head of Branch / Officer at the rank of Vice Head of Branch; Officer
12	Officer; Junior Officer
13	Junior Officer
14	Junior Officer
15	Junior Officer

Source: Department of Wage, Security and Welfare, Ministry of Personnel (ed.), *Yijiujiusan nian jiguan shiye danwei gongzi zhidu gaige gongzuo shouce*, p. 71.

Nevertheless, the new wage system is a more rational system of personnel management than the wage system adopted in 1985 was. There are four components in the salary: position salary, grade salary, seniority salary and basic salary. As shown in Tables 3 and 4, the range of salary for junior civil servants has been expanded to address the problem of "wage plateau." Because the overwhelming majority of civil servants in China are below the level of branch head, this measure will benefit officials at the lower levels. Now the maximum grade salary for a junior officer (*banshiyuan*) is equal to the lowest grade salary of a county head or a division head (*chuzhang*). This means that even without promotion, the salary of these officials will increase as their seniority grows.

Unlike the 1985 wage system reform, where wage increases were only laid down as a principle, the procedures for wage increase are now clearly spelt out. The mechanism for wage increase does not differ from the 1989 proposal described above, except that salary points are now linked to administrative positions. The first type of regular wage increase is through an increment of position salary given to officials every two years upon passing a performance appraisal. Secondly, for officials below the rank of vice-minister or equivalent, an increment in grade will be given to officials every three years (those scoring superior [*youxiu*] for three consecutive years in performance appraisal) or every five years (those passing performance appraisal). Of course, this does not apply to those who have already reached the top grade for a particular position. For officials at or above vice-minister level, an increment of grade is given every five years. Adjustment of overall wage level will be made every two years.

Apart from creating a new wage system with a focus on developing a regular mechanism for wage increase, another noteworthy aspect of the current wage system reform is the adjustment of the entire wage level. As the last large-scale wage system reform was taken almost a decade ago, many developments have accumulated to strain the system. The complication of the current wage reform stems from the fact that this is not a regular adjustment of the overall wage level, but an attempt to redress the problems accumulated over the past years. The issue, of course, centres on the question of the extent of salary increase, not for particular grades but for the civil service as a whole. At the heart of the question on the extent of wage increase are two issues: (1) the impact on state finances; (2) the extent to which the wage system can institutionalize the various subsidies and bonuses that have grown out of control in the old wage system.

The financial situation of both the central and local governments is possibly the biggest constraining factor in dealing fully with the problem of low wages for civil servants. It was suggested that this across-the-board wage increase for civil servants and employees in service units will cost the government more than 20 billion yuan a year.[63] This is quite a financial burden to both the central government and some local governments, although we do not know exactly how the amount is to be apportioned between the central and the local governments, except that the revenue is alloted according to the existing fiscal arrangement. Some poor localities obviously have difficulty in paying their employees according to the new scale. As a result, these localities are allowed to implement the new system step by step.[64] The financial situation of the governments at various levels is also likely to be an important factor in constraining the periodical adjustment of the wage scale in the future. Although it is now affirmed that the wage scale will be adjusted every two years, there is also a statement allowing the state to freeze the adjustment in special circumstances.[65]

Second, whether this wage increase is able to fully incorporate the various subsidies and bonuses into the wage should remain in doubt. Institutionalizing and regularizing such subsidies and bonuses are deemed necessary because they have made management and control difficult on the one hand, and have induced state organs to undertake undesirable "creative revenue earning" activities on the other (because not all of these subsidies and bonuses were paid by state revenue). However, these elements have become so important in the total remuneration that the wage increase in 1993 can only partially offset them. While some were removed, other forms of subsidies will continue to exist.[66] Over the long run, it remains to be seen if the wage adjustment can effectively keep up with the more than 20% inflation per year to prevent these subsidies and bonuses from emerging and running out of control again.

IV. Implementation Strategy and Issues

Students of Chinese politics have been keenly aware of the fact that policy outcome depends as much on how policy is implemented as it does on policy formulation.[67] Since it is still too early to comment on implementation, the discussion in this section should remain fragmentary and speculative.

Overall Strategy of Implementation

In September 1993, the Party Central and the State Council convened a national meeting to announce the implementation of the civil service system and wage system reform. The State Council issued an "Implementation Plan" in December 1993, which specified in greater detail such problems as implementation procedures and key issues only vaguely defined in the "Provisional Regulations." This plan bears on several issues. First, it tries to define in greater detail the scope of the civil service, i.e., where the civil service should and could be introduced. Appendix 1 to the plan lists the categories of the State Council organs falling into the scope of the civil service. Second, implementation is divided into three stages, namely, creation of positions on the basis of the result of administrative reorganization; filling the positions according to the requirements of these positions; and implementing the rules concerning recruitment, promotion and demotion, circulation, avoidance, retirement, etc., provided by the "Provisional Regulation." Third, the provisions of the "Provisional Regulations" are divided into two types: those which should be introduced immediately, and those (such as the contract system, setting the maximum age limit for positions at different levels, dismissal, removal and area avoidance) that immediate implementation is not required. Fourth, it sets some principles and measures governing the transition from the present framework to the civil service system (including filling positions and determining the grades and salary of individual members). Finally, the rules governing the creation of non-leading positions are set in great detail in Appendix 2.

Several observations can be made about these implementation arrangements. First, Appendix 1 only attempts to set the scope of the civil service at the central level, leaving the scope of the state civil service at local levels to be determined by provincial-level governments. Although the Ministry of Personnel still exercises final control in this regard by requiring local implementation plans to gain its consent, it is most likely to be the case that at the local level, the scope will be set differently according to the needs and interests of provincial governments (see discussion below). Moreover, Appendix I also allows considerable discretion. For example, it states that whether the service units directly under the State Council should fall into the scope of the civil service should be decided in due course according to the functions they perform.

The second feature is that the implementation of the civil service system at the local level is left to be decided by provincial governments. Although the national conference convened in September 1993 and the "Implementation Plan" demanded that the local governments should give priority to this task, whether it occurs, however, is an imponderable.

A third feature which will affect the implementation of the civil service system is that there are practically no rules governing how the present employees become state civil servants.[68] Conflicting principles are held simultaneously. On the one hand, it is required that a high standard should be maintained; on the other, it is suggested that the transition should not affect stability. Together with these conflicting principles, it is also stated that those becoming civil servants should go through appropriate legal procedures, the meaning of which, however, are not clearly defined. At a national conference on wage system reform, many participants demanded that clear guidelines and specific requirements about transition should be provided. In response to this demand, Vice Personnel Minister, Cheng Lianchang, insisted that different departments and localities should develop their own methods of transition according to their specific conditions.[69] Although Cheng Lianchang later suggested that transition might be based on the result of performance appraisal over the past two years, or on the result of a comprehensive evaluation,[70] the conditions concerning transition remain perhaps too "flexible."

Implementation in 1994

Although the Ministry of Personnel has urged a faster implementation of the civil service system, some supplementary regulations governing specific aspects have not been released. Only several such supplementary regulations were issued in 1994. These included the document governing position classification (released in January), the regulations on performance appraisal (released in March) and the regulations on recruitment (released in June).[71] Other regulations still remain on the drafting desks of the Ministry of Personnel. This situation has created a serious problem for the civil service system, because the "Provisional Regulations" only contain the abstract outlines. As an interim measure, Cheng Lianchang suggests that before the supplementary regulations are released, state agencies should follow rules which had already existed before the promulgation of the "Provisional Regulations."[72]

Partially as a result of a lack of interest and misunderstanding among the rank and file cadres, and partially as a result of the requirement for the civil service system to proceed according to the pace of administrative reorganization, implementation in 1994 has not made significant progress. At a national conference on the implementation of a civil service system held in August and September 1994, it was revealed that 40 out of the 58 organs designated to implement the civil service system under the State Council, and 21 provincial-level governments had drafted their plans for implementation. Only a few ministries were said to have almost completed the transition to the civil service system.[73] These included the Ministries of Civil Affairs and Construction. At the provincial level, Shaanxi, Jilin and Anhui seem to have moved the fastest. Shaanxi has been able to move faster because it was selected as early as January 1993 to be a site for the pilot scheme of administrative reorganization.[74] In April 1994, it was indicated that the transition of the Shaanxi provincial government to the civil service system would finish before the end of June 1994.[75] Anhui's implementation was announced by the provincial government in July 1994, and it became the first provincial implementation plan which was issued by the Ministry of Personnel throughout the country. This is probably because Anhui had set a faster schedule for implementing the civil service system in the province. According to the provincial schedule, implementation at the provincial and prefectural levels will start in the second half of 1994, and work at the county level will begin in the first half of 1995. By the end of 1995, the civil service system will basically be in place in the whole province.[76]

The implementation at the local level has not followed a single pattern. Some localities implement the system from the top down, i.e., first in the provincial government and later at prefectural and county levels.[77] Anhui appears to be a prime example of this pattern. Other localities have first implemented it at the lower levels where administrative reorganization has been completed. Shandong and Jilin seem to have followed this pattern.[78] Still some other localities, such as Hubei, have only experimented with a civil service system in selected localities.[79]

The most important development concerning the implementation of various above mentioned aspects of the civil service system in 1994 was the recruitment examination held in Beijing in September 1994. A total of 26 state agencies at the central level planned to recruit more than 400 junior civil servants (below the rank of branch head) through the examination. As the first such recruitment examination held since the promulgation of the "Provisional Regulations," this examination attracted widespread attention and publicity.[80] However, the practice of recruiting state officials through open examination is by no means a new thing in China. It has been in existence since 1982, though in a less institutionalized fashion, and more than 7 million officials have reportedly been recruited through various forms of examinations.[81] Since 1989 when the Central Organization Department and the Ministry of Personnel issued the regulations concerning the use of examinations to recruit officials in state agencies,[82] the Ministry of Personnel has organized 5 joint recruitment examinations for a total of 32 central state agencies.[83]

According to officials of the Ministry of Personnel, two features distinguish the September 1994 examination from previous recruitment examinations. First, it is the first recruitment examination which has explicitly used the term civil servant. Second, it is more formalized and is organized strictly according to the June 1994 regulations concerning recruitment. Whether these features really make a difference remains a question for further research. It is particularly noteworthy that most of these 400 plus positions were open only to Beijing candidates. Only two agencies (the Ministry of Railway and the State Marine Bureau) were open, to a limited extent, to candidates from outside Beijing. The reason for restricting the candidacy to Beijing is not hard to understand. Under China's present system of household registration, nationwide mobility, particularly for junior positions, is heavily constrained.[84] Although in theory the new recruitment code issued in June 1994 should come into force immediately, it seems that no open recruitment examination applying the new code has been held at the provincial level in 1994.

Implementation According to the Progress of Administrative Reorganization, and Implementation Bias

The *raison d'être* for requiring the implementation of the civil service system to follow the progress of administrative reorganization is that the latter will provide a sound basis for the former. Because the state bureaucracy is bloated and, more importantly, the development of economic structural reform has called for changing the role and functions of government, many features of the civil service system cannot be implemented without firstly addressing the problem through a reorganization exercise. For example, it is only after the main functions of an organ have been clearly defined that such tasks as job analysis and creation of positions can be performed. Another function of administrative reorganization is that, by deciding in advance such matters as the total establishment and the ratio of leading positions to total establishment of an organization, it tries to forestall runaway bureaucratic expansion commonly associated with the implementation of new policy initiatives. In this way, implementation of the civil service system should be carried out within the overall parameters set by administrative reorganization.

Although Chinese leaders have demanded that administrative reorganization and the civil service system be closely coordinated, these are in fact two separate exercises. Institutionally speaking, administrative reorganization has been supervised by the COEC and, in particular, its General Office (*zhongyang bianban*), while the civil service system is under the jurisdiction of the Ministry of Personnel. Although *zhongyang bianban* used to be "hooked to" the Ministry of Personnel, it has gradually moved away from it. Since last year, *zhongyang bianban* has formally been given an independent ministerial status and its organization has greatly expanded. Two departments responsible for organization and establishment originally instituted within the Ministry of Personnel were transferred permanently to *zhongyang bianban* in early 1994. Although the Personnel Minister, Song Defu, and Vice Minister, Zhang Zhijian, continue to be its director and vice director, it is evident from the development in the past two years that the work of *zhongyang bianban* and those of the Ministry of Personnel are increasingly separated.[85] As testimony to this, "The Main Tasks of Personnel Work for 1994" published by the Ministry of Personnel in January 1994 does not cover much about administrative reorganization.[86]

Requiring the implementation of a civil service system to follow administrative reorganization, and the institutional separation of the management of civil service system and administrative reorganization, however, have resulted in the neglect of the civil service system. Compared to administrative reorganization and wage system reform, the implementation of the civil service system gives rise to two problems. First, its objectives are not clearly set and cannot be fully operationalized. As indicated, many procedures remain poorly defined. The second problem is that the civil service system does not affect the interests of the implementors as directly and obviously as administrative reorganization and wage system reform do. The result is a common implementation problem in China: selective implementation or implementation bias. This concept, developed by Barry Naughton in his analysis of the implementation of central decisions concerning investment control, refers to situations when implementors selectively implement the policies favouring their interests.[87] Jilin's executive vice-governor, Liu Xilin, states this problem clearly when he speaks about civil service system implementation in his province:

> Especially because this reform [civil service system] comes out simultaneously with administrative reorganization and wage system reform, people normally care more about the latter. What they care about are such matters as which organs will be cut, who will be streamlined and how much wages will be increased. At the same time, they normally do not pay adequate attention to implementing the civil service system.[88]

Interim reviews of the implementation of the civil service system in the first year also reveal that "there is a problem of understanding." Some people have equated that system with wage system reform. They think that once they receive increased wages according to the new scale, that is all the civil service system is about. Another widely held view is that becoming a civil servant is nothing more than a new title, although Chinese leaders stress that this is an important measure of political structure reform.[89] To many central ministries and localities, the implementation of the civil service system is seen mainly as an opportunity to create more higher level positions or to fill the positions that are still vacant. This is because the transition to the new system necessarily entails such tasks as the creation of positions, determining the grades of individual officials, and deciding who is to fill what positions. Among others, the question of creating non-leading positions has received most attention from the rank and file cadres, because it gives state agencies opportunities (largely not available in the past) to create more high-level positions.[90] Because many people anticipate that control will become more stringent as the relevant rules of the civil service system are implemented, or the positions will be filled, they consider now the last opportunity to get promotion or move to a higher grade. Xu Songtao aptly describes this as the attempt to catch the last train (*gan mobanche*).[91]

These problems were fully reflected in Song Defu's August 1994 discussion of the problems in implementing the civil service system. He called for more propaganda to correct the misunderstandings identified above. The civil service system, he argued, should be implemented in a timely manner or else it would miss the right opportunity. He also emphasized that those measures contingent upon restructuring should be implemented immediately after restructuring was completed, implying that, in reality, many localities did not implement the civil service system enthusiastically. Song Defu also reiterated the persistent theme that most measures of the civil service system were not contingent upon administrative reorganization, urging state agencies to implement them as quickly as possible. In an attempt to change the not-very-enthusiastic attitude toward the civil service system, the Ministry of Personnel issued a brief speech by Premier Li Peng to reiterate the virtues of the civil service system in late 1994. However, Li Peng seemed not very enthusiastic about the implementation of the civil service system, as reflected in the following statement from the Premier's speech:

> It is very important that the implementation of the civil service system should be coordinated with administrative reorganization. Now some places [or departments] have implemented the civil service system and have also carried out wage system reform, but *have not yet carried out administrative reorganization. We should speed up the pace of administrative reorganization* (italic added).[92]

One cannot help but have the impression that Li Peng does not give as much importance to the civil service system as he does to administrative reorganization. This perhaps reflects the position of the leadership as well. In the 14th congress report, Jiang Zemin also went to considerable lengths in elaborating the importance of administrative reorganization, but only gave one short sentence to the civil service system.[93]

V. Concluding Remarks

Without rejecting wholesale the many improvements embodied in the "Provisional Regulations," this chapter has discussed the limitations of the civil service system by reviewing its origin and the process through which it has evolved. Although Chinese leaders still emphasize that the civil service system is a measure of political structure reform, this has taken on a very different meaning. While the uncertainty clouding the civil service system has already gone, the civil service system has perhaps lost the most opportune moment. Some of the problems in implementation can perhaps be traced back to the evolution of the civil service system from a relatively radical reform to a very modest one. Now, rank and file officials all over China tend to think that the civil service system contains nothing new and is just old wine in a new bottle.

At the same time, the civil service system is competing with administrative reorganization for scarce leadership attention. Li Peng's speech cited above suggests that the current leadership gives priority to administrative reorganization over the implementation of the civil service system. Although the civil service system and administrative reorganization are in many ways complementary to each other, in the implementation game, the zero-sum nature of elite attention means that there is considerable conflict between these two measures. The institutional separation between the management of administrative reorganization and that of implementation of the civil service system, i.e., between COEC and the Ministry of Personnel, makes it likely that administrative reorganization receives more leadership attention. At the same time, because the objectives of the civil service system can only be vaguely defined, and also because the civil service system is not directly and immediately related to the interests of the rank and file officials, strong leadership support is essential for successful implementation. At present, whether this is available is doubtful.

Notes

1. *Zhonghua renmin gongheguo guowuyuan gongbao* (Communiqué of the State Council of the PRC), No. 18 (2 September 1993), pp. 837–49.
2. *Renmin ribao* (People's Daily) (Beijing) (hereafter *RMRB*), 11 September 1993, p. 1; 22 September 1993, p. 1. The conference was officially convened in the name of the Party Central and the State Council to give the implementation efforts greater legitimacy and authority.
3. King K. Tsao, "Civil Service Reform," in *China Review 1993*, edited by Joseph Cheng Yu-shek and Maurice Brosseau (Hong Kong: Chinese University Press, 1993); John Burns, "Civil Service Reform in Contemporary China," in *China: Modernization in the 1980s*, edited by Joseph Y. S. Cheng (Hong Kong: Chinese University Press, 1989); John Burns, "Chinese Civil Service Reform: The 13th Party Congress Proposals," *The China Quarterly*, No. 120 (December 1989), pp. 738–70; Jean-Pierre Cabestan, "Civil Service Reform in China: the Draft 'Provisional Order Concerning Civil Servants'," *International Review of Administrative Science*, Vol. 58 (1992), pp. 421–36; Jean-Pierre Cabestan, *China News Analysis*, No. 1383 (15 April 1989), No. 1437 (15 June 1991); Anthony Cheung, "Civil Service Reform in the People's Republic of China: New Concepts and Old Limitations," revised paper presented at the conference on "Reform and Policy Implementation in China," The Hong Kong Institute of Asia Pacific Studies, The Chinese University of Hong Kong, 9–11 September 1991. See also United Nations,

Reforming Civil Service Systems for Development, TCD/SEM. 85/7-INT-85-R61, New York, 1985. Exceptions are, King Chow, "Reform of the Chinese Cadre System: Pitfalls, Issues and Implications of the Proposed Civil Service System," *International Review of Administrative Science*, Vol. 57 (1991), pp. 25–44; Hong Yung Lee, *From Revolutionary Cadres to Party Technocrats* (Berkeley and Los Angeles: University of California Press, 1991), pp. 374–84.

4. Harry Harding, *China's Second Revolution* (Washington, DC: The Brooking Institution, 1987), pp. 209–11; John Burns, "The Chinese Civil Service System," in *The Hong Kong Civil Service and Its Future*, edited by Ian Scott and John Burns (Hong Kong: Oxford University Press, 1988), pp. 205–206.

5. On the first theme, see John Burns (Note 3); Hong Yung Lee (Note 3); King Chow measures China's civil service system along the specific rules designed to ensure meritocracy in the federal government of the USA, see Chow (Note 3).

6. See, for examples, Zhao Ziyang, "Advance Along the Road of Socialism with Chinese Characteristics," *Beijing Review* (Beijing), Vol. 30, No. 45 (9–15 November 1987), pp. xviii-xix; "Editorial," *RMRB*, 22 September 1993, p. 1.

7. For a brief discussion of the term cadre, see A. Doak Barnett, *Cadres, Bureaucracy, and Political Power in Communist China* (New York: Columbia University Press, 1967), pp. 38–41.

8. Melanie Manion, "The Cadre Management System, Post-Mao: the Appointment, Promotion, Transfer and Removal of Party and State Leaders," *The China Quarterly*, No. 102 (June 1985), pp. 203–33; John Burns, "China's Nomenklatura System," *Problems of Communism*, September/October 1987, pp. 36–51; John Burns, "Strengthening Central CCP Control of Leadership Selection: the 1990 Nomenklatura," *The China Quarterly*, No. 138 (June 1994), pp. 458–91.

9. We use the term "reconsider" here because, as discussed below, views about whether this concept should continue to be used have changed.

10. Zhao Ziyang (Note 6), p. xviii.

11. See Tao-chiu Lam and Hon S. Chan, "Designing China's Civil Service System: General Principles and Realities," forthcoming in *International Journal of Public Administration*. In his speech to the national conference to start the implementation of the civil service system and the reform of the wage system in September 1993, Song Defu, the new Personnel Minister, continued to stress the importance of developing different personnel management systems for different types of institutions. See Song Defu's speech to the conference, reprinted in *Yijiujiusan nian jiguan, shiye danwei gongzi zhidu gaige gongzuo shouce* (1993 Manual of Reform of the Wage System of State Organs and Service Units) (hereafter *1993 Manual of Reform*), edited by Department of

Wage, Security and Welfare, the Ministry of Personnel (Beijing: Renmin chubanshe, 1994), pp. 15–30.

12. Susan Shirk, *The Political Logic of Economic Reform in China* (Berkeley and Los Angeles: University of California Press, 1993), pp. 65–66.

13. David Lampton, "A Plum for a Peach: Bargaining, Interest, and Bureaucratic Politics in China," in *Bureaucracy, Politics, and Decision-Making in Post-Mao China*, edited by Kenneth Lieberthal and David Lampton (Berkeley and Los Angeles: University of California Press, 1992), p. 56.

14. The group was called *Zhongyang zhengzhi tizhi gaige yantao xiaozu* (Central Small Study Group on Political Structure Reform). Other members of the group were Hu Qili, Tian Jiyun, Bo Yibo and Peng Chong, representing the Central Secretariat, the State Council, the Central Advisory Committee and the Standing Committee of the NPC respectively. Zhao's personal secretary, Bao Tong, headed the General Office, which supported the group. See Chen Yizi, *Zhongguo: shinian gaige yu bajiu minyun* (China: Ten Years' of Reform and 89 Democratic Movement) (Taipei: Lianjing, 1990), pp. 106–107; Chen Ruisheng, Pang Yuanzheng and Zhu Manliang (eds.), *Zhongguo gaige quanshu: zhengzhi tizhi gaige juan* (Encyclopedia of China's Reform: Political Structure Reform Volume), (Dalian: Dalian chubanshe, 1992), p. 32.

15. Deng Xiaoping, *Jianshe you Zhongguo tese de shehui zhuyi, zengding ben* (Building Socialism with Chinese Characteristics, Expanded Edition), (Hong Kong: Sanlian shudian, 1987), pp. 119, 121–33.

16. Chen Yizi (Note 14), p. 112; Chen Ruisheng, Pang Yuanzheng and Zhu Manliang (eds.) (Note 14), p. 32.

17. Deng Xiaoping (Note 15), pp. 121–23, 126 and 133.

18. For a description of the seven areas of reform, see Zhao Ziyang (Note 6), pp. xv–xxiv.

19. Dai Guangqian, "Proposing a Reform of the Cadre and Personnel System and the State," *Chinese Law and Government*, Vol. 23, No. 4 (Winter 1990–1991), pp. 61–73. This is an English translation of a speech originally given in June 1988. Dai was a member of the specialist small group on cadre and personnel system under Zhao Ziyang's task force and, before early 1994, the Director of the Department of Examination and Recruitment, Ministry of Personnel. He managed an office directly responsible for the design and implementation of the pilot scheme in the Ministry of Personnel. Since early 1994, he has become the director of the Department of Mobility and Deployment of the Ministry of Personnel.

20. There is no consensus on the political impact of the proposed civil service system. John Burns and Jean-Pierre Cabestan do not think that the proposed civil service system would significantly affect the *nomenklatura* system. See John Burns and Jean-Pierre Cabestan, "Editors' Introduction," *Chinese Law and Government*, Vol. 23, No. 4 (Winter 1990–1991), p. 6.

21. Interviews with officials from the Ministry of Personnel, Beijing, November 1994. Unless otherwise specified, analysis below is based on these interviews and therefore will not be further supported by reference to these interviews. We were also shown an excerpt of the "Overall Conceptual Scheme" relevant to the reform of the cadre and personnel management. See also Hu Zhenmin, "Guojia gongwuyuan de guanli tizhi" (The Management System of State Civil Service), in *Guojia gongwuyuan zhidu jianghua* (Lectures on State Civil Service System), edited by Liu Junlin and Dai Guangqian (Beijing: Nengyuan chubanshe, 1987), pp. 303–28.
22. Zhao Ziyang (Note 6), p. xviii. For a discussion of the number of officials falling into these two categories, see John Burns (Note 3).
23. Cao was deputy head of the Central Organization Department from 1984 to 1987. See Chen Yizi (Note 14), p. 108.
24. Chen Yizi (Note 14), p. 124.
25. Zhao established a Central Research Office for Political Structure Reform and appointed his personal secretary, Bao Tong, to be its head. A National Association for the Study of Political Structure Reform was also established in October 1987. Two key participants in the design of the reform programme headed the association. Zhou Jie, deputy director of the General Office of Central Committee (*zhongyang bangongting*) and head of one of the specialist small groups under the high level task force, became chairman. Chen Yizi was the deputy chairman. See Chen Yizi (Note 14), pp. 108, 113.
26. Ibid., p. 124.
27. Susan Shirk (Note 12), pp. 66–67.
28. Chen Yizi (Note 14), p. 119; Dai Guangqian (Note 19); Hu Zhenmin (Note 21); "Guojia gongwuyuan zhanxing tiaoli (di shiliu gao)" (Provisional Regulations on State Civil Servants [the 16th draft]) (May 1989), reprinted in *Guojia gongwuyuan zhanxing tiaoli (caoan) zhushi shuoming* (Explanatory Notes to Provisional Regulations on State Civil Servants [draft]), edited by Xu Songtao (Beijing: Zhongguo renshi chubanshe, 1989), pp. 209–23.
29. See *Renshi gongzuo wenjian xuanbian* (Selection of Documents on Personnel Work), Vol. 11 (1989), (hereafter *Selection of Documents*), (Beijing: Zhongguo renshi chubanshe), pp. 3–5, 6–9; *Zhongguo renshi nianjian, 1988–1989* (Chinese Personnel Yearbook, 1988–1989), (Beijing: Zhongguo renshi chubanshe, 1990), pp. 137–40; Chen Yizi (Note 14), p. 119.
30. Hu Zhenmin (Note 21), p. 326.
31. Interview with officials from the State Environment Protection Bureau, one of the organs selected to participate in the pilot scheme of implementing civil service system, Beijing, November 1994.
32. Interviews with officials from the State Environment Protection Bureau, the State Auditing Administration and the Ministry of Personnel, Beijing, November 1994.

33. *Zhongguo laodong renshi bao* (China Labour and Personnel Post) (Beijing), 2 August 1988, p. 1.
34. Deng Xiaoping, *Deng Xiaoping wenxuan* (Selected Works of Deng Xiaoping), Vol. 3 (Beijing: Renmin chubanshe, 1993), pp. 296–308, 324–27.
35. "Zhonggong zhongyang guanyu jiaqiang dangde jianshe de tongzhi" (Party Central Notice on Strengthening Party Construction), *Zhongfa*, No. 9 (28 August 1989), reprinted in *Selection of Documents* (Note 29), Vol. 12 (1990), pp. 12–23.
36. After State Councillor Li Guixian stepped down from the position of president of the People's Bank of China, Li Peng has passed some of the portfolio to him. However, Li Peng continues to be the head of the increasingly important Central Committee on Organization and Establishment, a post he has concurrently held since the organ was formed in early 1988. In the newest round of party and state organizational restructuring, the organ was elevated to become one of the 12 policy deliberation bodies (*yishixing jigou*) in the Party Central. Among these policy deliberation bodies are such influential bodies as the Central Leading Group on Economics and Finance, the Central Leading Group on Foreign Affairs etc. See "Guanyu dangzheng jigou gaige de fangan" (A Plan of Party and State Organizational Restructuring) (passed by the 2nd plenum of the 14th CC in March 1993), reprinted in *Jigou gaige, gongwuyuan zhidu he gongzi zhidu shiyong wenjian xuanbian* (Selection of Practical Documents on Organization Restructuring, Civil Service System and Wage System Reform), *Zhongguo renshi zengkan* (Supplement to China Personnel) (hereafter *Supplement to China Personnel*) (Beijing: Zhongguo renshi chubanshe, 1993), p. 4.
37. Interview with a scholar from Beijing University who visited Hong Kong in September 1993.
38. Xu Songtao, "Jiji wentuo de jianli shihe Zhongguo guoqing de gongwuyuan zhidu" (Actively and Cautiously Establishing a Civil Service System Aligned with China's National Situation), in *Guojia gongwuyuan zhidu shidian gongzuo yantao wenji* (Research and Discussion Articles on the Pilot Scheme of State Civil Service System) (Beijing: China Senior Civil Servants Training Centre, September 1991), p. 15.
39. Jiang Zemin's report was reprinted in *Wen Wei Po* (Hong Kong), 13 October 1992, pp. 19–20.
40. Burns and Cabestan (Note 20), p. 6.
41. See Zhao Ziyang (Note 6), p. xix where it is stated that "The implementation of the new system governing public servants will make it easier for the party to reinforce and improve leadership over personnel work, facilitate the growth of outstanding cadres in both categories who possess political integrity and professional competence, and help to improve the efficiency of government work and the stability of state administration." Article 1, Chapter 1, 16th

draft. See also the elaboration in Xu Songtao (ed.) (Note 28), pp. 9–12; Chen Yizi (Note 14), pp. 115–16.

42. Hugh Heclo, *A Government of Strangers: Executive Politics in Washington*, (Washington, DC: The Brookings Institution, 1977), pp. 19–21.

43. Therefore, this case resembles the "garbage can" view of policy making, which posits policy making as solutions looking for problems and means looking for ends. See Michael Cohen, James March, and Johan Olsen, "A Garbage Can Model of Organizational Choice," *Administrative Science Quarterly*, Vol. 17, No. 1 (March 1972), pp. 1–25. March and Olsen applies the model to analyze administrative reorganizations in the United States in "Organizing Political Life: What Administrative Reorganization Tells Us about Government," *American Political Science Review*, Vol. 77, No. 1 (March 1983), pp. 281–96.

44. See Xu Songtao, "Guojia gongwuyuan zhidu de xingcheng he fazhan" (The Formation and Development of State Civil Service System), in *Guojia gongwuyuan zhidu peixun jiangyi* (Lecture Notes for State Civil Service System Training), (Beijing: China Senior Civil Servants Training Centre, 1992), pp. 62–63. Li Peng's view on the importance of this has remained consistent. When he met local representatives participating in a conference on the implementation of the civil service system in September 1994, Li reiterated the same line of thinking, stressing that the civil service should develop a mechanism for enabling the new to supersede the old. Li's speech is reprinted in *Renshi zhengce fagui zhuankan* (Special Journal for Personnel Policy and Regulation) (hereafter *Special Journal*), No. 10 (1994), pp. 13–14.

45. Xu Songtao (Note 44), pp. 62–63.

46. See Luo Gan, Song Defu and Cheng Lianchang's speech in the conference kicking off the implementation of the state civil service system in September 1993, reprinted in *1993 Manual of Reform* (Note 11), pp. 3–30, pp. 48–60.

47. Charles Lindblom, *The Policy-making Process* (Second Edition), (Eaglehood Cliffs, NJ: Prentice-Hall, 1980), p. 24.

48. Zhao Ziyang (Note 6), p. xviii; Chen Yizi (Note 14), pp. 115–16; Xu Songtao (ed.) (Note 28), pp. 16–17.

49. Xu Songtao (Note 44), pp. 62–63.

50. Note that the corresponding chapter (Chapter 8) in the 16 draft contains nothing like this.

51. On discussion of these concepts, see Xu Songtao (ed.), *Guojia gongwuyuan zhidu chuanshu* (Encyclopedia of State Civil Service System) (Changchun: Jilin wenshi chubanshe, 1994), p. 1127.

52. The implementation of the "contract system" has been postponed until the "conditions are ripe." See Song Defu's speech in the September 1993 conference, reprinted in *1993 Reform of Manual* (Note 11), p. 19.

53. "Zhongyang zuzhibu guanyu 'zhonggong zhongyang guanlide ganbu zhiwu

mingcheng biao' de tongzhi" (Central Organization Department's Notice on Revising "The List of Position Managed by CPC Central") [10 May 1990], *Selection of Documents*, Vol. 13 (1991), pp. 35–53. See also John Burns, "Strengthening Central CCP Control of Leadership Selection: the 1990 nomenklatura," *The China Quarterly*, No. 138 (June 1994), pp. 458–91. On the 1984 decentralization, see John Burns (Note 8).

54. Interview with a well-connected scholar from Beijing in Hong Kong, February 1994 and with officials from the Ministry of Personnel, Beijing, November 1994.
55. "Guanyu guojia xingzheng jiguan buchong gongzuo renyuan shixing kaoshi banfa de tongzhi" (Notice on Using Examinations to Recruit Employees in State Administrative Organs) (9 January 1989), *Selection of Documents*, Vol. 12 (1989), pp. 40–42.
56. Chapter 11, "Provisional Regulations."
57. The text of the document appeared in *Special Journal*, No. 1 (1994), pp. 8–10.
58. *Special Journal*, No. 8 (1994), pp. 14–16.
59. Kang Yao, "Guojia gongwuyuan gongzi zhidu de jiben gouxiang" (The Basic Idea on the Wage System of State Civil Servants), in *Zhongguo gongwuyuan zhidu gousi* (The Conception of China's Civil Service System), (Beijing: China Senior Civil Service Training Centre, August 1989), p. 115.
60. Article 52, Chapter 11, 16th draft; Article 63, Chapter 13, "Provisional Regulations."
61. This discussion is based on Kang Yao (Note 59), pp. 111–29.
62. Kang Yao, "Guojia gongwuyuan gongzi zhidu" (Wage System of the State Civil Service System), in *Guojia gongwuyuan zhidu peixun jiangyi* (Note 44), p. 180.
63. Zhang Zhijian's speech at the September 1993 conference, reprinted in *1993 Manual of Reform* (Note 11), p. 42.
64. "Jiguan gongzuo renyuan gongzi zhidu gaige shishi banfa" (Implementation Method of the Wage System Reform for State Administrative Organ Employees), reprinted in *1993 Manual of Reform* (Note 11), p. 85.
65. *1993 Manual of Reform* (Note 11), p. 66.
66. Of all the subsidies and bonuses at the central level, only 64 yuan are offset by the salary increase. For a list of the subsidies and the like falling into the scope of 64 yuan and those falling outside, see the document issued by the State Council's Administrative Management Bureau, the Minister of Personnel and the Ministry of Finance in February 1994, reprinted in *Jiguan, qiye, shiye danwei xianxing gongzi zhengce ji jieda* (Wage Policy for State Organs, Enterprises and Service Units, and Answers), edited by Benshu bianjizu (Groups of Editors), (Beijing: Jingji guanli chubanshe, 1994), pp. 174–75.
67. David Lampton (ed.), *Policy Implementation in Post-Mao China* (Berkeley

and Los Angeles: University of California Press, 1987); Kenneth Lieberthal and David Lampton (eds.), *Bureaucracy, Politics, and Decision-making in Post-Mao China* (Note 13).
68. Note, however, that methods for determining grades and salary scales are meticulously set out. Please refer to Tables 2, 3 and 4.
69. Cheng Lianchang's speech at the conference, reprinted in *1993 Manual of Reform* (Note 11), pp. 52–53.
70. Cheng's speech at a conference held in December 1993, reprinted in *Special Journal*, No. 4 (1994), p. 26.
71. *Special Journal*, No. 8 (1994), pp. 17–20 (recruitment); No. 6 (1994), pp. 22–24 (performance appraisal); No. 4 (1994), pp. 14–16 (position classification).
72. Cheng Lianchang's speech at the conference, reprinted in *1993 Manual of Reform* (Note 11), p. 54.
73. *Zhongguo renshi* (China Personnel), No. 10 (1994), p. 4; *RMRB*, 16 August 1994, p. 3.
74. *Zhongguo renshi*, No. 1 (1994), p. 44.
75. *Zhongguo rencaibao* (China Talent Post) (Beijing), 24 April 1994, p. 1.
76. *Zhongguo rencaibao*, 17 July 1994, p. 1.
77. Xu Songtao, "Dui shishi gongwuyuan zhiduzhong jige wenti de renshi" (My Understanding of Several Problems in the Implementation of Civil Service System), *Zhongguo renshi*, No. 8 (1994), pp. 4–6.
78. *RMRB*, 21 August 1994, p. 3; 23 August 1994, p. 3; Xu Songtao (Note 77).
79. Xu Songtao (Note 77).
80. *RMRB*, 31 July 1993, p. 1; *Fazhi ribao* (Legal System Daily) (Beijing), 31 July 1994, p. 1; *Jingji ribao* (Economic Daily) (Beijing), 31 July 1994, p. 1; *Wen Hui Bao* (Shanghai), 31 July 1994, p. 1; *Jingji ribao*, 10 August 1994 (Special Issue), p. 1 and p. 3; *Gongren ribao* (Workers' Daily) (Beijing), 14 August 1994, p. 3.
81. *Jingji ribao*, 14 June 1994, p. 1; *Zhongguo rencaibao*, 19 June 1994, p. 1.
82. *Selection of Documents* (Note 29), Vol. 12 (1989), pp. 40–42.
83. *Zhonghua gongshang shibao* [zhoumoban] (Chinese Industrial and Commercial News [Weekend Edition]) (Beijing), No. 682 (27 August 1994), p. 1.
84. *Guojia gongwuyuan bao* (State Civil Servants Post) (Chengdu), 21 July 1994, p. 2.
85. Interview; see also Cheng Lianchang's speech at a conference held in December 1993, reprinted in *Special Journal*, No. 4 (1994), pp. 30–31.
86. Reprinted in *Special Journal*, No. 2 and 3 (1994), pp. 42–49.
87. Barry Naughton, "The Decline of Central Control over Investment in Post-Mao China," in *Policy Implementation in Post-Mao China* (Note 67).
88. Liu Xilin, "Gaige, bushi zai yizhang baizishang zuohua" (Reform: It Is Not

Drawing on a Piece of White Paper), *Zhongguo renshi*, No. 10 (1994), p. 11.
89. Li Peng's speech to the September 1993 conference, reprinted in *Supplement to China Personnel* (Note 36), pp. 131–32; Li Guixian's speech to a conference held in August 1994, summarized in *Zhongguo renshi*, No. 10 (1994), pp. 5–6.
90. Although non-leading positions at branch head and division head levels had existed in the past, it had not been formally legitimated.
91. Xu Songtao (Note 77).
92. *Special Journal*, No. 10 (1994), pp. 12–14.
93. *Wen Wei Po*, 13 October 1992, pp. 19–20.

3

Central-Provincial Relations

Jae Ho Chung

As many of the key reforms of the post-Mao era have generally been directed toward decentralization (*fangquan rangli*), the topic of central-local government relations has recently been given particularly close attention both in and outside China. Consequently, a large number of studies have been produced to revive some old debates and generate new ones. The core of these debates concerns state capacity of China, which is argued by many to have steadily declined over the years to produce a wide range of local perversities.[1] On the basis of such pervasive local anomalies, a multitude of perspectives have been proposed in an effort to understand the evolving relations between Beijing and the localities. Many point to the possibility of China being split up, although they differ significantly on the format and nature of such a division. Some argue that China has already been transformed into several "duke economies" (*zhuhou jingji*) which are not so easily susceptible to central intervention. Others suggest that China may well be on its way to national disintegration along the political and territorial dimensions. Still others take a more cautious approach by proposing that economic regionalism needs to be distinguished from political independence and that state capacity needs to be differentiated from the centre's capability to control local governments.[2]

Whichever perspective we might adopt, however, it would nevertheless point to a relatively similar assessment that, compared to the pre-reform period, the overall balance of power has relatively tilted toward localities. The key question is whether the central government has actually become so weak as to facilitate a situation where even political and territorial disintegration is a serious possibility. There is no doubt that the centre has long been tolerant of various local perversities due mainly to its vital concern with the hoped-for gains of the reform as a whole.[3] And the power of Beijing has indeed been reduced by a series of extensive decentralization. Yet, the question remains as to whether the prevalence of corruption, the breakdown of social order, and the relative fiscal decline of the centre — the three most commonly cited anomalies — constitute sufficient indicators of the central-local balance of power in China. Comparatively speaking, for instance, an increase of crime and social disorder at the street level in the United States would not necessarily render the federal government weak relative to its state and local counterparts.

One key problem with many state-capacity arguments originates from the superfluous use of fiscal measures as the sole indicator of central-provincial dynamics. By using fiscal measures expressed mostly in percentage terms, we are bound to adopt such clear-cut designations as winner and loser in describing central-local relations. Such a dichotomous conceptualization seems erroneous, or highly debatable at the least, since formal arrangements and transactions — i.e., fiscal and budgetary allocations and transfers — do not tell everything about the delicate balance between central control and provincial autonomy. Therefore, it is important to bear in mind that fiscal decentralization should not be construed as necessarily and automatically weakening the overall capacity of the centre. Furthermore, central-local relations are very often positive-sum games (probably more so during a period of rapid economic expansion) and their respective payoffs may vary greatly over different policy issues concerned.[4]

Any review of central-provincial relations in China is thus a very complex task not only because it overarches at least two different levels of government (and analysis) but because it is also concerned with a variety of policy issues. While the predominant majority of studies on China's central-provincial relations focus exclusively on their fiscal dimension (mostly on budgetary arrangement, and fewer on plan formation, investment decisions, grant distribution, project location, material allocation and subsidy provision), there is an increasingly acute need for us to adopt a more comprehensive perspective on the central-provincial dynamics that are themselves being highly diversified over time. Such a comprehensive perspective enables us to explore a multitude of key dimensions in which Beijing and the provinces most frequently interact.[5]

This chapter provides an overall review of central-provincial relations in the following eight dimensions. First, a set of quantitative and qualitative indicators are presented to illustrate certain trends toward the reduced power and influence of the central government, particularly in the economic sphere. The second section is devoted to the reform of tax-sharing system (*fenshuizhi*) adopted in January 1994 as a key case study of Beijing's renewed efforts to stem local economic autonomy. The third section provides discussions of the centre's evolving capacity to control information and statistics on local performance. The fourth concerns an organizational dimension, particularly the decision to cancel the "central economic cities" (*jihua danlie*) status for provincial capitals. The fifth discusses the changes introduced in the foreign economic relations sector and their impact upon central-local dynamics. The sixth explores key personnel changes that occurred in 1994, especially those of Jiangsu, Heilongjiang, Shanghai, and Shandong. The seventh section evaluates the possibility of an emerging relationship between the People's Liberation Army (PLA) and local governments. The eighth examines Beijing's dilemma derived largely from regional inequalities between rich and poor provinces, as well as increasingly strengthened horizontal ties among localities. The chapter will be concluded by shedding some light on the "imminent-crisis" thesis that presupposes a disintegrated China in the foreseeable future.

Central-Local Relations under Reform: Some Economic Indicators

One of the most significant changes that post-Mao reforms introduced to weaken the overall power of the centre is the significantly reduced role of central planning. Much of the centre's planning function was operationally decentralized to utilize provincial planning initiatives, and most of central planning instructions also became "guidance targets" rather than "compulsory targets."[6] Table 1 provides key indicators for the reduced role of central planning in four key policy arenas of agricultural production, industrial production, material allocation, and export control. As the table indicates, by 1985 the central government had already delegated a bulk of its planning authority to local governments. And by 1993, compared to the earlier years, central planning was limited to an extremely small portion: (1) zero compulsory planning in agricultural production (though some recentralizing measures were adopted in 1994); (2) less than one-fourth of the total number of products and about 7% of the gross value of industrial output; (3) less than 5% of the number of products formerly allocated by the centre; and (4) a mere 2% of the export items formerly under central control.

In addition to planning, four other arenas witnessed a gradual decline of central power *vis-à-vis* localities. First of all, enormous autonomy was granted to provincial-level governments in endorsing investment projects without obtaining Beijing's approval.[7] Second, with regard to price control, as of 1993 only 10% of agricultural products, 15% of industrial products and 30% of producer's goods were subject to strict government regulation.[8] In foreign trade, too, local initiatives and incentives were radically promoted as the number of foreign trade corporations increased from a centrally controlled dozen in 1979 to over 5,000 in 1990, and local governments were allowed to retain their foreign exchange earnings.[9]

Unlike the economic issue areas discussed above, the impact of post-Mao decentralization on non-economic areas is much more difficult to

Table 1. Reduced Role of Central Planning, 1979–1993

	Agricultural production	Industrial production	Material allocation	Export control
Pre-1979	27	—	256	—
1980	—	120+	—	900+
1981	20*	—	—	—
1982	13*	—	—	—
1985	0	60+	20+	31
1990	0	—	19	—
1991	0 (15)	—	—	—
1992	0 (9)	59	19	27
1993	0 (7)	36	12	19

Note: Figures refer to the number of products or items under the State Planning Commission's compulsory planning; figures in parentheses refer to the number of products or items under guidance planning.

Sources: * Terry Sicular, "Agricultural Planning and Pricing in the Post-Mao Period," *The China Quarterly*, No. 116 (December 1988), p. 677. Other figures are from State Planning Commission, "Wo guo zhongyang yu difang jingji guanli quanxian yanjiu" (Study of Boundaries of Economic Management between China's Central and Local Governments), *Jingji yanjiu cankao* (Reference Materials for Economic Research), No. 434/435 (1 March 1994), pp. 19, 21, 22.

assess not only because post-Mao reforms have been largely economic in nature, but because there are no readily available quantitative indicators with which to gauge their effect on political and administrative issue areas. We do have some scattered pieces of evidence as to the kind and magnitude of change in a few important non-economic arenas, especially concerning the expanded provincial autonomy in local legislation and personnel management. On the other hand, we have also witnessed how swiftly provinces complied with Beijing's political preferences in the immediate aftermath of the Tiananmen Incident in 1989.[10] It is thus extremely difficult to come up with a single balance sheet on the relative power of the central and local governments in China without considering the nature of various policy issues involved. We can, however, draw a sketch of central-local balance of power in a multitude of issue areas where central preferences and local priorities interact very often.

The Fiscal Dimension: The Implementation of the Tax-Sharing System[11]

In November 1993, a crucial decision was made at the Third Plenum of the

Fourteenth Party Central Committee to give an unprecedented boost to the centre's fiscal capacity. The importance of the decision lies in that the previous "system of fiscal contract" (*caizheng baoganzhi*) was to be abolished and replaced by the "system of tax sharing." And this significant change was ratified as a budgetary law (*yusuanfa*) at the second plenary session of the Eighth National People's Congress (NPC) held in March 1994. In a sense, the centre has finally drawn a last card to retrieve its long-lost fiscal control over the provinces, although its concrete implementation remains to be seen.

Background

Central-provincial budgetary arrangements in the post-Mao period have been extremely complex not only in their diversities among different provinces but also in their frequent changes over time. Such complexities may have been a manifestation of the experimental spirit of the central government in carrying out the fiscal reform. On the other hand, however, they may also have represented a series of efforts to redress the problems of the centre's loss of control over inter-governmental fiscal flows. On two crucial occasions, the centre failed to induce provincial compliance in implementing the much publicized transition from the overall-revenue sharing scheme (*zong'e fencheng*) to the specific-revenue sharing scheme (*fenlei fencheng*), first in 1980 and again in 1985.[12]

In 1988, there was another change designed to institutionalize the "fiscal contract system" which further expanded provincial autonomy in fiscal management. Under this arrangement, all the revenues raised within the province except for the taxes from the centrally owned enterprises and tariffs went to the provincial coffers, and a fixed sum negotiated by central and provincial governments was delivered to the centre or subsidized to the provincial governments in deficit. Since the transfer was fixed not by the ratio but by the amount, provinces had enormous incentives to raise more revenues, which would then be reinvested and retained within the region. Under this system, 16 budget-deficit provinces (including 8 ethnic minority and border provinces) received fixed central subsidies regardless of possible improvement in their fiscal positions. The annual rate of increase in the centre's subsidies for minority provinces was cut down to 5%, however. Second, the fixed-sum transfer arrangement was made with three fiscal-surplus provinces of Shandong, Heilongjiang and Shanghai. Third, Hebei, Liaoning, Beijing, Jiangsu, Zhejiang and Henan were to increase their contracted baseline figures at a rate ranging from 3.6 to 6.5% per annum while enjoying a 100% marginal retention rate. Fourth, Anhui, Tianjin and Shanxi would continue to implement the system of overall-revenue sharing. Fifth, Guangdong and Hunan would progressively increase its remittances according to the stipulated yearly rate of 9 and 7%, respectively.[13]

In 1990 the seventh plenum of the Thirteenth Central Committee pronounced a decision to leave the dominant fiscal contract system unchanged during the entire period of the Eighth Five-Year Plan (1991–1995). Despite such a decision to maintain the *status quo*, some experiments were already underway in the direction of strengthening the centre's fiscal capacity. In 1992, experiments of central-provincial tax-sharing were conducted in four province-level units of Liaoning, Tianjin, Xinjiang and Zhejiang as well as in five "central economic cities" (*jihua danlie shi*, hereafter CECs) of Wuhan, Qingdao, Dalian, Shenyang and Chongqing.[14] These experiments constituted an important prelude to the tax-sharing reform to come in 1994. Before we explore what this reform has proposed to change, it is necessary to understand some key consequences of the post-Mao fiscal reform, which were apparently perceived so grave that even the official promise made at the Seventh Plenum had to be reversed.

Propellants of *fenshuizhi*

As provinces have become very adept in taking advantage of the new central-local relationship characterized by negotiation and bargaining, the reform that had begun as an effective measure of reviving local incentives and promoting local initiatives instead produced a situation where it has become increasingly difficult for the centre to control the provinces. For instance, the share of total state revenues in gross national product (GNP) consistently dropped from 31.2% in 1978 to 16.2% in 1993, thus clearly indicating the tendency toward the reduced state power in revenue control. More importantly, Beijing successively failed to increase the centre's share of budgetary revenues, which went down from 57% in 1981 to 33% in 1993.[15]

There are various reasons why such a situation occurred. One important reason concerns the rapid increase in the size of extra-budgetary funds (EBFs) and "extra-establishment funds" (EEFs). EBFs are the revenues that fall outside the purview of the state budget and are collected by local governments according to set rules. EBFs increased eleven times from RMB 34.7 billion in 1978 to 385 billion in 1992, while the total budgetary revenues only tripled in the same period. EBFs as a percentage of budgetary revenues also grew from 31 in 1978 to 98 in 1992. As of 1992, the shares of EBFs of the central and local governments were 44 and 56%, respectively. EEFs are the revenues that are collected locally but not in accordance with rules agreed to between the central and local authorities. It is believed that by 1991, the sum of EBFs and EEFs accounted for almost three quarters of all revenue incomes collected by the entire government sector.[16]

Another important reason for the relative decline in state revenues as well as central revenues lies in the problem of tax evasion which has become increasingly pervasive in recent years. Local governments very often arbitrarily granted the privilege of "reduced taxes and tax exemption" (*jianmianshui*) to the enterprises under their jurisdiction. Many enterprises that were really locally funded often took on a false identity of foreign-invested firms in order to obtain favourable tax treatment. Furthermore, many foreign and domestic enterprises occasionally got involved in producing "artificial losses" by raising their costs to create losses and thus to reduce their tax liability. According to a report by the Ministry of Finance, a nationwide tax auditing conducted in 1989 alone produced RMB 95 billion of "penalty incomes" for the state. An internal source also confirmed that the yearly average of tax evasion in the 1990s may well reach RMB 100 billion.[17]

Despite the relative decline of both state and central revenues, the size of their expenditures continued to increase. One important fiscal burden that the state had to shoulder was to provide various subsidies in the process of reform, especially in the forms of price subsidies (*jiage butie*) and enterprise deficit subsidies (*qiyie kuishun butie*). On the average, various normal expenditures by the state — such as administrative expenditures, defence spending, payments for bonds and so on — have accounted for about 20% of national income at any given year. Currently, however, when the total state revenues could not reach this level (as of 1988, the ratio was already 19.2%), even the most indispensable expenditures of the state had to be provided in part by loans made both domestically and overseas.[18] Consequently, budget deficits became successive and the inflationary trends continued to intensify.

While the centre had occasionally implemented a variety of measures to secure funds, these largely *ad hoc* measures did not seem to have been highly effective in tackling the very source of the complex problems.[19] With the fiscal contract systems adopted in 1988 by a majority of provinces (among which 16 were the recipients of central subsidies), severe limits were put on how much the centre could increase its revenue income. Although the shared revenues (*fencheng shouru*) of 1990 increased over those of 1988 by RMB 46 billion, the amount remitted to the centre increased only by RMB 1.8 billion — a mere 3.9%.[20] In addition, when local governments did most of the collection of revenues for the centre, there was bound to be some room for potential problems. Furthermore, bargaining and negotiation were so pervasive in the entire budgetary process that the final outcomes (baseline figures or sharing ratios) have very often been in the direction of further reductions of central shares of revenues. Overly diversified patterns of revenue-sharing, which allowed provinces to engage in a one-to-one bargaining with the centre regarding the baseline figures or sharing ratios, contributed considerably to the weakening of the overall fiscal capacity of the centre. Consequently, in stark contrast with the centre experiencing successive deficits (throughout 1981–1993 except for 1989), local governments marked seven-year surpluses in the 1981–1993 period.[21]

Obviously, the ever-increasing size of the budgetary deficit, high levels of inflation, and the lack of sufficient central resources with which to implement effective macro-economic control must have been crucial to the centre's decision to introduce the *fenshuizhi* reform even at the expense of reversing its earlier commitment to the fiscal contract system at least for the 1991–1995 period.[22] According to the 1993 budget report by Finance Minister Liu Zhongli, China marked a budget deficit of RMB 89.9 billion, of which 38.5 billion were financed by domestic debts, 30.9 billion were financed by foreign debts, and the rest, 20.5 billion, remained unfinanced. Given that tax revenues constituted more than 80% of all budgetary revenues in 1993, readjusting the ways tax revenues were distributed between different levels of governments must have been most appealing to the centre.[23]

The Tax-Sharing Reform in 1994

The tax-sharing reform entails the following key measures. First, it involves a new scheme of classifying different categories of taxes to be retained or shared by the central and provincial governments. Table 2 provides a break-down of various taxes into three categories adopted by the 1994 tax-sharing reform. Four measures are particularly notable for their implications for central-provincial fiscal relations. One concerns the division of the consolidated industrial-commercial tax into the business tax (*yingyeshui*) as a local tax and the product circulation tax (*shangpin liutongshui*) as a part of the value-added tax to be shared between the central and local governments. Since the provinces' well-known preference for the overall-revenue sharing system originated largely from their wish to get a large share of the consolidated industrial-commercial tax which was more voluminous than any other single tax category, effective implementation of the new system would naturally require a change in this respect.

Table 2. Three Categories of Taxes under the *Fenshuizhi* Reform

Designation	Kinds of taxes
Central Taxes	custom duties; custom-levied consumption and value-added taxes; consumption tax; centrally owned enterprise income tax; business, income and urban construction taxes from railways, central banks and insurance companies; income taxes from local and foreign-invested banks and other financial enterprises licensed by the People's Bank of China; and profits remitted from centrally-owned enterprises
Local Taxes	business tax; locally owned enterprise income tax; individual income tax; urban land use tax; fixed-asset investment adjustment tax; urban construction tax; real estate tax; vehicle and vessel use tax; stamp tax; butcher tax; agriculture and animal husbandry tax; special agricultural product tax; farm land use tax; contract tax; inheritance tax; property gains tax; and profits remitted from the locally owned enterprises
Shared Taxes	value-added tax, securities transaction tax, resources tax

Source: "Guowuyuan guanyu shixing fenshuizhi caizheng guanli tizhi de jueding" (State Council's Decision on Implementing the "Tax-Sharing" System), State Council Document No. 85 issued on 15 December 1993, published in *Caizheng* (Finance), No. 2 (1994), p. 19.

Other noteworthy changes concern the establishment of three taxes of the shared category, the tighter control imposed on the profits from the production and sales of cigarettes and liquor, and the cancellation and merger of several taxes. First, the shared category includes the value-added tax (*zengzhishui*), securities transaction tax (*zhengquan jiaoyishui*) and resources tax (*ziyuanshui*). The value-added tax will be imposed on the entire process of commodity production and circulation, and shared between the central and provincial governments in the ratio of 7.5 and 2.5. The securities transaction tax will be equally divided by the central and provincial governments. The resources tax will mainly go into provincial coffers except for the tax levied on off-shore oil which will be retained exclusively by the centre.[24] Another key issue concerns the changes introduced to the cigarette and liquor sector. According to the new system, all the consumption taxes (newly levied on the sales of both tobacco products and liquor) that are collected will go into central coffers and 75% of value-added taxes levied on the production and circulation of these two products will be retained by the centre. Given that cigarette and liquor taxes amounted to almost 10% of the total state revenue incomes of 1993, this change is not at all of minor nature.[25] Finally, several minor taxes were merged with other taxes or simply cancelled to simplify the entire tax structure. Individual income tax, individual income adjustment tax and privately-run enterprise income tax were merged into one category of individual income tax. Salt tax was also merged into resources tax. And wage adjustment tax, animal trading tax and three others were abolished.[26]

Second, a standardized tax rate of 33% was imposed on all domestic enterprises since foreign-funded and foreign wholly-owned enterprises had already been enjoying this favourable rate (although certain enterprises in the Special Economic Zones and Economic and Technological Development Zones enjoyed a special rate as low as 15%). Before the reform, there were four different tax rates ranging from 35 to 55% depending upon the size and the ownership of the enterprises. Given the pervasive habit of domestic enterprises in seeking to evade taxes by creating artificial losses or assuming a false identity as foreign-funded enterprises in order to obtain favourable tax treatment, the adoption of a unified tax rate for all enterprises was designed to simplify matters and plug an important loophole in the collection of taxes. Furthermore, the authority to grant the privileges of "reduced taxes and exemption" was recentralized back to the State Council for many key taxes including the value-added tax and business tax.[27]

Third, in its efforts to monitor tightly the process of tax collection and prevent local attempts to evade taxes, Beijing has announced its intention to establish a bi-level system of tax collection: that is, to set up national-level tax bureaus (*guoshuiju*) as well as local tax bureaus (*difang shuiju*). Since the predominant role played by local governments in collecting taxes has long been perceived as contributing to the weakening fiscal authority of the centre, by establishing national tax bureaus Beijing hopes to improve its tax capacity. The division of labour between the two is such that the national tax bureaus are responsible for central taxes and local tax bureaus take charge in collecting local taxes. Interestingly, all shared taxes will first go to the national tax bureaus which then, according to the fixed ratio, distribute them to local governments.[28] This seems to constitute an important case of vertical (*tiao-tiao*) control reasserting itself over horizontal (*kuai-kuai*) management in the era of decentralization.

Finally, the central government made it explicitly clear that the most important purpose of the new policy is to increase the share of budgetary revenues in national income and the central share of budgetary revenues and, therefore, to improve the centre's overall macroeconomic control capacity. The centre also stipulated that the legislative powers over central, local and shared taxes are to be monopolized by the centre. While the official documents on tax-sharing did not specify the target figures, frequent references were made to a few influential studies that seem to have contributed significantly to the earlier adoption of the reform. According to these studies, the share of budgetary revenues in national income is to increase to 25% in the short run and to more than 35% in the longer run, while the central share of the budgetary revenues is to rise to 50% in the short run and more than 65% in the longer run.[29]

Provincial Reactions to the Tax-Sharing Reform

Since the most important goal of the new tax system lies in increasing the central share of revenue incomes, it is rather natural to expect negative responses from the provinces which are now placed in a losing position (although there may be certain side payments covering other policy issues). In order to ensure relatively smooth and effective implementation of the reform, the central government adopted two key measures aimed at mitigating provincial resentment and reducing potential problems of local foot-dragging. First, as mentioned earlier, since 1992 the tax-sharing system had been experimented with in four province-level units and five "central economic cities" as a sort of feasibility test. Second, before the decision to implement the new tax reform was made at the Third Plenum, Vice-premier Zhu Rongji, along with 62 high-level cadres, visited 16 provinces and municipalities including Guangdong, Shanghai, Shandong, Zhejiang, Jiangsu and Tianjin, for the purposes of exchanging opinions and persuading recalcitrant provincial leaders.[30]

Three additional arrangements were made to mitigate potential discontent on the part of the provinces. First, the central government made a pledge that it would reimburse or transfer cash back to the provinces in order to ensure that their total revenue incomes would not drop below the level of revenues obtained before the introduction of the new tax system. That is, the revenue incomes of 1993 are to be taken as the baseline figure, and if the revenue incomes of 1994 drop below this baseline figure, the balance between the two becomes the amount of cash transfer from the central government. Second, the central government made another pledge that, if the projected goal of the centre's share of budgetary revenues reaching 60% is accomplished, at least one-third of the central revenues will be dispensed to reduce interprovincial inequalities. If the first measure is aimed at relatively rich coastal provinces, the second measure seems geared toward poor, inland and minorities provinces. Finally, Beijing also introduced certain "transitional" arrangements (through 1995) such as honouring the decisions by the provincial authorities on reduced taxes and tax exemption as well as providing two transitional tax rates (27 and 17%) for enterprises with low profitability.[31]

Provincial responses to the new tax reform seem varied among different provinces. Obviously, provincial views voiced in various official publications were generally in support of the reform: 13 provinces and two "central economic cities" reportedly expressed their full support at the national fiscal work conference held in December 1993. On separate occasions, leaders of Hubei, Xinjiang, Guangxi and Qinghai gave their support for the reform. Unofficially, too, provinces like Shaanxi, Qinghai and Gansu are reported to have welcomed the reform as a crucial measure that will enable the centre to allocate more fiscal resources to poor inland provinces. For instance, Pu Xishou, Governor of Anhui, expressed his full support for the reform which, according to him, replaced a very "unfair" system of fiscal contract.[32]

If we follow the logic of Liu Zhongli, Minister of Finance, that the new system will make rich provinces contribute more to the national economy, poor provinces must welcome the policy. However, views seem quite dissimilar even among the poor provinces. Many provincial delegates to the second session of the Eighth National People's Congress held in March 1994 had a lot to say against the new system. Delegates from Xinjiang, Guangxi and Yunnan demanded that the new policy avoid the malpractice of standardization and have preferential arrangements for poor minority regions. Despite the support given by his provincial leader (Guan Guangfu), a Hubei representative completely downplayed the validity of the reform by asking "why can't localities make deficits while the centre does it all the time?"[33]

While many of the backward and inland provinces were generally resentful of the absence of any preferential arrangements for poor regions, Yunnan and Guizhou had particular reasons to be discontented with the reform. These two provinces specialize in the production of cigarettes and liquor and their provincial revenues have been heavily dependent upon taxing these products. However, as discussed earlier, the 1994 tax reform categorizes all the consumption taxes levied on the sales of tobacco and liquor products and 75% of value-added taxes levied on the production and circulation of these two products as central income. Furthermore, in the case of Yunnan, 60% of the marginal increase in provincial tax revenues will also have to be remitted to the centre. In the case of Guizhou, 92% of the marginal increase in provincial tax revenues from tobacco and liquor will also have to be remitted to the centre. Subsequently, it was reported that this year Guizhou might have to ask the centre to provide RMB 400 million as central subsidies and another RMB 500 million as loans.[34]

The views of coastal provinces were also negative and even confrontational. Relatively developed coastal provinces generally regarded the tax-sharing reform as "robbing the rich to help the poor" (*jiefu jipin*). According to a report, as early as October 1993, some leaders of coastal provinces allegedly said that they would "sabotage" the centre's efforts to reassert its fiscal control.[35] In the case of Guangdong, worries were not about this year since the centre would make a cash transfer if the provincial revenue income fell below the level of 1993. What concerns the provincial leadership is that, since Beijing will take away 75% of the shared taxes, the rate of increase in its budgetary revenues will significantly slow down to produce fiscal pressures on local expenditures.[36]

Officials from Fujian were more critical. With a very high level of indebtedness — as of 1993, RMB 9.1 billion of domestic debts as well as US$ 1.1 billion of foreign debts — Fujian perceived as very grave the potential effects of the reform on reducing the marginal rate of growth in provincial revenue incomes. Especially when such a high level of indebtedness was allegedly caused by the centre's demands for infrastructural development, Fujian might have felt almost betrayed by the centre. Given the prospect that the centre's budgetary subsidies to Fujian may not increase over that of 1993, Fujian had every reason to oppose the reform. Pan Xincheng, head of the Fujian Provincial Finance Department, went so far as to comment that "if our central government leaders do not support Fujian ... there will be a lot of regret.... The central government must give us more support if it expects Fujian to play a leading role in the unification of China."[37]

The generally negative views among many provinces on the tax-sharing reform were clearly manifested by the number of votes that opposed the legislation of the budgetary law at the second plenary session of the National People's Congress. According to Table 3, among the four key issues subjected to voting by the NPC delegates, two with budgetary implications got many more "no" votes than the other two issues. Particularly, with regard to the legislation of the budgetary law, almost one quarter of the delegates either voted against it or abstained from voting, clearly illustrating pervasive local dissatisfaction with the new fiscal arrangement.

Table 3. Number of Votes for Four NPC Decisions

Issues	Vote Yes	Vote No	Abstain	Invalid
Budgetary Law	2,110	337	225	49
Budget for 1994	2,403	178	129	11
National Economic and Social Development Plan for 1994	2,584	60	56	21
Government Work Report	2,655	23	25	18

Source: *Ming Pao*, 23 March 1994.

Scenarios for the Implementation of the Tax-Sharing System

Since the Third Plenum decision to introduce the tax-sharing system, the central government has displayed two contrasting positions regarding how the new system should be implemented. One position is to demand that all provinces consider the interests of the nation as a whole and strictly follow the regulations promulgated by the central government. At the National Financial Work Conference held in December 1993, Liu Zhongli stressed that provinces must implement the tax-sharing system as stipulated in the policy directives without arbitrary changes. According to Liu, implementation must proceed in accordance with the principles of "unified perception, unified behaviour and unified pace" (*tongyi renshi, tongyi xingdong, tongyi butiao*).[38]

Despite criticisms of "standardized implementation" (*yidaoqie*), the central government seemed determined to enforce strict implementation of the new system. Beijing's position became increasingly tough as various complaints were heard from provinces. *Guangming ribao* (Guangming Daily), for instance, made it clear that "those who argue 'localities have their own measures to block central policy' [*shangyou zhengce xiayou duice*] will be severely criticized ... [and] according to the discipline of our party, lower-level organizations must obey the directives of their superordinate organizations." Beijing's determination was manifested in part by the Ministry of Finance's dispatch of work-teams to provinces like Shanghai, Jiangsu, Shandong, Tianjin, Hebei, Henan, Heilongjiang, Shaanxi, and Sichuan to supervise local implementation. The tough position of the central government made localities increasingly resentful, and expressions like "iron-fist policy" (*tiewan zhengce*) and "when persuasion fails, imposition predominates" (*shuobufu jiuyafu*) were used to characterize the process of implementation.[39]

On the other hand, there have also been some signs that Beijing's attitude may have become more flexible over time. When the new tax system was first introduced, it was claimed that Beijing's share of total state revenues would increase up to 60%. Over time, however, such a target was deemed too ambitious. In December 1993, Feng Bing, Deputy Secretary-general of the State Commission for Restructuring the Economy, commented that the highly publicized target of 60% was only a "guess" which might not materialize at all. Again in January 1994, Jin Xin, director of the State Tax Administration, admitted that it might take five or more years to boost the central share to 60%.[40]

Given such contrasting positions displayed by the central government, it is very difficult to project which route the actual implementation of the tax reform will take. We can conceive of three possible patterns. First, if the first type of attitude dominates Beijing's dealing with the provinces, the new reform is very likely to be carried out to the original intentions of the reform despite provincial opposition. Given that Beijing had to reverse its own pledge to introduce the tax-sharing system during the Eighth Five-Year Plan period, we cannot preclude the possibility that the centre may opt for coercive means to induce provincial compliance. The more serious China's macroeconomic problems become, the more likely it will resort to political and administrative measures to carry out the reform to its original intention. As long as the centre holds on to the personnel mechanism of local control, Beijing's coercive capability can work quite effectively in inducing provincial compliance.

If Beijing employs a more flexible attitude in dealing with the provinces, we might see a protracted period of central-provincial bargaining,

Central-Provincial Relations 3.17

which may in turn produce two outcomes. The centre's stipulation made it clear that the new tax reform should "proceed gradually with occasional adjustments." Gradual implementation with occasional adjustments could produce all sorts of parochial incentives for the provinces to engage in bargaining with the centre, drag their feet and even bend central directives to accommodate local interests.[41]

Some evidence suggests that Beijing's will has already been stifled with regard to the "property gains tax" (*tudi zengzhishui*). According to its original scheme, all profits from real estate transactions were to be taxed by 30 to 60%. This policy immediately came under severe criticism by coastal provinces with utmost concern with foreign investment. Guangdong is reported to have filed strong complaints to Beijing, and Shanghai sent its mayor, Huang Ju, to Beijing at least twice in January alone to protest against this tax. By mid-April, the centre came up with a revised version, according to which profits from real estate transactions that did not exceed 20% of the original investment were to be exempted from the property gains tax. Only in February 1995 were the details of the tax finalized. According to the finalized regulation, overseas property developers who made agreements on their real estate projects before 1 January 1994 were to be given a five-year exemption period.[42]

Compared to the total number of issues that will be subject to bargaining, the property gains tax is perhaps only the tip of an iceberg. As the *modus operandi* of the current fiscal arrangement is only of a transitional nature, Beijing and the provinces will soon have to figure out how to reduce disagreements over such issues as (1) how to delineate the expenditure responsibilities of the central and provincial governments; (2) how to deal with local extra-budgetary funds; and (3) whether to continue to use the baseline-figure method (*jishufa*) or to adopt the factor-analysis method (*yinsufa*) in determining budgetary allocation to the provinces. In fact, some in-house policy recommendations of the Ministry of Finance reveal that central-provincial bargaining over these issues will be neither fast nor easy.[43]

A protracted period of bargaining may facilitate a process in which incremental readjustments have to be constantly made to accommodate provincial interests at the expense of the centre's goals. If this were the case, the outcome would very likely be a highly diversified system of fiscal arrangements, thus mooting one crucial intention of the entire reform — simplifying the central-provincial fiscal arrangements. Worse yet, we can also conceive of a situation where effective provincial foot-dragging and opposition put the entire tax-sharing reform in jeopardy. If the past experiences were any guide at all, the possibility of an aborted reform — i.e., going back to the fiscal contract system — cannot be completely precluded, although at this point it seems more a matter of possibility than of feasibility.[44]

Whichever route the tax-sharing reform may eventually take, its actual implementation will no doubt constitute a crucial indicator of the evolving balance of power between Beijing and the provinces. Considering the pervasive view that post-Mao reforms have gradually eroded the capacity of the central government to the extent that even political and territorial disintegration is a possibility, the success of this significant reform would contribute much to an alternate understanding of post-Mao China's central-local government relations. On the other hand, if the tax-sharing reform fails to accomplish its original goals, we will have more persuasive evidence as to Beijing's weakened capacity *vis-à-vis* the provinces (also on the 1994 tax reform, see the chapter by Christine Wong in this volume).

The Information Dimension: Statistical Control and Monitoring Capacity

In the policy arena many kinds of resources other than fiscal ones are important. Control of negotiations over resource allocation is more often than not dictated by the inequality of access to key information. Such inequality of access creates incentives for special interests to withhold or distort potentially damaging information.[45] In our context, these special interests refer to provincial and sub-provincial authorities that are often called agents, implementors, or middlemen. In implementing the centre's policy, these local officials are required to report regularly on their performance to the central authorities. The centre's aspirations for the "complete" control of information on local compliance (and performance) are very often frustrated, however, by peculiar local norms of implementation. The most prevalent norm of implementation — as a set of "culturally rational" choices available for implementors to choose from in the face of conflicts between the priorities of the centre and the preferences of the localities — is dictated largely by bureaucratic careerism based on the survival imperative.[46]

In socialist systems like China where key personnel decisions are still controlled solely by the highly centralized *nomenklatura* system, most of local leaders would not wish to produce an image of "lagging behind other provinces" or of "resisting the centre." While various decentralizing measures adopted in the post-Mao era have subsequently created abundant incentives and opportunities for local implementors to break out of the previously most common pattern of "suffering in silence," overt manifestation of resistance to the centre is not yet a popular alternative. On the other hand, the "hidden transcripts" of bureaucratic careerism seem to die hard, and one key manifestation of bureaucratic careerism is reporting distorted (both inflated and deflated) information on local performance.

Manipulating performance statistics has long been a key characteristic of the policy implementation process in China. The Great Leap Forward period is particularly notorious for the prevalence of inflated and distorted production statistics supplied by local authorities. Peasant stories of grave food shortages grossly contradicted official statistics showing abundance almost everywhere in China. Provincial implementation of the communization policy (*renmin gongshehua*) during this period also illustrates the same problem. Within only one month after the Beidaihe conference in August 1958 where the nationwide communization was decided upon, 97.2% of all peasant households in China were reported to have been incorporated into the communes with 15 provinces boasting 100%.[47] While no studies are available to confirm the continued prevalence of falsified statistics in the periods that followed, there is no indication that such malpractices were halted. Instead, many studies indirectly suggest that central leaders had to utilize various means of monitoring local performance — inspection trips, conferences and meetings, work-team dispatches, "squatting at a point" (*dundian*) and so on — mainly because of their deep-seated distrust of performance statistics submitted from below.[48]

Several policy measures adopted in the earlier years of the post-Mao era further testify that there were indeed considerable degrees of manipulation and manoeuvres of key production statistics on the part of local authorities. In 1977, for instance, the central government specifically called for immediate redress of the widespread practice of reporting inflated information by the localities on key production statistics. In October 1980, the State Planning Commission, Ministry of Agriculture and the State Statistical Bureau issued a joint circular calling for a halt in providing inflated production statistics. Furthermore, the circular presented five indices for grain production and four indices for animal husbandry to replace an overly simplified single index of "per mu grain output" and "the number of livestock in possession."[49]

There is no doubt that post-Mao decentralization measures were designed to supplement the weak monitoring capacity of the Beijing government by delegating decisional authority to local governments with abundant local information.[50] Yet, it should be noted that decentralization and strengthened central monitoring capacity are not necessarily mutually exclusive. As a matter of fact, post-Mao China has witnessed a gradual strengthening of the centre's control over information and statistics. Starting with the rehabilitation of the State Statistical Bureau in 1978, the tightening of the centre's control over statistics was further consolidated with the legislation of the "statistics law" (*tongjifa*) by the National People's Congress in 1983. In 1987, the central government forced provincial-level governments to draft legislation against statistical manipulations so that, by the end of 1992, 25 provinces, municipalities and autonomous regions adopted various penalties for the violators. The central government also occasionally carried out large-scale investigations and dug out over 50,000 and 70,000 violations of the statistics law in 1989 and 1994 respectively. Furthermore, the State Statistical Bureau has maintained more than 1,000 sampling-survey teams at the county- and city-level (*xianshi chouyang diaochadui*). In order to minimize the interference from the respective territorial (*kuai-kuai*) administration, the State Statistical Bureau was put in charge of directly handling personnel management and financial expenditures of local statistical bureaus at the county level and above.[51] The staff size of the State Statistical Bureau also radically increased from 280 in 1981 and 580 in 1988 to more than 1,000 in 1994.[52]

Such a tendency toward the strengthened central control over information and statistics was noted by some observers. Nina Halpern, for instance, argued that "[A]lthough the dispersal of other resources contributed to the fragmentation of authority in the post-Mao era, the changes stemming from changing information flows were more complicated and probably, on balance, produced greater centralization."[53] Despite some positive assessments of the centre's strengthened grip over information, problems of distorted reporting seem to continue. Various official and media reports confirm that such malpractices continue despite Beijing's efforts to curtail them. In February 1993, Zheng Jiaxiang, deputy director of the State Statistical Bureau, acknowledged that "for a variety of reasons, some localities and units have very serious problems of reporting manipulated and distorted information and statistics." Media reports, too, warn against the prevalence of inflated reporting on the part of key local officials who seek promotions and other benefits by claiming major successes in implementing the centre's policies. Warnings were also issued to provincial governments against the malpractice of providing deflated reports on enterprise profits and tax revenues collected by the local tax bureaus. Furthermore, frequent calls were made for the revision of China's outdated statistics law in order to prevent any deliberate falsification of economic statistics by local officials.[54]

A series of interviews the author carried out in Heilongjiang in the summer of 1994 revealed some instances of statistical manipulation in the "agricultural system" (*nongkou xitong*). According to the interviewees in Harbin, the State Statistical Bureau maintains an extensive information network over the local agricultural system utilizing various units ranging from the "rural economic investigation teams" (*nongcun jingji diaochadui*) under the provincial statistical bureaus to the "statistical survey personnel" (*tongjiyuan*) at the village level. All these units are subject to vertical control by the State Statistical Bureau and are financed through central government expenditures. Despite such mechanisms designed specifically to prevent interference from the local administration, however, interviewees noted that "many key statistical indicators — such as total grain output, per capital incomes, inflation rate, average birth rate and so on — have to be approved by the key leaders of the territorial administration before they can be reported upwards or published." They further added that "in most cases inflated statistics are the main problems although in some areas local leaders under-report their performance in expectation of more subsidies and support for poverty alleviation."[55]

At the Third and Fourth Plenums of the Fourteenth Central Committee in 1993 and 1994, Beijing strongly emphasized the role of macro-economic control over various problems the Chinese economy was facing. Macro-economic control, to be effective, however, requires a supply of highly reliable information and statistics. Unless Beijing is both determined and able to win this "war over statistics," the central government's efforts to take back some economic decision-making powers from local governments may prove futile. Considering the relative ease with which classified information about the centre is available — presumably, with the right connections, you might even be able to buy secret internal documents of Politburo Standing Committee meetings that have not yet adjourned — Beijing is indeed fighting a very tough war with the provinces.[56]

The Organizational Dimension: The Cancellation of the *Jihua Danlie* Status of Provincial Capitals

One crucial change introduced in the organizational dimension was the cancellation of the "central economic cities" status for the provincial capitals (*shenghui*). The CEC designation had been one of the most innovative developmental strategies devised by the post-Mao leadership. While formally still subject to provincial directing in administrative terms, the CEC status enabled cities so designated to enjoy provincial-level status in various economic policy issues.[57] With support from Zhao Ziyang and his think-tank, Dalian had constituted the first experimental city for the CEC policy, although it was Chongqing which was first approved in early 1983. In 1984–1985, Wuhan, Guangzhou, Xian, Shenyang, Harbin and Dalian also joined the list of a privileged few. Perhaps, the CEC designation was largely an administrative compensation Beijing provided for inland provincial capitals with limited access to foreign capital (with the exceptions of Guangzhou and Dalian). In 1987, however, Qingdao and Ningbo, too, obtained the privileged status, which were soon followed by Xiamen and Shenzhen in 1988, and Nanjing, Chengdu and Changchun in 1989 (see Table 4).[58]

Table 4. Distribution of 14 Central Economic Cities

Year of designation	Provincial capitals	Non-provincial capitals
1983	—	Chongqing
1984	Wuhan	—
1985	Shenyang, Xian, Harbin Guangzhou	Dalian*
1987	—	Qingdao*, Ningbo*
1988	—	Xiamen*, Shenzhen*
1989	Nanjing, Chengdu, Changchun	—
Total	8	6

Note: Asterisk (*) denotes coastal cities.

In the beginning at least, there were hopes that, despite the obvious loss of some important portions of revenues and tax incomes, provinces could nevertheless greatly benefit from CECs in their territories which might produce significantly expanded economic activities and thus play a crucial role as an agent of development for the entire province.[59] Later, however, all sorts of disagreements, tension and conflicts were generated between the provinces and CECs now enjoying provincial-level decision-making powers over a wide array of policy issues.[60] While this contradiction between the province's wish for continued control and the CEC's demand for more autonomy was common for all CECs, particular degrees of "unhappiness" on the part of the provincial governments seem to have been more considerable in the case of the eight CECs which housed both provincial and municipal governments.[61] The ensuing conflicts between the provincial and CEC governments became so serious and disruptive that the central government allegedly began to do extensive research on the particular problem as early as 1992. In the summer of 1993, the controversial CEC status was finally pronounced terminated with regard to the eight provincial capitals, thus allowing only six out of 14 CECs to remain. Subsequent justifications provided by Beijing further confirm the magnitude of the problem caused by the CEC designations of some provincial capitals:

> The State Council's recent decision is primarily aimed at preventing contradictions between the provincial governments and the provincial capital cities from intensifying and at restoring certain economic powers enjoyed by the provincial capital cities to the provincial governments.[62]

The cancellation of the *jihua danlie* status for the provincial capital cities, however, was granted a two-year grace period during 1994–1995 mainly for the purpose of allowing time for various readjustments and matching the five-year plan cycle (i.e., another transitional period granted to the "tax-sharing" reform also coincides with this period). By absorbing former CECs, some provinces (such as Hubei absorbing Wuhan) may be able to make up for the chronic shortage of funds facilitated by the increased expenditure responsibilities and the newly adopted tax-sharing system. It seems, however, that these eight former CECs are not going to lose all of their previous privileges. In administrative terms, they are still to be categorized as "deputy-provincial level" (*fushengji*) units. In addition to these eight former CECs, two more cities — Jinan in Shandong and Hangzhou in Zhejiang — were elevated to become "deputy-provincial level" cities in 1994.[63] The cancellation of the CEC status for provincial capitals provides key evidence on the "coastal bias" that the current leadership has continued to manifest: only one of the remaining six CECs — Chongqing — is an inland city. At the same time, it also testifies to the potential capacity of the centre in using administrative means to grant and withdraw certain privileges of both provincial and local government units.[64]

The Foreign Economic Relations Dimension: Reform Continues to Intensify

The reform of China's foreign economic relations in 1994 can be summarized by two key changes introduced in the areas of foreign exchange control and foreign trade. Stipulated in November 1993, the foreign exchange reform included the following key measures.[65] First, beginning on 1 January 1994, China's official and swap exchange rates were to be unified and the unified rate was to be set by the People's Bank of China in accordance with the daily market rate. Second, the nature of the yearly-plan for foreign exchange balance (*waihui shouzhi jihua*) was changed from "compulsory" to "guidance." Third, more importantly for our concern, significant changes were introduced into the foreign exchange retention system. Before 1994, enterprises had to remit large portions of their foreign exchange earnings to the state: the average retention rate was 25% in 1982–1989, and most of the province-level units enjoyed an average of 50% retention rate in 1990–1993.[66] Beginning on 1 April 1994 (after a three-month grace period), foreign currency was to be managed not by administrative means such as "remittances" but by an economic method. More concretely, Chinese exporters are supposed to sell all of their foreign currency earnings to 13 designated banks, from which they can also purchase foreign currencies with *Renminbi*. A key question concerns how to interpret this significant change within the central-local relations framework. It seems that the abolition of the retention system represents another key measure (the tax-sharing reform is one) designed to boost the centre's capacity for macroeconomic control over local behaviour. While the centre formally had to give up its fixed (20%) income from local remittances, it now commands a significantly expanded pool of foreign currency earnings deposited in the 13 banks which are subject to its tight control.

The key reform measures in foreign trade included a further reduction of 283 products in December 1993 and another 195 products in May 1994, which had formerly required import licenses. They also included a delegation of import-export authority to a large number of enterprises: the number of enterprises (excluding foreign-invested ones) with their own import-export authority grew from 1,360 in May 1993 to 7,010 in January 1994. Given Beijing's plan for 1995 and beyond, the overall number of enterprises with their own foreign trade authority will grow more significantly in the years to come.[67]

Two other issues merit attention due to their implications for central-provincial relations. One concerns the implementation of the newly introduced value-added tax (VAT). In addition to the general worry that the new VAT may produce heavier tax burdens than the old consolidated industrial and commercial tax it replaced, foreign-invested firms became resentful in August 1994 when Beijing announced that VAT refunds would not be made for goods using raw materials of local origin. Since then many local governments came up with innovative schemes to keep foreign investors happy: Guangdong, for instance, allowed foreign enterprises to pay only the amount of VAT that they ought to as opposed to paying the amount in full. Provincial authorities are thus faced with a serious dilemma between making foreign investors happy and complying with the centre's directives. Provincial authorities are also currently prevented by Beijing from breaking up large contracts into smaller deals to circumvent the need to obtain the centre's approval.[68]

The Personnel Dimension: Purge, Co-optation and Faction-Building

The significance of the personnel dimension in understanding the dynamics of central-provincial relations lies in various dimensions: (1) the centre wants provincial leaders to be faithful agents of central priorities, while localities want them to be sincere representatives of regional interests; and, (2) whose who succeed at the centre are important in determining which province's interests are more likely to be accommodated in the future. In 1994, there were many personnel changes in at least nine province-level governments including Jiangsu, Heilongjiang, Shanghai and Shandong, although the nature of these reshuffles may differ.[69]

The personnel change in Jiangsu concerned the transfer in December 1993 of its party secretary, Shen Daren, to the position of provincial People's Congress chairman. This particular change took place in the immediate aftermath of the Third Plenum where the key decision on tax-sharing reform was made. According to some media reports, Shen was an outspoken critic of the new tax reform and his opposition was well known during Zhu Rongji's tour to the province during August 1993. Although supposedly Shen was not the only provincial leader who spoke against the new policy, he was probably made a scape-goat by the centre which wanted to "kill the chicken to scare the monkey." In fact, after the transfer of Shen, Jiangsu and its new party secretary (and concurrently governor), Chen Huanyou, have been very cautious in expressing their views on the highly controversial tax reform.[70]

The personnel reshuffle in Heilongjiang also concerns the transfers of its provincial party secretary, Sun Weiben, to the chairmanship of the provincial People's Congress and of its governor, Shao Qihui, to become Vice-minister of Machine Industry, in August 1994. The main reason, according to the author's interviews in Harbin, was personal rivalries and conflicts between Sun and Shao which eventually invited arbitration by the central government. As a key consequence, the new party secretary did not come from within the province in order to avoid further complications with intra-provincial factional politics. Instead, the new party boss of Heilongjiang, Yue Qifeng, is a Hebei native with extensive work experiences in Hebei including its governorship. In line with the now popularized norm, the new governor still came from within the province, however. Tian Fengshan, a Heilongjiang native with extensive work experience in the province, is currently serving as the acting governor.[71]

Perhaps the most significant personnel change of 1994 occurred in Shanghai. First, Shanghai party boss and Politburo member, Wu Bangguo, was inducted into the Central Committee Secretariat at the Fourth Plenum in September 1994. Given that the induction of a provincial boss directly into the Secretariat was rare (at the 13th Central Congress, Li Ruihuan was the only such case), Wu's case is interpreted largely as part of the efforts by Jiang Zemin to elevate members of the so-called "Shanghai faction" in order to strengthen his power and influence on the central political stage. The change is also regarded by some observers as an effort by the centre to co-opt certain vocal provincial leaders so as to deprive localities of "heavy-weight" fighters against central policy, particularly with regard to the new tax policy. The position of the Shanghai party boss vacated by Wu, then, was taken over by its former mayor, Huang Ju, who was also promoted to be a member of the Politburo. The addition of Huang to the Politburo is thus considered as a clear indicator of the increased power of the so-called "Shanghai faction."[72]

A similar change took place in Shandong where the provincial party boss and Politburo member, Jiang Chunyun, was inducted into the Central

Committee Secretariat. Jiang was the first ever party boss of Shandong to serve concurrently as a Politburo member.[73] The same two perspectives — co-optation or factional politics — can also be applied to his new Secretariat position. While Jiang's promotion to the Politburo in 1992 is attributed to the positive assessment of his economic accomplishments in Shandong by Deng Xiaoping, some reports also imply his close connections with Chen Yun.[74] There is no question that these personnel changes in Shandong and Shanghai are closely related with succession politics in Zhongnanhai, but given the extent to which these two provincial-level governments had contributed to Beijing's coffers and were making strong demands for more preferential treatment in return, the co-optation perspective also seems to make sense. Perhaps, it may require a longer time-frame for us to assess more precisely the rationale of these crucial personnel changes.[75]

The Coercive Apparatus: The PLA and Regionalism

Other than the paraphernalia of party and government organizations, the military networks of the PLA provide crucial conduits of power and control in China. If this conduit is somehow blocked by tensions between central priorities and local preferences — say, by a collusion between provincial governments and local PLA units against central authorities — it may possibly signal an ominous beginning of the so-called "dynastic cycle." In contemporary China, however, there are certain key obstacles to the formation of such a local civilian-military collusion against the centre. While the most powerful sub-national PLA organization is the military region of which there are seven, its civilian equivalent resides one level down at the provincial level. It seems, therefore, that the chances for a meaningful collusion between the two distinct institutions are rather slim. On the other hand, provincial governments' teaming up with military districts at the provincial level poses a relatively insignificant threat as the latter have little control over regular PLA forces. Furthermore, military region commanders and political commissars now serve three years on average before being transferred to new posts in other geographical locations, while in the past they stayed in one place for as long as ten years or more. This change is perhaps reflective of the centre's concern about growing localism in the PLA.[76]

Despite such structural impediments to the emergence of anti-Beijing alliances between local government and military forces, concerns are currently generated with regard to the genesis and possible diffusion of regionalism in the PLA. The most important reason for such concerns lies in the fact that the PLA is now economically more active and more sensitive to the changes in the local market environments than ever before. The PLA's highly profitable "military-run businesses" (sarcastically labeled as *bingshang* or *junshang*) have become highly diversified not only in their sectors and products (which range from arms manufacturing and trade, restaurant and hotel management, and even to smuggling) but also in terms of their geographical foci (covering all provinces).[77] Among many problems related to these businesses, its strengthened economic status (its expanded financial ability to support itself) and a rather corresponding decline in professionalism and discipline have contributed to the increasing concern with the center's loss of control over local PLA forces which then might collude with local government authorities in order to demand more autonomy from Beijing's directing.[78]

To what extent is this possibility of the formation of local power blocs against Beijing real and feasible? Interestingly, it seems, while almost all studies mention the manifestation of regionalism in the PLA as a high possibility especially during a period of confusion and turmoil at the central political stage, they nevertheless restrain their argument in actually linking the PLA's regionalism with the political and territorial disintegration of China. As a matter of fact, many argue that PLA forces would still be highly compliant to central control even if they were to be subject to the same situation as that in June 1989.[79] Despite the rampant problems with military discipline, moral decay and other illegal activities like smuggling, no sufficient evidence is available to suggest that the emergent regionalism, if not organizational parochialism, is currently any real threat to the power of the central government in controlling the military. In fact, Beijing has recently further tightened its ideological and administrative grip over both local and grass-root party cells within the PLA, possibly as part of its efforts to curtail the spread of regionalism.[80] Whether the party will still be able to completely control the military in the post-Deng phase, as it did in the past, remains to be seen.

The Horizontal Dimension: Inter-regional Tension and Inter-provincial Cooperation

It has become a cliché that many of the post-Mao reform measures have been biased against non-coastal regions. A predominant majority of special policy measures — such as the "coastal development strategy" — were initially applied only to coastal provinces, municipalities and cities. For instance, such preferential policies as "Special Economic Zones" (SEZs), "Coastal Open Cities" (COCs), and "Economic and Technological Development Zones" (ETDZs) were initially granted only to selected coastal areas. It was only in the early 1990s that the Beijing government adopted an "all-round development strategy" by opening up border and inland areas including Heilongjiang, Xinjiang, Yunnan and others. Many view the widening gap of economic development between coastal and inland provinces as a key consequence of the belated granting of "special policies" to these non-coastal provinces.[81]

In response to the prevailing discontent among the inland provinces which had suffered from both the lack of overseas connections and the insufficient policy support from the centre, Beijing recently made a pledge to provide more funds for infrastructural development in these regions, to arrange various trade fairs, and to dispatch delegations to neighbouring countries for the purpose of luring more foreign investment. Inland provinces, however, did not stop at passively waiting for the centre's provision of preferential policies. Some of them went so far as to form regional blocs to present their "collective" demands to Beijing. In mid-1994, for instance, party bosses of the five northwest provinces of Shaanxi, Gansu, Qinghai, Ningxia and Xinjiang held a "summit meeting" where they agreed to join in efforts to obtain more preferential policies from Beijing which, in their view, had been too much biased toward coastal regions. They went further to produce a pledge that they would explore the possibility of an "economic cooperative zone" — a regional entity to cope with their economic problems.[82] As a matter of fact, this five-province bloc is only the most recent of China's more than 100 interprovincial or interregional multilateral organizations, which include, to name the principal ones, the Regional Economic Coordination Association of Southwest China, the Northeast Economic Zone Coordination Office, the Shanxi, Gansu and Sichuan Economic Cooperative Region, and the Nanjing Association for Regional Economic Coordination.[83]

Given that the horizontal link-up among local government officials had been rare in pre-reform China, what does the formation of these regional blocs imply?[84] As a matter of fact, this constitutes only one, though important, manifestation of "horizontal linkages" created at the sub-national level. Another relatively less known but crucial case concerns the annual meetings held by the then fourteen "central economic cities" where concrete strategies to deal with the centre on a collective basis were discussed and adopted. In addition, coastal provinces occasionally "team up with" (*jie duizi*) hinterland provinces on the basis of their respective comparative advantages, such as building power plants in Yunnan to provide electricity for Guangdong enterprises.[85] In the case of Tibet, Beijing specifically ordered 29 other provinces and municipalities to come up with at least one project for which "teaming up" would be made to promote infrastructural development in the autonomous region.[86]

Interprovincial and intercity diplomacy also looms large. Various provinces, SEZs, COCs, and CECs currently maintain several liaison offices in other provinces and cities. Take Qingdao for an example. After Qingdao became a CEC in 1987, Qingdao established its Beijing office under the approval of the State Council. Consisting of Secretariat, Information Department, Economic Liaison Department, a guest house and a trading company, Qingdao's Beijing Office carries out the following functions: (1) consolidate Qingdao's relationship with the State Council; (2) collect relevant information on political, economic and science-technology affairs and relay it to Qingdao; (3) implement "horizontal economic liaison" (*hengxiang jingji lianluo*) with other regional and functional organizations to attract capital, technology and human resources; (4) strengthen Qingdao's "influence" in the centre and enhance the city's reputation; and (5) carry out tasks given by the central party and government units.[87] Other than Beijing, Qingdao also maintains its liaison offices in Guangzhou, Shanghai, Shenzhen and Xiamen. Inland cities seem to have established more liaison offices than their coastal counterparts perhaps in order to make up for their relative lack of contact with the outside world. Compared to Qingdao with a total of five liaison offices, Harbin, Shenyang and Jinan, for instance, maintain 13, 8 and 7 offices in other provinces and cities.[88]

The more and the faster these horizontal linkages are created, the more difficult Beijing may find it to deal with groups of provinces and cities which put forward their demands on a collective and egalitarian basis. On occasions, the central government may find it very hard to persuade provinces on the issues that do not even lead to the formation of collective interests. For instance, the emerging parochialistic sentiments of "NIMBY" (not in my backyards) often facilitated a situation where Beijing had been consistently baffled in designating a few dumping sites for radioactive waste.[89] The process in which varieties of horizontal linkages are created and expanded and the ways in which they affect central-local relations will constitute very important research topics in the years to come.[90]

Succession Politics and Beyond: An Uncertain Passage

Given the nature and scope of changes introduced in the last 19 years since the death of Mao Zedong, leadership change seems to constitute a crucial factor affecting the entire polity in China including intergovernmental relations. Given that succession politics (and other political manoeuvres surrounding the succession issue) will necessarily favour those promoting policies that aim to enlarge the overall size of the "resource pie," we may presume that decentralization (as the most cost-effective way to utilize abundant local information) may continue to be an irreversible direction of China's reform. If the direction is set — although the pace of further decentralization may occasionally slow down depending upon the successor(s) and particular political contingencies (such as intermittent political efforts to reduce inter-regional inequalities) — the fundamental nature of the evolving relationship between the central and provincial governments (i.e., decentralizing) is likely to remain largely unchanged. If so, we need to be concerned about the situation where succession politics may operate as a key catalyst for the worst-case scenario — political and territorial disintegration of China.

How feasible is the "imminent crisis" thesis that predicts the political and territorial disintegration of China in a foreseeable future? Many who view it as a very feasible scenario compare China with the former Soviet Union. Regardless of certain apparent similarities between the two, the possibility of political and territorial disintegration seems fairly remote in the case of China. There are two major justifications for this view. First, it can be argued that China is not the Soviet Union at all. That is, with over 90% of its population being Han-Chinese (as opposed to the defunct Soviet Union where Russians constituted less than half the population) and most of her provinces integrated into the China Proper well over one millennium ago, it is not very likely for China to follow the Soviet Union's tumultuous path of total disintegration, although the possibility of limited secessionist struggles by Tibet and Xinjiang may not be completely precluded.[91]

Second, historical precedents of dynastic collapse in China seem to have been produced by an indispensable combination of three factors: the formation of peasant armies, the emergence of autonomous provinces with fiscal and military autarky, and foreign aggression and encroachment. For instance, the collapse of the Qing dynasty was facilitated largely by the troubles produced simultaneously by local peasant armies such as the Taiping and Nian Rebellions, the rise of regional militarists (and later warlords) with independent tax bases, and constant threats from foreign aggression since the Opium War.[92] In light of these three conditions, it is not very likely that post-Deng succession politics will constitute any significant catalyst for China's political and territorial disintegration. Not only is the Chinese perception of the international strategic situation more positive than ever before, but China also maintains the most friendly relations with other countries since 1949.[93] While the demonstrations by tax-crushed peasants in Sichuan in June 1993 and a few others that followed ignited a fear of peasant revolt, the likelihood of an enduring nationwide militarized revolt seems rather remote. This follows especially from Beijing's shrewd policy of providing more support for agriculture and peasants on the one hand, and on the other, of harshly clamping down on the formation of village clans, as well as from the absence of a significant linkage between political dissidents in the cities and discontented peasants. There is a possibility, however, that rural revolts may be ignited by excessive levies on peasants who, as in the past, may opt to challenge the *status quo* out of their subscription to millenarian beliefs.[94] Of the three aforementioned conditions that are likely to facilitate China's political and territorial disintegration, provincial autonomy is perhaps the one that most approximates the specified condition, although the development of provincial independent armies is highly unlikely.[95]

In sum, something that had begun as an effective measure of reviving local incentives and promoting local initiatives produced a situation where it has become increasingly difficult for the centre to control the provinces. The central government has made a series of efforts — including minor readjustments and macro-economic control measures — largely in vain. Beijing has recently begun to implement a variety of measures — one key example being the tax-sharing reform — designed to bring local autonomy under control. To what extent Beijing's recent confrontation with the provinces will be effective remains to be seen. As a matter of fact, the effectiveness of Beijing's reassertion of its control over the provinces may perhaps decline in proportion to the duration of decentralization reform. That is, decentralization may gather its own momentum over time so as to make a certain level of provincial autonomy difficult, if not impossible, to reverse. The future balance of power between the centre and the provinces is thus a very precarious one as central-provincial dynamics have become a half-open Pandora's box which can be flung open initially by succession politics and later by rampant socioeconomic contradictions that come with the reform. Then, again, the overall power of the centre in China had been somewhat excessive in the past, and various key reform programmes — marketization and privatization — may perhaps be better implemented by stronger provincial governments with more abundant local information.[96]

Notes

1. For the issue of state capacity, see Wang Shaoguang and Hu Angang, *Zhongguo guojia nengli baogao* (Report on the State Capacity of China) (Hong Kong: Oxford University Press, 1994; also from Shenyang: Liaoning renmin chubanshe, 1993); and contributions by Wang Shaoguang, Hu Angang, Yang Dali, Cui Zhiyuan, Shao Yuqing and Xiao Geng on "Zhongguo guojia nengli de bianlun" (Debates on China's State Capacity), *Ershiyi shiji* (The Twenty-First Century), No. 21 (February 1994), pp. 4–23.
2. Studies that point to the possibility of China's disintegration include Wu Guoguang and Wang Zhaojun, *Deng Xiaoping zhi hou de Zhongguo* (China after Deng) (Taipei: Shijie shuju, 1994), pp. 181–282; Edward Friedman, "China's North-South Split and the Forces of Disintegration," *Current History*, No. 575 (September 1993), pp. 270–74; Maria Hsia Chang, "China's Future: Regionalism, Federation, or Disintegration," *Studies in Comparative Communism*, Vol. 25, No. 3 (September 1992), pp. 211–27; and "Dalushehui maodun yu Deng Xiaoping hou zhengju yuce" (Contradictions in the Mainland Society and Some Predictions about Post-Deng Politics), *The Nineties* (Hong Kong), March 1994, pp. 49–57. For a foreign policy prescription based on the possibility of China's disintegration, see Harry Harding, *A Fragile Relationship: The United States and China since 1972* (Washington DC: The Brookings Institution, 1992), pp. 305–307. For "duke economies," see Qiu Honghui, "Zhonggong zhuhoujingji de xingcheng ji wenti" (The Formation and Problems of Mainland China's "Duke Economies"), *Zhonggong yanjiu* (Studies of Communist China), Vol. 24, No. 11 (November 1990), pp. 34–40. For more cautious approaches, see David S. G. Goodman, "Provinces Confronting the State?" in *China Review 1992*, edited by Kuan Hsin-chi and Maurice Brosseau (Hong Kong: Chinese University Press, 1992), pp. 3.2–19 and John Fitzgerald, "Reports of My Death Have Been Greatly Exaggerated: The History of the Death of China" and Dali L. Yang, "Reform and the Restructuring of Central-Local Relations," in *China Deconstructs: Politics,*

Trade and Regionalism, edited by David S. G. Goodman and Gerald Segal (London: Routledge, 1994), pp. 21–58, 59–98.
3. This logic is discussed in Barry Naughton, "The Decline of Central Control over Investment in Post-Mao China," in *Policy Implementation in Post-Mao China*, edited by David M. Lampton (Berkeley: University of California Press, 1987), pp. 76-77. As Dali Yang has correctly pointed out, however, "it is difficult to differentiate between the case of the centre choosing not to exercise its prerogat.ves and the centre being unable to do so." See Dali L. Yang, "Reform and the Restructuring of Central-Local Relations" (Note 2), p. 74.
4. See Douglas Durasoff, "Conflicts between Economic Decentralization and Political Control in the Domestic Reform of Soviet and Post-Soviet Systems," *Social Science Quarterly*, Vol. 69, No. 2 (June 1988), pp. 388–89; and Kenneth G. Lieberthal, " Introduction: The 'Fragmented Authoritarianism' Model and Its Limitations," in *Bureaucracy, Politics, and Decision Making in Post-Mao China*, edited by Kenneth G. Lieberthal and David M. Lampton (Berkeley: University of California Press, 1992), p. 20. For a fuller discussion on the issue of fiscal indicators and central-local government relations as positive-sum and issue-variant games, see Jae Ho Chung, "Studies of Central-Provincial Relations in the People's Republic of China: A Mid-Term Appraisal," *The China Quarterly*, No.142 (June 1995), pp. 173, 180–87.
5. Exemplary work which adopt "comprehensive approaches" include Jia Hao and Lin Zhimin (eds.), *Changing Central-Local Relations in China: Reform and State Capacity* (Boulder: Westview, 1994); and Jae Ho Chung and Shiu Hing Lo, "Beijing's Relations with the Hong Kong Special Administrative Region: An Inferential Framework for the Post-1997 Arrangements," *Pacific Affairs*, Vol. 68, No. 2 (Summer 1995).
6. See Thomas Lyons and Wang Yan, *Planning and Finance in China's Economic Reforms*, Cornell University East Asia Papers No. 46 (Ithaca: Cornell University Press, 1988).
7. Currently, with regard to the projects financed by domestic funds, the ceiling is set at RMB 200 million for Guangdong, Fujian, Hainan and Shanghai (Pudong). For foreign-invested projects, over 20 provincial-level governments in the coastal region (including "special economic zones" and "central economic cities") can approve projects with investments up to US$ 30 million. For most inland provinces, autonomous regions and central economic cities (except Wuhan), the ceiling is set at US$ 10 million. See State Planning Commission, "Boundaries of Economic Management between China's Central and Local Governments," pp. 20–21.
8. Ibid., p. 5.
9. Nicholas R. Lardy, *Foreign Trade and Economic Reform in China, 1978–1990* (Cambridge: Cambridge University Press, 1992), p. 39.

10. For local legislation, see Sen Lin, "A New Pattern of Decentralization in China: The Increase of Provincial Powers in Economic Legislation," *China Information*, Vol. 7, No. 3 (Winter 1992–1993), pp. 27–38; for an earlier effort of decentralization of personnel management, see John P. Burns, "China's Nomenklatura System," *Problems of Communism*, No. 5 (September–October 1987), p. 38; and for the recent recentralization attempt by Beijing, see John P. Burns, "Strengthening Central CCP Control of Leadership Selection: The 1990 Nomenklatura," *The China Quarterly*, No. 138 (June 1994), pp. 470–74. For Guangdong's compliant behaviour in the aftermath of the June Fourth Incident, see Yang Xiaohui, *Shengjizhengfu de zizhuxingwei — kaifang gaige shiqi de Guangdong zhengfu* (Provincial Autonomous Behaviour: Guangdong in the Period of Reform and Opening), (Master thesis to the Department of Politics and Public Administration, The Chinese University of Hong Kong, 1990), chapter 5.
11. This section is an abridged and updated version of "Beijing Confronting the Provinces: The 1994 Tax-Sharing Reform and Its Implications for Central-Provincial Relations in China," *China Information*, Vol. 9, No. 2/3 (Winter 1994–1995), pp. 1–23.
12. While the specific-revenue sharing scheme seemed generally attractive, provinces were more than willing to give up their share of the profits from locally owned enterprises as long as they could get a larger share of more stable and voluminous industrial-commercial taxes (*gongshangshui*) under the overall-revenue sharing arrangement. See Susan Shirk, "Playing to the Provinces: Deng Xiaoping's Political Strategy of Economic Reform," *Studies in Comparative Communism*, Vol. 23, No. 3/4 (Autumn/Winter 1990), pp. 245–46. As of 1989, the industrial-commercial tax was the largest tax source, comprising over 85% of the total tax revenues. In Shandong, for instance, the share of the industrial-commercial tax constituted 89% of the province's revenue incomes in 1985 and 91% in 1993. See *Shandong tongji nianjian 1993* (Shandong Statistical Yearbook 1993) (Beijing: Zhongguo tongji chubanshe, 1993), pp. 119–20; and 1994 issue, p. 117.
13. For various types of the fiscal contract system, see Song Xinzhong, *Zhongguo caizheng tizhi gaige yanjiu* (Study of China's Fiscal Reform) (Beijing: Zhongguo caizheng jingji chubanshe, 1992), pp. 59-62. For the provincial breakdown of the four categories of the fiscal contract system in 1991, see Ramgopal Agarwala, *China: Reforming Intergovernmental Fiscal Relations* (Washington DC: The World Bank, 1992), p. 68; and Lok Sang Ho, "Central-Provincial Fiscal Relations," in *China Review 1993*, edited by Joseph Cheng Yu-shek and Maurice Brosseau (Hong Kong: Chinese University Press, 1993), p. **12**.8.
14. Guo Yanzhong, "Fenshuizhi yanjiu zhuanji" (Special Edition on the Study of

the Tax-Sharing System), *Jingji yanjiu cankao*, No. 401 (1 January 1994), pp. 41–44.

15. *Zhongguo tongji nianjian 1994* (China Statistical Yearbook 1994; hereafter *ZGTJNJ*) (Beijing: Zhongguo tongji chubanshe, 1994), pp. 20–21.

16. For the data on EBFs, see *Zhongguo tongji zhaiyao 1994* (Statistical Survey of China 1994), (Beijing: Zhongguo tongji chubanshe, 1994), p. 40. Although three-fourths (76.4%) of all EBFs resided with enterprises in 1991, local governments easily tapped enterprise funds by imposing a variety of levies or by shifting various administrative costs to enterprises. See Lok Sang Ho, "Central-Provincial Fiscal Relations" (Note 13), pp. **12**.3, **12**.7; Wang Shaoguang, "Central-Local Fiscal Politics in China," in *Changing Central-Local Relations in China* (Note 5), p. 97; and Yu Tianxin, "Guibing he shudao yusuanwai zijin de gaige shizai bixing" (The Reform of Merging and Channeling the Extra-Budgetary Funds Is Inevitable), *Jingji yanjiu cankao*, No. 417 (7 May 1994), pp. 30–31.

17. See Xiang Huaicheng (Vice-minister of Finance), *Jiushiniandai caizheng fazhan zhanlue* (Strategies of Fiscal Development for the 1990s) (Beijing: Zhongguo caizheng jingji chubanshe, 1991), p. 65; and *Jingji cankao* (Economic Reference), 31 July 1993 cited in "Dangqian caishui gaige bage beijing jieshao" (Eight Backgrounds to the Current Fiscal and Tax Reform), *Caizheng yanjiu ziliao* (Fiscal Research Materials), No. 2 (20 January 1994), p. 2.

18. See Song Xinzhong, *Zhongguo caizheng tizhi gaige yanjin* (Note 13), pp. 63, 65, 68–70. A Finance Ministry source contends that the share of budgetary revenues in national income should be at least 28% in order to secure the absolutely necessary expenditures of the state. See Xiang Huaicheng, *Jiushiniandai caizheng fazhan zhanlue* (Note 17), p. 16.

19. For these measures ranging from specialized levies imposed on extra-budgetary funds and the distribution of provincial quotas for the purchase of national bonds to "forced loans" and other demands for fiscal contribution, see *Dangdai zhongguo caizheng* (Contemporary China's Finance) (Beijing: Zhongguo shehuikexue chubanshe, 1988), pp. 309–11; Christine P. W. Wong, "Central-Local Relations in an Era of Fiscal Decline: The Paradox of Fiscal Decentralization in Post-Mao China," *The China Quarterly*, No. 128 (December 1991), p. 701; Guo Yanzhong, "Fenshuizhi yanjiu zhuanji" (Note 14), p. 37; Peter Tsan-yin Cheung, "The Evolving Relations between the Center and Guangdong in the Reform Era" in *Changing Central-Local Relations in China* (Note 5), pp. 226–27; and Department of National Bond Management of the Ministry of Finance, *Zhongguo guozhai zhanlue wenti yanjiu* (Study of China's National Bonds Strategy) (Beijing: Jingji kexue chubanshe, 1991), p. 75.

20. "Dangqian caishui gaige bage beijing jieshao" (Note 17), p. 3.

21. Yuan Zhenyu, *Caizheng chizi yanjiu* (Study of Fiscal Deficit) (Beijing: Zhongguo caizheng jingji chubanshe, 1991), pp. 298, 301–302; Christine P. W. Wong, "Central-Local Relations in an Era of Fiscal Decline ..." (Note 19), p. 707; and Xiang Huaicheng, *Jiushiniandai caizheng fazhan zhanlue* (Note 17), pp. 16, 26, 65–66. For budgetary balances in 1981–1993, see *ZGTJNJ 1994*, p. 220.
22. See "Dangqian caishui gaige beijing jieshao" (Note 17), pp. 1–4; and Guo Yanzhong, "Fenshuizhi yanjiu zhuanji" (Note 14), pp. 14–16.
23. For the 1993 budget report, see "China's Finance Minister Hints at Dangers Ahead," *Far Eastern Economic Review*, 24 March 1994, p. 48.
24. *Renmin ribao*, 23 November 1993; and Cao Bolong, "Mingnian shixing de xinshuizhi yu xianxing shuizhi de bijiao fenxi" (A Comparative Analysis of the Current and New Tax Systems), *Baokan soyin ziliao: caizheng yu shuiwu* (Newspaper Index Materials: Fiscal and Tax Matters), No. 2 (1994), pp. 50–51.
25. See *Ming Pao* (Hong Kong), 14 March 1994. In 1994, tax revenues from the tobacco sector amounted to RMB 55 billion (14 billion up from 1993), accounting for 12% of all tax revenues. See *South China Morning Post* (Hong Kong), 17 January 1995.
26. For detailed discussions of each tax category and a useful collection of documents on "transitional arrangements," see *Xin shuishou zhidu jiangjie* (Discussions of the New Tax System) (Beijing: Qixiang chubanshe, 1994).
27. See the aforementioned State Council Document No. 85, p. 19; "Dangqian caishui gaige bage beijing jieshao" (Note 17), pp. 11–12; and "Mingnian shixing de xinshuizhi yu xianxing shuizhi de bijiao fenxi" (Note 24), p. 50.
28. State Council Document No. 85, p. 19; and *Renmin ribao*, 23 November 1993.
29. See, for instance, Wang Shaogang and Hu Angang, *Jiaqiang zhongyangzhengfu zai shichangjingji zhuanxingzhong de zhudao zuoyong* (To Strengthen the Primary Role of the Central Government in the Period of Transition to Market Economy) initially made available at Yale University in May 1993, pp. 76–77. For a little more modest prescription of 28 and 55%, respectively, see Xiang Huaicheng, *Jiushiniandai caizheng fazhan zhanlue* (Note 17), p. 16. Also see *South China Morning Post*, 20 December 1993.
30. *South China Morning Post*, 19 January 1994.
31. See State Council Document No. 85, p. 19; *Wen Wei Po* (Hong Kong), 3 February 1994; and Ning Xueping, "Ping caishui tizhi gaige fangan" (Commentary on the Fiscal and Tax Reform Measures), *Gaige* (Reform), No. 2 (1994), reprinted in *Baokan soyin ziliao: caizheng yu shuiwu*, No. 4 (1994), p. 60.
32. For the provincial views expressed at the national fiscal work conference, see

"Caizhengtingzhang tan fenshuizhi gaige" (Financial Bureau Chiefs Discuss the Tax-Sharing Reform), *Caizheng*, No. 2 (1994), pp. 11–13. For Hubei, Xinjiang, Guangxi and Qinghai, see "Shengqu dangzheng lingdao tan caishui gaige" (Provincial Leaders Discuss the Fiscal and Tax Reform), *Caizheng*, No. 4 (1994), pp. 2–3; for three inland provinces, *South China Morning Post*, 19 January 1994; and for Anhui, *Ming Pao*, 15 March 1994.

33. *Wen Wei Po*, 21 March 1994; and "Shixing fenshuizhi difang caizheng zenmeban" (What about Local Finance after the Tax-Sharing Reform?), *Caizheng yanjiu*, No. 7 (1994), p. 47.
34. *Ming Pao*, 14 March 1994; and *Wen Wei Po*, 22 March 1994.
35. *South China Morning Post*, 30 October 1993; and Guo Yanzhong, "Fenshuizhi yanjiu zhuanji" (Note 14), p. 18.
36. *Wen Wei Po*, 3 February and 21 March 1994.
37. *South China Morning Post*, 14 March 1994.
38. *Jinrong shibao* (Financial Times), 6 December 1993.
39. For warnings on standardized implementation, see *Renmin ribao*, 13 December 1993; for the rigid position of the centre, see *Guangming ribao* (Guangming Daily), 21 March 1994; for the expressions made by localities, see *Express News* (Hong Kong), 18 and 22 March 1994; for the dispatch of work-teams, see "Caishui gaige jinzhan qingkuang de diaocha" (A Survey on the Progress of the Fiscal and Tax Reform), *Caizheng*, No. 4 (1994), p. 4; and for the centre's warning against regionalism, see *Renmin ribao*, 29 November 1994.
40. *South China Morning Post*, 20 December 1993 and 19 January 1994.
41. State Council Document No. 85, p. 19 and *Renmin ribao*, 23 November 1993. Zhou Xiaochuan, Vice-president of the Bank of China, commented that, given the Japanese experiences with the consumption tax reform, the entire process in China will take at least three years of bargaining and adjustments. Information from his talk given at a seminar at the Hong Kong University of Science and Technology on 28 April 1994.
42. For criticisms from Guangdong and Shanghai of the property gains tax, see *South China Morning Post*, 17 February 1994; for the revised version, see *Ming Pao*, 16 April 1994; and for the finalized version, see *South China Morning Post*, 16 February 1995.
43. These recommendations include: (1) local governments' EBFs should be merged into official budgetary funds and EBFs residing in enterprises must be controlled solely by the firms as investment funds; (2) the enterprise income tax should become a shared tax divided in such a way that the centre retains 18% and localities get 15% of the 33% levied; and (3) in the long run, the shared-category should be abolished for the purpose of further enhancing the centre's fiscal capacity. See Yu Tianxin, "Guibing shudao ..." (Note 16), pp. 34–35; Ministry of Finance, "Dui gaige caizheng tizhi de ruogan zhengce

yijian" (Some Policy Opinions Regarding the Fiscal Reform), *Hubei caizheng yanjiu* (Hubei Fiscal Research), No. 2 (1994) reprinted in *Baokan soyin ziliao: caizheng yu shuiwu*, No. 4 (1994), p. 67; and "Lun fenshuizhi de zhidao yuanze ji qishishi yunzuo wenti" (On the Leading Principles and Implementation Problems of the Tax-Sharing Reform), *Caizheng yanjiu*, No. 3 (March 1994), p. 15.

44. In fact, there were fears that the whole reform might repeat the failure of the early 1980s. See "Fenshuizhi yu difang zuli" (The Tax-Sharing Reform Encounters Local Opposition), *Guangjiaojing* (Wide Angle), January 1994, p. 11. For the disagreements and concerns over the tax-sharing reform within the policy community of the government, see Policy Research Office of the State Planning Commission, "Wo guo zhongyang yu difang jingji guanli quanxian yanjiu" (Study of Boundaries of Economic Management between China's Central and Local Governments), *Jingji yanjiu cankao*, No. 434/435 (1 March 1994), pp. 58–66.

45. See Giandomenico Majone, *Evidence, Argument and Persuasion in the Policy Process* (New Haven: Yale University Press, 1989), pp. 102–103.

46. For bureaucratic careerism, see Joel S. Migdal, *Strong Societies and Weak States: State-Society Relations and State Capabilities in the Third World* (Princeton: Princeton University Press, 1988), pp. 239–42.

47. For the falsification of statistics in this period, see Kenneth Lieberthal, "The Great Leap Forward and the Split in the Yenan Leadership," in Roderick MacFarquhar and John K. Fairbank (eds.), *The Cambridge History of China*, Vol. 14, *The People's Republic*, Part 1: *The Emergence of Revolutionary China 1949–1965* (London: Cambridge University Press, 1987), p. 309; and Alfred L. Chan, "The Campaign for Agricultural Development in the Great Leap Forward: A Study of Policy-Making and Implementation in Liaoning," *The China Quarterly*, No. 129 (March 1992), pp. 57, 65. For the data on communization, see Frederick C. Teiwes, "Provincial Politics: Themes and Variations," in John Lindbeck (ed.), *China: Management of a Revolutionary Society* (Seattle: University of Washington Press, 1971), p. 172.

48. See, for instance, Michel Oksenberg, "Methods of Communication within the Chinese Bureaucracy," *The China Quarterly*, No. 57 (January–March 1974), pp. 1–39.

49. *Renmin ribao*, 16 November 1977; and Beijing Xinhua Domestic Service, 24 October 1980 in *Foreign Broadcast Information Service: Daily Report-China* (hereafter *FBIS*), 27 October 1980, pp. L4–5.

50. See, for instance, Yasheng Huang, "Information, Bureaucracy, and Economic Reforms in China and the Soviet Union," *World Politics*, Vol. 47, No. 1 (October 1994), pp. 124–29.

51. State Statistical Bureau, *Zhongguo tongji gongzuo nianjian 1993* (China Statistical Work Yearbook 1993) (Beijing: Zhongguo tongji chubanshe,

1993), pp. I-51–54, III-13–14; and *South China Morning Post*, 21 January 1995.

52. For 1981 and 1988, see Huang, "Information, Bureaucracy, and Economic Reforms in China and the Soviet Union" (Note 50), pp. 127–28; and for 1994, see *South China Morning Post*, 28 October 1994.
53. Nina P. Halpern, "Information Flows and Policy Coordination in the Chinese Bureaucracy," in Kenneth G. Lieberthal and David M. Lampton (eds.), *Bureaucracy, Politics, and Decision Making in Post-Mao China* (Note 4), p. 126.
54. For Zheng's acknowledgment, see his speech to the national conference of provincial-level statistical bureau chiefs published in *Zhongguo tongji gongzuo nianjian 1993*, p. I–52. For deflated reports on tax revenues and enterprise profits, see *Eastern Express* (Hong Kong), 2 March 1994. For calls for the revision of the law on statistics, see 8 December 1993. For other media reports warning against statistical manipulation, see *Renmin ribao*, 17 August 1994 and *China Daily*, 11 September 1994.
55. Author's interviews in Harbin in 11–15 July 1994. For a general discussion of the statistical work on rural areas, see He Huanyan, "Nongcun shehuijingji diaocha gongzuo de jianli yu fazhan" (The Establishment and Development of the Survey Work on the Rural Social Economy) in *Zhongguo bashiniandai tongji gaige yu fazhan*, edited by Zheng Jiaxiang (Reform and Development of China's Statistical Work in the 1980s) (Beijing: Zhongguo tongji chubanshe, 1992), pp. 86–95.
56. A Hong Kong report suggested that classified documents could be purchased for US$10,000. See *The Mirror* (Hong Kong), October 1994, p. 46.
57. CECs were allowed to negotiate directly with Beijing in setting the baseline figures for remittance or the ratios for revenue sharing; CECs no longer needed provincial licenses for exports, and they were authorized to approve foreign investment projects up to US$ 30 million; and in many cases, CECs took over large enterprises (56 in the case of Wuhan) formerly managed by the centre or the respective provincial governments.
58. For the backgrounds to the CEC policy, see Paul E. Schroeder, "Territorial Actors as Competitors for Power: The Case of Hubei and Wuhan," in Kenneth G. Lieberthal and David M. Lampton (eds.), *Bureaucracy, Politics and Decision Making in Post-Mao China* (Note 4), pp. 286–91. For the chronology of designation, see Dorothy J. Solinger, "The Place of the Central City in China's Economic Reform: From Hierarchy to Network?" in *China's Transition from Socialism: Statist Legacies and Market Reforms 1980–1990* (Armonk: M. E. Sharpe, 1993), p. 212.
59. Such reasoning applied to Hubei's initial acceptance of Wuhan's CEC proposal. See Schroeder, "Territorial Actors as Competitors for Power" (Note 58), p. 292.

Central-Provincial Relations 3.41

60. For a detailed analysis of these problems in the case of Wuhan, see Schroeder, "Territorial Actors as Competitors for Power" (Note 58), pp. 293–304 and Dorothy J. Solinger, "City, Province, and Region: The Case of Wuhan" in *China's Transition from Socialism* (Note 58), pp. 177–79. For a Chinese critique of this problem, see Zhu Limin et al., "Zhongyang yu difang zhengfu shiquan huafen yu zhineng peizhi wenti yanjiu" (Study of How to Distribute the Rights and Functions of Central and Local Governments) in *Difang jigou gaige sikao*, edited by Wu Peilun (Thoughts on the Reform of Local Organizations), (Beijing: Gaige chubanshe, 1992), pp. 182–87.
61. In the case of Qingdao, the delegation to the city of the ownership of certain key industrial enterprises — an important part of the CEC package — faced serious difficulties due to the unwillingness of some provincial organizations. For instance, the ownership of the Qingdao Steel Mill Corporation had not been devolved until 1991 due to the staunch opposition from the Shandong Provincial Metallurgical Corporation which was in turn under the control of the Provincial Metallurgical Bureau. In regional planning of economic reform, too, the provincial authorities have tended to give more support to Yantai and Weihai instead of Qingdao which, before the CEC designation, had been the only "dragon-head" (*longtou*) of Shandong's reform. Interviews in Jinan on 28 and 29 June 1994.
62. See *FBIS*, 12 August 1993, p. 16. Also see Ibid. 9 November 1993, p. 33.
63. Interview in Jinan on 28 June 1994.
64. It is not entirely inconceivable that the centre cultivates and utilizes these key cities as counterweights to the growing autonomy and regionalism of provincial authorities. This speculation has benefitted from Vivienne Shue, *The Reach of the State: Sketches of the Chinese Body Politic* (Stanford: Stanford University Press, 1988), pp. 54–55.
65. For this section, I am indebted to Liu Guangshan, "Yijiujiusi nian huizhi gaige ji zhanwang" (The 1994 Foreign Exchange System Reform and Its Prospect), *Jingji yanjiu cankao*, No. 591 (16 December 1994), pp. 9–11; and "Xinwaihui guanli tizhi de yunxing zhuangkuang ji cunzai de yixie wenti" (The Current Situation of the New Foreign Exchange Management System and Its Problems), *Jingji yanjiu cankao*, No. 601 (1 January 1995), pp. 40–52.
66. Information obtained from Lardy, *Foreign Trade and Economic Reform in China* (Note 9), pp. 55–56; and author's interview in Qingdao on 22 June 1994. Until 1990, the retention systems varied along the regional lines. With the announcement of the State Council Circular No. 70 (1990), retention rates were to vary according to the kind of items concerned. The figure of 50% was applied to most items. See "Wo guo zhongyang yu difang jingji" (Note 44), pp. 23, 46.
67. See Lo Jingfen, "Yijiujiusinian jingji gaige shiping" (An Assessment of the Economic Reform in 1994), *Jingji yanjiu cankao*, No. 592 (8 December

1994), p. 20; and "Yijiujiusinian zhongguo waimao jiben zhuangkuang de huigu yiji dui yijiujiuwunian zhongguo waimao qianjing de zhanwang" (A Retrospect on China's Foreign Trade in 1994 and Its Prospect for 1995), ibid. No. 601 (1 January 1995), p. 21.

68. For the VAT issue, see *South China Morning Post*, 27 January 1995. And for the break-up of large projects, see *Renmin ribao*, 21 January 1995.

69. In addition to these four provinces, the party secretary of the Inner Mongolian Autonomous Region, Wang Qun, was replaced in December 1993 by Liu Mingzu, formerly deputy party secretary of Guangxi. Hubei's party secretary, Guan Guangfu, retired in December 1993 to be replaced by Jia Zhijie, its governor. And at least eight more provinces received new governors in 1994-1995 (up to March) including Anhui's Hui Liangyu (formerly a deputy party secretary of Hubei), Shaanxi's Cheng Andong (formerly Xian's party secretary), Hunan's Yang Zhengwu (formerly its deputy party secretary), Hebei's Ye Liangsong, Henan's Ma Zhongchen (formerly Shandong's deputy governor), Liaoning's Wen Shizhen (formerly its deputy governor), Gansu's Zhang Wule, and Fujian's Jiang Zhuping. No detailed information is yet available for us to explore the backgrounds of each of these cases. For the changes, see *South China Morning Post*, 27 December 1994, and 23 January, 25 and 27 February, and 22 March 1995; and *Zhonggong yanjiu*, various issues in 1994–1995.

70. See *South China Morning Post*, 8 December 1993 and 19 January 1994, and *Ming Pao*, 12 March 1994.

71. For the changes and brief profiles of Yue and Tian, see *Zhonggong yanjiu*, Vol. 28, No. 5 (May 1994), p. 127; ibid., Vol. 28, No. 6 (June 1994), p. 114; and ibid., Vol. 28, No. 9 (September 1994), p. 122.

72. For these competing perspectives on the personnel changes in Shanghai, see *South China Morning Post*, 29 September 1994. Wu was recently appointed as a vice-premier in charge of industry at the National People's Congress session in March 1995. See *South China Morning Post*, 18 October 1994 and 18 March 1995. In February 1995, Huang Ju's mayoral position was succeeded by Xu Kuangdi, formerly Shanghai's deputy mayor and another close associate of Jiang Zemin. See *South China Morning Post*, 25 February 1995.

73. Jiang was succeeded by Zhao Zhihao — Shandong-native former governor — who was in turn succeeded by Li Chunting, the first deputy governor who is also a Shandong native. Jiang was appointed as a vice-premier in charge of agriculture in March 1995. See *South China Morning Post*, 25 November 1994 and 18 March 1995.

74. During his renowned southern tour in 1992, Deng is alleged to have praised Jiang's accomplishments in Shandong. See He Pin and Gao Xin, *Zhongguo xinquangui: zuixin lingdaozhe qunxiang* (China's Power Élite: The New Leadership Profiles) (Hong Kong: Contemporary Monthly, 1993), p. 260. For

Jiang's alleged connections with Chen Yun, see *South China Morning Post*, 12 October 1994. Others (especially many interviewees in China) suggest Jiang's linkage with Song Ping, a strong "organization man" of Shandong origin.

75. On the other hand, two other provinces merit attention by virtue of the absence of any personnel changes. First, despite being the most economically dynamic province, Guangdong was excluded from any involvement with key personnel changes. Second, Beijing was again silent on Sichuan, which had even failed to send its party boss, Xiao Yang, to the Politburo in 1992, unlike his two predecessors of Zhao Ziyang and Yang Rudai.

76. For an excellent discussion of structural constraints on the collusion between local civilian and military authorities, see Michael D. Swaine, "Chinese Regional Forces as Political Actors," in Richard H. Yang et al., *Chinese Military Regionalism: The Security Dimension* (Boulder: Westview, 1994), pp. 63–67. For the average duration of service by regional commanders, see *Hongkong Standard*, 9 October 1994.

77. According to an estimate, in 1993 alone the PLA is said to have made about US$ 5 billion from its industrial and commercial enterprises. This figure amounts to 83% of its officially allocated budget for 1994 (excluding those hidden spending). See *South China Morning Post*, 22 April 1994.

78. There is an emergent literature on this issue. See, for instance, Tai-Ming Cheung, "Profits over Professionalism: The PLA's Economic Activities and the Impact on Military Unity," in *Chinese Military Regionalism*, pp. 85–110; Mel Gurtov, "Swords into Market Shares: China's Conversion of Military Industry to Civilian Production," *The China Quarterly*, No. 134 (June 1993), pp. 213–41; and Thomas J. Bickford, "The Chinese Military and Its Business Operations: The PLA as an Entrepreneur," *Asian Survey*, Vol. 34, No. 5 (May 1994), pp. 460–74.

79. See, for instance, David S. G. Goodman, "The PLA in Guangdong Province: Warlordism and Localism," in Yang et al., *Chinese Military Regionalism* (Note 76), pp. 220–21; Gerald Segal, *China Changes Shape: Regionalism and Foreign Policy* (London: International Institute for Strategic Studies, 1994), pp. 24–25; and *Eastern Express*, 2 June 1994.

80. For this information, see *South China Morning Post*, 19 and 30 September 1994, and *Ta Kung Pao*, 15 October 1994.

81. For the opening of the border provinces, see Liu Baorong and Liao Jiasheng (eds.), *Zhongguo yanbian kaifang yu zhoubian guojia shichang* (The Opening of China's Border Areas and the Neighbouring Markets), (Beijing: Falü chubanshe, 1993) and Jude Howell, *China Opens Its Doors: The Politics of Economic Transition* (Boulder: Lynne Rienner, 1993), pp. 86–87, 93, 95–96, 112. And for a Chinese study of inter-regional inequalities, see Ma Lieguang et al., *Zhongguo geshengqu jingji fazhan bijiao* (Comparison of Economic Development among China's Provinces and Regions), (Chengdu: Chengdu

keji daxue chubanshe, 1993), chapter 5 which compares Sichuan, Hubei and Shandong.
82. See *South China Morning Post*, 20 May and 23 August 1994.
83. See Xu Bingwen et al., *Zhongguo xibei diqu fazhan zhanlue gailun* (Survey of Economic Development Strategies in China's Northwest Region), (Beijing: Jingji guanli chubanshe, 1992), pp. 246–50; Jia Hao and Wang Mingxia, "Market and State: Changing Central-Local Relations in China," in *Changing Central-Local Relations in China* (Note 5), p. 44; and Yong-Nian Zheng, "Perforated Sovereignty: Provincial Dynamism and China's Foreign Trade," *The Pacific Review*, Vol. 7, No. 3 (1994), pp. 316–18.
84. For a view that characterizes the key nature of China's provincial leaders as a "categoric group" rather than a political group, see David S. G. Goodman, "Provincial Party First Secretaries in National Politics: A Categoric or a Political Group?" in *Groups and Politics in the People's Republic of China*, edited by David S. G. Goodman (Cardiff: University College Cardiff Press, 1984), pp. 68–82
85. For the information on the annual meetings of the CECs, I am indebted to Dorothy Solinger, "Decentralization in Wuhan" (Draft) which was prepared for the "Decentralization in China" project of the World Bank, September 1994, p. 15. For the pairing of Yunnan and Guangdong, see Segal, *China Changes Shape* (Note 79), p. 18.
86. The centre's order was very effective since almost all provinces responded within two months. Rich provinces like Guangdong, Shandong, Shanghai, Jiangsu and Zhejiang made committed themselves to projects with investments ranging from RMB 39 to 60 million, while poor, backward and minorities provinces — like Qinghai, Jiangxi, Anhui, Gansu and Inner Mongolia — contributed RMB 3 to 6 million. *World Tibet Network News* (on Internet), 21 September 1994 and *Liaowang* (Outlook), No. 558 (26 September 1994), pp. 14–23. I thank Barry Sautman for sharing this information with me. For reports on the "cadre exchange programme" designed to transfer development experiences of the coastal regions, see *South China Morning Post*, 22 March and 1 April 1995.
87. These five functions are listed in Qingdao Municipal Office for Historical Research, *Qingdao nianjian 1992* (Qingdao Yearbook 1992) (Qingdao: Zhongguo baike quanshu chubanshe, 1993), pp. 70–71. Items (1) and (4) are particularly interesting since they make it no secret that the city wants to sustain a good working relationship with the central government and the State Council and to exert influence over the centre's policy.
88. These figures are from an interview in Qingdao on 14 December 1994.
89. For the NIMBY case, see *Eastern Express*, 7 February 1994.
90. Since many studies have already noted the diversification and localization of China's foreign (economic) relations, only a few references are made here.

See Segal, *China Changes Shape* (Note 79); contributions by Brantly Womack and Guangzhi Zhao, Michael B. Yahuda, Peter Ferdinand, and Ingrid d'Hooghe in *China Deconstructs* (Note 2); Colin Mackerras, *China's Minorities: Integration and Modernization in the Twentieth Century* (Hong Kong: Oxford University Press, 1994), chapter 7; Zhang Amei and Zou Gang, "Foreign Trade Decentralization and Its Impact on Central-Local Relations," in *Changing Central-Local Relations in China* (Note 5), pp. 153–77; Lilian C. Harris, "Xinjiang, Central Asia and the Implications for China's Policy in the Islamic World" and Gaye Christoffersen, "Xinjiang and the Great Islamic Circle," *The China Quarterly*, No. 133 (March 1993), pp. 111–51.

91. See, for instance, David S. G. Goodman, "The Politics of Regionalism: Economic Development, Conflict and Negotiation," in *China Deconstructs* (Note 2), pp. 3–4, 8–9, 12–14; David S. G. Goodman, "Provinces Confronting the State?" (Note 2), pp. **3.**15–17; and Wu and Wang, *Deng Xiaoping zhi hou de zhongguo* (Note 2), pp. 253–82.

92. See Frederick Wakeman Jr., *The Fall of Imperial China*. (New York: The Free Press, 1975), chapter 8. For a study that pointed out the aforementioned three factors contributing to dynastic collapse, see Wei-chin Mu, *Provincial-Central Government Relations and the Problem of National Unity in Modern China* (doctoral dissertation to the Department of Politics, Princeton University, 1948) (Ann Arbor: Universities Microfilms Inc., 1965), p. 25.

93. See, for instance, Li Luye, "The Current Situation in Northeast Asia: A Chinese View," *Journal of Northeast Asian Studies*, Vol. 10, No. 1 (Spring 1991), pp. 78–81.

94. In the first six months of 1994, state cash levies on peasants increased by 41% while their income rose just 9.5%. See *South China Morning Post*, 2 November 1994. Very recently, the central party and government called for the strengthening of rural grass-roots party cells and monitoring of religious activities in the countryside. See *South China Morning Post*, 11 October 1994 and *Renmin ribao*, 30 October 1994. The prevalence of religious cults in the countryside and Beijing's sensitivity to it are well illustrated in *South China Morning Post*, 22 February and 20 March 1995.

95. For a very cautious approach on this issue, see Ellis Joffe, "Regionalism in China: The Role of the PLA," *Pacific Review*, Vol. 7, No. 1 (1994), pp. 17–27.

96. While decentralization is not identical to privatization, local governments can play a much more direct and meaningful role in schemes of privatization reform due to their abundant local information. In this sense, as ownership reforms further progress in China, the decentralizing trend may also become more manifest. For this possibility, see János Kornai, *Highway and Byways: Studies on Reform and Postcommunist Transition* (Cambridge: MIT Press, 1995), p. 99.

4

From Confrontation to Compromise: A Historical-Structural Account of the Rapid Deterioration of Cross-Straits Relations in 1994

Timothy Wong

Introduction

The year 1994 witnessed fierce struggles between economics and politics in cross-straits relations, with the latter having triumphed over the former until the end of the year when Taipei and Beijing attempted to reconcile again to stop the rapid deterioration of their relations. For most of the year, in spite of the continuing rapid growth of cross-straits trade and other exchanges, mutual nasty worded salvoes from the two governments were often heard, threats of force from Beijing were repeatedly made, frequent military exercises in Taiwan were reported, and semi-official talks on strengthening economic and cultural exchanges and cooperation almost stagnated. This chapter will review and analyze the major developments of cross-straits relations in 1994. However, since these developments were closely related to the political conflicts between Taipei and Beijing that had accumulated over the past several years, and since the fallout from these conflicts eventually spilled over into the economic and cultural areas, this chapter will purposefully trace the historical-structural conditions in which these developments took place and against which they can be better understood.

The Changing Political Reality in Taiwan in Recent Years

Although political animosity across the straits has existed since the establishment of the People's Republic of China (PRC) in 1949, political conflicts between Taipei and Bejing in recent years were largely triggered by Taipei's radical mainland policy shift in response to the rapidly emerging democratic reality in Taiwan. As is widely known, Taiwan's democratic reform was started by Chiang Ching-kuo, the late President of the Republic of China (ROC), toward the end of his life in the early and mid-1980s. It was also a time when Taiwan's society and economy were moving toward a state of relative maturity. However, today very few scholars would monocausally attribute the reform to the endeavour of the ruling Kuomintang (KMT) or more specifically, of President Chiang. The general concensus is rather that it was a product of at least four interacting structural factors: (1) the rapid development and consolidation of political opposition forces openly and directly pushed the state toward democratization; (2) the rising civil society asserted itself as an autonomous unit and exercised pressures on the state to liberalize through various social movements; (3) part of the ruling KMT élites became increasingly willing and confident to introduce political reform; and (4) the reform and open-door policy beginning in the late 1970s in mainland China and the tides of political liberalization and democratization then taking place in most parts of the world generated pressures on the KMT state to reform itself and at the same time had demonstrative effects on the Taiwanese.[1]

Due to the interactive effect of these four structural factors, Chiang's sudden death in January 1988 did not alter Taiwan's democratization process. His successor, President Lee Teng-hui, continued the process and then accelerated it after his power was consolidated in the 1990 indirect presidential election where he was proclaimed the eighth ROC President by the National Assembly. Under the presidency of first Chiang and then Lee, Taiwan has managed to remove or alter many of the authoritarian structures of the past, including lifting martial law; broadening freedoms of press and expression; legalizing opposition political parties; releasing political prisoners and reducing the use of the judicial system to stifle dissent; and last, but not the least, introducing for the first time in forty years full elections for the National Assembly in 1991, the Legislative Yuan in 1992 and the Governor of Taiwan in 1994. In addition, direct election of the President of the ROC is scheduled to be held in 1996. Once this election is completed, Taiwan's political reform will have drawn to a close and a truly meaningful representative democracy operating through multi-party politics will come to preside over Taiwan's political future.

Among these political structural changes, the most important one should be the formation of the pro-independence Democratic Progressive Party (DPP) in September 1986. Since the formation of this new party, the KMT authorities have taken no repressive actions. With the lifting of martial law in July 1987, Taiwan has obviously begun a new political stage in which competitive multi-party politics and representative democracy become the most important driving force of political development. Under the new rules of the game, the DPP had rapidly emerged as a significant opposition party by gathering strength in elections of the following years: in the 1989 Legislative Yuan supplementary elections, it captured 33% of the popular vote; in the 1991 National Assembly full elections, 24%; in the 1992 Legislative Yuan full elections, 36.9%; in the 1993 Mayors and County Magistrates elections, 41%; and in the 1994 Mayors of Taipei and Kaohsiung and Governor of Taiwan elections, 38%.[2] Especially in the 1994 elections, the DPP candidate Chen Shui-bian even won the Mayor of the capital city Taipei, putting the KMT incumbent candidate Huang Ta-chou into a humiliating third place. The victory not only provided the DPP with its strongest foothold ever in government; it also meant that the DPP was a step closer on its road to rule.

The development of multi-party politics and representative democracy has led to the institutionalization of political conflicts and significantly reduced political instability caused by the rising political confrontations characteristic of the KMT's later years of authoritarian rule. This can be attested to the fact that political confrontations have declined rapidly both in number and magnitude since the early 1990s.[3] In fact, as time goes by, the political state in Taiwan is increasingly popularized, drawing its mandate from, and holding responsibility to, only the people of Taiwan rather than people in the whole of China.

Nevertheless, democratization inevitably complicates Taiwan's unresolved status in the international community. In the modern framework of nation-states, the development of multi-party politics and representative democracy also means the development of popular sovereignty.[4] If Taiwan were an independent nation, this would certainly consolidate the cohesiveness of its people and strengthen the legitimacy of the ruling state. In fact, as democratization deepens, Taiwan increasingly looks more like a popular nation-state with its own sovereignty than a regional government under a higher sovereign state. However, due to its unique history the KMT state still adheres to the ideal of one China and claims that the ROC on Taiwan represents one of the two divided Chinas while aiming at future reunification. This is in spite of the fact that most parts of the world do not recognize its Chinese sovereignty even in a limited sense. The PRC on the mainland even claims that Taiwan is only a province of China. It also threathens that it may resort to force to bring Taiwan back into China under the PRC sovereignty if it considers this necessary, especially should Taiwan opt for *de jure* independence.

Continuing international isolation, the PRC's threat of force, and rapid local democratization have intertwined with and lent momentum to a separatist movement which owes its origins to the previous fifty years of Japanese colonial rule and the subsequent mainlander political domination until very recently.[5] According to the poll results conducted by the Taiwan Public Opinion Research Foundation, the percentage of pro-independence supporters had increased steadily since the late 1980s, from 8.2% in 1988, 12.5% in 1990, 15% in 1992, to 23.7% in 1993.[6] Another independent survey done in 1992 by a researcher of the Institute of Ethnology,

Academia Sinica, indicated that 47.9% of the respondents accepted or would not oppose *de jure* independence, while 52.1% opposed.[7] In a recent poll done in April 1994, people opposing *de jure* independence further dropped to 45.6%.[8] Even among those who opposed *de jure* independence, most of them did not accept rapid reunification.[9] Instead, they strongly favoured the current separation from the mainland, fearing that the communist system there might damage the freedom and prosperity they enjoyed in Taiwan.[10]

Taipei's New Approach to Its Relations with the PRC and the International Community

The changing political reality in Taiwan has inexorably altered the rules of the game for cross-straits interaction. As Andrew Nathan succinctly said in 1990:

> Political reform in Taiwan has changed the fundamental assumption on which China's Taiwan policy has hitherto been based, that the Kuomintang has the power single-handedly to negotiate the future of the island with the CCP. Democratization has so complicated the internal politics of Taiwan that it is now impossible for any deal to be struck with the mainland that does not command popular support in the island. Given the enormous risks that unification would pose for the people of Taiwan, this new political reality bodes ill for reunification on anything like the terms that have hitherto been offered by Peking.[11]

What democratization has done to Taiwan is that it has given rise to a popular state whose interests must more or less coincide with those of its citizens and whose activities must follow the new democratic norms. Besides, the development of such a popular state should enhance Taipei's ability to deal with the sensitive issue of reunification. The delegation at the bargaining table can always say to its Beijing counterpart: "I would like to agree, but this won't be acceptable at home."[12] Hence, it is not surprising that Taipei is so eager to accelerate Taiwan's political reform.[13] By means of democratization, Taipei is now acquiring more room to steer the development of cross-straits relations in a more desirable direction and at a more controllable pace.

In response to the emerging democratic reality driven by popular support, Taipei has moved toward a new, active approach to the mainland

and international relations. The overall approach is often referred to as "flexible" or "pragmatic" diplomacy, which aims to discard the previous strait-laced ideology of claiming sovereignty over the whole of China. More specifically, while still formally adhering to the ideal of reunification, Taipei attempts to reverse the trend of international isolation brought about by derecognition of the ROC by the United Nations in 1971. To achieve this objective, it engages in a long-term two-fold campaign: toward the mainland on the one hand and the international community on the other.

Taipei's new approach to the mainland is to normalize cross-straits relations by making the PRC recognize Taiwan as a political equal. Toward this end, Taipei unilaterally went ahead and relaxed its historically antagonistic relationship with Beijing. In May 1989, Shirley Kuo, Taiwan Minister of Finance, led a delegation to attend the annual meeting of the Asian Development Bank in Beijing, the first time ever in forty years that high-ranking KMT government officials made their appearance on the mainland. In October 1990, President Lee set up the National Unification Council to delineate Taiwan's new policy toward China. In the same month, the cabinet-level Mainland Affairs Council (MAC) was established, and in November the semi-official Straits Exchange Foundation (SEF) was founded under the authority of the MAC to carry out "unofficial" contacts with the PRC authorities and deal with "non-governmental" matters.

In February 1991, the National Unification Council announced its "National Unification Guidelines" in which short-, intermediate- and long-term policies toward China were clearly spelt out. The "Guidelines" particularly underlines that equal recognition is the most important objective of the short-term policy, without which any transition to the intermediate term would be impossible. In May 1991, President Lee officially abolished the "Temporary Provisions during the Period of Mobilization against the Communist Insurgency" and, in effect, announced that the Chinese Communist Party (CCP) is no longer a "bandit" organization and the PRC no longer an "illegitimate" government.

The above measures and actions reflect Taipei's new, emerging policy toward mainland China as a result of its changing political reality and growing confidence and eagerness to normalize its relationship with Beijing. In September 1992, the MAC finally issued its long-awaited report on "Issues and Prospects of Direct Transportation Links across the Taiwan Straits." The report states that the ROC is willing to open direct air and sea links with China, on the condition that the Chinese Communists renounce the threat of force against Taiwan and recognize the ROC as an equal political entity. The opening of direct transportation links has been repeatedly proposed by the PRC since 1979. This report indicates Taipei's baseline of reunification which is equal political recognition.

At the same time, while working hard to make Beijing negotiate on the unification issue on equal terms, Taipei is well aware of the importance of military might in determining the game.[14] Hence, although the defence budget has steadily decreased since the 1950s, it still amounted to around 25% of the total government budget during the past three years.[15] Apart from the regular budget, there is also a special budget line called "Procurement of High Performance Fighters." In 1993 and 1994, this budget amounted to 4.38% and 3.75% of the total government budget respectively.[16] In 1992, Taipei also published its first *1992 National Defence Report, ROC*.[17] The publication was both a response to popular pressure for transparency and an attempt to make clear to the Taiwanese people as well as to the PRC its new defence policy. The *Report* contains four major points: (1) Taiwan repudiates and opposes the use of force to achieve reunification. (2) The thrust of Taiwan's defence policy is deterrence, not aggression. (3) Taiwan will continue to strengthen its defence capability in accordance with the PRC's military development. (4) The focus of Taiwan's military development is a modernized, self-sufficient defence system based upon quality rather than quantity. In summer 1994, the second biannual report, *1993–1994 National Defence Report, ROC*,[18] came out, reiterating all the major points of the previous one and showing serious concern for Beijing's recent military expansion.

While seeking equal recognition from the PRC and strengthening its defence capability, Taipei also endeavours to tear down its international isolation. For Taipei, open and equal international participation is a presupposition of the development of an independent Taiwanese state. As a strategy, Taiwan's internationalization also exercises pressure on Beijing. In 1993, Taipei openly expressed its interest in re-entering the United Nations. This idea was first put forward by the DPP in 1988. At that time, the KMT refused to entertain the DPP's proposal because it was considered to be unrealistic and conflicted with the policy of one China. After five years of rapid democratization, the KMT radically changed its position on the question, and this to a certain extent reflected the KMT's ability to use the emerging democratic forces to its advantage in dealing with the unification issue. It also signified the emergence of a popular state in

Taiwan rallying for its own identity and autonomy. In June 1993, President Lee endorsed the idea by referring to the models of Germany and Korea, arguing that the ROC's changed position was not inconsistent with the policy of one China. At about the same time, Taipei's Foreign Ministry successfully mobilized a number of Latin American states to sponsor a resolution admitting Taiwan in the name of the ROC on Taiwan into the United Nations as one of the two independent states in a divided nation. However, the resolution was vetoed by the United Nations General Committee before reaching its General Assembly.

Despite the failure of the attempt, Taiwan continued to pursue its policy of attaining wider international recognition. One recent strategy has been the "vacation diplomacy," which aims not only at wider international recognition but also at redirecting part of the excessive Taiwanese investment in mainland China to other countries to avoid over-dependence on the mainland. The latter objective is widely known as the government-directed "Southward" (Southeast Asia) policy versus the individually initiated "Westward" (China) tendency of capital movement. In December 1993, Premier Lien Chan spent his "private vacation" in Singapore and met a number of Singaporean officials. Then in February 1994, President Lee took a bolder step visiting Thailand, Indonesia and the Philippines. During the visits, Lee signed a number of trade and investment agreements with the hosting countries. Naturally Beijing launched its protests and accused Taipei of attempting to divide China, but it could do nothing concrete to stop these "private" visits. Although both the hosting countries and Taipei claimed that these visits were "private," they were in reality official in all but name, and the willingness of these Southeast Asian nations to receive Lien and Lee in spite of Beijing's strong protests has to some extent testified to the rising, unignorable importance of Taiwan in Asia. At the end of 1993, Taiwan had more than US$90 billion in foreign reserves (the second highest in the world after Japan), a per capita income of US$11,000 and escalating investment outflows.[19] As today's international political economy is so interdependent and differentiated, it appears that to continue to keep a nation as economically significant as Taiwan outside the normal activities of regional life is not rational and even detrimental to Southeast Asian development in general. In addition, Southeast Asia has demonstrated that even under the one-China constraint, there are creative ways to form ties with Taipei.

In May, Lee extended his international tour to visit Nicaragua, Costa Rica, South Africa and Swaziland — four of the 29 countries that officially recognize the ROC on Taiwan. Lee met with more than 20 of the foreign leaders who attended Mandela's inauguration, most of them from countries with no formal ties to Taipei. He also met most Central American leaders and even shook hands with US Vice-President Al Gore.[20]

In July 1994, Taipei once again successfully mobilized 12 Latin American countries to fight for its re-entry into the United Nations, though like the one in 1993, the resolution was vetoed by the United Nations General Committee. Of course, Taipei was very certain that their campaign would not succeed as long as Beijing continued to oppose it, but they still carried it out as a routine ritual because they must in some way satisfy the rising popular demand for an internationally recognized Taiwan. Otherwise, frustrated citizens might turn to the DPP, which not only looked for Taiwan's re-entry into the United Nations but also consistently pursued its *de jure* independence as a totally new nation.

Two months later, Taipei found another opportunity to break its international isolation when President Lee Teng-hui was invited by the Olympic Council of Asia (OCA) to attend the opening of the Asian Games in Japan. To flout Beijing's 22-year ban on such visits since Japan established diplomatic ties with the PRC in 1972, Lee accepted the invitation and looked set to go. To show their solidarity, a majority of Taiwan's lawmakers and many local organizations also rallied behind the President. It appeared that the majority of Taiwanese also supported the idea. During a half-hour TV programme, more than 50,000 people telephoned to express approval for the visit; only 400 opposed it.[21] In Beijing's view, Taipei's move was no less than a bid for *de facto* independence from China, which would have an adverse effect on the cause of ultimate reunification. Hence, it warned of boycotting the event if Lee attended, together with a series of harsh statements it made about Taiwan. Under Beijing's overwhelming pressure, the OCA implicitly withdrew Lee's invitation on 12 September, saying that "No political figure will be invited to or accommodated at the 12th Asian Games."[22] Once again, Beijing's diplomatic might triumphed. However, Taipei was no loser, because the incident further strengthened Taiwanese determination to campaign for a greater international recognition.

To put all that has been discussed in perspective in respect of Taipei's new approach to its relations with mainland China and the international community, it is not difficult to find that Taipei was very firm on its baseline in dealing with Beijing. Taipei knew very well about Beijing's potential threat and international influence, but it also did not overlook the popular demand for greater recognition abroad for Taiwan. Especially in the face of Taiwan's rapidly emerging democratic reality, the KMT-controlled state must listen to the voices of an increasingly articulate population if it wants to continue to stay in power.

Internal Developments on the Mainland

Some internal developments on the mainland have also strained Taiwan-mainland relations. Although the PRC has been liberalizing its economy since 1979, politically it remains close to what Edwin A. Winckler (1987) called "hard authoritarianism" characterized by the ruling regime's unhesitant suppression of all forms of democratic and political liberalization movements attempting to challenge its rule.[23] In China's past fifteen years of economic development, large-scale political suppressions occurred almost once every three to five years. The most notorious and brutal one of course is the "June 4 Incident" of 1989 in which thousands of civilians were injured and killed in a government military crackdown on the democracy movement then taking place in Beijing as well as in other major Chinese cities. The crackdown, as well as other suppressions of smaller scales, strengthened years of KMT propaganda about the evils of communism. Besides, Beijing's post-June 4 effort to deny what the world had watched on television further undermined the confidence of Taiwanese in PRC's credibility.[24]

The "June 4 Incident" not only underlined the Chinese Communist regime's "hard authoritarianism"; it also aggravated China's long-standing problem of power succession after the supreme leader Deng Xiaoping. After the incident, the CCP General Secretary Zhao Ziyang, who was chosen by Deng himself as his successor, was formally sacked for dividing the party, and the former city boss of Shanghai Jiang Zemin was called in to take over Zhao's place. Over the past five years, with the support of Deng, Jiang gradually established and consolidated his own power base. However, until very recently it has been the general view among Taiwanese leaders that Jiang's position was still not firm and that there is a high possibility of a violent power struggle after Deng's death. In fact, President Lee Teng-hui has instructed Taiwan's local officials several times in recent months to pay close attention to changes in the CCP leadership. He also openly expressed his wish of a stable post-Deng China.[25] On 8 February 1995, a study entitled "China in the Near Term" done by the US Secretary of Defence was fully reported by a major Taiwanese newspaper. According to the newspaper's report, the study concludes that "disintegration" is the top possible scenario in the post-Deng era, followed by a "linear future of authoritarianism."[26] This conclusion, in conjunction with Taipei's existing concern, would certainly increase Taipei's hesitation to enter any hasty negotiations with Beijing on the reunification issue before the political scene on the mainland is clear.

Apart from their concern with mainland political development, the "Incident of Lake Qiandao" that occurred last spring also restrains the Taiwanese from an early reunification with the mainland. In the incident, all 32 people, of whom 24 were Taiwanese, on board a vessel touring Lake Qiandao were found dead after a fire. For more than a week, mainland authorities insisted that it was an accident. Unauthorized autopsies were performed and relatives were compelled to accept the cremation of the victims. Although Beijing later acknowledged that the fire was a "man-made incident," it refused SEF's request to represent on behalf of the relatives of the victims in dealing with the incident. All of this outraged the Taiwan public. Amid the popular anger, President Lee criticized the Beijing government as an "evil force" acting like a "group of bandits that the people should remove as soon as possible."[27] Such words have not been heard from Taiwan's leaders in years. At the same time, Taipei suspended cultural and educational exchanges with the mainland, froze the further liberalizarion of imports of semi-finished goods from China, and put off reviewing some applications for indirect investment there by major Taiwanese companies. Moreover, Taiwan's travel agents agreed to cancel all group tours to the mainland from 1 May. Even though these actions were all relaxed later as mainland authorities eventually managed to deal with the incident in a more transparent and rational way, it appears that the increasing friendly relations gradually developed between the two areas over the years are still very fragile and that for reunification to occur, there is still a long way to go.

The immediate effect of the incident was that it further strengthened a consensus against unification with communist China. Two separate opinion polls conducted two weeks after the incident showed a rapid rise in pro-independence sentiment, from a stable 20–23% before the incident to the historic peak of well over 27%.[28] Besides, according to a survey done by the National Chengchi University in early July (about three months after the incident), although the pro-independence supporters had declined to 24%, there were 52.1% of the respondents preferring to maintain the present *status quo* of Taiwan, including 42.2% "preferring to maintain the *status quo* and to postpone consideration of the unification issue" and 9.9% "preferring to maintain permanent separation from the mainland."[29] In other words, if this survey has some degree of representativeness, over 75% of the Taiwanese are separatists of some kind. To the policy-makers on both side of the straits, this is certainly an unignorable percentage.

There is no doubt that the Lake Qiandao Incident was an accident. However, if we locate it in the structural context of the existing cross-straits relations, the meaning it carries extends far beyond that of any ordinary accident. As the mainland is still very backward in many areas, such incidents will inevitably continue to occur. Hence, to the Taiwanese, what the Lake Qiandao Incident reveals is not simply a serious accidental crime, nor an administrative mistake unintentionally committed by the PRC authorities. Instead, it reflects wide discrepancies in thinking, legal customs, government administration and living standards across the straits. These discrepancies, none of which will be easy to overcome in the near future, are obviously important forces pulling Taipei as well as the Taiwanese away from an early reunification.

Hong Kong's Experience of "One Country, Two Systems"

Since 1984 when the Sino-British Joint Declaration was signed in which the model of "one country, two systems" was stipulated for recovering China's sovereignty over Hong Kong, Beijing has continuously insisted that the model should also be the basis for its future reunification with Taiwan, except that more favourable conditions might be granted to Taiwan by negotiation. Owing to that fact, the experience of Hong Kong in its scheduled reversion to PRC sovereignty in 1997 by means of this model becomes an important reference for Taiwan.

According to Beijing's explanation, the concept "one country, two systems" refers to "a country with a unified system, which according to specified rules of its constitution and law, allows one or more of its regions to adopt political, economic and social systems that are basically different from the country at large. Yet the governments of these regions are the regional governments of the country. Unless exceptionally permitted by the government according to law, the regional governments cannot exercise state sovereignty."[30] Based on this understanding, Beijing issued the Draft of the Basic Law of the Hong Kong Special Administrative Region

(SAR) in 1988 and passed it into the Basic Law in 1990 with little change in respect to the relationship between the central authorities and the future Hong Kong SAR.

The Basic Law states that the central government will only be responsible for Hong Kong's defence and foreign affairs and that Hong Kong will enjoy a high degree of autonomy. But contrary to the popular will in Hong Kong, the Basic Law also purposefully limits Hong Kong's democratic development to the extent that it can be easily manipulated by China.[31] As to the first SAR Legislature to be formed in 1997, only 20 out of the total 60 seats are allowed to come from direct popular election. In October 1992 when the newly appointed Governor Chris Patten exploited the grey areas of the Basic Law and put forward to Hong Kong people his political reform proposals to broaden the Legislature's democratic basis, Beijing was extremely angry and condemned Mr Patten with abusive language. After almost half a year of continuing wrangles, both the British and Chinese governments eventually entered a long process of negotiations on Hong Kong's future political and constitutional arrangements. The negotiations, however, broke off in December 1993, with both governments accusing each other of lacking sincerity. Since then, Mr Patten has proceeded to implement the political reform.

On the other hand, openly declaring that representative councils of all three levels (Legislative, Urban, and District) in Hong Hong would be disbanded and reorganized in 1997 and ignoring Hong Kong's pro-democracy organizations' accusation of violating the Basic Law, the Chinese government has begun to participate directly and actively, in all aspects of the preparation for Hong Kong's scheduled reversion through the Preliminary Working Committee for the SAR Preparatory Committee (PWC) founded in Beijing in July 1993.[32] Composed of both pro-China local élites and Chinese officials, the PWC met regularly in 1994 and made many controversial proposals regarding the post-1997 arrangements in Hong Kong, including setting up an appointed temporary Legislative Council on 1 July 1997. In a survey done in late September 1994 by the Chinese University of Hong Kong and the Cable TV, only 14.7% of the 1,012 respondents indicated that they still had confidence in "one country, two systems" promised by China and Britain ten years ago, while over 68% answered no confidence (38.7%) or a little confidence (29.7%).[33]

Given all the above in Hong Kong's experience, the "one country, two systems" model for reunification seems to have turned Taipei and its people away rather than drawing them closer. In Taipei's view, the experience of Hong Kong has very much confirmed its suspicion that the model would only lead to the annexation of the ROC by the PRC and the subjugation of Taiwan to Beijing.

From a practical point of view, not only has the experience of Hong Kong frightened the Taiwanese; as a concept "one country, two systems" is also by itself not attractive to them. As Professor Kuang-sheng Liao cogently said in 1991 in the first volume of *China Review*,

> Taiwan has far more choices than Hong Kong with regard to its future political destiny. First of all, Taiwan is separated from the mainland by the Straits. Taiwan is thus more separated from China than Hong Kong in terms of the physical environment. It is no simple task for mainland China to use force against Taiwan. Secondly, the Taipei government has a relatively stable political organization. Although Taiwan is in a political transition, the KMT still wields considerable power to maintain political order and promote economic prosperity. To overthrow KMT rule by the mainland now would be very difficult. Thirdly, although Taiwan is now isolated internationally, its international trade has developed rapidly. Its total foreign trade value already reached US$88 billion, ranking thirteenth worldwide. The annual average per capita income has topped US$7,000. Its people enjoy a comfortable and peaceful life, with higher living standards than those of the mainland Chinese. These objective conditions have made the Taiwanese and their government resist the idea of being led by and unified with China.[34]

Professor Liao's comments were still based upon the conditions of 1991. Since then, four years have passed and during the period Taiwan experienced many profound changes, especially on the political front. As pointed out earlier, Taiwan's democratic reform is today close to completion. It is very difficult for a state, which is popularized and has its own *de facto* sovereignty, to accept the subordinate arrangements defined by the model of "one country, two systems," not to mention the fact that mainland China is still very backward both politically and economically. This explains to a large extent why the Taiwanese are so hesitant to embrace reunification.

Changing Attitudes of the International Community

The changing attitudes of the international community also play a role in ROC-PRC relations. When Washington established formal diplomatic relations with the PRC in 1980, the US Congress passed the Taiwan Relations Act (TRA) that linked the future of Taiwan with American security in the Western Pacific.[35] The TRA indicated that the US was pursuing a policy that allowed Taiwan to decide its future relations with the mainland on peaceful terms. Under the TRA, the US had the legal obligation to stop any aggression against the peace of Taiwan by supplying Taiwan with adequate self-defence articles and services. In other words, the US would not accept any attempt by the PRC to solve the question of Taiwan by means of force.[36] This policy has been carefully carried out since the US-PRC normalization. Although the August 1982 Sino-US Communiqué imposed constraints on US arms transfers to Taiwan,[37] in the following years Washington managed to replace Taiwan's obsolete systems with advanced ones, including "a fleet of frigates with antiship, antisub, and antiair capabilities; advanced fighter aircraft; modernized battle tanks; and a range of ground-to-air, air-to-air, and antiship missiles."[38]

International political developments in the 1980s and early 1990s further strengthened US commitment to Taiwan's security. In the international arena, the strategic importance of the PRC to the US had diminished rapidly since the USSR under Mikhail Gorbachev introduced political reform and endeavoured to improve its relations with the West in the mid-1980s. The June 4 Incident of 1989 on the mainland also destroyed Western optimism about the PRC's peaceful transformation to a democratic society under its economic reform and open-door policy. Moreover, the rapid democratization of Taiwan plus its economic might create moral and practical difficulties for the West in continuing to maintain a rigid one-China policy.[39]

As a result of all the above developments, the US agreed to sell 150 F-16 fighter aircraft to Taiwan in September 1992. At almost the same time, a similar deal of 60 French Mirage 2000-5 fighters was concluded by the French government. The PRC, of course, reacted to the sales angrily because they not only signaled the West's moving away from the one-China policy, but also would improve Taiwan's defence capability significantly and thereby lower Taipei's willingness for reunification under the model of "one country, two systems." However, both the US and French governments had more or less anticipated the PRC's anger and opposition.[40] Apart from economic considerations, that they still went ahead with the deals in spite of the PRC's opposition, to a certain extent signifying the increasingly sympathetic tendency of the international community toward the existing situation in Taiwan.

In September 1994, Washington further announced the upgrading of its relations with Taiwan. Under the new policy, several important improvements can be observed, including: (1) The name of Taiwan's representative mission in the US will be changed from the Coordination Council for North American Affairs to the more official-sounding Taipei Economic and Cultural Representative Office. (2) US personnel in Taiwan will be able to meet with their local counterparts up to deputy level; they will also be allowed to visit Taiwan's Foreign Ministry. (3) High-level US officials will be able to visit Taiwan to discuss economic and cultural matters. (4) Taiwanese representatives will be allowed transit visas, though they still cannot go to the US in an official capacity. While having received all these improvements, Taipei was still very much disappointed, because Washington maintained that it would not support Taipei's bid to re-enter the United Nations. Without this support, Taipei's road to formal international recognition inevitably remains long and bumpy. Nevertheless, as Washington reiterated that the TRA would continue to be the basis of US-Taiwan relations, this should somehow console Taipei's concern about its national security.[41]

All these developments point to the emerging trend that the international community, though it is still far from giving Taiwan formal recognition, is increasingly reluctant to see the island being forced toward reunification with the mainland simply because it is militarily inferior.[42] In view of all the changes in Taiwan and mainland China, the international community begins to take a more flexible, sympathetic approach to its relations with Taiwan. It wants to let Taiwanese people decide their future free of threat and force instead of pressuring them to settle with the PRC before the conditions are ripe.

From Confrontation to Compromise

Although Taipei's various campaigns for greater international recognition, driven more or less by Taiwan's recent historical-structural changes, have drawn attention and sympathy from the international community, they unavoidably engage Taipei in direct confrontation with Beijing. Up until now, Bejing still maintains that Taiwan is an inseparable part of China and must be unified under the sovereignty of the PRC in accordance with the prescribed model of "one country, two systems." In other words, in Beijing's view, there is only one China which is the PRC, and therefore

Taipei's internationalization attempt, no mattter in what form, is no less than an open separatist move and must be stopped. Such directly conflicting positions of Taipei and Beijing on the political front have eventually pushed them into what Gerrit W. Gong calls the "dilemma of polarized leverage," in which both Taipei and Beijing attempt to enhance their own bargaining leverage by means of polarizing their political situations.[43] For some Taiwanese leaders, to act in an increasingly separatist way can exercise pressure on Beijing, and this in itself is a way to strengthen Taipei's bargaining power. On the other hand, from the viewpoint of some Beijing leaders, as long as they do not give up the use of force as a possible means of achieving reunification with Taiwan, they are still able to maximize their bargaining leverage. The outcome of these divergent interpretations, however, is paradoxically dangerous: if the PRC does not give Taiwan greater international recognition, separatist voices in Taiwan will increase; and if Taipei pursues greater international recognition and therefore becomes farther away from mainland China and closer to separatism, Beijing will be more likely to resort to force to solve the conflicts across the straits.

The developments of cross-straits political relations in recent years have precisely fallen into the above dangerous dilemma. In fact, almost all of Taipei's internationalization campaigns (the major exception is the "vacation diplomacy" which did establish some informal ties with some Southeast Asian countries) end in failure as a result of Beijing's opposition and pressure. To further show its determinacy, Beijing also published a *White Paper* on the question of Taiwan in August 1993, both clarifying its own position on reunification and criticizing Taipei's recent internationalization campaigns. Some major points include: (1) Since "any sovereign state is entitled to use any means it deems necessary, including military ones, to uphold its sovereignty and territorial integrity," Beijing will never give up the use of force in the pursuit of reunification as demanded by Taipei. (2) As Taiwan is part of China and has no independent sovereignty, Beijing strongly opposes Taipei's bid to return to the United Nations in any form. (3) Besides United Nations Organizations, Taipei is "ineligible for membership in other categories of intergovernmental organizations" without Beijing's prior approval. (4) The international community — especially the US — should not attempt to interfere in China's reunification without facing serious political and other consequences.

Taipei has become increasingly frustrated by Beijing's intransigence and the continuing international suppression. Such frustration was acutely revealed in a rather emotional interview given by President Lee Teng-hui to a Japanese newspaper in May 1994. In the interview, Lee made many controversial remarks, such as: "the term 'China' is very ambiguous"; "Taiwan is the country of Taiwanese"; "the PRC's claim of Taiwan as one of its provinces is a dream"; "the KMT had been an external regime to Taiwan until very recently"; "to be a Taiwanese is miserable"; and "like the exodus in the Old Testament, the Taiwanese have been on their road."[44] These remarks, as well as others made by Lee at previous times, were interpreted by Beijing as Lee's separatist intention turned public. On 14 June, the Xinhua News Agency openly condemned Lee for moving toward an independent Taiwan.[45] Two days later, the *People's Daily* (overseas edition) published a signed article, both questioning Lee's Chinese attachment and criticizing his separatist tendency.[46] Besides, in the days that followed, many CCP commentaries and seminars repeated an identical message: danger is near; and an editorial of a pro-China newspaper in Hong Kong even implied the possibility of using force to stop Taiwan from moving further toward real separatism.[47] To the Taiwanese, however, the worst came when their Defence Ministry reported in the same month the discovery of a CCP submarine lingering for more than 45 hours in the vicinity of Penghu, a ROC-controlled island some 60 miles off central Taiwan.[48]

While cross-straits tensions rapidly escalated under Beijing's frequent charges and suspicious moves, Taipei showed no intention of backing down. In July, it formally issued its first official *White Paper on Relations with the Mainland*, repeating its position that the PRC should recognize the authority of the ROC government. On the whole, the Taiwanese *White Paper* contains seven major points on reunification which Taipei had developed and articulated in recent years: (1) The present split of China across the straits is a result of the establishment of the PRC in October 1949 and the subsequent retreat of the ROC government from Nanjing via Guangzhou to Taipei. Since then, the two governments have maintained separate rule over the two sides of the Taiwan Straits. (2) The existence of a divided China is not simply a power struggle between the KMT and CCP; it has been heavily shaped by international politics and external ideological domination, both of which eventually gave rise to the confrontation between a Nationalist China and a Communist China. (3) Taiwan has relinquished the use of force as a means of reunification. (4) The model of "one China, two equal political entities," not "one country, two systems," should be employed to resolve present ROC-PRC conflicts. The ROC-PRC relations are neither international nor purely internal to a sovereign nation. (5) The model of "one country, two systems" proposed by the PRC does not work because "one country" means annexation of the ROC by the PRC and "two systems" implies subjecting Taiwan to the PRC's arbitrary determination. (6) ROC-PRC relations should be based upon the principles of reason, peace, equality and reciprocity. (7) If the PRC moves to practice democracy, people in Taiwan will support reunification rather than separation.

Alongside the publication of the *White Paper*, Taipei also increased the frequency of military exercises of varying scales to counter the military threat from Beijing. On 28 September, the second large-scale "Hanguang" integrated military exercise in the year was held, only four months after the first one.[49] On 14 November, during a small-scale military exercise on Jinmen the ROC soldiers mistakenly hit the countryside of Xiamen and wounded four mainland Chinese. Although the ROC Defence Ministry apologized almost immediately to the PRC government and said it would bear all the responsibilities, the incident had provoked among the Taiwanese extensive fear of a possible straits war if cross-straits relations continued to deteriorate. A fictional account of a military attack on Taiwan published in August 1994 soon became a bestseller, selling over 100,000 copies in only a few months after its publication.[50]

The rapid deterioration of cross-straits relations on the political front quickly affected other areas. To go back a bit, since the mid-1980s when cross-straits economic exchange began to experience rapid growth, Beijing and Taipei had gradually moved away from their long historical antagonism, showing signs of willingness to establish a stable, working relationship to regular cross-straits economic and cultural activities. In 1985, Taipei relaxed its tight control of trade and investment activities on the mainland, even though direct trade was still prohibited. Two years later, it lifted its restrictions on visiting the mainland and allowed Taiwan residents to visit their relatives on the manland. In 1990, Taipei also began to allow mainland residents to visit Taiwan, though on a restricted basis. Most importantly, as pointed out earlier, in the same year the SEF was founded to manage cross-straits affairs. In response, Beijing set up the Association for Relations Across the Taiwan Straits (ARATS) in 1991. While both SEF and ARATS nominally claim that they are non-governmental in order to avoid political dealings, they actually represent their government on each side of the straits and under their governments' direct command. In April 1993, a symbolic breakthrough was made when a high-level meeting between the Presidents of the two organizations, Koo Chen-fu of SEF and Wang Daohan of ARATS, was held in Singapore. At the meeting, a number of agreements were signed including those on document verification and registered post.

After the Koo-Wang meeting, however, eight lower-level meetings of the two organizations followed later in the year and in 1994, but none of them achieved a significant breakthrough. In the second secretary-level meeting held in Taipei in August 1994, a high degree of consensus was eventually reached on the issues of extraditing airplane hijackers and illegal immigrants and settling fishing disputes; yet tremendous difficulties appeared when two deputy secretary-level meetings held at later times attempted to translate the consensus into language agreeable to both parties. State sovereignty remained the centre of dispute. Under the rapidly deteriorating political mood across the straits, mutual suspicion ruled. Beijing was extremely careful of forming any agreements with Taipei that would imply equal recognition, whereas Taipei was afraid of being trapped in any subordinate status with potentially adverse political implications and therefore strongly insisted that some formal recognition of Taiwan's independent political status by Beijing was the basis for any important bilateral agreements to be formed.

Nevertheless, ironically throughout the year, the rising political tension between Beijing and Taipei did not slow down the development of other areas of cross-straits interaction, especially the economic one. According to Beijing's estimate, cross-straits trade in 1994 would amount to US$17 billion, an increase of US$2.6 billion from last year.[51] Besides, in spite of Taipei's active promotion of the "Southward policy" early in the year, approved Taiwanese investment in mainland China rose from some US$10 billion in 1993 to US$22.261 billion in 1994, more than doubling itself in one year.[52] Investment in 1994 also made Taiwan the second largest foreign investor in China (only after Hong Kong), and in the same year over 25,000 Taiwanese companies and enterprises were operating on the mainland.[53]

Such rapid growth of cross-straits economic exchange indirectly announced the failure of Taipei's "Southward policy." It also forced the governments on both sides of the straits to rethink the potential disaster of the continuously escalating tension between them. Especially in Taiwan, President Lee Teng-hui was heavily criticized by the newly founded New Party (NP) for directly causing the conflict. During the elections of Mayors of Taipei and Kaohsiung and Governor of Taiwan, the NP leaders even openly claimed that Lee had had a timetable for Taiwan's independence, producing further damage to Lee's political image as well as to the KMT's ruling status. In the economic sector, business and industrial leaders also expressed their concern that the continuing confrontation between Beijing and Taipei on the political front would significantly constrain their ability to compete with other countries in developing the mainland market, which is now the fastest growing region in the world. They also worried that if Taipei could not sit down as soon as possible with Beijing to negotiate the post-1997 arrangements, the reversion of Hong Kong to PRC sovereignty in 1997 would put much of their business in jeopardy. For under the existing no-direct-trade policy, their business activities with the mainland are largely done through Hong Kong. All these criticisms and concerns had a negative impact on the KMT government's popularity. According to a Gallup Poll survey conducted in late December 1994, satisfaction with Lee's administration in Taiwan dropped from a record high of over 90% some years ago to a historical low of 65.5%.[54]

Under pressures of varying degrees from all fronts, Taipei began to adjust its mainland policy in the final quarter of the year. In October, Lee expressed his willingness to meet with Jiang Zemin in international settings to discuss the issue of reunification. Besides, during the entire course of the year-end elections, Lee and his KMT administration repeatedly emphasized that opposition to independence was their unchanged national policy. The most important breakthrough, however, came in late December with Taipei's announcement of its plans for building Taiwan into a high-tech, multi-purpose operation centre. In the announcement, Taipei also specifically put forth its plans to open Taiwan's major ports to essentially direct trade with China, revealing its willingness to strengthen economic ties with the mainland. Several days later, in his new year speech Premier Lien Chan further stressed that the coming year would be an economically-led year for both sides of the straits and that his government would actively and practically continue talks with Beijing to improve cross-straits relations.

Seeing Taipei's softening position, Beijing also lowered its confrontational gesture. In November, Jiang Zemin responded to Lee's earlier summit proposal in a friendly way by saying that he was very willing to meet with Lee, but since cross-straits relations were Chinese affairs, the meeting should be held in Chinese societies. In early January, on Taipei's request Beijing quickly and cooperatively arranged the third SEF-ARATS secretary-level meeting which was held at the end of the same month. Athough there were still no agreements signed at the end of the meeting, the mood during the entire meeting was exceptionally friendly, showing the urgent desire of both governments to return to an improved relationship. Several days after the meeting, in a ground-breaking Lunar New Year's address Jiang further sent a highly conciliatory message across the straits. In the address, Jiang reaffirmed the notion of one China, but emphasized concrete arrangements of future reunification would be negotiated on equal terms. He also softened Beijing's longstanding threat of force by saying that Chinese would not attack Chinese. Moreover, Jiang indicated that party leaders and representatives of local political groups on both sides of the straits could participate in future reunification talks.

As to Jiang's address, Taipei's response was careful but friendly. As Lee said several days later, it was an important document of policy change that deserved Taipei's thorough analysis and careful responses.[55] By now, a year of escalating tension has largely subsided. The two governments seem finally to have realized the extreme danger of the "dilemma of polarized leverage," and want to work toward mutual benefits instead of zero-sum solutions.

Conclusion

Given the current trends of Taiwan's deepening democratization and growing economic might, China's unchanged authoritarian communist system, Hong Kong's experience of "one country, two systems," and the international community's emerging politically neutral attitude toward the China reunification issue, cross-straits reunification under Beijing's proposed scheme of "one country, two systems" will be extremely difficult, even if the PRC wants to resort to force. Under the almost completed democratic reform, the Taiwanese state is no longer single-handedly controlled by the ruling KMT. Instead, it must take care of the general interests of its citizens in accordance with the new democratic norms. Hence, not surprisingly, the DPP Chairman Shih Ming-teh also said in a magazine interview last year that the KMT increasingly shared a similar view with his party on international and defence policies.[56] Shih's comment should not be interpreted as a conspiracy between the KMT and the DPP. He only pointed out the fact that the ruling KMT must work within the confines of a democratic Taiwan. For the KMT administration, they either actively respond to the growing popular pressure for greater international recognition or choose to be pushed from power. At the same time, in a world where democracy is a sacred norm, it is also very difficult for the international community to continue to keep a democratic Taiwan outside the normal activities of international life simply on the basis of the abstract principle of one China, not to mention that the economic opportunities Taiwan offers are also irresistable to many countries.

It was under these conditions that Taipei began its internationalization campaigns. Such campaigns, however, were in conflict with Beijing's one-China policy, and the struggles on the political front, typically expressed in the form of the "dilemma of polarized leverage," inevitably influenced other areas. Hence the rapid deterioration of cross-straits relations characteristic of 1994. In particular, the development of the "dilemma of polarized leverage" across the straits not only paralyzed all the semi-official talks between the two sides held in 1994; it also rapidly enhanced the dangerous possibility of a violent Taiwan-mainland clash. In the final quarter of the year, both Taipei and Beijing gradually realized that such dangerous development would benefit neither side, especially in consideration of the ever growing economic and other activities across the straits. As a result, they both shifted back to a more conciliatory position in dealing with one another, attempting to look for solutions of mutual benefit to their existing conflicts.

To look for solutions of mutual benefit is where Taipei and Bejing stand today at the beginning of 1995. Yet, this is only a beginning, not just for the year 1995, but also for the two governments to return to talks as the fundamental approach to solving their conflicts. As Taiwan continues to democratize and press for greater international participation, and as the international community tends to be increasingly sympathetic to Taiwan's situation, the road ahead for Taipei and Beijing in peacefully settling their conflicts will still be extremely rough. Exceptional patience and wisdom will be needed to avoid a reversion to the "dilemma of polarized leverage" which would lead nowhere but to a tragic end.

Notes

1. Hsing-huang Hsiao, "The Reorganization of the State-Society Relations in a Pluralistic Process," in *The Taiwan Experience in a New Stage: Continuation*

and *Breakthrough*, edited by Michael Y. M. Kau (Taipei: 21th Century Foundation, 1991), pp. 375–400.
2. *Ming Pao* (Hong Kong), 4 December 1989; 22 December 1991; 22 December 1992; 18 November 1993; 4 December 1994.
3. Hung-Mao Tien, "Taiwan's Evolution Toward Democracy: A Historical Perspective," in *Taiwan: Beyond the Economic Miracle*, edited by Denis Fred Simon and Michael Y. M. Kau (Armonk: M. E. Sharpe Inc., 1992), pp. 3–24; Parris H. Chang, "The Changing Nature of Taiwan's Politics," in ibid., pp. 25–42.
4. Liah Greenfeld, *Nationalism: Five Roads to Modernity* (Cambridge: Harvard University Press, 1992), p. 10.
5. Thomas Gold, *State and Society in the Taiwan Miracle* (Armonk: Sharpe, 1986); Thomas W. Robinson, "Beijing-Taipei Relations Approaching the Year 2000," in *Taiwan: Beyond the Economic Miracle* (Note 3), pp. 369–86; Allen Chun, "From Nationalism to Nationalizing: Cultural Imagination and State Formation in Postwar Taiwan," *The Australian Journal of Chinese Affairs*, No. 31 (1994), pp. 49–69.
6. *Ming Pao*, 10 May 1993.
7. Nai-teh Wu, "Provincial Consciousness, Political Support and National Identity," in *Ethnic Relations and National Identity*, edited by Chang Mau-kuei et al. (Taipei: Institute For National Policy Research, 1993), p. 47.
8. *Ming Pao*, 18 April 1994.
9. *Ming Pao*, 10 May 1993.
10. Kuang-sheng Liao, "China's State Structure and National Reunification," in *China Review 1991*, edited by Kuan Hsin-chi and Maurice Brosseau (Hong Kong: Chinese University Press, 1991), p. **4**.14.
11. Andrew Nathan, *China's Crisis: Dilemmas of Reform and Prospects for Democracy* (New York: Columbia University Press, 1990), p. 153.
12. Robert D. Putnam, "Diplomacy and Domestic Politics: The Logic of Two-Level Games," *International Organization* 42, No. 3 (Summer 1998), pp. 427–60.
13. Richard C. Bush, "The Role of the United States in Taiwan-PRC Relations," in *Taiwan: Beyond the Economic Miracle* (Note 3), pp. 345–68.
14. Martin L. Lasater, *Policy in Evolution: The US Role in China Unification*, (Boulder: Westview Press, 1989).
15. *The Republic of China 1992 National Defence Report* (Taipei: Li Ming Cultural Enterprise Co., Ltd., 1992), p. 121.
16. Ibid., p. 126.
17. Ibid.
18. *The Republic of China 1993–1994 National Defence Report* (Taipei: Li Ming Cultural Enterprise Co. Ltd., 1994).
19. *Asiaweek*, 28 September 1994, p. 31.

20. *Far Eastern Economic Review*, 9 June 1994, p. 18.
21. *Asiaweek*, 28 September 1994, p. 30.
22. *Far Eastern Economic Review*, 22 September 1994, p. 14.
23. Edwin Winckler, "Institutionalization and Participation on Taiwan: From Hard to Soft Authoritarianism?" *The China Quarterly*, 3 (September 1987), pp. 482–99.
24. Bush (Note 13), pp. 358–59.
25. *United Daily News*, 9 February 1995.
26. *China Times*, 8 February 1995.
27. *Far Eastern Economic Review*, 21 April 1994, p. 24.
28. Ibid.; *Ming Pao*, 18 April 1994.
29. *United Daily News*, 4 August 1994.
30. Byron Weng, "One Country, Two Systems," in *The Future of Taiwan*, edited by F. K. Guo and Zhao Fushan (Beijing: China Friendship Publishing Co., 1986), p. 351.
31. Hsin-chi Kuan, *Hong Kong After the Basic Law* (Nova Scotia: The Institute for Research on Public Policy, 1991), pp. 15–18.
32. Joseph Yu-shek Cheng, "The Sino-British Conflict and Hong Kong's Ruling Crisis," in *Politics and Elections in Hong Kong*, edited by Joseph Yu-shek Cheng and Kin-Sheun Louie, (Hong Kong: Oxford University Press, 1995), p. 122.
33. *Ming Pao*, 29 September 1994.
34. Liao (Note 10), p. 4.5.
35. Martin L. Lasater, *The Taiwan Issue in Sino-American Strategic Relations* (Boulder: Westview Press, 1984); Lasater (Note 14); Ramon H. Myers, *A Unique Relationship: The United States and the Republic of China Under the Taiwan Relations Act* (Stanford, CA: Hoover Institution Press, 1989).
36. Martin L. Lasater, "Taiwan's International Environment," in *Democracy and Development in East Asia*, edited by Thomas Robinson (Washington: The AEI Press, 1991), p. 92.
37. The August 1982 Sino-US Communiqué stipulates that "the United States Government states that it does not seek to carry out a long-term policy of arms sales to Taiwan, that its arms sales to Taiwan will not exceed, either in qualitative or in quantitative terms, the level of those supplied in recent years since the establishment of diplomatic relations between the United States and China, and that it intends to reduce gradually its sales of arms to Taiwan, leading over a period of time to a final resolution" (Quoted from Lasater [Note 14], p. 89).
38. Bush (Note 13), p. 352.
39. Lasater (Note 36), p. 97.
40. In real political terms, the PRC could do little to retaliate against the United States, because the Sino-US economic ties had developed rapidly in favour of

China and Beijing needed to continue the most-favoured-nation trade status from the United States. On the other hand, France was less fortunate as its economic ties with mainland China were comparatively weak. As a result, on 23 December 1992, Beijing closed down the French Consulate-General in Guangzhou to show its anger.

41. *United Daily News*, 9 September 1994.
42. Bush (Note 13), p. 355.
43. *China Times*, 15 January 1995.
44. *The Nineties* (Hong Kong), July 1994, pp. 42–43.
45. Ibid., p. 104.
46. *People's Daily* (overseas edition), 16 June 1994.
47. *The Nineties*, July 1994, p. 38.
48. Ibid., pp. 38–39.
49. *United Daily News*, 28 September 1994.
50. Long-ping Cheng, *T Day: The Warning of Taiwan Strait War* (Taipei: China Times Publishing Co., Ltd., 1994).
51. *Hong Kong Economic Journal*, 30 December 1994.
52. *Overseas Chinese Daily News*, 3 January 1995.
53. Ibid.
54. *China Times*, 4 January 1995.
55. *United Daily News*, 4 February 1995.
56. *Far Eastern Economic Review*, 23 June 1994, p. 23.

5

Calling the Tune without Paying the Piper: The Reassertion of Media Controls in China

Joseph Man Chan

Introduction

In my previous review of media development in China, I stated that 1992 would be remembered as the year of commercialization.[1] Indeed, commercialization in the field of communications has made rapid strides since then. Once dependent on state subsidies, the mass media increasingly rely on advertising revenue and derive income from non-media activities. The competition within and across the media are intensifying. To attract audiences, the mass media go beyond their traditional functions of propaganda and education and venture into entertainment and information. Communications outlets ranging from periodicals to cable television have multiplied exponentially to meet the needs of advertisers and audience. China has even witnessed the growth of alternative distribution networks, coproductions, joint ventures, and private production houses.

While the trend of media commercialization persists at the time of writing in early 1995, 1994–1995 will be remembered more as the period during which China sought to reassert control over its mass media. Development within this period represents the Chinese Communist Party's (CCP) attempt to resolve the inherent contradiction between economic reform and authoritarianism. It illuminates the pendulum-like pattern of media development in China, oscillating between relaxation and tightening. The focus of this chapter is to review the CCP's tightening measures as China completes another oscillation in media development. How media control is possible or impossible in an increasingly commercialized setting will also be analyzed.

Containing the Forces of Media Commercialization

Associated with media commercialization are signs indicating that the CCP's tight controls over the media and ideology are weakening. Some of the complaints often cited by CCP leaders include: (1) China Central Television (CCTV) and other TV stations show too many foreign programmes and movies, thus negating the party's ideological work. (2) Domestic movies have lost their appeal whereas reactionary coproductions

---

The author is grateful to the South China Programme at The Chinese University of Hong Kong for its financial support for this research.

Calling the Tune without Paying the Piper 5.3

persistently receive international recognition. (3) Opening up more radio channels has rendered the situation almost uncontrollable. Direct phone-in programmes tend to deviate from the party line and have undesirable influence over the audience. (4) Hong Kong and Taiwan singers are heavily promoted by the Chinese media, thus turning them into idols for the young and undermining the popularity of domestic singers. (5) Writers, artists and propaganda workers put money above everything else. They have become callous to ideological work.[2]

To consolidate and to regain its control over the media and ideological work, the CCP held the largest national propaganda conference since 1957 between 24–29 January 1994. It was attended by virtually all the central party leaders, including Jiang Zemin, Li Peng, Ding Guan'gen, Qiao Shi, Li Ruihuan, the propaganda chiefs at the national and provincial levels, as well as heads of the national media. At the conference, Jiang Zemin reiterated the primary importance of propaganda and ideological work for achieving both revolutionary and construction purposes.[3] He urged that ideological work had to be applied with both hands. The most important task, according to Jiang, was "to arm the people with scientific theory, to lead people with the right opinion, to shape people with noble spirit and to encourage people with good works."[4]

Media control did not begin with the national propaganda conference.[5] In late 1993, the Public Security Department, Ministry of Radio, Film and Television, and the CCP's Propaganda Department banned the unauthorized reception of foreign satellite television. After April 1994, all satellite operators, installation workers and manufacturers would have to apply for licences. The new rules tightened controls over the equipment installation workers and manufacturers, instead of the viewers. As the ban was found not very effective, the Beijing authorities later released another set of rules for implementation. China also raised objections to the beaming of the BBC World Service Television by STAR TV, a regional satellite service based in Hong Kong.[6] Rupert Murdoch, STAR TV's owner, wanted to expand satellite television into China and dropped the BBC service in 1994.

The CCP was particularly concerned over the leakage of confidential information to foreign journalists in 1994. While publications were not allowed to reprint overseas articles, all units and individuals were barred from granting interviews to Hong Kong and Taiwan journalists without authorization.[7] The CCP's Propaganda Department and the State Bureau of Secrecy held a conference in mid-1994 to tighten the gag on the press as

China's concern about defusing social unrest became a top priority.[8] New orders were issued to the Chinese press to avoid divulging state secrets and to steer clear of "sensitive" matters.

Related to the leakage of so-called confidential information are the two well-known cases of Xi Yang and Gao Yu in 1994. Xi Yang, a *Ming Pao* reporter from Hong Kong, was sentenced to 12 years imprisonment for allegedly publishing national secrets. His informant Tian Ye, an employee of People's Bank of China, received a sentence of 15 years.[9] Another journalist Gao Yu and her informant also received heavy sentences for publishing confidential information in Hong Kong publications. Many journalists viewed these cases as the CCP's attempt, in the words of a Chinese proverb, to scare the monkey by killing the rooster.[10]

The monitoring of media performance was stepped up when propaganda departments at different levels charged a team of censors to detect reports deserving party discipline. For instance, the CCP's Propaganda Department had appointed 20-odd censors to scan the national press for deviations from the party line.[11] These sensors were mostly senior and retired editors seconded from major newspapers. The *People's Daily*, *Beijing Youth Daily*, and *Workers' Daily* are reported to have been criticized as a result of complaints brought forth by these censors.

Meanwhile, the propaganda heads periodically convened meetings with the chief editors to tell them what to report and what not to report.[12] In places as liberal as Guangdong, the chief editors in 1994 were forbidden to report on the dark side of birth control, the high unemployment rate, peasant protests, or the health of party leaders, as well as the critical comments made by deputies to the People's Congress and Political Consultative Conference. They were warned not to over-report inflation and corruption. They had to seek clearance before they could expose the corruption of the security forces and the military.

The CCP dreads the influence of foreign culture, especially that from Hong Kong and Taiwan, as a cause of "peaceful evolution." To reduce the visibility of Hong Kong and Taiwan singers, they were not given an important role in the big New Year's eve CCTV variety show in 1994. They were at one time even barred from performing in China. But the ban met with strong opposition from overseas and was replaced by some strict rules.[13] In early 1995, several major newspapers in Beijing and Shanghai originally planned to have heavy coverage of the American Academy Awards. But the CCP's Propaganda Department directed that they should play down the event and could only report the final Oscar results.[14] The rationale was that heavy coverage would undermine the official media's effort to establish socialist aesthetics and values.

A joint circular issued by the CCP's Central Committee and the State Council pointed out that weak management and inadequate legislation had allowed China's "cultural market" to be flooded by publications that were pornographic, excessively violent and politically reactionary.[15] It set limits on the growth of printing houses and audio-visual production lines for the following two years. Cable television stations would be limited by an annual quota while the number of outlets lending publications and videos would be strictly controlled. In the first half of 1994, the Chinese authorities seized nearly 6 million books and magazines which violated copyright laws or were deemed too violent and pornographic.

In spite of growing pressure for coproductions and joint ventures from within and without, the CCP continued its careful approach to foreign media capital. In 1982, China had only two movie coproductions whereas 54 of the 154 movies made in 1993 were coproductions. By the new rules released in mid-1994, the annual quota for coproductions was limited to a total of 30.[16] China would have to hold majority control in any joint project. The rules of the Ministry of Radio, Film and Television would apply equally to these joint projects. All the post-production work must be done in China to ensure that the final product would be the same as the script endorsed by the authorities. No coproduced movies would be allowed to enter international competitions without the prior consent of the Ministry of Radio, Film and Television.

In recent years, many coproduced films that were not endorsed by the Chinese authorities have received international awards. For instance, Tian Zhuangzhuang's *Blue Kite* was voted the best picture at the Tokyo International Film Festival. Chen Kaige's *Farewell My Concubine* won the top honor at the Cannes Film Festival and a Golden Globe trophy for being the best foreign-language picture. Some of the delinquent directors, including Tian Zhuangzhuang and Zhang Yuan were singled out and denied employment and professional help by China's movie studios.[17]

Although China had allowed some joint ventures in magazine publication, the launching of *Modern Mankind Daily* (*Xiandai ren bao*) in 1994 was the first newspaper joint venture. But that same year, the CCP reasserted its ban and closed down *Modern Mankind* for allegedly lacking a sponsor.[18] The paper was under the Guangdong branch of the China Council for the Promotion of International Trade (CCPIT). Originally considered a pilot test of media reform, it had received the blessing of the provincial propaganda department and government publication bureau.[19] But CCPIT severed the relationship in July 1994. The paper then approached several potential sponsors and all appeared to be positive at first. They began to back off when pressures from above mounted. It was observed that the closure was a result of the CCP's attempt to tighten its grip over joint ventures and to delink the paper from Yu Pun-hoi, the owner of *Ming Pao*, who had protested over the Xi Yang case. The ban on newspaper joint ventures also applies to Sing Tao Ltd. whose proprietor, Sally Au, is high on the CCP's cooperation list. Sally Au's paper the *Hongkong Standard* was initially allowed to be printed in Beijing. But this arrangement only lasted for three months after which the *Standard* was told to stop printing "due to technical and print capacity problems."[20] Nor did her plan to launch a joint venture *Shenzhen/Hong Kong Economic Times* materialize as originally scheduled.[21]

Not all the CCP's measures are geared toward ideological control. It has also introduced ethical guidelines and legislation in response to various problematic situations. As complaints over paid journalism (advertising disguised as news) multiplied, the Propaganda Department and News and Publication Administration appealed to all journalists to put an end to this unacceptable practice and to develop professional ethics. Journalistic ethics is in general not taught in Chinese journalism schools. It is the first time the Beijing authorities formally place such an emphasis on ethics in dealing with the excesses of media commercialization. However, the call has fallen mainly on deaf ears.

While China has failed repeatedly to introduce journalism laws, it did pass the Advertising Law in 1994. This law bans the advertising of cigarettes in the mass media and imposes penalties on false advertising. It does, however, allow local media to accept more foreign advertisements and will gradually phase out the three-tier rates system for local firms, Sino-foreign joint ventures and foreign companies. China will also test the system of restricting advertisement placement to agencies that are organizationally and financially independent of the mass media.[22] Although these changes do not directly affect the ideological sphere, they will have an impact on the media's advertising revenue and operating environment.

Media Oscillation

Media development in China has followed the swing of the political pendulum during the reform era.[23] Three major political and cultural swings occurred prior to the 1990s: the CCP's campaigns against "spiritual pollution" in 1983, against "bourgeois liberalization" in 1987, and against "peaceful evolution" in 1989. In each case, the perceived threat was the influence of Western culture, particularly its conception of press freedom and democracy. These campaigns resulted in tightened ideological policy, stagnation in media reforms, and reduced media import. The campaigns were preceded by periods of relatively relaxed ideological and press control, as manifested in increased diversity and boldness of opinions.

The current tightening policy completes another cycle of the pendulum-like pattern of media development in China since 1989. In the wake of the prodemocracy movement and the collapse of communism in Europe, the CCP tightened its ideological and communications policies. Such controls began to relax somewhat after Deng Xiaoping pushed for greater economic reform and warned that the major threat to the CCP was "leftism" in 1992. His talks and consequential economic reforms resulted in rapid commercialization in the media and various attempts at reforming the media. However, the relaxed period was rather short-lived. By the end of 1993, the CCP began to retighten its media controls.

The pattern of the current left turn can be characterized in several ways: first, rather than imposing media controls primarily as part of a brief political campaign as they were in the past, the current effort to control the media is sustained and systematic. It began in late 1993 and continued well into 1995. The restrictive measures range from banning the reception of foreign satellite television, restricting concerts held by Hong Kong singers, condemning paid journalism, and deregistering undesirable publications, to holding the largest national propaganda conference since 1957.

Second, the use of restrictive measures is mixed, including legal limitation, policy directives, administrative rules, mini-campaigns, and normative guidelines. This speaks to the diverse motivations behind the CCP's controls: While the CCP's overriding concern is with social stability and social control, it attempts to introduce ethical norms to tame paid journalism and to increase the cost of pornography by campaigns. It appears that media controls take on new dimensions as society increases in complexity.

Third, the media controls are reasserted without attempting to eradicate commercialization which is the economic base of problems such as the rise of pornography, paid journalism, and the commodification of publication permits. This shows that economic reforms in the realm of communications have reached a point where it is difficult, if not impossible, for China to revert to total media control. The state simply cannot afford to subsidize the numerous media that have cropped up in the last decade. In addition, economic growth requires effective advertising channels to bridge the gap between suppliers and consumers. As we shall observe later, media commercialization continues to serve as a liberating force on media control in China.

That media reforms in China occur in a pendulum-like manner begs an explanation. An examination of the context that leads to the current cycle shows that several factors are at work:[24]

(1) Policy Disjunction

China's approach to development is disjoined: Led by Deng Xiaoping, the CCP wants to achieve economic modernization without yielding political control. It has gone so far as being willing to marketize China's planned economy. But politically, it has insisted on the Four Cardinal Principles, the essence of which is to maintain the dictatorial rule of the CCP. As mass media are considered to be political-ideological institutions, they are among the very last to undergo reform. All the media reforms have stopped far short of full autonomy. Whenever the media are perceived to have gone too far and contributed to social instability, the CCP will not hesitate to tighten its reins.

(2) Power Struggles and Policy Swings

The history of the CCP is marked by periodic intraparty struggles in the change of central leadership. As the mass media are a function of the political will of the CCP, media controls fluctuate as such power struggles take sudden turns. The current media oscillation took place in the context of diverging political tendencies, resulting from Beijing's attempts to consolidate its authority over the regional powers, to maintain its power over macro-economic adjustment, and to prepare for the post-Deng succession. Since the inception of the reform period, there has been a gradual shift of power from the center to the regions. This shift accelerated as economic reforms took off after Deng made his southern tour in 1992. Meanwhile, the central government had been taking macro measures to regulate the overheated economy which were met with only partial success. As Deng Xiaoping becomes increasingly senile, it is natural for Jiang Jemin to consolidate his control over the communication channels to prepare for the transfer of power.

(3) Lack of Rule of Law

Media controls in countries which practise the rule of law are relatively stable. They do not fluctuate as the government changes leadership. But China's legal rule is in its infancy. Communications law are overarching and general. While the constitutional rights of freedom of expression are often denied for political reasons, the ultimate power of interpreting laws remains in the hands of party leaders.

(4) Perceived Cultural and Ideological Threats

The reassertion of media controls is also prompted by the prevalence of foreign media fare, the adverse effects of media commercialization, and public loss of faith in socialism and the party. In recent years, the media in China have been internationalized as a result of the diffusion of foreign satellite television, pirated videos and music tapes, television programmes, and coproductions.[25] The influence of popular culture from Hong Kong and Taiwan is particularly strong, so strong that party leaders have called for limitation, if not suppression. As mass media become more profit oriented, media operators tend to distance themselves from the party when economic considerations clash with ideological allegiance. Media licences are sometimes transacted as commodities, thereby undermining the party's control over the media's property rights and the authority to make key personnel appointments. Other excesses of media commercialization such as the rise of pornography and paid journalism are also conducive to the reimposition of media controls.

Why Is Media Control Possible

As evidenced by the systematic constraints that the CCP has exerted over the media during 1994–1995, the party still has the political will and strength to maintain a tight hold over the propaganda machine. How and why media controls are still possible in an increasingly commercialized environment is an intriguing question.

The possibility of continued media control can best be explained by the CCP's rather effective organizational apparatus. Media commercialization in China has stopped short of privatization. Owned by the party-state, mass media are controlled by the propaganda department at the corresponding and higher levels. All media workers are considered to be cadres or employees of the party state. Although some media have assumed economic independence, they still owe their survival to the CCP which has the ultimate control over their licences. In the last instance, whether a medium can exist or not, and in what form it should exist, depends on the evaluation of the party leaders.

The CCP also controls the media by holding onto the power of making key personnel appointments, ranging from chief editors and publishers to the heads of broadcasting stations. Since the leading media personnel owe their position, authority and privileges to the CCP, one should not expect them to be independent in making their decisions. In fact, they are criticized, transferred, or demoted if they are found to deviate from the party line. There is therefore a political incentive for them not to overstep ideological boundaries and to obey party directives.

At the media level, there is a hierarchy of gatekeepers. Reporters learn to know what is politically correct through socialization as well as by trial and error. What they report is screened by editors who were promoted for their seniority and political loyalty. There is a tendency for them to avoid making political mistakes which will affect their career prospects. As the leading journalists and media cadres are held accountable, they will take pains to ensure that their subordinates abide by the rules and regulations. To deviate from the party line will not only open oneself to criticism from above but also to power struggles within the media organization. One's colleagues may report lapses to propaganda authorities out of ideological or selfish considerations.[26]

However, the above explanation should not be interpreted to mean that the Chinese communication system is a monolithic whole that agrees with the party center in total. Mass media may show deviation from the official party line as a result of intraparty struggles, relaxed control from the party center, existence of liberal local leadership, vested interest in particular issues, genuine beliefs on the part of journalists, as well as attempts to lure audience and advertising money. But political deviations are more the exception and toeing the party line is more the rule.

Market Forces vs. Ideological Controls

No figure is available as to the exact proportion of Chinese mass media that have become financially independent. But virtually all mass media realize that they will have to stand on their own feet sooner or later. Some newspapers and television stations are known to have made huge profits. In 1993, eight newspapers had an annual profit of over 100 million yuan.[27] However, their economic independence has not earned them corresponding editorial autonomy. They still have to play to tunes called by the CCP.

At the time of this writing, ideological controls appear to have contained the liberating force of media commercialization in the political arena. But the reassertion of ideological controls has failed to check this force on other fronts. In response to the social needs for information, entertainment and advertising, broadcasting outlets and publication outlets continue to increase. The *Guangzhou Daily* has expanded to 20 pages in early 1995. Indeed, more than 150 newspapers increased their newsholes (that is, news coverage) in 1994. The multiplication of weekenders and infotainment supplements have spawned the growth of freelancers and professional writers who make their living by contributing articles.[28] As they are less dependent on a single media outlet, they tend to have somewhat more independent views.

The sovereignty of the market is redefining the yardsticks of journalism. The golden rules of journalism, according to the *Xinmin Evening News*, are to make its news "shorter and shorter, softer and softer, and broader and broader."[29] The editor-in-chief of *Wen Wei Po* is reported to have said: "News comes first, ideological education is secondary." CCTV has given its journalists much greater autonomy in arranging the news order in all but the official national news broadcast (*xinwen lianbo*). Journalists working in Guangzhou TV are rewarded for reporting exclusive and influential stories. Meanwhile, news media have diluted their dependency on journalism by diversifying their investment in consultancy, real estate, entertainment, tourism, public relations, advertising, and other businesses forming conglomerates.

Continuing commercialization has intensified media competition across regions. For instance, the *People's Daily* plans to launch its east China edition from Shanghai in 1995.[30] This will post competition for *Liberation Daily* which has responded by including more news about east China. The competition is particularly strong between the newspapers of provincial capitals and the provincial newspapers. The latter are usually more tightly controlled than the former because of their political status, thereby undermining their responsiveness to audience needs. The provincial papers have to serve the needs of a much more diverse population over a much larger region. This tends to reduce their relevancy to the population of provincial capitals. In addition, the audience profile of the provincial capitals are more attractive to advertisers because of their homogeneity and higher purchasing power. While national and provincial newspapers continue to command a higher political status, they are losing their circulations to city newspapers and evening newspapers.

Television competition across the national, provincial and city lines is becoming equally strong. For instance, the battle for viewers in Beijing involves CCTV, Beijing TV, and the neighbouring provincial station of Hebei. The Ministry of Radio, Film and Television has newly set up the Center for the Management of Satellite Television to supervise the project of broadcasting 10 provincial channels by satellite in 1995–1996.[31] Satellite has been used by provincial channels from Yunnan, Guizhou, Xinjiang, Tibet, Shandong, and Zhejiang to overcome the obstacles of signal transmission caused by rugged terrain. Now provinces such as Guangdong and Hubei also want to broadcast their television signals via satellite, presumably for the same reason. However, a natural outcome of satellite transmission is to make the provincial channels accessible to the national audience through cable networks or reception dishes. As some provincial stations have rather strong programming, the satellite project will in effect break down the national monopoly now enjoyed by CCTV. That is why CCTV has been lobbying to have the potentially competitive satellite service of Guangdong restricted to the Cantonese dialect while the latter insists on broadcasting in Mandarin. The gradual breaking down of media monopolies over administrative areas is expected to have great repercussions for media development in China in the years to come.

In a competitive environment, there is a greater tendency for journalists to test the CCP's ideological boundaries. *Beijing Youth Daily* is an outstanding example in this regard.[32] Originally, it was an official newspaper for students. But under the leadership of a few highly motivated journalists, it has become an influential newspaper in recent years. It is now known for its insightful comments and coverage of social problems. In 1994 it published a report criticizing the organizational weakness of Shanghai's East Asian Games. Consequently, its chief editor Chen Qi lost his job. But in other cases, self-criticism sufficed. By 1994, Hongze Lake, China's fourth largest, was severely polluted, resulting in the demise of the local fishing industry and in widespread illness.[33] The *Beijing Youth Daily* broke the news and narrowly escaped punishment. This is a noted instance in which journalists have successfully struck what is usually called a "line call" (*ca bian qiu*), a reference to reports that have stretched to the very limit of the CCP's tolerance.

Competition is not limited to domestic media products. The Chinese film industry has to compete directly with foreign countries. In 1993, the first 9 of the 10 best selling movies in Shanghai were coproductions with Hong Kong or Taiwan.[34] Foreign media products are expected to continue to compete with the domestic media industry through piracy, satellite television, trade, and coproductions.[35] Following the 1995 Sino-American accord on the protection of intellectual property, all quotas and licensing requirements for software and audio-visual products, including films, will be removed. It appears that China will at best harness rather than cut off foreign audio-visual products.

The multiplication of communications outlets creates immense demands for new information and entertainment. Cable television that has cropped up rapidly in China since the early 1990s is a good example. The large number of cable networks and channel capacity require feeding by numerous programs. As the domestic production capacity is low, there is a strong tendency for cable networks to import foreign programs, legally or illegally.[36] By the same token, it is difficult to resist joint ventures and coproductions as they are instrumental in securing capital and technology which are much needed for media development.

The CCP cannot afford subsidizing all the mass media. Economic loss and market competition have rendered reform necessary. The continuous drop of box office revenues in China is conducive to important changes in the Chinese movie industry. Cinema attendance has drastically dropped over the last ten years. The number of movie shows dropped by about 50% between 1992 and 1993, with revenue down by 37%.[37] The natural way out was to end the separation among production, distribution and exhibition. Different forms of revenue sharing are now allowed to spread the risk among various parties in the movie production chain. Since February 1995, foreign movies can also be distributed in China on the basis of splitting the revenue by pre-negotiated proportion.[38]

It appears that the CCP is trying hard to prevent the force of commercialization from cracking its organizational control over the media. Since it cannot afford to finance them all, it has to satisfy itself with harnessing rather than controlling the media in total. A sense of realism has probably led the Propaganda Department to focus its control on just 8 institutions — the Xinhua news agency, *People's Daily*, *Qiushi* magazine, *Economic Daily*, *Guangming (Enlightenment) Daily*, CCTV, Central People's Radio,

China International Radio and in important areas such as Beijing, Shanghai, Guangdong, Sichuan, Shaanxi, Hubei, and Liaoning.[39]

To conclude, media commercialization represents an erosion of ideological control in China.[40] The reassertation of media controls is an attempt to contain its liberating forces and excesses and to maintain social stability. The growing marketization and internationalization of China's economy have put structural pressures on the mass media to follow suit.[41] Although the CCP remains quite effective in policing political deviations, it has begun to accept that some changes such as media commercialization and competition across regions are irreversible. The relatively effective organizational control that the CCP now still enjoys will not last forever. As indicated by the only partial observance of the ban on unauthorized reception of foreign satellite television, its effectiveness has been eroded to some extent in the reform era. Its effectiveness will be further undermined as corruption of the CCP grows and as the incentives for deviation increases. Those incentives will be both economic, as benefits grow and the competition for audience intensifies, and political, as pressure for democracy heightens.

Notes

1. Joseph Man Chan, "Commercialization without Independence: Trends and Tensions of Media Development in China," in *China Review 1993*, edited by Joseph Cheng and Maurice Brosseau (Hong Kong: Chinese University Press), pp. 25.1–21.
2. Ming Hua, "Guangdianbu huanma you neiqing" (The Inside Story of Personnel Changes in the Department of Film, Radio and TV), *The Nineties* (Hong Kong), June 1994.
3. Qi Xin, "Qiangying luxian juanlin Zhongguo dalu" (Hard line Policy Reigns Mainland China), *The Nineties*, May 1994, pp. 40–43.
4. As quoted in Cheng Ying, "Zhonggong wenhua xuanchuan da zhengsu" (The CCP's Purge of Culture and Propaganda), *The Nineties*, March 1994, p. 40.
5. Staff, "Weixing dianshi shoufa shijian buduan" (Continuous Penalties for Satellite TV), *Open Magazine*, Hong Kong, June 1994, p. 53.
6. Dough Holden, "BBC Looks for Satellite Link," *South China Morning Post*, 11 August 1994. For the penetration of STAR TV in China, see Joseph Man Chan, "Accessibility and National Responses to STAR TV in Asia," *Journal of Communication*, Vol. 44, No. 3 (Summer 1994), pp. 112–33.
7. Wu suli, "Zhonggong shoujin yishi xingtai kongji" (The CCP Tightens

Ideological Control), *Open Magazine* (Hong Kong), February 1994, pp. 10–11.
8. Willy Lam, "State Tightens Gag on Press to Head Off Unrest," *South China Morning Post*, 6 October 1994.
9. Joseph Man Chan and Yiu-ming To, "Interplay Among Democratization, Reunification, and Press Freedom in Hong Kong: A Critical Event Analysis," a paper presented at International Communications Association, 11–15 July 1994, Sydney, Australia.
10. He Daping, "Gao Yu shijian de lailongqumai" (The Story of the Gao Yu Incident), *Contemporary Monthly* (Hong Kong), 15 January 1995, pp. 24–26.
11. Willy Lam, "Censors to Crack Down on Papers," *South China Morning Post*, 1 November 1994, p. 1, 7.
12. Li Yue, "Zai jiacengzong tiaodong de xinwen liangxin" (The Conscience of Journalism Struggles under Pressure), *Ming Pao Monthly* (Hong Kong), April 1995, pp. 52–54.
13. See Note 7.
14. Li Desheng, "Guanfang jin chuanmei dazuo Aosika dianyinjiang xinwen" (Officials Ban Heavy Coverage of Oscars), *Ming Pao* (Hong Kong), 1 April 1995, p. B1.
15. Agence France Presse, "Crackdown on Printing Firms to Stop Pornography," *South China Morning Post*, 4 December 1994, p. 7.
16. He Xinming, "Yuren hepai dianying chang shoupian, dalu xuezushishilu yuyi xianzhi" (Mainland China Limits Movie Coproductions to Reduce Cheats), *Pai Shing Bimonthly* (Hong Kong), 16 May 1994.
17. Yu Jiwen, "Dalu yingshi zhizuo jingru susha de yandong" (China's Movie Production Enters A Severe Winter), *The Nineties*, May 1994, pp. 56–58.
18. Staff, "Hezuo banbao zhong yaozhe" (Joint Publications Die Finally), *Yazhou zhoukan*, Hong Kong, 15 January 1995, p. 20.
19. Wai-fing Chan, "Beijing's Paper Chase," *South China Morning Post*, 26 January 1995.
20. As quoted in Peter Stein, "China to Stop Printing Hong Kong Paper," *The Asian Wall Street Journal*, 6 January 1994, p. 8.
21. Staff, *Yazhou zhoukan* (Note 18).
22. Staff, "Guanggao jingyin jizhi he guanli tizhi gaige de zhongda jucuo" (Important Reforms of Advertising Operation and Management), *Zhongguo guanggao*, February 1994, pp. 3–8.
23. Joseph Man Chan, "Media Internationalization in China: Processes and Tensions," *Journal of Communication*, Vol. 44, No. 3 (Summer 1994), pp. 70–88; Chin-Chuan Lee, "Mass Media: Of China, About China," in *Voices of China: The Interplay of Politics and Journalism*, edited by Chin-Chuan Lee (New York: Guilford Press), pp. 3–18.

24. I had raised the issue of why Chinese media development oscillated with Dr He Zhou, then a colleague at The Chinese University of Hong Kong. He later wrote a newspaper article entitled "Shi fang shi shou — Zhongguo chuanmei nanyi baituo de guaiquan" (Alternating between Relaxation and Tightening: The Strange Cycle That Chinese Media Cannot Break). I shared with him the observation that media oscillation can be partially attributed to the lack of rule of law and the periodic occurrence of power struggles.
25. Joseph Man Chan (see Note 23).
26. Lin Haike, "Zhonggong kongzhi xinwen de muhou mangluo" (The Scenes Behind the CCP's Journalism Controls), *Ming Pao Monthly*, April 1995, pp. 55–57.
27. Staff, "Zhengzhi yazhi yinying xia shanshan jinguang" (The Sparkling Gold in the Shadow of Political Suppression), *Yazhou zhoukan*, 15 January 1995, pp. 14–18.
28. Staff, "Jiyou zhuangaoren liangyou buqi" (The Uneven Freelancers), *Yazhou zhoukan*, 15 April 1995, pp. 18–19.
29. Staff, "Media Looks on Lighter Side," Reuter, *South China Morning Post*, 28 January 1995, p. 6.
30. See Note 27.
31. Interview with a Chinese television executive.
32. See Note 12.
33. See Note 27.
34. Ma Shi Tu, "Zhongguo dianying ruhe tupo kunju?" (How Can the Chinese Movie Industry Breakthrough?), *Hong Kong Economic Journal*, 16 July 1994.
35. See Note 23.
36. Ibid.
37. Lan Ning, "Dianying faxing fangying shichang: Ruhe yingjie mingtian" (How to Face up to the Future Movie Market), *Liaowang* (Outlook), 21 February 1994, pp. 37–39.
38. Staff, "Shouci chaizhang fencheng waiguo dianying" (Splitting the Revenue of Foreign Movies for the First Time), *Ming Pao*, 20 October 1994, p. D4.
39. Gong Guangzheng, "Zhonggong xuanchuan sixiang gongzuo de jiben silu" (The Basic Ideas of the CCP's Propaganda Work), *The Mirror* (Hong Kong), August 1994, p. 48.
40. See Note 1; Leonard Chu, "Continuity and Change in China's Media Reform," *Journal of Communication*, Vol. 44, No. 3 (Summer 1994), pp. 4–21.
41. See Note 23.

6

The Legal Reform

Edward J. Epstein and Chong Tin Cho

1. Introduction

Since our last review of legal developments in China, negotiations intensified to make it possible for China to rejoin the General Agreement on Tariffs and Trade (GATT). With almost all of its trade conducted with members of the GATT, China expects a number of concrete benefits from membership. It is also a matter of national pride that China should become a founding member of the World Trade Organization (WTO). Therefore, although they failed, the tireless GATT negotiations from 1993 to 1994 were accompanied by new economic laws and legal developments which purport to commit China irrevocably to the post-Mao market reforms and prepare her for full participation in the WTO's system of international trading obligations.

Watching these developments, students of modern Chinese legal history will feel a sense of *déjà vu*. At the turn of the century, the Qing's response to the West was to reform and meet the West on its own terms. This resulted in systematic transplants of Western law which continued throughout the Republican period. Today, China is not humiliated by extraterritoriality but the object of much legal reform is unchanged, that is, to appease the West with laws which look familiar, to comfort investors with a legal system that disguises the real sources of legitimate power and so ultimately to be able to take full advantage of the international trading system established and run according to Western rules. At the same time, there have been a number of developments in public law which are directed at some of the problems not addressed in economic laws, such as tense labour relations within enterprises, the widespread practice of corruption and the ineffective and disorganized government bureaucracy. Administrative law refocusses on the professionalism and integrity of cadres and the rights of individuals aggrieved by the wilful or negligent conduct of cadres.

2. Law in the Market Place

Fair Competition and Consumer Protection

Since the early 1980s, China has attempted to regulate many types of unfair and fraudulent trading activities with piecemeal legislation, including prohibitions on corrupt payments and kickbacks from monopolistic

Legal System 6.3

transactions, and sanctions against hoarding and speculation. There are also consumer protection statutes on foodstuffs and public health, pharmaceuticals, advertising and product quality. There have also been some measures aimed directly at particular monopolistic practices, such as "sealing off" areas from competing goods and services by the levy of discriminatory charges and fees.

China's *Anti-Improper Competition Law* (Competition Law), *Consumer Protection Law* and *Product Quality Law* have four principal objectives:[1]

— elimination of corruption;
— protection of consumers from defective or substandard products;
— protection of business reputation and trade secrets;
— prohibition of coercive and monopolistic trade practices.

In the Competition Law, bribery is a proscribed improper trade practice and is defined as the use of goods or other means to induce the sale or purchase of goods or services. Bribery includes secret commissions but discounts and wholesaler commissions that are given openly and are properly entered into business accounts are excepted. Bribery is punishable by an administrative fine of up to RMB200,000 (US$25,000) and the bribe itself may be confiscated. The parties may also be investigated for criminal liability according to the circumstances.

Like its regional predecessors, the Competition Law addresses unfair trade practices which directly affect consumers. The consumer protection provisions are divided into two parts. First, there are four prohibited types of deceptive practice:

— forgery of trademarks;
— passing off goods or services or otherwise imitating product names, packaging or design;
— misusing another's name so as to mislead consumers as to the identity of the product's maker;
— mislabelling goods so as to mislead consumers regarding quality.

Second, there are comprehensive provisions against fraudulent advertising which prohibit false and misleading advertising as to quality, composition, function, use, maker, durability and place of production. Liability for fraudulent advertising extends jointly to the advertiser as well as those who produce, design, market advertisements or act as agents of the advertiser.

Similar protection is given by the Consumer Protection Law and Product Quality Law. Historically, product quality in the People's Republic of China was primarily a question of administrative regulation. That is, administrative authorities were responsible for setting quality standards, overseeing quality control and penalizing breaches of quality standards. However, in the early 1980s the authorities began to lose control over quality due to the enormous increase in industrial output which led to the production of shoddy and often dangerous goods in large quantities. Sometimes, even good products were damaged during transportation or bailment but were still sold to the unsuspecting public who were keen to buy all kinds of consumer goods. When the goods did not work or caused loss to property or person, nobody wanted to take responsibility.

Therefore, in 1986 the first legislation was introduced to create "product quality liability." Product liability in the West means civil liability for loss caused to property and person by defective products. However, the concept of Chinese product quality liability is much wider and includes administrative, civil and criminal liability for products which do not satisfy administrative standards on a wide variety of manufacturing issues, including safety, labelling, instructions and warnings.

The Product Quality Law applies to all goods circulated in China whether they are made in China or not. The law places duties on both manufacturers and retailers. Manufacturers are required to ensure that their products:

— comply with applicable administrative or trade standards;
— are free from "unreasonable danger" to persons or property;
— have the properties that should be possessed by the products except for defects clearly brought to the consumer's attention;
— conform with samples or packaging and labelling descriptions.

"Defect" is defined as "an unreasonable danger existing in the product that poses a threat to the safety of person or property or products which do not comply with applicable administrative or trade standards." This represents an important departure from earlier law under which the criterion for product liablity was that the product was substandard in an administrative sense.

Several defences are available to manufacturers. Manufacturers are not liable if:

— they did not put the product into circulation;

- the defect did not exist at the time the product was put into circulation (i.e. the defect was caused by a third party by improper handling etc.);
- the defect in the product could not have been discovered at the time the product was put into circulation due to limited scientific or technological knowledge.

Although manufacturers bear primary responsibility for defective products, to prevent sellers from abdicating responsibility the Product Quality Law places them under basically the same liability as manufacturers. However, the Consumer Protection Law provides that sellers have a right to seek indemnity from the manufacturer where it is responsible for the defective product. Sellers also have a duty to:

- examine the goods to verify the genuineness of product quality certificates and marks;
- maintain the quality of the products and not sell products after their expiry date;
- ensure the product labelling conforms to labelling legislation.

In addition to a right to compensation for personal injury or damage to property, consumers have the right to require the seller and/or manufacturer to repair, replace or refund the price of a product which is defective. The Consumer Protection Law establishes a system for the resolution of consumer disputes through consumer associations, which have been growing in China since the late 1980s, administrative mediation, arbitration, if agreed by the parties, and the courts.

China has developed a formidable array of legislation protecting intellectual property but the general law has limited ability to protect trade secrets which do not fall into the categories of patents, trademarks and copyright. The Competition Law protects trade secrets which are broadly defined as any technological or trade information that is not in the public domain and that is kept secret by its proprietor who has an economic interest.

Trade secrets may not be acquired by theft, inducement, force, industrial espionage or other improper means and may not be leaked or used, or permitted to be used, in breach of any confidentiality agreement with the proprietor or by a third party who knows or ought to know that the information was obtained unlawfully. The enforceability of these provisions may, however, depend more on how important a foreign investor is to China than the inherent value placed by China's legal system on the rights and interests protected. Thus, Coca-Cola has seen its products successfully manufactured in China for many years without legislation protecting its secret formulas but other investors may find it impossible to enforce the law against even the most flagrant violators of intellectual property.[2]

Although it is possible that China may in the future establish a specialist authority to supervise improper trade practices, for the present the Competition Law will be enforced by the already overworked State Administration for Industry and Commerce (SAIC) which is China's central regulatory authority for domestic and foreign trade. Like other administrative authorities in China, the SAIC does not rely on the criminal process to enforce the law. Instead, the SAIC will investigate and penalize breaches of the Competition Law of its own motion. Only in exceptional circumstances will it refer the matter to judicial authorities for criminal proceedings to be initiated.

There are three types of penalties the SAIC can impose. First, there are administrative fines ranging from RMB100,000 to 200,000 (about US$12,500 to $25,000). Sometimes the fine may be calculated according to the income derived from the unlawful activity. Second, in addition to levying a fine, the SAIC can confiscate illegal gains, such as secret commissions and profits from illegal use of trade secrets. Third, the SAIC may also order the unlawful activity to cease, to suspend trading in goods or services under investigation and can impose fines if this order is disobeyed.

The imposition of a penalty by the SAIC is not final and can first be reviewed within the SAIC and if the aggrieved party is not satisfied with the outcome of review he may bring an action for judicial review under the Administrative Litigation Law.

In addition to penalties, the Competition Law confers a right on parties to sue for compensation to recover losses incurred as a result of improper competition. Where it is difficult to calculate the loss, compensation may be based on profits made by the violator during the period it was engaged in improper competition with the claimant. The creation of civil liability is becoming increasingly common in Chinese laws which protect private economic actors. Civil liability may also prove a more effective deterrent than administrative sanctions and gives the courts a more creative role in upholding market forces.

The final version of the Competition Law reveals a faltering will to address the underlying causes of China's unlevel playing field. As a result, the only attempts to deal with coercive trade are to prohibit the misuse of prizes to stimulate sales and "tied" or conditional sales, that is the sale of highly marketable goods tied to the sale of some useless or undesirable goods. Similarly, the regulation of market manipulation and monopolies has been reduced to three provisions on disparate matters: dumping (i.e. selling at below cost to drive out competitors), collusive or exclusionary bidding practices, and impeding the purchase by third parties of goods produced under an exclusivity arrangement with a state-owned enterprise.

Finally, the question of regional protectionist trade practices has been side-stepped. In post-Mao China, the devolution of economic decision-making power and rapid economic growth in a competitive environment has frequently led to intense trade rivalry and, in the absence of a level playing-field, has caused many localities to set up trade barriers to outsiders. Previous legislation against protectionism has not been successful. This is most probably due to the difficulty of enforcing anti-protectionist measures against local authorities. Perhaps for this reason, the anti-protectionist provisions in early drafts of the Competition Law were dropped from the final version.

Whereas earlier drafts of the Competition Law came closer to regulating monopolistic and restrictive practices in the manner of anti-trust legislation, the final version is primarily concerned with consumer protection or unfair competition. The new law is therefore disappointing in its failure to address underlying causes of China's unlevel playing field.

Real Property Transactions

Land in China is owned either by the State or by rural collectives. Enterprises and individuals may only acquire rights to use land but not ownership of land. However, buildings may be privately owned whether they are constructed on state or collectively-owned land. Registration of both land use rights and ownership of buildings will soon become mandatory but it may take time for registers to be set up. Most land in urban areas is owned by the State and, as with all publicly-owned assets in post-Mao China, there is a policy to put land into the hands of developers who will realize its potential more efficiently than the government. The result of this policy in recent years has been an explosion of real estate development in China's major cities.

To facilitate real estate development every legal system must have some basic rules to define rights in land and buildings and to create a reasonably safe system for freely transferring and mortgaging these rights. To cope with the real property boom many localities in China, particularly in Guangdong, made their own regulations. But at a national level, relatively little was done to regulate real estate development.

Developers, banks and consumers should therefore all feel more secure once China's new *Urban Real Property Administration Law* (Real Property Law) comes into effect on 1 January 1995.[3] The law does little more than to codify basic principles which can already be found in local legislation but these principles will now apply uniformly throughout China. They should also ensure that their existing property interests conform with the new law or they may be headed for problems in the future.

In China, there are two systems for acquiring land use rights from the state: either by direct allocation for free or at cost; or by purchase for value at auction and by tender or agreement with the local land administration authority. The rules for allocation of land use are set out in Part 2 of the Real Property Law. Although both systems of acquiring land are regulated by a land supply plan, direct allocation of land is heavily subsidized and therefore limited to low-cost housing or infrastructure development. There are many provisions in the new law to prevent and punish the exploitation of subsidised land for commercial development. Where land use rights are granted, the price is determined by negotiation but may not be less than the price fixed by the state.

From their inception, joint ventures between foreign and Chinese investors often involved the Chinese side providing a site as its contribution to the capital of the joint venture. The new law has made it clearer what rights come with that site. If the site has been acquired by the Chinese party (or the joint venture) by way of a grant and is transferred to the joint venture enterprise, it will have full land use rights to the site for the duration of the grant. That is, the joint venture will be able to sell, assign and mortgage the land use rights and as part of the assets of the joint venture the land use rights can be liquidated. If the site is acquired by way of allocation, however, the joint venture will be able to use the site but not otherwise deal with it, e.g. mortgage it. As Article 47 only permits the mortgage of buildings along with the land which they occupy, as a matter of general principle it will be impossible for the joint venture even to mortgage premises occupying allocated land. However, in Shanghai a compromise has been made to allow buildings on allocated land to be mortgaged providing that the mortgagee pays the premium which would have been paid to acquire granted land use rights at the time building property is liquidated.[4]

Part 3 deals with who can develop land and the conditions for development. There is a provision for incentives to housing development, including preferential tax treatment. If construction does not commence within one year of acquiring the land, a 20% penalty may be imposed and if the delay lasts two years the land may be resumed without compensation.

From a transactional point of view, Part 4 of the Real Property Law is the most interesting. It is also the longest, containing 27 articles describing real property transactions (i.e. transferring ownership in buildings and the user rights to the land they occupy from one party to another), setting out the manner of the transfer, the conditions, basic rules for mortgages and leases of buildings or apartments. The price of real property is not exactly determined by the market but set according to an appraisal system based on market indicators as well as replacement cost. It may come as a surprise to foreign developers that there is no mention that developments sold on the overseas market (including Hong Kong) are exempt from these rules. It remains to be seen how the appraisal system will work in practice and there has been more than one Chinese delegation to Hong Kong to study the territory's property market.

The Real Property Law includes provisions for the pre-sale of uncompleted flats. Like existing regulations in south China these rules attempt to bring some order into the excessive enthusiasm to develop property for the Hong Kong market and protect consumers. They have been supplemented by the more detailed *Measures for the Administration of the Pre-Sale of Urban Commodity Housing* which were introduced late in 1994.[5] Many Hong Kong purchasers of uncompleted flats on the mainland have found that the construction of their new homes has been delayed or has never commenced because their deposits have been the only source of financing construction (or have just disappeared). The Measures therefore introduce more control over pre-sales, including systems for the issue of pre-sale development permits, which should ensure developers have paid for the right to use the land in full and have complied with other legal requirements, and for the registration of pre-sale agreements. The Measures also require developers to have committed 25% or more of the total investment in the development but this does not seem to reduce the developer's reliance on pre-sale deposits.

The rules on mortgaging real property and leasing buildings in the Real Property Law are scanty but confirm existing practices and local rules. Banks will be relieved that China has finally enacted even scanty rules on mortgages although it should be noted that a mortgage in China does not give the lending bank an ownership interest in the mortgaged property. By registering the mortgage all the bank gets is a priority in time to recover the loan from the proceeds of sale. However, except for insolvency proceedings (which do not apply to individuals), there are still no procedural rules on he v to realize such a priority in the case of default. Registration of a mortgage is mandatory under the new law as well as local regulations and failure to register it may be fatal for the lender even if the borrower does not become insolvent.

Finally, there are penalties for both officials and developers who carry out land development in contravention of the law. Apart from fines, discipline and possibly prison for criminal offenders, the main penalty, developers should note, is the confiscation of all profits thereby earned.

The new *Urban Real Property Administration Law* has not attracted much attention since it was published in August 1994. This is probably because it only reflects the existing law and practice in localities which have already experienced a property boom such as in much of eastern Guangdong. But it should be considered a welcome development to regularise property development throughout China and a step toward a more market-orientated system in general.

Companies Law

After ten years on the drawing board, China's new Companies Law took effect on 1 July 1994. It has been received amidst some fanfare abroad but disappointment awaits anyone who thinks that China now has a unified and accessible set of rules governing the conduct of more than a million existing domestic companies. On the contrary, in the short term the Companies Law will simply add to the existing complexity which bedevils Chinese entrepreneurs and foreign investors alike. But the new law promises ultimately to simplify the web of legislation which now governs six different types of enterprises.

The real importance of the Companies Law is its commitment to securitising enterprises, including state-owned enterprises, which was the cornerstone of reformist economic policy thwarted after 4 June 1989 and revived only after Deng's "Trip to the South" in 1992. Owing to the failure of the factory manager responsibility system, licensing, contract management and other less radical policies for reforming China's enterprise system the Companies Law now promises gradually to allow all types of enterprises to convert to limited liability companies, in effect to privatize, and to allow larger companies to issue shares.

Unlike the system in most Western countries whereby promoters can register any company which satisfies the legal conditions, China's Companies Law requires administrative approval to create a company. Once the company has been established, however, there is no provision for interference by the state in the company's management or winding up, except where the company is a wholly state-owned company. Therefore, the new law's commitment to entrepreneurship and ultimately to privatization seems irrevocable.

Under China's existing economic system the ownership of enterprises is the key regulatory factor. There are thus six different types of enterprises: state-owned, collectively-owned, privately-owned, wholly foreign-owned and partly foreign-owned, that is equity and cooperative joint venture enterprises, and each is governed by separate laws and regulations. To complicate matters further, some of these enterprises have already been legally converted into companies under special legislation, such as has existed since 1988 for foreign-owned enterprises in Guangdong's Special Economic Zones or under the 1992 *Opinions of the State Commission for Reform of the Economic Structure for the Standardization of Limited Liability* and *Joint Stock Companies*. Still other companies have been created by administrative action, although their status is uncertain, and "briefcase companies" for mainly fraudulent transactions have become prevalent.

The Companies Law will allow existing enterprises to convert to companies regardless of their system of ownership. In the long term it is hoped that the new law will thus ultimately unify China's corporate system as well as regularize the status of existing companies, legal and illegal. In the short-term, however, it will mean that the complex enterprise system will coexist with the company system and thereby create a formidable maze of corporate structures.

The two possible new corporate forms are the "limited company" and a "company limited by shares." Both are companies with limited liability and the key differences are how they are established, held and governed. The limited company is like a private company: it is established by application of the prospective shareholders and its membership may not exceed fifty persons. For the time being, state, collective and even foreign investment enterprises which convert to limited liability companies will remain closely held although technically the directors are responsible to the shareholders in general meeting. The company limited by shares is more like a public company. It shall be promoted by at least five persons except for state enterprises converting to companies, half of whom are resident in China, who may either hold all the shares or hold part of the shares and offer the rest for public subscription. Although the shareholders in general meeting are also the organ of authority of a company limited by shares, the activities of the directors are monitored by a supervisory board which includes shareholder and employee representatives. The supervisory board idea was borrowed from European public companies and has long been favoured in China because it will allow the state to retain a supervisory function over the activities of state enterprises which "go public."

The Companies Law has no immediate effect on wholly or partly foreign-owned investment enterprises. Although they have long been recognised to be limited liability companies, their establishment and corporate governance is regulated by separate legislation, for example, the Equity Joint Venture Law and its Implementing Regulations which date back well over a decade. At this stage, there can be little advantage in foreign-owned enterprises applying for registration as limited companies but there is no doubt that larger enterprises or enterprise groups will now contemplate conversion to joint stock companies so as to be able to issue shares on Chinese and foreign securities markets.

The new provisions on the registration of foreign companies in China will be of interest to foreign investors and Chinese entrepreneurs alike. Once implementing rules are passed, they will allow companies incorporated abroad to operate branches within China which do not bear independent liability. Although registration is not automatic and is subject to the Chinese branches having sufficient operational funds, it will be possible for both Chinese and foreign business people to have a corporate presence in China without establishing a Chinese company. This presence appears more substantial than a representative office but what real benefits accrue from registration in China will depend on whether the authorities and institutions such as banks treat Chinese registered foreign companies any differently from representative offices.

There is no doubt that the ability to establish a company limited by shares, by issuing shares, will prove to be the most important aspect of the new law. There are two reasons for this. First, public issues will allow economically sound enterprises to recapitalize without resort to

China's tightly controlled banking system. Secondly, allowing state-owned enterprises to issue shares to the public will irrevocably change the socialist system of ownership which has traditionally been big, public and pure. Of course, it will be the securities law, expected later this year, which will decide just how far and how fast capitalisation and ownership reform will really go but the Companies Law is a necessary foundation and points optimistically forward.

Whereas the assets of state enterprises are owned legally and politically by the state, the Companies Law has separated the ownership of company property in a legal sense from the state's political interest. The organization of companies, however, has not yet rid itself from the vestiges of state (and party) bureaucratic intervention. Where large state enterprises become companies they will remain subject to a Board of Supervision which will be dominated by the major shareholder, the State. However, by abandoning the factory manager system in favour of a board of directors and general manager (managing director), the Companies Law has removed external interference by one stage. Ultimately, as the state divests or dilutes its shareholdings in companies, the capacity of remnant state economic bureaucracy to interfere in a company's business affairs will diminish. The final draft of Companies Law ominously restored the status of the Communist Party's grassroots in company affairs but this role is not defined and this provision may merely have been a sop to party ideologues.

With 230 articles, the Companies Law is one of China's most detailed laws but it still lacks some important features of modern company law, such as details about debt administration and security for loans. The ten articles on insolvency and winding up are also disappointing because they add little to existing piecemeal provisions. If China is going to have a successful company system it must be understood that adequate legislation for the eventuality of corporate failure is just as important as laws for the successful establishment and management of a company. The Companies Law requires the State Council to produce further detailed regulations on almost every important topic. Reports in May 1994 indicated that the State Council had commenced drafting regulations on the administration of Chinese branches of foreign companies and several regulations on share issues by companies limited by shares, including overseas listings, issue of shares at a premium, preferential shares, employee shares and special RMB shares.[6] It can only be hoped that these regulations will be issued without delay.

Amendments to the Economic Contract Law

When it was first enacted in 1981 the Economic Contract Law introduced some post-Mao innovations which reflected the increasing autonomy of enterprises and the decreasing role of mandatory state plans but it was nevertheless a codification of contract principles and practice based on central economic planning. Contracts and contract law continued to move away from economic planning with the introduction, in 1985, of the Foreign Economic Contracts Law and, in 1988, of the Technology Contracts Law. By the end of the 1980s, changing economic policy had made the Economic Contract Law partly outmoded and in 1993 China's official commitment "to a socialist market economy" was accompanied by amendments to the law.[7] These changes purport to make the law suitable for a market-based economic system and compatible with the expectations of foreign investors who are increasingly subject to China's domestic contract regulation.

Thirteen references to state economic planning have been deleted from the Economic Contract Law. The purpose of the law is no longer to "guarantee fulfilment of state plans" but rather "to ensure the healthy development of the socialist market economy." (Article 1) Reference to the bank settlements system, whereby the banks supervised contract performance by controlling the transfer of payments between contracting parties, has been deleted. So too has the reference to the economic management bureaucracy monitoring the economic performance of enterprises by regulating their contract behaviour. The "arbitration plus litigation" system for the resolution of contract disputes has been replaced by an "arbitration or litigation" system like that available to the parties of foreign economic contracts and technology contracts. This allows parties to an economic contract to exclude the courts and choose arbitration as the only and final means of settling a contract dispute.

Although these changes are obviously more than cosmetic, appearances are still apt to mislead. The amended Economic Contract Law is preparing for the further decline in central economic planning and management in China but economic planning has not ended by a mere stroke of the pen. On the contrary, many references to making and performing contracts according to economic plans in the old Economic Contract Law have merely been replaced by references to administrative regulations. It is quite likely that for the time being these regulations will reproduce policies once formulated as economic plans. The fact that they now appear in the form of legislation may increase their transparency but could also make them more rigid and more rigorously enforced. Moreover, references to mandatory planning have not disappeared altogether. For example, whilst commodity prices have been rapidly deregulated in recent years, Article 17(3) still refers to contracts which must adhere to prices fixed by the state. "Contract administration," that is the process by which state regulatory authorities supervise the making and performance of contracts as well as assist in the mediation of disputes, has been circumscribed but not completely abandoned.

The fact the Economic Contract Law remains wedded to state economic planning reveals a contradiction underlying many of China's legal reforms when trying to adapt a law originally conceived as a "tool of state planning" to facilitate market reforms. Outwardly, the law appears to be a radical departure from the central planning model and this is no doubt an impression China hopes to convey to the outside world. In fact, even where parts of the planning system are dead they continue to rule the law from the grave. To be legally committed to the market system China needs to abandon the concept of economic contracts altogether and unify its contract legislation with reference to civil law. A unified national contract law is now being drafted and this may help to resolve many of the outstanding problems.

Arbitration Law

Disputes are an inevitable part of doing business and an effective system for settling disputes is as important for preventing disputes as it is for resolving them. China has been conscious of this for a long time but whilst building apparently respectable legal structures and institutions for resolving disputes, China has not been able to ensure that they work effectively. A credibility gap has therefore been growing between the theory and practice of settling disputes in China and nowhere has this become more apparent than in arbitration.

Arbitration is effectively the only choice for settling commercial disputes in China. Litigation in foreign courts would usually be a futile exercise because foreign judgements cannot be enforced in China and most Chinese parties have few if any assets abroad. Litigation in China will be equally futile because outside major Chinese cities most Chinese judges are not equipped to understand let alone judge complex commercial transactions. Even arbitration outside of China may be futile if the Chinese courts will not enforce the foreign award.

In recent years, China has therefore attempted to improve its system of commercial arbitration. In 1994, China enacted its first Arbitration Law.[8] The new law governs both domestic and foreign-related arbitration and is a missed opportunity to standardise the arbitral process in China. In fact, the terms of the new law are very vague and it is up to individual arbitral bodies to regulate their procedures in detail. In 1994, new, more comprehensive rules were made to govern arbitration by the China International and Economic Arbitration Commission (CIETAC). CIETAC enjoys a monopoly on arbitrating international and foreign related trade disputes in China. In 1994, CIETAC received a record 829 cases, even more than the Paris-based International Council on Commercial Arbitration.[9] However, CIETAC has earned a mixed reputation in the foreign business community. Grumbles against CIETAC include lack of legal and technical sophistication, bias in favour of the Chinese party, failure to observe basic procedural fairness and the difficulty of enforcing awards. Unfortunately, these are all symptoms of underlying institutional problems which cannot be dealt with by the stroke of a pen and there are therefore many examples of how the new Arbitration Law and Arbitration Rules fail to appease the grumblings.

In arbitration the problem of enforceability looms large. China acceded to the *New York Convention for the Recognition and Enforcement of Arbitral Awards* in 1987 and since then foreign courts, especially in Hong Kong, are regularly enforcing CIETAC awards. However, China's own courts are reluctant to enforce CIETAC awards. In recent years, the situation has become so embarrassing that statistics and discussion of enforcement are conspicuously absent from CIETAC's yearbooks and other publications. The difficulty of enforcing awards is part of a larger and much older problem of regional protectionism in China's courts. Although the Supreme People's Court has recognized the problem for some time, it appears impotent to correct it.[10] China's court system is locally funded and judges, who frequently have roots in the local community, have a low status and poorly paid job without security of tenure. Not surprisingly, the courts in one locality are loath to enforce a judgement or an award which is in favour of another locality (let alone a foreigner) but is contrary to local interests.

Another vexing problem is the choice of CIETAC as a forum for arbitration. Although Article 2 of the Arbitration Rules has expanded

CIETAC's jurisdiction from "international" disputes to "international or foreign-related" disputes, the important question of CIETAC's jurisdiction over cases between a foreign investment enterprise and a domestic enterprise still has not been resolved. In a 1992 case, the Beijing Intermediate People's Court refused to enforce a CIETAC award on the grounds that CIETAC had no jurisdiction to determine a dispute between a Sino-foreign equity joint venture and a domestic enterprise because both were Chinese legal persons and their dispute was therefore not "international."[11] CIETAC officials maintain that since the Rules were changed in 1994, CIETAC has jurisdiction because such a dispute would be "foreign-related." However, it is difficult to imagine that a Chinese court will conclude that a dispute between a joint venture and a locally owned enterprise becomes "foreign-related" simply because a foreign investor owns a share (possibly as little as 25%) of the joint venture enterprise.

Foreign investors are concerned that they are being forced to arbitrate in China's even more unsophisticated domestic arbitration system and that such arbitrations further lack sophistication and enforceability. This particular issue is only part of the underlying problem China created in the 1980s by developing two parallel legal systems, domestic economic law for domestic transactions and foreign economic law for foreign-related transactions. The rationale for this distinction was that rapidly making foreign economic law would help to create an hospitable environment for foreign trade and investment and act as a temporary interface between the international market system and China's planned economy. Over time, China's whole legal framework has become more sophisticated, state economic planning has declined and the two systems of law are slowly converging. However, the two systems of arbitration have been kept separate.

Finally, neither the Arbitration Law nor the new CIETAC Rules resolves the old problem about the timely filing of the defence in preparation for the hearing. Although the Arbitration Rules provide that the respondent shall file a defence within 45 days of receipt of the arbitration claim, in practice the tribunal will allow the respondent to present his defence at any time up to and including the day of the hearing. This is very unfair to the claimant who has no chance to prepare a reply to the defence in advance of the hearing and it is contrary to common practice around the world. However, it has become an acceptable practice in China because, it is argued, a defence is a right not an obligation. In fact, it is a good example of the Chinese attitude that procedural niceties should not be permitted to get in the way of the substantive issues, especially where that would affect the Chinese party to the arbitration who is usually the respondent.

There is some good news. At the same time the new CIETAC Arbitration Rules came into effect a new list of CIETAC arbitrators was published which includes 86 foreign arbitrators, increased from a mere 13 foreign arbitrators first placed on the panel in 1989, but still a small minority among a total of 289 arbitrators. Also, article 40 was added to give the parties an opportunity to examine and give their opinions on expert reports commissioned by the arbitral tribunal. This is certainly in response to the Hong Kong High Court's refusal to enforce a CIETAC award, the only such case thusfar, on the grounds that it was procedurally unfair for the tribunal not to give both sides the opportunity to refute adverse evidence contained in such a report.[12] It is a good sign that CIETAC responds to criticisms from outside China and it is more the pity the Hong Kong High Court has not been stricter about the enforcement of CIETAC awards tainted by procedural irregularities.

Legal Change and the World Trade Organization

It has been eight years since China formally applied to re-join the GATT. China's failure to do so before the GATT became the World Trade Organization was ignominious and mostly due to US opposition. However, since recently settling its intellectual property disputes with China, the US has promised to support China's entry to the WTO as a founding member. China has had observer status in the GATT since 1971 and 85% of her trade is conducted with GATT members. The Chinese government therefore expects a number of benefits from full participation in the WTO. However, these benefits will come at a price because China's trading partners, particularly the European Unions (EU) and the US, have their own expectations of China.

Apart from the obvious issues of reducing tariffs and increasing market access, Western countries expect China to continue building a system of law and government which is market-based and more transparent. China has responded with a number of new laws and revisions of old ones. A number of these have already been discussed above. In addition, in 1994 China passed the Foreign Trade Law as well as introducing a number of taxation and foreign exchange reforms based on legal regulations rather than mere administrative fiat. This is designed to bring China's system of economic regulation into line with international expectations and is consistent with the direction established in recent years to move away from central economic planning.

The most desperate attempt to appease Western trading partners in 1994 was China's adoption of the Foreign Trade Law which came into effect on 1 July 1994.[13] According to China's Foreign Trade Minister Wu Yi, the new law represents a fair and free trade policy which commits China to the international trading system but judging by their quiet response, Western trading partners remain unconvinced. The Foreign Trade Law purports to establish a liberal trade regime where the import and export of goods and technology is "free" (Article 15) and the "gradual development of international service trade is promoted" (Article 22). In fact, the law does nothing to reduce the trade restrictions currently imposed by China's trading system. Like the amended Economic Contract Law, it refers repeatedly to "relevant laws and administrative regulations" which shall regulate trade and prescribe the restrictions on trade freedom. Contrary to China's official press, this does not bid farewell to the old system of government managed trade. All it means is that some restrictive administrative policies will be transformed into legal regulations. Assuming the administrative regulations are thus adequately published (and there is no provision in the new law requiring their promulgation) this may enhance the transparency of restrictive trade policies but will not diminish their restrictive impact on trade.

Article 4 says that China implements a "unified system of foreign trade." Of course, this has never been true and probably never will be true. China's post-Mao trading policies have always been based on uneven development between different parts of China, especially between coastal and inland regions. Law making and regulatory powers have been devolved to localities and the competition between China's rapidly developing regions has created local protectionism. This has been most clearly illustrated by the inability of the central government to overcome local resistance to crackdowns on intellectual property piracy in south China.[14] As we have already seen, it is also evident in the protectionism practised by the courts when enforcing judgments and arbitral awards. We have also seen that the central government failed to address local protectionism in the Anti-Improper Competition Law, probably because it realized it was powerless to control protectionist practices. The WTO, like much contemporary public international law, is based on the ideal of the Western nation state which has a strong central government capable of complying with international obligations. In fact, as the long standing intellectual property dispute between China and the US shows, this ideal is not applicable to China and the West is naive to expect a comparable degree of compliance.

Two new direct tax laws came into effect in 1994. The *Chinese Enterprise Income Tax Law* unifies direct taxation of the many types of Chinese business entities which were formerly taxed on the basis of whether they were owned by the state, collectives or by private companies or individuals.[15] Although the new law does not apply to foreign investment enterprises, it unifies the standard tax rate for Chinese and foreign investment enterprises at 33% and thus signals a move toward a level playing field. Similarly, the new Individual Income Tax Law is clearly aimed at bringing more Chinese taxpayers into the net.[16] Four new indirect taxes were also introduced. The old system of Consolidated Industrial and Commercial Tax (CICT), essentially a turnover tax which had existed in China since the 1950s, has been abolished. CICT has been replaced by three indirect taxes: a Value-added Tax (VAT) with a standard rate of 17% which is comparable to EC countries,[17] a Consumption Tax at a rate between 3% and 45% for "luxury" items such as cars, liquor and tobacco,[18] and a Business Tax on services at a rate of between 3% and 20%.[19] A controversial capital gains tax on the sale of land use rights and buildings was also introduced to reduce speculation in China's booming property sector. However, the outcry against the new tax, especially from the many Hong Kong property developers with projects in China, delayed its enforcement until implementing regulations were published early in 1995.

Reforms in China's tax system were mirrored in the system of foreign exchange control.[20] Again the predominant theme is to create a level playing field by equalising access to foreign exchange and thus prepare China's currency for free convertibility without losing control over foreign exchange expenditure. The foreign exchange retention system, whereby every foreign currency earner was allowed to retain all or a portion of earnings in a designated account for future expenditure, is being replaced by a foreign exchange settlements system. Under the new system, all foreign exchange income must be sold to authorised banks at the quoted rate. At the same time, foreign exchange is conditionally available for *Renminbi* at the quoted rate. The approval procedures are being simplified to allow foreign exchange to be purchased with *Renminbi* on the basis of supporting documents, such as a contract for the sale of goods. This reform was accompanied by a devaluation of the *Renminbi* to the rate prevailing in the swap markets. It is intended that the official rate will be maintained by an national unified inter-bank foreign exchange market.

Article 10 of the GATT provides that parties shall promptly publish legal and administrative provisions relating to almost any kind of trading interests. In recent years, China has, sometimes willingly and sometimes not, opened up its legal system. More collections of laws, regulations and cases have been published in the last five years than in thirty years previously. Yet China's highly centralised political system militates against disclosure. If a powerful person does not give approval for publication, the information remains a state secret. This principle applies to information about economic and trade policies as well as the law. Whilst major laws are published, many rules, decisions and directives which tell us about practice under these laws remain *neibu* or "internal only." Even a fact as important but harmless as the investment project approval limits on various authorities will not be found in a published document. Of course, economically sensitive information such as the import plan and, in some areas, rates for land-use fees are state secrets.

3. Developments in Public Law

Whilst China has achieved a great deal in accelerating market-based economic reform and has enacted numerous economic laws, regulations and rules both at the national and local levels, the government is encountering problems in the public economy, such as low productivity in state-owned enterprises, tense labour relations within enterprises, widespread practice of corruption and ineffective and disorganized government bureaucracy. The government understands that unless these serious problems are also dealt with, the economy cannot continue to prosper.

Reform in the public law sphere has been put on the agenda but only modest progress has been made thusfar. Civil service reform has been discussed for at least a decade and the first legal step was taken in 1994 with the enactment of the first Civil Service Regulations which are designed to establish a well organised and ethical civil service system. It has also enacted the first national Labour Law covering almost every aspect of labour affairs. The role of the courts is also being enhanced, in particular, the trial of administrative and economic cases. In 1994, the Standing Committee of the National People's Congress (NPC) also enacted the State Compensation Law to provide redress to victims of maladministration.

Building a Legal Framework for Labour in the "Socialist Market" Economy

Before the open-door policy and economic reform, China did not officially recognize unemployment and firing was never heard of because individuals were somehow to be employed and fed by the state. The public economy offered almost all workers cradle-to-grave welfare. This is known as the so-called "iron rice bowl" system. On the other hand, there was little or no incentive to increase productivity and the advancement of employees was based mainly on their loyalty to the Communist Party. With the introduction of economic reform, other types of enterprises were introduced to supplement the state-owned enterprise system. Diversity in the enterprise system has brought with it new complexities in labour affairs and new problems in labour relations. Managers and owners of private enterprises are primarily concerned with how to extract the highest profits. At the same time, the rights and welfare of workers have not been given adequate legal protection. Excessive overtime, workers locked in factories and even physical abuse have thus become commonplace. Inadequate protection of workers has also resulted in some disastrous industrial accidents, affecting social stability and economic development.

In 1993, the PRC Constitution was amended for the second time to recognise the official ideology of establishing a "socialist market economy." Thereupon, a new, comprehensive national labour law was needed to replace the obsolete methods of regulating labour affairs. The national Labour Law (*Laodongfa*) was promulgated on 5 July 1994 and came to effect on 1 January 1995. The Law is designed to solve new labour problems and facilitate the development of the so-called socialist market system.

The Labour Law is also a codification of existing regulations, rules and guidelines. Its 107 articles deal with a range of issues including promotion of labour contracts and collective contracts, wages and salaries, protection of female staff and underage workers, labour disputes and legal liability. According to Article 2, the law applies to workers (*laodongzhe*) with whom a labour relationship is created and applies to enterprises, including foreign investment enterprises, and individual economic organisations (employing unit, *yongren danwei*) inside the PRC, which means, it applies to all the staff working in all the enterprises in PRC. The law also applies to state authorities, institutions, social organisations if they have a contractual labour relationship with the workers. In effect, it applies to most employers and workers throughout China.

Legal System

The Labour Law reflects China's socialist ideology. Protection of rights of workers is the basic aim of the Labour Law and is given a prominent place. Article 3 stipulates several fundamental rights of workers, most of them reiterate the existing rights guaranteed by the Constitution and other laws. The rights include the right to choose an occupation, the right to rest and take vacations, the right to wages, the right to vocational training, the right to social insurance and welfare, the right to strike and so on.

Chapter 3 of the Law stipulates the principles governing labour contracts (*laodong hetong*). A labour contract can be for a fixed term, an open term contract or a term determined on a job-to-job basis (Articles 16 and 20). Phasing out the iron rice bowl system has proven a heavy burden for economic development and the government responded by introducing the labour contract system in state-owned enterprises in 1986. By 1994, 35 million persons or some one-third of the workers in state-owned enterprises were employed under the labour contract system.[21] Enterprise workers now have more freedom to choose their occupation under the Labour Law since the iron rice bowl has been broken because the state no longer guarantees employment. However, because a social security system has not been fully established and workers with longer employment history with the state-owned enterprises are resistant to the labour contract system, Article 106 allows provincial governments to determine the implementation of the labour contract system in accordance with the actual situation in their own regions. This is designed to allow for gradual change in the state-owned sector and mitigate the effects of unemployment and social instability.[22]

The Labour Law also specifies the provisions of collective contracts, rules relating to enterprises discharging their employees and the right of workers to resign. Approval of the labour contract by the government is no longer required. However, the failure of employers to comply with the requirements of the Labour Law will make them liable to pay compensation to the employee.

The controversial issue of minimum wages is not fully explored in the Labour Law. Article 48 simply states that the state shall implement a system of guaranteed minimum wages, specific standards for minimum wages shall be formulated by the provincial governments and submitted to the State Council for the record. The provincial governments must refer to the following factors when deciding and adjusting the minimum wage:

a. the minimum cost of living of workers themselves and of the average number of dependants of such workers;
b. the average wage and salary level in society;
c. labour productivity;
d. the overall employment situation; and
e. differences in the level of economic development between regions.

Since the situation in each province varies greatly, it is reasonable that the standards for minimum wages should be determined by the provincial government. However, it is highly likely that provincial governments will set their minimum wage as low as possible so as to compete with other provinces. Further, as standards for minimum wages and salaries do not require its approval, the State Council may not control the minimum wages according to the provisions of the Labour Law.

The right of enterprises to hire and fire workers is also expressly provided for. Where an employing unit genuinely needs to reduce the number of its staff during statutory restructuring on the verge of bankruptcy or when major production or operation problems arise, it should explain the situation to the trade union or staff 30 days in advance, listen to the opinions of the trade union or the staff, and may reduce the number of its staff after submitting a report to the labour administration department. Thus, redundancies are now clearly provided for. This provision has the potential to increase enterprise productivity and the survival of the state enterprise system but will, no doubt, prove unpopular with workers accustomed to a high degree of job security.

The Labour Law also sets out the powers of labour administration at all levels. Chapters 11 and 12 contain the powers and duties of the labour administration which include carrying out inspections and enforcing the labour law, the power to give warnings, to order offending units to correct malpractices, to impose fines, to order the employing units to pay the workers' remuneration or to pay compensation for economic losses. In the light of the serious industrial accidents which have occurred in recent years, the Labour Law grants extensive powers to the labour administration to enforce conditions for worker safety and health. Article 92 provides that where an employing unit's safety facilities or health conditions do not comply with state regulations the labour administration or the relevant authorities should order remedial measures to be taken and may impose a fine. Where the circumstances are serious, the department can apply to a people's government, at or above the county level, for a decision to order suspension of production pending remedial measures. Where workers suffer loss of life or property due to a major accident resulting from the employing unit's failure to adopt measures against a latent danger, the persons responsible should be held criminally liable. Criminal liability should also be imposed on the persons responsible where serious consequences arise due to a major accident involving death or injury as a result of workers being forced to engage in dangerous activities which violate rules and regulations. Workers are also allowed to terminate their labour contracts at will where the employing units have coerced them into employment by means of violence, threats or illegal restriction of personal freedom.

Where an employing unit illegally recruits minors who have not reached the sixteenth year of age, the labour administration department has the power to impose a fine. Where the circumstances are serious, the Administration for Industry and Commerce shall revoke the employing unit's business licence. Penalties are clearly provided throughout the law but it remains to be seen to what extent they will be imposed by the government officials in practice. Further eleven sets of labour regulations are being drafted.

Establishing a "Clean and Efficient" Civil Service System

The NPC, its Standing Committee and the State Council have enacted more than 20 laws and regulations providing for penalties against embezzlement, bribery and corruption. Nevertheless, in practice, these laws and regulations have not been strictly implemented and enforced. Corrupt government officials with support from high levels are still out of the reach of the law. It is generally believed that only junior government officials will be punished by law. There were 27,463 cases of economic crime in 1993 out of which 22,106 persons were convicted. Out of the 22,106 convicted, however, only 69 were government officials at the grade of county heads or division heads (*xianchu de ganbu*) and only 7 were at the grade of department heads under a ministry or bureau heads (*siju de ganbu*).[23] Apart from well known corrupt practices, the government is also faced with overstaffing of officials and overlapping of the structure of government departments.

In 1987, the civil service reform (*gongwu gaige*) was launched to fight against corruption and building up of an efficient and clean government.

With six years experience in a few central and provincial departments, the government understands that a comprehensive reform should be carried out not only to alleviate symptoms of corruption but also to work out a permanent cure. It also realizes that legislation should be intensified and application of laws should be strict.[24]

There are hundreds of regulations, rules, notices and departmental guidelines regulating the activities and working procedures of the civil servants. They cover most aspects, including government structure, training, documentation, and even the use of government vehicles. Almost a hundred of them dating back to the 1950s are still in force.[25] For more than forty years, the enormous civil service system has been governed by these musty documents which lack a unified and detailed legal structure for civil servants to follow.

After around 10 years' drafting with twenty-one drafts, the *Provisional Regulations of the State Civil Servants* came into effect on 1 October 1993. With 18 chapters containing 88 articles, the Regulations lay down the general guidelines for almost every aspect of the civil service from recruitment and selection, performance appraisal, training, rules on the avoidance of conflict of interest, service grades and discipline.

It is remarkable that in Chapter 2 it is provided that civil servants are allowed to criticize and give suggestions to government departments and their senior officials. They are also allowed to express their grievances and make complaints. It is well known in China that if one criticizes or complains about senior officials in government departments, one will have a difficult time and it seems doubtful that this express provision can protect outspoken civil servants in the current cadre culture.

The civil service system is divided into leading staff (*lingdao zhiwu*) and non-leading staff (*feilingdao zhiwu*). Leading staff are those who carry out managerial duties, such as minister and department head; non-leading staff are specialists, such as researchers or economists. It is hoped that this division can streamline civil servants so that there will be fewer leading officials in the system and help to develop professional grades in the government.[26] Civil servants are further divided into 15 grades, ranging from the premier of the State Council to clerical staff. Article 11 sets out the criteria in assigning the grades, including their ability and moral standard, actual performance and work experience. In light of the fact that the "Four Cardinal Principles" are laid down in Article 2 of the Regulations, it seems inevitable that moral standard should include political correctness and loyalty to the CCP and the socialist system.

Article 31 expressly lists 14 types of proscribed behaviour. Not surprisingly, "spreading ideas damaging the reputation of the government, organising and joining illegal organisations, and attending anti-government meetings, demonstrations and strikes" is on the top of the list. One may recall during the 1989 Democracy Movement, thousands of civil servants bearing the names of their departments on banners joined in the student demonstrations. It is also not surprising that the meaning of "anti-government" is not defined in the Regulations. Despite some attempts to separate Party and government it does not require much imagination to stretch the meaning of "anti-government" to opposition to the party.

In addition, corrupt practices, embezzlement, suppression and revenge (*daji baofu*), waste of public resources and disobeying orders are also on the list. Moreover, "doing business, establishing enterprises and joining other business" is not allowed. This is part of the existing attempt to separate the government from enterprises thus clearly distinguishing political activities from economic activities. It is also part of the existing, largely unsuccessful attempt to prevent official powers being used to achieve economic ends. In practice, a web of economic relations have been established between parts of government and economic enterprises. Existing prohibitions make it rare nowadays for an official to hold office in an enterprise but officials formally leaving the civil service are informally continuing to serve in a government sponsored enterprise. Every department that can be involved in this activity is involved, including powerful parts of the state apparatus such as the police, army and organs for the administration of justice. Therefore, it seems doubtful that this provision can be enforced against the existing system of abuse.

Article 33 stipulates five administrative penalties for misbehaviour by civil servants, namely, warning, demerit, serious demerit, demotion, discharge from leading duties and dismissal. Since relevant regulations for reward and punishment have not yet been promulgated, the 1957 *Temporary Rules for Reward and Punishment* and 1988 *Tentative Measures for Investigating and Hearing Administrative Discipline Cases by the Supervisory Organs* are still applicable.[27]

Chapter 12 lays down the rules of avoidance of conflict of interests in the civil service system. There are three rules. The first one is civil servants with close family relationships are not allowed to have a leading relationship (*lingdao guanxi*) or be in a supervisory, auditing, personnel and financial role in the same organ. Secondly, where a civil servant is executing his duties, and he or she realizes that his job is related to his own interest or interest of his close family members, he or she should withdraw to avoid conflict of interest. Finally, civil servants who assume leading posts under the level of county people's government are not allowed to be posted to their home locality. However, the last rule is not applicable to autonomous regions as Article 114 of the Constitution expressly permits otherwise. The purpose of these rules is to circumscribe favouritism in the civil service system but their implementation will definitely be an arduous task and will encounter strong resistance from existing civil servants who benefit from the old practices.[28]

Apart from corrupt practices at all levels, the government is also faced with enormous waste of state resources at all levels. It was reported that government officials have used more than RMB100 billion in public revenues for entertainment and business trips in 1992.[29] To reduce the waste of government resources and to perfect the government's auditing system, the former Auditing Regulations were replaced by the more detailed Auditing Law. The latter was promulgated on 31 August 1994 and come into effect on 1 January 1995. This law states the establishment of national and regional auditing authorities and implementation of an auditing supervision system by the State Council. It also stipulates the limits of power of auditing authorities and their responsibilities, auditing procedures and penalties for violation. The Auditing Law applies to all the state organisations and all state-owned financial institutions, enterprises and institutional organisations.

The "iron rice bowl" system is also broken in relation to the civil service. Civil servants may be dismissed if they breach Article 31, as discussed above, or if their performance is unsatisfactory or they refuse to accept another job assignment (Article 74). By dismissing deadwood in the government, it is believed that the civil service system will be more efficient and manageable. On the other hand, where a civil servant is allowed to resign, the approving authority should approve within 30 days after submission of the written application. Nevertheless, there are two provisos in relation to resignation. First, a government department may set down the minimum years of service (3–5 years) and a government department may refuse a resignation application if the civil servant has not yet completed the minimum years of service. Secondly, civil servants occupying posts connected to national security and confidential information are not allowed to resign.

From the contents of the Regulations, it can be seen that the government is cautious about reforming the civil service system as the stability

Legal System 6.29

and continuity of the system are top priorities. Further, the nature of the civil service system which emphasises principles of merit, neutrality and promotion according to examinations, are incompatible with the party's fundamental right of control. The government knows that a competent and honest civil service is crucial to economic development but there is no plan or indication at least in the Regulations to build up political neutrality within the system. As these regulations are temporary it is still too early to speculate their effect and how the government will amend them. Since the Regulations only set out the guidelines, further detailed rules (*peitaofagui*) in relation to every aspect of the civil service are needed to complete the whole picture.

Strengthening the Role of the Court in Administrative Cases and Economic Crimes

With an increasingly prosperous market economy in China, the focus of the criminal courts has shifted to fighting economic crime. Speculation and profiteering (*touji daoba*) which were the main targets in the planned economic system are no longer relevant. Most decided cases now involve crimes of selling imitation, fake and inferior products, which differ markedly from previous economic crimes such as reselling controlled price items at a profit. In 1993, 314 people were convicted of crimes of selling imitation, false and inferior products.[30]

With increasing popular pressure to combat corrupt practices, embezzlement and bribery have become the current focus. Nevertheless, it is increasingly a challenge to define current economic crimes in a market economy due to the increasing complexity and variety of economic behaviour. In the past few years, conflicts have often occurred between the courts, procuracies and government departments on how to enforce the law. At a national working conference on the handling of economic crimes cases, eight criteria were advanced for defining economic crimes in relation to business activities of enterprises and technical staff.[30] These criteria require a distinction to be made between corruption and business practices which are improper or even normal and do not constitute crimes.[31]

After the conference, the people's courts acquitted a group of technical staff for alleged economic crimes in light of the last two certeria discussed in the conference. The change of attitude of the people's courts with more clear guidelines in implementation of law has played an important role in the promotion of a market economy and of technology development. This change is important as far as the stability of the laws is concerned.

In the *China Review 1992* we explored the lingering traditional vision of authoritarian justice in China and the introduction of the Administrative Litigation Law which allows the individual to seek redress in the courts against unlawful state interference with his personal freedom and property. Currently, China's administrative cases involve most administrative fields including land, industrial and commercial administration, environmental protection and taxation.[32] In the 1990s, the number of administrative cases has increased dramatically but even the central court leadership understands that the lower courts have difficulty in trying such cases without interference from the executive. In 1987, the courts accepted 5,240 administrative cases. The figure increased to 8,573 in 1988 and 27,911 in 1993. Of the administrative cases heard and judged in 1993, 23.56% of the government's decisions were affirmed, 20.39% of the government's decisions were amended or discharged, 41.31% of the cases were withdrawn by the applicants. The withdrawal rate is very high indeed. One may speculate that the low success rate and the high withdrawal rate are due to the influence and suppression of the government. Ren Jianxin, the president of the Supreme People's Court in his 1994 Supreme People's Court Working Report admitted that some judges were afraid of affecting the relationship with the government and thus did not hear the administrative cases properly. Ren further said that one of the objectives of the court is to promote the Administrative Litigation Law and help more people understand their rights.[33]

Ren in his speech known as "The relations between the court and government of the PRC" at the conference marking the 200th anniversary of Australian Law said,

> The people's court and people's government are two parallel systems of State organs that carry out different functions under the unified supervision of the people's congress and its standing committee.[34]

It was the first time Ren as the president of the Supreme People's Court tried even cautiously to express in an open forum his idea of the courts being independent from the government. Apart from mapping out the relationship with the government, Ren also expressed his intention to raise the status of the judges.[35]

From 1995, the people's courts have another law to enforce and further protect the rights and interests of the applicants in administrative cases. The State Compensation Law came into effect on 1 January 1995. The law is enacted to supplement the existing laws as the existing laws only allow an aggrieved person to claim civil liability against the wrongful government official. Article 7 states that the state should take up the liability of the wrongful government official and assume the responsibility of compensation, known as state's tortious liability (*guojia qinquan zeren*).

Apart from supplementing the existing law, the legislative purpose of the State Compensation is to solve two existing problems. First, an aggrieved person can directly receive compensation from the wrongful government department instead of the wrongful official who may not be capable of paying compensation. Secondly, it is hoped that the government officials can perform their duties more freely without the fear of being sued for compensation.[36]

The law divides state compensation into two types, namely administrative compensation (*xingzheng peichang*) and criminal compensation (*xingshi peichang*). Administrative Compensation means that where the administrative departments and their officials, when exercising their powers, have infringed the rights and interests of the people, legal persons and other institutions, the aggrieved persons have the right to claim compensation. The aggrieved person or his successor can directly apply to the wrongful government for compensation (Articles 6 and 18). Or, he or she can start administrative proceedings in the court claiming compensation from the wrongful government departments at the same time. Criminal compensation is catering for the tortious liability of the public security organisation, court, procuratorate. In order to settle the disputes of criminal compensation, the intermediate people's court or above should set up a Compensation Committee to hear the cases. The decision of the committee is final and can be enforced immediately. If the court can make full use of its powers under the law, it surely can strengthen its role and powers in protecting the people from maladministration and abuse of the powers of the government.

4. Conclusion

Recent legal developments are clearly linked to China's desire to participate in the world trading system and to remain attractive to foreign investors. The new legislation which gives effect to China's so-called "socialist market economy" must therefore be understood as a response to the West. It should not be taken at face value because obviously the law cannot by itself create a market, even a "socialist market," without accompanying changes to the economic and political systems. As the legislation on competition, contracts and companies demonstrates, however, China's policy-makers have only been willing (or able) to go a certain distance toward economic deregulation and even these "progressive" laws harbour vestiges of the planned economy.

Meanwhile, developments in public law have been directed at some of the problems not addressed in economic laws, such as tense labour relations within enterprises, the widespread practice of corruption and the ineffective and disorganized government bureaucracy and individual grievances against the state arising from the wilful or negligent conduct of state cadres. By embracing the contract system, the Labour Law also affirms the market but at the same time attempts to create a fair system of labour relations. The government understands that unless these serious problems are also dealt with, the economy cannot continue to prosper.

Notes

1. (Competition Law) *China Law & Practice*, 18 November 1993, pp. 31–37; (Consumer Protection Law) *China Law & Practice*, 16 May 1994, pp. 33–43; (Product Quality Law) *China Law & Practice*, 3 June 1993, pp. 21–33.
2. Carl Goldstein, "Legal Aid: China Develops Business Law by Looking to Guangdong," *Far Eastern Economic Review*, 4 November 1993, pp. 71–72.
3. *China Property Review*, 18 October 1994, pp. 8–14.
4. "Regulations of Shanghai Municipality on Mortgage of Real Estate," *China Economic News*, 16 January 1995, pp. 7–9 (pt. 1); 23 January 1995, pp. 7–9 (pt. 2).
5. *China Law and Practice*, 27 January 1995, pp. 41–43.
6. *Wen Wei Po* (Hong Kong), 2 May 1994, p. F6 and 19 May 1994, p. C4.
7. *China Law & Practice*, 18 November 1993, pp. 41–46.
8. *China Law & Practice*, 7 November 1994, pp. 23–37.
9. *China Daily Business Weekly*, 26 March 1995, p. 2.
10. Ren Jianxin, "Zuigao renmin fayuan gongzuo baogao" (Working Report of the Supreme People's Court), *Zhonghua renmin gongheguo zuigao remin fayuan gongbao* (PRC Supreme People's Court Gazette), No. 2 (1994), p. 67.
11. See *China International Construction Consultant Corporation v. Beijing Lido Hotel Company* cited in Kaplan et al., *Hong Kong and China Arbitration: Cases and Materials* (Butterworths: Hong Kong, 1994), p. 316.

12. *Paklito Investment Ltd. v. Klockner East Asia Ltd.* [1993] 2 HKLR 39. [this is the correct legal citation: 2 refers to volume 2 and 39 is the first page of the report.]
13. *China Law & Practice*, 25 July 1994, pp. 20–27.
14. See Note 2.
15. *China Daily Business Weekly*, 13–19 February 1994, p. 2.
16. *China Law & Practice*, 31 January 1994, pp. 23–29.
17. Ibid., pp. 30–36.
18. Ibid., pp. 38–42.
19. Ibid., pp. 44–48.
20. See "Public Announcement of the People's Bank of China on Reform of Foreign Exchange System," *China Daily*, 16 January 1994, p. 4 and its various implementing regulations.
21. Zhang Shicheng, "Laodongfa zhong de ruogan wenti" (Several Problems in the Labour Law), *Zhongguo lüshi* (China Lawyer), October 1994, p. 29.
22. Ibid.
23. Note 10, p. 65.
24. At the Fourteenth National Congress of the CCP held on October 1992, Party Secretary Jiang Zemin in his report declared that the government was going to introduce further civil service reform in the coming years.
25. By conducting a search on the term "gongwu" (civil service) in the Zhongtian Chinese Law Index System, 95 regulations, rules, notices and departmental guidelines are found in effect as of November 1994.
26. Pi Chunxie (ed.), *Zhongguo gongwuyuan tiaoli shiyong jiangzuo* (Practical Speeches on the Chinese Civil Service Regulations), (Beijing: Metallurgy Industry Press, 1993), pp. 47–48.
27. Ibid., p. 99.
28. Ibid., p. 185.
29. Li Ping, "Jingren de langfei" (Incredible Waste), *Jingji ribao* (Economic Daily), 10 May 1993.
30. Note 9, p. 65.
31. Distinguishing: (1) embezzlement of public funds through exercise of powers by enterprise officials, from excessive shares and distributions due to improper measures of the enterprise officials; (2) the taking of bribes by enterprise operation and marketing personnel, from obtaining their due rewards using improper means; (3) embezzlement of enterprises' public properties, from acquiring their due contracted rewards by contractors in improper means; (4) enterprises' necessary treatments with courtesy, from personal misappropriation, embezzlement and freely spending of public funds; (5) the offering of bribes to seek improper benefits, from the payment of commission and service fees to win business deals and lawful benefits; (6) seeking private gains at the units' expense, from obtaining rewards after

reporting to the units when obtaining commission and service fees; (7) accepting bribes, from obtaining reward in unreasonable ways by technical staff who offered technical services entrusted by the units; (8) technical staff asking for and taking bribes by use of the units' key technology and power for approval, from taking rewards and technical labour rewards as moonlighters without infringing the units' interests. 1993 *Law Yearbook of China*, pp. 89–90.
32. Note 10, p. 67.
33. Ibid.
34. Ren Jianxin, "Zhonghua renmin gongheguo fayuan ji qi yu zhengfu de guanxi" (Reflections between the Courts and Government in the PRC), *Renmin fayuan nianjian 1988* (People's Court Yearbook 1988), p. 737.
35. Ren Jianxin, "Zai quanguo gaoji fayuan yuanzhang huiyi kaimu shi de jianghua", (The Opening Speech at the All China Higher Courts Presidents Conference), *Zhonghua renmin gongheguo zuigao renmin fayuan gongbao* (PRC Supreme People's Court Gazette), No. 1 (1994), p. 26.
36. Zhu Weijiu, "Tantan woguo de guojia peichangfa" (Discussing our Country's State Compensation Law), *Zhongguo lüshi*, July 1994, p. 30.

7

China and International Organizations

Gerald Chan

The end of the Cold War has ushered in many new developments in world affairs. One of these is the recognition among political analysts that, within the field of international relations, international organizations are playing a greater role in enhancing cooperation amongst states and in settling their differences. China, on the other hand, is assuming greater importance in global affairs. Its open-door policy, adopted since the late 1970s, has guided the country in increasing contacts with various actors in the world, including international organizations (hereafter sometimes referred to as IOs).

As a research area, China's relations with international organizations have remained relatively under-explored, compared with other areas of China's international relations, especially its inter-state relationships with other countries. The volume of published works has remained relatively small.[1] The main reasons are the research preference of scholars and the scarcity of source-materials.[2]

This chapter tries to present an up-to-date account of China's participation in international organizations. It describes some theoretical work in the field and analyses some empiricial evidence mainly from a macro-perspective.

Although the chapter concerns primarily China's participation in international organizations, I have included as far as possible the participation of Taiwan and Hong Kong in these organizations as well, for the sake of comparison. This comparison is interesting in several ways. First, China and Taiwan are competing with each other in gaining membership of some organizations, especially intergovernmental organizations where sovereignty is under severe contention between the two. The competition had been particularly fierce before 1979 when the so-called "Olympic formula" was devised to accommodate both China and Taiwan as members of the International Olympic Committee. Subsequently both China and Taiwan have been eligible to participate in Olympic activities on a more or less equal footing. This formula has been adopted by a large

---

I am grateful to Dr Tsui Kai-yuen, Dr Henry M. K. Mok, and Mr Paul S. L. Wong for their comments on an earlier draft of this chapter made in a workshop held at The Chinese University of Hong Kong on 7 January 1995. I am also thankful to Professor Joseph Y. S. Cheng, Dean of the Faculty of Humanities and Social Sciences, City University of Hong Kong, and his faculty office staff for providing various facilities during the final stage of my writing-up.

number of international sporting organizations, international non-governmental organizations (INGOs), and a few intergovernmental organizations (IGOs) in admitting both China and Taiwan as members.[3] However, there are limits to the applicability of the formula, and Taiwan's effort to increase its participation in international organizations has come under constant political pressure from China.

Secondly, Hong Kong is to revert to China's sovereignty in 1997 and its scope of participation in international organizations is laid down by the Hong Kong Basic Law, promulgated by China's National People's Congress in 1990. In a way what happens to Hong Kong's participation close to 1997 may serve as a harbinger of things to come for Taiwan.

Thirdly, it is interesting to compare the participation in international organizations of the so-called "three Chinas" — mainland China, Taiwan, and Hong Kong. They have different political systems: China is a socialist state in transition; Taiwan is in a speedy process of democratization and it is in direct conflict with China over sovereignty claims; and Hong Kong is still in the main a British colony soon to become a Special Administrative Region of China. The Chinese government has promised the people of Hong Kong a high degree of autonomy and a continuation of its present economic and social systems for fifty years, under the "one country, two systems" arrangement. Increasingly, economic integration has brought southern China, Taiwan, and Hong Kong together to form one of the world's fastest growing economic regions.

A Theoretical Overview

The theoretical study of China's relations with international organizations has so far remained largely at the behavioural level. At the decision-making level, how Chinese leaders make decisions and adjust their policy towards international organizations are still largely unknown. Wang Jie, a member of Peking University's Department of International Politics, has offered a broad-brush description of China's policy adjustments under four headings: (a) China's pursuit of an independent foreign policy; (b) its adherence to the Five Principles of Peaceful Co-existence; (c) its solidarity with the Third World; and (d) its "give-and-take" approach to develop China's economy.[4] This "give-and-take" approach refers to the loss of some aspects of China's independence in return for the benefits that can be derived from its interdependence with the outside world.

In reviewing China's behavioural approach to international organizations since 1949, Samuel Kim has identified three patterns, namely, symbolic/normative behaviour, security behaviour, and functional behaviour.[5] These three patterns of behaviour are of course not mutually exclusive of each other. Rather they exhibit different emphases during different periods of development in China's relations with the outside world. In the 1950s the symbolic/normative behaviour was more prominent as the newly-established communist China was trying to establish its international identity. During the Cold War period of the 1960s and 1970s, the security behaviour was more apparent as China was trying to find its proper strategic balance in its conflictual relationship with either or both of the superpowers. Since the adoption of the open-door policy in the late 1970s, China has adopted an increasingly functional approach to its participation in international organizations.[6]

The above three time periods tie in well with China's effort to deal with the world of international organizations. The symbolic/normative behaviour in the 1950s was the outward expression of China's (unsuccessful) revolutionary effort to *transform* the system of international organizations so that they could be freed from the domination by the West, especially the United States. The security behaviour in the 1960s and 1970s was reflective of China's effort to *reform* the system, often calling on the cooperation of other developing countries in seeking changes to the exploitative way in which major international organizations were being run. The functional behaviour since the late 1970s to the present bears witness to China's endeavour to *conform* to the present system of international organizations and to derive the maximum advantage therefrom.[7]

Underlying China's participation in international organizations is the pursuit of its national interests, which change over time with its prevailing ideology. The staunch Marxist-Leninist-Maoist ideology of the 1950s and 1960s dictated that China was to be in severe conflict with the West and the system of international organizations dominated by the West. The United Nations system was a prime example. China perceived that international organization and law were used by the imperialists to exploit the communist and the developing countries. The split with the Soviet Union in the late 1960s meant that China was also excluded from nearly all international communist mass organizations in the fields of youth, women, journalism, and development controlled by the Kremlin. Isolation and anti-foreignism gave way to the open-door policy after the Cultural Revolution and the fall of the Gang of Four. Interaction with the outside world steadily increased in speed and intensity from the late 1970s up to the present, although with intermittent bouts of retrogression typified by a kind of two-steps-forward and one-step-back movements, like the crackdown on the Democracy Wall and the June 4th Tiananmen Incident. However, the general trend is clear: China has become increasingly interdependent with the outside world. Socialist ideology is mixed with free market forces and ideas. National interests are defined more and more in terms of economic returns. A neo-functional approach is gradually replacing a socialist approach to the running of China's political economy. This neo-functional approach is different from the usual understanding of functional approach. In the former, the state is heavily involved in guiding and controlling the process of integration or cooperation. In the latter, however, the same process is allowed to develop more or less freely with minimal government intervention.

The present Chinese style of participation in international organizations bears several unique characteristics: first, the state is by far the most dominating actor in such participation, much more so in IGOs than in INGOs. Given the political culture and economic situation in China, the actors involved in the Chinese participation in INGOs are mostly government officials or representatives of elite groups or mass organizations. These groups and mass organizations are usually funded by the government, so although they are being regarded sometimes as non-governmental bodies, they are in fact quasi- or semi-governmental in nature. The influence of the government on the Chinese participants is considerable. Secondly, the level of participation by Chinese individuals in INGOs is low, especially when measured against China's vast population. This low level of participation can also be attributed to Chinese culture as well as its economy. In China, as in many other Asian societies, social organizations are structured in a hierarchical way. The bringing together of individuals as independent equals to discuss social issues in an open forum is alien to the traditional Chinese thinking and customs. The fact that the average income of the people is still very low bears a correlation too with the low level of Chinese participation in international organizations. Thirdly, as a result of its political culture and its low level of participation, the Chinese input into important policy processes in international organizations is minimal compared with countries of similar standing in the international political economy.

Considering these three characteristics, the most appropriate theoretical base of Chinese participation in international organizations seem to be neo-functionalism, although it is a kind of neo-functionalism tainted with Chinese characteristics, in particular the heavy state involvement in the pursuit of China's national interests through participation in international organizations.

An Empirical Analysis

According to the *Yearbook of International Organizations*,[8] there are 5,102 conventional international organizations as of 1993, of which 272 are IGOs and 4,830 INGOs. These are the major international organizations in the world, of which China is a member of 47 IGOs and 900 INGOs. The comparable figures for Taiwan are 8 IGOs and 733 INGOs, and in the case of Hong Kong, 11 IGOs and 921 INGOs.

If the scope of IOs is widened to include other international bodies, such as organizations emanating from places and persons, organizations of special form, subsidiary and internal bodies, and religious orders,[9] then there are 11,643 IOs as of 1993, of which 1,683 are IGOs and 9,960 INGOs. Of this widened scope of IOs China is a member of 222 IGOs and 1,507 INGOs. The corresponding figures for Taiwan are 19 IGOs and 1,196 INGOs, and that for Hong Kong are 56 IGOs and 1,517 INGOs.

Compared with China or many other countries, Taiwan and Hong Kong have a very low level of participation in IGOs. In the case of Taiwan the reason is simple: China objects strongly to Taiwan's involvement in these organizations, saying that Taiwan is a part of China and therefore has no right to be represented. In the case of Hong Kong, a British colony and a free trading port, it has comparatively little direct interest in involvement in international politics.

If the INGO membership figures are measured in terms of per capita basis, then it becomes apparent that both China's and Taiwan's participation in INGO activities are lacking far behind that of Hong Kong. This may serve as an indication of Hong Kong's relatively more liberal social system, leaving the people greater freedom of association.

As of 1993, a number of 511 international organizations (widened scope) have both China and Taiwan as members. Eight of these are IGOs and the rest INGOs. (There are no major IGOs which have Taiwan, and not China, as a member, according to the *Yearbook*.) The eight IGOs are:

- Asia-Pacific Economic Cooperation Council

- Asian Development Bank
- European Foundation for the Improvement of Living and Working Conditions
- International Centre for the Study of the Preservation and the Restoration of Cultural Property
- International Institute of Refrigeration
- International Seed Testing Association
- International Sericultural Commission
- World Ocean Circulation Experiment

Of these eight IGOs, the first two are more well-known than the other six. The Asia-Pacific Economic Cooperation (APEC) forum, grouping together eighteen countries along the Pacific Rim, represents one of the world's most dynamic economic power-houses. Collectively the member countries account for about 60% of the world's population and half its production and trade. Initiated by former Australian Prime Minister Bob Hawke, it was inaugurated in 1989 as a forum to discuss trade and economic cooperation among some major Asia-Pacific countries. Over the years it has gradually expanded and institutionalized in the form of an annual summit meeting among economic ministers and since 1993 the head of states of the member countries. A permanent secretariat was set up in Singapore in 1993 to coordinate the work of the forum.

The summit held in Bogor, Indonesia, in November 1994 marked a milestone in APEC's development. Leaders at the meeting agreed to form a free trade area by the year 2020. Malaysia is the only country to have expressed a different view. It wants to reserve its own right to adjust itself to the timetable of trade liberalization. Although details of the trade liberalization measures have yet to be worked out, the fact that a near consensus was reached on such an important issue cannot be underestimated.

China was reported to have harboured reservations at first because it was concerned that APEC might turn into an institutionalized form and that the rigid timetable might be disadvantageous to developing countries like China. The fact that China eventually went along with the agreed timetable means that a triumphant outcome for the group as a whole was reached. President Jiang Zemin, like most other leaders attending the summit, made use of the opportunity to meet other leaders on a bilateral basis and to make side trips to neighbouring countries before and after the summit.

The Bogor summit was the second such summit after the one held in Seattle in the United States a year earlier. At both summits Taiwan was represented by Vincent Siew, the then chairman of the Economic Planning and Development Council.[10] President Lee Teng-hui of Taiwan wanted to attend both the Seattle and Bogor summits but was unable to do so because of China's objections. Organizers of the Seattle summit avoided inviting Lee claiming that APEC was an economic grouping, not a political one; Taiwan could send an economic minister but not the president. The Indonesian government cited the Seattle summit as a precedent to bar Lee from attending. Likewise Hong Kong could only send its financial secretary, Hamish MacLeod, to attend both summits.

When China, Taiwan, and Hong Kong were admitted to the APEC forum in 1991, China's objections to the admission of Taiwan and Hong Kong were suppressed because, first of all, APEC was an economic grouping, not a political one. Member countries felt that Taiwan and Hong Kong were two important economies that could not be ignored in an integrated development in the Asia Pacific region. More importantly to China, however, was that a suitable name was adopted for Taiwan following the precedent set by the "Olympic formula."[11] So APEC provides yet another important example of the spill-over effect of the Olympic formula from a non-governmental level to an intergovernmental level, apart from the Asian Development Bank.

The conflict between China and Taiwan over their membership of the Asian Development Bank (ADB) produced a big row at the IGO level, partly because Taiwan had a stronger position in the ADB. It was a founding member of the bank and had a strong economic base. But China too was a strong country, politically and economically, which members of the bank wanted to include. A "compromise" was reached when China was admitted to the bank in 1986 under its official name, People's Republic of China, and Taiwan could retain its seat under the name of "Taipei, China." This is a name that the Republic of China on Taiwan continues to protest, although with a muted voice over the years.

Some Comparisons: China, Taiwan, and Hong Kong

It would be useful to analyse the types of international organizations, both IGOs and INGOs, of which China and Taiwan are members.[12] Table 1 shows the nature of the functions of these organizations.

China and International Organizations

Table 1. Functional Breakdown of IOs Having China and Taiwan As Members, 1993

Grouping*	UIA Classification	Membership	Subtotal
Political	International relations	10	
	Politics	4	
	Law, administration	8	22
Economic	Professions, employers	18	
	Trade unions	4	
	Economics, finance	9	
	Commerce, industry	16	
	Agriculture	21	
	Transport, travel	20	88
Education/	Documentation, press	11	
communication	Education, youth	39	
	Arts, literature, radio	16	66
Religion	Religion, ethics	14	14
Scientific/	Technology	56	
technical	Science	80	136
Social/health	Social sciences	14	
	Social welfare	29	
	Health, medicine	87	
	Sport, recreation	55	185
Total			511

* The grouping system is borrowed from Werner J. Feld and Roger A. Coate, *The Role of International Non-governmental Organizations in World Politics* (New York: Learning Resources in International Studies, 1976), p. 3.
Source: Compiled from the Union of International Associations (UIA) (ed.), *Yearbook of International Organizations 1993/94*, Vol. 2, China and Taiwan.

The table indicates that organizations within the social/health grouping have the highest number of memberships from both China and Taiwan, followed by the scientific/technical, economic, education/communication, political, and religion groupings, in that order. According to the Union of International Associations (UIA) classification, the international organizations with the most number of memberships from both China and Taiwan are those in health and medicine, followed by science, technology, sport and recreation, and education and youth. International organizations with the least number of memberships from both are those in politics and trade unions. This demonstrates quite clearly that the technical and sporting areas are the ones in which there is more room for accommodation or even cooperation between the two countries, whereas much less room for accommodation or cooperation exists in the political area. To a certain extent this vindicates the validity of one of the premises of the theory of functionism that there is a distinction between low politics (technical, functional) and high politics (strategic, power).[13] The policy implication that can be drawn is that China and Taiwan should develop more cooperation in areas of low politics so that trust and confidence can be built to allow their cooperation to proceed to areas of high politics.

It is interesting to compare the situation depicted in Table 1 to the situation about a decade ago in order to see what have been the changes over the years. Overall there is a substantial increase in the number of international organizations of all functional natures, mainly INGOs, having both China and Taiwan as members. The number in the political grouping increases from 9 in 1984 to 22 in 1993. The corresponding numbers for other groupings are: economic (from 14 to 88); educational/communication (from 16 to 66); religion (from 8 to 14); scientific/technical (from 35 to 136); and social/health (from 50 to 185).[14] It is difficult to pin-point the reasons for the various increases. Several observations can be made, however. First, the increases are due mainly to the substantial expansion of China's participation in international organizations in general subsequent to the open-door policy and to its fast economic growth. China was a member of 51 IGOs in 1983 and 358 INGOs in 1984, but in 1993 the corresponding figures are 222 IGOs and 1,507 INGOs. The rise in the case of Taiwan is less spectacular. The number of IGOs of which Taiwan is a member has remained more or less stagnant: about 10 to 20 throughout the last decade. The number of INGOs, however, has increased from 441 in 1984 to 1,196 in 1993. This serves to demonstrate the result of Taiwan's concerted effort to expand its so-called "international space," but it is still under immense political pressure from China in intergovernmental organizations. The second observation is that the rate of increase is faster in the economic, education/communication, scientific/technological, and social/health groupings than in the political and religion groupings. This shows that China is more willing to open up and liberalize activities in the economic and technical areas while maintaining a tight control over political and religious affairs. Thirdly, and more specifically, the most spectacular increases in IO participation where both China and Taiwan are members are in the functional areas of professions/employer (from nil in 1984 to 18 in 1993), agriculture (from nil to 21 over the same period), and health/medicine (from 12 to 87).

One way to measure how active a country is in its involvement in the activities of international organizations is to see how many headquarters or secretariats of these organizations are based in the country. In the case of China there are 36 principal secretariats (headquarters, main offices) and 13 secondary (regional) secretariats, making a total of 49 as of 1993.[15] The corresponding total figures for Taiwan and Hong Kong are 35 and 77 respectively.[16] The fact that the Hong Kong figure is higher than the China figure serves to demonstrate to a certain extent that Hong Kong is more vibrant in its involvement in IO activities. This is not too surprising given the fact that Hong Kong is far more cosmopolitan than China. The low Taiwan figure is due to the pressure exerted by China to exclude Taiwan from involvement in IOs.

How do the "three Chinas" compare internationally in providing home bases for international organizations? The *Yearbook of International Organizations 1993/94* gives a table of countries where the greatest number of principal secretariats of the major IOs are located.[17] In a decreasing rank order of 34 countries, Hong Kong stands at the 30th. Neither China nor Taiwan can make it to the table. The top ten countries are Belgium, France, the United Kingdom, the United States, Germany, Switzerland, the Netherlands, Sweden, Denmark, and Italy. In Asia, Japan, the Philippines, and India rank ahead of Hong Kong. Japan is of course comparatively more internationalized; the Philippines and India, former colonies of the US and the UK respectively, are more westernized than most other Asian countries.

Hong Kong offers an interesting case in that its participation in international organizations is affected by its being absorbed into Chinese rule. The Hong Kong Basic Law, which is regarded as the mini-constitution of Hong Kong, stipulates that China may allow Hong Kong to participate in international organizations by using the name "Hong Kong, China."[18] This name is apparently a derivative of the name "Taipei, China" first officially formulated under the Olympic formula to show that Taipei is a part of China.

Since Hong Kong is not going to challenge China's sovereignty over itself, it is most unlikely that it will reject the use of the name "Hong Kong, China" in international organizations. In fact Hong Kong is using this name in its association with the Asian Development Bank and the Asia-Pacific Economic Cooperation Council.

As far as INGOs are concerned, China is unlikely to raise any objections to Hong Kong's participation even if the name used is not strictly adhered to. After all Hong Kong is not challenging China in any way in non-governmental activities. However, IGOs may prove to be a bit tricky and China will be more cautious towards Hong Kong's activities in them. According to the *Yearbook of International Organizations*,[19] Hong Kong is a member of 37 IGOs. Most of these are economic and technical in nature, and it is unlikely that China will object to Hong Kong's continuing involvement in them. However, Hong Kong is a member of a few IGOs which belong to the family of British Commonwealth organizations, by dint of its colonization by Britain. Examples are the Commonwealth Legal Advisory Service, the Commonwealth Scholarship and Fellowship Plan, the Commonwealth Secretariat, and the Conference of Commonwealth Surveyors. Whether or not China will voice its objections to Hong Kong's continuing participation in the activities of these organizations remains to be seen. The most probable scenario is that China will stop Hong Kong's participation or instruct Hong Kong to phase out its involvement, because China is not a member of the British Commonwealth and the idea that Hong Kong still maintains its links with the Commonwealth might smack of imperialism. In fact Hong Kong took part in its last Commonwealth Games held in Canada in 1994. Similarly the Hong Kong Red Cross Society will cease to be a branch of the British Red Cross and will become a branch of the Chinese Red Cross, in constitutional terms if not in the day to day running of Red Cross activities. Likewise, Hong Kong's membership of Interpol (International Criminal Police Organization) will be subsumed under that of China and become an arm of the criminal police operation in Beijing.

Another very important IGO that Hong Kong is a member of while China is not (as of early 1995) is the General Agreement on Tariffs and Trade (GATT). To place the case of GATT in global context, Table 2 gives a comparison of the participation of China, Taiwan, and Hong Kong in some important international organizations.

China and GATT

Taiwan, under the name of the Republic of China, was a founding member of GATT in 1947. After the communist victory in mainland China, it withdrew in 1950 and returned as an observer in 1965. Upon China's entry to the United Nations in 1971, it was forced to withdraw from GATT as well as other specialized agencies of the United Nations system.

In 1986 China started to apply to "renew" its membership. The long drawn-out application process led a senior Chinese trade official to protest

Table 2. "Three Chinas" in International Organizations, 1994

	China	Taiwan	Hong Kong
United Nations	Yes admitted 1971	No expelled 1971	No
IMF/World Bank	Yes	No	No
GATT	Applying	Applying	Yes
Asian Development Bank	Yes admitted 1986	Yes founding member 1966	Yes admitted 1969
Asia-Pacific Economic Cooperation Meeting	Yes attended by president	Yes not attended by president	Yes attended by financial secretary
International Olympic Committee	Yes	Yes competes as Chinese Taipei	Yes competes as Hong Kong
Asian Games	Yes	Yes	Yes
FIFA*	Yes	Yes	Yes
Diplomatic Relations	159 countries	29 countries	Nil

* FIFA: French acronym for International Federation of Football Association.
Sources: Adapted from *Newsweek Bulletin*, 6 September 1994, p. 51. Information on Hong Kong is taken from the *Yearbook of International Organizations* and other sources.

strongly in November 1994, that if China was not admitted by the end of 1994, China would not abide by its previous commitments to free trade. A Chinese scholar in the West has aptly dubbed this situation as "politics of frustration" from the Chinese perspective.[20]

The main source of Beijing's frustration is the long list of demands of the West, led by the United States, to force China to liberalize its trade. The principal cause of the deadlock is that China is being treated as a near developed country for the purpose of assessing its eligibility to become a contracting party (member). By that categorization, Beijing has to commit a further substantial opening up of its market to the outside world. The United States wants to extract concessions from China in the areas of increasing the "transparency" of China's trade relations, the "national treatment" of foreign investors, foreign access to its market, and liberalization of its services sectors, among others. To China, this seems extremely unfair treatment that no GATT applicants have had to endure before. China argues that it is still very much a developing country, particularly in view of China's huge population which puts China's economic indicators on a per capita basis at a very low level when compared with other countries.[21]

Underlying these conflictual stands are the fears of a potentially huge influx of cheap Chinese goods into Western countries, in particular the United States. For example, if China is admitted to GATT, then Europe has to cut its tariffs on Chinese made clothing and shoes from 23% to 5% and Australia has to cut its from 49% to 5%![22] At present, China is the world's sixth largest trading nation. Its total export amounts to some US$100 billion per year, 30 to 40% of which is destined for the United States.[23] The World Bank estimates that if China can gain greater access to the world's big markets as a member of GATT, its exports could soar by as much as 38%.[24] China has the second-largest trade surplus with the United States after Japan, some US$28.9 billion in the first seven months of 1994.[25] To ensure that they can even the score with China, countries in the West are trying to secure better terms to enter the China market. Hence the whole commercial issue has become politicized.

The latest round of negotiations between Chinese and GATT officials in Geneva broke down in mid-December 1994, and talks were scheduled to resume in February 1995.[26] A likely timetable for China to enter the World Trade Organization (WTO), which replaced GATT on 1 January 1995, is in July 1995, according to Robert Cassidy, the United States trade representative for Asia and the Pacific.[27] Still, China can be retroactively granted the status of a founding WTO member, a status China desires and one the West can afford to give.

Conclusion

Two overall observations can be made, one concerning the theory and practice of China's participation in international organizations and the other concerning the study of international relations in the West in general and the study of international organizations in particular.

China's participation in international organizations since the adoption of its open-door policy in the late 1970s shows several major characteristics. First, there is a significant increase in China's participation in both IGOs and INGOs. Several reasons account for this: (a) China's increasing interaction and interdependence with the outside world; (b) its fast economic growth and, in some coastal areas of China, growing affluence; and (c) the eagerness of the outside world to engage China in international and regional affairs.

Secondly, China's participation is becoming less restrained by the "two-China" issue. Beijing has established itself as the sole representative of all China, including Taiwan; at least it is so ackowleged by most countries and international organizations in their bilateral agreements with China. This international status of China meets with decreasing challenge from Taipei. Now Taiwan is not challenging the existence of a mainland China regime ruled by the Chinese Communist Party; it is only trying to establish itself as a separate independent political entity. China, however, continues to voice its strong protest against any Taiwanese move to assert its separate diplomatic identity and against any other countries trying to improve or upgrade their political relations with Taiwan.

Thirdly, the role of Chinese culture and tradition remains a significant factor in shaping China's participation. Chinese society is still organized along authoritative, hierarchical lines. The country is under *renzhi* (rule of man) rather than *fazhi* (rule of law). Respects for individual equality and privacy are still primitive and foreign to most Chinese in the mainland. All these domestic conditions effect the style of China's participation in international organizations, the great majority of which are established along Western liberal, democratic lines. Therefore, by casting the increase in China's participation in the last two decades against its huge population, China's membership of international organizations is very limited. Its participation is mainly dominated by the state, the government, or individuals representing the state or government. This is the case even in some major INGOs. Participation by Chinese individuals representing their own selves is very rare.

As the state is the major actor in China's involvement in IO activities, the pursuit of national interests has become the main objective of China's participation, despite the functional nature of many IOs of which China is a member. Existing theories of international organizations in the West that come close to describing and explaining the Chinese way of participation are realism and neo-functionalism. However, given the significant influence of Chinese culture and tradition on its style of participation, it would be more appropriate to call the Chinese way of participation "neo-functionalism with Chinese characteristics."

This leads to the second observation. John W. Burton, one of the leading theorists in the British tradition of international relations, once estimated that about 90% of the self-proclaimed international relations scholars were male in the United States.[28] Although there is a growing tendency, mainly championed by élite women in the West, to promote the study of gender politics, clearly the contemporary study of international relations is dominated by male elites in the West, especially in the United States. This is equally true in the study of international organizations.

International organizations as functional institutions grew out of European experiences, and the study of them is naturally biased towards the Western view. There is no systematic study of the growing networks of overseas Chinese businesses and organizations, nor are there any major studies on Islamic organizations from an international organization perspective. These are often not treated, and therefore not defined, as international organizations according to the Euro-centric view. Although the Union of International Associations, the editorial office of the *Yearbook of International Organizations*, has published a reference on Islamic organizations and another on African organizations,[29] there is as yet no equivalent publication on Asian international organizations, let alone Chinese international organizations. The lack of study and research in these areas is an indication of the neglect or ignorance on the part of mainstream international relations scholarship in the West. Until something is done to address this issue, a huge gap will remain in the study of international relations and organizations.

Notes

1. Book-length treatments include, for example, Samuel Kim, *China, the United Nations, and World Order* (Princeton, N.J.: Princeton University Press, 1979); Gerald Chan, *China and International Organizations* (Hong Kong: Oxford University Press, 1989); Harold K. Jacobson and Michel Oksenberg, *China's Participation in the IMF, the World Bank, and GATT* (Ann Arbor, Michigan: University of Michigan Press, 1990); Lin Cheng-i, Yeh Kuo-hsing and Chang Jui-meng (eds.), *Taiwan jiaru guoji jingji zuzhi celue fenxi* (An Analysis of Taiwan's Strategy in Entering Into International Economic Organizations) (Taipei: Institute for National Policy Research, 1990); and Chu Yun-han and Jennifer Arnold (eds.), *The Role of Taiwan in International Economic Organizations* (Taipei: Institute for National Policy Research, 1990). There is little work done on Hong Kong's participation in IOs. Two related articles are: James T. H. Tang, "Hong Kong's International Status," *The Pacific Review*, Vol. 6, No. 3 (1993), pp. 205–15 and Bernard H. K. Luk, "Hong Kong's International Presence," in *The Other Hong Kong Report 1994*, edited by Donald H. McMillen and Man Si-wai (Hong Kong: Chinese University Press, 1994), Chap. 23, pp. 429–41. Apart from these, there are a few published articles on a similar subject. Apart from those written by

Samuel Kim, see also Byron S. J. Weng, "Divided China and the Question of Membership in International Organizations," HKIAPS Reprint Series No. 6 (The Chinese University of Hong Kong, 1991); and Dennis Van Vranken Hickey, "Coming in from the Cold: Taiwan's Return to International Organizations," *Issues & Studies*, Vol. 30, No. 10 (October 1994), pp. 94–107. A mainland Chinese scholar has recently published a descriptive, normative essay on some aspects of China's policy adjustments towards IOs. See Wang Jie, "Guoji zuzhi de xingcheng fazhan he woguo zhengce de tiaozheng" (The Formation and Development of International Organizations and Our Country's Policy Adjustments), in *Guoji zhengzhi lunji* (Essays on International Politics), edited by Liang Shoude et al. (Beijing: Beijing chubanshe, 1992), pp. 25–44. See also Wang Jie, *Guoji geju yu guoji zuzhi* (International Structure and International Organizations) (Beijing: Peking University Press, 1993).
2. See Chan, *China and International Organizations* (Note 1), pp. 1–3.
3. Ibid., chap. 3 and 9.
4. Wang, "The Formation and Development of International Organizations" (Note 1), pp. 40–43.
5. Samuel S. Kim, "China's International Organizational Behaviour," in *Chinese Foreign Policy: Theory and Practice*, edited by Thomas W. Robinson and David Shambaugh (Oxford: Clarendon Press, 1994), Chap. 15.
6. For China's functional approach to its participation in IOs, especially INGOs, since 1971, see Chan, *China and International Organizations* (Note 1).
7. Kim, "China's International Organizational Behaviour" (Note 5), p. 431.
8. Union of International Associations (ed.), *Yearbook of International Organizations 1993/94* (Muchen; New Providence; London; Paris: K. G. Saur, 1993), Vol. 2. All the 1993 statistics quoted in this chapter are taken from this latest edition of the yearbook available at the time of writing.
9. See the latest issue of the *Yearbook of International Organizations* for the definitions of these organizations.
10. Siew is now heading the Mainland Affairs Council.
11. Taiwan's name in APEC is Chinese Taipei, which is based on the precedent set in the Pacific Economic Cooperation Council in 1986 and the International Olympic Committee in 1979. See Lawrence T. Woods, *Asia Pacific Diplomacy: Nongovernmental Organizations and International Relations* (Vancouver: UBC Press, 1993), pp. 129–36.
12. Membership of IOs serves only as a crude indication of the depth of participation in IOs. Better ways to measure how active a country is in its participation in IOs include monetary, personnel, and policy contributions towards the working of these organizations. However, to do this would involve a detailed, micro-analysis of each individual organization, which is beyond the scope of this chapter. Also, different organizations carry different weights in

international affairs. For example, the United Nations system is much more important than an international sporting organization. Membership of IOs therefore conceals the relative importance of these organizations. None the less membership counts do serve as a handy indicator at a higher level of analysis.
13. For a discussion of the theory of functionalism in international relations, see David Mitrany, *The Functional Theory of Politics* (New York: St. Martin's Press, 1975), and A.J.R. Groom and Paul Taylor (eds.), *Functionalism: Theory and Practice in International Relations* (London: University of London Press, 1975).
14. The figures for 1984 are taken from Chan (see Note 1), p. 156, Table 9.1. All the figures quoted in this chapter are culled from the various issues of the *Yearbook of International Organizations*.
15. *Yearbook of International Organizations 1993/94*, Vol. 2, p. 1,722.
16. Ibid., pp. 1,772–73.
17. Ibid., p. 1,736.
18. Articles 150 and 151.
19. *Yearbook of International Organizations 1993/94*, Vol. 2.
20. My personal communication with Zhang Yongjin of Auckland University's Political Studies Department on 8 December 1994 in Wellington, New Zealand.
21. *Beijing Review*, 14–20 November 1994, pp. 10–11.
22. *Time* magazine, 19 December 1994, p. 40.
23. *Asian Wall Street Journal*, 2–3 December 1994, pp. 1 and 14; and *Australian Financial Review*, 8 December 1994, p. 12.
24. *Asian Wall Street Journal*, 2–3 December 1994, p. 1.
25. *Mainichi Daily News*, 12 April 1995, p. 6.
26. Voice of America news broadcast, 21 December 1994.
27. *Dominion*, Wellington (19 November 1994), p. 9.
28. Quoted by Jindy Jan Pettman in her plenary address "Worlding Women" to a conference on "New World Order/New International Relations/New Zealand" held at Victoria University of Wellington on 8 December 1994.
29. *African International Organization Directory 1984/85*, 1st ed., and *Arab-Islamic International Organization Directory 1984/85*, 1st ed.

8

China's Foreign Relations in the Asia-Pacific Region: Modernization, Nationalism and Regionalism

Quansheng Zhao

Three key words, *modernization, nationalism,* and *regionalism,* can be used to illuminate the basic trends of foreign relations of the People's Republic of China (PRC) in the 1990s and future direction of Chinese foreign policy. Modernization refers to China's concentration on economic growth. The modernization drive has served as a basic guideline in China's both internal and external activities. Nationalism has emerged as a leading ideological current behind China's drive toward modernization. In the post-Cold War era, nationalistic feeling appears particularly strong among Chinese intellectuals and government officials as well as other circles of Chinese society. Regionalism emphasizes that China has remained a regional power. Despite its global aspirations, Beijing has concentrated its political and economic activities in the Asia-Pacific area, including East and Southeast Asia, as well as Russia and the United States (US). And indeed, the PRC has remained a major player in East and Southeast Asian regional affairs.

This chapter will concentrate on China's foreign relations in the Asia-Pacific area, namely Japan, the Korean Peninsula, Southeast Asia, Russia, and the United States, as well as the issue of Taiwan. Other regions will not be the focus of this study. Nor will it cover China's relations with international organizations, such as General Agreement on Tariffs and Trade (GATT) and Asia-Pacific Economic Co-operation (APEC), which is the focus elsewhere in this book (see Gerald Chan's chapter). One should notice that the purpose here is not to provide comprehensive pictures of China's bilateral relations with these countries; rather it highlights three basic trends — modernization, nationalism, and regionalism — that can demonstrate the influences that act upon Chinese foreign policy. To elaborate these points, some historical backgrounds will also be discussed.

In the 1994 "Year in Review" article, the *Far Eastern Economic Review* states that, "China continued to play its now-familiar role as a leading magnet for investment and diplomatic attention."[1] This comment is quite accurate about China's international role in the post-Cold War era. The most obvious evidence is China's rapidly growing economic power. According to a widely publicized International Monetary Fund report (*World Economy Outlook*, 1993) and other similar reports, China's economy is poised to overtake that of Japan in absolute size and China will be a larger economy than the United States "shortly after the turn of the century."[2] Based on these accounts, two *New York Times* reporters and Pulitzer Prize-winners, who spent 1988–1993 in Beijing, have made the following comments about "Greater China"[3] consisting of the PRC, Taiwan, Hong Kong, and Macau:

> The global economy is sometimes said to be tripolar, revolving around the United States, Japan and the European Community. But Greater China is rapidly becoming a fourth pole, a new pillar of the international economy. According to World Bank projections using comparable international prices, Greater China in the year 2002 is projected to have a gross domestic product of $9.8 trillion, compared with $9.7 trillion in the same year for the United States. If those forecasts hold, Greater China would not just be another economic pole. It would be the biggest of them all.

The two reporters continue to argue that China "has a chance to grow and prosper and become a major international power, perhaps eventually a superpower such as the world has never known."[4] Although there are many far-less optimistic predictions about China's future, particularly in the forthcoming post-Deng era,[5] these reports have reflected the picture of China's concentration on its economic growth for the past decade.

In addition to the growing attractions of the Chinese market, China's strategic importance has been increasingly recognized when the world entered the 1990s. The PRC has appeared more assertive in dealing with its neighbouring countries and establishing its leading role in East Asia. For example, influential US Senator Sam Nunn forcefully advocated in early 1994 that the US should accord the most-favoured-nation (MFN) status to China, simply because the strategic relationship between the two countries is "too important to sacrifice."[6] It is believed that the major considerations behind US President Bill Clinton's decision in May 1994 to renew China's MFN status and to delink the issue from human right are strategic and economic factors.[7]

From Beijing's perspective, East and Southeast Asia has remained one of the most important areas for China's foreign policy objectives. The importance is not only in the military and political dimensions, but also in the economic dimension, directly related to China's modernization drive.

From Table 1, one can see that according to geographical locations China's trading partners' rankings in 1993 are: Asia ($115.2 billion), Europe ($40.4 billion), North America ($30.2 billion), Latin America ($3.7 billion), Oceania ($3.6 billion), and Africa ($2.5 billion). It is clear that China's foreign trade with Asian countries is more than that with all the countries outside of Asia combined. Furthermore, East and Southeast Asia, as shown in Figure 1, constitute the bulk of trading activities, and

Table 1. China's Major Trading Partners (1993)

(Unit: US$ 1 million)

Region and selected countries	Export	Import	Total value
Asia	52635.91	62575.86	115211.77
Japan	15779.41	23253.30	39032.71
Within Greater China	24050.02	23559.71	47609.73
Hong Kong	22063.91	10472.65	32536.56
Macau	524.33	153.92	678.25
Taiwan	1461.78	12933.14	14394.92
Korea (North)	602.35	297.29	899.64
Korea (South)	2860.19	5359.90	8220.10
ASEAN	4683.32	5995.82	10679.17
Brunei	10.64	0	10.64
Indonesia	691.57	1451.35	2143.02
Malaysia	704.28	1083.95	1788.24
Philippines	281.30	213.47	494.76
Singapore	2244.96	2645.61	4890.57
Thailand	750.47	601.44	1351.91
Burma	324.70	164.82	489.53
Cambodia	20.32	1.21	21.53
Laos	37.12	3.51	40.63
Vietnam	276.00	122.63	398.64
Africa	1527.43	1003.13	2530.56
Europe	16428.59	23985.74	40414.33
EEC	11693.10	14411.59	26104.69
United Kingdom	1928.57	1663.67	3592.25
Germany	3968.46	6039.78	10008.25
France	1290.54	1645.17	2935.71
Italy	1304.90	2737.42	4042.32
Former USSR	3092.76	5927.06	9019.82
Russia	2691.82	4987.44	7679.25
Latin America	1776.21	1930.95	3707.16
North America	18163.18	12071.29	30234.77
Canada	1197.69	1375.12	2572.80
USA	16964.00	10688.06	27652.06
Oceania	1231.58	2361.14	3592.72
Australia	1060.93	1948.98	3009.90

Source: *China's Latest Economic Statistics*, February 1994, pp. 19–23.

accounted for 55% of China's foreign trade. That within "Greater China" — Taiwan, Hong Kong, and Macau — also ranked high. One should notice that China's trade with Hong Kong is largely a function of re-export to other countries, many of them in North America and Europe.

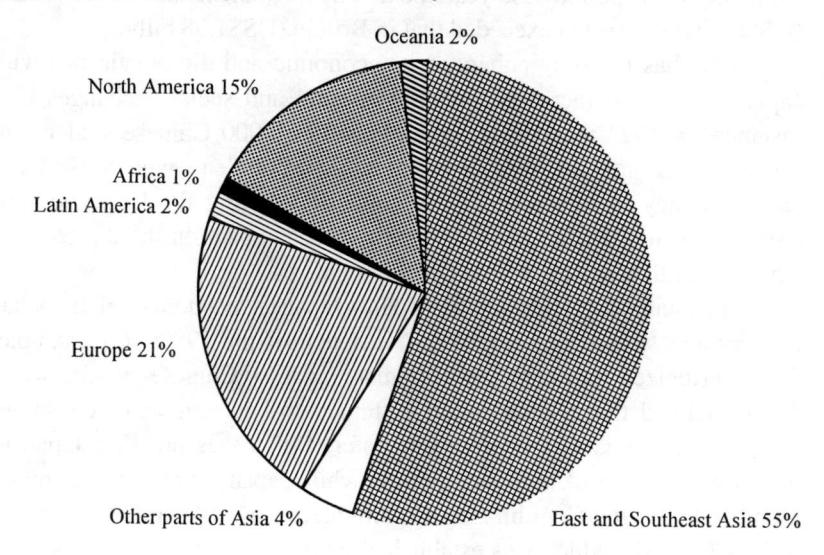

Figure 1. China's Foreign Trade of 1993 — by Continent

- Oceania 2%
- North America 15%
- Africa 1%
- Latin America 2%
- Europe 21%
- Other parts of Asia 4%
- East and Southeast Asia 55%

Source: Compiled from *China's Latest Economic Statistics*, February 1994, p. 19.

Nevertheless, the extensive economic transactions within the "Greater China" area have been impressive. Now, let us examine China's major foreign relations in the Asia-Pacific region with special reference to the three basic trends — modernization, nationalism, and regionalism.

Relations with Japan

Since the early 1970s, Japan has been a major source of capital, technology, and manufactured imports to China, and bilateral trade has been flourishing. In 1993, for example, Japan was China's foremost foreign trading partner. Sino-Japanese trade was about one-third higher than the size of Sino-US trade. Japan has a large share of Chinese markets in virtually every field except aircraft technology, which is dominated by US companies. Entering the 1990s, Japanese direct investment in China has also picked up momentum. In the first six months of the 1994 fiscal year (April to September), China was the second largest destination for Japan's overseas direct investment. It reached US$1.14 billion, a 63.5% increase from the same period last year, next only to that in the United States (US$6.60 billion), and exceeded that in Britain (US$1.08 billion).[8]

China has not only enhanced its economic and diplomatic ties with Japan, it has also increased bilateral cultural and social exchanges. For instance, in 1992 there were approximately 50,000 Chinese students in Japan. About one-half were so-called language students who worked and earned money in Japan under the guise of studying the language.[9] Increased bilateral exchanges will have a direct impact on the direction of China's political and economic development.

Understandably, the increase in Sino-Japanese economic relations has also brought about some problems. In much of the 1980s, for example, China criticized Japanese protectionism against Chinese goods, while Japan claimed that China should better control its import of consumer goods. In the area of technology transfer, China was pressing Japan to increase its export of high technology, while Japan was restrained by its membership in the Coordinating Committee for Multilateral Export Controls (COCOM), which was established in 1949 to control transfers from Western countries to the Communist bloc. Even after the COCOM's disbandment with the end of the Cold War, China is still not satisfied with Japan's practice in terms of technology transfer.[10] In addition to the economic areas, other prominent conflicts include the territorial dispute over Diaoyu Islands, the status of Taiwan, and Japanese militarism.

The issue of "Japanese militarism" is an important subject characterized by Beijing's changing interpretation of Tokyo's intention. Due to the bitter memory of the World War II Japanese invasion, China's fears of Japanese militarism are sincere and enduring. However, Beijing has shown itself prepared either to play down or to emphasize those fears, depending on China's changing policy agenda. In the 1960s and 1970s, Beijing's concern about Japanese militarism was primarily motivated by international-diplomatic considerations. In response to the international environment which was marked by competition and hostility between the United States and the Soviet Union, Mao Zedong eventually came to view Japan and Western Europe as intermediate zones between the "revolutionary forces" of the Third World countries and the two "reactionary" superpowers. China sought to cultivate friendly relations with Japan and Western European countries. Beijing's need for economic development also prompted it to seek closer relations with Tokyo and to reduce the Chinese media's criticism of "Japanese militarism." Such criticism disappeared completely after Kakuei Tanaka became Japanese prime minister in 1972.

Entering the 1980s, Beijing's concern about Japanese militarism was rooted chiefly in China's domestic development, namely the rising nationalism of Chinese intellectuals and other circles of Chinese society, an ideological current that the drive toward modernization was strengthening. In 1982, the issue of militarism reappeared as a result of the "textbook controversy." Japan's Ministry of Education was sharply criticized for revising the description of Japan's wartime behaviour in school textbooks. Rather than stating that Japan had "invaded" China and other parts of Asia, the wording was changed by the Japanese Ministry of Education to "entered," provoking protests throughout East and Southeast Asia. Beijing launched a full-scale campaign attacking Japan's militaristic tendencies. The textbook controversy resurfaced in 1985 and 1986, when revised editions of textbooks describing Japan's actions in World War II were published. China's news media launched a new wave of criticism against Japanese militarism, triggering student demonstrations in Beijing, Shanghai, and other major Chinese cities, and giving expression to popular nationalistic sentiments.

A more recent concern about Japan's militarism came in the summer of 1994. A Chinese navy-sponsored magazine *Xiandai Jianchuan* (Modern Naval Vessels) published an article warning that Japan's navy was no longer exclusively defence-oriented and the country's capability to project military power ought to be monitored carefully. In citing Japan's dispatches of forces abroad for UN peacekeeping operations and minesweepers for operations in the Persian Gulf area, it further suggested that "Japan is probing world opinion regarding its embarkation on a new militaristic path."[11]

At the APEC summit meeting held in November 1994 in Jakarta, Chinese President Jiang Zemin had a 45-minute meeting with Japanese Prime Minister Tomiichi Murayama. Jiang made a clear warning to Japan, "Militarism sometimes comes to the surface inside Japan," — referring to the repeated gaffes by Japanese ministers as they attempted to whitewash Japan's wartime history — "Japan must reflect on its history and it is important that you educate your youth on this."[12] On the other hand, as a close neighbour of China, Japan has also felt uneasy about China's military development. In October 1994, Japanese Defence Agency Chief Tokuichiro Tamazawa told US Defence Secretary William Perry that Japan was "anxious about [the increase in] the transparency" of China's defense budget,[13] so that Japan will have precise information about China's military development.

The issue of Taiwan is another key factor in Sino-Japanese relations, simply because it relates to the vital issue of regime legitimacy from Beijing's perspective. Even though Japan issued a number of official statements in 1972 declaring Taiwan to be Chinese territory, Taiwan has continued to remain a potentially volatile issue between China and Japan. During the Asian Games in Hiroshima in October 1994, Taiwan's Vice-Premier Hsu Li-teh was invited to attend the Games, after a failed attempt by Taiwan's President Lee Teng-hui to visit Japan. The episode brought about strong protests from Beijing.[14] At one point, China even considered boycotting the Asian Games because of the Taiwan problem.[15] At the APEC summit in Jakarta the following month, Tomiichi Murayama in his meeting with Jiang Zemin reiterated that Tokyo did not support "two Chinas," attempting to ease strained ties with Beijing. "Frankly speaking, opposition (against Japan) appeared among the Chinese people following Hsu's attendance at the Asian Games," Jiang told Murayama. "But the Chinese government has been coping with the problem with restraint."[16]

When one looks at the future directions of Chinese foreign policy toward Japan, one should remember that the most important bilateral relationship in East Asia is that between China and Japan. Despite such contentious issues as Japanese militarism, the facts that Japan is China's foremost trading partner and that China's market will become increasingly important to Japan will ensure that Sino-Japanese relations remain close. A recent development in this regard is the agreement between the two countries in December 1994 on the fourth Japanese aid package to China (the first package was started in 1979). This is a yen loan of 580 billion yen (US$ 5.8 billion) covering the three-year period of 1996 to 1998.[17]

Policy toward the Korean Peninsula

Strategic and political calculations have consistently dominated Beijing's policy toward conflict in the Korean Peninsula. From the 1960s to the mid-1980s, Pyongyang was able to play the "Beijing card" against the "Moscow card," effectively preventing China from moving closer to Seoul. As the international situation changed, especially after the Soviet Union and Eastern European countries established diplomatic relations with South Korea, the PRC gained more freedom and confidence in expanding its relations with South Korea. Beginning with the late 1980s Beijing has had strong incentives to develop relations with Seoul, because a closer relationship might increase China's leverage in dealing with the Korean problem and with East Asia as a whole. As one US official in Washington suggests, "Having good relations with both [Koreas] puts China in the best possible situation" in world politics as well as regional affairs.[18]

Nevertheless, one should not overlook other factors such as domestic politics and economic conditions which have also played an important role in the evolution of China's policy toward Korea. The policy was significantly altered in September 1992 when China finally agreed to establish diplomatic relations with South Korea. It had taken more than two years for Beijing to follow Moscow's lead in establishing relations with Seoul.

At the same time, economic development was a major incentive for the PRC to normalize its relations with South Korea. China's modernization programmes cannot be realized without extensive external support and exchanges from industrialized countries that can provide advanced technology, capital, markets, and managerial skills. South Korea possesses most of these resources.

South Korea has become increasingly important as a trading partner for China. In 1993, Sino-South Korean trade reached US$8,220 million, far exceeding trade with North Korea of US$899.6 million. As a newly industrialized country and a close neighbour, South Korea can provide China with valuable experience and lessons in terms of economic development strategy, especially in "export-led" industrialization. South Korean businessmen have set up direct investment and joint ventures in China, most notably in Shandong province. In April 1994, for example, South Korean Technology Minister Kim Si Joong announced that conglomerates including Samsung and Hanjin (the owner of Korean Air) would help China produce mid-sized commercial airplanes.[19]

Yet, China has managed also to maintain a warm relationship with North Korea. Regarding the controversial issue of nuclear development in North Korea, China has held a cautious, yet positive, position. On the one hand, China, the United States, Japan and Russia have all agreed that the development of nuclear weapons in the Korean peninsula should be prohibited. On the other hand, while admitting that China did not have accurate information regarding North Korea's nuclear weapons development programme,[20] Beijing opposed economic sanctions on Pyongyang. Moreover, China also demanded that the United Nations Security Council downgrade its demand for inspections of North Korea's nuclear installations from a resolution to a non-binding "statement." A vote on a resolution would require China to go on record with either a veto or an abstention. A statement did not require a vote.[21]

In the spring of 1994, the International Atomic Energy Agency (IAEA) under the United Nations unearthed fresh evidence of North Korea's clandestine nuclear programme. Pyongyang was under tremendous pressure from Washington and Seoul to further open up its nuclear installations for international inspection.[22] In meetings with South Korean President Kim Young Sam and Foreign Minister Han Sung Joo during their visit to Beijing in 26–30 March, Chinese leaders made it clear that they would oppose any economic sanctions on North Korea, and even be reluctant to go along with a resolution from the United Nations Security Council. Rather, Beijing would like to have more time to "work its persuasion on Pyongyang before any UN sanctions are imposed."[23]

The death of Kim Il Sung in July 1994 and his succession by his son Kim Jong Il did not change China's policy toward the Korean peninsula. In his visit to Seoul in October–November 1994, Chinese Premier Li Peng assured South Korean President Kim Young Sam that China was positive toward the Geneva nuclear accord signed between North Korea and the United States in September.[24] Soon after, Chinese President Jiang Zemin also expressed "strong support" for the nuclear deal to US President Bill Clinton when they met at the APEC summit in Jarkata.[25]

China and South Korea will probably work closely in regional and global affairs. Each side regards the other as a counterweight to the increasing economic and military strength of Japan. However, there will be problems between the countries; their differing political systems and levels of economic development will inevitably contribute to friction. The ground for cooperation will, however, be much greater than that for conflict.

PRC–Taiwan Rivalry in the International Community

The Taiwan issue has occupied high priority in Beijing's foreign policy. Although both Beijing and Taipei have officially regarded the status of Taiwan and the question of its reunification with the mainland as domestic issues, these clearly have international implications, given the long period of separation and the involvement of the major powers. For Beijing, the issue concerns national sovereignty and regime legitimacy. Since Wong Ka-ying's chapter in this book is concentrated on the evolution of mainland-Taiwan relations, this chapter will only concentrate on the PRC-Taiwan rivalry in the international community.

While bilateral relations, particularly economic relations, across the Taiwan Strait have strengthened since the late 1980s,[26] the Beijing-Taipei rivalry in the international community has been primarily caused by the Taiwan independence movement which has support among some sectors of Taiwanese society, particularly within the opposition Democratic Progressive Party (DPP). For Beijing, the most unwelcome scenario for the future of Taiwan is that Taiwan might opt to become a legally independent state — *taidu* in Chinese. Such a prospect appalls the leadership of the PRC, who, like the Chinese people as a whole, are deeply ingrained with Chinese nationalism.

At the 28-member General Committee of the United Nation's 49th General Assembly in late September 1994, there was a debate on whether to establish an *ad hoc* committee to analyze "the exceptional situation of Taiwan's status and recommend a solution at the 50th session." Beijing unambiguously opposed this move. There were only seven delegations addressing the General Committee in favour of Taiwan (the draft was originally sponsored by 14 countries outside of the committee). The proposal was then defeated without a vote.[27] Thus, another Taiwan-launched UN campaign was lost.[28] Nevertheless, it is expected that this kind of campaign will continue for years to come as long as there is a phenomenon of Beijing-Taipei rivalry in the international community.

The PRC was alarmed by Taiwan's diplomatic efforts in promoting its international status, such as President Lee Teng-hui's nine-day diplomatic tour in early 1994 to Indonesia, the Philippines, Thailand under the guise of a "golfing holiday";[29] and his May 1994 visit of Nicaragua, Costa Rica, South Africa and Swaziland — four of the 29 countries that officially recognize Taiwan;[30] and Premier Lien Chan's June 1994 secret visit to Mexico after an official visit to Central America.[31] Soon after, Beijing started to openly criticize Lee's "*taidu* tendency." A series of articles in the *People's Daily* and in pro-Beijing newspapers in Hong Kong charged the native Taiwanese leader with discriminating against Chinese mainlanders in his government and obstructing unification. "Lee Teng-hui should rein in the horse at the edge of the precipice just before committing a serious blunder," the *People's Daily* warned.[32]

The PRC's Taiwan policy has been further complicated by the internal dynamics of power politics. No Chinese leader, conservative or reformers alike, can afford to be cast as *lishi zuiren*, or the people condemned by history for splitting the nation; such an appellation would be a lethal blow in Beijing's continuing power struggles. It is, therefore, not groundless for the best-seller fiction book in Taiwan to predict that there will be a military takeover by mainland China once the island declares its independence.[33] When facing the situation of *taidu*, the choices that decision makers in Beijing may have are indeed quite limited.

On the other hand, Beijing is well aware that the political situation on Taiwan is more complex than before. In his visit to Taiwan in August 1994, Tang Shubei, the highest-ranking Beijing official ever to visit Taiwan, recalled a comment by paramount leader Deng Xiaoping that China's modernization has to precede unification.[34] There are two messages: first, Beijing realizes that the unification with Taiwan is a prolonged process, therefore Beijing would have to be patient; second, the PRC would try to make every effort not to let the Taiwan issue hurt its modernization drive.

Out of fear of *taidu*, Beijing has consistently refused to pledge not to use force against Taiwan. Jiang Zemin, stated in December 1992 that the "PRC will adopt resolute measures if Taiwan declares independence."[35] The pursuit of *taidu* would, in other words, involve the risk of war. Indeed, after the death of Chiang Ching-kuo in 1988, Beijing has seen an increasing likelihood of *taidu*. Based on this analysis, Deng Xiaoping has suggested that between the two methods for China's unification — peaceful and military means — the latter is a more likely outcome for Beijing to prepare; and the timing for military action is when Taiwan openly declares independence.[36] Beijing's latest effort to prevent *taidu* is a high-profile eight-point statement made by Jiang Zemin in January 1995. Jiang emphasized that under the "one China" principle, the two sides should formally end hostilities; and that President Lee Teng-hui was welcome to visit China "in an appropriate capacity." At the same time, Lee Teng-hui confirmed the importance of the direct talks across the Strait by saying, "Regardless of whether it takes 100 times or 100 years, the two sides should continue to talk."[37] These statements are widely believed as mutual efforts at the highest level in Beijing and Taipei to prevent the possible military actions in the Taiwan Strait caused by the increasing *taidu* tendency on the Island.

To Beijing's advantage, international conditions make *taidu* unlikely to occur in the near future. General opinion in the international community has been unfavourable toward *taidu* since the PRC entered the United Nations in 1971. No major power in today's world would openly support a declaration of Taiwan's independence at the expense of breaking relations with the PRC and triggering an international crisis. There is serious doubt that the United States will send troops in once such a crisis occurs. This doubt was echoed by Taiwan's foreign minister Frederick Chien who told the Taiwanese parliament in 1994, "The US Government will not send troops to help us to fight in a war.... At most, it could offer us defensive weapons."[38]

Nonetheless, despite the unpropitious international environment, Beijing remains acutely sensitive to the issue of *taidu*. As long as Taiwan maintains *de facto* separation from the mainland, political forces within and outside the island will continue to demand *taidu*. The longer that separation continues, the stronger Taiwan's tendency toward independence will become. This tendency will be enhanced if further political turmoil occurs on the mainland akin to the Tiananmen Incident. Under such circumstances, public opinion in the international community might take a more sympathetic attitude toward Taiwan.

Southeast Asia

The transformation of China's relations with the nations of Southeast Asia exemplifies the shift from an ideologically rigid, isolationist policy under Mao to a less doctrinaire, more pragmatic and cooperative approach favoured by Deng. Indeed, whereas for Mao isolationism was desirable, for Deng the very threat of international isolation was sufficient to inspire a rapid improvement in China's relations with its Southeast Asian neighbours.

Southeast Asia comprises the six countries of the Association of Southeast Asian Nations (ASEAN — Brunei, Indonesia, Malaysia, the Philippines, Thailand, and Singapore), Vietnam, Cambodia, Laos (the three countries together are also known as Indochina), and Burma. Vietnam is scheduled to become ASEAN's seventh member in July 1995, and Laos has an observer status.[39] There is a likelihood that Cambodia and Burma may join the team in the near future.[40] In the 1950s and 1960s, China dismissed the members of ASEAN as mere "running dogs of US imperialism." Although Beijing changed its view of the nature of ASEAN in the 1970s, it remained suspicious of Indonesia, which broke relations with Beijing in 1964 after a failed *coup* attempt by the Indonesian Communist Party. In addition, anti-Communist Singapore had refused to establish diplomatic relations with the PRC for more than two decades.

China's relations with the countries of Indochina have likewise been far from smooth. Until the early 1970s, the PRC enjoyed a "comrade-plus-brother" type of relationship with Vietnam, fighting first against France (the early 1950s) and then against the United States (the 1960s and early 1970s). But after the Vietnamese Communists defeated the South and achieved national unification, Sino-Vietnamese relations worsened rapidly, primarily due to Vietnam's occupation of Cambodia and the territorial disputes along the border and in the South China Sea. To deny Vietnam's ambition of dominating the entire Indochina area, China launched a punitive war against Vietnam in 1979. On the other hand, Vietnam's joining ASEAN in 1995 has been regarded as a counter to China's weight, reshaping the balance of power and political and strategic relations in East and Southeast Asia. Vietnam's armed forces of more than 850,000 people have remained much bigger than those of Thailand and Indonesia (300,000 soldiers each), which have the biggest ASEAN forces.[41]

A number of disputes between China and some of the Southeast Asian countries remain unresolved, notably territorial claims over some of the South China Sea islands (disputes with Vietnam, the Philippines, Malaysia, and Brunei). The bulk of the disputed areas are Xisha (Paracel) and Nansha (Spratly) Islands. In the past two decades, China had three major actions. In January 1974, the Chinese army and navy took Xisha from South Vietnam. In March 1988, the Chinese navy took six atolls in Nansha archipelago from Vietnam. And in February 1995 China moved further south and planted its flag on Meiji (Mischief) Reef, which the Philippines claimed was part of its Kalayaan group of islands while Beijing disputed that claim. The PRC has repeatedly called for negotiations on the joint economic development of the Nansha area, but received no warm reaction so far from the contending nations. China's most recent action in the Meiji Reef area rung alarm in several Southeast Asian capitals.[42] Philippine President Fidel Ramos, for example, immediately made a protest against Beijing and then announced the creation of a taskforce that would strengthen its territory claim in the Nansha area.[43]

A number of studies have been conducted regarding Beijing's policy choices facing the South China Sea disputes. By applying a formal model approach, for example, Samuel Wu and Bruce de Mesquita have conducted a study on the likelihood China will use military forces over the dispute in the South China Sea. They conclude that since reformers in the

PRC will have a much better chance to implement their agenda, "policies that emphasize a stable international environment are expected to prevail in the near future." Therefore, China is "unlikely to engage in any significant uses of force" to pursue its agenda in the South China Sea "over the next few years."[44] On the other hand, however, one cannot overlook the driving force of nationalism that is behind China's territorial claims. While Beijing may try its best to avoid a major war, it may also conduct limited military actions, or "local war," to enhance its positions in the area.[45]

Although China's relationship with Southeast Asia began to improve steadily from the early 1980s, the turning point was the Tiananmen Incident of 1989. Because of the diplomatic and economic sanctions imposed by Western nations, Beijing faced isolation from the international community. The collapse of the Soviet and East European Communist regimes further exacerbated Beijing's international isolation. Beijing was forced to adjust its foreign policy to face the challenges of the post-Cold War era.

One of China's new initiatives was an Asian-oriented foreign policy, and Southeast Asia was a major focus of its diplomatic overture. Beijing has accomplished four concrete steps in this direction in the wake of Tiananmen. First, in August 1990, Beijing normalized relations with Indonesia. Second, two months later, China established diplomatic relations with Singapore. Third, Beijing has been actively involved in the UN peacekeeping forces in Cambodia since 1992. And fourth, Beijing normalized relations with Hanoi in 1991, leading to a visit to Vietnam by Premier Li Peng in December 1992, at the end of which Li announced "we have much more common points than disputes."[46] By the end of 1994, there were three rounds of talks between Beijing and Hanoi on disputes over their common 1,130-kilometre land border. Some progress was reportedly made during these talks.[47]

This improvement of relationship with Southeast Asian countries was highlighted by the visit of Jiang Zemin to Singapore and Malaysia in November 1994, on his way to the Indonesian APEC meeting. On the return trip home, Jiang stopped off in Vietnam making the first official visit to that country by China's highest leader in several decades. At the visit's end, China and Vietnam agreed to form an expert group to negotiate a settlement of their dispute over the Nansha (Spratly) Islands. Chinese Foreign Minister Qian Qichen also stressed that both countries felt they should shelve their disputes and concentrate on economic development.[48]

The recent development of bilateral relations between China and

Burma is also noteworthy. Since the beginning of the 1990s, trade between Burma and southern China, Yunnan province in particular, has been flourishing as never before. Bilateral trade reached US$ 490 million in 1993. There has also been simultaneous growth in military ties between Rangoon and Beijing.

The development of further military cooperation between China and Burma worried Southeast Asian neighbours, who were alarmed by the massive Chinese shipments to Burma's army, air force, and particularly the Burmese navy. Indonesian military sources, for example, considered that granting China military access to Burmese bases would present a threat to the Straits of Malacca, a major waterway for Southeast Asia's sea-borne trade. Although Beijing denied that it intended to project its influence into Southeast Asia, many regional governments feared China was using Burma to expand its military and political reach.[49] The visit of Li Peng to Burma in December 1994 marked the first such high-level visit since 1981, aiming to enhance the so-called *baobo qingyi*, brotherly relationship, between the two countries.[50]

The boom brought unwelcome aspects, too: a surge in logging, opium production and illegal Chinese emigration. The Mekong River has become the leading conduit out of China for illegal migrants to the West. Snakeheads, the merchants of migration, charged about RMB 220,000 (US$26,000) in 1994 for passage overseas. At the same time, thousands of Chinese were content to stay in Burma, most of whom engaged in commercial activities.[51] Sometime down the road, Beijing will have to seriously deal with these problems. Indeed, one of the major issues discussed during Li Peng's 1994 visit was how to cooperate to repress drug smuggling along the Sino-Burmese border.[52]

For future direction, Beijing will likely continue to cooperate in the international arena, particularly with regional nations, in the post-Cold War era. A larger regional coordinating organization may be necessary to prevent military and political crises and to coordinate economic activities in East and Southeast Asia. The PRC, along with Taiwan and Hong Kong, would be expected to play an active role in such an organization, as would North Korea, South Korea, Japan, the ASEAN states, and possibly Vietnam. The participation of the United States and Russia would also be helpful and would ensure that their interests will not be jeopardized. Among existing organizations, the APEC group, which includes the PRC, Taiwan, Hong Kong, South Korea, Japan, Australia, Canada, New Zealand, the United States, and the ASEAN countries, seems to be a particularly promising instrument for enhancing trade between the nations of the region.

Relations with Russia and the United States

An examination of China's foreign relations in the Asia-Pacific region would be incomplete without discussing Russia and the United States, given these two powers' respective immense impact on this area. This brief discussion, however, concentrates on the more recent development without elaborating on historical legacies.[53]

Although the collapse of the Soviet empire and Communist ideology profoundly upset the Beijing leadership,[54] the decline of the Soviet threat has also presented new possibilities in China's security thinking, particularly in the Asia-Pacific area. If China and Russia continue to follow a pragmatic line, they may further improve their bilateral relations. Indeed, following three summits — Mikhail Gorbachev's visit to Beijing in 1989, Jiang Zemin's visit to Moscow in 1991, and Boris Yeltsin's visit to China in 1992 — bilateral relations have significantly improved. Some Western observers pointed out as early as 1988, that the Chinese "have little to lose from inching toward Moscow in order to gain a bit more leverage."[55]

Yeltsin's visit to Beijing produced meaningful results in Sino-Russian relations. By signing 24 joint statements, documents, and memoranda of understanding in areas including military and technological cooperation, space exploration, and nuclear energy development, China would be able to upgrade its military equipment significantly, while Russia would receive much needed food supplies.[56]

In September 1994, Jiang Zemin paid another visit to Moscow. With a much more comfortable and stabilized bilateral relationship than the previous years, Jiang and Yeltsin signed a declaration confirming that China and Russia agreed not to aim nuclear missiles at each other, never to use force against each other, and to sharply limit the number of troops stationed along their border. An equally important result of the visit was the economic agreement signed by the two leaders. Yeltsin told Jiang, "We pay much attention to studying the experience of economic reforms in China," referring to China's successful reform policies and remarkable economic growth over the past decade. Indeed, the bilateral economic relations between the two countries had developed rapidly. China became Russia's second largest trading partner after Germany. The total trade volume reached US$7.68 billion in 1993, having doubled in the last three years.[57]

Nevertheless, China's *rapprochement* with the former Soviet Union would not lead China to abandon its cooperation with the United States and Japan. To the contrary, the powers may find more reasons to cooperate than to confront each other. In the early 1990s, for example, Beijing, Washington, Tokyo, and Moscow reached a consensus on prohibiting the development of nuclear weapons in the Korean peninsula, particularly in North Korea. Such cooperation serves not only China's economic interests, but also its security interests. The advanced military equipment from Russia has now become a new source for the upgrading effort of the PLA (People's Liberation Army). In November 1994, for example, China signed a $1 billion deal with Russia to buy four Kilo-class patrol submarines, a major upgrade for the Chinese navy.[58]

The downturn in Sino-American relations since Tiananmen has serious implications for all three major fields of bilateral relations: political, economic, and strategic. Political and economic disputes had caused the relationship to become "prickly" even before Tiananmen.[59] Nevertheless, the Beijing leadership attached great importance to its relations with Washington, and was pleased to host US Secretary of State James Baker in late 1991. His visit was called "a success,"[60] despite the serious disagreements voiced during his stay. China also regarded the United States, with Japan and the European Community, as its major source of advanced technology, capital, and markets.

Since the early 1990s we have witnessed a gradual warming up of the brisk relationship between Beijing and Washington. Although having criticized the PRC on such issues as human rights and unfair trading practices in his presidential campaign, President Bill Clinton made a critical decision in 1994 to delink the human rights issue from the renewal of China's most-favoured-nation status, thereby removing a major obstacle to bilateral relations.[61]

On the other hand, as long as the future of Taiwan remains unsettled, the potential for Sino-American conflict will continue. Furthermore, the Republican victory in US congressional elections in November 1994 has produced what one specialist called the "most pro-democracy, pro-Taiwan, pro-Tibet, anti-Chinese Communist Party and anti-People's Liberation Army" Congress in recent memory.[62] Senator Jesse Helms, the new chairman of the powerful Senate Foreign Relations Committee, reportedly claimed that, "Given the choice of Chinas, I would take Taiwan every time." And Helms' counterpart in the House Foreign Affairs Committee Benjamin Gilman, an old friend of Tibet's exiled leader, the Dalai Lama, was the sponsor of a bill declaring Tibet an occupied country.[63] Furthermore, the Alaska senator Frank Murkowski, also the new chairman for the Senate Energy Committee, issued an open invitation to Lee Teng-hui to visit Alaska for the 1995 US–ROC (Republic of China) Business Council meeting.[64] These statements will certainly create problems for the future development of Sino-American relations. Indeed, the first incident in 1995 was the trade war threats caused by the clash over intellectual property rights.[65] One may expect that the clashes between the two countries in political, economic, and cultural dimensions will continue for years to come.

From the perspective of world politics, however, the two countries' national interests are not fundamentally in conflict. Indeed, the strategic foundation that brought the two countries together in 1972 is still largely in place. Washington has consistently recognized the importance of Beijing's cooperation on East and Southeast Asian regional affairs, such as Korean unification and the Cambodian peace settlement.[66] The international competition for the China market is also a major consideration for US foreign policy toward China. One such example is the aircraft industry. There has been air-traffic congestion at ground level in Beijing as the world's three main aircraft manufacturers — Boeing and McDonnell Douglas of the United States, and the European consortium Airbus Industries — compete for the China market which expected to spend US$66 billion over the period of 20 years after 1994.[67] American companies, such as Boeing and McDonnell certainly would not like to see the loss of business opportunities over political factors. After all, many other Western countries have put economics ahead of politics when dealing with China. One fresh memory for the Americans was the decision made by the French government in early 1994: to cut off future arms sales to Taiwan and to mend fences with Beijing, so that France can tap into China's booming economy.[68] The last-minute settlement between Beijing and Washington over the copyright protection disputes in February 1995, avoiding a major trade war worth more than US$2 billion, seemed to demonstrate the importance the two capitals attach to each other. Although not directly linked, this settlement may also clear the way for China to join the World Trade Organization with "developing country" status which was previously blocked by the United States.[69] These kinds of considerations with economic (as well as strategic) factors behind them will continue to play important roles in Sino-US relations during the years to come.

More recent efforts to improve bilateral relations were made at the APEC summit in Bogor in November 1994, when Jiang Zemin met with Bill Clinton. This meeting was reportedly more smooth than last year's meeting in Seattle, where Jiang delivered a blunt rebuff to Clinton's overtures on human rights. While expressing his deep concerns about the possible US support to Taiwan independence, Jiang made some conciliatory proposals including that the two countries "should step up consultation and cooperation for resolving environmental issues, the proliferation of weapons of mass destruction, terrorism and drugs."[70]

Future Directions and Choices

Although it is always risky to predict the character of a country's foreign policy and its choices, general trends in China's recent foreign policy — modernization, nationalism, and regionalism — are evident and seem likely to continue into the post-Deng era.

Beijing's commitment to modernization as its first priority goal will more then likely to remain. Even though Deng's policy of "reform and openness" has not always progressed smoothly, the Beijing leadership in the first half of the 1990s, centred around Jiang Zemin, seems confident that periods of slow economic growth and political instability, such as that following the 1989 Tiananmen Incident, would only be temporary. In the early and mid-1990s, China was relatively stable politically and is prospering economically.

According to the Asian Development Bank, China's economy grew 7% in 1991 and 12% in 1992, an "exceptional strength" in the recessive world economy.[71] It seems most likely that "Chinese economic growth until the turn of the century might even match the 9% annual rate of expansion achieved in 1980–93."[72] Given this apparent dedication to modernization, the only circumstance under which China might readopt a Maoist policy would be a drastic internal political shift toward radicalism akin to that of the Gang of Four. Such a shift would necessarily isolate China from the outside world and damage its modernization drive. However, a return to isolationism seems highly unlikely for a variety of reasons.

One major factor is China's bitter experience in the ten-year Cultural Revolution (1966–1976), which produced a consensus among the Chinese people as well as its leaders — never again! Radical revolutionary ideas no longer appeal to the majority of the people; instead, the drive toward a market economy now enjoys widespread support. In addition, the policy of reform and openness launched by Deng has gained a momentum of its own and has already transformed the Chinese policy-making structure from vertical to horizontal authoritarianism.[73] Those forces that inspired Deng's policy continue to grow stronger. Chief among them are the many supporters and beneficiaries of economic development and modernization efforts; the technocratic bureaucrats that are emerging among the élites; the passing away of the revolutionary generation; China's opening up to the outside world; and the enormous increase in the diversity and complexity of foreign-policy decisions. Although the struggle to succeed Deng seems certain to be fierce (the removal of the brothers Yang Shangkun and Yang Baibing from top military positions at the 14th Party Congress in 1992 highlighted another round of the power struggle), the transformation process from vertical to horizontal authoritarianism will continue, ensuring that political inputs and interests are considered in the formulation of Chinese foreign policy.

China's top foreign-policy priority is likely to remain, as Robert Sutter has stated, "the pragmatic quest for a stable environment needed for effective modernization and development."[74] Or as Donald Zagoria has expressed the matter, China's foreign policy will "continue to be subordinated by its powerful desire to modernize the Chinese economy and the need to maintain a peaceful international environment."[75] China's foreign policy will remain pragmatic, economically oriented, and cooperative yet independent. However, even though the general direction of China's future development will be toward economic modernization and greater political participation, it will most likely follow a zig-zag pattern such as China has experienced in the past.

Internally, nationalism has been one of the driving forces behind China's modernization efforts. Power politics within the ruling élites will more than likely remain a major factor for the decision makers' calculations in formulating Chinese foreign policy. Therefore, highly sensitive issues, such as the issue of Taiwan (particulary its independence), the dispute over the South China Sea Islands with several Southeast Asian countries, and the dispute with Japan over the Diaoyu Islands, are potential areas for the internal power struggle, leading a variety of policy choices for the Beijing leadership including both diplomatic means and the use of military force.

Faced with the changing dynamics of the post-Cold War era, the PRC must address a number of issues concerning its present and future policies. Here, China's primary foreign policy goal is in line with its domestic priority — economic modernization. To promote economic development and to control problems (such as the confusion over the currency exchange rate in 1994, and inflation caused by an overheated economy in the early 1990s)[76] arising from economic reform, has become a central task for all PRC leaders, old and new alike, and will continue to be a basis for foreign policy decisions.

To combat the uncertainty in its post-Tiananmen relations with the United States, Beijing has developed a multi-direction strategy, centred on regionalism, to prepare for any undesirable future developments. While trying hard to restore relations with the United States to the pre-1989 level, China has made manoeuvring in three directions. First, China has further expanded its influence in East and Southeast Asian regional affairs by cultivating relations with capitalist economies such as Japan, South Korea, the six ASEAN countries, Burma, as well as its relations within the other parts of Greater China — Taiwan, Hong Kong, and Macau.

Second, China has improved or enhanced its relations with the other two Asian socialist countries — Vietnam and North Korea, and the two former socialist neighbours — Russia and Mongolia. The PRC has also strengthened its footing in Central Asia. In May 1994, Li Peng paid a swing through central Asian countries including Turkmenistan, Uzbekistan, Kazakhstan and Kirgyzstan, further enhancing Beijing's position in this area.[77] Although it is unlikely at present, China may, if the domestic and international moods change, even set up an informal Asian-socialist alliance consisting of China, North Korea, and Vietnam to resist Western pressure for political and economic liberalization.

Finally, Beijing has continued to develop cooperative relations with industrialized countries (other than the United States) such as Japan and the Western European countries. As discussed earlier, China has always attached great importance to its relations with Japan. A stable Beijing-Tokyo relationship will serve as a key to regional stability in East Asia. Beijing has also managed to maintain cordial relations with the Europeans, particularly since the early 1990s. This was further demonstrated by the European Union's Trade Commissioner Leon Brittan's visit to Beijing in November 1994, showing a different attitude from the "harder American position" in terms of such controversial issues as China's membership in the World Trade Organization.[78]

As the PRC's international status is gradually restored and strengthened in the wake of Tiananmen, Beijing's leadership will become more confident in world affairs, enabling China to exhibit a more positive behaviour. If the Chinese regime perceives itself as less threatened by foreign powers, particularly the United States, Russia, and Japan, it will become more cooperative in international affairs, and will behave more like an insider and a partner than an outsider or challenger. But if the world seems more threatening, considerations of national security and the issue of regime survival will take top priority in Chinese foreign policy, which may push Beijing to extreme directions.

China will remain a regional power with global aspirations. Regionally it will concentrate its external activities in the Asia-Pacific area. On global matters, China will go along with the mainstream of world opinion while seeking to advance its own independent policy. Given the rapid decline of Soviet/Russian power, the collapse of communism, and the advent of a more cooperative relationship between Moscow and Washington, the extent to which China can pursue an independent course is questionable. The concept of an independent foreign policy is perhaps more useful for China with regard to the North-South divide; China would like to play a leading role in the Third World and will act more independently in its relationships with industrialized countries on behalf of Third World countries. As the only Third World member of the UN Security Council, China may follow the policies of the major powers on some occasions, but may also act as a protector of Third World interests on some other occasions.

The struggle for the transition of power prepared for the post-Deng era is looming large. Despite the popular speculation that the fate of the current Chinese top leader Jiang Zemin will be similar to that of Hua Guofeng, a transitional leader from 1976 to 1978 between the era of Mao and the era of Deng, Jiang has made every effort to secure his leading position. It is believed that the strengthening of Jiang's power base will likely make China's domestic and foreign policies stable in the post-Deng era. Yet, nobody can be sure what would happen after the death of Deng, since Chinese politics at both institutional and individual levels are so uncertain and unpredictable. However, as long as the dust remains unsettled, a bold and imaginative change to the current foreign and domestic policies is likely since the major concern for each individual leader in

Beijing is the potential succession crisis in Chinese politics. This assessment was shared by many China watchers both inside and outside of the country. For example, right before US Secretary of State Warren Christopher's visit to Beijing in March 1994, Chinese authorities in Beijing and Shanghai grabbed a string of at least 13 high-profile political activists, including China's best-known dissidents Wei Jingsheng and Wang Dan. This action, however, was viewed by foreign observers as "largely a result of domestic political struggle," not a diplomatic show.[79]

The decline of communism, however, will enable Chinese foreign policy to become more flexible in many areas. Chinese foreign policy behaviour in general will continue to be a mixture of flexibility and rigidity,[80] the balance varying according to the changing dynamics of domestic politics, the Beijing leadership's perception of the outside world, and the international environment.

Notes

1. "Year in Review: Free Trade: Key Asian Value," *Far Eastern Economic Review*, 29 December 1994 and 5 January 1995, p. 27.
2. Nicholas Lardy, *China in the World Economy* (Washington, DC: Institute for International Economics, 1994), pp. 106–10.
3. There are different definitions for the concept of "Greater China." In a broad way, it refers to the "rapidly increasing interaction among Chinese societies around the world as the political and administrative barriers to their intercourse fall." In a much narrower sense, it focuses "exclusively on Hong Kong, Macau, Taiwan and mainland China." See Harry Harding, "The Concept of 'Greater China': Themes, Variations and Reservations," *The China Quarterly*, No. 136 (December 1993), pp. 660–64. For example, *Business Week* (10 October 1988, pp. 54–55) referred to "Greater China" as the prospective result of the three-way economic integration of Hong Kong, Taiwan and the mainland.
4. Nicholas Kristof and Sheryl WuDunn, "China's Rush to Riches," *The New York Times Magazine*, 4 September 1994, p. 54.
5. In a study commissioned by the US Defense Department, for example, half the panel of China experts argued that China would experience a "Soviet-style break-up" within seven years of Deng's death. For details see, Nigel Holloway, "For Whom the Bell Tolls," *Far Eastern Economic Review*, 2 February 1995, pp. 14–15.

6. See Carl Goldstein, "Jerky Movements: U.S.–China Ties See-Saw on Human Rights," *Far Eastern Economic Review*, 17 February 1994, p. 20.
7. Susumu Awanohara and Lincoln Kaye, "Full Circle," *Far Eastern Economic Review*, 9 June 1994, pp. 14–15. For a detailed accounts of the Clinton Administration's considerations on China's MFN status, see D. Lampton, "America's China Policy in the Age of the Finance Minister: Clinton Ends Linkage," *The China Quarterly*, No. 139 (September 1994), pp. 597–621.
8. "Direct Investment in China Soars," *The Japan Times* (weekly international edition), 12–18 December 1994, p. 12.
9. *Renmin ribao*, 27 November 1992, p. 4.
10. *The Japan Times* (weekly international edition), 5–11 September 1994, p. 3.
11. Quoted from "China Snipes at 'Offensive' Maritime SDF," *The Japan Times* (weekly international edition), 13–19 June 1994, p. 3.
12. Simon Beck, "Jiang Presses Leaders Over One-China Policy," *South China Morning Post* (Hong Kong), 15 November 1994, p. 13.
13. "Tokyo Ready to Talk Defense with Beijing," *The Japan Times* (weekly international edition), 31 October–6 November 1994, p. 2.
14. For details, see Julian Baum, "Regrets Only," *Far Eastern Economic Review*, 22 September 1994, pp. 14–16; and Lincoln Kaye, "Lip Service: China-Taiwan War of Words Heats Up," *Far Eastern Economic Review*, 20 October 1994, p. 20.
15. "China May Boycott the Asian Games," *The Japan Times* (weekly international edition), 12–18 September 1994, p. 2.
16. "Tokyo Sticks to One-China Policy Line," *The Japan Times* (weekly international edition), 21–27 November 1994, p. 5. Also see Simon Beck, "Jiang Presses Leaders Over One-China Policy," *South China Morning Post*, 15 November 1994, p. 13.
17. Charles Smith, "Eager to Please: Tokyo Sets Aside Own Rules in China Aid Package," *Far Eastern Economic Review*, 26 January 1995, pp. 25–26.
18. Nayan Chanda, "Chinese Welcome North Korea's Kim, But Relations Are Subtly Changing," *The Asian Wall Street Journal Weekly*, 21 October 1991, pp. 24 and 26.
19. "South Korea: Aircraft for China," *Far Eastern Economic Review*, 21 April 1994, p. 83.
20. "South Korea: Information Gap," *Far Eastern Economic Review*, 21 April 1994, p. 13.
21. "Making Haste Slowly: Seoul, Tokyo, Play Up to Beijing on North Korean Issue," *Far Eastern Economic Review*, 7 April 1994, p. 16.
22. Nayan Chanda, "Seal of Disapproval," *Far Eastern Economic Review*, 31 March 1994, pp. 14–15.
23. Note 21.

24. Shim Jae Hoon, "Sitting on the Fence," *Far Eastern Economic Review*, 10 November 1994, p. 15.
25. "Beijing Backs North Korea Pact," *South China Morning Post*, 15 November 1994, p. 1.
26. An encouraging sign came from the Taiwan side toward the end of 1994 when Vincent Siew, former chairman of the Council of Economic Planning and Development, was appointed head of the Mainland Affairs Council replacing Huang Kung-huei, whose conservative approach to mainland policy kept the lid on cross-straits relations. With a reputation of being flexible and economic-oriented, Siew proposed setting up "offshore centres," located probably inside the port districts of Kaohsiung and Taichung, that would process trade with the PRC. Premier Lien Chan also gave his blessing by stating, "in the current stage, trade should play a primary role in the government's mainland policy." Although nothing definite yet, it appears that with strong push from Taiwan's business community, Taipei is prepared to open direct trade with the mainland. See Julian Baum, "China Bound: Odds Improve for Direct Trade Links," *Far Eastern Economic Review*, 29 December 1994 and 5 January 1995, pp. 15–16. For economic incentives for the improvement of the across strait relations, also see Yu-Shan Wu, "Mainland China's Economic Policy Toward Taiwan: Economic Needs or Unification Scheme?" *Issues & Studies* 30, No. 9 (September 1994), pp. 29–49.
27. Ted Morello, "Hearing Problems: Taiwan's UN Feeler Squashed by Beijing," *Far Eastern Economic Review*, 6 October 1994, p. 29.
28. At the 1993 General Assembly of the United Nations, there were seven countries which sponsored the draft item in favour of Taiwan. They are all Central American nations: Belize, Costa Rica, El Salvador, Guatemala, Honduras, Nicaragua and Panama. Of these countries, only Nicaragua upheld its stance in 1994.
29. Julian Baum, John McBeth, Rodney Tasker, "In His Private Capacity: President Lee Scores Points in Holiday Diplomacy," *Far Eastern Economic Review*, 24 February 1994, pp. 18–19.
30. Julian Baum, "Fast Friends: Lee's Tour Staves Off International Isolation," *Far Eastern Economic Review*, 9 June 1994, p. 18.
31. "Taiwan: Secret Visit," *Far Eastern Economic Review*, 16 June 1994, p. 13.
32. Julian Baum, "Dire Straits: Beijing Frets Over a More Independent Taiwan," *Far Eastern Economic Review*, 21 July 1994, pp. 19–20.
33. A best-seller book entitled *August 1995: China's Violent Invasion of Taiwan*, which is a fiction about China's take over of Taiwan after the latter declares independence, sold 60,000 copies in less than two months in the summer of 1994, further indicating the sensitivity of the issue. For details, see Julian

Baum, "Fear of Falling: Prophet of Chinese Invasion Makes Many Nervous," *Far Eastern Economic Review*, 13 October 1994, pp. 24–26.
34. Julian Baum "Charm Offensive," *Far Eastern Economic Review*, 18 August 1994, pp. 14–15.
35. *Renmin ribao*, 16 December 1992, p. 1.
36. This strategy has been confirmed by the recollections of Xu Jiatun, *Xu Jiatun huiyilu* (The Memoirs of Xu Jiatun) (Hong Kong: Lianhebao, 1993), pp. 561–62, who was a former member of the CPC central committee, the highest ranking Chinese official in exile abroad.
37. Julian Baum, "Jiang Talks Strait," *Far Eastern Economic Review*, 16 February 1995, pp. 14–15. Also see *Yazhou zhoukan* (The International Chinese Newsweekly), 19 February 1995, pp. 18–24.
38. "Taiwan: Standing Alone," *Far Eastern Economic Review*, 17 November 1994, p. 13.
39. "A Seventh for ASEAN," *Far Eastern Economic Review*, 8 December 1994, p. 12.
40. By the end of 1994, Laos was an observer, Cambodia was waiting for approval of its application for observer status in ASEAN, and Burma expressed its interest in becoming an observer. See Frank Ching, "Growing ASEAN Faces Strains," *Far Eastern Economic Review*, 29 December 1994 and 5 January 1995, p. 23.
41. Saritdet Marukatat, "Vietnam in ASEAN Will Counter China's Weight," *The Japan Times* (weekly international edition), 28 November–4 December 1994, p. 8.
42. For details, see Nayan Chanda et al., "Territorial Imperative," *Far Eastern Economic Review*, 23 February 1995, pp. 14–16.
43. "Ramos Sets Up Territory Taskforce," *South China Morning Post*, 23 February 1995, p. 11.
44. Samuel Wu and Bruce de Mesquita, "Assessing the Dispute in the South China Sea: A Model of China's Security Decision Making," *International Studies Quarterly* 38, No. 3 (September 1994), pp. 398–99.
45. For the idea of "local war," see Lee Ngok, "The People's Liberation Army: Dynamics of Strategy and Politics," in *China Review*, edited by Kuan Hsin-chi and Maurice Brosseau (Hong Kong: The Chinese University Press, 1991); and Guan Jixian, *Gaojishu jubu zhanzheng zhanyi* (High-tech Local War), (Beijing: Guofang daxue chubanshe, 1993).
46. *Renmin ribao*, 1 December 1992, p. 1; 2 December 1992, p. 1; 3 December 1992, p. 1.
47. Philippe Agret, "Hanoi Beats the Drum to Solve Tense Border Disputes," *Eastern Express*, 25 October 1994, p. 8.
48. "Vietnam: Spratly Negotiations," *Far Eastern Economic Review*, 1 December 1994, p. 13.

49. Bertil Lintner, "Enter the Dragon," *Far Eastern Economic Review*, 22 December 1994, pp. 22–24.
50. *Wen Wei Po* (Hong Kong), 27 December 1994, p. 1.
51. Bertil Lintner and Chiang Saen, "River of Dreams: Chinese Emigrants Pour Down the Mekong," *Far Eastern Economic Review*, 22 December 1994, p. 26.
52. *Ta Kung Pao*, 28 December 1994, p. 6.
53. For detailed accounts of China's changing relationships with the United States and the Soviet Union from a historical perspective, see Gordon Chang, *Friends and Enemies: The United States, China and the Soviet Union, 1948–1972*. (Stanford, Calif.: Stanford University Press, 1990).
54. Faced with dramatic changes in the former Soviet Union and East Europe, Beijing drew grim conclusions about how to defend socialism in China. An internal Chinese Communist Party document outlined five lessons learned from the failed Soviet *coup* of August 1991:
    (a) Proletarian dictatorship should be maintained.
    (b) No multiparty system should be allowed.
    (c) State-owned enterprises and the state-controlled sector should be the basis of the economy.
    (d) The party must command the army.
    (e) The campaign against "bourgeois liberalism" should be stepped up.
    See Nayan Chanda, "This Week's Sino-Vietnamese Summit Crown the Emergence of China as the Regional Power," *The Asian Wall Street Journal Weekly*, 4 November 1991, pp. 2 and 20.
55. "Moscow, Meet Peking," *The Christian Science Monitor*, 30 September 1988.
56. *Renmin ribao*, 19 December 1992, p. 1; also see "Talks Open New Russia-China Era," *The Virginian-Pilot and the Ledger-Star*, 19 December 1992, p. a11.
57. Michael Specter, "Russia and China Act to Cut Arms, Widen Ties," *The New York Times*, 4 September 1994, p. 8.
58. "China: Subs from Russia," *Far Eastern Economic Review*, 23 February 1995, p. 13.
59. Adi Ignatius, "China-U.S. Relationship Is Still Prickly," *The Wall Street Journal*, 14 July 1988, p. 11.
60. "Baker's China Mission Called a Success," *Beijing Review* 34, No. 47 (25 November–1 December 1991), pp. 7–8.
61. For detailed accounts of the controversy around the MFN treatment of China by the United States, see Qingshan Tan, "The Politics of U.S. Most-Favored-Nation Treatment to China;" also Sheree Groves, "Sino-U.S. Relations: The Battle Over MFN Status," *Current Affairs Notes*, No. 22 (31 May 1991), pp. 1–6.

62. Nayan Chanda, "Storm Warning," *Far Eastern Economic Review*, 1 December 1994, pp. 14–15.
63. Ibid.
64. Nigel Holloway and Melena Zyla, "Collision Course," *Far Eastern Economic Review*, 19 January 1995, pp. 14–15.
65. Kari Huus, "Back to Normal: U.S.-China Trade War Looms Closer," *Far Eastern Economic Review*, 19 January 1995, p. 52.
66. For the evolution of American foreign policy toward China, see Banning Garrett, "The Strategic Basis of Learning in U.S. Policy Toward China, 1949–1988," in George W. Breslauer and Phili E. Tellock, *Learning in U.S. and Soviet Foreign Policy*. (Boulder, Col.: Westview Press, 1990), pp. 208–63.
67. Nury Vittachi and Michael Westlake "Tribute Time: Western Aircraft Companies Woo China," *Far Eastern Economic Review*, 25 August 1994, p. 42.
68. Lincoln Kaye, "Learning to Bow," *Far Eastern Economic Review*, 27 January 1994, pp. 12–13.
69. Lincoln Kaye, "Trading Rights," *Far Eastern Economic Review*, 9 March 1995, p. 16.
70. Simon Beck, "Jiang to Push New US Deal," *South China Morning Post*, 15 November 1994, p. 1.
71. "Asian Economies Continue to Be Star Performers," *The Japan Times* (weekly international edition), 7–13 December 1992, p. 17.
72. See Nicholas Lardy, *China in the World Economy* (Washington, DC: Institute for International Economics, 1994), pp. 18–22. Lardy's predictions are based on his analysis of following elements of Chinese economy: strong agricultural foundation, high rates of saving and investment, effective human capital formation, relatively low income inequality, rapid demographic transition, rapid growth of manufacture exports, and high productivity growth.
73. For detailed analyses, see Quansheng Zhao, "Domestic Factors of Chinese Foreign Policy: From Vertical to Horizontal Authoritarianism," *The Annals of the American Academy of Political and Social Science*, No. 519 (January 1992), pp. 159–76.
74. Robert Sutter, "Implications of China's Modernization for East and Southeast Asian Security: The Year 2000," in *China's Global Presence: Economics, Politics, and Security*, edited by David M. Lampton and Catherine H. Keyse (Washington, DC: American Enterprise Institute in collaboration with the Institute of Southeast Asian Studies, 1988), p. 206.
75. Donald Zagoria, "The End of the Cold War in Asia: Its Impact on China," in *The China Challenge*, edited by Frank J. Macchiarola and Robert B. Oxnam (New York: The Academy of Political Science, 1991), p. 11.
76. For China's economic problems, see Lincoln Kaye, "Deafened by Decree: China's Currency and Tax Reforms Spread Confusion," *Far Eastern*

Economic Review, 13 January 1994, pp. 80–81; and Carl Goldstein, "Doctor's Orders: Beijing Tries Again to Cool China's Economy," *Far Eastern Economic Review*, 17 February 1994, pp. 44–45.

77. Ahmed Rashid, "Chinese Challenge: Li Peng Visit Highlights Beijing's Growing Role in the Region," *Far Eastern Economic Review*, 12 May 1994, p. 30.
78. Shada Islam, "Friendly Signals: Europe Wants Its Own Pow-Wow with East Asia," *Far Eastern Economic Review*, 17 November 1994, p. 30.
79. For details, see Lincoln Kaye and Carl Goldstein, "Bluff and Bluster," *Far Eastern Economic Review*, 17 March 1994, pp. 16–17.
80. For detailed analyses, see Quansheng Zhao, "Achieving Maximum Advantage: Rigidity and Flexibility in Chinese Foreign Policy," *American Asian Review*, Vol. 13, No. 1 (Spring 1995), pp. 301–33.

9

China Defence Budgeting: Structure and Dynamics

Ka Po Ng

One of the main issues in the recent debates about the emergence of a "China threat" in the Asia-Pacific region has been the continuous and marked increase in China's defence budget since 1990. The defence budget is, indeed, an important indicator of the defence posture of a state but is, however, only part of defence economic activities.

National defence and economics interact at three levels: (1) the present and future availability of national resources for national defence purposes; (2) the share of national defence in resource allocations; (3) the efficient utilization of allocated resources.[1] The first level is essentially a structural problem and concerns the grand strategy and economic planning policies as well as higher level decision making. In the name of national security, this level of defence economic relations usually remains stable unless dramatic changes occur in the international security environment and the leadership at home.[2] The second level is mainly a problem of budgetary allocations and, to a large extent, is affected by the first level decisions. The third level is essentially the business of military logistics as well as research and development (R&D), acquisition of military hardware and defence industrial production.

Defence economics, as understood by the Chinese military, is the intersection between economics and military science. It covers a wide range of economic activities, including human resources planning, communications and transport, stockpiling of strategic materiel, military-run businesses, arms transfer, wartime mobilization of economic resources.[3]

Given the interlocking relationship between defence budgeting and other levels of defence economy, this chapter follows the three levels of defence-economic interactions with primary focus on the defence budgeting. It begins with a brief discussion of China's defence economic decision making. In the section on the defence budget, we will look into the issue of reading the budget, determinants to China's defence spending behaviour, attempts to solve budget problems and the other side of the official defence outlay — the hidden budget.

This chapter is a revised version of a chapter in the author's M.Phil. dissertation presented to the University of Hong Kong in 1994. The author wishes to thank Professor Lee Ngok, Dr N. J. Miners and Col. John Corbett for their comments on an earlier draft of this essay.

I. Defence Economic Planning

The availability of resources for national defence depends on defence economic planning in the long term and the grand strategy of the state because the future amount of resources available is the result of present decisions. Likewise, today's available resources are determined by yesterday's policy choices.[4] This level of defence economic activities is particularly important to China because of its political peculiarity.

Decision Making

At the apex of China's power structure, the boundaries between the party, government and military leadership (Central Military Commission [CMC] and Ministry of National Defence) are deliberately blurred by overlapping membership to ensure party control and the interrelationship is never made clear.[5] Despite the provision for the establishment of a state CMC in Section 4 of the 1982 Constitution, the Chinese have not been specific in their reference to policies and decisions made by the "CMC," not even on such important occasions as the CMC enlarged meeting in 1985 when a new doctrine for peacetime defence planning was adopted.[6] Today, both the party and state CMCs remain intact but their memberships continue to overlap. The relationship between these two CMCs is still ambiguous. The defence industrial and Science and Technology (S&T) sector has also been under joint party, state and military leadership. Its policies toward civil-military integration, for example, were decided and elaborated in 1983 at a conference of the State Planning Commission, the State Economic Commission (which was merged into the State Planning Commission in 1988) and the Commission in charge of Science and Technology and Industry of National Defence (COSTIND).[7] Besides, the conversion efforts have been coordinated and supervised by a coordination group formed by the State Planning Commission, the State Science and Technology Commission (SSTC) and the COSTIND.[8] The State Planning Commission, the SSTC and the COSTIND have played significant roles in defence economic policy making.

However, the institutional approach does not depict the full picture of China's defence economic planning because the politico-military authority is highly personalized. A small group of senior revolutionary veterans with experience as both military and party leaders has formed an informal leadership and wielded the supreme power.[9] In the group, Deng Xiaoping has been "the first among equals" after 1977 and has been hailed as the "chief architect" of post-Mao reforms. It was he who had urged structural reform of the People's Liberation Army (PLA) since 1975, who had pushed for a civil-military integrated defence economic strategy, and who had brought China from war preparation to peacetime construction.[10] This personality factor makes more ambiguous the scene at the first level of defence policy making which determines the availability of resources allocated to national defence, and leaves the stability of modernization programmes in question. In order to ensure the continuity of his policies, Deng Xiaoping has already endeavoured to put his men in control of the institutional leadership, for example the appointments of Zhao Ziyang as the CMC's First Vice-Chairman in 1987 and Jiang Zemin as its Chairman in 1990.[11]

The Grand Strategy

Deng Xiaoping asserted that economic development was the general interest (*daju*) of the country and that "all branches of the armed forces should devise ways to support and participate in this national construction programme." The concept of national power, somehow crude, was introduced to China's defence planning: "once the national economy is improved and national power enhanced, it will not be difficult to produce more atomic bombs, missiles and other equipment, whether for air, sea or land."[12]

When this grand strategy is put in more precise terms, the then Director of the Military Economic Institute, Professor Wang Qikun, argues, there are four relational aspects of defence economics which deserve attention. The first is the relations between input and output. The logistical management and defence funding allocation system must be improved in order to achieve economic efficiency (*xiaoyi*) which implies the optimization rather than maximization of available resources. Secondly, mutual support between the military and local governments is essential but, he points out, that some civilian authorities have undermined the resources for military facilities. Thirdly, the strategy to build a civil-military integrated industrial base is validated by experience. Yet, some purely military production capacities should be maintained since these are cumulative and cannot be achieved overnight. Fourthly, despite the financial contribution of military-run businesses, they should be subordinated to military training.[13]

However, Wang Qikun's remarks focus primarily on the optimization of resources and the balance between elements within the national defence system but neglect those external to it. Externally, there is, again, mainly a problem of balance — the relationship of national defence *vis-à-vis* other elements of national power, especially economics. The policy of civil-military integration which had been inaugurated in the mid-1950s was soon reversed as a result of the adoption of a war preparation doctrine in the Cultural Revolution. From the mid-1960s to the 1970s, defence planning was divorced from and given excessive priority over civilian construction and economic development. Thus, to avoid repeating past mistakes and too radical a swing in the opposite direction, the post-Mao leadership has to find a balance between national defence modernization and the development of other elements of national power although economic growth has been made the "general interest" of the country. Its answer has been a return to civil-military integration.[14]

The balance, internal and external to the national defence system, must be set with a view to fulfil the system objective — the expansion of strategic choices. Precisely, it must, in the short term, enhance the military to deal with local war which is regarded by Chinese leaders as the most probable form of threats to national security. The next step is to go beyond immediate needs. National defence economic development should promote a flexible national defence system to handle a wide range of threats.[15] The achievement of this objective has to rely on rational resource allocations in the national defence system between expenditure on equipment and other defence spending, the production and R&D of equipment as well as key equipment and other equipment.[16] These balancing decisions are indicated in the defence budget.

II. The Defence Budget

Defence budgeting reflects the first level decisions — the grand strategy. The low priority accorded national defence in the Four Modernizations has led to a continuous decline in defence spending, both as a fraction of state expenditure and of GNP, until the fiscal year of 1989 as shown in Appendix C. Putting it in Weida and Gertcher's three-level analytical framework, the CMC makes the first level decisions and determines the guidelines for allocation priorities in the defence budget while second or intermediate level distributions of resources among different service arms are left to the three general departments of the PLA. Microscopic decisions, the third level, involve redistribution internal to each of the services and military units.[17]

Defence Spending Behaviour/Determinants

Many PLA senior officers have long complained about the continuous decrease since the 1980s in the defence budget in real terms. A cadre in the Navy Service Academy, in his survey of the defence budget in the 10 years since 1979, argues that the first phase, 1979–1983, had witnessed a normal decline but the second phase, 1984–1988, had seen excessive shrinking. With 1978 as base index 100, the defence budget declined, on average, by 1.6% annually in the first phase except in 1979 and 1980 (due to China's conflicts with Vietnam and the aftermath) but the budget decrease averaged 4% in the second phase.[18] Why did this happen? How does Beijing view the relationship between military spending and the national economy? What are the factors for China to consider when it makes its choice in defence budgeting?

Some defence analysts suggest a correlation between national wealth and force ratios in defence spending. James Payne puts forward an equation:

$$F = E*D$$

F is military forces, E military effort (i.e. "the impulse of sacrifice for military preparations") and D the discretionary resources available. E and D are regarded as independent variables: E is a psychological factor and D economic. According to this equation, "the wealthier a nation, the higher its force ratio."[19]

However, contrary to the economic development of the state, the Chinese troops, on the one hand, had grown dramatically by 3.6 million between 1959 and 1971 when the national economy was first struck by the Great Leap Forward and later disrupted by the Cultural Revolution; on the other, they have not become bigger despite the increasing GNP since the 1980s. China's defence burden (military expenditure as a fraction of GNP) has not varied with changes in GNP either. China's defence burden has followed a rather consistent pattern, particularly since 1979.

Defence spending has also not reflected the state's financial situation. The curves in the appended graphs indicate that China's defence budgeting has little inclination for annual adjustments but shows consistency over various periods. From the post-Korean War period to the 1960s, defence expenditure was maintained at almost the same level (Graph A) while its proportion in national expenditure (Graph D) had continuously declined with only one exceptional increase in 1955. In the 1960s, defence expenditure began to grow quickly until 1971 (Graph A) and its proportion in national expenditure was kept at a high level (Graph D). Only between 1972 and 1978 did an obvious w-shaped defence expenditure curve occur when dramatic changes took place in the state leadership. Yet, the very bad deficits in 1960, 1967 and 1975 did not affect military expenditure (Graphs A, C). Even a closer study of the defence spending behaviour after 1979 demonstrates similar consistency.[20] Defence expenditure has increased by two different set of paces in the periods 1982–1988 and 1989–1993, one gentle and other fast (Graphs 1, 2). While defence expenditure over national expenditure continuously declined in 1982–1986 and, after a rest in 1986–1987, picked up after 1988, the defence burden showed a similar trend (Graphs 5, 7). The changes in military spending, defence expenditure as a fraction of national expenditure and GNP, have not corresponded to the fluctuations in state budget balances and retail price levels (Graphs 4, 8). Particularly from 1988 onwards, China's defence burden and the share of defence spending in national expenditure has continued to climb although the pressure of price increases had been alleviated and came to a low 2.1% in 1990.

Three observations are derived from China's defence spending behaviour. Firstly, market economic theories have their limitations to interpret defence economic decisions. Such concepts as disposable income and the propensity to spend, which in Payne's equation are represented by D and E, cannot be applied without qualifications. Secondly, adjustments of defence expenditure (to reflect official retail price changes) would not help much in understanding the Chinese defence spending behaviour. It is, to a certain extent, due to the little changes prior to the 1980s. But, more importantly, the army has had its own channels of material supply and procurement pricing system.[21] And as the country gradually reforms its economic system, the special treatment for the military is also being removed bit by bit. Market forces will therefore have a greater impact on China's defence spending. Thirdly, China's defence spending is very much characterized by plans, not annual budgeting and fine adjustments. However, this does not imply that economic factors are irrelevant. While economics defines the "affordable force structure," it leaves to the politico-military leaders to assess the security environment and work out the "desirable force structure." The result is a compromised "producible force structure."[22] But since the state has "to produce, trade and accumulate efficiently, under a reasonable degree of security," and national defence is a costly means to ensure security, the government has to make its "first-level" decisions which are "analogized to insurance choices by individuals."[23] Defence spending is similar to buying insurance against possible damages in the failure of peace. In the final analysis, the compromise still depends on the leaders who weigh the economic factor and threat perception.

Despite James Payne's recognition of the psychology factor of defence planners, his definition of "military effort," variable E, is oversimplified. Professor William Shepherd proposes an alternative formula which exemplifies the role of threat perception in making defence economic choices.[24] Given E is the exposure to loss, p, the probability of loss, and I, the payment for loss avoidance or compensation, the maximum efficient defence spending should be:

$$I = p*E$$

China's defence budgeting has reflected the changing balances between economic factors and strategic considerations which include war preparations or real armed conflicts with foreign countries (see Graphs A–D). The high defence spending between 1951 and 1953 was obviously related to the Korean War. The stability in defence expenditure in the following years showed that nation building, particularly economic development, was dominating in the grand strategy. It was broken only after the removal of Peng Dehuai, who masterminded the first stage of China's defence modernization, and his replacement in 1959 by Lin Biao to take charge of the CMC. This change in military leadership and the calls for "rectifying the army and preparing for war" led to steep increases in defence spending in the 1960s. The country again entered a stage when the military factor, based on real and exaggerated threats, was dominant. Moreover, the military in the 1960s was gradually drawn into political power struggles and the state decision making apparatus.[25] That period saw a series of crises and military actions, the Sino-Indian War in 1962, the sour relations with the former Soviet Union which finally culminated in skirmishes in 1969, the sending of troops to Vietnam in 1965. It was not until 1972, after Lin Biao had died and China reorganized its military leadership, that the trend for high defence spending was reversed. Moreover, the "normalization" of relations with the United States, as signalled in the signing of the

U.S.–China joint communiqué in 1972 and the subsequent establishment of diplomatic relations in 1979, meant a less hostile international environment for China.[26] Although the Chinese fought the South Vietnamese over the Paracels in 1974, the armed conflict was of very low intensity and thus did not push up the cost.[27]

In the late 1970s, the balance again swung back in favour of economic development although, in 1979, military expenditure was increased to finance the Sino-Vietnamese border war. The Deng leadership adopted a grand strategy for defence modernization which significantly changed the pattern of defence spending — the second-level defence economics. It began to re-evaluate the security environment and modify (and eventually abandon in 1985) the doctrine which had prepared the country and the army to fight an "early, all-out nuclear war." Instead, the new grand strategy has emphasized balanced development of the various elements of national power and given economics the top priority. Step by step, the post-Mao leaders started a demobilization of military personnel and industrial resources by passing rules on the early retirement of veteran army cadres, personnel reductions and by implementing a civil-military integrated defence industrial policy.[28] Not surprisingly, defence expenditure as a proportion of national expenditure and GNP dropped steadily between 1982 and 1989 (see Graphs 5, 7).

However, dissatisfaction with the declining budget was also brewing among the military officers who had been eager to close the gap between the PLA and the armed forces of other great powers. As a result, defence expenditure was reset on a rising trend. A study conducted by National Defence University researchers prior to the military suppression of the democracy movement in 1989 had suggested that China's defence burden should not go below 2.2% while the proportion of defence spending to the state expediture should not be lower than 12%. After the military suppression, the army's bargaining position was strengthened because the incident showed that the party had to rely on the gun to maintain law and order. The increase in defence expenditure after the suppression may well be the result of plans to make up for the previous losses and accelerating defence modernization.[29] Besides, the preparations for post-Deng succession have added weight to the PLA as a political leaverage. In 1994, the army became more vocal in its demand for a stable share of the nation's economic growth. At the National People's Congress in March 1994, 104 military deputies signed a proposal which asked for a fixed proportion of defence expenditure to GNP.[30] Generals and soldiers also publicly expressed similar opinions.[31] The PLA was demanding that national defence should be given a larger weight in the accumulation of national power.

How much is enough? Many scholars and analysts would like to have an estimate of how much the Chinese government has "actually" been spending on national defence and how much the army is asking. But, before we understand the structure of the budget, any estimates would be meaningless and would not be accurate.

The Structure of the Budget

Defence budget (*guofangfei*) in China is a larger concept than military budget (*junfei*). While the latter is allocated by the logistics, the former includes also money spent on the militia and stockpiling of strategic materiel which are controlled by the state.[32] The structure of the Chinese defence budget is usually divided into 3 parts: costs in living expenses, maintenance expenses and development expenses.[33] But, based on the "Account Headings of the PLA Budget," the defence budget falls into 11 categories and 59 items. The 11 categories are: living (including salaries, wages and retirement pensions), official business, administration and operations, education and training, equipment procurement, logistical equipment procurement, maintenance and management of equipment, capital constructions (including civil air defence), scientific R&D, war preparation and others.[34] A comparison between these 11 categories and the items in Appendix 3a, however, shows that these two classifications are not conflicting.

No matter how the defence budget is categorized, the structure and allocation priorities in the defence budget have been a subject of complaint in the PLA. Military modernization has been hindered by a vicious circle: as a result of reliance on outdated weapons and quantitative superiority in manpower and equipment, expenses on maintenance and living take away an undue proportion of the budget leaving little for military hardware development. While replacement of old hardware is slow, the army has to use the obsolete equipment inventories which in turn consume a large share of the budget.[35]

Since 1978, the predominant position of living expenses in the defence budget has been mitigated only during China's armed conflicts with Vietnam which consumed a large amount of ammunition; expenses on equipment maintenance increased from 14.21% to 33% in the warfighting budget while living expenses decreased from 38.23% to 18%.[36] But the situation was seriously aggravated in the 1980s mainly for four reasons. Firstly, inflation pushed up expenses on food as well as on wages and allowances; after the pricing reforms, retail price increases went up to an unprecedented 8.8% in 1985 and the worst years were 1988 and 1989 when prices, according to official statistics, rose by 18.5% and 17.8% respectively. In view of the return of serious inflation in 1994, the CMC decided to increase, from 1 October 1994 on, the daily food allowance of each soldier by an average of one yuan. Assuming the number of soldiers at two million, the government would have to pay an extra 730 million yuan yearly.[37] Secondly, streamlining the military establishment and demobilization created a large number of retired or demobilized officers who continued to be fed from the PLA's coffers (see Table 1).[38] Thirdly, such extra burdens as kindergarten and primary school education for the officers' children was imposed on the army. Fourthly, since the introduction of volunteers to the army in 1978, their ratio *vis-à-vis* conscripts has increased; but volunteers, who are usually technical and skilled personnel, receive higher wages than conscripts (although the effect on defence spending is marginal).[39] By 1992, expenses on food have doubled since 1986, after four increments during the period.[40] It is estimated that over 35% of the defence budget is spent on personnel but less than 27% on the procurement of equipment.[41]

This dilemma in defence economics is the result of the loss of balance over the inner-directed and other-directed approaches as well as over resource allocations in the national defence system. The Maoist

Table 1. Number of Cadres Resettled/"Transferred" 1979-1994

(in Thousands)

Year	1979	1980	1981	1982	1983	1984	1985	1986
Number of Cadres	184	199	Unkn	42	76	75	134*	179
Year	1987	1988	1989	1990	1991	1992	1993	1994
Number of Cadres	130	75	40	25	27	30#	58#	50#

* discharged in 1985 but resettled in June 1986.
# People's Armed Police officers included.
Sources: Cadre Department, GPD, & Military Institution Studies Department, AMS. *Zhongguo renmin jiefangjun ganbu zhidu gaiyao* (An Outline of the PLA's Cadre System) (Beijing: Junshi kexue chubanshe, 1988), pp. 386-88. *Jiefangjun bao*, 5 May 1989, p. 1; 6 October 1990, p. 1; 15 December 1991, p. 1; 24 March 1992, p. 1; 19 May 1993, p. 1; 5 and 6 April 1994, p. 1. *Renmin ribao*, 7 May 1989, p. 2; 17 March 1991, p. 3.

inner-directed approach, which was incorporated in the People's War doctrine, relied heavily on quantitative superiority as the Red Army had done in the revolutionary war. This left the leadership in 1977 an inflated army. Besides, in view of American "hegemonism" and Soviet "social imperialism," industries had been moved to the strategic depth of interior China, the so called "third front."[42] To redress the imbalance in defence planning or, more specifically, the irrational structure of the defence budget, the new leadership under Deng Xiaoping had to adopt a new grand strategy and turn to structural reforms in the PLA for a way out of the difficult situation.

The plan was later elaborated by Yang Shangkun in 1985, "Through reform and streamlining, we should reduce the number of troops, eliminate obsolete equipment, slash expenses on food, clothing and daily expenses of personnel as well as on the maintenance of equipment. We should spend more money on the development of urgently needed weapons."[43] The high command expected that structural reform of the army would lead to a more balanced allocation of defence funds.

Structural Reforms and Demobilization: Defence Economic Implications

Demobilization includes the concepts of discharge (*tuiwu*), retirement (*tuixiu/lixiu*), and "transfer" (to civilian positions) (*zhuanye*). Except for discharge, which is applied to soldiers, the latter three concepts are used for officers. Serving officers who reach the retirement age may opt for retirement (*tuixiu*) while *lixiu* are retired officers who joined the army and "participated in revolution" prior to the establishment of the PRC. Officers who retire from or leave the army to reasons of force reduction (*caijun*) and health reasons are transferred to civilian assignments in state administrative and business units (*zhuanye*). It seems that demobilization is understood in China to include all forms of leaving the army.[44]

The PLA, which had been dramatically expanded in the 1970s to almost six million became a heavy burden on the national economy in the post-Mao era.[45] In his capacity as party CMC Vice-Chairman, Deng Xiaoping criticized the PLA in an enlarged CMC meeting of 1975 as overstaffed, lax, arrogant, extravagant, lazy. After the fall of the Gang of Four, a plenary session of the CMC in 1977 confirmed Deng Xiaoping's remarks in 1975 and drew up "A Plan for the Readjustment of the Military Organisation." A series of streamlining measures began with focus on administrative units (*jiguan*) at various levels and their subordinate organs. Then in an enlarged meeting of the Standing Committee of the CMC, Deng Xiaoping made clear the interactions between the economic and military elements, and explicitly called for reductions in military expenditure in the interest of economic reforms:[46]

> Our considerable spending on the military is not good for national construction; overstaffing in the army also hinders the modernisation of equipment. Our policy is to use the money saved from reductions in army personnel to replace old equipment with new one.... During this period, we should do our best to reduce military expenditure in order to strengthen national construction.

The climax of streamlining came in 1985 when a demobilization of one million servicemen was announced at an enlarged CMC conference and this was reportedly completed in two years.[47] The demobilization has annually saved 2.14 billion yuan of living expenses.[48]

The lessons of the Gulf War against Iraq in 1991 intensified the quantity versus quality debate which had begun among Chinese military leaders in the late 1980s. Those who favoured a smaller but better equipped standing army gradually gained the upper hand.[49] At an enlarged CMC conference in April 1992, the military leadership decided on a further reduction of 300,000–500,000 troops.[50] This demobilization programme was on the one hand a triumph of the "qualitative development school" and, on the other, of the grand strategy which gave the development of national power top priorities. The defence forces had to sacrifice numbers for improvement in the quality of their equipment.

But it is recognized that force reduction or demobilization is not a panacea for the problem of an unbalanced budget and that its effect will be slow to come. It takes time for the money saved from personnel reductions to be relocated for procurement or R&D purposes.[51] Besides, at least in a short period of time after demobilization, the burden of personnel on national defence will actually increase. Soldiers receive demobilization allowances (*fuyuan zizhujin*) from their army units, usually the companies, according to their rank and seniority. And, officers, subject to individual qualifications, receive the benefits of retirement or transfer. Retired officers (*tuixiu*) are given pensions; based on a circular issued by the CMC and State Council in 1987, those who have served in the army for 10 years or less get 70% of their salaries and others who have served for more than 10 years get 1% more for each additional year up to 90% of their salaries.

They also receive a lump sum for resettlement subsidies and living subsidies as well as other allowances. Retired veteran officers (*lixiu*) receive monthly living allowances and other subsidies for such items as resettlement, transportation and clothing. Some of them are also provided with "retired cadres apartments" (*ganxiushuo*) which are regimental level units and number over 1,100 across the country in 1992. Whereas, transferred officers are given living allowances and demobilized allowances. Of course, when they are transferred to civilian administrations, these ex-officers receive salaries according to their new jobs. The relatives of demobilized officers also get various forms of subsidies.[52]

The effectiveness of force reduction to save money from personnel is quite limited, given the low wages and salaries in the Chinese military which provides its soldiers with free food, bedding and clothing. Besides, demobilization itself incurs costs in resettlement. In the PLA which combines conscription with voluntary military service, the conscript earns the least. But a volunteer does not fare much better. The highest monthly wage, grade 8, for voluntary service is 108 yuan and the lowest, grade 1, is only 36 yuan (see Appendix E).[53] In February 1980, the CMC introduced a "structural salary system" (*jiegou gongzi zhi*). From 1980 to 1989, there have been reforms in the officer's salary structure in 1980, 1985, 1988 and 1989. In 1985, seniority was made a formal component of the officer's salary. As of 1989, the proportion of "post salary" (*zhiwu gongzi*) accounted for 70% of the total salary, "ranking salary," (*junxian gongzi*) 21% and "seniority salary," 9% (see Appendix D1 and D2 for the salary scale). Despite these reforms, the salary of an officer had increased by 29% only between 1985 and 1988.[54] Since servicemen do not get much from the army, their reductions of course do not contribute much to redress the bias in the budget. Moreover, large scale personnel reductions are limited by the minimum requirement for maintaining a credible defence force and the national economic capacity to absorb the demobilized soldiers. Therefore, demobilization must be coordinated with other reforms in the army, such as the military hardware R&D and production, in order to optimise the use of the defence budget.

The Problem of Reading the Budget

Since "defence burden" is defence expenditure expressed as a proportion of GNP, analysis of defence spending appears to require only some mathematical exercise. However, the use of defence burden for cross-national comparison is made difficult by the problems of defining and measuring the numerator (defence spending) and the denominator (GNP).[55] The scope and content of the outlay vary among countries and this problem has led to controversies over the reading and interpretation of the defence burden. Of course, the unavailability of information further complicates analysis.[56] Therefore, there are many approaches to measure and read defence spending and a discussion of defence economics in terms of the defence burden must start with a clear definition of the structure of the budget.

The "factor cost" method has been used by the US Central Intelligence Agency to assign US prices to all military goods and services consumed. By contrast, the "residual" approach measures the defence budget by counting the estimated value of all industrial production and then subtracting that used for civilian purpose.[57] These methods, if applied to China, will certainly cause double distortions, firstly in the estimate of the costs and secondly in the conversion of Chinese costs to US currency.[58]

Added to the problem of measurement is that of content. Different countries and major international organizations have their own definitions for the inputs and not necessarily for purposes of concealment.[59] For example, expenditure on stockpiles of strategic materials, which forms part of the Chinese budget, is not counted by the Stockholm International Peace Research Institute (SIPRI).[60]

The Chinese Hidden Defence Budget

In China, there are four main sources, both quantifiable and non-quantifiable, of the hidden defence budget and these sources are far from exhaustive. The first is military spending placed under civilian categories in the state budget. The second is the distorted pricing system for the production of military equipment. The third is military expenses funded by civilians under various names and in various forms. The fourth includes the income earned by military economic activities and other activities that defray costs in the army.

The first source is the result of different definitions, as discussed above, but also of deliberate attempts to hide real military spending. This part of the hidden budget is, in other words, both intentional and otherwise. In China, the defence budget does not include spending on foreign military assistance, civil air defence, or space and atomic projects for military use. The funds for the paramilitary People's Armed Police (PAP), which was established in 1983, is put under administrative expenditure. In the 1992 budget, "Air Traffic Control under Military Aviation" was put in the section of "Other Expenses" while, in the 1993 budget, "Expenses on PAP Capital Construction" came under "Capital Construction," and "Pension for Retired Servicemen" under "Pension."[61] Expenses on the militia are split between the central and local administrations.[62]

The procurement prices of military equipment have been a major source of hidden defence budget. As James Payne argues, "to the extent that coercion is used to command resources for military purposes, the defence burden statistic will understate the true military effort."[63] It is particularly true in China where transactions between army consumers on the one hand and military hardware producers and R&D units on the other are under strict control by the state. The PLA's expenses on procurement do not reflect the actual value because pricing is distorted by political measures. The procurement prices have long been set at 5% profit on top of production cost although the reforms in recent years have gradually led to divergent pricing systems.[64]

In the course of national defence modernization, the defence system has been moving toward greater civil-military integration in order to accumulate national power and rationalize the structure of the defence industrial base. The differentiation between investment in civilian and military projects has become blurred as in, for example: the construction of the 73,000 km border defence road network, the army's first optical fibre communication trunk line in Shenyang, and the Shenyang-Dalian Highway which can be used as airstrip for combat aircraft.[65] Civil-military integration is also implemented in army logistics. The Nanjing Military Region established a new logistical system in June 1992 for joint supply of universal automobile parts by the army and localities.[66]

Additionally, given the peculiar civil-military tradition in China, financial contributions from civilian administrations in the name of "cherishing the army and giving preferential treatment to their relatives" (*yongjun youshu*) are not revealed in the annual defence budget. The people or local governments may provide military service allowances, various kinds of subsidies, free housing, transport, materials and other gifts. For instance, in 1987–1992, the Liaoning government alone paid 9.2 million yuan of subsidies, supplied 2,497 housing units and waived 1.4 million yuan of taxes and 1.37 million yuan of transport expenses.[67] However similar figures are not always made available by local governments. This has made the quantification of this source of defence funding extremely difficult.

Economic production has been one of the three main responsibilities of the PLA (the other two being warfighting and mass work). Since the founding of the PRC in 1949, the army has taken part in agricultural production. Following various reforms, the General Logistics Department adopted a strategy for high yield, high economic efficiency and small manpower in a conference on agricultural sideline production in 1982.[68] In 1982–1991, the army produced 5.5 million tons of grain, 0.15 million tons of oil, 0.68 million tons of meat and 6.8 million tons of vegetables. In 1992 alone, sideline production was valued at 580 million yuan.[69] This agricultural production certainly saved a large sum of living expenses.

However, expense reduction is not enough and extra funding sources must be explored. Lucrative arms sales have formed one of the major extra-budgetary funding sources for the Chinese army. Already in the 1980s, Beijing revised its arms transfer policy. The CMC in 1980 approved the "Request for Instructions on Military Assistance and Arms Sales," by which military assistance was administered by the General Staff Department and sales of weapons by individual defence industrial ministries under the coordination of the then National Defence Industry Office.[70] By 1985–1989, China had exported about US$7 billion worth of weaponry.[71] The arms transfer agreements between China and the developing countries in 1990 were valued US$2.59 billion and China became the third largest conventional arms exporter to these countries.[72] The military trading companies appear to have high autonomy over the profits. The General Logistics Department's Xinxing Corporation has been able to retain 100% of its foreign exchange earnings.[73] However, the role of arms export as a funding source for military modernization should not be exaggerated. Given the low price of Chinese weapons, production costs, and the number of government and military agencies which share the profits, the PLA will not have much left.[74] Other funding sources include army production and business activities.

At first, the military production and business units, after providing services to the army, utilized their residual capacity to make money. However, in the 1980s, they developed rapidly and some of them operated as commercial units; "getting subsidies from the market" became the mainstream opinion.[75] One of the famous legends was the First Military Medical University in Guangzhou which ran a pharmaceutical factory and a profit-making clinic. By 1990, the output value per worker in the factory reached 320,000 yuan and the clinic also earned some HK$40 million in foreign exchange.[76] In 1991, production and business units in the Xinjiang

Military District alone achieved an output value of 396 million yuan and earned 108 million yuan. It was also reported in early 1993 that the PLA owned about 10,000 businesses which had an annual output value of over 30 billion yuan and an annual profit of five billion yuan.[77] There seem to be arrangements for profit retention in the military and the retained profits are used in individual military units at their own discretion.[78]

Although this extra-budgetary income has improved the financial situation of the army, the military involvement in business activities has soon led to problems in civil-military relations, administration, morale and corruption. There have been more and more reports about conflicts between army units and civilians, soldiers breaching discipline and committing "economic crimes." Political work in recent years has been to ensure not simply ideological orthodoxy, but dedication to military professionalism and clean practices. Military legal work has also been promoted to combat various malpractices. But these efforts have appeared too weak in the face of the shocks brought by Deng Xiaoping's economic reforms.[79]

III. Conclusion

Since the defence budget is determined by the accumulative results of "first level decisions" which define resources available for national defence, Chinese politico-military leaders will continue to face two important problems in the years to come. One is the reform of a rational budget structure, which allows the allocation of more funds to military hardware development and acquisition without hurting individual interests. The other is the balance between national economic growth and the build-up of a modern national defence system.

Despite structural reforms and demobilizations since the late 1970s, the PLA remains a huge army. The high command has to make a difficult choice between feeding and equipping its soldiers. On this question, the CMC has voted for the former.[80] This policy implies that stability and morale are given priority over the procurement of equipment. The significant increases in the defence budget since 1990 have been largely a kind of compensation — for soldiers who have lost the opportunity to profit from the economic boom and for the military for its subservience to economic development. Thus, the focus of analyzing the Chinese defence budget should not be on the increases *per se*, but on the movement among the military to urge a link between the budget and GNP growth. The PLA is not content with adjustments and compensations; it demands a stable and long-term increase in funding. Obviously, it has learnt how to benefit from the intricate relationship between economics and national defence.

On this question, Deng Xiaoping has answered with a grand strategy which urges civil-military integration. The military is encouraged to alleviate its financial constraints at the third level of defence economic activities — logistics, including the use of dual-purpose infrastructure and organization of supply networks which rely on civilian resources. Since these are at best mid- to long-term measures, the political leaders have also devised expedient policies. Extra-budgetary channels have been expanded to raise funds and have proved effective. A direct result of a growing hidden defence budget is increasing difficulties in reading the Chinese budget. But China has to pay its costs also. On the one hand, civil-military integration requires an efficient mobilization system to convert and organize resources for national defence use;[81] on the other, low morale and corruption has begun to plague the PLA and arouse concern. The problem is that the Chinese national defence system is slow to adapt to these new challenges — the accounting and auditing systems are obsolete, civil-military relations require re-definitions, political education has proved to be ineffective, inflective, and the mobilization system is underdeveloped. However, as the army acquires a taste for the market economy, it will be difficult for the government to reverse the trend.

When the buck is eventually passed back to the "first-level" decision makers, the real problem in China's defence budgeting becomes clear. It is the political leadership itself. Without changes in the highly personalized authority structure, stable reforms will be impossible; not until the regime can rule legitimately without reliance on coercion, can a rational balance between national defence and economics be found. In the final analysis, the three levels of defence economics are closely integrated; national defence cannot be divorced from other elements of national power, politics and economics. The interaction of these factors will continue to shape the course of China's national defence modernization.

Appendix A: China's Defence Budget Allocations

Category	Proportion	Items
Development expense	30%	Scientific research and development Equipment and weaponry procurement Logistical equipment procurement Education and training Military installations Others
Maintenance expense	33%	Equipment and weaponry maintenance Fuel Hygiene and medicine Political work Management of material Operating cost Official business External relations Others
Living expense	36%	Salaries and wages Allowances Food Welfare Bedding and clothing Others

Sources: Jiang Baoqi (chief ed.), *Zhongguo guofang jingji fazhan zhanlüe yanjiu* (A Study on China's National Defence Economic Development Strategy) (Beijing: Guofang daxue chubanshe, 1990), p. 51. *Dangdai* (Contemporary Weekly), Hong Kong, 31 March 1990, p. 17.

Appendix B: China's Defence Spending 1950–1978

(in billion RMB)

Year	DE	Change over previous year	NE (balance)	DE over NE	Social product	Retail price changes
1950	2.801	N/A	6.81 (–0.29)	41.13%	68.30	N/A
1951	5.264	87.93%	12.25 (+1.07)	42.97%	82.00	12.2%
1952	5.784	9.88%	17.60 (+0.77)	32.86%	101.50	–0.4%
1953	7.538	30.33%	22.01 (+0.27)	34.25%	124.10	3.4%
1954	5.813	–22.88%	24.63 (+1.61)	23.60%	134.60	2.3%
1955	6.500	11.82%	26.93 (+0.27)	24.14%	141.50	1.0%
1956	6.117	–5.89%	30.57 (–1.83)	20.01%	163.90	0%
1957	5.511	–9.91%	30.42 (+0.60)	18.12%	160.60	1.5%
1958	5.000	–9.27%	40.94 (–2.18)	12.21%	213.80	0.2%
1959	5.800	16.00%	55.29 (–6.57)	10.49%	254.80	0.9%
1960	5.800	0.00%	65.41 (–8.19)	8.87%	267.90	3.1%
1961	5.000	–13.79%	36.70 (–1.11)	13.62%	197.80	16.2%
1962	5.694	13.88%	30.53 (+0.83)	18.65%	180.00	3.8%
1963	6.642	16.65%	33.96 (+0.26)	19.56%	195.60	–5.9%
1964	7.286	9.70%	39.90 (+0.05)	18.26%	226.80	–3.7%
1965	8.676	19.08%	46.63 (+0.70)	18.61%	269.50	–2.7%
1966	10.101	16.42%	54.16 (+1.72)	18.65%	306.20	–0.3%
1967	8.302	–17.81%	44.19 (–2.25)	18.79%	277.40	–0.7%
1968	9.409	13.33%	35.98 (+0.14)	26.15%	264.80	0.1%
1969	12.618	34.11%	52.59 (+0.09)	23.99%	318.40	–1.1%
1970	14.526	15.12%	64.94 (+1.35)	22.37%	380.00	–0.2%
1971	16.947	16.67%	73.22 (+1.26)	23.15%	420.30	–0.7%
1972	15.939	–5.95%	76.64 (+0.02)	20.80%	439.60	–0.2%
1973	14.539	–8.78%	80.93 (+0.04)	17.96%	477.60	0.6%
1974	13.339	–8.25%	79.08 (–0.76)	16.87%	485.90	0.5%
1975	14.246	6.80%	82.09 (–0.53)	17.35%	537.90	0.2%
1976	13.445	–5.62%	80.62 (–2.96)	16.68%	543.30	0.3%
1977	14.904	10.85%	84.35 (+3.09)	17.67%	600.30	2.0%
1978	16.784	12.61%	111.10 (+1.02)	15.11%	358.81	0.7%

Note: DE = Defence Expenditure
NE = National Expenditure
Source: *Zhongguo tongji nianjian* (Statistical Yearbook of China, 1993) (Beijing: Zhongguo tongji chubanshe, 1993), pp. 215, 223.

Graph A. Defence Expenditure 1950–1978

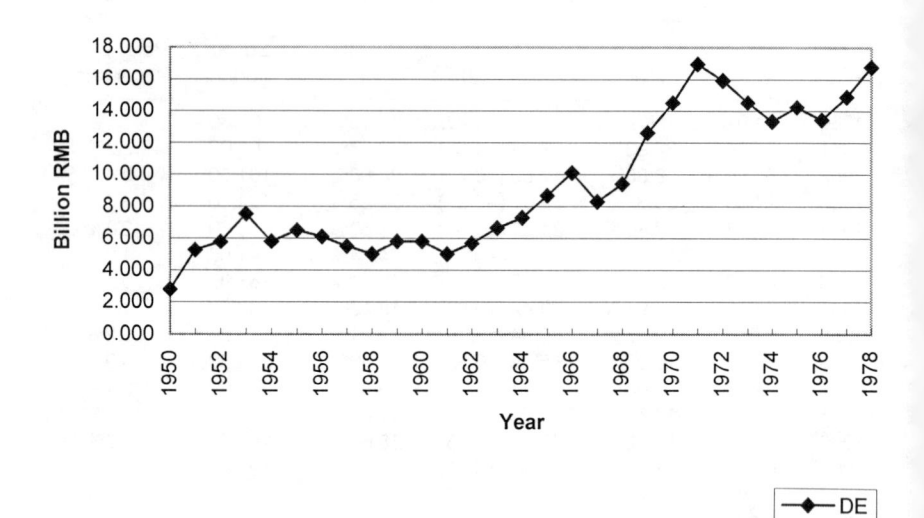

→ DE

Graph B. National Expenditure 1950–1978

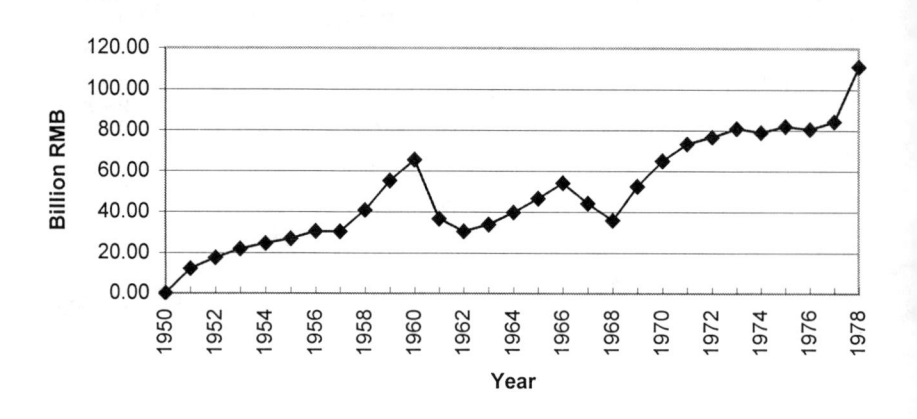

→ NE

China's Defence Budgeting: Structure and Dynamics

Graph C. State Budget Balance 1950–1978

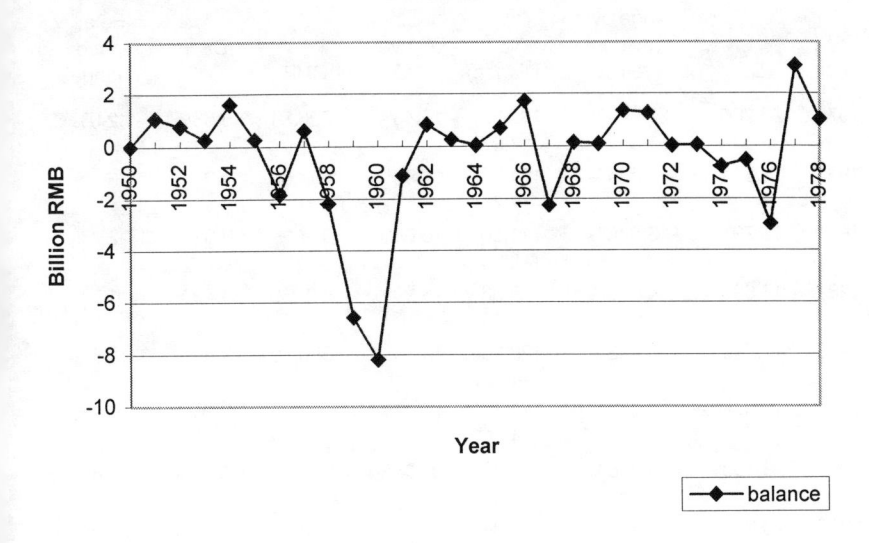

Graph D. Defence Expenditure over National Expenditure 1950–1978

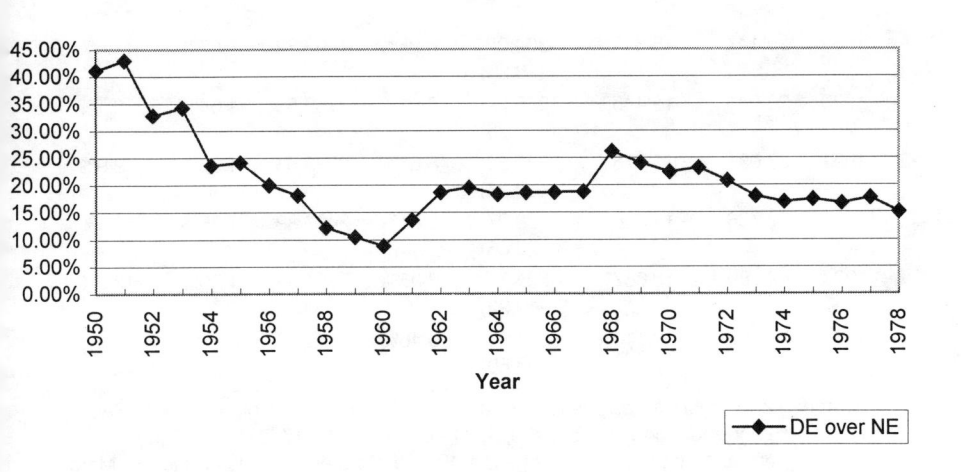

Appendix C: China's Defence Spending since 1979

(in billion RMB)

Year	DE	Change over previous year	NE (balance)	DE over NE	GNP	DE in GNP	Retail price changes
1979	22.266	32.662%	127.39 (−17.07)	17.48%	398.81	5.58%	2.0%
1980	19.384	−12.944%	121.27 (−12.75)	15.98%	447.00	4.34%	6.0%
1981	16.797	−13.346%	111.50 (−2.55)	15.06%	477.30	3.52%	2.4%
1982	17.635	4.989%	115.33 (−2.93)	15.29%	519.30	3.40%	1.9%
1983	17.713	0.442%	129.25 (−4.35)	13.70%	580.90	3.05%	1.5%
1984	18.076	2.049%	154.64 (−4.45)	11.69%	696.20	2.60%	2.8%
1985	19.153	5.958%	184.48 (+2.16)	10.38%	855.76	2.24%	8.8%
1986	20.075	4.814%	233.08 (−7.06)	8.61%	969.63	2.07%	6.0%
1987	20.962	4.418%	244.85 (−7.96)	8.56%	1130.10	1.85%	7.3%
1988	21.800	3.998%	270.66 (−7.86)	8.05%	1401.82	1.56%	18.5%
1989	25.147	15.353%	304.02 (−9.23)	8.27%	1599.33	1.57%	17.8%
1990	29.031	15.445%	345.22 (−13.96)	8.41%	1769.53	1.64%	2.1%
1991	33.031	13.778%	381.36 (−20.27)	8.66%	2023.63	1.63%	2.9%
1992	37.786	14.396%	438.97 (−23.66)	8.61%	2437.89	1.55%	5.4%
1993	42.580	12.687%	528.74 (−19.92)	8.05%	3134.23	1.36%	13.2%
1994	55.060	29.310%	581.98 (−63.80)	9.46%	4380.00	1.26%	N/A

Source: *Zhongguo tongji nianjian* (Statistical Yearbook of China, 1994) (Beijing: Zhongguo tongji chubanshe, 1994), pp. 32, 213, 217, 231. The figures of DE, NE and Retail price changes in 1994 are based on *Jingji ribao*, 21 March 1995, pp. 2–3.

China's Defence Budgeting: Structure and Dynamics

Graph 1. Defence Expenditure since 1979

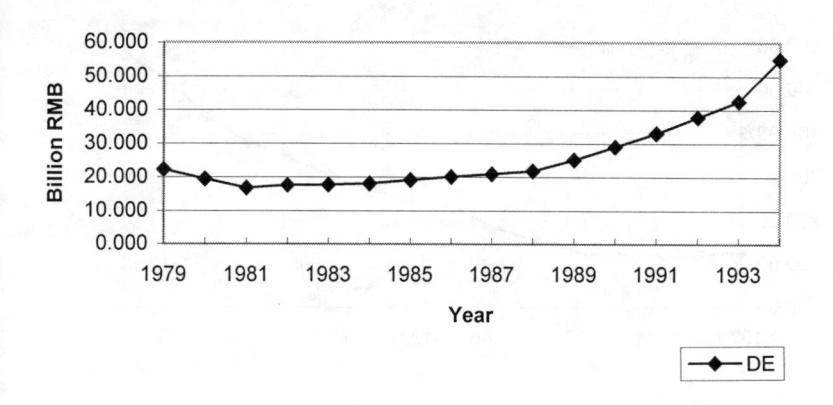

Graph 2. Defence Expenditure Changes since 1979

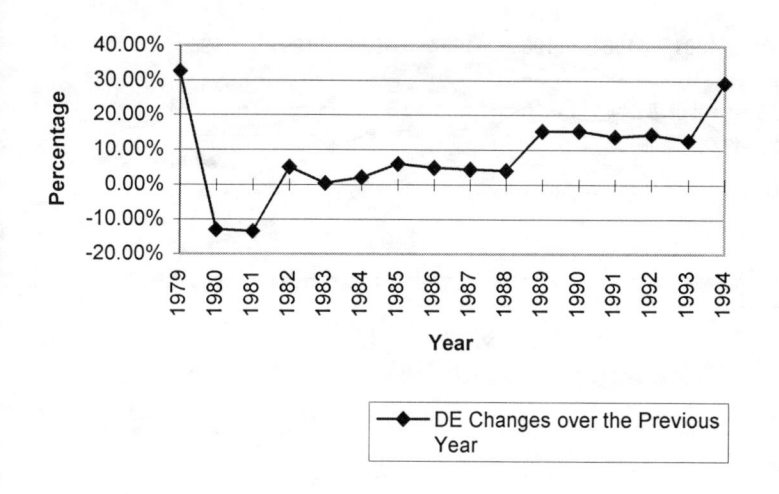

Graph 3. National Expenditure since 1979

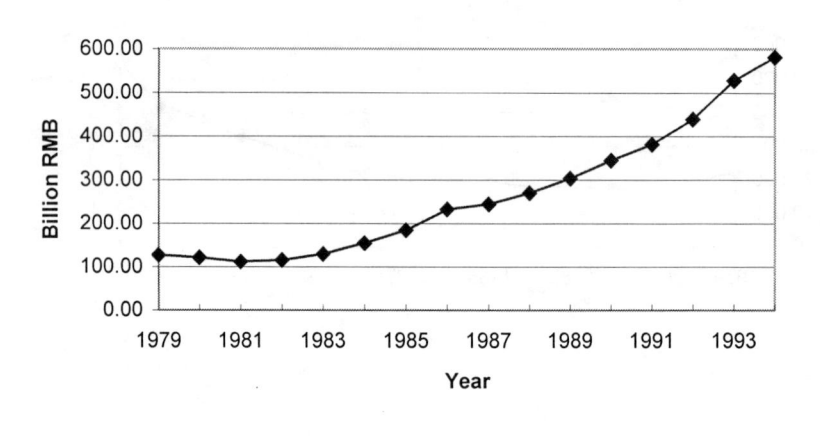

Graph 4. State Budget Balance since 1979

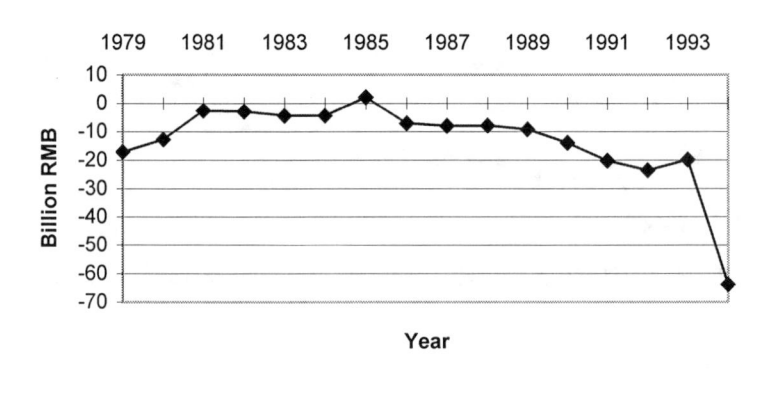

Graph 5. Defence Expenditure over National Expenditure since 1979

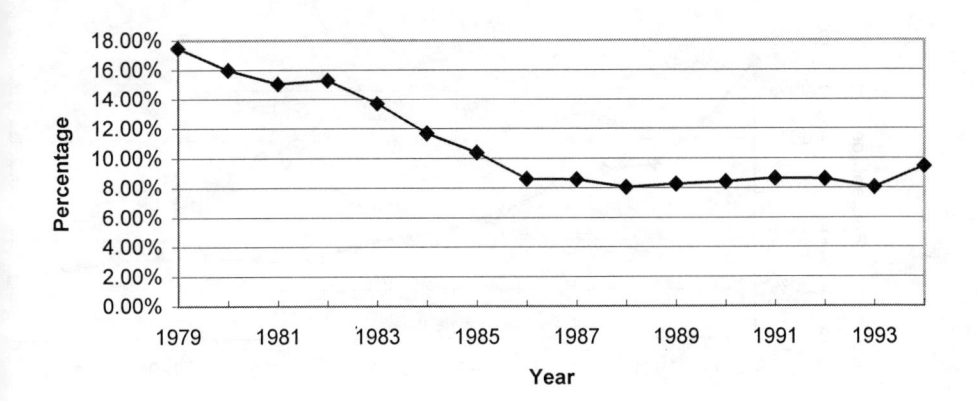

Graph 6. Gross National Product since 1979

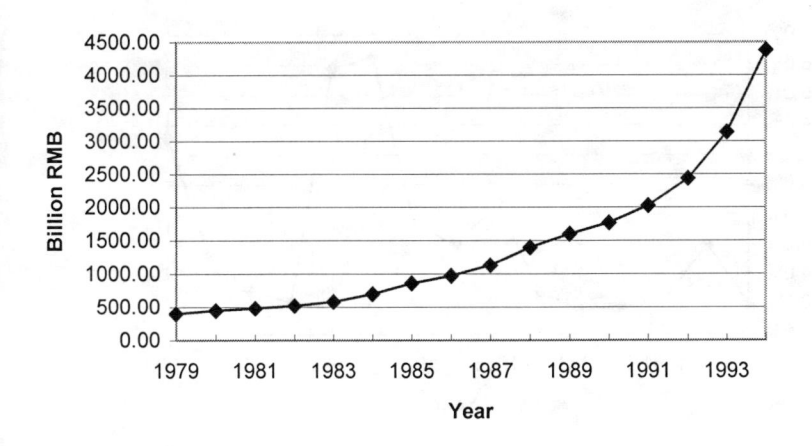

Graph 7. Defence Burden since 1979

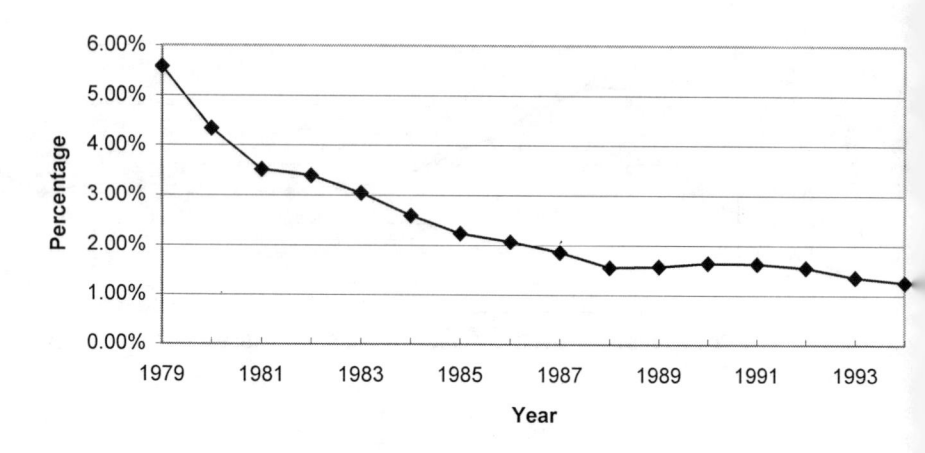

— DE over GNP

Graph 8. Retail Price Changes since 1979

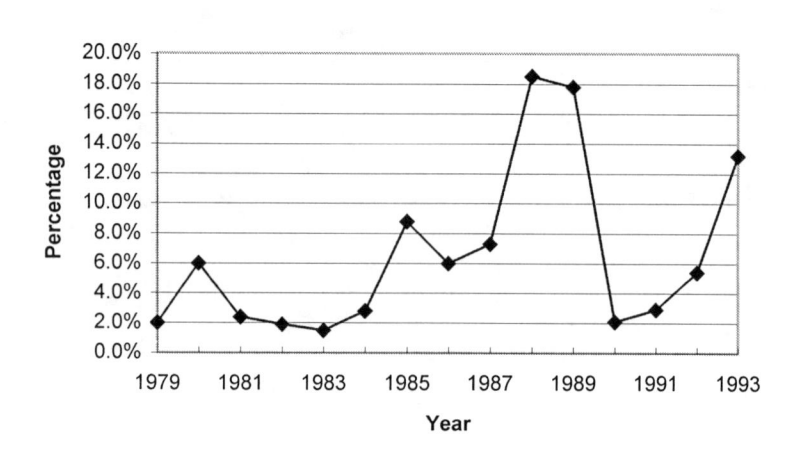

— Retail Price Changes

Appendix D1: Salaries Scale of Officers as Effective from 1 July 1985

	Post salaries			Ranking salaries	
Post (or Equivalent)	Technical/ Art grading	Sport grading	Monthly salary (*yuan*)	Executive grading	Monthly salary (*yuan*)
CMC chairman/ vice-chairmen			340	Grades 1, 2 and 3	240
				Grade 4	200
CMC members			230	Grade 5	184
MR commands	Grade 1		206	Grade 6	170
				Grade 7	156
				Grade 8	144
MR deputies/ Corps commands	Grade 2		186		
Deputies	Grade 3		170	Grade 9	134
				Grade 10	126
				Grade 11	118
				Grade 12	110
Army commands	Grade 4		156		
Deputies	Grade 5	Grade 1	143		
Division commands	Grade 6	Grade 2	130	Grade 13	102
				Grade 14	94
				Grade 15	86
				Grade 16	78
Deputies	Grade 7	Grade 3	117		
Regiment commands	Grade 8	Grade 4	105		
Deputies	Grade 9	Grade 5	94	Grade 17	70
Battalion commands	Grade 10	Grade 6	83	Grade 18	63
Deputies	Grade 11	Grade 7	74	Grade 19	56
Company commands	Grade 12	Grade 8	66	Grade 20	50
Deputies	Grade 13	Grade 9	58	Grade 21	44
Platoon commands	Grade 14	Grade 10	50	Grade 22	39
Deputies	Grade 15	Grade 11	42	Grade 23	34

* Seniority Allowance: 0.5 yuan for each service year with a maximum of 40 years. For active officers, their seniority will be counted until June 1985.

Source: Cadre Department, GPD, and Military Institution Studies Department, AMS, *Zhongguo renmin jiefangjun ganbu zhidu gaiyao* (An Outline of the PLA's Cadre System) (Beijing: Junshi kexue chubanshe, 1988), p. 313.

Appendix D2: Revised Salaries Scale of Non-Commissioned Officers*

	Post Salaries		Ranking salaries	
Post (or equivalent)	Technical grading	Monthly salaries (yuan)	Rank	Monthly salaries (yuan)
Battalion commands	Grade 10	121–175 (6 Increments)	Lieutenant-Colonel	46
Deputies	Grade 11	110–160 (9 Increments)	Major	40
Company commands	Grade 12	105–146 (8 Increments)	Captain	34
Deputies	Grade 13	95–133 (8 Increments)	Lieutenant	29
Platoon commands	Grade 14	85–121 (8 Increments)	Second Lieutenant	24

* The source did not specify when this salaries scale was effective but claimed that it was "recent." Since the book was published in June 1993, it can be assumed that the data were based on information in 1992.

Source: Zhang Zhujun, *Jundui jicheng zhengzhi gongzuo zhinan* (A Guide to Political Work at Grassroots Army Units) (Shandong: Shandong daxue chubanshe, 1993), pp. 201–202.

Appendix E: Wage Scale for Volunteers as in 1989

(in RMB)

Gradings	1	2	3	4	5	7	8
Wages	36	44	54	64	74	96	108

Source: Shi Shanyu and Wang Zhiqiang (chief eds.), *Junren wanshi wen* (Questions and Answers for the Servicemen) (Beijing: Changzheng chubanshe, 1989), p. 84.

Notes

1. William J. Weida and Frank L. Gertcher, *The Political Economy of National Defense* (Boulder, CO: Westview Press, 1987), p. 6.
2. John Kenneth Galbraith, *Economics and the Public Purpose* (Middlesex: Penguin, 1975), pp. 199, 315.
3. *Jiefangjun bao*, 17 April 1991, p. 3. Gao Dianzhi, *Zhongguo guofang jingji guanli yanjiu* (A Study of China's Defence Economic Management) (Beijing: Junshi kexue chubanshe, 1991), p. 1.
4. Karen Berney, "Aspects of Modernisation," in *Chinese Defence Policy*, edited by Gerald Segal and William T. Tow (London: Macmillan, 1984), p. 145.
5. Paul H. B. Godwin, *The Chinese Communist Armed Forces* (Maxwell Air Force Base, Alabama: Air University Press, June 1988), pp. 37, 46. Michael D. Swaine, *The Military and Political Succession in China: Leadership, Institutions, Beliefs* (Santa Monica, California: RAND, December 1992), p. 15.
6. CMC Legal System Bureau, *Zhonghua renmin gongheguo junshi fagui huibian* (A Compilation of the People's Republic of China Military Legislation, 1949–1988) (Beijing: Zhongguo minzhu fazhi chubanshe, 1991), p. 25. *Renmin ribao*, 11 June 1985, p. 1.
7. Xie Guang (chief ed.), *Dangdai Zhongguo de guofang keji shiye* (Contemporary China's National Defence Science and Technology Undertakings), Vol. 1 (Beijing: Dangdai zhongguo chubanshe, 1992), p. 176. Paul Humes Folta, *From Swords to Plowshares? Defense Industry Reform in the PRC* (Boulder, CO: Westview Press, 1992), p. 66.
8. Huai Guomo, "A Decade of China's Defence Industrial Conversion," *Conmilit*, No. 165 (October 1990), p. 22.
9. Michael Swaine (Note 5), pp. 18 and 172.
10. Wang Chengbin (chief ed.), *Deng Xiaoping xiandai junshi lilun yu shijian* (Deng Xiaoping's Modern Military Theory and Its Practice) (Nanchang: Jiangxi renmin chubanshe, 1991), pp. 1 and 73.
11. Ngok Lee, *China's Defence Modernisation and Military Leadership* (Canberra: Australian National University Press, 1989), pp. 224–26, 258.
12. Deng Xiaoping, *Build Socialism with Chinese Characteristics*, (rev. ed.; Hong Kong: Joint Publishing Co., 1987), p. 78. Ku Guisheng, "Deng Xiaoping guofang jingji sixiang chutan" (A Preliminary Research on Deng Xiaoping's Defence Economic Thinking), *Junshi jingji yanjiu* (Military Economics Studies), No. 2 (1988), pp. 8–9.
13. *Jiefangjun bao*, 17 August 1990, p. 2.
14. Jiang Baoqi (chief ed.), *Zhongguo guofang jingji fazhan zhanlüe yanjiu* (A Study of China's National Defence Economic Development Strategy)

(Beijing: Guofang daxue chubanshe, 1990), pp. 13–16. Sun Zhenhuan, *Zhongguo guofang jingji jianshe* (China's National Defence Economic Development) (Beijing: Junshi kexue chubanshe, 1991), pp. 155–62.
15. Jiang Siyi, *Mao Zedong junshi sixiang lun — jieshao Mao Zedong junshi wenji* (Discussions of Mao Zedong's Military Thinking — An Introduction to *A Collection of Military Works by Mao Zedong*) (Beijing: Zhonggong zhongyang dangxiao chubanshe, 1994), p. 239.
16. Jiang Baoqi (chief ed.) (Note 14), p. 18. Sun Zhenhuan (Note 14), pp. 162–66. *Guofang fazhan zhanlüexue jiaocheng* (A Course on National Defence Development Strategy, hereafter as *National Defence Development Strategy*) (Beijing: Guofang daxue chubanshe, 1990), p. 231.
17. Liu Qing, "Youhua guofang jingfei fenpei jiegou, tigao junshi xiaoyi" (Improve the Defence Funding Allocation Structure, Increase Military Efficiency), *Lun woguo xianjieduan guofang jingji wenti* (Our Defence Economic Problems at the Present Stage, hereafter as *Defence Economic Problems*) (Beijing: Guofang daxue chubanshe, 1990), pp. 230, 233 and 234.
18. Chen Bingfu, "Zhongguo guoqu shinian guofangfei jingji fenxi" (An Economic Analysis of China's Defence Expenditure in the Last Ten Years), *Jingji yanjiu* (Economics Research), No. 6 (1990), p. 77.
19. James L. Payne, *Why Nations Arm* (Oxford: Basil Blackwell, 1989), p. 37.
20. Deng Xiaoping was reinstated in 1977 and became the paramount leader in 1978. But, since the defence budget is usually planned one year in advance, the effect of Deng's military policies on defence spending was reflected only in the 1979 budget.
21. The author wishes to thank Dr Tsui Kai-yuen for pointing this out to me. Gao Dianzhi, *Zhongguo guofang jingji guanli yanjiu* (A Study of China's Defence Economic Management) (Beijing: Junshi kexue chubanshe, 1991), p. 48.
22. Richard J. Latham, "Implications of the Post-Mao Reforms on the Chinese Defense Industries," in *China's Military Reforms: International and Domestic Implications*, edited by Charles D. Lovejoy, Jr., and Bruce W. Watson (Boulder, CO: Westview Press, 1986), p. 40.
23. Murray Weidenbaum, *Small Wars, Big Defense: Paying for the Military After the Cold War* (New York: Oxford University Press, 1992), pp. 20 and 21. William G. Shepherd, "The Economics of Arms Race: Self Interest and National Security," *American Economic Review*, May 1988, p. 52.
24. William G. Shepherd (Note 23), p. 52.
25. Li Junting et al., *Zhongguo wuzhuang liliang tonglan, 1949–1989* (Survey of China's Armed Forces, 1949–1989) (Beijing: Renmin chubanshe, 1990), pp. 408–12.
26. Jonathan D. Pollack, "China and the Global Strategic Balance," in *China's Foreign Relations in the 1980s*, edited by Harry Harding (New Haven: Yale University Press, 1984), p. 153. Liu Pei, "Zhongmei jianjiao yilai de liangguo

anquan guanxi" (Sino-American Security Relations since the Establishment of Diplomatic Relations), *Zhongmei guanxi shinian* (A Decade of Sino-American Relations) (Beijing: Shangwu yinshuguan, 1989), pp. 53 and 54.
27. Military History Studies Department, Academy of Military Science (ed.), *Zhongguo renmin zhiyuanjun kangmei yuanzhao zhanshi* (A History of the Chinese People's Volunteers 'Resist the United States and Support Korea' War) (Beijing: Junshi kexue chubanshe, 1990). Li Ke and Hau Shengzhang, *Wenhua dageming zhong de renmin jiefangjun* (The PLA in the "Cultural Revolution") (Beijing: Zhonggong dangshi ziliao chubanshe, 1989), pp. 226, 352, 364. Zhang Guiping, "Xisha qundao ziwei huanji zuozhan" (Self-defensive War over the Paracels), in *Jubu zhanzheng yu haijun* (Local War and the Navy), edited by Xu Xikang (Beijing: The Haijun chubanshe, 1988), pp. 236–38. Jiang Baoqi (chief ed.) (Note 14), p. 36.
28. Military History Studies Department, Academy of Military Science (Note 27), pp. 711–12, 721–22. Guo Shouhang, *Deng Xiaoping guofang xiandaihua sixiang yanjiu* (A Study of Deng Xiaoping's Thoughts on National Defence Modernization) (Beijing: Guofang daxue chubanshe, 1989), p. 37.
29. Jiang Baoqi and Zhang Shengwang (eds.), 1990, p. 40. Gerald Segal, "China and the Disintegration of the Soviet Union," *Asian Survey*, No. 9, Vol. 32 (September 1992), p. 851.
30. *Jiefangjun bao*, 17 March 1994, p. 1.
31. Liu Jingsong, "Shiying shehui zhuyi shichang jingji, nuli tigao junshi jingji xiaoyi" (Enhance Military Economic Benefit to Adapt To Socialist Market Economy), *Junshi jingji yanjiu* (Military Economics Studies), July 1994, p. 9. Li Huaixin, "Shehui zhuyi shichang jingji tiaojian xia junshi jingji gongzuo de dasilu" (Train of Thought of Military Economic Work under the Condition of Socialist Market Economy), ibid., p. 55.
32. Jiang Baoqi (chief ed.) (Note 14), p. 25.
33. Ibid., p. 51. *Dangdai* (Contemporary Weekly), 31 March 1990, p. 17.
34. Chen Bingfu, "Guofang feiyong guoji duibi de zhangwai ji tiaozheng" (Obstacles and Adjustments to International Comparison of Defence Budget), *Defence Economic Problems*, 1990, p. 439.
35. Zhang Kundeng, "Dui jianshe jinggan changbeijun jiben mubiao he tujing de sisuo" (Deliberation on the Basic Objectives and Methods for the Building of a Crack Standing Army) in Planning and Organization Department, Academy of Military Science, *Xinshiqi changbeijun jianshe yanjiu* (A Study of the Standing Army Building in the New Era) (Beijing: Junshi kexue chubanshe, 1990), p. 56. Zhou Cun, "Zou jingbing liqi daolu, jianshe jinggan de changbeijun" (Take the Road of a Crack Army and Efficient Equipment, Build a Capable and Slim Standing Army), ibid., p. 99.
36. Xu Guangyi (chief ed.), *Dangdai Zhongguo jundui de houqin gongzuo*

(Logistical Work of Contemporary Chinese Army) (Beijing: Zhongguo shehui kexue chubanshe, 1990), p. 305.
37. *Jiefangjun bao*, 3 October 1994, p. 1.
38. It is impossible to quantify the financial burden imposed on the army by the resettlement of discharged officers because the arrangements between the state, local authorities and the army have changed many times since 1979 (for example, see *Jiefangjun bao*, 18 April 1992, p. 1). The benefits of demobilized officers are discussed later in the text and, for details, see Cadre Department, General Political Department, and Department of Military Institution Studies, Academy of Military Science, *Zhongguo renmin jiefangjun ganbu zhidu gaiyao* (An Outline of the PLA's Cadre System) (Beijing: Junshi kexue chubanshe, 1988), chaps. 17–18. However, the sheer number of demobilized officers suggests that resettlement has been very costly.
39. Jiang Baoqi (Note 14), p. 49.
40. *Jiefangjun bao*, 30 July 1992, p. 1.
41. Note 18, p. 81.
42. Ngok Lee (Note 11), p. 140. Sydney Jammes, "Military Industry," in *Chinese Defense Policy* (Note 4), p. 118. Jin Zhude et al., *Guofang jingji lun* (On Defence Economics) (Beijing: Jiefangjun chubanshe, 1987), pp. 48 and 49.
43. *Hongqi* (Red Flag), No. 15 (1 August 1985), pp. 1–7.
44. Chen Liheng and Wang Jingjie (chief eds.), *Junshi zhishi cidian* (Dictionary of Military Knowledge) (Beijing: Guofang daxue chubanshe, 1988), p. 624. Shi Shanyu and Wang Zhiqiang (chief eds.), *Junren wanshi wen* (Questions and Answers for the Servicemen) (Beijing: Changzheng chubanshe, 1989), pp. 114, 131, 147 and 161. For details of the rules and regulations as well as the definition of various terms concerning demobilization, see CMC Legal System Bureau, 1991, pp. 514–85.
45. Li Ke and Hau Shengzhang (Note 27), p. 364.
46. Deng Xiaoping, 1983, pp. 15 and 249. Han Huazhi (chief ed.), *Dangdai zhongguo jundui de junshi gongzuo* (The Military Work of the Contemporary Chinese Army), Vol. 1 (Beijing: Zhongguo shehui kexue chubanhse, 1989), pp. 74 and 75. Lonnie D. Henley, "China's Military Modernization: A Ten Year Assessment," in *China's Military Modernization: International Implications*, edited by Larry M. Wortzel (New York: Greenwood Press, 1988), pp. 97 and 98.
47. *China Daily*, 2 September 1989.
48. Zhou Cun (Note 35), p. 100.
49. "Reforms of China's Total Force," *China News Analysis*, No. 1460 (15 May 1992), p. 2.
50. *Jiefangjun bao*, 24 March 1992, p. 1. *Wen Wei Po* (Hong Kong), 25 April 1992, p. 2. Hua Zhen, "Jundui jingxin Dagaizu" (The Army Is Undergoing Major Reorganization), *Contemporary Weekly*, 15 May 1992, p. 15.

51. *Jiefangjun bao*, 31 January 1992, p. 3.
52. Shi Shanyu and Wang Zhiqiang (chief eds.) (Note 44), pp. 127 and 151. Cadre Department (Note 38), pp. 396, 402, 411, 439, 443–45, 458–67, 478. Xiang Xu (chief ed.), *Zhongguo renmin jiefangjun junguan shouce: lujun bufen* (The Chinese PLA Officer's Handbook: The Army) (Qingdao: Qingdao chubanshe, 1991), p. 709. *Jiefangjun bao*, 24 September 1992, p. 4.
53. Shi Shanyu and Wang Zhiqiang (chief eds.) (Note 44), p. 84.
54. Cadre Department (Note 38), pp. 312–14. *Zhongguo renmin jiefangjun ganbu renshi guanlixue* (The PLA Cadre Management) (Beijing: Junshi kexue chubanshe, 1993), pp. 301–302. Pang Zhifei, "Shenru yanjiu woguo shehui zhuyi chuji jieduan junshi jingji lilun yu shijian — junshi jingji lilun taolunhui zongshu" (Study in Depth Our Military Economic Theories and Practice at the Early Stage of Socialism — A Review of the Seminar on Military Economic Theories) *Junshi jingji yanjiu* (Military Economics Studies), No. 6 (1988), p. 9.
55. James L. Payne (Note 19), pp. 19–20.
56. Abraham S. Becker, *Military Expenditure Limitation for Arms Control: Problems and Prospects* (Cambridge, MA: Ballinger, 1977), pp. 11 and 12.
57. James Payne (Note 19), pp. 21 and 22.
58. US Arms Control and Disarmament Agency, *World Military Expenditures and Arms Transfers 1990* (Washington, DC: Government Printing Office, 1990), p. 29.
59. For details, see Abraham S. Becker, 1977, pp. 12 and 13.
60. Note 18, pp. 437–40. At present, there are about three million kinds of military materials in China. Pang Zhifei, "Junshi wuzi" (Military Material Resources), *Junshi jingji yanjiu* (Military Economics Studies), No. 3 (1988), p. 46. *Jingji cankao bao* (Economic Information Daily), 20 June 1992, p. 1. *Zhongguo tongji nianjian* (China Statistical Yearbook 1993) (Beijing: Zhongguo tongji chubanshe, 1993), p. 223.
61. Huang Daxiao and Xu Yonghua, "Yijiu jiuernian guojia caizheng yuxuan xiangmu jianjie" (A Brief on the Account Headings of the 1992 State Budget), *Caizheng* (Finance), No. 1 (1992), p. 24. Chen Yonghua and Chen Xinhua, "Yijiu jiusannian guojia caizheng yuxuan xiangmu jianjie" (A Brief on the Account Headings of the 1993 State Budget), *Caizheng* (Finance), No. 12 (1992), p. 22.
62. *Jingji cankao bao*, 20 June 1992, p. 1. *Fazhi ribao* (Legal System Daily), 20 March 1993, p. 1.
63. James L. Payne (Note 19), p. 20.
64. You Qianzhi et al., *Zhongguo guofang jingji yunxing fenxi* (Analysis of China's Defence Economic Operations) (Beijing: Zhongguo caizheng jingji chubanshe, 1991), p. 85.
65. *Jiefangjun bao*, 28 August 1990, p. 1. *Liaoning ribao*, 4 May 1992, p. 1. In

1989, for the first time, a Chinese combat aircraft successfully landed on a highway. See *Zhongguo kongjun* (China Air Force), No. 1 (1990), pp. 18–20.
66. *Jiefangjun bao*, 25 September 1992, p. 2.
67. *Liaoning ribao*, 23 July 1992, p. 1.
68. Xu Guangyi (chief ed.) (Note 36), pp. 562–65.
69. *Nanfang ribao*, 20 July 1992, p. 2. *Jiefangjun bao*, 8 January 1993, p. 1.
70. Xie Guang (chief ed.) (Note 7), p. 172.
71. Richard A. Bitzinger, "Arms to Go: Chinese Arms Sales to the Third World," *International Security*, No. 2, Vol. 17 (Fall 1992), p. 84.
72. R. Bates Gill, "Curbing Beijing's Arms Sales," *Orbis*, No. 3, Vol. 36 (Summer 1992), pp. 379–80.
73. Shirley Kan, "China's Arms Sales: Overview and Outlook for the 1990s," in *China's Economic Dilemmas in the 1990s: The Problems of Reforms, Modernization, and Interdependence*, Vol. 2 (Washington, DC: Government Printing Office, 1991), p. 707.
74. The author wants to thank a veteran China watcher who pointed this out to him.
75. Cheng Kuaile, "Zhunque bawo houqin shichang xingwei de jiben tezheng" (On Correct Understanding of the Characteristics of Logistic Marketing Behaviour), *Junshi jingji yanjiu* (Military Economics Studies), No. 12 (1994), pp. 53–54.
76. Ye Peng, *Xiwang zai nanfang* (The Hope Resides in the South) (Beijing: Jiefangjun wenyi chubanshe, 1991), pp. 4, 86–91, 186. *Jiefangjun bao*, 7 May 1992, p. 1.
77. *Xinjiang ribao*, 16 June 1992, p. 4. *Zhongguo qingnian*, No. 2 (1993), p. 14.
78. Nicholars R. Lardy, *Foreign Trade and Economic Reforms in China, 1978–1990* (Cambridge: Cambridge University Press, 1992), p. 55. For example, see *Jiefangjun bao*, 9 February 1993, p. 1.
79. Qiu Keren (chief ed.), *Jundui zhengzhi gongzuoxue lilun xintan* (New Approaches to Army Political Work Theories) (Beijing: Junshi kexue chubanshe, 1993), pp. 194–207. "The Army: A New Stage in the 'Fish-and-Water' Relationship," *China News Analysis*, No. 1423 (1 December 1990), pp. 1–9.
80. "Shenru tantao Deng Xiaoping junshi jingji sixiang cujin junshi jingji lilun yanjiu jinyibu fazhan" (Making a Thorough Discuss of Deng Xiaoping's Military Economic Thought, Develop Military Economic Theory Study Further [sic]), *Junshi jingji yanjiu* (Military Economics Studies), September 1994, p. 8.
81. *Jiefangjun bao*, 2 June 1991, p. 3.

10

China-Hong Kong Relations

T. L. Tsim

The relationship between China and Hong Kong in 1994 was characterized by economic integration and political confrontation. The schizophrenia of economic liberalization and political repression which is the hallmark of Deng Xiaoping's China, has taken control in China's relations with Hong Kong. On the one hand, the fear that Hong Kong might be turned into a counter-revolutionary base intensified after 4 June 1989. On the other hand, the fact that Hong Kong will be particularly useful in meeting China's capital needs became more and more apparent after the flotation of the first H share on the Hong Kong Stock Exchange on 15 July 1993. This was the issue of Tsingtao Brewery which raised HK$889 million. Until Shanghai develops the laws and infrastructure necessary for an international financial centre, Hong Kong's usefulness to China cannot be easily replaced. But Hong Kong is also a hotbed of Western ideas about democracy, freedom, human rights, the rule of law and the separation of government powers. Events leading up to June 4 have shown that such ideas could fire the imagination of Chinese youths and lead them down the path of political reform, a path the Communist Party leadership was loath to take on its own accord. In her dealings with Hong Kong, therefore, China's objectives are twofold. She is going after political control and she believes this could be achieved without jeopardizing Hong Kong's long cherished prosperity. The underlying theme in China-Hong Kong relations is, therefore, bifurcation.

Economic Integration

The economic integration of Hong Kong with China is taking place everyday and seems to be supported by people on both sides of the border. At least there have been few arguments against the movement of goods, money and people from Hong Kong to China and vice versa. The increase in two way traffic between China and Hong Kong over the last 16 years since the beginning of China's open-door policy has been nothing short of spectacular. Take the movement of people. In 1978, before the open-door became a policy, 1,290,000 people travelled to China from Hong Kong and 24,800 people made the journey in the opposite direction. In 1994, Hong Kong residents made 24,798,140 trips to China. The increase over a sixteen year period was 19 times. During this same period, the increase in the number of Chinese visitors to Kong Kong is even more remarkable. From 24,800 visits in 1978, the number shot up to 1,943,678 visits in 1994, or an

China-Hong Kong Relations

increase of 78 times. The figures for the movement of people are given in Table 1. Figures for the year 1984 are included to give an idea of the growing momentum in the last 10 years since the signing of the Sino-British Joint Declaration that year.

Table 1. PRC Resident Arrivals and Hong Kong Resident Departures

	1978	1984	1994
Hong Kong resident departures for PRC	1,290,000	8,040,000	24,798,140
Visitor arrivals from PRC to Hong Kong	24,800	114,000	1,943,678

Source: *Hong Kong Monthly Digest of Statistics*, published by the Census and Statistic Department of the Hong Kong Government, 1995.

What has been even more impressive is the movement of goods. In 1978, China's imports from Hong Kong amounted to a paltry HK$81 million. In 1994, this had shot up to HK$61 billion, an increase of 753 times. The growth of China's exports to Hong Kong tells the same, although less spectacular story. From a base of HK$10.5 billion in 1978, China's domestic exports to Hong Kong grew to HK$470.8 billion last year, an increase of some 45 times. Table 2 shows conclusively how China has emerged from an insignificant trading partner in 1978 to Hong Kong's leading export market, re-export market and source of most of Hong Kong's supplies over a period of 16 years. The increase in Hong Kong's re-exports to China over this period is a staggering 1,509 times while the growth in re-exports from China is 149 times.

Economic integration is perceived to be beneficial to both sides. Hong Kong needs cheap labour, cheap raw materials and low rentals. Hong Kong also needs a readily accessible market for its goods and products. China provides all of these. On the other hand, China needs capital,

Table 2. China's Trade with Hong Kong

(Unit: HK$ million)

	1978	1984	1994
1. China's exports to Hong Kong	10,550	55,753	470,876
2. China's imports from Hong Kong	81	11,283	61,009
3. Hong Kong's re-exports to China	214	28,064	322,835
4. Hong Kong's re-exports from China	3,659	28,107	545,831

Source: *Hong Kong Monthly Digest of Statistics* (see Table 1).

technology, management expertise and market sense; and Hong Kong provides all of those. The synergy is perfect and the combination has worked to both sides' advantage with the workers of Hong Kong's manufacturing industries possibly the only losers. What has made 1994 special is the fact that this economic integration, particularly in the area of financial services now seems to be not just welcome but positively encouraged by the highest echelons in Beijing. China fever, in particular, has gripped Hong Kong's financial services sector with the introduction of H shares and the takeover of Hong Kong shell companies by Chinese mainland concerns. Although toward the second half of the year the shares-for-capital fever seems to have abated, the trend of the People's Republic of China (PRC) companies coming to Hong Kong to raise money is now well established and Hong Kong has become the preferred destination ahead of New York and London or indeed China's own bourses in Shenzhen and Shanghai themselves.

When China's doors opened in 1979, it was the Hong Kong businessmen who first seized the opportunity to invest across the border. Hotels, factories, office buildings and apartment blocks have sprung up over the years financed largely by Hong Kong money. The trend intensified after the signing of the Sino-British Joint Declaration in 1984 when it became clear that Hong Kong will become part of China again in 1997. There was a dramatic slowdown in the aftermath of the Tiananmen Incident but as memories of the brutalities faded and as China's economy came out of recession toward the end of 1991, Hong Kong businessmen renewed their interest in China with a vengeance and huge amounts of money were poured into the mainland. This time around, the flow is no longer one way or in one direction. As China recovered her composure after the June 4 debacle, Chinese companies and entrepreneurs began to find their way into Hong Kong in ever greater numbers. They established companies or branches in Hong Kong, bought offices and residential properties and bought into Hong Kong companies or took them over outright. The result of this development which intensified after Deng Xiaoping's call for faster reform in China in the spring of 1992 is that China's investments in Hong Kong are now estimated to be in the region of US$25 billion as against Hong Kong's direct investment in China of around US$40 billion at the end of 1993. China has overtaken both Japan and the United States as the leading investor in Hong Kong. At the end of March 1994, Japan's investment in Hong Kong was estimated to be US$12.7 billion and the United States had US$10.5 billion's at the end of

1993. China with US$25 billion in the territory, has more investments than both these two countries combined. (All the above figures are taken from the March 1995 issue of *Hong Kong Business*).

Where China-Hong Kong relations are concerned, the picture which emerges in 1994 is one of accelerating integration in the economic sphere. The cross-holding of assets is extended to the financial industry as the following table released by the Hong Kong Monetary Authority will make clear.

Table 3. External Claims and Liabilities of Authorized Institutions in Hong Kong vis-à-vis China

(Unit: HK$ billion)

	Position as at the end of 1980	1984	1994	Average annual growth rate 1980–1994
1. Claims on banks in China	7.1	10.7	176.6	26%
2. Claims on China's non-bank sector	0.5	1.8	61.6	41%
3. Liabilities to banks in China	1.0	23.2	225.8	47%
4. Liabilities to China's non-bank sector	N/A	N/A	7.8	
4. Net claims on China	6.6	–10.7	4.6	

At the end of 1994, Hong Kong had claims on China's banking sector of US$176.6 billion, an increase of almost 25 times on the figure for 1980, the first year when such statistics became available. Also in 1994, Hong Kong's claims on China's non-bank sector stood at US$61.6 billion, an increase of some 123 times on the figure for 1980. In the same year, Chinese companies raised HK$2,838 million, or close to US$364 million, through the flotation of nine H shares in the Hong Kong stock market. H shares are so named because they are PRC companies with PRC assets but listed on the Hong Kong Stock Exchange, hence the initial H. These figures give a true picture of the importance of Hong Kong's capital raising function for China.

Guangdong province has been a major beneficiary of such integration as this enables Guangdong to plug into Hong Kong's superb infrastructure and to raise much needed capital for her own developments in the Pearl River Delta. In justifying her fast growth to the central government,

Guangdong has argued that she is able to grow much faster than the national average because there are no bottlenecks which might lead to overheating. The Daya Bay nuclear plant is in operation and is supplying electricity to the southern part of Guangdong; the super highway which links Guangzhou and Hong Kong has been opened to traffic and Hong Kong's container terminals will become even more accessible to Guangdong's exporters. There are more airports, first class roads, and port facilities in the Pearl River Delta area than anywhere else of comparable size in China.

Political Confrontation

So far the success stories are in the economic arena. On the political front, 1994 was a year of continuing confrontation. Britain's long search for an agreement with China over Governor Patten's electoral package for Hong Kong's Legislative Council election in September 1995 ended in failure. Mr Patten's proposals were passed by Hong Kong's Legislative Council on 29 June 1994. Prior to that, when it became clear to the Chinese side that agreement on the issue was out of the question, Beijing had set up what is known as "a second stove" in the form of the Preliminary Working Committee (PWC). The Committee is appointed by the Chinese government, the majority of its membership is made up of Hong Kong people. Its functions almost as a shadow Legco, hence the words "second stove." China also made it clear that the three-tier structure of Legislative Council, Urban and Regional Councils, and District Boards as constituted under Mr Patten's proposals will be dismantled and re-constituted after the change of sovereignty in 1997. There will be no through train for Councillors. As a result, Beijing argues, there will be a need for a provisional Legislative Council and members of this provisional body will also be appointed by the Chinese government. It should be noted that both China's action — the creation of the Preliminary Working Committee and Mr Patten's own — the introduction of his electoral bill — were unilateral decisions. The two, taken together, finally spelled the end of convergence. There was no meeting of minds between Britain and China over Hong Kong's electoral system.

The Chinese side was not going to leave things at that. They deliberately cold-shouldered Alastair Goodlad when the British Minister with special responsibility for Hong Kong visited Beijing on 14 July 1994.

They also decided to extend non-convergence to other areas as they made it plain that there would be no through train for either senior civil servants or judges. Aside from taking quite divergent views over the concept of "elections," there were other differences between the British and Chinese sides, and some of these differences were quite substantial. The 22 September meeting of the Joint Liaison Group in Beijing achieved very little for either side. While the British delegation wanted to devote time to the definition of who is a Hong Konger, the Court of Final Appeal, Container Terminal Number Nine and the proposed old age pension scheme, their Chinese counterpart was more interested in discussing Hong Kong's public finance, the structure of Hong Kong's civil service and the hand over of civil servants' files. Not the first time, this meeting ended without agreement as Hong Kong drifted closer and closer to the date of transition. As if to remind the British that their days are numbered, the Chinese installed a count-down clock at Tiananmen Square and set it ticking away with the last thousand days to 1 July 1997.

Minimal Cooperation

It would be an over-simplification to say that the political *impasse* has led to non-cooperation in all other areas. The suspicion that China was linking the political arguments with the disputes over the financing of Hong Kong's airport which might have been true at one stage finally evaporated on 24 June 1994. On this day, five days before Legislative Council passed Mr Patten's electoral proposal, China and Britain reached agreement on the financial arrangement for the airport. This was subsequently confirmed on 4 November when the minutes were approved. There were other notable successes which indicated that the Chinese side was fully capable of taking a pragmatic approach if such an approach was in their own best interests. At the June meeting of the Joint Liaison Group (JLG), for instance, the British and Chinese sides reached agreement over the use of military land in Hong Kong after 1997, in particular which parcels of land were to be handed over to the People's Liberation Army and which might be kept by the Hong Kong authorities. A year earlier, in the middle of 1993, on 1 April, the Hong Kong Monetary Authority came into being. This development could not have taken place without the blessing of Beijing. Hong Kong's reserves and foreign currency holdings in the form of the Hong Kong Exchange Fund are a matter of top priority for the Beijing government because the stability and convertibility of the Hong Kong dollar depend on it and Hong Kong's position as an international financial centre could be put at risk if mistakes were made. Over the years, it should be noted, there is a good record of cooperation between the two sides on monetary policy.

In the second half of 1994, as China decided to come to terms with Mr Patten's electoral package, Vice-Premier Qian Qichen was put in charge of China's policy toward Taiwan, Hong Kong and Macau. With this change, a more pragmatic approach emerged. Mr Qian indicated that he was prepared to work with the British on other transitional matters even if they could not agree on the electoral package. There was a reciprocal and noticeable softening on the British side as Mr Patten announced that he would not object to "informal meetings" between Hong Kong's civil servants and members of China's Preliminary Working Committee provided these meetings take place in accordance with certain guidelines, and these were published in October. The Hong Kong government also took on board the PWC's suggestion that there should be an Infrastructure Coordination Committee between the two sides so that each will know what the other is doing across the border in such things as roads, ports, bridges, airports, railways, power stations, container terminals and telecommunication installations. This body which was created on 2 December 1994 will remove duplication of effort and ensure that any addition to the infrastructure on one side of the border will be brought to the attention of the other side and due notice taken of each other's views on the matter. Late in 1994, it was announced that Vice-Premier Qian will visit Britain next year. This was taken by many as an indication that politics aside, there will be better cooperation and better coordination on practical matters from here on.

China's Objectives

When the Sino-British Joint Declaration was signed in September 1984 and the return of Hong Kong to Chinese sovereignty in July 1997 became a reality, there were people who believed, naively, that now that Chinese honour had been satisfied and Chinese national pride assuaged, Beijing would or could really live up to her promise of giving Hong Kong a high degree of autonomy for 50 years under Deng Xiaoping's concept of one country two systems. The British government had encouraged this false sense of security until events at Tiananmen Square in 1989 rudely shattered such carefully nurtured false pretences. Those who were in the know or who read between the lines of newspaper reports knew that the most difficult part of the Sino-British negotiations had been over the concept of sovereignty, with the Chinese insisting that sovereignty entails administration and that the two are inseparable. After the signing of the Joint Declaration which promised the people of Hong Kong that the future legislature of the Special Administrative Region shall be returned by election, the most difficult part of the Joint Liaison Group's work had been to arrive at a form of election which is acceptable to the people of Hong Kong, the British government and the Chinese government, with the latter always opting for a more restrictive franchise or a less democratic form of government for the future Special Administrative Region. It was because of China's objection that the British government decided not to introduce direct elections in Hong Kong in 1988.

After the Tiananmen Incident of 4 June 1989, the Chinese government, alarmed that Hong Kong people had been so supportive of the students and dissidents, became even more determined to exercise effective control over the territory. The Basic Law for Hong Kong promulgated by the National People's Congress in April 1990 contains clauses which will enable the central government to intervene in Hong Kong with or without the Hong Kong government's consent. Article 18 says, "In the event that the Standing Committee of the National People's Congress decides to declare a state of war or, by reason of turmoil within the Hong Kong Special Administrative Region which endangers national unity or security and is beyond the control of the government of the Region, decides that the Region is in a state of emergency, the Central People's Government may issue an order applying the relevant national laws in the Region." Article 23 of the Basic Law also requires the Hong Kong government to pass laws "to prohibit any act of treason, secession, sedition, subversion against the Central People's Government." The operative word is not "two systems" but "one country."

China's fears of democracy sprang from the fact that many members of the democratic parties in Hong Kong also had overlapping membership in the Hong Kong Alliance in Support of the Patriotic Democratic Movement in China, the group which raised a lot of money to support the democracy movement in China in 1989. These democratic parties had a strong showing in the first direct election in Hong Kong in 1991, winning 15 of the 18 seats while pro-China candidates lost in every constituency in which they competed. Clearly, if the people of Hong Kong were allowed to choose freely in a truly democratic system of government, they would opt for parties and candidates who would not toe Beijing's line and who would champion forcefully Hong Kong's own best interests. This explains Beijing's intransigence over Governor Patten's new electoral package which varies only slightly from the so-called "understanding" that the Chinese side claimed to have reached with the British government when Lord Wilson was Governor.

If gaining political control were the only objective, however, China would have taken a different strategy in the way she dealt with Britain and Hong Kong. But this was not all. China has a second objective, this is to maintain Hong Kong's stability and prosperity, in particular Hong Kong's status as an international financial centre. The Chinese leaders have had to accept, albeit reluctantly, that while Shanghai is China's leading city, business centre, port and manufacturing centre, Shanghai still has a long way to go before it could turn itself from a domestic financial centre into an international financial centre. For that to happen, Shanghai needs to have sophisticated laws on banking, the securities industry and insurance industry, as well as professionals in the fields of law and accounting. Shanghai also needs a legal system which is perceived to be fair and equitable and not loaded in favour of the state; and China needs a fully convertible currency. There can be no international financial centre without a convertible currency, the rule of law, the free flow of information and the confidence of the international financial community. Shanghai still has quite a way to go. In the meantime, Hong Kong is China's only city that can fulfil such a role. The takeover of Hong Kong cannot be a hostile takeover. Unlike Kuwait whose wealth is in the rich oil reserves underground which can be taken over physically, the wealth of Hong Kong is in its people and in its systems. A hostile takeover will drive away the people who know how to run the systems; and once these people leave, the systems will collapse by default. Above all, international financial centres are strange creatures which depend for their continued survival on international business confidence. It takes years to build up such confidence but a simple, elementary mistake could ruin it.

Having grasped the nettle of Hong Kong's peculiar situation, the Chinese leaders' strategy, therefore, is not to stonewall Britain on every issue but to offer cooperation where necessary and to confront and browbeat only if these should serve useful purposes and provided that such confrontation does not go beyond the limit of endurance on the part of the international business community. In pursuing this strategy, Chinese leaders seem to take advice from their own business interests in Hong Kong as well as from Hong Kong and international businessmen operating in the territory rather more than from the New China News Agency (NCNA). Politically, China's strategy in 1994 was to isolate Governor Patten by undermining his credibility in Hong Kong and the support he enjoyed in Britain. PWC members some of whom were drawn from the Hong Kong government's own former appointees to Legco and Exco spearheaded many of the attacks, whether they were directed against Mr Patten himself or his policies. Where Britain was concerned, China's strategy was to tempt British businessmen with the prospect of more trade and service contracts if only Mr Patten would play ball. In dealing with the democratic parties in Hong Kong, Beijing employed united front tactics on the one hand and the classic divide and rule approach on the other. The New China News Agency actively cultivated its relationship with Meeting Point and the Association for Democracy and People's Livelihood while snubbing the United Democrats. To cite but one case in point, Mr Anthony Cheung, the Chairman of Meeting Point, was invited to become a Hong Kong Affairs Advisor while overtures from members of the United Democrats to the New China News Agency were continually rebuffed. When Meeting Point joined up with the United Democrats to form the Democratic Party, Mr Cheung also found probably to his chagrin, that the invitation to him to serve as an Advisor had been withdrawn.

In the meantime, China did everything she could to nurture the party that is closest to herself, the Democratic Alliance for the Betterment of Hong Kong (DAB). Members of this party have better access to NCNA, some of them are Hong Kong Affairs Advisors, some are PWC members and they are regularly invited to visit Beijing and regularly come back with messages for the Hong Kong people from Chinese leaders. The idea is to build up the DAB's status and credibility by giving them exposure at the expense of the other political parties. In spite of this, the DAB's election fortunes have been mediocre which once again illustrates the fundamental point that there is no popular support for China and her handmaidens in Hong Kong. If this is correct, it explains why the Chinese side would want to load the dice in its favour by means of an electoral process which would, in Mr Patten's words, be tantamount to rigging the elections. As Mr Patten declined to be an accomplice in this conspiracy and as public opinion in Hong Kong is not on their side, Chinese leaders decided to back track. Sir Percy Cradock had once contended that China would not honour the Joint

Declaration and would take over Hong Kong before 1997 if Britain insisted on giving more democracy to the territory. Mr Patten decided to do exactly that but nothing untoward happened; the People's Liberation Army stayed on their side of the border. This was because the Chinese leaders, mindful of Hong Kong's useful position and her particular weaknesses, have decided against taking things too far. The confrontation with Mr Patten having passed into the history books, the Chinese officials were content to contain the damage by issuing the threat that they would change everything after 1997 until the political system conforms with the Basic Law. It is interesting to note in passing that while in 1982 at the start of the Sino-British negotiations, the Chinese leaders had let it be known that China would take over Hong Kong to serve as an example for Taiwan, these days they are no longer talking about this. It is as if this is no longer an objective or no longer deemed to be important. Either the overall strategy has been changed or the Chinese leaders never meant what they said.

Britain's Objectives

As far as Britain's side of the story goes, basically, on 29 June 1994 Mr Patten called China's bluff and won. In so doing, he has also exposed the shifty nature of many of Hong Kong's politicians and civil servants. Having demonstrated a willingness to stand by his own judgement and Britain's obligation, Mr Patten has exorcized once and for all the charge that Britain was conniving at China's attempt to sell Hong Kong people down the river. The aged eagle has spread its wings. Without this gesture, there was always going to be the suspicion that Britain did a deal with China behind Hong Kong people's backs and would do it again. With this probably final gesture, Britain's conscience is clear. She can now depart with honour in 1997, and it will be some of the people in Hong Kong who stand accused if things do not work out. The passage of the electoral package has not harmed Hong Kong's stability and prosperity and the onus is now on China to prove that it has. Britain has attempted, in the final years of British administration, to secure for Hong Kong the rule of law, the freedoms people here have always enjoyed, and the rights that have sometimes been taken for granted. A Bill of Rights was passed by Legco in 1993, and other laws have had to be amended to take cognizance of this development. The restrictive Public Order Ordinance which was passed when Lord Wilson was Governor, was amended in 1994 to give back to the press the freedom to report that journalists crave. This was not enough, however, to stop self censorship on the part of the two terrestrial broadcasters.

It is in the way that Governor Patten deals with the Court of Final Appeal that criticism might still be levelled against him. Final appeal, traditionally, has been dealt with by Britain's Privy Council. After 1997, as Britain will no longer be the sovereign power, this arrangement could not continue. It has became necessary to create a Court of Final Appeal in Hong Kong and, right from the start, the composition of the judges who will sit on that court became a matter of heated debate between the Chinese and British delegations to the Joint Liaison Group. The British side argued for 3 local judges and 2 others from common law jurisdictions outside Hong Kong. The Chinese side insisted on a 4 to 1 split. In 1991, after many years of fruitless discussion and on the advice of the then Governor-in-Council, the British side agreed to the 4–1 composition at a meeting of the JLG. In late 1991 when this agreement was the subject of a motion debate in Legco, it was defeated by a sizeable majority and Britain has not been able to make good on its side of the bargain. Mr Patten is now prepared to give the bill a second try and a stormy session is expected ahead. He will be charged with having softened his stance now that his place in history is secure. He will probably argue that he had inherited this situation which was not of his making and that having a Court of Final Appeal now, even one that is less than completely satisfactory, is better than not having one at all and leaving things to after 1997. Courts after all, need a good breaking-in period. The Chinese side will not make things any easier for Mr Patten by either keeping quiet or by endorsing the proposal he is putting to Legco after consultations with the Bar Association and the Law Society. This case will show that while Mr Patten is prepared to take on China over some issues he regards as vital, he is fully capable of seeking an accommodation with the future sovereign power if he perceives this to be necessary. In the last remaining two and a half years of British administration, the government in Hong Kong seems to be fighting a rearguard action before the Union Jack is lowered for the last time.

As 1994 drew to a close, many important issues remained unresolved. The definition of who is a Hong Konger is one of them. The sharing of civil servants' files is another. The localization of laws is a third, and getting China to endorse international treaties affecting Hong Kong is a fourth. The work of the Joint Liaison Group had been stalled on many occasions and in spite of optimistic noises by the Foreign Secretary and

Foreign Minister of both countries, progress remained illusive and differences ran deep. China might be overplaying her hand by insisting on a role for her and her advisors in the drafting of the 1996–1997 budget and in making civil service appointments.

The people of Hong Kong who lived through these times have seen a lot. China's anti-democratic nature throughout the months and months of bilateral talks on the electoral package now stands fully exposed. The promise of not interfering in Hong Kong's affairs except as they relate to defence and foreign policy has gone out of the window as one mainland official after another pronounced on textbooks for Hong Kong's schools, civil servants' files, amount of land for auction, Hong Kong's old age pension scheme, Container Terminal Number Nine, and the Hong Kong government's budget. While part of the blame could be levelled at some Hong Kong Affairs Advisors and members of the Preliminary Working Committee who encouraged the Chinese officials to intervene and occasionally over-step the line, the point of it all is that such encouragement has a willing audience and as such bodes ill for the future. The significance about 1994 is that much of the criticism against Britain and Britain's role in acting as China's handmaiden has disappeared after Mr Patten took the stand that he did.

Many people are still prepared to stay in Hong Kong after the Chinese government disclosed its hand and its plans. But they are doing so because the money is good, because they call Hong Kong home, or because they think they could live with a diminution of freedom, rights and democracy, and not because they have any illusion about what the future entails. The conspiracy of euphoria Italian journalist Tiziano Terzani once accused the British, Hong Kong and Chinese governments of fostering is here no longer. For as long as the economic integration with China is bringing positive, tangible benefits to Hong Kong and Hong Kong people, there will always be those who think an erosion of democracy, freedom and rights is something they can live with and probably the price they will have to pay if they stay in the territory beyond 30 June 1997. Many are now learning *putonghua*, the *lingua franca* in China, while arguing for more Chinese to be used in Hong Kong's schools, and generally reasserting their Chinese identity.

A second group, those who either do not believe in "one country two systems" or who do not believe that the Chinese government will live up to her promises and who do not wish to live in a Hong Kong with its freedoms and rights curtailed, are leaving the city at the rate of some

60,000 a year, for countries like Canada, Australia, the United States, Britain or Singapore. Economic integration may be beneficial to Hong Kong but if this leads to the takeover of Hong Kong's mass media by China or business interests which are beholden to the Chinese government, there is no escaping the diminution of press freedom which will follow. It remains to be seen whether Hong Kong can continue as an international financial centre when the free flow of political as well as economic information which it has enjoyed so far is brought to an end or modified to take account of China's political sensitivities.

A third group who provide the mainstay for the democratic parties in Hong Kong are organizing themselves for a protracted battle against the new sovereign power and her minions. They are going to contest the elections in March and September of 1995 and win by a large, convincing margin. If they were really free to choose, the great majority of the people in Hong Kong would probably not support the imposition of Beijing's rule on Hong Kong. If they see voting for the Democratic Party as their best chance of achieving such an objective, then it is to the Democrats that they will turn.

Given this diversity of views and reaction, it is fair to say that Hong Kong has become a more and more political city. There is now some genuine articulation of interests and there is a growing need for the resolution of conflicts and differences in ways which are conducive to the continuation of a stable, sensible and workable government. Hong Kong is now clearly a city divided and a city living in danger of losing its best assets and its most attractive appeals. Most Chinese leaders, barring Wang Daohan perhaps, do not even understand this. Wang used to be the mayor of Shanghai and is now in charge of negotiations with Taiwan on reunification across the Taiwan Straits. He was at his perceptive best when he spoke about the need to win over the people of Hong Kong and not simply lord it over them. He alone seems to realize that winning over the hearts and minds of people in the territory has not been done and needs to be done. As Mr Patten has said on many occasions, after 1997 it is China's responsibility to reassure the people of Hong Kong and the international business community that all will be well and that Hong Kong will continue to function as a going concern; it is no longer Britain's watch. This will not be an easy task. China's leaders, the Hong Kong and Macau office and the New China News Agency, still seem more interested in wrestling political control than addressing this vital question.

11

Inequality and Stratification in the Nineties

Deborah S. Davis

Introduction

Over the decade of the 1980s, decollectivization of agriculture and operational reforms in urban industry substantially altered the distribution of resources. Wealth became more concentrated in coastal provinces, and income inequalities within rural and urban communities were greater than they had been at the start of the decade.[1] The gap between male and female wage earners widened[2] and social welfare benefits became more skewed in favour of the urban minority.[3] However, despite such reallocation of resources and privilege, core principles of remuneration which generated these inequalities and supported the process of stratification remained surprisingly similar to those of the late Mao years. As in the 1970s, material rewards were distributed according to a hierarchy of job statuses which consistently favoured urban over rural enterprises, state over collective units, and offered the most generous social welfare to those of highest rank rather than those in greatest need. Thus, for example, using national data comparing the situation of 1978 to that of 1988, Azizur Khan and his colleagues discovered that not only had the urban-rural income differential widened as the structural reforms gained momentum, but that rural residents had assumed a heavier tax burden. In 1988, 39% of per capita average urban income (or RMB 720) came as net subsidies or income in kind; in the same year, each rural resident made a *net payment* of 2% of income as a tax to the state. Or put another way, every urban resident annually received government subsidies worth 95% of total rural per capita disposable income.[4]

During the early 1990s the economic reforms dramatically accelerated once again and market-like principles of distribution began to undermine the basic assumptions of the Maoist reward structure. As a result, the significance of job hierarchies declined, and personal attributes and inter-unit differences began to affect occupational achievement more directly than had been true in the early 1980s. For rural residents the most critical element of the accelerated reform was reduced control over rural to urban migration. In response, millions who had been disadvantaged by virtue of their place of birth or first job placement quit villages or enterprises with

---

The author wishes to thank the following colleagues for their criticism of an earlier draft of the this essay: Bian Yanjie, Chen Xiangming, Suzanne Pepper, Tsui Kai Yuen, Wang Gao, Wang Shaoguang, and Zhou Xueguang.

depressed wages and moved to jobs in other locations with higher rewards. Growth in the scale and number of private (*siying*) enterprises as well as a surge of foreign investment also had an immediate impact. Offering wages and benefits according to performance rather than bureaucratic criteria and disregarding past privileges of rank, these non-state employers attracted those who felt stultified or trapped and job switching became common.

However, the retreat from state socialism remains incomplete. Especially in urban areas, economic reform has largely been incremental; political reform has barely begun. Thus it is not surprising that in the early 1990s when one searches for underlying patterns and principles of social stratification, the institutions and ideology of the Communist Party-state still exercise enormous influence. In the pages that follow I will first describe the most salient dimensions of inequality, paying particular attention to the ways in which old and new disparities complement or contradict each other, and then conclude by identifying nine emergent patterns shaping the process of social class reproduction in the early 1990s. By focusing on these underlying societal processes, I hope a review of the past will provide insight into a future Chinese society which will be even further removed from the one created by the Maoist regime than is the contemporary market-socialist hybrid.

Primary Dimensions of Inequality

Rural-Urban Inequality

As in earlier decades, during the early 1990s the primary inequality within the Chinese population is between rural and urban residents.[5] Despite massive out-migration from impoverished rural areas and from jobs in low paid agriculture to higher wage positions in industry and construction, the gap between rural and urban residents which had narrowed during the first years of post-Mao reform widened in the 1990s. In 1990 average rural per capita income had been 45% of mean urban per capita income;[6] by 1993 it had fallen to 39%.[7] Moreover growth rates of real income (that is nominal growth less inflation) was lower during the 1990s for rural than for urban households, thereby suggesting that the inflation problems about which urban residents were so outraged, were much more burdensome (and potentially destabilizing) in rural areas.[8]

Substantial and growing rural-urban inequalities are also present in all areas of social welfare spending. During the commune era, provision of medical, educational, and welfare services was primarily the responsibility of each brigade, which relied on village specific standards of living to determine the size and allocation of collective expenditures. At the commune level rural residents enjoyed some state services provided by national or provincial tax revenues, but usually made significant levels of co-payment. For example, for the minority of village children continuing to senior high, parents were responsible for room and board, as well as a portion of tuition. At the commune hospital many procedures and most medicines required some cash payment by the patient. If rural patients were referred to county or city hospitals, their brigade health cooperative paid a fraction of the bill, and the family took out loans to cover the balance. Childless elderly, orphans, and disabled without responsible kin (*wubaohu*) were entirely a village responsibility; only the minority who moved to old age homes drew on commune or state funding. Throughout the post-1949 decades all rural residents bore total financial responsibility for building and maintaining their homes.

By contrast urban residents consistently received these services free or at below cost. Urban children by virtue of their household registration enjoyed higher quality schools — more professional teachers, better textbooks, better equipped classrooms — for which parents paid a far lower share of costs than rural parents. Most urban adults had easy access to hospital procedures and medications, yet paid little more than a registration fee. Never-employed adults and children with a working relative paid a fraction of the bill, while those without a kin tie to an urban employee became wards of the municipalities not the responsibility of their neighbours. In addition all urban residents received ration tickets entitling them to buy foodstuffs at prices below those charged to rural residents and the majority lived in housing rented for less than 5% of their monthly salary.

In the first decade of the post-Mao reforms the rural-urban gap in services persisted and in situations where commune level structure and funding were critical, the disparities actually widened. For example, in 1975, 40% of hospital beds and 42% of doctors (as opposed to paramedics) were based in city areas. By 1989 the percentage had risen to 52% of hospital beds and 64% of doctors, with the greatest shifts occurring between 1987 and 1989 when there was no further redrawing of rural and urban boundaries.[9] In the mid-1980s, only 14% of urban residents paid their own medical bills, by contrast in rural areas 81% of patients were entirely self-paying and 44% of all rural clinics were run as private (*geti*) enterprises.[10]

After 1990 as national policy encouraged further commodification of welfare goods and services, rural-urban disparities became even more acute because withdrawal of subsidies and direct state services went farthest and fastest in rural areas while change in cities was marginal and incremental. Thus in the area of medical reforms, rural innovations have focused on collective health insurance policies with relatively high individual premiums for a fixed amount of hospital fees. Moreover, nothing has been done to re-establish the low cost village paramedic system of barefoot doctors which had been so successful in reaching the poorest of rural inhabitants.[11] In urban areas by contrast local clinics continue to provide cheap paramedic care and reform concentrates on co-payment of insurance fees, with a cap placed on the percentage of basic wage which can be deducted for premiums.[12] In 1994 the government unveiled a more radical reform which would require urban employees to contribute to a national insurance plan to cover major illness and establish individual medical accounts modeled on provident funds. Should this plan which is to reach 800 cities and counties by December 1995 be nationalized, urban residents may finally experience a radical departure from past practice.[13]

Even in the area of housing where the rhetoric of commercialization (*shangpinhua*) is most insistent in urban areas, the inequalities between urban and rural residents remains particularly stark. Rural families still assume total responsibility for building and maintaining their homes. Most draw water from local wells, haul coal or charcoal from rural markets, and pay the entire cost for installing electric service. By contrast, urban families receive housing and utilities as public services. In 1993, the average city household still spent only 5.4% of monthly income on rent, water, electricity and gas.[14] Thus even in a city like Beijing where commodification of housing has been pushed vigorously and a sizeable number of residents have access to overseas money or high incomes, only 7% of the housing stock was in private hands as of July 1993.[15] In addition when urban families did participate in the new market for private housing, they often bought their flats at subsidized rates far below market or replacement cost, thereby creating new inequities among the urban population as well as widening the rural-urban gap.[16]

During the early 1990s one also observed increased suffering among the poorest households, and as with other components of social welfare reform in the early 1990s, the gap between services for rural and urban areas widened in favour of city residents. In the commune era, poverty-stricken rural residents had multiple sources of aid. If their hardship was the result of natural disaster they were eligible for national emergency relief, usually in the form of grain deliveries, tax forgiveness, and sometimes building supplies and small amounts of cash. If they were destitute because they could not support themselves and had a spouse, child, or parent who had been a revolutionary martyr or soldier killed while on duty, they received government stipends. If they did not live in a devastated area or had no connection to a military or party casualty, they turned to their fellow villages. Households unable to feed themselves were permitted to borrow basic foodstuffs and sometimes cash on long term interest free "loans" if they were considered by the village to be worthy *kunnanhu* (households in difficulty). Individuals who were physically weak and had no village kin to care for them could be designated a "five guarantees household," (*wubaohu*) and became wards of the village. In exchange for handing over their homes to the brigade, they would be provided basic food, clothing, shelter, medical aid, and a funeral. In 1978, there were 2.676 million *wubaohu*.[17]

In urban areas, most social welfare was provided through the work place if an individual's or family's destitution had been caused by the loss or disability of the primary wage earner. The minority with no connection to a work unit, turned to the municipal government. If they were the dependent of a service man or revolutionary cadre, they received a dependents allowance. If they were destitute and had no kinship link to someone who had been disabled or killed while employed by an urban enterprise, the military, or the Chinese Communist Party (CCP), they became wards of the city, receiving a monthly stipend to support them in their home or maintaining them in a public facility paid for by municipal or ministry revenues.

After the collapse of the commune and brigade welfare organizations, the varieties and levels of support declined. Rural *wubaohu* continued to be protected, if necessary through intervention of the Bureau of Civil Affairs (Min Zheng Ju), but the percentage of those designated *wubaohu* by their village who then actually received all five guarantees steadily declined from 99% in 1984 to 75% by 1992.[18] The system of brigade level loans to *kunnanhu* collapsed with the disappearance of the commune and even relief to those suffering from natural disasters was cut back. Officially the policy was to substitute relief payments which had been used for consumption with development grants which would spur private entrepreneurship and industry, and the press frequently trumpeted this shift as a key explanation for lower rates of extreme poverty after 1985.[19] The decline was real and did reflect the success in the reform policies of allowing outmigration from the poorest areas and sponsorship of new family enterprises and sidelines. Yet although the number of rural residents living at or below subsistence fell from 125 million in 1985 to 80 million in 1992,[20] the reality was that nearly 10% of the rural population remained mired in intractable poverty for which the government took little responsibility.

By contrast in the cities, not only did food, housing, fuel, and medical benefits continue through the units for dependents of former employees and through municipal governments for the wards of the state, but unemployment insurance was introduced to help cover the costs of dislocation among urbanites let go from bankrupt or deficit ridden state enterprises.[21] Thus Table 1 which traces fluctuations in the number of needy who regularly received fixed amounts of aid between 1985 and 1992 shows that the urban poor not only received a disproportionate share of state resources but also that by 1992 they had an absolute advantage despite their much lower percentage in the total population, by contrast with rural destitutes.

Table 1. Rural *Wubaohu* (WBH) and Urban *Kunnanhu* (KNH) Receiving State Aid*

(in millions)

	1985	1988	1990	1991	1992
Rural WBH	0.226	0.221	0.218	0.207	0.186
Urban KNH	0.182	0.176	0.164	0.161	0.192

* *dingqi dingliang*, that is at fixed time intervals a fixed amount of aid.
Source: *Zhongguo tongji nianjian 1993* (Chinese Statistical Yearbook, 1993) (Beijing: Zhongguo tongji chubanshe, 1993), p. 808.

While not denying that the economic reforms and the push to commodify social services increased the risk of poverty among urban residents after 1990, it is also the case that the government has created a "soft landing" and basic safety net for urbanites, while leaving the rural poor to fend for themselves under the new rules of "market-socialism."

Inequalities within the Rural Sector

As a result of the decentralization of the economy and the new tolerance for private commerce and enterprise, farm families all over China are theoretically able to deploy their household labour in agricultural and non-agricultural tasks, and by appointing different members to a range of non-farm activities increase total income over that of the late 1970s. Households can also turn themselves into private enterprises specializing in a range of service and trade activities. In fact, it is suburban farm families living near urban markets and especially in the rapidly developing coastal areas which have gained the most. For example in 1993, when average per capita net income of all rural residents was RMB 921, in Zhejiang province the average was RMB 1,745, in Guangdong RMB 1,674, in Jiangsu RMB 1,266 while in Gansu it was only RMB 550 and in Guizhou RMB 579.[22]

Another illustration of the same phenomena which begins to capture the cumulative impact of regional inequalities is a comparison of ownership of key consumer durables, whose purchase requires several years of surplus income. Thus we see in Table 2 that despite larger mean household size (MHS), rural families as a group have yet to approach urban families in terms of access to such basic durables as bicycles, fans, washing machines, and refrigerators, and that inter-provincial differences — even after excluding the cities of Beijing, Shanghai, and Tianjin — uniformly exceed those between urban and rural areas.

Table 2. Household Consumption (items owned per 100 households)

		1990	1991	1992 (range by province excluding Beijing, Shanghai, Tianjin)
MHS	rural	4.80	4.71	4.67
	urban	3.50	3.43	3.37
Bikes	rural	118	121	125 (19–206)
	urban	188	151	190
Electric fans	rural	41	53	60 (1–212)
	urban	135	143	146
Washing machines	rural	9	10	12 (1–36)
	urban	78	80	83
Colour TVs	rural	4	6	12 (1–24)
	urban	59	68	78
Refrigerators	rural	1	1	2 (0.04–11)
	urban	42	48	52

MHS = Mean Household Size.
Source: *Zhongguo tongji nianjian 1993* (Chinese Statistical Yearbook, 1993), (Beijing: Zhongguo tongji chubanshe, 1993), pp. 286, 289, 311, 320, 321.

Male-female Disparities

One of the accomplishments of the Mao years in contrast to the pre-communist decades was reduced levels of inequality between working men and women. Particularly during the 1970s, CCP policies of leveling the top and equalizing the bottom, so compressed the reward structure that among young adults who entered the work place after 1965, male-female differences in terms of education, professional training, and income dramatically narrowed. In the realms of power, as measured by membership on high level CCP organs or in leadership of factories or brigades, women remained inferior to men. But in everyday life it was noteworthy how similar were male and female life chances when compared to those of men and women of their parents' generation.[23]

By the late 1980s, the shift to a more individuated reward structure and the retreat of the bureaucratic state spawned a resurgence of gender inequalities. In urban firms where the Cultural Revolution policy had produced the most decisive convergence in wages, men at first began to gain over their female age peers and then women ten or more years their senior.[24] The official press reported that female graduates of prestigious universities had difficulty in securing jobs in their specialties, and in some cases were "returned" to their departments for a second job assignment (*fenpei*) when units refused to accept them after discovering they had hired a woman.[25] Such discrimination was not unknown before 1980, but during the reform period it appears to have become more flagrant.[26] Women were also far less likely than men to set up as private entrepreneurs and in rural areas were more likely than men to stay in low wage farm work.[27]

In the political realm, women also fell further behind male peers. The pre-existing gender gap in Communist Youth League and CCP membership widened,[28] and the percentage of women taking leadership at the local level fell below that of the 1970s.[29]

Cohort and Generational Inequalities

Over the decade of the 1980s the Chinese population aged and by the early 1990s nearly 10% of the population was over age sixty. Nevertheless, as is clear from Table 3, the demographic centre of gravity remained with the young and therefore one might expect that state resources and policies would favour those who represented China's future.

In practice, however, the Chinese government both before and after

Table 3. Size and Age Distribution of Chinese Population

(in percentage)

	1953	1964	1982	1987	1992
0–4 years	15.6	14.4	9.3	9.3	9.2
5–9	11.4	13.6	10.9	9.0	9.6
10–14	10.1	12.4	13.0	10.3	8.8
15–19	9.2	8.9	12.4	11.9	8.8
20–24	8.4	7.3	7.3	11.3	10.7
25–29	7.5	7.3	9.1	6.9	10.2
30–34	6.8	6.7	7.2	8.4	6.9
35–39	6.2	5.9	5.3	6.6	7.9
40–44	5.5	5.1	4.8	4.9	6.2
45–49	4.9	4.4	4.7	4.4	4.5
50–54	4.2	3.8	4.0	4.3	4.0
55–59	3.5	3.2	3.3	3.7	3.9
60–64	2.6	2.5	2.7	2.9	3.2
65–69	1.9	1.7	2.1	2.2	2.4
70+	2.1	1.9	1.7	3.2	3.6
Total population (in millions)	574m	705m	1015m	1072m	1155m

Sources: Judith Banister, *China's Changing Population* (Stanford: Stanford University Press, 1987), pp. 25, 27 and 34. For 1987, *Zhongguo tongji nianjian 1988* (Chinese Statistical Yearbook, 1993), (Beijing: Zhongguo tongji chubanshe, 1988), pp. 105–107, *Zhongguo renkou tongji nianjian 1993*, (Chinese Demographical Statistical Year Book 1993), (Beijing: Zhongguo tongji chubanshe, 1993), pp. 6–8, 352.

1980 has favoured the old, in particular the urban old, when it has come to distribution of welfare benefits. Between 1978 and 1992, the number of people collecting life-time pensions rose from 3.14 million to 25.98 million. By 1992 retirement costs exceeded those for medical care,[30] and were taking 17.6% of the entire wage bill.[31] This special attention to the needs of pensioners can also be seen clearly by tracing the percentage of state budgets that went to programmes targeted at the urban old versus those targeted at national defence or education. Thus in Table 4 one observes how in less than fifteen years pension expenditures rose from 1.5% to 15.8% of the state budget while military expenditures fell from 15.8% to 8.5% and those for education stalled around 12% from 1983 onward.

However, in other dimensions, the acceleration of the Deng reforms

Table 4. Comparison of Expenditures for Pensions, Military, and Education as Percentage of State Budget 1978–1992

	Pensions	Military	Education	State Budget as % of NI
1978	1.5%	15.0%	6.7%	37%
1979	2.5%	17.5%	7.3%	38%
1980	4.1%	15.9%	9.4%	33%
1981	5.5%	14.9%	10.9%	28%
1982	6.3%	15.2%	11.9%	27%
1983	6.7%	13.6%	12.0%	27%
1984	6.8%	11.6%	11.8%	27%
1985	8.0%	10.3%	12.4%	26%
1986	8.3%	8.5%	11.5%	30%
1987	9.7%	8.5%	11.0%	26%
1988	11.8%	8.0%	12.2%	23%
1989	12.5%	8.2%	12.4%	23%
1990	13.6%	8.4%	12.0%	24%
1991	14.5%	8.6%	12.4%	23%
1992	15.8%	8.5%	N/A	22%

Source: *Zhongguo tongji nianjian 1993* (Chinese Statistical Yearbook, 1993), (Beijing: Zhongguo tongji chubanshe, 1993), pp. 33, 215, 223–24, 808, 817.

has worked to the disadvantage of the old and created an environment in which the young have reaped the largest gains. For example in rural China, the highest incomes have accrued to those who excel at producing for the free markets and those who have left agriculture entirely and found wage work in new industries or construction. Rarely are these high earners old; often they are unmarried or newly married young adults who in the commune years had languished in brigade work teams earning at best the wage of their fifty or sixty year old fathers. Thus for rural youth the reform decades dramatically increased their earning power and their economic contribution to the household.

Among urban employees, the gains of the younger generations are less uniform. Through the early 1990s, the principle of seniority persisted within most state enterprises and it was only in the private sector or foreign-owned joint ventures that the young consistently pulled ahead of their elders.[32] Yet even here youth in and of itself did not confer a complete advantage. Thus, one study of joint ventures in Guangdong found that the best educated middle-aged staff drew the highest salaries and although young adults in production jobs earned more than older line workers, they still earned less than older workers in the state sector if the value of medical care and housing was included.[33]

Occupational Cleavages within the Urban Population

One of the issues that brought people into the streets in May and June 1989, and fueled public outrage across the nation was the sense that the reforms of the 1980s had unfairly enriched a minority with special connections, leaving the majority to struggle with nominally higher wages seriously eroded by inflation.[34] Urban professionals and others with advanced education were often the most outspoken because, despite positions of authority, their salaries tended to be only marginally higher than those they supervised, and sometimes were lower.[35] Also by the late 1980s the managerial and technical strata knew what their peers outside of China in Taiwan and Hong Kong earned and they chafed at the Chinese wage scales whereby young and middle-aged physicians or university professors earned less than privately employed artisans. Within the blue collar ranks there was also a strong sense that the reforms had failed to create an equitable pay scale. In particular blue collar workers were angry that in most enterprises wage scales remained compressed and that the key to financial gain was assignment to an especially profitable enterprise not individual achievement or expertise.[36]

After 1990, income inequality further increased and dissatisfaction among urban residents again intensified.[37] High rates of inflation eroded nominal wage gains and created severe hardship for those on fixed incomes or those dependent on the generosity of others.[38] In response, enterprise leaders constrained by the government to index salaries to productivity gains increased non-wage subsidies in order to placate a restless work force.[39] As a result, inequality in urban areas grew but clear disparities among different occupations did not immediately emerge. Instead the resources of the work place decided reward levels and because of greater enterprise autonomy, wage and benefits among enterprises which previously had been quite similar became more unequal. Hence urban residents doing similar, even identical jobs, received widely different incomes.[40] However because in many cases "rich" enterprises owed their wealth to favouritism, access to state monopolies, connections to export licenses, or upwardly biased state prices for their product, managers as well as staff viewed the new reward structure as unfair. In addition because it continued to be difficult for employees to move from one enterprise to another, many felt trapped and further resented the good "luck" of colleagues who had been fortuitously placed in a wealthier unit at the time of their first job assignment or had the connections to get them high paid jobs in joint ventures.

Patterns and Processes of Social Stratification

At the end of the Mao era there were "two Chinas." First there was the China of the vast majority, where despite the elimination of private property and the nationwide system of People's Communes, households and communities were required to be self-sufficient. The diet was restricted almost entirely to what villagers themselves produced. Homes were built by each household using materials family members personally accumulated. Medical, education, and welfare benefits were paid by village funds. In the "Second China," lived the urban minority for whom the communist revolution had created a socialist society. Most urban adults were guaranteed life-time employment with regular monthly salaries, free medical care, subsidized housing, and pensions which replaced 75% of their last wage. Urban children went to school at little direct cost to parents and everyone enjoyed cheap public transportation and state subsidized food rations. In short urban residents of China had reaped more material benefits from the communist victory than had their peers living in the countryside.

Certainly those living in the First China would have preferred to move to the Second China and enjoyed the advantages of socialism. However, after 1955 police controls over domestic migration blocked rural-to-urban migration as an individual strategy of economic advancement. Therefore, rural residents remained socially "inferior" to urbanites — regardless of occupational or political status of the city resident. Operating rather like a caste system, the policy curbing migration to cities created an historically anomalous situation. Traditionally the Chinese peasantry had not been bound to the land or the landlord, and during the decades immediately before the communist victory, both élite and impoverished rural residents moved frequently between rural and urban areas. In contrast, during the Mao era, the fluid relation between city and countryside had been replaced by a polarized environment where urban and rural social hierarchies rarely intersected and neither marriage nor apprenticeship, itinerant peddling nor sojourning, could be used by rural born residents to become permanent urban residents. Rather an individual's status in this bipolar world was established at the moment of birth.[41] A small minority who entered the army and were granted urban *hukou* or the status of state cadre (*guojia ganbu*) upon their demobilization did move from the self-contained villages to the socialist cities. An even smaller group became urban residents through entry into university and assignment to a state enterprise after graduation. However, the majority of rural men remained in the villages of their birth following in the occupational footsteps of their fathers; most rural women, did leave their parents' village, but moved no farther than the village of their husband.

For those born to urban parents the overall pattern of social class reproduction also was distinctive. As in other communist nations, the party-state officially discriminated in favour of the sons and daughters of the pre-communist and contemporary proletariat. However, until the early 1960s those who excelled at competitive exams, rarely were refused access to higher education or professional jobs solely on the basis of class background. As a result, because "competitive" exams tended to favour children with well educated parents, non-proletarian children of politically mediocre class prestige routinely were more successful than children with less educated or illiterate parents. Consequently, until the early 1960s middle class children were able to get the educational credentials that guaranteed a white collar or professional job comparable to that of their parents even though supervisory or leadership posts might be closed to them on political grounds.

During the Cultural Revolution decade (1966–1976) CCP leaders made deliberate efforts to break this reproduction of middle class and professional status by replacing competitive entrance exams based on academic achievement with a screening procedure based on political purity. The short term result was downward mobility for children from the non-CCP middle and upper-middle classes who upon completion of secondary school became manual workers.[42] However, after the onset of the Cultural Revolution in 1996 and the relocation of 17 million urban teenagers to the countryside during the decade thereafter, it was not just children of the middle-class or those with bad class backgrounds who were downwardly mobile. Millions of sons and daughters of unskilled and skilled workers, of party members and even army officers also were prevented from matching or surpassing their parent's occupational status.[43]

Social Prestige

Class position is not defined solely by the distribution of job titles, wages or benefits. Social prestige and access to positions of power are also critical, and here the Maoist revolution — even prior to the Cultural Revolution — did not produce even partially egalitarian outcomes. On the contrary, the legacy of political mobilization and struggle between 1950 and 1957 against "landlords," "rightists," "anti-socialist elements," and other "enemies of the people" distinctively stratified Chinese society along lines of political purity and power. At the pinnacle were revolutionary heroes and national level political leaders or those who traced their ancestry to revolutionary martyrs and/or high party leaders. At the bottom of this politically defined status hierarchy (and clearly inferior to all others) were the "five types" (*wulei fenzi*) (landords, rich peasants, counter revolutionaries, bad elements, and rightists), a strata which might best be described as "the communist sub-proletariat." This strata, which could (and was) on occasion further subdivided into relative degrees of shame and ignominy, were excluded from professional work during the frenzied heights of the Cultural Revolution class struggles, and in some cases denied medical care, housing, and permanent employment. Furthermore, in most cases the stigmatized identity was extended to their children and grandchildren. Thus, just as rural infants were denied access to opportunities in the city because their mothers' were born in the countryside, so children whose parents or grandparents had been politically stigmatized were excluded from full participation in Chinese society and denied any chance to improve upon the occupational or social status of their family of origin.

Stratification and Re-stratification in Contemporary Urban China

The impact of increasing — if still partial — marketization on inequality and stratification has been discussed above. The distribution of incomes has become more skewed and employment in the new sectors and in jobs where individuals bargain for higher pay on the basis of scarce skills has altered the prestige and wage hierarchies. Thus by the early 1990s, it was not unusual for graduates of technical schools, who even as late as 1985 would have been very satisfied to accept a technician's job in a state radio factory, to search desperately for jobs as porters at a new Hilton or Sheraton. Positions as cadres or party workers which had previously been desirable became second and third choices, while the professions of medicine or university research which had attracted many of the brightest students in the early 1980s routinely lost staff to jobs in the commercial sector. In the short term, teachers and nurses of retirement age were kept on because there were no young successors to teach their classes or care for their patients.

Without comprehensive national data comparing financial returns on different occupations over time it is premature to generalize about the emergent hierarchy of prestige and wealth. But drawing on Chinese publications and interview sources — especially those that focus on student choices for post-secondary study and for first jobs — a preliminary structure of status and power has merged. Manual work in the state sector which for 30 years provided job security, decent wages, and social prestige, has lost status.[44] Commercial positions which previously had been denigrated have become respectable, and if they promise access to foreign resources, they offer higher salaries than those in industry. By 1993 there were a significant number of domestic millionaires, and throughout China, a new class of wealth openly flaunts their success with a confidence that would have been inconceivable during the 1970s. At nightclubs, discos and karaoke bars the newly rich routinely spend the equivalent of a university professor's monthly salary on one night's entertainment. Mercedes, Lexus, and BMWs fill the parking lots of joint venture hotels. Cellular phones and Rolex watches appear in the dining rooms of even middle sized county seats. Body-guards and prostitutes operate with only the most minimal efforts to be invisible to police.

Emerging Parameters and Principles of Social Stratification

The social structure of contemporary China remains fluid, at times even chaotic. Yet because patterns of inequality have persisted for almost a decade, one can identify parameters and principles of stratification which distinguish late Deng society from that of the final Mao years and thereby establish a framework within which other recent shifts in cultural and social life can be analyzed. They are summarized here both as a conclusion to this chapter and are reflected in several of the chapters on contemporary society in this volume.

1. *While agricultural labour has a far lower rate of return than industrial labour, and welfare benefits have become more concentrated in*

cities, urban residence no longer as automatically confers economic superiority as it did between 1955 and 1980.

During the decades of severe restraints on rural to urban migration and generous subsidies and guaranteed employment to urban residents, the top earners in rural areas could not approach those on the bottom rungs of the urban wage and benefit ladder. As we have seen in the materials analyzed above, urban-rural inequalities overall have persisted and deepened after 1990. Yet because of the spectacular gains in suburban areas and new emiseration among some segments of the urban population, the two ladders of compensation overlap, and those at the lower end of the urban ladder, stand below the most prosperous 15–20% of the rural population. To a large extent the new wealth of rural China is the result of the incorporation of the suburbs into a metropolitan economy where state assets are concentrated. But because those who accumulate the wealth in rural areas do so through non-state firms and individual family enterprise, suburban wealth represents a structural transformation.

2. *Cohort inequalities of the late Mao era have eroded and in some instances have been reversed.*

The weakening of a redistributive state which allocated rewards on the basis of seniority and blocked inter-cohort competition for leadership has permitted newcomers to compete more successfully with the old timers. As a result the financial advantages which those in their fifties and sixties enjoyed over those in their thirties and forties during the late 1970s have eroded. In the political arena where there is still neither open competition nor routinized procedures of succession, gerontocracy prevails. But for the majority whose work does not require political capital or endorsement, the greatest rewards go to the quickest and most adroit and to the extent that age and cohort are good predictors of financial success, it is the young, newcomers who are favoured.

3. *Inter-unit profit levels have widened in both urban and rural areas creating a mosaic of inequality which is not easily explained by a bureaucratically defined hierarchy of job statuses or by returns to individual level human capital.*

In rural areas, coastal villages have in general done better than those in the interior, but even in coastal provinces one finds dramatic disparities among similarly located villages as a result of a fortuitous investment by a joint venture or a favoured relationship with a state enterprise concentrating its contract work in one location. However because markets for labour and inputs are more active and pervasive in the decollectivized rural areas, inter-unit inequalities within single geographical locales are less stark than those in cities where bureaucratic privilege is more enduring and labour mobility is more constrained.

4. *Gender inequality is pervasive in all occupations.*

As the affirmative action policies of the Cultural Revolution are renounced, as wages are set by "a market" which discriminates against those presumed to bear heaviest family obligations, males are encouraged to assume high risk jobs which demand mobility and leadership and women are encouraged to take primary responsibility for domestic comfort. In urban areas, this may mean that wives remain in near-bankrupt state enterprises that guarantee housing and medical insurance while the husbands move to joint ventures or start out as *getihu*. Throughout rural China, it encourages a division of household labour where married women assume major responsibility for low paid farm work and men in the household become traders, long distance sojourners, or members of a roving construction team. Whichever scenario prevails, women's individual incomes fall below those of male peers and the association between female gender and low wage, low prestige work is strengthened and serves an underlying principle for the allocation of societal rewards and authority.

5. *Urban manual workers are increasingly disempowered and disenfranchised*

As layoffs and job loss to low wage rural industries create the specter of widespread unemployment, the urban proletariat sees the end to its secure and privileged past. Yet because of the continued ban on non-state political mobilization and the importance of inter-firm inequalities, manual workers find it difficult to assert their interests within the hybrid economy of "market-socialism" or to build class solidarity based on their shared occupational status.

6. *The number of paths to power and wealth have multiplied.*

As political purity becomes increasingly irrelevant, and opportunities for capital investment and self-employment expand, the number of pathways to power and wealth multiply and rural and urban residents can choose among several strategies of social advancement. For example, when one observes rural households, it is clear that families explicitly mix risks to maximize total opportunity sending one member off to work in a distant city, another to a nearby factory, but still keeping at least one member on the land should the off-farm investments collapse or go sour. However because such flexibility is available primarily to that segment of rural residents in the rapidly industrializing coastal areas, this proliferation of opportunities is also another axis along which the 1990s are generating new inequalities. For those living in desolate terrain far from good transportation or urban markets, decentralization and reduced state supervision means persistent poverty.

In urban areas as noted in statement No. 3, sectoral and inter-firm inequalities combined with barriers to the free flow of labour have reinforced firm-specific privilege. However, urban individuals now enjoy a range of choice incomparably richer than that faced during the 1970s. In coastal cities, every year there are more joint ventures recruiting skilled workers, accountants, computer experts, engineers, and marketing staff. Chinese private companies and individual practices have begun to appear in significant numbers. Since 1990, second and even third jobs have proliferated and urban residents expect several job changes over their work lives.

7. *Technical expertise and managerial talent grants authority independent of membership in the Communist Party, and thereby lays the foundation for the emergence of a new middle class comparable to those which emerged in Taiwan and Hong Kong during the 1960s.*

Despite recent efforts to recruit engineers, intellectuals and top scientists into the Communist Party, overall the trend is to separate political and technical leadership. Moreover in the private or foreign affiliated sectors, no demands are made that experts join the party. Money has new independence, and to the extent that an increasing percentage of young technocrats and factory level leaders remain outside of the party and are allowed to develop shared professional and financial interests, a foundation for a fundamental realignment of social class power has been established.

8. *Despite the multiple paths to success, there appears to be a trend toward higher rates of social class reproduction.*

Because personal resources and connections are often decisive for getting jobs in joint ventures or in providing start-up capital for either investment or self-employment, family wealth and political power determine a young adult's occupational position more directly than they did in the 1970s when the best a parent could do was prevent their children from being assigned the worst jobs. Now in the less politicized and more diversified and commercial economy of the 1990s, parents can actively advance a child's career rather than simply exercise damage control. Conversely, where collective controls and resources have been reduced, children whose parents lack resources are at a disadvantage, particularly when it comes to starting a business or moving into rural industry. If this pattern persists one would expect to see high levels of social class reproduction.

In occupations where tertiary education leads to the best paid jobs, competitive exams of mastery initially favoured adolescents from the best educated families. This trend suggested that China by the year 2000 would experience a process of social class reproduction among the professional strata quite similar to that of the decades immediately before and after 1949 when university education was accessible primarily to children of the upper-middle class. After 1990, however, the social background of those taking the university entrance examinations shifted and by 1994, the authorities could claim that a majority were of "rural" origin.[45] It is premature to generalize from this recent change, but what it suggests is that as market opportunities favour those from better endowed families or more economically advanced regions of the country, those who lack family capital or come from remote areas will turn to universities as a location where individual performance is more directly rewarded.

9. *At the pinnacle of Chinese society a few thousand offspring of the highest echelons of the CCP are reproducing their élite class status through strategies rooted in monopolies of political power and privileged access to state property.*

Able, for example, to broker arms sales or currency speculation due to their access to the highest level of state power, this strata of "princes and princesses" have the potential to fundamentally alter the special interests of the élite. They also stand in opposition to the emergent managerial-technical strata and make no ideological claim for the loyalty of the proletariat as did their parents. In many ways they are reminiscent of the powerful cliques of the Nationalist era who built personal fortunes during years of great emiseration by using public resources for personal gain.

A Glance Forward

The parameters and principles of social stratification in the early 1990s are fragmented and overlapping. As a result, neither a dichotomized model of class interests nor a hierarchical continuum of class segments captures the reality of contemporary China. What is clear is that patterns of inequality and tensions among different strata are developing along a trajectory distinct from that of the Mao years, and that the situation is too fluid for one to know how — or when — it will stabilize. Identification of the most salient

Inequality and Stratification in the Nineties 11.21

patterns of differentiation, however, provides an initial framework within which to contemplate the immediate future. Partial and incomplete, it is offered here as one means of encouraging a preliminary dialogue.

Notes

1. There is an enormous literature on shifts in the degree of income inequality and no single measure or standard data set is used by all sources. Nevertheless there is agreement about these broad trends, which can be documented by simple measures that show rural per capita income steadily dropping as a percentage of urban incomes after 1983 (Kang Chen, "China's Economic Reform and Social Unrest," in *China Report*, Vol. 1, No. 1 (March 1990) or those that document rural losses in real income after 1988 (Barry Naughton, "Inflation in China," in *China's Dilemmas in the 1990s*, edited by the Joint Economic Committee, Washington DC Government Printing Office, Vol. 1 [April 1991], p. 142). Similarly more elaborate studies such as Shamus Mok's doctoral study of Shiyan over the entire decade ("China's Motor Cities," unpublished PhD. dissertation, Michigan State, 1994) or the extensive reanalysis of the State Statistical Bureau data by a group of international experts (see Azizur Rahman Khan, Keith Griffin, Carl Riskin, and Zhao Renwei, "Household Income and Its Distribution in China," *The China Quarterly*, No. 132 [December 1992], pp. 1029–61) show increased inequality despite steady increases in aggregate incomes.
2. For example in 1978, while males working in state sector industry earned more than females within each age group, women who had ten years seniority consistently out earned more junior males. By 1988, this was no longer the case; both women over fifty and those under forty earned less than or approximately the same as men under thirty. *Zhongguo laodong gongzi tongji nianjian 1989* (Chinese Yearbook of Labour and Wages 1989) (Beijing: Laodong renshi chubanshe, 1989). See also Khan et al., "Household Income …" (Note 1).
3. See for example the shift in the urban:rural ratio of hospital beds, doctors, nurses, or upper-middle school entrants and graduates between 1975 and 1990. *Zhongguo tongji nianjian 1993* (Chinese Statistical Yearbook 1993) (hereafter *ZGTJNJ*) (Beijing: Zhongguo tongji chubanshe, 1993), pp. 736–40, 797–98, 808; *Zhongguo shehui tongji nianjian 1993* (Yearbook of Chinese Social Statistics 1993) (Beijing: Zhongguo tongji chubanshe, 1993), p. 208.
4. See Khan et al., "Household Income and its Distribution," (Note 1), p. 1037.

For a discussion of the bias in welfare benefits see, Deborah Davis, "Chinese Social Welfare Outcomes," *The China Quarterly*, No. 119 (1989).
5. Over the decade of the 1980s the official definition of urban and rural populations shifted making comparisons using government statistics difficult. In particular the 1984 decision to include millions of agricultural households living in metropolitan areas annexed to cities inflated the size of the urban population and made data which used this definition of urban actually include many individuals and households who lived a self-sufficient rural life with few of the subsidies and social services available to non-agricultural populations resident in urban cores. To correct for this redefinition of urban and rural I have attempted to limit my discussion of urban conditions to the non-agricultural population. When I must rely on secondary sources for reports of change over time or official statistics do not specify whether urban averages include agricultural households, there is no way to guarantee precision over time. However to the extent that comparisons are between rural and urban groups after 1990, one can be reasonably sure that one is capturing real shifts between comparable units of analysis.
6. As measured by per capita *shenghuofei*.
7. *Renmin ribao* (People's Daily) (hereafter *RMRB*), 23 February 1991, p. 2 and 1 March 1994, p. 2.
8. In 1990 real rates of income growth were 1.8% in rural areas and 8.6% in urban areas. By 1993, there was some improvement in both areas, but the urban residents maintained their lead, gaining 10.2% as opposed to only 3.2% for rural residents. *RMRB*, 23 February 1991, p. 2 and 1 March 1994, p. 2.
9. *ZGTJNJ 1993*, p. 798.
10. *Zhongguo weisheng nianjian 1987* (Chinese Health Yearbook 1987) (Beijing: Renmin weisheng chubanshe, 1987), pp. 497, 524, and 526.
11. *RMRB*, 29 September 1992, p. 2.
12. *RMRB*, 7 August 1992, p. 8.
13. Mu Chuan, "Developing Modern Labour Markets," *Zhongguo wuxi bao*, 13 July 1994, trans. in *JPRS*, 15 September 1994, pp. 60–62.
14. *Zhongguo xinxi bao* (Chinese Scrupulous Daily), 4 March 1994, p. 1, trans. in *JPRS*, 24 May 1994, p. 51.
15. *RMRB*, 7 January 1994, p. 2.
16. For example, in 1993 Beijing commercial housing cost between RMB 3,000 and 4,000 per square meter, or between RMB 120,000 and 140,000 for an apartment of average size. *RMRB*, 15 January 1993, p. 2. However it was not unusual in that year for apartments to be sold at RMB 140, or even RMB 80, per square meter. *RMRB*, 15 January 1994, p. 2.
17. *Zhongguo shehui tongji ziliao* (Chinese Social Statistics) (hereafter *ZGSHTJNJ*), (Beijing: Zhongguo tongji chubanshe, 1985) p. 132.
18. *ZGTJNJ 1985*, p. 799; *ZGTJNJ 1993*, p. 808.

19. *RMRB*, 2 June 1994, p.2.
20. *Ming Pao* (Hong Kong), 13 October 1993, A15.
21. *RMRB*, 15 July 1994, p. 2.
22. *Nongmin Pao* (Peasant Gazette), 17 February 1994, trans. in *JPRS*, 17 March 1994; *Zhongguo xin bao* (China News), 4 March 1994, trans. in *JPRS*, 19 April 1994.
23. Martin K. Whyte, "Sexual Inequality under Socialism," in *Class and Social Stratification in Post-Revolution China*, edited by James Watson (Cambridge: Cambridge University Press, 1984), pp. 198–238.
24. Typical of the shift is the data reported in two large surveys of average monthly wage (including bonus and subsidies) for employees of state industry in 1978 and 1988:

	1978		1988	
	male	female	male	female
under 30	34	34	122	111
30–39	43	40	148	127
40–49	57	49	164	144
50+ yrs.	71	57	174	127

Source: *Zhongguo laodong gongzi tongji nianjian 1989*, p. 346.

25. *Beijing Review*, 10 August 1987, p. 9; *RMRB*, 31 July 1987, p. 4.
26. Drawing on interview material, Suzanne Pepper has documented this phenomenon among Beida graduates in 1976.
27. Whereas women were 37% of all *zhiyuan* in urban areas and 40% of all workers in rural industry, they were only 24% of all *getihu*. *Beijing Review*, 31 October 1988, p. 6. In a seven provinces survey of rural households investigators found that number of men not number of adult women significantly increased the likelihood of the household establishing a private business, that if a household sets up a business men are most likely to be in charge, and that even when rural families ran businesses, women remained almost exclusively in agriculture. Barbara Entwisle et al., "Gender and Family Businesses in Rural China," *American Sociological Review*, Vol. 60, No. 1 (February 1995), pp. 36–57.
28. Nan Lin and Wen Xie, " Occupational Prestige in Urban China," *American Journal of Sociology*, Vol. 93, No. 4 (1985), pp. 793–832.
29. *RMRB*, 1 May 1989, p. 4; 18 August 1990, p. 3.
30. *ZGSHTJNJ 1993*, p. 114.
31. *ZGTJNJ 1991*, pp. 119, 130, 790; *ZGTJNJ 1993*, pp. 132, 817.
32. Feng Tongqing, "Zou xiang shichang jingji de qiye zhigong" (Industrial Workers and Staff Turn toward a Market Economy), *Zhongguo shehui kexue* (Chinese Social Science), No. 3 (1993), pp. 101–20.

33. Ibid. Critical to the lingering rural-urban gap is the vast subsidies for housing, food and medical care which state employees received outside of their wage packet, items for which the rural migrant labourers would have to pay market prices.
34. *RMRB*, 26 June 1989, p. 4; 8 August 1990, p. 5.
35. *Ming Pao*, 21 September 1988, p. 8; *RMRB*, 4 March 1990, p. 1; Cheng Zhongyen, "Butong bumen de daxue wenhua chengdu zhigong shouru" (Income of University Graduates in Different Sectors), *Shehuixue yu shehui diaocha* (Sociology and Social Investigation), No. 1 (1990), pp. 34–35.
36. Hu Fengyun, "Zhengxun jingji zhixu huanjie fenpei bugong" (Restore the Economic Order by Making Economic Distinctions More Just), *Shanghai gaige* (Shanghai Reform), No. 2 (1989); "Guanyu zhigong de kanfa" (Investigation of Worker and Staff Attitude to Work), *Zhongguo laodong kexue* (Chinese Labour Science), No. 2 (1989), pp. 21–25.
37. *Ming Pao*, 27 July 1991, p. 7; *Far Eastern Economic Review*, 24 June 1993, p. 34; Bian Yanjie, John Logan, Pan Yukang, and Guan Ying, "Income Inequality in Tianjin 1978–1993," paper prepared for conference on Civil Society in Tianjin, University of California-San Diego, 5–9 June 1994.
38. *Ming Pao*, 31 July 1994, B6.
39. *RMRB*, 30 June 1994, p. 4; Christian Henriot, Françoise Ged, Jean-Louis Rocca, Shi Lu, "Entre Etat et Marche: Radioscopie des Industries Shanghaiennes (1980–1992)" (Between State and Market: Survey of Shanghai Industry [1980–1992]), (Lyon: Institut d'Asie Orientale [CNRS URA 1579], September 1994), pp. 171–79.
40. Li Jiangtao, "Danwei zai shehui fenceng zhong de yiyi" (Significance of *Danwei* in Social Stratification), paper at conference on Social Stratification in Chinese Societies, The Chinese University of Hong Kong, December 1993.
41. But the communist rules that designated residential status — unlike traditional inheritance practices — required that infants assume the (residential) status of their mothers. Consequently, if a rural woman married an urban man, neither she nor her children could move to join him in the city. If a rural man married an urban woman, he would not be able to move to the city, but his children could be raised by their mother in the city. However, the likelihood of an urban woman choosing to marry a poorly paid villager from whom she would have to maintain a separate urban household if she wished her children to share the advantages of urban residence made such marriages extremely rare.
42. Deborah Davis, "Skidding: Downward Mobility among Children of the Maoist Middle Class," *Modern China*, October 1992, pp. 410–37.
43. Ibid.
44. *RMRB*, 28 October 1990, p. 8; Wang Fengyu, "Attitudes and Expectations of Chinese Urban Youth towards Employment and Training," in *Social Security*

in the *People's Republic of China*, edited by Renate Krieg and Monika Schaedler (Hamburg: Mitteilungen des Instituts fuer Asienkunde, 1994).

45. This observation was made to me by Zhou Xueguang in a personal communication, and by Suzanne Pepper. See her chapter in this book and her citation to an article in *Zhongguo jiaoyu bao*, 7 July 1994.

12

The Family Status of Chinese Women in the 1990s

Jean K. M. Hung

The year 1994, international year of the family, witnessed the highest profile given to the family and women in the 45 years history of the People's Republic of China (PRC). For the first time, the State Council published a White Paper, *The Situation of Chinese Women*. It is just one of many projects designed to prepare for the Fourth World Conference on Women, which will take place in Beijing in 1995. Other projects include the publication of two large-scale surveys on women, activities concerned with the election of the "model family," etc. From 1 March 1994, urban employees in China started to enjoy two-day weekends every other week and had their working hours reduced from 48 to 44 hours per week. The slogan, "Leave your Sundays to your family," was publicized in the press repeatedly and soon became a pet phrase among city residents.

After coming to power in 1949, the communist government promoted an ideology which held that the loyalty once belonging to the family should be shifted to the party and its highest leader: "Father is dear, mother is dear, but they are not as dear as Chairman Mao." It was unimaginable during the Mao era that family values would be emphasized again.

The de-politicization and secularization of society in post-Mao China has changed the role and image of women as well as offered "a variety of role options for Chinese women."[1] The economic and social changes have also significantly accelerated the "family revolution," started at the beginning of this century in urban China and extended during the early 1950s to rural areas. The aim overall was to eliminate patriarchal domination and establish a more democratic family system.[2] To what degree have these goals been reached? What is the impact of the top-down movement on women's family status? What is the cost to women themselves of their higher status at home?

In response to these questions, this chapter examines the changing family status of Chinese women from three perspectives: (1) women's position in the home as shown in national surveys; (2) the comparative family status of rural and urban women; and (3) the legal protection of women's family status *vis-à-vis* structural and cultural constraints in the society. In addition to the findings of two surveys conducted in China in the early 1990s, this chapter is also based on my own study of family relationships in a southeast Chinese city,[3] as well as my observations during field trips to 18 villages in Fujian, Shandong and Guizhou from 1992 to 1994.

The Family Status of Chinese Women in the 1990s

The Two National Surveys on Women's Status

The National Women's Federation and the National Statistics Bureau jointly conducted a survey (hereafter, WF survey) on women's situation and status in 1990. The survey was designed and carried out according to national survey standard requirements. Two thousand trained investigators interviewed more than 45,000 people in 23 provinces. The respondents are both men and women from 18 to 64 years old, selected by multi-stage, dual sampling with stratified unequal probability. The preparation of the survey started in 1989, the standard survey time was 15 September 1990. The first volume of the survey findings at the national level was published in 1993.[4] Almost concurrently, another large-scale survey was conducted by the Institute of Population Studies (hereafter, IPS survey). The sample of 4,509 urban couples and 4,524 rural couples cover 30,088,886 couples in Shanghai, Shanxi, Shandong, Guangxi, Ningxia and Jilin. The IPS survey was sponsored by the Chinese government and the UN Population Fund. It is the most sophisticated survey study of this kind in terms of sample frame, questionnaire design and investigation method. The results were published in a 1994 volume dedicated to the Fourth World Conference on Women.[5] Together these two surveys constitute the most extensive investigations on women in Chinese history. What follows is a small selection of the findings from these surveys.

Table 1 illustrates public opinion on gender equality from the WF survey. This table shows that women's legal status is highest compared to their status in other respects, while women's family status is second highest. Fifty-nine percent of women and 55.7% of men think that men and women have equal status at home. Seventeen percent of women and 18.3% of men believe that women's family status is higher than men's, while 23.7% of women and 26% of men think that men's family status is higher. In urban areas, 58% of people think men and women enjoy equal status at home and 21.4% of them say that women's family status is higher; 20.1% say the opposite. The finding comes as no surprise to people and scholars in China. Considering the long history of China's patriarchal kinship system and the traditional women's position of *san cong* or three obediences (which stipulate that a woman should obey her father before marriage, her husband when married, and her son when widowed), the change in women's family status within half a century is significant. Women's inferiority, imposed by social norms and women's submissive, supporting role in the family are fading away.

Table 1. Public Opinion on Gender Equality by Sexes

(in %)

		Women very high	Women higher	Equal	Men higher	Men very high
Political status	women	0.1	0.9	51.0	35.8	12.1
	men	0.1	1.7	56.6	31.4	10.0
Legal status	women	0.2	4.0	81.3	11.5	2.9
	men	0.2	5.9	82.4	8.7	2.7
Economic status	women	0.3	6.4	49.7	38.7	4.8
	men	0.3	6.6	51.0	38.1	3.9
Family status	women	0.9	16.3	59.0	21.0	2.7
	men	0.8	17.5	55.7	23.2	2.8
Social norm	women	0.2	1.9	39.3	50.4	8.2
	men	0.4	2.3	40.3	49.1	7.8

Source: WF survey, p. 340.

As noted, men's opinion regarding women's status is very much the same as that of women themselves. Women's satisfaction with their family status is also demonstrated by their positive response shown in Table 2.

Table 2. What Do You Think of Your Family Status?

(in %)

	No answer	Very high	Rather high	Ordinary	Low	Very low
Urban women	0.5	16.6	41.3	40.3	1.0	0.3
Urban men	0.3	19.5	42.8	36.2	1.0	0.1
Rural women	0.4	9.2	36.2	51.6	2.3	0.3
Rural men	0.4	21.8	37.4	38.8	1.3	0.3

Source: WF survey, p. 245.

One may doubt the degree to which personal feelings reflect reality. Nevertheless, if we compare what women think of their status in the public domain (see for example, Table 3), it is obvious that women are more satisfied with their status at home than with their status in society. Not surprisingly, men agree with them.

While only 1.3% of urban women think that they have low or very low family status, 62.5% (10.3% + 52.2%) of urban women believe that men have better promotion opportunities in their work unit.

Table 3. Promotion Opportunities

(in %)

	Men very high	Men higher	Same	Women higher	Women very high	Not clear
Women	10.3	52.2	16.5	0.6	0.0	19.6
Men	8.8	50.3	22.2	1.8	0.1	16.7

Source: WF survey, p. 457.

Rights of Income Management and Allocation

The IPS survey which focuses specifically on women's family status, finds that the wife's management and joint management of family income between husband and wife in the cities account for 86.6%, 6.6 points more than the husband's management and joint management.[6] Income management used to be and still is mainly the woman's responsibility. It reflects the tradition of *nan zhuwai, nü zhunei*, women take care of family matters, men of those outside. The women I interviewed in both rural and urban areas usually have clearer ideas than men about family income and expenses.

According to the survey, the allocation of income by men and women is almost the same. Thus, 66.25% of men and 66.06% of women in the cities can allocate 11–100 yuan. The proportion of wives who can allocate 51–100 yuan is 34.4%, slightly higher than husbands (34.16%).[7]

Women's increasing involvement in family decision-making reflects the tremendous change in Chinese women's family status. However, responsibility for family funds does not necessarily mean rights or power over their family affairs and by extension higher family status of wives. The situation also depends on how well-off the family is. In the countryside, the housewives do not enjoy their "right" of income management and allocation because they are responsible more than their husbands for how to make the ends meet. A middle-aged woman in Shandong told me that she could not sleep at night, worrying about the betrothal money for her two sons.

Marriage and Fertility Decisions

In the IPS survey, 94.64% of urban women and 70.88% of rural women had married of their own independent will. And, 79.91% of fertility decisions were made jointly by wife and husband in the city, 82.87% in the countryside.[8] The statistics also show that both urban and rural women had more control over fertility decisions than men. Freedom to choose a mate is the most important thing for the emancipation of Chinese women in the domestic sphere. In that sense, about 20% of rural women have not yet been "liberated." As for women's right over fertility, it is not easy to certify whether the wife or the husband has greater decision-making power. As a matter of fact, under the one-child policy, a family's fertility decisions have already been made by the government unless the family or one spouse decides not to have a child at all or to defy the government's regulation by having another child. Unfortunately, neither of these two surveys inquired about who made decisions in those extraordinary circumstances.

The IPS survey also covers rights of decision for consumption, individual development and children's development. Generally speaking, most couples make these decisions jointly, while the wife has more say in some situations and the husband's opinion counts more in others. The Chinese emphasize harmonious family life rather than individual autonomy at home. Women may willingly let husbands make decisions on certain things and vice versa. Again, I would argue that unless there is disagreement between wife and husband, the fact of who makes decisions does not directly reflect the distribution of power in the family. However, both surveys were cleverly designed to test women's status at home on matters other than women's "rights."

Table 4. Does Your Spouse Ignore Your Opinion during Conversation

(in %)

	No answer	Often	Sometimes	Occasionally	Almost never
Women	0.4	2.6	5.7	11.2	80.1
Men	0.4	2.0	5.3	9.9	82.5

Source: WF survey, p. 226.

Less than 2.6% of women and 2% of men often pay no attention to their spouses and 80.1% of women said that their husbands never ignore their opinion during conversation. *Furen zhijian*, or opinion of women used to mean narrow-minded in Chinese. It was impossible for couples in "old" China to draw equal attention during their conversation. Compared with urban men, those in the countryside pay less attention to their wives.

The issues will be discussed later. The survey also shows that the oldest age group (60–64) draws less attention from their husbands and the youngest group (20–24) draws more attention from their husbands.[9]

Table 5. Who Should Be the First to Have Good Food in the Family

(in %)

	Son	Daughter	Children	Wife	Husband	Wife and Husband	The old	Whole family
Urban wife	11.79	12.14	27.11	0.68	6.91	22.32	17.39	1.66
Urban husband	10.96	11.14	27.15	5.53	2.01	23.65	17.73	1.79
Rural wife	8.26	3.74	41.64	0.53	8.70	10.75	19.31	7.07
Rural husband	7.72	3.38	46.23	1.74	2.11	11.82	20.01	6.57

Source: IPS survey, p. 500.

Privileges within the family constitute an interesting set of indicators in the IPS survey. Among the family's expenditures, money for food accounts for the greatest outlay and allocation for food reflects the focus of the family life. The survey shows that in both urban and rural areas, children are the most privileged family members. Of husband and wife, more women think the husband should be treated better than the wife in terms of food. It is generally believed that men need more nutrition because they are responsible for heavier work. More urban parents think that the girls deserve better food than the boys, while the rural parents think the opposite. In both rural and urban areas, people who think that the children should eat the best food, outnumber people who still believe the elderly deserve better food. This attitude clearly reflects a decline of the age hierarchy. As for who should be the one to wear the best clothes in the family, 25.63% of urban men said the wife, while only 4.48% of rural men agree with the view. Children come first again in this respect.[10] Not surprisingly, more urban parents like to dress their girls better than their sons. My own study also shows that discrimination against girls in these respects is almost non-existent in cities but still very common in the countryside.

How time is spent is another important indicator illustrating the division of labour at home between the wife and husband. Surprisingly, urban men spend almost the same amount of time as do women on domestic chores, as well as on caring for children and the elderly. This finding seems contradicted by the answers to another question, "Who is the main bearer of housework?" in the same survey. For instance, in 80.44% of the families, the wife is mainly responsible for washing clothes.[11] Yet as shown on Table 6, the time the husband and wife spend on laundry is one hour for the wife and 0.81 hour for the husband. The men may have exaggerated the time they spend on domestic chores and perhaps the time goes much slower for them when they are doing laundry. But modern Chinese men at least do not treat their wives as domestic helpers like their father's or grandfather's generations did.

According to the WF survey, however, in urban areas, men spend 2.16 hours per day on domestic chores, while women spend 3.75 hours, more than one-third longer than men. The time rural women spend on domestic chores is much more than the time spent by men, 5.18 hours by women and 2.23 hours by men.[12]

The average time spent on domestic chores by men and women in my case study in one city coincides with the result of the WF survey, and the time spent by young couples is almost the same as the result shown by the IPS survey. A survey conducted in 1994 on married life in Beijing shows that in 40% of families, the wife and husband share the domestic chores equally or the husband does more.[13] In any event, the findings of the WF and IPS surveys indicate that Chinese women's status at home has improved greatly. Some Chinese scholars even argue that Chinese urban women's family status is actually among the highest in the world, including developed countries such as the United States.[14]

Time spent can be calculated, but mental and physical energy cannot be measured. Generally speaking, the family means more to women than to men, and the women are more devoted to family life. Table 7 is the

Table 6. Time Spent by Urban Husband and Wife on Daily Activities

(in hours)

	Work	Travel on the way	Cooking	Laundry	Tutoring children	Taking care of children	Taking care of the old	Film or TV	Sleep	Study
Husband	7.96	0.94	1.37	0.81	1.07	1.53	1.15	2.07	7.96	1.40
Wife	7.90	0.96	1.76	1.00	1.06	1.88	1.27	1.97	7.99	1.15

Source: IPS survey, pp. 242–43.

Table 7. What Do You Think Is the Most Important Thing in Your Life?

(in %)

	Health	Family	Career	Contribution to society	Others
Men	21.07	16.49	18.88	17.29	26.32
Women	26.34	29.84	10.57	9.95	23.30

Source: *Sample survey.* Wen Xianliang, "Lun shichang jingji zhong funü de shiyinxing" (The Women's Adaptation to the Market Economy), *Funü yanjiu* (Women Study), No. 2 (1993), pp. 8–14.

result of a sampling survey conducted in Sichuan in 1991 among 722 employees in the electronic industry.

One fact is usually overlooked by most analysis, namely, that women's status is based on their commitment and contribution to the family. The patriarchal authority in the traditional family system was bestowed and determined by the culture. Men were superior to women simply because they were men. The women's family status, however, is achieved mainly through the women's own effort. Women's contribution to the family costs them not just their leisure at home but also their equal opportunities and status in the public sphere. The theoretical hypothesis of the IPS study, following the mainstream of Western studies on family power, does not pay enough attention to the cost of women's family status. First, women bear more family responsibility, which demands time and energy; secondly, women are considered by society as family-oriented. Therefore, for the long term interest of the work unit, women should not be hired nor given serious responsibility such as supervising other people if men are available.[15] Table 3 also illustrates this phenomenon. Thirdly, women for whom their career is at least as important as their family life are influenced by this kind of social prejudice. According to the IPS survey, 72.87% of urban women still believe that a wife should sacrifice her own career for her husband's.[16] About one-third of women do not agree but the family-oriented stereotype nevertheless affects all. The woman's personal career development is therefore handicapped, which helps explain why women's family status might cost them the equal opportunities in the public domain.

In China, as in most countries, gender equality at home may also be affected by the unequal education level and income of husband and wife. Looking at the socio-economic and educational structure, Chinese women are still at a disadvantage, compared to men. According to the WF survey, rural working women's annual income is 1,235 yuan and the men's is 1,518 yuan, with women getting 81.4% of the men's earnings.[17] Urban women earn 1,788 yuan and men 2,316 yuan a year, with women receiving only 77.4% of the men's pay.[18] The expectation of marriage, another special social notion, also attributes an unequal relationship between husband and wife. A woman is usually looking forward to marrying somebody who has at least the same education level, is smarter and has more abilities than herself. The man is reluctant or afraid to marry a woman with higher education or who earns more money than himself.

Comparison of Urban and Rural Women's Family Status

During my field study in a southwest Chinese city in 1993, I noticed that in many families talkative teenage girls always dominated the lunch table. In the countryside, however, conditions were very different. For example, when only women were available, both the village cadres and the women themselves would tell us that nobody was at home. In some villages in northern Fujian, to our questions on how many children they had or how many labourers the family had, the answer usually did not include girls and the women.[19] The women do not count at all. Why is the contrast between city and the countryside so sharp? I will examine the reasons from the perspectives of the economic structure, social norms, the family kinship structure and inheritance. The aim is to see whether and how the patriarchal family system still functions in the cities and countryside and what are the economic, social and legal bases of urban women's family status.

The Economic Structure

The above-quoted income indicator shows the difference between women and men, but cannot demonstrate the real income levels of the rural and urban sectors. The welfare situation in urban areas has diversified during the last decade. But generally speaking, compared to the rural population, the urban employees benefit greatly from the bonuses of their work units in addition to the welfare system of the government. Urban residents and farmers are actually living in two different societies.

For example, family reproduction in the cities is sponsored by the government. In addition to the medical care of mother and child, most women employees enjoy three months' maternity leave, nurture break during working hours for mothers of infants and other welfare amenities. Rural women, however, are excluded from these health care programmes. Compared to urban women, rural women are less independent economically, their income is not as stable as urban women employees and their old age is not secured by any welfare system.

Table 8. Access to the Welfare System of the Rural and Urban Women

(in %)

		Retirement pension	Medical care	Sick leave	Maternity leave
Urban women	yes/no	82.6/17.3	71.0/29.0	79.9/20.0	85.3/14.7
Rural women	yes/no	5.6/94.2	8.0/91.9	9.2/90.7	12.1/87.7

Source: WF survey, p. 90.

Table 8 illustrates comparative access to welfare as of 1990. The respondents were women 18 to 64 years old, some of whom would not have been employed. Hence, the actual rate of urban working women who had access to the welfare system was probably higher than the survey indicated. Also, the small percentage of rural women who had access to the welfare system actually belonged to the rural non-agricultural population rather than to farm families. Among the benefits, retirement pensions matter most because the life-time income frees both women and men from having to depend on their children for support in old age. Thus, for the first time ever, pensions eliminated in the cities marriage's function of producing sons for old-age protection. But rural women have remained throughout responsible for giving birth to sons in order to provide security, and women are still blamed if they fail to give birth to a son. The pressure on women has also become greater under the government's compulsory birth control programme.

Rural women's family status is also negatively influenced by the fact that farming is the least rewarding job in China. Due to unfair terms of trade between industry and agriculture, the farmers are at a great disadvantage economically. But it has been estimated that women now account for 70% of the total agricultural labour force since only women perform agricultural labor in more than one-third of all farm families. In such families, husbands are engaged in more economically rewarding non-agricultural occupations. Hence, the wife usually works longer hours and does heavier work than her husband but earns less money than him.

After decollectivization in the early 1980s, the family became an independent economic unit again and patriarchal domination still prevails therein. The migration of rural labour, which started in the mid-1980s, however, has made a big impact on the farmers' family life although the situation varies. In some areas, the men migrate, leaving women to manage the family farm alone. In a Shandong village I visited in 1994, 70% of men were engaged in non-agriculture jobs for the whole year or seasonally. Women complained about the heavy burden they could hardly bear. From the perspective of family power, the cost of their new predominance in production may therefore be greater than the benefits.[20] Comparing women's situation in two villages, one in Fujian and another in Shandong, I found that the Shandong women certainly worked longer hours and had tougher responsibilities than the Fujian women. Hence, even though Shandong women have more economic responsibilities, it is difficult to conclude that they are in a better position than Fujian women. Again, women's status comes at a price.

In areas where women have a better chance of being employed by the newly developed industries or service enterprises, however, the improvement of women's family status is obvious. In a village in northern Fujian, I was told by some proud fathers about their daughters' financial contribution to the family. The most important occasion in this township in 1993 happened a few days before Chinese New Year, when eight buses chartered by the township government brought the girls back home from Guangdong for the festival and family reunion.

Social Norms

Social notions and culturally determined social phenomena are changing along with economic development. Chinese patriarchal power used to be based on the patrilineal kinship system. When parents in urban areas no longer have to depend on their children's support for old age protection, the once very strong belief in the importance of *xiangyan*, or continuance of the family line, is weakened. According to the WF survey, only 34.9% of urban residents do not agree that the children may take their mother's surname, 49.7% do not care and 13.2% agree to let their children be named after their mothers.[21] According to a survey in five big Chinese cities, 18% of newly married couples choose to live together with the wife's family.[22]

The surveys also show that in the big cities more women want to have daughters than sons. "You get a name by giving birth to a son and get

The Family Status of Chinese Women in the 1990s

lucky by giving birth to a daughter." "You will lose your son when he marries, you will have a new son when your daughter marries." These popular sayings reflect the changed notion in urban areas. But the situation in the countryside is not the same for the reasons discussed above.

Nevertheless, since it is now politically wrong not to respect a woman until she has given birth to a son, men especially would hesitate to give the "wrong" answer. Hence, there should probably be more in the "agree" group than these figures show. Even so, more than one-fifth of the men openly admitted that a woman would not be respected unless she gave birth to a son.

Patriarchal domination in rural areas is also reflected in women's secondary role in the family. In the WF survey, to the question, "Who makes decisions on the family's economic allocation?" in urban areas, 57.7% of the interviewees said the wife and the husband jointly, 10.9% said mainly the husband and 20.2% said mainly the wife, 5% said other men in the family and 6.1% said other women in the family. By contrast, in rural areas the rate was 48.1% jointly, 23.2% mainly the husband, 11.8% mainly the wife, 11.5% other men in the family and 4.9% other women in the family.[23] The IPS survey shows that most domestic chores, like cooking, washing, and taking care of children, are still done mainly by women in rural areas.[24]

Other much more serious kinds of discrimination against women, which are determined largely by social norms, include the drowning and abandonment of female infants and the trafficking in women. These phenomena are all primarily rural. So too are the high drop-out rates among female students, as well as arranged and mercenary marriages. All these issues are directly or indirectly related to women's low family status.

Table 9. A Woman Can Earn Respect of the Family Only by Giving Birth to a Son

(in %)

	Urban area		Rural area	
	Agree	Disagree	Agree	Disagree
Wife	6.68	93.32	30.40	69.60
Husband	7.12	92.88	21.26	78.74

Source: IPS survey, p. 428.

The Kinship Network and Support to and from the Natal Family

In urban areas, women's status at home is secured by the close bond between mothers and their married daughters. A married daughter may continue to be considered as a member of her natal family and function as such. She still involves herself in her natal family's affair and continues to fulfil her obligation as a daughter. Her mother may also associate herself with her daughter's family by providing help in child-rearing.[25]

The urban couple usually has closer relationships with the wife's family than with the husband's family. A *xiangsheng*, funny talk, "Go to the Zoo," which was popular in 1994, made jokes about city boys, saying that all the engaged and married men were busy on Sundays because they had to do domestic chores for their in-laws.

The long-term supporting relationship between and mutual commitment of the mother and daughter also prevail in the countryside.[26] Nevertheless, rural communities in China are still structured according to the continuing norms of exogamy. Most rural women leave their home villages after they marry.[27] The geographical distance between the mothers and their married daughters makes substantial involvement in each other's family life impossible. But women's status at home is related to the degree of support she can obtain from her natal family. A common comment on some woman's high or low family status is that she has/does not have her natal family standing behind her, *kaodezhu niangjia*.

The Rights and the Practice of Inheritance

Patrilineal inheritance is an important attribute of the patriarchal kinship system which has been practiced in China for thousands of years. The women's inheritance rights were clearly stipulated by the laws in both mainland China and Taiwan as well. However, Taiwanese women still find it difficult to inherit their share of property without being accused of being greedy women by their family and relatives. They may have to choose between the inheritance right and their good relationship with their relatives. In most cases, the women would sign a waiver to give up their inheritance rights "voluntarily." The mainland urban Chinese family, however, did not have to deal with the problem for a simple reason: there was almost no private property left for the family to inherit after socialist reform in the early 1950s. Therefore, in the cities at least, one of the most complicated problems was resolved by the dramatic change in socio-economic structure.

For farmers, their most important property is the land. It was assigned to them by the state in the early 1950s, collectivized a few years later, and redistributed to them again for individual use in the early 1980s. When a women marries, she usually moves to stay with her husband and in-laws in another village and she cannot bring the use of her share of land with her. She then has to wait until the next land readjustment in the village to be allocated her a portion of land. Yet in some areas, land has never been readjusted since decollectivization in the early 1980s. A woman usually would not be discriminated against for not being able to contribute her land to the family she marries into. But neither has her status been enhanced by the additional property she can bring with her.

In the early 1990s, most urban residents were still living in houses owned by their work units or by the local government, but the farmers do not have access to any housing welfare system. For farmers, the house owned by the family may be its most valuable property, which is inherited by the son only. In interviews, male farmers told me that the daughters are nevertheless treated fairly because they receive dowries and do not have to support aged parents. In theory, rural women enjoy the same inheritance rights as urban women. Nevertheless, despite decades-old equal inheritance laws, women's rights are still neglected by both the people and the local government. It is widely reported in the press that women are not even aware of their equal rights of inheritance, to say nothing of being able to fight for them through legal procedures.[28]

Table 10 shows a majority of rural people against the idea of a married daughter's inheritance rights; only 20.7% (10.1% + 10.6%) of the urban population think similarly.

Structural and Cultural Constraints against Legal Protection

As mentioned above, compared to women's status in other aspects, their legal status is considered to be highest by the public. Gender equality in the family is stipulated by the constitution as well as many fundamental laws, including the *Marriage Law*, the *Law of Inheritance*, the *Civil Law*, and the *Criminal Law*. From the late 1980s, national and local laws and regulations on the protection of rights and the interests of women were enacted one by

Table 10. What Do You Think about the Inheritance Rights of Married Daughters?

(in %)

	Rural area			Urban area		
	Total	Women	Men	Total	Women	Men
Should be equal with brothers	13.8	11.4	16.5	40.6	36.4	45.5
Should be less than brothers	9.7	9.4	10.1	7.9	7.2	8.6
Should be more than brothers	0.5	0.6	0.4	0.6	0.6	0.6
Better not to have any	15.6	16.0	15.2	10.1	12.0	7.9
Should not have	40.5	44.0	36.7	10.6	11.8	9.2
Do not care	19.8	18.5	21.1	30.1	31.8	28.2
No answer	0.1	0.1	0.1	0.1	0.1	0.1

Source: WF survey, p. 453.

one. Socio-economic and cultural constraints on the protection of women's family rights are important topics in the Chinese context, where women's emancipation has been carried out by a top-down movement. We have discussed some cultural obstacles to the practice of inheritance rights in rural China. Here we are only going to examine three other instances: domestic violence, the sexual relationship, and divorce.

Domestic Violence

Maltreatment of women and violence against women are prohibited by law. In the survey conducted by the National Women's Federation, domestic violence is classified as "the women's position in the conflict between husband and wife."

Table 11. Did You Ever Strike the First Blow in a Conflict with Your Spouse?

	No answer	Often	Sometimes	Seldom	Never
Urban women	0.4	0.9	4.6	15.8	78.4
Urban men	0.2	0.3	3.0	13.2	83.3
Rural women	0.3	1.0	9.1	21.3	68.3
Rural men	0.1	0.5	4.7	15.4	79.3

Source: WF survey, p. 237.

About 80% of urban men and 70% of rural men never struck the first blow in a conflict between husband and wife. But the survey did not provide a clear picture about how serious domestic violence is in China because there is no clear cut distinction between "often" (0.9%) and "sometimes" (8.2%). The IPS survey found that in rural areas 4.68% of husbands often beat their wives, 1.22% of wives often beat husbands. The proportions in cities are 1.57% and 0.49% respectively.[29] A survey conducted by the Beijing Association of the Study of Marriage and the Family in February and March 1994 had a surprising finding: 20.4% of wives were beaten by their husbands and 14.3% of husbands were beaten by their wives.[30]

The surveys conducted in the early 1990s should be regarded as pathbreaking since domestic violence has never been considered a serious social issue in China. Some survey conductors themselves argue that only a small percentage of women are beaten by their husbands. Considering the huge population of China, however, the absolute number of the victims of domestic violence is significant. Taking Shanghai for example, 0.9% of married women will be about 36,000 and 4.68% means there would be 187,200 family violence victims. Also, there are almost no community facilities to protect the victims of domestic violence. Nevertheless women's studies, women's organizations, and especially the women's hot lines,[31] which have emerged during the last ten years, have drawn attention to the issue. Unfortunately, their influence, weak as it is in the cities, cannot reach rural areas, where domestic violence is more frequent. There the situation can be very serious. Wives are still considered the property of their husbands. Some farmers treat their wives like chattel, whom they believe they have bought through the paying of betrothal gifts or money. "I beat the wife I married just like I ride the horse I bought."[32]

Looking at domestic violence from men's perspective, it seems hard to believe that one-fifth of women strike the first blow in domestic conflicts. Unfortunately, we cannot find similar research on historical China or Western societies with which to compare. But, perhaps the high rate of "violence against men" is an indicator of women's improved family status.

Sex and Status

It is believed that the surveys still underestimate the degree of violence against women due to the traditional attitude that "domestic shame should not be made public." Violence caused by the wife's refusal to have sex with the husband might be the "dirtiest linen" for the family. One intellectual woman, who has been married for more than twenty years, told me that she had been agonizing all those years because her husband wanted to have sex with her almost every night. Believing it was her duty as a wife to fulfil her husband's desire, she had tried to cooperate until she found that she had contracted a venereal disease from her husband. But when she started to reject her husband's sexual requests, he forced her violently. She did not tell her closest relatives about her suffering because of the shame. This woman, like other women I interviewed, never used the word "rape" to describe domestic sexual violence. Rape within marriage is basically not recognized in China.[33]

As Table 12 shows, 46.6% of rural women and 62.40% of urban women believe that a woman can deny her husband's request for sex. The survey also provides tables with age and education difference. An interesting phenomenon is that the women's age and education level do not influence substantially their attitude toward the husband's right to sex.[34] A woman's obedience in the sexual relationship certainly helps the couple to maintain superficial harmony. When a woman feels reluctant to have sex with her husband but still tries to meet his request she suffers psychologically. It could be considered a part of the price she pays for her family status and harmonious married life. When a woman feels strongly against her husband's sex request and is not aware of her right to refuse, she suffers more. Her own happiness and the marriage might be jeopardized consequently.

The survey also shows that 58.53% of rural husbands and 67.26% of urban husbands agree that a wife can turn down her husband's sex request. Considering the traditional obedient role of women, the improvement is significant. According to the survey, more men than women actually agree that women have the right to turn down a request for sex from the husband.

Table 12. May a Wife Turn Down a Sex Request from Her Husband?

(in %)

	Rural wife	Rural husband	Urban wife	Urban husband
Yes	46.60	58.53	62.40	67.26
No	35.59	27.39	18.66	19.84
Yes but difficult	17.81	14.07	18.94	12.90

Source: IPS survey, p. 404.

It is questionable whether they really believed so or they thought that it was the right answer.

Divorce and Housing

For centuries, a Chinese woman could not divorce her husband, but could only be divorced by him. The divorce sometimes was based on the order from their in-laws, though it may not have been the husbands' own wish. Women's right to divorce, guaranteed by the *Marriage Law* of the PRC, is a great breakthrough in terms of the women's family status. In recent years, the divorce rate has increased rapidly, from about 4.7% in 1979 to 9.97% in 1993.[35] About 70% of divorce cases in China during the last few years were initiated by women. Nevertheless, divorce is often difficult due to the housing problem.

Article 44 of the *Law on the Protection of Rights and Interests of Women* stipulates that "the problem of the house jointly rented by the husband and wife should be resolved through negotiation according to the principle of concern for the rights and interests of the wife and children." The stipulation is ambiguous but it recognizes the women's disadvantage in divorce. In most cases as a result of the housing policy in urban China, the house belongs to the husband's unit, because the women employees usually have no access to housing.[36] The law, therefore, says: "When the husband and the wife live in a house belonging to the husband's unit and the wife has no place to live after divorce, the husband should help to resolve the problem if he is able." Because the problem of housing in divorce cases has become very troublesome, the People's Supreme Court issued its Document No. 32 in 1993, which gave more detailed stipulations on the right to housing in divorce disputes. But no laws can change the fact that for women, divorce often means having no place to stay.

The National Confederation of Trade Unions conducted a survey in 1993 on the housing situation in 277 units in 11 provinces and cities. Their findings were just as expected. The allotment of dwellings was unfair to genders in 85.6% of the units. In the 70 units investigated in Dalian City, 100% of women employees had no right to be allotted any housing.[37] Some divorced couples were still living together; many divorces had been delayed or were being reconsidered because one spouse could not afford to leave the housing unit.

In the rural areas, houses are private property belonging neither to the collective nor to the state. Rural parents are obligated by cultural tradition to build a house for each son in the family. When all the sons are married, the parents either live by themselves or with one of the sons' families. The houses are owned and inherited patrilineally. If a woman wants to divorce her husband she will have no place to stay. She may go back to live, inconveniently of course, with her brother or parents. But unfortunately, the state of divorce as well as women's family life in the rural areas are under-reported and under-researched by empirical studies.

Conclusion

An old Chinese woman told me that she did not like the Communist Party but that she was grateful to the party for one thing. "If the party had not come," she said, "I would have been a housewife all my life and my husband would probably have found a concubine." As many Western studies have pointed out, women's liberation has never been treated as a top priority by the Communist Party.[38] But in spite of the fact that Mao's communist regime failed to achieve many of its original goals such as building a prosperous socialist country, it has succeeded in raising significantly women's status at home by changing the economic structure, by enacting laws and by promoting the ideology of gender equality. Without this top-down movement for changing the status of women, it would have been impossible for the Chinese women to achieve their present position. This argument just reflects the reality but does not intend to justify the radical socio-economic reforms which have caused great damage to the society.

In the home at least, Chinese urban women today enjoy greater equality than Chinese women of previous generations or women in many other countries. Chinese women's family status is no longer determined by the family order of the patriarchal kinship system. Nevertheless, women's family status costs them greatly both at home and in society. Women contribute more than men to the family by spending longer hours on domestic chores and children as well as by devoting more attention to family. Many Chinese women also work full time outside the family. Yet they are less welcomed by employers and have less opportunity for promotion because of family-oriented stereotyping.

According to the surveys quoted above and my case study, the younger the couple is the more equal women seem to be in the family. The phenomenon is attributed to the dramatic cultural transformation of

Chinese society. The patriarchal family order is declining significantly in rural China and is being replaced by husband-wife equality in urban China. However, women's lower status in the public domain, reflected in access to education as well as in labour and political participation has a negative influence on women's status at home. There are also some factors almost beyond the reach of social reform, such as people's conception of the choice of a mate. Both women and men still wish the husband to be a more capable person than the wife. Under the structure of exogamy, which is still practiced in many rural areas, girls are bound to leave their native village and go to a strange environment with many negative consequences for their status in the family and society.

In Chinese society, the family rather that individual is considered the basic "cell" of the community. Family values are still respected by ordinary people, and for most of them harmonious family life is more important than personal autonomy. In many families, women are expected to sacrifice their own interest for the sake of their families or husbands and some women willingly do so. The government and the Women's Federation have been advocating *sizi* or four selves: self-respect, self-confidence, self-reliance and self-strengthening. Since the early 1980s, women's magazines and newspapers have held a few forums to discuss whether a woman should be satisfied with her role as *xian neizhu* or good assistant to her husband if she enjoys this kind of life. Also discussed is the question of whether women's status should be judged only by Western standards and values. Such questions remain controversial among scholars and non-scholars alike.

The woman's status at home and the woman's situation in general are very much different between rural and urban women. The reasons for the differences also explain why urban women have achieved today's status at home. Due to the economic structure, rural women are not as independent economically as urban women. They have much less access to welfare benefits provided by the government. The family revolution started in the cities almost a century ago, and the movement was introduced in the Chinese countryside four decades later. Moreover, the process of cultural transformation takes a longer time in the countryside than in the cities because the reform in agriculture has never departed from its original mode of production, in which the household still plays the role of an economic entity. The patriarchal order of the family relationship has therefore not been fundamentally challenged.

The improved family status of women discussed in this chapter is a result of forty years' "family revolution." But since the early 1980s, Chinese society has become more pluralistic but also more stratified along with its economic reform programme. The changed social conditions have also diversified women's individual positions. Liberal feminists emphasize the opportunities that society can provide for women. Marxist feminists advocate equalization. The socio-economical changes happening in China in recent years are characterized by more opportunities and less social equality. The two theories will be tested by the future development of women's situation in China.

Notes

1. See Stanley Rosen, "Chinese Women in the 1990s: Images and Roles in Contention," in *China Review 1994*, edited by Maurice Brosseau and Lo Chi Kin (Hong Kong: Chinese University Press, 1994), pp. **17**.1–**17**.28.
2. See C. K. Yang, *The Chinese Family in the Communist Revolution* (Cambridge, Massachusetts: Harvard University Press, 1959).
3. Jean Hung, *Mother-daughter Relationships in Contemporary Urban China* (M.Phil thesis, The Chinese University of Hong Kong, 1994).
4. For the WF survey, see Tao Chunfang and Jiang Yongping (eds.), *Zhongguo funü shehui diwei gaikuan* (An Overview of the Social Status of Chinese Women), Vol. 1: National-Level Data (Beijing: Zhongguo funü chubanshe, 1993). Also, Stanley Rosen (Note 1), p. **17**.17.
5. For the IPS survey see Sha Jicai, *Sampling Survey Data of Women's Status in Contemporary China* (Beijing: International Academic Publishers, 1994).
6. Ibid., p. 22.
7. Ibid., p. 23.
8. Ibid.
9. WF survey (Note 4), p. 227.
10. Ibid., p. 520.
11. Ibid., p. 250.
12. Ibid., pp. 182–83.
13. Li Yinghe, "Beijing ren, hunyin ruhe?" (Beijing People, How Are Your Marriages), *Zhongguo funü bao* (The Chinese Women's News), 6 July 1994, p. 3.
14. Shen Anqi, "Zhongwai funü jiating diwei bijiao" (The Comparison of Family Status of Urban Women between the Chinese and the Western societies), *Shehui* (Society), No. 1 (January 1992), pp. 12–15.
15. Tang Shen, "Zhongguo dangqian zhiye xingbie fenghua toushi" (Analysis of

the Present Gender Differentiation in Occupations in China), *Funü yanjiu luncong* (Women Studies), No. 3 (May–June 1993), pp. 35–38.
16. IPS survey (Note 5), p. 337.
17. According to the statistics announced by the National Statistical Bureau, the farmer's per capita income in 1990 was 630 yuan. The survey cited here refers to those rural women with remunerated income and therefore yields a substantially higher average annual income figure.
18. WF survey (Note 4), pp. 85–88.
19. The same situation was encountered by other researchers who conducted investigation in rural areas. See Wang Shuxin, "Pinkunxian shang de nuren men" (Women in Rural Poverty), *Nüxin yanjiu* (Women's Studies), No. 2 (March and April, 1993), pp. 4–8.
20. Liu lang, "Laoqu you yiqun 'liushou nü'" (A Group of 'Left-behind Women' in the Revolutionary Base), *Funü shenghuo* (Women's Life), No. 4 (April 1994), pp. 9–11.
21. Ibid., p. 311.
22. Zhang Minjie, "Cong fu ju: jiating de fazhan qushi" (Matrilocal Residence: the Trend in Family Development), *Zhongguo funü bao*, 4 April 1994, p. 3.
23. WF survey (Note 4), p. 202.
24. IPS survey (Note 5), pp. 270–71.
25. Jean Hung (Note 3).
26. See E. Judd, "*Niangjia*, Chinese Women and Their Families," *The Journal of Asian Studies*, Vol. 48, No. 3 (1989), pp. 525–44.
27. E. Judd, *Gender and Power in Rural North China* (Stanford: Stanford University Press, 1994), p. 51.
28. See Xu Xun, "Huan renjian yi gongzheng" (Return Justice Back to Human Society), *Funü shenghuo*, No. 6 (June 1994), pp. 4–5.
29. Ibid., p. 157.
30. Li Yinhe, "Beijing jiating baoli diaocha" (A Survey on Domestic Violence in Beijing), *Hunyin yu jiating* (Marriage and the Family), No. 8 (August 1994), p. 39.
31. Li Yang, "Cong nü qi xianxiang yinqi de sikao" (Thoughts Stimulated by Violence against Wives), *Funü Shenghuo*, No. 4 (April 1994), pp. 12–14.
32. Cao Mingsheng, "Ai de huangyuan" (Wasteland of Love), *Zhongguo funü bao*, 8 August 1994, p. 2.
33. Li Dun, *Xing yu fa* (Sex and Law), (Zhengzhou: Henan renmin chubanshe, 1993), pp. 402–404.
34. IPS survey (Note 5), pp. 405–408.
35. For the figures from 1979 to 1991, see Tian Han, "Lihun ka zai Zhongguo ren shou zhong" (The Divorce Card in the Hand of Chinese), *Nüxin yanjiu*. No. 2 (February, 1992). The figure of 1993 was provided by the Wang Xinjuan at the USC seminar on 22 November 1994.

36. Yan Jiangfeng, "Lihun funü gai zhu nali?" (Where the Divorced Women Can Live), *Zhongguo funü bao*, 4 January 1994. p. 3.
37. Women Employee Section, the National Trade Unions, "Zhufang fenpei: nannü ren bu pingdeng" (Housing: Still Unfair between Men and Women), *Zhongguo funü bao*, 11 February 1994, p. 3.
38. See P. Andors, *The Unfinished Liberation of Chinese Women, 1949–1980* (Bloomington: Indiana University Press, 1983) and M. Wolf, *Revolution Postponed: Women in Contemporary China* (Stanford: Stanford University Press, 1985).

13

Reforms in the Social Security System

Chack Kie Wong

Introduction

The Chinese Ministry of Labour has set 1995 as the year for launching comprehensive reforms in the social insurance system for retirement protection and unemployment benefits.[1] Reforming the provision of enterprise medical benefits is also underway, albeit only on a pilot-project test basis. In addition, the State Council is preparing to establish a ministry which will oversee matters related to social security. And the National People's Congress is considering the creation of a committee on social security as well as relevant draft legislation.[2] In general, the central government gave high priority to reforms in social security, particularly in social insurance for retirement protection and unemployment benefits.

Nevertheless, these measures can be regarded as coming a bit too late. 1995 is the 18th year of the reform era since the path-breaking third plenary session of the Eleventh Central Committee of the Chinese Communist Party (CCP), at which the focus of work shifted to economic development. In the past, reform initiatives for retirement and unemployment protection were not lacking, but only in recent years has the central government stepped up its efforts in these two areas. The initiatives on retirement protection and unemployment benefits are considered important because they are instrumental to the reform of state-owned enterprises, the crucial hurdle for the success of Deng Xiaoping's economic reform. One reason for this of course is the serious losses currently being incurred by state-owned enterprises. According to recent estimates, 15% of all such enterprises are beyond hope of economic recovery,[3] while 41.4% of them suffered losses during 1994.[4] Since the most obvious solution is to dissolve all such enterprises; the establishment of a comprehensive unemployment insurance system becomes essential for maintaining social stability. This would also facilitate labour mobility by establishing a universal system of protection and benefit entitlement for workers from enterprises of different ownership types. In any event, the equalization of work-related welfare would not discourage job changes.[5]

Clearly, reform in the social security system is essential to economic reform, and should be perceived as part of China's institutional transformation in the process of incorporating market mechanisms and values into its predominantly state-controlled economy. In China, the social security system is generally seen as composed of three major categories. They are: (1) social insurance which includes retirement protection and unemployment insurance, as well as medical and work-related injury benefits; (2) social welfare including compulsory basic education, public health care, public housing, rent and price subsidies; and (3) social assistance which includes assistance to the poor, disaster relief, and aid to veterans and their families.[6]

Social security in China thus comprises nearly all the components of social policy in the West, but this chapter will focus on retirement protection and unemployment benefits. It begins with a further brief explanation as to why China's incorporation of market mechanisms and values requires corresponding reforms in the social insurance system. This will be followed by an illustration of the problems within these reforms due to the lack of additional resources injected by the state. Finally, we will look into why and how the state is assuming a strong regulatory role.

The Interdependence between Institutional Transformation and Social Insurance Reform

The principal aim of social security is to prevent or alleviate poverty by providing people with an income or tangible benefits to help them cope with an interruption in or loss of earning power, or to meet special needs such as those arising from illness, death, marriage or birth.[7] To achieve this aim, social insurance schemes for protection against old age, unemployment, illness and work injury are established to spread the risk among the insured members. For those unable to support themselves, the government must intervene by providing cash or in-kind benefits of various kinds. These state-provided benefits are usually called social welfare and/or social assistance, and are regarded as a secondary mechanism of distributing a society's social resources. Unlike social welfare and social assistance, social insurance operates by requiring employers and employees to contribute to insurance funds. In some cases, the state may be partly or wholly responsible for the funds, for example, in old age pensions that cover non-contributors such as the handicapped or housewives as beneficiaries. Therefore, social insurance for old age protection in China is, in fact, a labour insurance scheme for retired workers who have made contributions during their working life. In other words, retirement protection, as well as unemployment benefits, are a form of work-related welfare in China. In terms of financing, social insurance funds for the retired and the unemployed operate either on a "pay-as-you-go" basis or on the "forced saving" system. The former is based on the principle of inter-generational redistribution while the latter is a form of redistribution of income among an individual's different life stages.

Before Deng Xiaoping's economic reform, China's institutions were radically different from those of the West. Social insurance provisions in the urban regions were mainly financed by state-owned enterprises. Some Chinese scholars questioned the enterprise-based system of income protection and benefit entitlements as a "social" system.[8] The reason for the "non-social" nature of enterprise-based welfare was an institutional set-up in which the state and the economy overlapped. In this system, enterprises lacked economic autonomy because they were under the direct financial and managerial control of the state through the CCP and government command structures. In pre-reform China, under the socialist system of comprehensive protection for employees, employment meant life-long entitlement to a package of benefits including housing, medical care and retirement protection; some large enterprises even provided day care and education for workers' children. This is the "iron rice bowl" system, with its notion of inducing the disincentive to work and near non-existence of job mobility. Enterprises did not have to worry about cost efficiency in providing welfare for their workers, as the state absorbed all "reasonable" costs.

However, the incorporation of market mechanisms into the economic system has forced the state and the economy to disengage from each other. And this disengagement, or segregation, aims to generate a new environment to help enterprises make cost efficiency and profit maximization their primary economic considerations. In this respect, social security contributions have been transformed into a factor which inhibits the enterprises' capital accumulation. On the other hand, unprofitable enterprises go into bankruptcy to relieve the state from injecting further revenues to ensure their survival. This institutional transformation is only one side of the story. It logically forces the state to set up social insurance funds to maximize risk-spreading.

However, there is another side to the story. In new ventures, such as privately-owned enterprises and those with overseas investment, the relatively younger labour force would likely discourage enterprise participation in social insurance funds without state coercion. Therefore, newly emerging enterprises might not see the need to participate in any social insurance fund. Only those state-owned enterprises which would definitely benefit from participation because of their ageing work force are likely to join. For instance, the total number of retired workers was equal to 17.4% of the total labour force in state-owned enterprises in 1993;[9] in cities like Shanghai which have an ageing population, retired workers accounted for 31.25% in 1990, and are expected to reach 42.4% in the year 2000.[10] The ageing of the labour force has naturally caused financial difficulties for state-owned enterprises. In view of the younger labour force in newly created enterprises of the private-ownership type, their participation in the social insurance system would reduce the contributions from state-owned enterprises. Furthermore, contributions from individual workers is also viewed as an additional source. Nevertheless, comprehensive coverage of enterprises of all ownership types has not been a practice in the reform era which suggests the need for new legislation in this area.

Reforms of Social Insurance as a Resources Extraction Project

By 1995, the process of seeking additional resources remained unfinished. This is the reason for launching comprehensive reforms in the realm of social insurance for retirement protection and unemployment benefits. The reform strategies are simple and straightforward. Firstly, to coerce enterprises with all types of ownership to be insured by means of a collective pool managed by government agencies; and secondly, to incorporate individual contributions by setting up personal savings accounts. These strategies aim at taking advantage of two social insurance systems: "pay-as-you-go" and "forced savings." For retirement protection, the collective pool generated by the "pay-as-you-go" method forms the first tier of minimum protection while "forced savings" in personal accounts constitutes the second tier for additonal protection. In fact, at present, the second tier of protection might be mere rhetoric contrived to attract individual contributions because "personal accounts" exist only in name at this time, according to one official.[11] Due to a lack of additional resources from the state to finance social security, contributions from "personal accounts" might be used to cover inadequate funding in the "pay-as-you-go" system.[12] In other words, reforms in social insurance have a practical function, that is, to raise additional resources to smooth the institutional transformation from a state-controlled economy to one which incorporates market mechanisms and values.

The Paradox of Under-benefits and Over-contributions

As the state lacks the revenue for such institutional transformation, it has to maximize intergenerational redistribution by including enterprises of all ownership types and individual workers as contributors to the system. These measures aim at establishing a "social" insurance system with adequate coverage and benefits without revising the state's financial priorities. Until 1995, this resource extraction project was far from successful; the Chinese government was thus forced to step up its efforts to tackle the issue of reform as regards retirement protection and unemployment benefits. Three major issues are described below to illustrate the paradox of under-benefits and over-contributions in social insurance for retirement protection and unemployment benefits.

First is the issue of inadequate coverage. Not all enterprises participate in social insurance funds. For instance, report undertaken by the Shandong Federation of Trade Unions revealed in late 1994 that only 45% of all urban workers in that province were covered by retirement insurance; those not covered were largely workers from collectively-owned enterprises, private enterprises and the self-employed.[13] The same report also found that less than 1% of workers from non-state-owned enterprises below the city and township level participated in any retirement social insurance scheme in Shandong.[14] In Guangdong province, only 66.4% of all urban workers were covered by retirement insurance by the end of 1990.[15] In terms of unemployment insurance, it was estimated that in 1993 only 46.5% of all urban workers in China were covered.[16]

Secondly, the issue of inadequate benefits. The present parameters for minimum retirement benefits is 50% of a city's average wage.[17] However, this is not an easy standard to achieve; for example, retired workers in collective- and state-owned enterprises in Guangzhou only received benefits equivalent to 33% and 44% respectively of the city's average wages in 1993. In terms of unemployment benefits, the minimum standard was fixed at 120–150% of a city's poor relief level[18] which was usually less than 30% of the average wage. It was even difficult to attain this minimum standard. For example, in Guangzhou, monthly minimum unemployment benefits for the year 1994 were lower than the city's relief payment to the poor.[19] A household survey conducted in 1993 of the city also found that the retired and the unemployed had a greater chance of falling into poverty: 32.9% of retired workers and 29.7% of the unemployed fell below the poverty threshold, defined as 50% of the monthly median household income; while among the employed, the respective percentage was only 6%.[20]

Thirdly, the issue of requiring heavy contribution by participating enterprises. Despite inadequate benefits, however, participating enterprises, mostly state-owned, contributed a substantial share of their revenues to social security in general, and social insurance in particular. In 1993, one estimate put the total for social security expenses, including rent subsidies, at about RMB310 billion, or 10% of China's gross domestic product. This was also the equivalent of 63% of all enterprises' total gross wages, of which 54% was covered by employers and the other 8% by employees.[21] Social insurance contributions amounted to about 34% of gross wages;[22] in cities like Guangzhou, which have an ageing labour force, the respective contribution from enterprises was 41% of their gross wages in 1994, of which 24.5% went toward retirement protection, and 1% for unemployment benefits.[23] In Shanghai, 25.5% went toward retirement protection, whereas in Wuhan and Chongqing, it exceeded 27%.[24]

The Paradox and the Quick Solution by Indexing

A paradoxical situation has emerged: although participating enterprises assign a substantial share of their revenues for social insurance payments, their retired and unemployed workers could not receive a comfortable return. This is obvious in regards to retirement insurance, as some state-owned enterprises contributed a quarter of their gross wages toward the scheme; with unemployment insurance, the standard contribution is only 1% of gross wages. However, this paradoxical situation is also the case in medical and work injury insurance, albeit to a different extent.

Inadequate coverage is clearly the manifested cause for this. Might the indexing of benefit levels to prices or wages solve this problem ? In China today, a worker's wages are composed of the basic wage, price subsidies and bonuses. The second and third components in the wage structure are a response to the incorporation of market mechanisms: The provision of bonuses links benefits to work performance, and the provision of price subsidies off-sets inflationary pressure on workers' living standards because of the inability or inexperience of the government at all levels to control price speculation. During the reform era, the percentage of basic wage versus total wage has continued to decline, for example, it was 85.7% in 1978 but dropped to 46.6% in 1993.[25]

The drastic decline in this ratio has kept retirement benefits, in particular, at low levels in comparison to average wages because the former are linked to a ratio of the basic wage. While some enterprises may provide price subsidies to their retired workers, the employed have to receive their basic wages and subsidies, plus a bonus as well. Since bonuses were provided as a performance-related mechanism to motivate workers, retired workers were not entitled to receive them. Besides, not all enterprises are profitable enough to link retired workers' benefits to wage or price variations. Given that 40% of state-owned enterprises endure losses, retirees in these loss-making enterprises will be left behind in regards to their benefits staying abreast of average living standards.

Thus, due to the changes in wage structure, retirement benefits, primarily calculated on the basis of basic wages were adversely affected.[26] But linking benefits to average wages as a hedge against inflation and economic growth also will not work. Other things being equal, the possible outcome of indexing to either average wages or consumer prices is the lowering of benefit levels. Nevertheless, the linking of benefits, for example in retirement insurance, to average wages has recently become the prevailing practice in most cities. For example, in Guangzhou since October 1993, one-third of basic retirement benefits are indexed to average wages;[27] in Shanghai since 1993, a portion of retirement benefits has also been linked to price changes.[28] Despite these measures, if additional resources are not injected into the schemes, maintaining benefits even at present levels will be impossible. One way out of this paradoxical situation if the state does not contribute additional resources, is to increase risk-spreading by including young and profitable enterprises in the scheme.

The Dilemma in the Design of Coverage Scope — The Prudent Use of State Regulatory Power

In fact, it is unfair to suggest that the state has not injected revenue into "ailing" state-owned enterprises. For example, subsidies to loss-making enterprises in 1993 amounted to RMB41.13 billion, or 9.7% of government revenue from taxes;[29] from this the retired derived indirect benefits. However, there is no indication that the state is willing to take part in the direct financing of social insurance, although it has already done so in the form of tax exemptions. In this regard, the only feasible way is to extend coverage scope to enterprises of all ownership types and to incorporate individual contributions with the objective of maximizing the intergenerational redistributive effects of the "pay-as-you-go" system. Obviously, the state must play a new role in adjusting for this new economic reality in order to ensure a smooth transition to a "Chinese-style socialist system."[30]

On the basis of the above discussion, economic reform does not mean the withering away of the state; on the contrary, the state has to take up a more active regulating role than before. In the pre-reform era, enterprises were an extension of the state apparatus in the economic arena. However, reform has created a new economic reality: the emergence of non-state-owned enterprises and the use of market principles in measuring economic performance, which enable the state to retreat from direct involvement in productive activities and to concentrate on its regulatory role in the establishment of institutional arrangements compatible with market mechanisms and values. Reform in the social security system is heading in this direction. But the choices are limited: the state has to use coercion backed up by new legislation, despite the danger of invoking disincentives to invest and work. However, the investment situation in China nowadays is hospitable to carrying out social security reforms by these means. For despite the fact that a large share of wages has to be put into social insurance funds, total wage levels are still low compared with other developing countries in the Asia-Pacific region. Moreover, China not only has cheap labour, it also offers a vast market to foreign investors. On the part of individual employees, it seems that the low contribution rates might have kept resistance to the change at a low level.

One important step the Chinese government has taken in assuming a greater role in regulation was the recent promulgation of the new Labour Law (*Laodongfa*) in mid-1994. The new law symbolizes the shift of the state's role from the management of workers to the protection of their rights.[31] This shift is necessary because the state cannot assume that profit-oriented enterprises, either state-owned or non-state owned, will represent the interests of the working class. Between 1986 and 1994, the Labour Ministry recorded more than 60,000 labour disputes; and in the first quarter of 1994 alone, more than 3,000 cases were filed.[32] The new law was the last of more than 30 revisions since Deng Xiaoping urged its promulgation in 1978.[33] The law stipulates that workers have the right to various forms of social security protection such as retirement, unemployment and sickness benefits; furthermore, workers and their employers are compelled to join social insurance schemes and to pay the subscribed fees.[34] Enterprises not covered by the retirement and unemployment system are liable to prosecution by law-enforcing agencies.[35] In the initial stage, workers' contributions to retirement insurance funds are limited to a maximum of 3% of their standard wages according to a 1991 State Council document.[36] For cities like Shenzhen, which is in the vanguard of economic reform, workers' contributions varied from 5% to 10% of their basic wages. However, workers' contributions are for their "personal accounts," in a system modeled after Singapore's Central Provident Fund.[37]

In light of the low rates of workers' contributions and the seemingly self-beneficial nature of personal accounts, the aim of the new Labour Law seems to have been promulgated principally to require the compliance of enterprises, especially those of non-state ownership types. The objective is clear: to maximize the redistributive effects.

The assumption of a stronger role by the state is, in fact, an equalization project for contributions and benefits including a wider scope of "good" contributors. Nevertheless in terms of the scope of coverage, the process of inclusion has to stop somewhere to ensure that benefits are set at an acceptable level. Indeed, the selection of the coverage scope was pragmatic.

Firstly, in retirement protection, because of low benefit levels, the state has to encourage enterprises to set up second-tier protection exclusive to employees of individual enterprises by establishing "personal accounts." Workers must also be urged to invest in private insurance as a third tier of retirement protection. These steps should lower expectations for the first tier of the collective pool which is compulsory and redistributive.

Secondly, it is necessary to preclude retirement protection from becoming a social insurance system for all of the aged. As suggested above, the present system of retirement protection is labour insurance; the non-working population in cities and towns are excluded, and must rely upon their working family members for welfare. The Confucian ethic of intergenerational responsibility emerges as the moral justification for such pragmatic considerations of benign neglect in the design of old-age protection.[38]

Lastly, due to wide income disparities between the prosperous coastal provinces and their underdeveloped counterparts in the southwestern hinterland, old-age protection schemes have to stop short of becoming a national insurance system, otherwise benefits will be reduced to unacceptable levels. The discriminatory inclusion and exclusion of participating members in the coverage design of old-age protection is necessary to attain a designated "optimum." At present the regional coverage is therefore set at the provincial level.

Reflecting these difficulties, it was recently revealed that only 13 out of 30 provinces, including province-equivalent municipalities and autonomous regions, had achieved the pooling of contributions at the provincial level for redistribution. Vested interests have to be blamed for this situation because cities with younger labour forces were unwilling to participate in the pooling without considerable coercion from higher authorities. This is understandable for by doing so, they contribute more and receive less than cities with an older labour force. However, cities like Guangzhou, with an older labour force, also resisted the provincial level coverage scope because by contributing, their direct control of the "piggy bank" was at stake.[39] Apparently, the bureaucracy has vested interests of its own.

The primary intervention tool used by the Chinese government in engineering social insurance reform is the wielding of regulatory power due to a lack of additional resources to facilitate this aspect of institutional transformation. Without adequate statistics, however, it is difficult to estimate the success of the "single" state regulatory tool for the extraction of additional resources to deal with the contradiction of under-benefits and over-contributions in social insurance. If intervention fails, the case for the state to become a third partner in directly financing social insurance might prevail. Several arguments for this follow:

Firstly, the state has a moral obligation to finance social insurance because state-owned enterprises and retired workers do not create the problem of old age protection and unemployment by themselves. They are victims of economic reform.

Secondly, reform in retirement protection and unemployment benefits is perceived as contributing to the reduction of losses of state-owned enterprises. For example, when social insurance reforms in retirement protection and unemployment benefits were actively pursued, the state's subsidies to loss-making state-owned enterprises were reduced drastically from 22% of the government's total tax revenues in 1988 to only 9.7% in 1993.[40]

Lastly, economic reform has also created new sources of revenue and taxes, for example, land sales, personal income tax and sales tax. These revenues and taxes are generated as a result of the incorporation of market mechanisms. However, the same mechanisms also create the impoverishment of the retired and the unemployed. The argument for compensation is therefore not totally groundless.

Conclusion

Although 1995 has been designated as a year in which the Chinese government is going to undertake "comprehensive" reforms of the social security system, in fact, the primary focus is on reform of labour insurance for retirement and unemployment protection. These initiatives are instrumental to the success of economic reform and particularly the reform of state-owned enterprises. While this narrow focus is undesirable, it is practical because the state does not have to inject valuable resources to finance this phase of institutional transformation. In this regard, the inclusion of the non-working population and the peasants in a national scheme for old age pensions was considered impractical. Therefore, the government only sought the inclusion of those "good" participants who could reinforce the financial viability of the insurance system through the application of the state's regulatory power. The promulgation of the Labour Law in 1994 symbolizes the changing emphasis of the state's role. However, whether this is sufficient remains crucial to the future reform of the social security system. Otherwise, there is a good argument for the state to become a third partner in the financing of social insurance. The need for state finance is more obvious in terms of extending the present coverage scope from urban workers to peasants, despite the unlikelihood of this in the near future.

In this respect, the reform of the tax system is clearly an important question. And from this point of view, 1995 is not a crucial year; but rather just another interlude in the long process of reform. In essence, social security is about the redistribution of social resources as a secondary mechanism for the rectification of social inequalities and problems generated by the market system. In the reform of the social security system, specifically that of social insurance for retirement protection and unemployment benefits, the state has precluded the redistribution by revenues generated from taxes which is often the case in the West's welfare states, and extended the coverage scope to "good" participants to solve the problem of inadequate protection. But this strategy has its limits. In the long run, the issue of using tax revenues to finance social security in general, and social insurance in particular, will be raised.

Notes

1. *Ming Pao* (Hong Kong), 27 September 1994 and 14 November 1994; *Renmin ribao* (People's Daily), overseas edition, 7 December 1994.

2. *Ming Pao*, 27 September 1994.
3. Ibid.
4. *Wenhui bao* (Shanghai), 12 January 1995.
5. *Renmin ribao*, overseas edition, 9 July 1994.
6. See an article which reports an experts meeting, "How to Perfect China's Social Security System," *Qunyan* (Popular Tribune), No. 10 (1992), pp. 4–12.
7. William Beveridge, the founder of British's post-war welfare state, in his classic text about social security, offers the classic definition of this sort. See *Report on Social Insurance and Allied Services*, 1942, Cmd. 6404, HMSO.
8. Huang Xiaojing and Yang Xiao "From Iron Ricebowls to Labour Markets: Reforming the Social Security System," in *Reform in China*, edited by B. Reynolds (New York: M. E. Sharpe, 1987).
9. The actual figures were: 18.95 million retired workers, and a total labour force of 109.2 million. See State Statistical Bureau, *Statistical Yearbook of China, 1994* (Beijing: China Statistical Publishing House, 1994), pp. 94–95, 665.
10. Zhang Guangming, "Reflections on the Reform of Worker's Retirement Insurance System," *Huadong jingji guanli* (Economic Management of Eastern China), No. 4 (1992), pp. 87–89.
11. *Ming Pao*, 31 October 1994.
12. Ibid.
13. Ibid.
14. Ibid.
15. Zhang Jun and Dong Bingguang, "Social Pension Reform Insurance in Guangdong: System Selection and Policy Operation," paper presented to the International Conference on the Establishment and Improvement of the Guangzhou Social Security System, 4–7 July 1994, Guangzhou.
16. It was disclosed to the press that in 1993, 74 million employees in urban regions were covered by unemployment insurance. See *Wenhui bao*, 14 January 1994; whereas there were a total number of 159 million persons in urban employment in the same year according to the *Statistical Yearbook of China, 1994* (Note 9), p. 84.
17. *Ming Pao*, 14 November 1994.
18. *Wenhui bao*, 21 April 1993.
19. Guangzhou Federation of Trade Unions, "Tentative Plan for the Reform of Guangzhou's Social Insurance System," paper presented to the International Conference (Note 15).
20. Chack Kie Wong, "Measuring Third World Poverty by the International Poverty Line: The Case Example of Guangzhou in Reform China," mimeo, The Chinese University of Hong Kong, 1994.
21. *Hong Kong Economic Journal*, 23 December 1994.
22. *Statistical Yearbook of China, 1994* (Note 9), p. 665.

23. Guangzhou Restructuring Committee, "The Present Situation and Future of Guangzhou's Social Security and Insurance System," paper presented to the International Conference (Note 15).
24. *Wenhui bao*, 2 September 1993, p. 2; *Ming Pao*, 14 November 1994, p. A2.
25. Tabulation based on State Statistical Bureau, 1994, p. 115.
26. Fei Weilin, "The Challenge and Strategies of Ageing Protection under Socialist Economic Market System," paper presented to the Annual Conference of China's Sociological Association, May 1994, Shanghai.
27. *Guangzhou ribao* (Guangzhou Daily), 31 October 1993.
28. *Wenhui bao*, 23 April 1993.
29. Note 22, p. 216, Table 7–5.
30. The third plenary session of the 14th Central Committee of the CCP held in November 1993 proclaimed the goal of establishing a market system with socialist characteristics. The establishment of a compatible social security system was being considered, for the first time, as important to the attainment of this goal.
31. *Wenhui bao*, 17 August 1994.
32. *Wenhui bao*, 16 July 1994.
33. Ibid.
34. *Renmin ribao*, overseas edition, 7 July 1994.
35. Nevertheless, local governments have to set their own schedules in the implementation of the new law. Since social security is only one of several components of the new Labour Law, another law dealing specifically with social security is being drafted by the National People's Congress and will be tabled in 1995.
36. The State Council, "State Council Decision on the Reform of Enterprise Workers' Retirement Insurance System," State Council Policy Statement No. 33, 26 June 1991.
37. Shenzhen seems to be the first city in China to use Singapore's experience with a central provident fund in reforming its social insurance system. For instance, provident fund schemes for housing are set up, workers and their employing enterprises contribute to the schemes, and the accumulated funds are used to build low-cost housing for members to purchase.
38. Note 26.
39. Note 15.
40. Tabulation based on State Statistical Bureau, 1994, p. 216, Table 7–5.

14

China's New Labour Law: Forging Collective Bargaining from the Rusting Iron Rice Bowl

David Peetz

On 1 January 1995, the *Labour Law of the People's Republic of China* came into force.[1] This is a momentous step in Chinese labour relations for several reasons. It establishes a set of minimum standards in key conditions of employment. It signifies a major effort by the authorities to end the iron rice bowl whereby Chinese employers provided cradle-to-grave welfare for their employees, from whom they expected and mandated life-long loyalty. And, perhaps most significantly, it puts in place the start of the framework for the encouragement of collective bargaining, hitherto unnecessary in the context of the iron rice bowl. In this chapter I will report upon the main provisions of the labour code, place it in the context of recent developments in the Chinese political economy and assess its strengths, weaknesses and prospects.[2]

The Political and Economic Context

The Labour Law is the latest of a series of market-based reforms that have been initiated since the early 1980s, as China moves toward what is now called market socialism. Perhaps the greatest impediment to market socialism was the "iron rice bowl." This term referred to the system whereby the state allocated jobs to workers and workers had permanent job tenure at least in state-owned enterprises (SOEs). These actually still employ the great majority of the urban workforce and employers provide a range of social welfare benefits such as old age pensions, housing and health insurance. Several of these benefits are, in advanced market economies, more commonly provided by or through the state. The rigidity of this system not only deprived managers of the right to fire or lay off unwanted or unneeded workers, it also deprived workers of the right to quit or transfer jobs and locked them into a stifling dependency relationship with that employer.[3]

In 1986 the State Council issued regulations that introduced a system of labour contracts, which was intended to apply to newly recruited permanent employees.[4] Labour contracts would divorce new employees from the iron rice bowl, by putting them onto fixed term (but renewable) individual contracts. The individual contracts could be long term (5 to 20

The views expressed in this chapter are those of the author and do not purport to represent the views of the Department of Industrial Relations.

years) or short term (1 to 5 years). Contract workers were to be entitled to the same rights as existing employees in terms of conditions, access to training, union membership and involvement in workers congresses, though there was considerable evidence of discriminatory treatment against them.[5] The effect of this reform has varied between provinces. In Hainan, for example, all workers were on labour contracts by the end of 1994, but the penetration in many other provinces was much lower.

Such changes were occurring in the context of substantial reforms to the product markets in which SOEs operated. Subsidies and central controls over production and markets were being released and removed. Nearly one half of SOEs were claimed to be operating at a loss in 1994. China's administrators were having to deal with substantial layoffs and rising unemployment and some subsidies were hastily reintroduced, though the general direction of reform remains unchanged.[6] The ownership status of SOEs is under review, with an increasing number either having been changed to private companies with shareholders or scheduled for privatization. Changes of ownership status are, amongst other things, clarifying the distinction between the separate interests of workers, employers and the state. Such clarification is seen as a pre-condition for enabling collective bargaining to occur, though collective bargaining is also possible in SOEs.

Over the same period, the expansion of the private sector, and in particular of foreign-owned firms and joint foreign-Chinese ventures, led to evidence of growing mistreatment of employees.[7] Workers in the foreign-owned sector were poorly unionized and were offered little protection, especially in the special economic zones (SEZs). In the Shenzhen SEZ, for example, 84 workers died in a November 1993 factory fire where the windows had been locked by the employer, while 93 died after a Hong Kong-owned factory caught fire and collapsed.[8] The incidence of organized industrial unrest has increased significantly and in the foreign-owned sector, wildcat strikes by workers, without any union presence or organization, have been reported.[9] Worker dissatisfaction is reported to have increased.[10] Pressure on unions and the state to develop an active union presence in the foreign-owned sector has intensified, and with it a recognition by policy-makers that collective bargaining must follow. There have been some earlier efforts at collective bargaining, for example, in the Beijing jeep manufacturing joint-venture founded in 1984. But for the most part foreign companies operating in China especially the smaller ones have, as in other Asian SEZs, managed to avoid effective union activity.

The Labour Law

The Labour Law was adopted at the eighth meeting of the Standing Committee of the National People's Congress on 5 July 1994.[11] It is the first legislative expression of an official decision to promote collective bargaining, and is also the final word on the introduction of a labour contract system. The Law contains 107 articles grouped into 13 chapters.[12]

Under the Labour Law, labour contracts should be applied to all employees. They should be written and should, as a minimum, contain clauses dealing with the duration of the contract, the contents of work, labour protection and working conditions, remuneration, discipline, termination conditions and responsibility for the violation of a labour contract.[13]

The duration of a contract may be fixed, flexible or dependent upon the completion of a specified amount of work (e.g., a building project), and it may contain a probation period of no more than six months. (§20, 21) A contract can be revoked with 30 days notice if the employee is: redundant (in an organization in deep financial difficulties); unable to work after having completed treatment for an illness or injury (excluding those suffered at work); still unqualified for his/her work even after receiving training or a transfer; or is unable to reach agreement with the employer after a significant change in the environment means that the original contract can no longer be carried out. (§26) It can be terminated without notice if the employee seriously breaches his or her duty or fails the probation period. (§25) But it cannot be revoked if an employee is off work due to work-related illness or injury, is still receiving medical treatment for a non-work related illness or injury, is pregnant or breast-feeding, or in other circumstances stipulated by law, administrative rules and regulations. (§29) An employee may leave immediately if the employer fails to pay agreed wages or uses violence, intimidation or illegal restriction of personal freedom. Otherwise, an employee may leave on 30 days notice. (§31, 32)

The Labour Law also enables workers to conclude a collective contract with their enterprise on matters relating to wages and benefits, hours, leave, occupational health and safety, insurance and welfare. In unionized workplaces, the trade union should negotiate the contract. In non-union enterprises, representatives elected by staff and workers conclude the contract. (§33)

Collective contracts, unlike (individual) labour contracts, should be submitted to an administrative labour department. The department has 15 days in which to raise any objections. Otherwise, after 15 days the agreement comes into effect. (§34)

Collective contracts bind the employer and all its employees. An individual labour contract cannot undercut conditions specified in a collective contract. (§35)

The Labour Law applies a distinction between disputes of interest (referred to in the law as disputes arising from the conclusion of a collective contract) and disputes of right (referred to as disputes arising from the implementation of a collective contract). Interest disputes concern the process of negotiating a new contract, and the labour law provides that if no settlement can be reached, the local government labour bureau may organize the relevant departments to handle the case in coordination. (§84)

Rights disputes concern the interpretation of an existing agreement. In the case of rights disputes, if no settlement is reached then the dispute may be referred to as a tripartite, external labour dispute arbitration committee for arbitration. The decision of the arbitration committee can be appealed to a people's court. The arbitration committee can also conciliate before it arbitrates; and be used by parties to an interest dispute for conciliation. Indeed, an internal labour dispute mediation committee, chaired by a union representative, can also be set up to conciliate disputes before they are referred externally. (§79, 80)

The Labour Law establishes a set of minimum employment conditions. The maximum working week is 44 hours, the maximum working day is 8 hours, and workers must have at least one day off per week, though other rules can be adopted with the approval of the labour bureau. (§36, 38, 39) Overtime should be no more than three hours per day (provided the health of workers is guaranteed) and no more than 36 hours per month, except where prompt rush repair is required. (§41, 42) Penalty rates (additional payments for working outside standard hours) apply at rates of 150% of ordinary pay for overtime, 200% for work on days of rest when no deferred rest can be taken, and 300% on public holidays. (§44) Workers are entitled to annual leave, the amount to be determined by the State Council. (§45)

The state is to implement a set of minimum wages, taking account of living expenses, average wage rates, productivity, employment and regional economic differences. (§47, 48, 49) But above these minimums the state does not get involved in wage fixing. The state, however, is to exercise macro-regulation and control of the total payroll. (§46)

Wages are to be set on principles of equal pay for equal work, and females are to enjoy equal rights to males in employment and recruitment. (§13, 46) Discrimination on the grounds of race, ethnic community, sex and religious belief is disallowed. (§12) Juniors under the age of 16 should not be employed except in cultural and sporting activities. (§15) Certain restrictions on the employment of juniors and of women, particularly pregnant, breast-feeding or menstrual women, are provided for. (§58 to 65) Paid maternity leave is available. (§62)

As explained in Note 13, minimum conditions of employment, like most other elements of the Labour Law, are expressed in terms of *yingdang*, that is, the law says that certain things *should* rather than *must* be done. A major exception to this is in occupational health and safety. Employers must establish and perfect the system for occupational safety and health (including through the provision of training) and must abide by the safety standards set by the state. Employees must abide by rules of safe work. (§52 to 56) Employees have the right to refuse to work in unsafe conditions that violate rules. (§56) The state is to establish a monitoring system for work-related injuries, deaths and diseases. (§57)

The minimum entitlements are, however, supported by a regime of orders and penalties for firms that disregard them. Hence orders can be made on, and/or fines or compensation are payable by, firms which pay below minimum wages, deduct wages without reason, breach maximum hours limitations, fail to pay penalty rates for hours above standard hours, encroach on the legitimate rights and interests of female and juvenile workers, or breach occupational health or safety laws. (§89 to 96)

Employers and the state have broad obligations placed upon them to establish and expand systems of vocational training. The state is also to establish skill standards and job classifications. (§66 to 69)

The state is to develop social insurance in the areas of retirement incomes, unemployment insurance, workers compensation, medical insurance and child-bearing. It is also to encourage employers to set up supplementary insurance. (§71 to 76)

Labour departments at national, provincial and county levels are instructed to establish inspection services with rights to enter premises. (§85, 86) Trade unions are to safeguard workers interests and supervise implementation of laws and rules. (§88)

Provincial and municipal governments are to work out the implementing measures for the labour contract system and report their measures to the State Council for the record. (§106)

Assessment

The developments of the past decade in China have revealed three models of the labour market: the directed model, in which the allocation and price of labour is determined by the state; the individual contracting model, in which the allocation and price of labour is the outcome of bargaining between individual employees and firms; and the collective bargaining model, where it is the outcome of bargaining between employees acting together, usually represented by a union, and a firm or groups of firms.[14]

Clearly the Chinese government has sought to move away from the directed model as being incompatible with market socialism in product markets. The success of these efforts will, in the first place, depend upon the extent to which the iron rice bowl can be dismantled.

In this respect, recent national legislation requiring provincial administrations to establish several systems of social insurance will be critical. Unemployment insurance, old age pensions, workers' compensation (work-related accident or illness insurance) and health insurance are all to be provided through the state, financed through mandatory contributions by employers and, to a lesser extent employees. At a minimum, provincial systems must cover employees of SOEs, but they may cover employees from all enterprise types (as they do, for example, in Hainan). Certainly, the move from a directed model to a more open labour market would be better achieved if social insurance were to cover all employees.

The capacity to move away from the iron rice bowl will also be determined by the strength and sustainability of the opening up of SOEs to market forces. As SOEs become more immersed in markets, including through collectivization and privatization, there needs to be adequate employment growth to absorb the labour that is displaced by SOE layoffs and even closures. If the rate of change is too fast, the threat or reality of social disturbance may lead to a revision of policy. But change still has to be rapid enough to support a change in organizational culture within SOEs. The faster employment growth occurs in the private (including foreign-owned) sector, and the more compatible employment conditions are between the private sector and SOEs, the better will be the prospects for reform of SOEs. So far, economic growth has been strong — an estimated 13% in 1994 — but growth has been uneven between regions and some provinces may find particular difficulties in absorbing employees laid off through SOE modernization.

If the move away from the directed model succeeds, the critical question is, of course, which model is to take its place. At present, the legal infrastructure is much stronger in support of labour contracts than of collective contracts. The former have been provided for and operated since 1986, while the latter are a new concept in law, practised effectively in only a small number of firms. The Labour Law deals more comprehensively with labour contracts than with collective contracts,[15] many details of which are left to regulations yet to be promulgated. Collective contracts are entirely voluntary, but the legislation makes clear its intent that all workers should be covered by labour contracts. The individual contracting model would appear to have a head start on the collective bargaining model.

Yet a system based around individual contracting would hardly be able to be described as market socialism. A collective bargaining model would seem more consistent with this guiding philosophy, and it appears that this model is what Chinese policy-makers have in mind for the SOE sector after the demise of the directed model.

The foreign-owned sector, however, has provided an even stronger impetus for policy-makers to pursue a collective bargaining model, for it is here that the excesses of capitalism have already shown the individual contracting model to be inadequate. It is in this sector that policy-makers and unions wish to see collective bargaining develop first.

Collective bargaining, if it is to be effective, will face different but closely related problems in the state-owned and private (especially foreign-owned) sectors. In the SOEs, unions have to change their focus from being welfarist — concentrating on assisting employees resolve problems with their housing, health care pay and the like — to being independent bargainers, negotiating with management over pay and conditions and organizing employees to act collectively in support of claims. This requires the extrication of management and party interests from union interests. If workplace union officials hold management positions, or continue to be appointed by management or the party, it is doubtful that they could perform an independent advocacy and organizational role.[16] They must be truly responsive to the interests and expressed wishes of their members, and exercise leadership — not in ensuring that discipline is maintained and that work is performed as specified in the labour contract,[17] but in explaining to members their strength in acting collectively and the costs and benefits of options available to them.

This does not mean that Chinese unions must or can become confrontationist to become independent. The experience of Australian unions have shown that they can lose the support of their membership either if they are confrontational toward management when employees do not seek confrontation, or conversely if they acquiesce to management agendas when their members want something different.[18] Indeed, confrontationism for its own sake would severely contradict the cultural norms that have developed in Chinese workplaces.

As the Chinese market system evolves, and/or the ownership status of SOEs changes, the distinct interests of management and unions are becoming more apparent. This is a necessary, but not sufficient, condition for trade unions to become autonomous, representative and responsive. Much of the rest will depend upon the strategic choices made by the Chinese union movement. There are already signs that the union movement, at the national level, has been taking a more independent stance from state and party since 1989.[19] This trend would need to continue and accelerate if collective bargaining is to have any chance in those enterprises which, for the moment at least, are in the state-owned sector.

In the foreign-funded enterprises (FFEs) union problems are not so much in identifying their interests as separate from employers, as they are in gaining entry to and representation in the enterprises. By October 1994, it was estimated that a union presence had been established in a third of FFEs in Beijing, a significant increase on a year earlier but still leaving the majority of workers in FFEs without coverage.[20] The All China Federation of Trade Unions (ACFTU) aims to unionize all FFEs in less than a year.[21] But management of FFEs, especially in SEZs are averse to union coverage and especially averse to active unionism. Throughout China, the use of SEZs to promote foreign investment has been premised on the availability of generous taxation concessions, fast-tracked project approval procedures and an appropriately qualified but industrially docile labour force. Unionization is thus antithetical to the motives many foreign investors have in setting up operations in the SEZs.

The problem for unions has not just been one of employer resistance. In many FFEs, reports have arisen of non-union workers undertaking wildcat industrial action.[22] Sometimes, unions have been able to subsequently recruit members from these enterprises. The pattern of unorganized industrial action partly reflects FFE managements' ability to prevent unionization, but it probably also reflects inadequacies in the abilities of many existing official unions to reflect and be responsive to employees' interests and wishes. The response of Chinese law to this problem has been interesting: collective contracts can be negotiated between an enterprise and either a union or, in non-union firms, employees within a workplace acting collectively. The allowing of non-union collective contracts appears to be aimed at encouraging collective organization for the improvement of employee conditions where unions lack the ability to organize them directly.[23]

The Labour Law itself is silent on what happens if non-union employees acting collectively, wish to organize themselves into a formal body which they may wish to call a union, even if it is not recognized as part of the existing official union structure centred around the ACFTU. The 1992 *Trade Union Law*, however, effectively prevents workers from establishing new trade unions outside the official structures. To date, the Chinese authorities have not responded kindly to attempts to establish competing organizations. We could expect that, in at least some cases, employees may wish to retain the organizational form established for negotiating a collective agreement as an ongoing mechanism for the protection of employee interests. If they were allowed to do so, and to call these groups unions, then it would increase the pressure upon existing unions to develop their representativeness, responsiveness and autonomy.

In turn, the encouragement of non-union collective bargaining through the Labour Law is likely to put increased pressure on the authorities to eventually accept or even recognize groups of employees in FFEs who wish to organize collectively and to call themselves a union.

Any more detailed assessment of the Labour Law can only at this stage, be preliminary as several major sets of regulations have yet to be finalized. These include the *Rules on Examination and Management of Collective Contracts* and the *Rules on Settlement of Disputes Arising Out of Conclusion of Collective Contracts* as well as *Regulations regarding the Settlement of Collective Disputes and the Setting of Minimum Wages*. Indeed, it appears likely that it will be at least a year before regulations are promulgated. These regulations will provide many of the details that, in Australia, might be provided by legislation itself. Local labour bureaus, in turn, will be asked to formulate local regulations in relation to each of these issues.

The detail in these regulations will be critical. The Labour Law, for example, states that labour contracts must be for a defined period but makes no such requirement upon collective contracts. This, it is likely, would be dealt with through regulation. Without such an obligation, it would be impossible to clearly identify when a dispute is a rights dispute and when it is an interest dispute.[24] It would therefore be difficult for the parties to maintain commitment to collective contracts once they were made. Parties could not be expected to treat a collective contract as having indefinite duration, and so without a specified duration they would be entitled to seek to reopen it at any opportune time.

Indeed, the treatment of disputes of right and disputes of interest in the regulations will be of special interest. Practice across most advanced market economies is that parties engaged in disputes of interest have a right to take industrial action in support of their claim, subject only to restraints of one form or another in essential services or, sometimes, core public services. On the other hand, there are often legal restrictions on the taking of industrial action in support of rights disputes (where a collective agreement is already in place), and arbitration rather than industrial action is usually the course of last resort for parties in rights disputes.

The Chinese treatment of rights disputes appears to be in line with this international practice. On the other hand, the treatment of interest disputes seems likely to be different to the treatment of rights disputes, but in precisely what way is not yet clear.

It appears that a strong emphasis will be placed on mediation in rights disputes, and that, when no agreement has been reached, labour bureaus will be encouraged to undertake mediation or create joint working parties involving those concerned. Parties will be prohibited from engaging in strikes or lockouts while mediation is underway. It has yet to be determined when mediation is activated, and what happens to the parties' rights to undertake industrial action before mediation, or afterwards if mediation is unsuccessful. It is not uncommon for leadership in developing countries to be wary of enabling a legal right to take industrial action, due to fear of the consequences for industrial stability and foreign investment. Yet, as shown by the Australian experience to 1993, the absence of a formal right to take industrial action is, itself, no guarantee that strikes will not occur — or even that strike levels will be kept low by international standards.[25] Moreover, if parties are unable to take legal industrial action (with whatever qualifications are necessary) in the course of an interest dispute, it is difficult to envisage the mechanisms for collective bargaining maturing. This is because the potential to undertake collective industrial action is a key element in the distinction between collective bargaining and individual contracting. Likewise, if the regulations do not make it clear that there is a real and important distinction between rights and interest disputes, then commitment to agreements necessary to preserve the integrity of collective bargaining will be difficult to develop.

Other aspects of the legislation appear to be well suited to the development of collective bargaining. The establishment of minimum standards in wages, leave, hours and penalty rates for non-standard hours; the development of commitments in relation to training, discrimination and occupational health and safety; the external scrutiny of collective contracts and of premises; and the protection of conditions under collective contracts from being undermined by labour contracts, would appear to have the potential to ease workers' fears about the possible consequences of collective bargaining.

Whether this potential is realized may depend on two factors. The first is the levels at which minimum wages are finally set. The second and more important is the enforceability of the standards. Prior to the introduction of the Labour Law, contravention of those standards that had existed was commonplace. Overseas Chinese investors from Hong Kong and Taiwan knew how to bypass any Chinese labour regulation.[26] The problem, according to Mobo Gao, arose from local authorities being either unwilling or unable to enforce existing regulations.[27] To the extent that local authorities see advantage in ignoring labour decrees in order to attract or retain foreign investment, national policy-making will be undermined.

In the SOEs, the greatest problem will be in persuading employers and employees, particularly those used to a system in which the manager was regarded as almost a father figure to the employee, that there is something to be gained for both of them in engaging in collective bargaining. This paternalistic workplace culture is, in many ways, more conducive to individual bargaining (which may merely reinforce the pseudo-parent-child power relationship) than to collective bargaining (in which conflicting interests may be more overt and, to those workers comfortable with a paternalistic culture, threatening). The atomization of workers born of a tradition of authoritarian relationships between leaders and led make it difficult to organize workers collectively.[28]

To say that the development of a culture of collective bargaining in China will be a major task is a bit like saying that there are significant technical issues involved in sending a person to Mars. Nonetheless, the national level Chinese authorities are approaching the issue systematically and seriously. The Ministry of Labour has decided to pilot the move in six major centres: Beijing, Shenzhen, Dalian, Qingdao, Chengdu and Xian. A cross-section of enterprises by industry and firm size is included in this pilot. The experience of the pilots will then be used to generate lessons on how collective bargaining can be spread more widely through the rest of China. Workplace surveys will be undertaken in non-SOEs to identify patterns of workplace relations and attitudes to collective bargaining, and in firms involved in the pilot projects to evaluate their experiences.

The Ministry of Labour has established a Department of Labour Relations and Inspections to oversee collective contracts. Provincial labour bureaus are to set up comparable bodies, which will also collect statistical data on collective contracts. Training programmes are planned for participants in collective bargaining, and these may be tailored to suit the distinct interests of managers, union officials and bureaucrats. The ministry may also offer consultancy services to those involved in collective bargaining. The bureaucrats enthusiastically seek information from other countries on their experiences and what this may mean for the spread of collective bargaining in China. Clearly, however, they are not interested in importing a model but will instead, if they succeed, adopt some uniquely Chinese version of bargaining.

Conclusion

As the directed model of labour relations inevitably falls away, the individual bargaining and collective bargaining models will compete for dominance in the labour market outside the true collectives. The outcome of this contest will be critical in determining whether China ends up with something that could genuinely be called market socialism.[29] Should the market exposure of the Chinese economy expand too rapidly, and collective bargaining develop too slowly, a new culture of individual contracting may take such a strong hold that it would be difficult for collective bargaining ever to dominate. The attempted introduction of collective bargaining first in the foreign-funded enterprises will test the ability of this concept to take hold in that part of the economy where workers may be most sympathetic to collective organisation and action, though management may equally be most active in their opposition.

Six key factors will determine whether collective bargaining can develop with sufficient force to play a significant role in the socialization of the emergent market forces. These are: the ability of existing unions to adapt (or new unions to coalesce) to autonomously organize for collective bargaining; the enforceability of the Labour Law; the nature of the regulations, in particular their treatment of interest disputes and industrial action; the durability of the culture of paternalism; the extent to which management will acquiesce (or be made to acquiesce) in the development of trade unionism and collective bargaining; and the ability of the labour bureaucrats to provide the necessary infrastructure to support the move to collective bargaining. Some of the early indications on this last point are promising. But Chinese trade unions face a major task in reconstructing themselves into autonomous, representative and responsive bodies capable of organizing members for the purposes of collective bargaining. If they cannot do this, collective bargaining will remain peripheral to Chinese labour relations. The new Labour Law provides unions with some support in the encouragement of collective bargaining. But to do this, it also needs to be enforceable. Whether the combined intentions of the bureaucrats, the unions and some employers will be sufficient to overcome the cultural barriers in Chinese workplaces to collective bargaining — and the resistance that many managers will no doubt show — is at this stage too early to determine.

Notes

1. Legislative Affairs Commission of the Standing Committee of the National People's Congress of the People's Republic of China, *Labour Law of the People's Republic of China* (Beijing: Ministry of Labour, 1994). Adopted at the Eighth Meeting of the Standing Committee of the Eighth People's Congress on 5 July 1994, promulgated by Order No. 28 of the President of the People's Republic of China.
2. Much of the data for this chapter were collected before and during a four day tripartite national seminar on collective bargaining held in Haikou City, Hainan in October 1994, attended by senior officials from the Ministry of Labour, provincial labour bureaus, the All China Federation of Trade Unions (ACFTU) and employer bodies, and organized by the International Labour Organization (ILO) and the Chinese Ministry of Labour. Funding was provided through the Australian government's programme of Support for ILO Activities (ASILO). Many thanks to Anita Chan for numerous helpful comments on an earlier draft.
3. Pat Howard, "Rice Bowls and Job Security: the Urban Contract Labour System," *Australian Journal of Chinese Affairs*, No. 25 (January 1991), p. 94; see also, Andrew Walder, *Communist Neo-Traditionalism: Work and Authority in Chinese Industry* (Berkeley: University of California Press, 1986).
4. A form of labour regulation, also referred to as labour contracts, had been

introduced, less than successfully, as far back as the 1950s. However, it bore only limited resemblance to the modern system of labour contracts. See Howard (Note 3).
5. Howard (Note 3), p. 100.
6. Carl Goldstein, "Elephants' Graveyard," *Far Eastern Economic Review*, 5 May 1994, pp. 77–78.
7. For example, Anita Chan, "Revolution or Corporatism? Workers and Trade Unions in Post-Mao China," *Australian Journal of Chinese Affairs*, No. 29 (January 1993) p. 42; and Anita Chan, "The Emerging Patterns of Industrial Relations in China — and the Rise of Two New Labour Movements," *China Information* (Spring 1995).
8. *Asia Labour Update* (January–March 1994) p. 5; *China Labour Bulletin* (July 1993) p. 7.
9. See Ching-kwan Lee, "Production Politics and Labour Identities: Migrant Workers in South China," this volume; Goldstein (Note 6), p. 77; Lincoln Kaye, "Labour Pains," *Far Eastern Economic Review*, 16 June 1994, pp. 32–33.
10. Howard (Note 3).
11. The Labour Law applies to labourers (*laodongzhe*), a term not defined in the law but actually referring to all non-agricultural employees. This contrasts with the Australian use of the term labourers, which in official publications refers to a class of mainly unskilled manual employees.
12. With the exception of the treatment of *yingdang* (see next footnote), this analysis is based on the official English-language version, translated by the Legislative Affairs Commission of the Standing Committee of the National People's Congress. As noted in the text, in case of discrepancy between the English translation and the original Chinese text, the Chinese text shall prevail.
13. Articles 16, 19. According to the English-language version, a labour contract shall be concluded where a labour contract is to be established. In Western law, this would be interpreted as requiring a labour contract, that is, indicating a labour contract *must* be established. However, the original Chinese version of the law uses the word *yingdang*, which is better translated as *should*. Hence, a labour contract should be established. This is a less forceful imposition than is implied by the English-language version of the law. I am indebted to Anita Chan for alerting me to this.
14. There is also a fourth model, one which has long been established in parts of the labour market: the worker co-operative model, in which the workers themselves are the owners of the means of production. Co-operatives receive various forms of preferential treatment by the state by comparison with privately-owned firms, and so in recent years there has been a growth of bogus co-operatives which are fronts for privately-owned firms. In the true

co-operatives, the distinction between the interests of the owners and those of labour is meaningless, as they are one and the same. For these firms, collective bargaining cannot be a real issue unless a management cabal has somehow expropriated power from the owners and workers. Perhaps the most legitimate expression of market socialism could be worker co-operatives freely operating in an open product market. In practice, the co-operatives have tended to be as much under the planning hegemony and personnel directives of the state as have been the SOEs, and the differences between collectives and SOEs have been of degree rather than of kind (e.g., Mayfair H. Yang, "Between State and Society: the Construction of Corporateness in a Chinese Socialist Factory," *Australian Journal of Chinese Affairs*, No. 22 [July 1989], p. 41). The extent to which this form of market socialism will expand will be a function of policies regarding reform of ownership patterns, product markets and planning. For these reasons, we do not consider the issue of collective bargaining in relation to the collectives any further in this chapter.

15. There are 17 articles in the Labour Law relating to labour contracts, and 2 relating to collective contracts.
16. For the conflict of union and party interests, see Yang (Note 14), p. 50; on union and management interests, see Anita Chan, *Chinese "Socialism" with Capitalist Characteristics: the Rise of Two New Proletarian Movements*, mimeo, Contemporary China Centre, Australian National University, 1994, pp. 12, 33. The *China Daily* of 20 October 1994 reported the case of the Xue Jingwen, who had been sentenced for life imprisonment for taking personal advantage of his positions as director of a paper mill and as a senior trade union official.
17. For examples of weaknesses in union performance at the workplace, see Ching-kwan Lee (Note 9).
18. D. Peetz, "Union Membership, Labour, Management and the Accord," (Ph.D. thesis, School of Industrial Relations and Organisational Behaviour, University of New South Wales, Sydney, 1995).
19. Chan, *Chinese "Socialism"* (Note 16).
20. *China Daily*, 20 October 1994.
21. Chan, *Chinese "Socialism"* (Note 16), p. 32.
22. Chan, *Chinese "Socialism"* (Note 16), p. 38; Kaye (Note 9), p. 32; Ching-kwan Lee (Note 9).
23. There is thus an analogy with Australia's *Industrial Relations Reform Act of 1993*, which enables a firm to negotiate enterprise flexibility agreements (EFAs) directly with employees acting collectively. However, in Australia, EFAs can be negotiated even in unionized enterprises, although a union in such instances has a right to be involved in negotiations. The government introduced EFAs largely as a means of encouraging collective bargaining

amongst non-union employees, but the main political pressure for the introduction of EFAs came from employer organizations and it is apparent that some employers and employer organizations see EFAs as a means of bypassing unions to achieve changes in the conditions laid down by industrial awards.
24. These are defined above, in the discussion of articles 79, 80 and 84.
25. Australian dispute level was at or above the OECD average for much of this century, arguably because of the failure of the system to distinguish the treatment of different disputes. Strictly speaking, few of those disputes were "legal," though it was until recently rare for legal action to be taken against unions following an industrial dispute. Following the introduction of a formal right to strike in many interest disputes in March 1994, there has been no major increase in Australian dispute levels. Australian Bureau of Statistics data only cover the four months to July 1994, but they show that working days lost for that period were 23% lower than over the same four month period a year earlier and 34% lower than for the same four month period in 1992. This cannot be explained by slackness in the labour market, as employment grew and unemployment fell substantially between the two periods.
26. Mobo Gao, "Migrant Workers from Rural China: Their Conditions and Some Social Implications for Economic Development in South China," in *Entrepreneurship, Economic Growth and Social Change*, edited by David Schak, Australia-Asia Papers No 7, (Brisbane, Queensland: Centre for Study of Australia-Asia Relations, 1993), pp. 29–30.
27. Ibid., p. 30.
28. Yang (Note 14), p. 57. Yang also points, in this 1989 article, to the difficulty caused by the fear of informers and the residues of surveillance under the cultural revolution.
29. It will also be affected by policies affecting the spread, environment and genuineness of co-operatives, including reform of ownership patterns, product markets and central planning.

15

Production Politics and Labour Identities: Migrant Workers in South China

Ching-kwan Lee

Politics of Identity in Shenzhen: State and Labour

The economic significance of Guangdong for the Chinese national economy goes much beyond what staggering statistics reveal. The 15% annual economic growth average over the past 12 years for the province as a whole and the 31% average economic growth for Shenzhen over the past four years have put to rest doubts about the south China region as another economic miracle in Asia.[1] Yet, a more invisible but no less salient dimension of Shenzhen's importance is that it has become the medium through which Chinese state officials articulate a new national economic identity. Shenzhen, along with other "special economic zones" in the southern provinces, epitomizes prosperity, novelty and liberation. It provides the linkage between some parts of China with the idea of East Asian newly industrialized countries, or NICs. Emerging from explicit comparison made between the "East Asian Tigers" and China's special economic zones, the official image of Shenzhen in the 1990s is that it is a model for a neo-authoritarian and economically dynamic China and represents an emerging East Asian Chinese economic identity.[2]

While the history of official debate over the meanings of special economic zones has been documented elsewhere,[3] a more complete grasp of this new national economic identity requires an account of "views from below." Even when state leaders construct understandings of the present and visions for the future to bolster their legitimacy, there remains the question of popular acceptance and the possibilities for alternative interpretations arising from society. This chapter offers a partial answer to this question by focusing on Shenzhen's migrant workers who have literally manufactured the economic success of Shenzhen. Their collective experiences and practices are constitutive of the polysemous East Asian Chinese economic identity, not in spite of but because of their divergence from official imaginaries.

To depict the collective identities and cultures of migrant workers in Shenzhen, I draw on the "culture-in-action" or "culture-as-practice" approach to the study of labour consciousness and action.[4] In this approach, workers' identities and consciousness are conceived less as the sum of individual attitudes and ideas abstracted from the context of social actions. Rather, labour identities are "maps of meaning" that emerge from the dynamic process of collective interactions, and are objectivated in social relations, institutions and practices. Ethnography replaces survey as the methodological tool to uncover labour's collective identities. Another advantage of such a conception of collective identities is that it allows for the discovery of paradoxes, oscillations and contradictory lines of thought and actions.[5]

There are three forms of labour practices or politics through which I analyze migrant workers' collective identities. The first form of labour politics, which takes place in what Marx calls the "hidden abode of production," is politics at the point of production. Specifically, it refers to (1) politics in the labour process, or the technical and social organization of tasks in production, and (2) the political apparatuses, like the state and the union, that regulate workplace politics.[6] The second form of labour politics is collective mobilization by workers, sometimes but not necessarily at the instigation by unions, in events of strikes, work stoppages and protests. Compared with production politics in which workers' resistance and consent are immersed in everyday production activities, workers' collective mobilizations are "crisis moment" events that take on more organized, visible and confrontational formats.[7] Finally, the third type of labour politics occurs outside the factory gate and consists of extra-production relations, behaviour and subjectivities. This form of labour politics can be understood as "cultural struggles" engaged in by workers as they defend themselves against various modes of control in their daily lives. Workers negotiate and contest meanings and values of their class, gender and ethnicity in a wider social field, not confinable to the factory.[8] In this form of labour politics, collective identities of workers are formed through consumption, leisure activities, social networking, and exposure to the urban way of life.

Political Economy of Migrant Labour

Migrant labour in this chapter refers to that portion of the floating population whose main reason for changing residence is the search for employment opportunities. Whether they are called migratory labourers, temporary workers, civilian workers, circulatory migrants, or sojourners, there are no official statistics on the exact number of migrant workers. One can only estimate, based on estimates from diverse sources, the scale of probably one of the world's largest migrant labour systems. Solinger has estimated that there were some 80 million "floaters" throughout the country by 1990.[9] Because the majority of these floaters migrate for reasons of gainful employment,[10] for the sake of estimation, one can simply equate the size of migrant workers with that of floaters. In Guangdong, by the end of 1993, there were 10 million migrant workers, a three-fold increase from the 3.69 million in 1990.[11] One official from Sichuan province reported that by 1993, there were 3 million Sichuan migrant workers in the Pearl River Delta, an area within Guangdong where most foreign-funded out-processing factories are located.[12] In Shenzhen, out of a total population of 1.7 million in 1990, a total of 980,700 were temporary migrants.[13]

The phenomenon of migrant labour is hardly new in China. Skinner has documented the pattern whereby particular localities cultivated specific occupational skills, ranging from academic and administrative talents, military specialists, traders, businessmen to carpenters, barbers and blacksmiths, for export to other localities in late Imperial China.[14] During the pre-1949 era, with the opening of treaty ports along coastal provinces and the establishment of manufacturing enterprises, peasant workers migrated from the countryside into Tianjin and Shanghai.[15] Like these previous sojourners, those who swarm train stations during the Lunar New Year month in the 1990s become migrant workers under specific political economic contexts. Two developments in the political economy of south China have played prominent roles in shaping the politics of migrant labour: rural economic reforms in the mainland and economic restructuring in Hong Kong.

The story of rural reforms in China is by now well-known. Most relevant to the present discussion is the release of massive surplus labourers, many of whom became migrant labourers after the demolition of the commune system in the early 1980s. Numerous articles in the Chinese press asserted by the mid-1980s that some 30–40% of China's rural labour force was redundant.[16] It was widely estimated that by 1993, there were between 150 million and 260 million surplus labour in rural China and it was predicted that by the year 2000, the figure would reach 300 million.[17] Gradual erosion of the Household Registration Regulations, which had for four decades restricted the movement of peasants into cities, also facilitated rural-urban migration. The year 1994 has seen further development in the loosening of the registration system. A proposal has been drafted by the Public Security Ministry allowing peasants to obtain residence registration in small towns and cities provided that they could find stable accommodation and employment.[18]

This massive supply of labourers is most welcome to foreign investors who are keen to take advantage of China's open-door policies, another key aspect of China's economic reform since 1979. Guangdong, which attracted 50% of all kinds of foreign investment in China in 1991 alone, became the meeting point of mobile labour and mobile capital. From 1979 to 1991, the province absorbed 38% of total foreign direct investments and 47% of total out-processing projects and compensation trade in China.[19] Among foreign investors, those from Hong Kong accounted for 60.5% of total foreign investments in China from 1979 to 1990.[20] There were by 1993, some 30,000 Hong Kong-funded out-processing establishments in Guangdong, producing 50% of Guangdong's export.[21] The enactment of preferential provisions for foreign investors, the supply of cheap land and labour are all important pull factors drawing in foreign investments.

Yet, the exodus of capital from Hong Kong into the mainland result also from endogenous economic forces of the Hong Kong economy and the policy of the colonial state. Specifically, since the 1980s, manufacturing industries in Hong Kong have had to respond to rising costs of production, protectionism from overseas markets, and growing competition from manufacturers in Southeast Asia and in other East Asian newly industrialized countries. Confronted with the challenge of economic restructuring and given the non-interventionist policy of the Hong Kong government, local manufacturers, predominantly small and medium enterprises, have limited capabilities to pursue technological upgrading unlike their counterparts in Taiwan, Singapore and South Korea where governments invest in these endeavours.[22] Their survival strategy has been to take advantage of the new availability of the massive supply of cheap labour and cheap industrial land in south China. This strategy has allowed Hong Kong manufacturers to continue to compete internationally on the basis of low cost mass production.

The combined effect of de-collectivization in rural China, industrial restructuring and relocation of Hong Kong manufacturing industries, and the opening of special economic zones is the influx of migrant labour from rural areas in different provinces into factories in south China. The main demographic characteristics of migrant workers are that they are young (mostly in the 15–29 age group),[23] single,[24] having a junior high education.[25] In a number of studies, it was found that women slightly outnumbered men among migrant workers, especially in Shenzhen and the neighbouring Pearl River Delta region. For instance, a number of surveys done among factory workers in the region found that 70% of the sampled subjects were females.[26]

The Hidden Abode of Production: Despotism and Localism

In Chinese official/élite discourses about migrant workers, workers' "plight" and "hardship" are given occasional short shrift, amongst more standard reports on their criminal involvements and the threats they pose to the social order.[27] For instance, in a plea for respecting the rights of workers as the "masters of the country and the society," a report in Beijing's *Fazhi ribao* (Legal Daily) summarized the findings of several surveys on migrant workers' conditions in Guangdong's foreign enterprises. Working hours in these enterprises were long: 9.3 hours a day on average, sometimes 12–16 hours, or even 24 hours on particular occasions. Some enterprises had no Sundays off and allowed only two days off every month. Overtime work was compensated for only 0.2–0.5 Hong Kong dollars per hour. Internal rules of these factories stipulated wage deduction and dismissal of workers if they failed to show up at work for two consecutive days in a month or 10 days in a year, forcing workers "to work like real robots manipulated by others."[28] Besides, workers were made to work in overcrowded, hot and suffocating work sites, with inadequate dust-, poison-, and fire-prevention facilities and water supply. Dormitories were crowded: a "70-square-meter dormitory in a Zhuhai based garment factory housed 86 people, while more than 180 staff and workers of a Zhuhai-based electronics factory were forced to live in a very small dormitory of a little over 100 square meters.... Some female staff and workers even complained about being insulted and sexually harassed."[29]

Reports like these shed light on the physical conditions of work, seen and evaluated by observers as appalling. Yet, they miss the processes of cultural mediation, processes through which physical conditions take on subjective and collective meanings.[30] To understand how migrant workers collectively experience and apprehend these conditions requires analyses on the interplay of workers' background, the constitution of shopfloor interests in everyday production work, the strategies of managerial control and the social organization of the labour market. In the rest of the section, I draw on ethnographic studies by myself and others to argue that the despotic factory regime set up in south China's foreign-funded sector is mediated by a culture of localism among workers and management. The co-existence of despotism and localism characterizes the lived experience of migrant workers at the point of production.

Despotism refers to a type of factory regime in which labour control works through coercion rather than consent.[31] In a Hong Kong-owned electronics factory in Shenzhen, where I have done fieldwork in 1992–1993,[32] workers were subjected to overt, visible, punishment-oriented and publicly displayed control. The factory grounds were fenced on four sides by high concrete walls and the main entrance gate was guarded around the clock by security guards carrying batons. Along production lines, there were many notice boards tabulating the daily and hourly output targets, the names of the "best" and the "worst" workers assessed on a weekly basis, and daily cleanliness scores of each line. Mottos saying "No spitting," "Ask your superiors when you have problem," "Quality comes first" were painted in bold Chinese characters on the walls. Visible display of rules showed only the tip of the regimental iceberg. New recruits were asked to read a 10-page handbook of elaborate regulations. The environment was strikingly similar to the prototypical factory in Karl Marx's time, when all punishment naturally resolved themselves into fines and deductions from wages. This factory's regulation book was filled with such despotic codes and penalties proscribing workers' demeanours and attire. For instance,

> Workers must put a factory identity card on their uniforms. Violators are fined 5 yuan. Workers who wear slippers at work, spit or litter are fined 10 yuan.... Workers punching cards for others are fined three days' wage. Workers who do not line up for punching time cards, do not change shoes according to rules, do not wear headscarves, have long nails, or roll up uniform sleeves are fined 1 yuan. Workers must apply for a "leave card" when going to the bathroom. Each violation is fined 1 yuan.... Leave of absence without prior permission is fined 30 yuan for the first day and 15 yuan for the second. Leave of absence with prior permission is fined 15 yuan ...

Similar disciplinary regime of work is found in other foreign-funded factories employing migrant workers in the Pearl River Delta region. In a rapidly developing township employing 50,000 to 60,000 workers in over 500 Hong Kong financed factories, one researcher found that factory compounds were usually locked up after a certain hour so that workers could not stay out late unless they are in the company of one of the managers or have the permission to do so. The actual working hours were almost always[33] longer than the 8 hours a day dictated by the contract. Surveillance and explicit threat of wage deduction (for damage to material due to poor workmanship) and dismissal are commonly utilized to ensure the quality and quantity of work effort. Status differentiation between Hong Kong management and the local workforce was reflected in the differential allocation of accommodation and food: local workers were assigned a bunk bed in sexually segregated dormitories whereas Hong Kong managers had better equipped quarters; local workers were served food of subsistence quality, while Hong Kong staff enjoyed greater variety of choice out of a different menu.[33]

Workers' critique of capitalist employment relations centred not so much on the unequal reward distribution but more on the dehumanizing aspects of factory work. Their critique of capitalism was made with reference to family agricultural production rather than socialist industrial production. Three aspects of factory work stood out as inflicting most pain on migrant workers who came to factories directly from the fields. Of all the rules in the factory I studied, the most detested was that of docking wages for all kinds of leave, including sick leave with doctor's notifications. This was considered the most "unfair" and "inhumane" practice in "boss' factories" (a term workers used to distinguish foreign-owned enterprises from state and collective enterprises). One woman complained,

> There is inequality in the villages too. Some peasant families have larger houses and more lands, and some earned more in their sidelines trades and production. We who come out to work know managers get higher pay than us workers. But it's really unfair that supervisors will not believe in you when you're really sick. They treat us like we are all liars even when some of us even nearly fainted at work.

Secondly, it was not so much the length of the workday or the high temperature of the shopfloor which provoked discontent. Rather, it was management's total control over workers' time that was experienced as despotic. Because overtime was demanded at the discretion of management, who gave only an hour's notice prior to the overtime shift, it was impossible for workers to make plans for their non-work hours. A worker further explained,

> It's actually more exhausting at home, with the blazing sun. Here at least, we have a shelter above our head. Yet, even though tending the field is very busy and hard work, we have a lot of free time. When your work is done, you can play with village friends. Here you have to hold your urine until they give you the permit to go to the bathroom.

Finally, workers' movement around the shopfloor was strictly circumscribed and was completely determined by management according to production and disciplinary needs. Many new recruits to the factory staunchly and openly resisted management's transfer instructions. Being moved from one assembly line seat to another, or "being kicked around like a football," was unacceptable to workers because it was an assault on their personal dignity.

Within the factories, despotic practices are mediated by a culture of localism. Localistic networks assume cardinal importance in determining migrant workers' social relations, daily practices, imagination and interests. Localistic networks are organized according to workers' native place village, county or province, and incorporate different ranks of workers and managerial staff. In the factory I studied, workers came from 14 different provinces and very diverse local dialects were heard on the assembly lines. Localistic practices by lineleaders, foremen and supervisors abounded and impinged poignantly on workers' material interests. Hong Kong managers were aware and tolerant of such practices by their junior staff. From the duration of bathroom visits, the assignment of difficult and easy tasks, application for home-visit leave, to the transmission of skills, promotion opportunities, and the ability to bring in locals, preferential treatments were given to locals. Depending on the interest at stake, membership criteria for locals shifted. The most basic distinction divided all workers into two groups: "northerners," i.e. those originated from provinces north of the Yangtze River, and "southerners," i.e. those from south of the River. Each group constructed the other in derogatory terms: "northerners" were bumpkinish, silly, rude and miserly; "southerners" were cunning, promiscuous, dishonest and spendthrift. More often, workers made finer distinctions among themselves by county origins. Petty favouritism was distributed mostly along county lines while scarcer resources like promotion or introduction of locals were limited to locals of the same village or kinship group.

In another ethnographic study of a joint venture electronics enterprise in Shekou, Shenzhen, the researcher noted the prominence of "regionalism" as the primary identity among migrant workers coming from different counties in Hunan and Guangdong. "Social interaction on the shopfloor to a large extent hinges on one's place of origin.... Relations of native place... are seen as natural and premodial, and fellow natives are tied to one another by pan-familial rights and obligations."[34] Regional groups also constructed stereotypes for each other. Shantou men were known to be astute petty traders while Shantou women were considered manipulative of men; *kejia* women were peasant-like, while Hunanese were hot-tempered. Not only were regional sentiment and hostility expressed through graffiti in restroom doors, incidents of verbal fighting and outbursts among regional groups were also found. As in the factory I studied, localistic tensions were related to material interests of workers. For instance, because Hunanese occupied positions of managers and engineers, Hunanese workers considered themselves superior to their Cantonese co-workers. "On the other hand, Cantonese are mainly workers and lower level clerks, and are resentful towards their Hunanese counterparts whom they feel to be less competent but are able to remain in the job or even get promotions simply because of *tongxiang* relations. Thus, without fellow natives in the workplace, Cantonese workers believe that promotion is impossible. The regional-occupational cleavage reinforces this idea and deepens the sense of helplessness among workers. They believe that their lack of 'good fortune' is a variable of regionalism rather than class. With class consciousness suppressed, regional differences become particularly conspicuous in the individuals' daily encounters."[35]

In short, ethnographic evidence shows that within the factories, workers are subjected to despotic regulations often exercised through localistic networks. Management consciously incorporates these networks onto the shopfloor as a way of attaining more efficient control over the workers, while workers participate in this culture of localism for reasons of protecting their work related interests. The emergence of this regime of localistic despotism is not random but is related to a set of institutional conditions, i.e. the political apparatus of production.

First of all, the state bureaucracy leaves a high degree of autonomy for management to deploy methods of labour control. Clientelist connections, or *guanxi*, between foreign investors from Hong Kong and Taiwan on the one hand, and local officials in the mainland are common.[36] These connections render whatever minimal labour regulations that exist ever more flexible and negotiable. There are no explicit laws defining a minimum wage level for workers in out-processing factories where most migrant workers are employed, no social insurance legislation and no compulsory trade union recognition to protect workers from arbitrary firing. With a state that nurtures managerial autonomy, workers resort to their own localistic networks for surviving the fluid labour market in Shenzhen. Locals provide critical resources for migrant workers, ranging from financing their first trip to Shenzhen, getting and changing jobs, obtaining the three permits necessary for sojourning in Shenzhen, to making loans in case of employers' late wage payment, and caring in times of sickness. Under these conditions of the labour market, management finds it convenient to exploit such localistic dependence to facilitate despotic control within the factories.[37]

Outbursts of Collective Action

I have argued that labour control over migrant workers in foreign-owned out-processing factories is accomplished by a regime of localistic despotism. In everyday production activities, class conflicts between foreign investors and migrant workers are mediated by or experienced as conflicts of interest among localistic groups. Yet, workers' culture is not a coherent piece and their general acquiescence to the regime of production does not preclude occasional and spontaneous outbursts of collective action. During these episodes, workers' class consciousness lends itself to public and collective expressions.

Official statistics offer a glimpse into the magnitude and the rate of increase of labour actions in Shenzhen. For instance, it was reported that in 1991, foreign-funded enterprises accounted for one-third of the total number of enterprises in Shenzhen and these enterprises witnessed a total of 834 labour disputes, or 68.6% of the city's total labour disputes.[38] Whereas there were only 21 work stoppages in Shenzhen in 1986–1987, the figure rose to 69 in 1989–1990.[39] Then, in 1992, there were a total of 255 cases of suspended production. In 1992, Shenzhen City Labour Bureau and Shenzhen City Federation of Trade Unions received more than 4,000 complaints about enterprises delaying or deducting payment of wages to staff and workers, involving nearly 30,000 staff and workers and 5 million yuan.[40] Another report observed that in January 1994, in just 10 days, Shenzhen City's Labour Bureau received over 160 complaint letters sent by workers and met with 370 people who came to complain. These complaints mainly involved unpaid wages, resignation allowances and security deposits not paid to workers after they resigned, barbaric management, and maltreatment of workers.[41]

Many more incidents of collective actions by workers escape the purview of labour officials, either because management successfully quenches unrest at an early stage or because workers find officials more an obstacle than a resource in their confrontation with managers. The dire scarcity of detailed information on the unfolding of these "crisis moment" events makes it difficult to examine workers' emerging consciousness as they engage in collective mobilization. Nevertheless, I offer two preliminary observations that may serve as pointers for further analysis. The two observations pertain to the role of localism and the role of official unions in labour activism.

If migrant workers' localistic networks can function to absorb the brunt of despotic rules within the factory and allow workers to satisfy mundane needs at the expense of other workers, localism can also be a facilitating factor for workers' mobilization against employers. As abundant labour historiography worldwide have documented, localism is a powerful cement contributing to the formation of worker solidarity necessary for collective actions.[42] Among Shenzhen's migrant labourers, there is also evidence that divisions along lines of native place origin serve as a powerful catalyst for labour militance. A press report noted that "workers from the outside have formed 'regional gangs' which often create social disturbances and could become a factor of social instability in the long run. For instance, 15 strikes took place in Longgang Town in Shenzhen, with eight of them instigated by Sichuan workers, three by Guangxi workers, two by workers from south of the Yangtze River, and two by Hunan workers."[43] Elsewhere, an observer also remarked, after interviewing workers involved in several work stoppages in Shenzhen, that localistic sentiments among migrant workers coming from the same native place contributed significantly to worker solidarity. When locals were maltreated by management, other locals would be infuriated and would protest against management on behalf of their locals.[44]

In the factory where I did research, workers passed on to new recruits the story of an incident in which a Hubei woman was fired after being caught stealing some ball-point pens from the office building. She accused the managers for not paying her the appropriate dismissal compensation. A few days later, a group of her Hubei locals attacked the personnel manager and her husband, who were then hospitalized. This incident was an important one in workers' collective memory in the factory. When they retold it to me and to others, it was very often in the context of expressing their discontent towards an "inhumane" management and their reliance on localism as a means of defense. Therefore, localism is a double-edged sword: while it may fragment class unity of the migrant workforce as a whole, it may also provide the collective identity spurring labour activism.

If localistic networks can contribute to labour's collective consciousness and actions, labour unions and labour officials in the state bureaucracy have worked towards the reverse direction of putting a lid on any emerging class confrontation between migrant workers and foreign investors. Trade union officials in Shenzhen see their role as educating workers to be cooperative with foreign management. The chairman of the Shenzhen Municipal Federation of Trade Unions once explained that they were "opposed to strikes, because that will harm the ultimate interests of the workers and the country as a whole."[45] During the several widely reported work stoppages in Shenzhen in 1993–1994, unions and labour officials' mediation efforts have aimed to thwart labour actions.

For instance, in March 1994, in a Taiwan-funded shoe factory in Shenzhen, management suddenly demanded a room-and-board fee (150 yuan per month) and had deducted that amount from workers' paychecks. Workers had long grievances towards management's tight control: among other rules, workers were required to follow fixed routes from the shopfloor to the dormitories and canteens, or else the punishment would be to stand for long hours in a public area inside the factory. On pay day, some workers posted a notice, undersigned by "Temporary Union," expressing their objection to the new room and board fee, low wage rate and unreasonable factory rules. Work stoppages among the 3,000 migrant workers lasted for three days. While workers stayed inside the dormitory, Public Security officials were called into the factory premises. Labour Bureau officials declared that the temporary union was illegal and they came in to mediate with management. Fearing reprimands, no workers dared to come out as representatives. After two days of negotiation between management and officials, an agreement was reached: management was to repay each worker the docked 150 yuan and workers were required to sign new contracts stipulating the deduction of the new room-and-board fee. Interviews with workers revealed that leaders of the incident refused to sign the new contract and quit the factory.[46]

In May 1994, some 2,000 workers in a Hong Kong-owned factory in Zhuhai participated in work stoppages and demanded a 30% pay rise to cover the 21% inflation rate and shortening of working hours from 12 to 8 a day. On the second day of the incident, union and labour officials intervened, while public security officials entered the factory premises to prevent an escalation of conflicts. According to a report of the incident, union officials told workers that their demand for a 30% pay increase was unreasonable because these officials themselves were only given a 10% raise. The result of union mediation was that workers would have a 13% pay raise. Activists in the incident were dismissed by management after negotiations were concluded.[47]

Officials involved in these incidents were toeing the official line when they largely assumed the role of suppressing class mobilization and confrontation. State regulations ordaining the establishment of unions in foreign enterprises have been in place since 1985 but were not effectively enforced, so much so that only some 20–25% of these enterprises were unionized.[48] And for out-processing factories, there is no law stipulating the formation of unions. Much is left to the discretion of foreign investors some of whom do not even sign contracts with workers, much less establish unions.[49] Among those which have unions, like the aforementioned joint venture electronics factory in Shekou, the main responsibilities of the union are to indoctrinate (e.g. disseminating the Communist Party's interpretation of the 1989 pro-democracy movement and the Tiananmen Incident) and entertain workers (organizing basketball and table tennis tournaments, film shows, New Year party, etc). Even when the company violates Chinese labour law — like when a woman worker was fired because of her pregnancy, or when workers were forced to work overtime beyond the 48 hours per week limit, or when women were fired because of deteriorating eye-sight after several years of working intensively with microscopes — union officials look on helplessly.[50]

In short, there is no lack of class consciousness and attempts at collective mobilization among Shenzhen's migrant workers. However, the institutional context, characterized by dependence of local officials on foreign investments and the suppressor role of trade unions, is not conducive to the development of sustained and organized labour activism. On top of these factors, the highly mobile and fluid labour market in Shenzhen encourages migrant workers to seek individual rather than collective means of resistance to redress whatever grievances they have at work. Job hopping, in view of the persistent demand for unskilled labour in Shenzhen, is a more effective way to improve one's livelihood and work conditions than collective resistance and bargaining. Likewise the seemingly unlimited supply of labourers which keep pouring into the cities in Guangdong convince employers that there is no shortage of workers to replace problematic ones. Under these conditions, migrant workers' collective identity *as an exploited class* is thwarted as often as and as soon as it emerges in episodes of open resistance. On the other hand, their collective, albeit fragmented, identity as *localistic groups* is reinforced every time they activate their localistic connections in their search for better job opportunities, and as they then enter anew into the routines of production, as documented in the last section.

Youth at Border Zones

For the generation of rural youth coming of age in the 1980s, going to Shenzhen is an once-in-a-lifetime odyssey that marks their transition to adulthood. Becoming a *dagongzai* or *dagongmei*, i.e. workers labouring for the bosses, brings a hotchpotch of contradictory but novel experiences, of which exploitation by foreign investors is only one of its many elements. Paralleling migrant workers' collective experience of hard and dehumanizing factory life are the new-found freedom in dating, an independent cash income, contact with people other than locals, exposure to an urban way of life and participation in various forms of popular culture. That is why no matter how often migrant workers are nostalgic of their home villages and families, they are reluctant to resume peasantry. For many of these young workers, Shenzhen offers challenges that allow them to grow, try and enjoy, even if it is not a place to stay. A migrant worker from Hubei, after surviving a blaze killing 68 workers of a raincoat factory in Guangdong in 1991, expressed her decision to come south again, saying "it's like going through a reincarnation, and you still choose to be a human being."[51] Migrant workers' contradictory love-hate sentiment about their identity as migrant workers finds expression in the lyrics of a popular song entitled "Dagongzai," well known among migrant workers in Guangdong:[52]

> Dagongzai come from five lakes and four seas, from all places and directions;
> Dagongzai are all young, seventeen or eighteen;
> Dagongzai come from all walks of life: cowboys, horseboys, PhDs, poets and singers;
> Dagongzai work hard selling their strength, working extra hours and extra shifts;
> Dagongzai make a lot of money for other people, bosses from Hong Kong and Japan;
> Dagongzai have good and bad tempers, missing their families and preserved vegetables at home;
> Dagongzai's life is hard: they are fired by the bosses;
> Dagongzai's life is free: they fire their bosses;
> Dagongzai always write home, saying how good their life is;
> Dagongzai always sigh, during quiet hours at night;
> Dagongzai keep their words at heart, to nobody's knowledge;
> Dagongzai like to sing the song "I wish I had a family";
> Dagongzai are strong, never shed tears when others are here;

Dagongzai have no residency in the Special Economic Zones, where they make every piece of brick with their sweat;
Dagongzai are a group of Chinese cowboys who can survive in any corner of the world ...

It is obvious that Shenzhen offers unprecedented economic opportunities for rural youths with limited education. Many workers confess that their monthly income of 200–300 yuan (as of 1992) is several times more than that of an average peasant in their home village. Yet, beyond this economic pull factor, the attraction of Shenzhen also lies in its "border zone" character. By this I mean not only the geographical location of Shenzhen as bordering that of Hong Kong which supplies migrant workers with an avalanche of consumption goods and leisure practices. Shenzhen is also a border land in a sociological sense: it is a place where people cross social and cultural borders as they negotiate and blend old and new norms and values in their everyday life. In short, migrant workers in Shenzhen "were no longer what they once were and not yet what they could become."[53] Everyday life is itself a creative process of cultural production[54] through which collective identities emerge. When young migrant workers explore the worlds of romance, consumption and urban popular culture, they simultaneously invent new identities of gender, locality and generation.

One of the most consequential challenges migrant workers pose, wittingly or unwittingly, to their family is their capability to erode patriarchal authority. This is so especially, though not exclusively, for women who are subjected to more patriarchal decisions at home than their male siblings. Many young women become migrant workers as a means to escape arranged marriages their parents impose on them. Once in Guangdong, their physical distance from home and earning abilities allow them to renegotiate with their parents about these marital arrangements. The story of a 22-year-old Hubei woman is typical of many others,

> The guy (the prospective groom) had an *hukou* and a job in a state unit in the city of Wuhan. My parents knew him through a match-maker. I saw him only once and my parents agreed to the engagement. I was only 17 and it was customary that the engagement would last several years before the marriage took place. I objected but they asked me where else could I find a city husband. So I came to Shenzhen. My parents had sent me telegrams a couple of times urging me to go back to help the guy's family business. I just neglected the telegrams. By now, I have repaid the 1,100 yuan he gave my parents over the past few years.

This woman met her present boyfriend, a Hubei local and co-worker of her brother in a furniture workshop in Shenzhen. They had gone back together for mutual home visits and their parents accepted their relationship. Other women workers express similar desire to get away from anticipatory parental imposition about their marriage. Working in Shenzhen allows them to fend off suggestions of match-makers. A 20-year-old Guangdong woman described what she expected to see during her up-coming home visit for the Lunar New Year and the kind of response she would say to her match-maker,

> All those match-makers are extremely busy during the two weeks of New Year when all young people return home from Shenzhen. They will ask mothers of every household if they want to meet some nice young men or women to be their potential son- and daughter-in laws.... I don't want to get married so soon, and so I can tell them either that 'I'm too young' or 'I already have a boyfriend in Shenzhen'.... Actually, the ideal situation is for us to get to know boyfriends ourselves while working here. Usually, we can meet people from the same county or nearby villages after coming here, like in gatherings with native folks. If we stayed home, we'd never have the chance to meet people outside the village.

Migrant workers' exploration of romantic relations sometimes cross localistic boundaries. These cases of "double crossings," i.e. deviating from parental arrangement and deviating from the norm of localistic homogamy, are subjected to severe gossip and negative opinion. Women involved in inter-provincial relationships are conscious of the difficulties these relations entail but also find excitement and satisfaction in having these experimental practices. Therefore, while workers may talk disapprovingly about their Guangxi forelady's relationship with a young man from Shanghai, saying "she would not get used to eating noodles everyday," or that "he's just fooling around with her," workers also see how another inter-provincial couple (a Guangdong woman and a Hubei man) get married after working together in the same factory for several years. So marriage norms are more fluid than those at home and young workers' dating practices are influenced by a confluence of factors: parental preferences, migrant peer culture and exigencies of Shenzhen.

For women workers, the new-found freedom of romance is not an unequivocal blessing and they have to walk a tight rope between redefining (urban and modern) femininity and being branded as promiscuous.

There is the widely shared view that romantic freedom also brings danger, and it is reflected most clearly in popular literature written by women workers on women workers. The genre of *dagong wenxue* is considered a type of popular culture specific to the Special Economic Zones and includes reportage and fiction concerning the lives of migrant workers. One very popular name is Anzi whose stories are mostly about *dagongmei* in Guangdong. The theme of romance is the most prominent one in her work, reflecting women workers' aspiration and fear for romantic experiences in their lives in Shenzhen. A recurring message from their stories is that romantic love enriches young women's lives. Although men in this age of frequent mobility are not always trustworthy, having experiences in love affairs is a necessary *rite de passage* on the way to modern womanhood. One story is about a young Guangdong woman worker who fell in love with a technician in the factory. She worked as hard as a robot and gave her boyfriend all her savings so that he could start a small business. She dreamed about becoming his bride one day while he could become a successful businessman. The man did make big money later but then fell for some other more glamorous woman. Recovering from her despair with the whole affair, the woman picked up tailoring and within three years had become a famous fashion designer in Shekou, Shenzhen. The author concluded the story by remarking that, "experience is enculturating. Perhaps because of the affair, she has transformed herself from a common *dagongmei* into a modern woman as she is today."[55]

In another story about the danger of emotional involvement, the author encourages young women to take that as a learning experience and to have the courage to quit unworthy relationships with dignity. A Hunan woman came to Guangdong in order to escape from an arranged marriage. She and her local workmates were attracted to their boss, who was "mature and had an irresistible masculine attraction." In a business trip, the boss taught one of them to dance and slept with her. Later, the woman found that he was not serious about the relationship and that he had started chasing other women. In the end, both women decided to quit their job, "for the sake of integrity and self respect."[56]

For many young women, the possibility for them to re-negotiate their gender identity through romantic and marital choices is such a cherished gain of becoming *dagongmei* that it outweighs the meaninglessness and exhaustion of factory work. Women make frequent reference to the fate of their mothers when they talk about how their lives are hard but better than the older generations. Thus, in dating and making choices about husbands, young women workers are re-defining their gender *and* generational identities. A 16-year-old Sichuan woman worker said proudly that "My mother never left our village. She has to work in the field all her life. But I can work in factories, away from the scorching sun. And I keep my own wage, though that's not much money." Four decades of imposed immobility for Chinese peasants and of "village involution" in all aspects of peasant life[57] make migration to cities an attractive move for peasants in general. For women peasants, the opportunity can mean more, if only because of women's subjugation to men. In a short story written by a woman worker, the author deplores her home village in Chaozhou, Guangdong, where the sons of one family force their sisters to marry into households which would exchange them with women as their wives. She also wrote of the gossip she heard about the sale of women for twenty to thirty thousand yuan each. The story ended with a plea to other women workers, "Sisters, let's be brave to alter women's fate!"[58]

Like dating, practices and experiences in the realm of consumption give public expressions to workers' gender, class and localistic identities. Firstly, workers have to balance the competing claims of fulfilling filial obligation and of personal satisfaction. How much of their wage is spent on personal consumption and sent home as remittances depends on the degree of their identification with the family. There seems to have emerged a gender differentiated practice in which women sent more than men. Secondly, even though cash income allows them to participate in the consumer market, without regard for workers' class or locality of origin, workers are often frustrated by their meagre income and by localistic prejudices of local businesses.

Research on migrant workers found that workers consistently and regularly sent remittances home. For instance, in a study on temporary migrants in Kaiping County, Guangdong, 64% of the subjects remitted between 14% and 50% of their earnings. Some of these migrants who became rural entrepreneurs reported that they had brought back luxury items and paid for the building or repair of the village home.[59] In another study on women workers in Shekou, women sent home some 20–25% of their monthly wage as remittances. Many of these women made every effort to save up, by working overtime, spending less and eating more cheaply in order to fulfil their responsibilities towards the family.[60] There was also evidence suggesting that female migrant workers sent more than their male counterparts. In a study of northern migrant workers in the Pearl River Delta, while women workers regularly sent home on average one-third to one-half of their income, men only did so on an irregular basis and only sent an average of 20% of their income.[61]

Beyond this aggregate quantitative difference, women and men hold diverse conceptions about remittances, a difference which is in turn related to their gendered objective of migration. Female migrant workers are concerned about saving up for their dowry, an independent economic resource at marriage, as well as contributing to the coffers of their family of origin. A Hubei woman's notion that her remitted money and her family's money are intermeshed but separable is characteristic of other women workers:

> My brothers never asked me to send money home in their letters. But still, I sent money three times since I came here two years ago. Everytime, I sent about 1,500 yuan. When my third brother got married, he used up 500 yuan and my eldest brother used some of the rest for building a house.... When I went home for the New Year, my brothers said they would repay me when I return later.... It's embarrassing to ask them not to use my money when I sent it home. If I did, they would blame me in their heart. But they know it's my money, and in the future, I will need that money, for my dowry. Normally, the bride needs about 2,000 yuan to buy furniture and electrical appliances for the new household ...

Among male migrant workers, not only do they send less or no money at all, they actually take pride in the fact that they spend as much as they earn. The gendered expectation for young men is that they should come to Shenzhen to accumulate skills and worldly experiences so that when they eventually return home, they can operate small workshops or retail businesses. Their expression of home orientation does not necessarily take the form of remittances for family expenses. Developing the drive and ability for future upward mobility are more important. Pursuit of a non-agricultural career in the future is the goal of many young men who come to expand their horizons and search for opportunities:

> My family does not expect me to work on the land. No one hopes to work on the land.... In our family, we often talked about how farming was hopeless, difficult.... Engaging in other business outside or doing something else could earn more money.[62]

Spending patterns are gendered and reflect emerging conceptions of femininity and masculinity. Women spend on adornments like hair pins, dresses and snacks while men spend on beers, dinning outside the factory, and patronizing beauty salons for haircuts and massages. The emphasis for women is on outlooks and men on new experiences. However, workers also experience class frustration and localistic discrimination at the point of consumption as much as, if not more than, at the point of production. Double digit inflation rates have grown faster than the increase in wage rates. That is why demands for pay increases have been the predominant cause triggering workers' collective action. As consumers, workers are frustrated by their meagre income with which they can purchase only limited goods and services. On the pay day of each month, workers in the factory I studied went to the downtown shopping district almost as a ritual. Yet, most just window shopped or bought minor goods like shampoo, soap, a pair of pants to replace the old ones, or a 5-yuan poster of Hong Kong television stars. More expensive items like radios, cameras or dresses — commodities beyond daily survival needs — were beyond workers' affordability, unless they cut corners elsewhere in their monthly budgets or sacrificed part of their remittances. In another study of Shenzhen workers, it was also found that the cost of living was so high that workers could ill afford to pay for frequent entertainment. Material constraints limited workers' leisure activities to those that did not cost much or anything at all: strolling, playing badminton or basketball in open spaces, reading for free in book stores, visiting friends and relatives, window shopping or simply taking a rest.[63] Therefore, although cash income opens up a sense of financial independence and allows for expression of new feminine and masculine identities through consumption, workers are constantly reminded of the limits set by their class inferiority in Shenzhen when they realize that afterall, there is so little they can afford and so much more beyond their reach.

Besides the formation of class consciousness, everyday consumption and exploration of urban public space are occasions for the recreation and reinforcement of workers' localistic identities. Sights of the urban landscape — modern airport, clean streets, high-rises, city lights and stores — provide the most affordable entertainment for workers. However, there are forbidden zones where workers, especially northerners, fear to tread or are maltreated. Northern workers reported hostile attitudes by local store keepers and restaurant waitresses once they found that workers spoke Mandarin rather than Cantonese. When I was doing my fieldwork and went strolling with Hubei or Jiangxi workers, they refused my invitation to sit down to chat in a newly-opened cafe, saying that was a place where they were not welcome. They enjoyed themselves most when in the end, we came into a public park where no one served or was served. Likewise in shopping malls, shop-keepers set the price for their merchandise according to whether the customers speak Mandarin or Cantonese. Working under the assumption that northerners only look and do not buy, these local store-keepers deliberately set a higher price when they are asked in Mandarin, so that they can get rid of northerners quicker. In retaliation, when northerners make major purchases, like buying gifts for New Year home-visits, they choose those shops which are more honest and are consistent in their quotation of prices. Given this everyday localistic hostility, some northern workers find the factory dormitory a temporary and relative haven where they are shielded from harassment of strangers.

Sometimes employers organize dance parties and karaoke contests for migrant workers. Workers of different localistic origin participate to varying degrees and always take on different roles in such events. Those who take to the dance floor and enter singing competition are mainly young Guangdong men and women, while northerners usually resign themselves to the role of spectators, remaining shy and foreign to these urban entertainments. Cantonese popular songs, broadcast from Hong Kong radio channels, can be heard on every floor of the dormitory but are hardly comprehensible for northern workers who cannot understand Cantonese. While Guangdong workers develop the habit of watching (or chasing) Hong Kong television drama series, northern workers are frustrated by not having the chance to tune in to a Mandarin channel. In their gatherings with locals, workers sing country songs in their dialects and play poker using Jiangxi or Hunan rules.

Therefore, although popular culture can draw migrant workers together, they constitute separate groups of audience. However, localistic boundaries are not static and unbridgeable. Boundary crossings in young workers' social life in Shenzhen do occur. In inter-provincial romantic relationships, both parties will each bring along their locals in birthday parties or Sunday outings. Workers thereby mingle with non-locals and exchange information about crops, customs and people in each others home province and county. Inside the dormitories, too, non-locals may be arranged to live together in the same room and sometimes endearing friendships develop. A Guangxi woman told me her interesting story of befriending a Guangdong woman by initially pretending to be a Guangdong woman. Only after they became good friends did she reveal her Guangxi origin, and both found each other's localistic prejudices laughable.

In short, Shenzhen is a land of insecurity as well as inspiration, hardship and novelty. It is not the place for permanent residence, but it offers new horizons for youthful transients. And, during the years of sojourning, as they toil along assembly lines, strike and protest, fall in love, dance and play, young migrant workers collectively apprehend, re-negotiate and at times even contest their class, gender and localistic identities. Afterall, becoming *dagongzai* is the dream of many Chinese youths in the 1990s. In an autobiographic account, a young worker wrote what could reflect the mentality of many of his contemporaries:

> At the beginning, with utter despair after failing the high school entrance examination, I was at a loss. I thought it was degrading to be a migrant worker. I found it pitiful and shameful for them to labour only for money.... Now, I realize it is these workers who produce more and more goods with the "Made in China" label.... I want to be an outstanding *dagongzai*, a star among them. I want to actualize the meaning of life as a *dagongzai* ...[64]

Conclusion: Migrant Workers as Emergent Communities

Through migrant workers' engagement in production politics and the creation of new cultural identities, a popular, unofficial view of Shenzhen, Special Economic Zones and south China emerges. Workers know of a more complicated, contradictory and multi-dimensional Shenzhen than official ideology likes them to see and believe. If hegemonic constructions of Shenzhen and south China accentuate prosperity, progress, and national pride (inherent in the emphasis on the Chinese characteristics of modernization),[65] the emergent, alternate culture constituted by the lived experience of the labouring masses adds to this positive imagery a mosaic of class exploitation, state suppression of labour rights, despotism and localistic prejudices, as well as opportunities to re-negotiate gender, localistic and generational identities.

What official ideology finds inconvenient or negligible can well be sociologically significant. This study of migrant labourers has shed light on the unfolding interplay of political struggles, social inequalities, and cultural differences in the "space between order and chaos."[66] As China in the 1990s undergoes large scale reforms and social change, "emergent communities"[67] like those of migrant labourers in south China are pockets of new practices, new identities and new social relations in the making. The notion of "emergent communities" differs significantly from that of "civil society" which some China scholars have used to describe the migrant population, private entrepreneurs, intellectual-students community, etc. Dorothy Solinger, for instance, suggested that the "floating population" is a form of civil society because it stands apart and against the state as well as supports and perpetuates state domination.[68] Yet, I find this interpretation problematic. As Heath Chamberlain has maintained, it is a flawed conception of civil society if its existence and viability are assumed to vary directly with the distance of state power. Rather, "civil society" denotes a community of individuals qua citizens, and is sustained by widely shared moral visions concerning relations among individual citizens and between this community of citizens and the state. Moreover, in the process of civil society formation, the state plays an important role in liberating people from the constraints of traditional family and social bonds, and in institutionalizing the ground rules for collective public life.[69] Yet, my discussion of south China's migrant labourers has shown that both their collective identities and their interaction with the state fall short of the ideals of civil society. Among migrant workers, individual and parochial interests typically take precedence over the common good and the state has so far been reluctant to assist workers' pursuance of their citizen rights, especially *vis-à-vis* foreign investors.

In describing migrant workers as "emergent communities," I intend to direct analytical attention not only towards the newness of their social relations and practices but also to their collective identities. Because workers have mutual orientation towards each other and they cohere to a certain degree, theirs are communities in the making. Although not yet or not necessarily in the direction of civil society, the significant question remains what kinds of collective visions and logic of action are generated. These emergent communities chart the course of social change as do those of state officials, foreign investors and other social groups. Social analysts neglect these emerging communities at their own peril. Yet, to take them seriously implies the need to rethink meta-theoretical assumptions in Chinese studies, based as they are on old models of economic and political development, prioritizing state institutions with scant attention paid to cultural transformation and social practices.[70]

Notes

1. State Statistical Bureau, *Statistical Yearbook of Guangdong*, 1987–1994.
2. George T. Crane, "'Special Things in Special Ways': National Economic

Identity and China's Special Economic Zones," *The Australian Journal of Chinese Affairs*, No. 37 (June 1994), pp. 71–92.
3. Ibid.
4. Ann Swidler, "Culture in Action," *American Sociological Review*, Vol. 51 (1986), pp. 273–86.
5. Rick Fantasia, *Cultures of Solidarity* (Berkeley: University of California Press, 1988).
6. Michael Burawoy, *Politics of Production* (London: Verso, 1985).
7. For an exemplary work, see Rick Fantasia (Note 5).
8. Aihwa Ong, "The Gender and Labor Politics of Post-Modernity," *Annual Review of Anthropology*, Vol. 20 (1992), p. 281.
9. Dorothy J. Solinger, *China's Transients and the State: A Form of Civil Society*, USC Seminar Series No. 1 (Hong Kong: Hong Kong Institute of Asia-Pacific Studies, Chinese University of Hong Kong, 1991). For breakdown of 25 cities from 1986 to 1989, see Roger C. K. Chan, "Challenges to Urban Areas: The Floating Population," in *China Review 1992*, edited by Kuan Hsin-chi and Maurice Brosseau (Hong Kong: Chinese University Press, 1992).
10. Li Mengbai, *Liudong renkou dui dachengshi fazhan de yinxiang ji duice* (The Impacts and Policies of the Floating Population on the Development of Big Cities) (Beijing: Jingji ribao chubanshe, 1991).
11. FBIS-CHI-93-242, 20 December 1993, p. 29. Also, Si-ming Li and Yat-ming Siu, "Population Mobility in Guangdong Province," unpublished manuscript, Hong Kong, Baptist College, 1992.
12. *Ming Pao* (Hong Kong), 10 July 1993.
13. T. K. Liang (ed.), *Shenzhen zhanzhu renyuan bidu* (A Guidebook for Temporary Employees in Shenzhen) (Guangzhou: Tongji daxue chubanshe, 1991), p. 46.
14. G. William Skinner, "Mobility Strategies in Late Imperial China: A Regional Systems Analysis," in *Regional Analysis Volume 1: Economic Systems*, edited by Carol A. Smith (New York: Academic Press, 1990).
15. Gail Hershatter, *The Workers of Tianjin, 1900–1949* (Stanford: Stanford University Press, 1986); Emily Honig, *Sisters and Strangers: Women in the Shanghai Cotton Mills, 1919–1949* (Stanford: Stanford University Press, 1986); Elizabeth Perry, *Shanghai on Strike: The Politics of Chinese Labor* (Stanford: Stanford University Press, 1993).
16. Jeffrey R. Taylor, "Rural Employment Trends and the Legacy of Surplus Labour, 1978-86," *The China Quarterly*, Vol. 116 (1988), pp. 736–66.
17. FBIS-CHI-93-162, 24 August 1993, p. 50; FBIS-CHI-93-135, 16 July 1993, p. 40; *Far Eastern Economic Review*, 10 March 1994, p. 27.
18. *Ming Pao*, 27 October 1994; *Far Eastern Economic Review*, 10 March 1994, p. 28.

19. Pak-wai Liu et al., *Zhongguo gaige kaifang yu Zhujiang sanjiaozhou de jingji fazhan* (China's Open Door Reform and Economic Development in the Pearl River Delta: A Research Report) (Hong Kong: Nanyang Commercial Bank, 1992).
20. Yun-wing Sung, "Non-institutional Economic Integration via Cultural Affinity: The Case of Mainland China, Taiwan and Hong Kong," Occasional Paper No. 13 (Hong Kong: Hong Kong Institute of Asia-Pacific Studies, The Chinese University of Hong Kong, 1992), p. 28.
21. *Hong Kong Economic Journal*, 5 August 1993.
22. T. L. Lui and S. Chiu, "Industrial Restructuring and Labour Market Adjustment Under Positive Non-Interventionism," *Environment and Planning A*, Vol. 25 (1993), pp. 63–79.
23. Alan P. Liu, "Economic Reform, Mobility Strategies, and National Integration in China," *Asian Survey*, Vol. 31 (1991), p. 402; Li and Siu (Note 11), pp. 21–22.
24. Dorothy Solinger (Note 9).
25. Ibid.; Li and Siu (Note 11).
26. Si-ming Li, "Labour Mobility, Migration and Urbanization in the Pearl River Delta Area," *Asian Geographer*, Vol. 8 (1989), p. 50; Siu-mi Maria Tam, "The Structuration of Chinese Modernization: Women Workers of Shekou Industrial Zone" (Ph.D. dissertation, Department of Anthropology, University of Hawaii, Manoa, Hawaii, 1992), pp. 230–31.
27. JPRS-CAR-90-083, 9 November 1990, pp. 6–39; FBIS-CHI-93-162, 24 August 1993, p. 51; *Far Eastern Economic Review*, 10 March 1994, p. 27.
28. FBIS-CHI-92-181, 21 September 1993, pp. 48–50.
29. Ibid.
30. E. P. Thompson, *The Making of the English Working Class* (New York: Vintage Books, 1963); William H. Jr. Sewell, *Work and Revolution in France* (Cambridge, MA: Cambridge University Press, 1980).
31. For the concept of "factory regime" and its two generic types, despotic and hegemonic, see Michael Burawoy (Note 6).
32. For a comparison between the Shenzhen plant and the Hong Kong plant of the same enterprise, see Ching-kwan Lee, "Engendering the Worlds of Labor: Women Workers, Labor Market, and Production Politics in the South China Economic Miracle," *American Sociological Review* (in press, 1995).
33. Josephine Smart, "Coercion, Consent, Reciprocity and Exploitation: Labour Managements in Hong Kong Enterprises in China," paper presented at the Centre of Asian Studies, University of Hong Kong, Hong Kong Studies Seminar Programme, 1993.
34. Siu-mi Maria Tam (Note 26).
35. Ibid., p. 137.
36. Josephine Smart and Alan Smart, "Personal Relations and Divergent

Economies," *International Journal of Urban and Regional Research*, Vol. 10 (1989), pp. 29–45; Chi-kin Leung, "Personal Contacts, Subcontracting Linkages, and Development in the Hong Kong-Zhujiang Delta Region," *Annals of the Association of American Geographers*, Vol. 83 (1993), pp. 272–302; Ching-kwan Lee (Note 32); You-tien Hsing, "Blood, Thicker Than Water: Transnational Networks Between Taiwanese Investors and Local Bureaucrats in Southern China," paper presented at the Pacific Rim UC Berkeley-National University of Singapore Conference on "The Transnationalization of Overseas Chinese Capitalism," 8–13 August 1994, Singapore.

37. For a detailed discussion, see Ching-kwan Lee (Note 32).
38. FBIS-CHI-93-181, 21 September 1993, p. 49.
39. FBIS-CHI-88-148, 2 August 1988, p. 32; FBIS-CHI-91-020, 30 January 1991, p. 67.
40. FBIS-CHI-93-181, 21 September 1993, p. 49.
41. FBIS-CHI-94-000, 2 February 1994, pp. 52–53.
42. For a thoughtful summary of this vast literature and especially on the role of localism in Chinese labour activism, see Elizabeth Perry (Note 15).
43. FBIS-CHI-91-020, 30 January 1991, p. 67. I thank Elizabeth Perry for giving me this citation.
44. Ying-yue Wang, "Mingong zai Zhujiang sanjiaozhou" (Civilian Workers in the Pearl River Delta), unpublished manuscript, 1994, p. 12.
45. Wing-yue Leung, *Smashing the Iron Rice Pot: Workers and Unions in China's Market Socialism* (Hong Kong: Asia Monitor Resource Centre, 1988), p. 177.
46. Ying-yue Wang (Note 44), pp. 10–11.
47. Ibid., pp. 11–12.
48. *Far Eastern Economic Review*, 3 November 1988, p. 38.
49. FBIS-CHI-94-035, 22 February 1994, pp. 53–54.
50. Siu-mi Maria Tam (Note 26), Chap. 5.
51. *Cheng Ming*, November 1991, p. 22.
52. A woman worker from Sichuan wrote me the lyrics of the song during my fieldwork in Shenzhen.
53. Renato Rosaldo, *Culture and Truth* (New York: Beacon Press, 1989), p. 208.
54. Paul Willis, "Cultural Production Is Different from Cultural Reproduction Is Different from Social Reproduction Is Different from Reproduction," *Interchange*, Vol. 12 (1981), pp. 48–67.
55. Anzi, *Qingchun yizhan* (The Station of Youth) (Shenzhen: Haitian chubanshe, 1992), p. 86.
56. Ibid., p. 130.
57. Mark Sheldon, "Family Strategies and Structures in Rural North China," in

Chinese Families in the Post-Mao Era, edited by Deborah Davis and Steven Harrell (Berkeley, CA: University of California Press, 1993), pp. 153–54.
58. *Gongren xin yidai* (A New Generation of Workers), No. 2 (March 1994), p. 1.
59. Yuen-fong Woon, "Circulatory Mobility in Post-Mao China: Temporary Migrants in Kaiping County, Pearl River Delta Region," *International Migration Review*, Vol. 27, No. 3 (1994), pp. 594–95.
60. Siu-mi Maria Tam (Note 26), pp. 243–46.
61. Iam-chong Ip, "Industrial Employment, Gender, and Transformation of Individual-Familial Economic Ties" (unpublished master thesis, The Chinese University of Hong Kong, August 1994), Chap. 5.
62. Ibid., p. 81.
63. Siu-mi Maria Tam (Note 26), pp. 213–18.
64. See Note 58, p. 2.
65. Aihwa Ong, "Why Chinese Modernity? The Narratives of Chinese Capitalism," paper presented at the Pacific Rim UC Berkeley-National University of Singapore Conference on "The Transnationalization of Chinese Capitalism," 8–13 August 1994, Singapore.
66. Renato Rosaldo (Note 53), pp. 105–106.
67. I develop this notion from the works of Raymond Williams. In *Marxism and Literature* (Oxford: Oxford University Press, 1977), he uses the term "emergent" as one element of the tripartite typology of a cultural system: the dominant, the residual and the emergent. He defines the "emergent" as "new meanings and values, new practices, new relationships ... which are substantially alternative or oppositional to [the dominant culture]" in p. 123. While Williams is talking about cultural formation, my usage here is more about social formation.
68. Dorothy Solinger (Note 9).
69. Heath B. Chamberlain, "On the Search for Civil Society in China," *Modern China*, Vol. 19, No. 2 (April 1993), pp. 199–215.
70. For a similar review, see Philip C. C. Huang, "The Paradigmatic Crisis in Chinese Studies," *Modern China*, Vol. 17, No. 3 (July 1991); Leo Ou-fan Lee, "Chinese Studies and Cultural Studies: Some (Dis-)Connected Thoughts," *Hong Kong Cultural Studies Bulletin*, No. 1 (December 1994), p. 22.

16

Community Festivals in Post-Mao South China: Economic Transformation and Cultural Improvisation

Helen F. Siu

In the last few years, I have observed various community rituals in the New Territories of Hong Kong, Shantou and the Pearl River Delta.[1] On the surface, these festivals appear strikingly similar in character. Most of them are religious in nature, centreing around particular community deities and their temples. At times, ancestral halls are involved. Local notables and non-local officials, like the deities, are put on centre-stage, highlighted with elaborate public ceremonies. There are also enthusiastic overseas participants. The usual crowds with their baskets of food and gifts to the gods come in boatloads, and jostle one another along the roads leading to the temples; the open spaces in front of the temples are often lined with large colourful placards announcing patrons and well-wishers from far and near; local vendors have a heyday selling food, incense, and religious charms; the air is thick with incense smoke; the chanting of Daoist priests and Buddhist nuns joins the orchestra of bustling noises from fire-crackers, operatic singers, the gongs and drums of lion-dance troupes. Communal feasting and the playful cheers of children add substance to the joyous occasions.

In the New Territories of Hong Kong, these community festivals have long been taken for granted by the general public as a colourful, seasonal part of the cultural landscape.[2] The government has rarely intervened, except for a few occasions when the competitive "snatching flower rockets" (*qiang huapao*) among the local young toughs in martial arts clubs led to fights and casualties.[3] In recent years, enthusiasm for religious rituals has been on the rise among the territory's residents, drawing in the prosperous middle classes. The government, in unusually enterprising ways, has helped to convert community and temple festivals into large-scale tourist attactions.[4] The annual dragon boat races are now an international affair, promoted both in Hong Kong and New York by the Hong Kong Trade and Development Office.[5] The Bun Mountain Festival in Cheung Chau, the annual birthday celebrations for the Empress of Heaven (*Tianhou*) at Joss House Bay, the opening (*kaiguang*) ceremonies for the new Buddhist image at the Pulian Temple on Lantau Island, were attended by high ranking officials and local notables, and made into media events.

The communities across the border seem to have caught up with tremendous speed in the staging of their local festivals. Although there is a hiatus of forty years when popular religious events were strictly forbidden by Communist Party ideology, the resources of the local organizers and the fervour of the participants today quite surpass those in Hong Kong. The phenomenon is intriguing because more than a generation's memory of these events and their cultural meanings have been cleansed by Maoist politics. Furthermore, party ideologues maintain an ambiguous attitude toward what they denounce as feudal superstitions, and are threatened by any hint of local sentiments.

In an earlier paper, I have argued that the reemergence of popular religious rituals in the post-Mao era cannot be seen as traditional sentiments frozen during the Maoist era, revived as the state machinery attempted to retreat in the 1980s. Instead, these rituals appear to be an ingenious recycling of fragments of popular culture, shrewdly pursued by a young generation to capture new economic and political opportunities. Moreover, knowingly or not, the practitioners and their popular agendas continue to take the power of the state for granted.[6]

In the seven years since I wrote the paper, south China has projected itself further into the global orbit of finance, manufacturing and trade. The momentum for economic transformations both in the villages, towns and cities has not been dampened by the events of June 4th, 1989. Amid the dazzling wealth generated in the region beyond anyone's wildest dreams, community festivals and popular religious rituals are pursued with intensity and marked by increasing scale. Energies have snowballed despite the awkward warnings of the state propaganda czars against feudal superstition, extravagence and waste. The connection between the economic and the ritual events is obvious. The new developments point to the direction of my general argument that these popular festivals do not represent the cultural nostalgia of an older generation attempting to relive the past. Instead they are the aggressive creations of *nouveaux riches* and local officials who know or care little about culture and tradition, and who are desperately capturing a window of opportunity to construct their future.[7]

The crucial questions remain as to who these entrepreneurs are and why they use community rituals for their purposes. Granting that these events are created by different people pursuing their own agendas, and that the resultant cultural landscape captures layers of meaning and imagination, the complicity of local officials is an important issue. They are major players in the recent economic transformation of south China, and it will be fruitful to see how they juggle between their interests, those of their community, and the conflicting messages of a state machinery which continues to be a vital source of power and connections.[8] How do officials at different levels of local government create a niche for themselves and open a public space where they can comfortably play both state, market, and society in order to tap the unprecedented economic resources? In the post-Mao "cultural nexus of power," where are their respective places? As this region is spinning into the world orbit through Hong Kong, they rapidly become part of a rising "bourgeoisie" in China, pursuing every consumer item they consider conspicuously "Western," and thriving on foreign connections. How then do their manoeuvres in local cultural events contribute to the complex meanings of being both Chinese and cosmopolitan, an issue looming increasingly large over the political horizon of both the governments in Beijing and Hong Kong?

One often finds the juxtaposition of the religious, secular, commercial and political in communal festivals. But could the events' precipitous rise to official attention in Hong Kong and south China be the interactive outcome of sustained social mobility in the region, accessibility to high-tech media in a society which builds on information intensity, an increasingly global network of affluent immigrants and emigrants whose identities are in flux, and the competitive efforts of the governments of Hong Kong and China to ground the cultural commitment of a worldly population? To highlight the issues, I shall analyze two recent community festivals, one in Shantou Municipality of eastern Guangdong and one in Jiangmen Municipality of the Pearl River Delta.[9]

Community Festivals in Shantou

In February 1993, I went with Dr Choi Chi-cheung and two other research students to Qianmei township (*xiang*), Chenghai county of Shantou Municipality. Since 1986, in connection with the Lunar New Year, the *xiang*'s various villages have staged parades of their local deities or earth gods. These are the male *Fude gong*, also known to the villagers as the master (*laoye*), and female *Fude ma*.[10] The festivities we saw, like the ones in the previous years, lasted several days. In the Chen surname village of Jumei within the Qianmei *xiang*, they took place in front of an old ancestral temple where only the *Fude gong* sat. On the same platform was an incense burner for deities of a nearby temple, *Jumei gumiao* which had been destroyed during the Cultural Revolution. Worshippers started to come with their offerings the night before the parade, and the festivities reached a climax by noon the next day, when women and children jostled their way through the crowd to burn incense at the main altar. One saw a sea of offerings: geese, heads of pigs, cakes, fruits, and paper money stuffed in colourful baskets, all set up on small tables guarded by each family. There was the usual all day puppet show with its gongs and drums for the deity's entertainment.

The parade of *Fude gong* began in the afternoon amid the noise of fire-crackers. The route covered all the settlements within the village boundary. Oddly enough, the old incense burner belonging to the old temple, which was paraded with *Fude gong*, was given unusual attention. Worshippers waiting in front of their houses along the route rushed forward to put incense in the burner. From the recollections of the old villagers, rituals for the deities of the old temple were conducted by a slightly different cluster of village settlements before the revolution. Today, memories of the old temple and its deities were vague. Neither the villagers nor the organizers distinguished rituals for the *Fude gong* from those for the deities represented by the incense burner, as the former village alliances had been transformed by administrative realignments in the last few decades. What we saw appeared to be rituals belonging to two separate temples being collapsed into one.[11]

During the rest of the afternoon, worshippers retired to their homes. However, villagers hurried out again after dinner, carrying lanterns. The lanterns, representing each household, were lit in the ancestral hall, and the *Fude gong* and the incense burner were hurried through the neighbourhoods once more with the crowd following closely behind. This time, it was the show for *Fude gong*. Lighting the lanterns for each household at the ancestral hall to ask for recognition and blessings resembled lineage rituals in the Pearl River Delta around Lunar New Year. The tightly packed schedule came to an end only after the crowd rushed back into the ancestral temple with *Fude gong* to make a final round of incense offerings.

The parade at the village of Qianxi took place on the next day, where both the *Fude gong* and *Fude ma* were taken from their temple and paraded. The day before, when offerings were made to the *Fude gong* at the focal ancestral hall of the Chens at Jumei, residents of Qianxi participated as members of lineage branches. However, they conducted their own parade, which involved the seven neighbourhoods (*she*) that made up the village with the Chen surname at Qianxi. Worshippers waited at designated public areas of each *she* with their tables of offerings. After a dramatic rush to the altar by local women to burn incense and paper money, the deities were carted off to the next site accompanied by drums and gongs and fire-crackers. The final resting place for the deities in the evening was the Chen ancestral shrine (*gonting*), at Zainei *she* of the village, home of a member of the lineage who had acquired the highest literati honours in imperial times.

A few observations are worth mentioning here. It is clear that the festival was orchestrated by local people for themselves, although some overseas relatives were involved. When we volunteered monetary contributions, we posed an obvious problem for the organizers. It is revealing that after much discussion, they wrote our names (my colleagues are male) on the poster of contributors as "married daughters," having found no other appropriate category.[12]

Moreover, although the worshippers were largely women, the organizers were male village elders, whom local people referred to respectfully as members of the elders' group (*laoren zu*).[13] There was no official headquarters, but the scheduled events proceeded without much fanfare. The villagers seemed to know where exactly the parade would pass and what was to be done. The village elders sat around the ancestral temple sipping tea, with a few seated at the entrance of the temple to take contributions.

Members of the *laoren zu*, not village officials, were in charge of the occasion. They were elderly men in the village. Judging from their backgrounds, they were not the powerful village leaders nor were they from local "literati" families of pre-revolutionary days. As ordinary retirees, they socialized in a semi-public area, often the house of a former landlord or a small ancestral temple which had been confiscated by the administration decades before. The post-Mao era of economic liberalization seems to have given these social groups a unique role to play. According to Choi Chi-cheung, the village administration attempts to attract the attention of natives overseas but lacks the resources to do so. Furthermore, with the history of the class struggles in the area, cadres find it more congenial to use a neutral group to reach the overseas relatives. The elders, by virtue of their history in the village, have a wide social network. In the eyes of the local officials, they become convenient conduits to new economic goals. On the other hand, villagers have viewed these elders as repositories of local traditions and would defer to them on matters of community rituals and cultural sentiments. This ambiguity has given the members of the *laoren zu* room for manoeuvre.

In contrast, our host who was a local cadre had not shown his face in any of the activities. I only saw his wife darting out of an alley far away from their house to put incense on the burner, and his daughters brought the household lantern to the parade at night. One may argue that in the

Shantou region, the physical presence of officials had never been strong. The newly elected generation of village cadres, being young and relatively ignorant of local traditions, would find themselves more marginal than ever. They could at best tag along.

Nor could these local officials be the indispensable link to resources from overseas at this point in time. From our conversations with villagers and cadres alike, there is a certain pride as well as ambivalence with regard to their overseas Chinese (*huaqiao*) connections. Some overseas Chinese have contributed to local roads and schools, but we saw only a few families returning to participate in the festivities. There was no sign either of a lineage association or a native place association (*tongxianghui*) organizing activities. The tension expressed itself when we unexpectedly wandered toward the former mansion of a prominent overseas Chinese merchant, the history of whom had been discussed with enthusiasm by the village elders. But the house had been given to some poor villagers after the Communist revolution. The occupant of the house tried to prevent us from paying even a short visit. My colleagues and I being visible outsiders might have led him to suspect that we would make claims to the house on behalf of the former owner. It remains to be seen how the *laoren zu* can activate community sentiments while reaching out to overseas relatives.

Community Festivals in the Pearl River Delta

The events in the Pearl River Delta contrasted sharply with those in Shantou. Three weeks after the festivals in Jumei and Qianxi, I attended community activities at Chaolian town (*zhen*), an island off the coast of Jiangmen Municipality on the western edge of the Pearl River Delta.[14] The invitations for an "Arts Festival" (*yishu jie*) were jointly issued by the *zhen* government and the Chaolian *tongxianghui* in Hong Kong. The organizers also provided ferry tickets from Hong Kong, local transportation, meals and accomodations in Jiangmen's best hotels. Over three hundred guests were invited from abroad, mainly Hong Kong. Another five hundred were notables from various official and non-official units (*danwei*) in the region. Together with hundreds of participants and workers for the parade, plus relatives and friends, the quiet, scenic island all of a sudden bustled with people, cars, noise and movement of all kinds. The island's ferry pier was jammed with traffic, and cars without a special permit were not allowed through. While local cyclists watched with bewilderment, chicken and ducks which were used to taking leisurely tours of their muddy territories literally fled for their lives.

Although termed an arts festival by officials, the festivities planned were identified by local talk as the traditional parading of the Hongsheng deity. Hongsheng temple in Chaolian is well known in history. It was a prosperous regional pilgrimage centre during the Qing. Fifteen stone stele erected from the reign of Qianlong to Guangxu recorded patrons of its renovations from far and near. There were officials, prominent merchants from Guangzhou and Jiangmen, and local ancestral trusts.[15] Large boats from various parts of the delta used to moor along the wide stone landing in front of the temple. With the Ou ancestral hall, the village office and community school clustering beside the temple, the area was the cultural, social and political centre of Chaolian. Once a year at the time of his birthday, the Hongsheng deity was paraded with elaborate rituals among the villages of the *xiang* in a prescribed order. The last parade was staged in 1946.

Since 1985, the temple has been restored with a donation of over a million Hong Kong dollars from the Chaolian *tongxianghui*. Part of the donation was used to widen the main road leading from the ferry pier to the centre of the *xiang*, and to build a small park in front of the temple. Various activities, largely non-religious in nature, have been staged by the *zhen* government in the park since then. After the *zhen* government authorities consulted educated members of the *xiang* in 1991 about the history and procedure of *youshen* or parading the diety, local "literati" families were excited at the prospect of reviving such tradition.[16] Fortunately for the organizers, a prominent scholar of the Lu lineage had recorded it in detail when he compiled the *Chaolian Village Gazetteer* (*Chaolian xiangzhi*) in 1946.[17] However, there were the expected difficulties. Few people remembered the details since the last event was conducted in the wake of the Japanese surrender and matching the written record with the present political realities required some stretching of the imagination. One obvious problem had to do with the much transformed power relationships among the lineages of the *xiang* after the revolution. The author of the document wrote with the bias of a scholar from one of the major old lineages and their ritual significance duely occupied central place. The Maoist revolution had long reduced the public impact of the traditional leaders of the rituals, scholarly members of the Lu, Chen, Ou, Pan, and Li lineages. However, in the post-Mao era, they were the ones securing the best connections with wealthy relatives overseas. The local cadres who have dominated the political scene in the last decades were from the poor households who had traditionally been excluded from the festivities because they did not belong to any ancestral hall and were thus categorized as members of the mixed surnames.[18] If the rituals were to be revived according to the book, serious compromises had to be made.

Tradition, nonetheless, could be reinvented in creative ways to satisfy all concerned. The festivities surrounding the Hongsheng temple and in particular, the parading of the deity's image, were embedded carefully by the *zhen* government in a chain of events included in the arts festival. In the evening before the parade, solemn ceremonies celebrating the deity's birthday were to be performed at the temple by leading members of the *tongxianghui* (as they were conducted in the *tongxianghui* headquarters in Hong Kong over the years). In the evening after the parade, *tongxianghui* members and overseas guests were to be invited to an auction of art objects in front of the temple. This was part of the tradition in pre-revolutionary times, but the elaborate ceremonies today were organized and conducted by the *tongxianghui* and not by the *zhen* government. The objects were lanterns, paintings and calligraphy donated by prominent scholars somewhat connected to Chaolian.[19]

The *zhen* government, on the other hand, issued a programme where centre place was given to the ground-breaking ceremonies of the building of a bridge linking Chaolian *zhen* to Jiangmen. In addition was an invitation to attend the exhibition of a major real estate project on the island, a joint venture between a group of developers in Hong Kong and the Chaolian *zhen* government. These projects were closely related. Local cadres had been working for years toward building the bridge, which could turn the island into prime real estate on the outskirts of Jiangmen. They had secured one-third of the required funds from the provincial and municipal governments. The rest was to be raised through joint-ventures and appeals to members of the Chaolian *tongxianghui*. The auction organized by the *tongxianghui* had an explicit fund-raising agenda. The *zhen* government also successfully sold land on the island at a low price to relatives and friends overseas through the *tongxianghui*, with the promise to buy the land back at a high price in a few years.[20] The cadres were banking on the prospect that once the bridge was built, the rise in real estate prices would more than compensate the costs.

The role of the villagers was ambiguous in the larger schema of things. Given the power and influence of the *zhen* government, it could proceed with the events without general spectators. In fact, for most of the official functions — the ceremonies at the temple the night before, the feasts, and the auction, local villagers were more or less excluded. There had been campaigns against local superstitions and the Jiangmen Municipal government was watchful. Chaolian *zhen* officials were warned that if popular religious sentiments went out of control, the *zhen* would have to explain to the higher ups themselves. Anything that had to do with the temple was to be conducted in the name of the Chaolian *tongxianghui*, and no cadres would show up. During the ceremonies at the temple the night before, the *zhen* government was to post non-local guards at the temple gate explicitly to prevent villagers from entering. Furthermore, in preparation for the parade the next day, the image of Hongsheng was to be transported from the temple to the front of the *zhen* government office by a few villagers under the direction of some local teachers. The plan was to be executed in the middle of the night without fanfare in order not to attact a following that would embarrass the officials. Moreover, the parade of the deity would be accompanied by displays of colourful floats and dragon dances, and preceeded by musical bands from local schools. Major enterprises and joint ventures of the *zhen* were invited to sponsor the floats, which were designed with the most forward-looking, politically-correct slogans.

But the sentiments of the villagers could not be totally ignored. The *zhen* government allowed a Hong Kong television crew to interview some village elders and local historians who helped with the organizing, but it also invited the Jiangmen television studio to do another version for video taping. The official functions of the festival were set on a weekend, a few days before the deity's actual birthday, supposedly for the convenience of guests from Hong Kong. But the schedule allowed villagers to bring their offerings on the actual anniversary of the deity's birth a few days later. By then these popular religious sentiments would be safely beyond the notice of municipal cadres. A believer or not, one of the organizers deemed it necessary to go quietly to the temple a few nights before the festival to pray for good weather.

It was a cold drizzly afternoon when my colleagues and I, together with a boatload of Chaolian "natives," arrived at the Jiangmen ferry pier after a three-hour ride from Hong Kong. The *zhen* government mobilized over twenty buses to transport the three hundred guests to the various hotels and restaurants in Jiangmen. A few buses took visitors directly to the ferry for Chaolian. They were mainly members of the *tongxianghui* and they were to stay with friends and relatives on the island. We were grouped together with professionals and business people to ride in mini-vans. The major developers and donors to the bridge-building project were promptly escorted by the party secretaries to the fleet of Mercedes Benz and Lexus "taxis" owned by the *zhen*, and driven off to the most exclusive hotel in Jiangmen.

Our hotel was also where the developer staged a sales-exhibition of Chaolian's real estate project. Over lunch and dinner, we were able to befriend a strange mix of guests who had distant connections with the *zhen*. These included Li Zhengtian, an artist/philosopher from Guangzhou who was one of the three authors of the "Li Yi Zhe" big character poster (see Note 19); a Mr Chen was once a guard for Mao Zedong; and a Chaolian woman with good connections in Beijing. The cadres who socialized with us were eager to inform us of the press conference about the bridge and the ground-breaking ceremonies. Although they were reluctant to disclose information on the rituals to be held by the *tongxianghui* at the Hongsheng temple, a cadre did arrange for a driver to take us there in the evening.

It was a solemn occasion in full "literati" style. While curious villagers peeped through the closed iron gates of the temple in the rain, the all-male cast of managers of the Hong Kong Chaolian *tongxianghui* celebrated the deity's birthday with the reciting of texts, and elaborate offerings of food and incense. While the Hong Kong television crew busied themselves recording the process, members of the *tongxianghui* watched in silence, broken only by the noise of firecrackers. The scene was ironic: for such an important community occasion, the local temple was enclosed for selected outsiders to perform the rituals which had been kept away from natives for over forty years. The cadres, in a hotel at Jiangmen, had conveniently chosen to hold a press conference on the same evening promoting their "Arts Festival."

Events in the morning were reserved for another group of spectators. To the relief of officials, the drizzling rain had stopped, quite contrary to the weather forecast. After giving a sumptuous breakfast at the hotel, the *zhen* government transported business friends and guests to the sites where the bridge and the villas were to be built. After speeches by party secretaries, the ground breaking ceremonies were performed smoothly. Major donors and overseas dignitaries were displayed on stage, and lion dances troupes and firecrackers added the usual commotion, noise and colour. As the sites were at the northern end of the island away from any sizable settlement, only women and children from nearby villages, and migrant labourers having nothing else to do came to watch the spectacle.

Some managers of the *tongxianghui* were present, but centre stage was given to overseas commercial developers.

Events of the day reached a climax after lunch, when the *zhen* government staged the formal opening ceremonies of the "arts festival" in front of the new government offices. All the municipal officials and political dignitaries were comfortably seated on the platform, facing a mixed audience made up of local villagers. A small truck carried the image of Hongsheng, surrounded by old village men dressed in traditional costumes as his "guards" and "servants." While the dozen or so colouful floats were examined and admired, the attention of local villagers focused on the image of the deity and his entourage. To the surprise and embarrassment of the cadres, local women came with baskets of incense and surged forward to pay their respects to Hongsheng as soon as the parade started, blocking the processions temporarily. It was obvious that the festival meant different things to different participants. For the old women kneeling in front of the truck, they reclaimed the important moment which had been denied the community for half a century.

For the next six hours, the parade moved through village after village along a route only more or less prescribed in the historical documents. As the floats mounted on small trucks had to pass through paved roads, certain small villages of mixed surnames in between the established settlements were able to view the parade. Moreover, ceremonies to receive the deity at the village of Zaigang was more elaborate than ever before. Although the village was traditionally looked down upon by other major surnames, it has become the home of several Communist Party secretaries and thus could not be ignored.

The parade was a continuous chain of traditional and modern spectacles. The entire community appeared to be watching, but what local villagers and their overseas relatives and friends drew meaning from were strangely compartmentalized. At the very front of the parade were several school bands and students carrying colourful banners. Parents proudly cheered the children on. The school bands were followed by the deity and his entourage. As soon as the deity appeared, households which had set up small tables of offerings in front of their homes started burning incense. The noise of firecrackers filled the air. The diety drew the largest crowds in front of major ancestral halls, where people rushed forward with incense. However, a twenty-six section dragon dance troupe separated the deity from the colourful floats sponsored by various joint-ventures and *zhen* enterprises. The floats were the least interesting to adults, but greeted with excitement by children and migrant labourers in a holiday mood. The cadres, on the other hand, had retired to the temple to prepare for the auction and dinner where the dignitaries, local entrepreneurs, and members of the *tongxianghui* would be brought together.

According to tradition, donated art objects and lanterns with the blessings of Hongsheng were auctioned to the highest bidder. The *tongxianghui* in Hong Kong had conducted the auction of lanterns for years. The proceeds were then used for the upkeep of the shrine at the headquarters of the *tongxianghui*. In Chaolian, the *zhen* government had been pursuing various local enterprises and joint-ventures for contributions to the bridge project. The auction this year at the temple became a happy arena for such purpose. The *tongxianghui* and overseas patrons donated objects, which were mostly acquired by heads of local enterprises with extraordinary bids throughout the evening.[21] In a festive mood, the *zhen* government netted over seven million Hong Kong dollars. The festival and the auction were publicized in some Hong Kong newspapers afterward. The developers were sufficiently encouraged by public response to their real estate projects that prices were raised another ten percent.[22]

It was only after the overseas guests left Chaolian that the temple livened up for the local population. Throughout the week, villagers came from far and near with their offerings. During the night of the actual birthday of Hongsheng, the temple caretaker counted over 130 roast pigs offered. The organizer who had prayed before went alone to the temple after the commotions to make offerings and, thank the deity for having granted good weather at the crucial moments.

Concluding Remarks

The two community festivals described in this chapter represent different processes by which local society "recycled" cultural resources and their sense of the past in order to join larger currents of social, economic and political change. Given a different history of political transformation, economic development and emigration, the roles of local cadres and entrepreneurs, returned natives, and overseas associations differ sharply in the two communities. Although in neither case can one argue that the interests of the representatives of the state are opposed to popular sentiments, the positions of the local cadres in relation to their communities could not have been farther apart.

In Jumei and Qianxi, local cadres stayed conveniently away while village elders in the *laoren zu*, itself a product of the revolution, carved out their sphere of influence and realigned community interests. Without much influence from the cadres or from overseas patrons, the villages seem curiously inward looking. In the post-Mao era, the area is just beginning to break out of an isolated existence previously imposed. It will be interesting to see if more economic resources could be brought into the local community through the connections between the *laoren zu* and the overseas natives. Would such an enterprising turn give the cadres leverage within the village power structure or would it further marginalize them? What independent channels could the cadres tap in order to give themselves a more positive role in the emerging economic landscape?

In the first decade of economic transformation after Mao, various counties in the Pearl River Delta have shrewdly rekindled sentiments of native place among their overseas relatives in order to generate much needed investments. These developments ironically reinforced the power and legitimacy of local governments especially at the level of market towns.[23] Inspired by such successes, cadres in Chaolian have taken the lead in weaving a new social and cultural tapestry that can accommodate varied identities and promote forward-looking economic agendas. However, before local enterprises can develop autonomous capital and networks on their own terms, the *zhen* government, together with an established overseas *tongxianghui*, continue to play an important role as brokers. They created the appropriate arenas for vital community concerns to be known regionally and overseas, and skillfully tapped available resources.

In an age of economic liberalization, ordinary villagers can appeal to the gods for good fortune and prosperity, and hope for favourable outcomes however intangible they may seem. For the officials, "selling" native place and community festivals with good political sense and overseas connections can reap real and immediate profits. At a historical juncture where asserting "Chineseness," however coarse and superficial it is, seems to be the politically correct thing to do, the promotion of community rituals is a convenient expression.[24] Popular religion and rituals with their malleable meanings can, afterall, be good business.

Notes

1. I visited the community cleansing (*jiao*) festival at Lai Chi Wo near

Shatoukok of Hong Kong, the birthday celebrations of Hongsheng at Kau Sai village of Sai Kung, the Bun Mountain Festival and the birthday of the Tianhou at Cheung Chau, the Dragon Boat Festival at Taipo, the community festivals at Jumei and Qianmei villages of Shantou, the new year festivities in the neighbourhoods in Chenghai, Shantou, the birthday of the founder of the Sanyi Jiao at Putian in Fujian province, the birthday of the Hongsheng and the Arts Festival at Chaolian zhen, and the Chrysanthemum Festival at Xiaolan Zhen. I missed the Beidi birthdate at Shawan of Panyu county. Some of the trips were partially funded by the South China Programme of The Chinese University of Hong Kong.
2. Volumes of historical and fieldwork materials have been compiled by Issei Tanaka on village festivals and theatre in Hong Kong and Guangdong. See *Ritual Theatre in China*, 1981; *Lineage and Theatre in China: Interdependence of Festival Organization, Ritual and Theatre in the Lineage Society of South China*, 1985; *Village Festivals in China: Backgrounds of Local Theatres*, 1989; all published by the Institute of Oriental Cultures, The University of Tokyo.
3. The late Barbara Ward has written on the "qiang huapao" in Kau Sai of Hong Kong. See Barbara Ward and Joan Law, *Chinese Festivals in Hong Kong*, (Hong Kong: Guidebooks Company Ltd, 1993 [first published in 1982]). See an essay by Choi Chi-cheung on the Bun Mountain Festival of Cheung Chau, in "Down to Earth: The Territorial Bond in South China," a book manuscript edited by David Faure and Helen Siu (Stanford: Stanford University Press, forthcoming).
4. Colourful bilingual booklets published by the Hong Kong Government Information Service and the Hong Kong Museum of History have described some of these festivals and sites in detail.
5. See materials put out by the Hong Kong Office of Trade and Development in New York on the Dragon Boat Festival as part of the Hong Kong–USA programme.
6. See Helen Siu, "Recycling Rituals: Politics and Popular Culture in Rural China," in *Unofficial China: Essays in Popular Culture in the People's Republic*, edited by Perry Link, Richard Madsen, Paul Pickowicz (Boulder: Westview Press, 1989), pp. 121–37.
7. See also Orville Schell, *The Mandate of Heaven: A New Generation of Entrepreneurs, Dissidents, Bohemians, and Technocrats Lay Claims to China's Future* (New York: Simon and Schuster, 1994), for emerging social groups in the era of reform.
8. On the marriage between power and market in the post-Mao era, see a collection of essays entitled *Fubai: huobi yu quanli de jiaohuan* (Decadence: The Exchange Between Currency and Power), edited by the editorial board of Jingji shehui tizhi bijiao (Beijing: Zhongguo zhanwang chubanshe, 1989).

For an overview of development in the Pearl River Delta, see Liu Pak-wai, Wong Yue-chim, Sung yun-wing, and Lau Pui-king, *Zhongguo gaige kaifang yu Zhujiang sanjiaozhou de jingzhi fazhan* (Liberalization in China and the Economic Development of the Pearl River Delta) (Hong Kong: Nanyang Commercial Bank, 1992).

9. For rituals emerging in Fujian, see also Kenneth Dean, *Daoist Ritual and Popular Cults of Southeastern China* (Princeton: Princeton University Press, 1993).

10. Choi Chi-cheung, a historian at the Hong Kong University of Science and Technology, had arranged for us to go with him to observe the festivals in Shantou. Details of the festivals have also been recorded by him. See Choi Chi-cheung, "Chuantong de yansu yu gaibian: Chaozhou Chenghai xian Longdu Qianmei xiang de youshen" (Continuity and Change in Tradition: The Parade of Deities in Longdu Qianmei Village of Chenghai County in Chaozhou), a paper presented at the conference on "Temples and Popular Culture," 18–20 March 1994, Center for Chinese Studies, Taiwan.

11. We asked about the old temple and its deities and were led to the site where it used to stand. Nothing there would inspire any definite memory.

12. For entry into the community, it was useful to have Choi Chi-cheung as a Chaozhou native. He speaks the local dialect.

13. Choi Chi-cheung stresses the importance of the village elders in his paper.

14. This time, I went with Choi Chi-cheung, Ma Mu-chi (a research student at Hong Kong University of Science and Technology), and my colleague Liu Zhiwei, a historian from Zhongshan University.

15. For a description of the temple's importance in the making of local community, see Helen Siu, *Agents and Victims in South China: Accomplices in Rural Revolution* (New Haven: Yale University Press, 1989), chap. 4.

16. These were educated members of the Lu, Ou and Chen lineages which were the largest landlords in the area. They have formed groups to play traditional Cantonese music and opera, and have helped the *zhen* government to compile local histories.

17. See Lu Zijun (Shangfu), *Chaolian xiangzhi* (The Gazetteer of Chaolian Village) (Hong Kong: Lam Shui Ying Press, 1946). Lu Shangfu was a Confucian scholar of some national repute. He was a student of Kang Youwei, and together with another Chaolian native son, Chen Zibao, were active in promoting education for both men and women in Guangdong and Hong Kong.

18. The party secretary of the *zhen* is from the Ou lineage of Zaigang, a village at the southern tip of the island. The Ou's had some ancestral halls, but had been considered by the major surnames as uncouth and *dan*. The head of the festival organizing committee is a member of the party committee. She comes from an old lineage of the Ma surname but the surname has few members left

in the *zhen*. Her husband and father-in-law are all cadres in the *zhen* government, and families bearing their surname are considered the *zaxing* (mixed surnames) with no ancestral hall.
19. Three paintings were donated by Li Zhengtian, a nationally known artist-philosopher in Guangzhou, who was a member of the team who wrote the tabloid "Li Yi Zhe" big character poster (*dazibao*) against the radical followers of Mao Zedong in the mid-1970s. A friend of mine commissioned several pieces by the Hong Kong calligrapher Wong Kam-cheung, and the head of the Chaolian *tongxianghui*, Lo Chi-lap, also donated some of his.
20. According to a *zhen* official, the difference between the selling prices and the promised buy back price was more than 50%. The latter was still far below the price of real estate across the river in Jiangmen.
21. The lanterns were ordered from a factory in Foshan. The four pieces of calligraphy by Wong Kam-cheung yielded HK$600,000. Li Zhengtian's calligraphy were given the highest bids.
22. This of course could be a publicity device, as the price increases were announced in the midst of speculations concerning the central government imposing profits taxes and other restrictions on real estate development.
23. See Helen Siu, "Socialist Peddlers and Princes in a Chinese Market Town," *American Ethnologist*, Vol. 16, No. 2 (May 1989), pp. 195–212.
24. See Margaret Ng, "The Importance of Being Chinese," *South China Morning Post*, 3 January 1995, p. 13 on the implications of Chinese identity as Hong Kong approaches 1997. For similar treatment of how Chinese identity is negotiated in Hong Kong, see Helen Siu, "Cultural Identity and the Politics of Difference," *Daedalus* (Spring 1993), pp. 19–43, and a paper under review by the same author, "Remade in Hong Kong: Weaving into the Chinese Cultural Tapestry."

17

Bringing Religion into the Socialist Fold

Chan Kim-kwong

Introduction

Chinese society is becoming ever more complex and volatile, with its mixture of consumerism, economic growth, corruption, liberalization, and authoritarian government. In this turbulent environment, China's religious communities face new challenges, and have responded in a variety of ways. This chapter highlights important developments in the state control of religion, and an overview of the religious groups themselves.

In the early 1950s, the government established a framework for the control of religion in China. The Chinese Communist Party (CCP), strongly influenced by Soviet Marxism, was hostile to all religions, which it saw as reactionary, feudalistic and, in the case of Christianity, pro-imperialist. Its policy was firmly predicated on the need at least to control, and preferably to eliminate, all religious belief and activity. The administrative structure reflected this. Religious groups were strictly monitored by at least three state agencies, the Religious Affairs Bureau (RAB), the United Front Work Department (UFWD), and the security forces (PSB). Moreover, the religious groups were obliged to re-organize themselves into national organizations (given the epithet "patriotic") that undertook a role of self-policing and self-censorship. From 1949 to 1979, all religious groups suffered severe persecution. Those who refused to join the patriotic organizations were treated as underground subversives, while even the patriotic groups were disbanded during the Cultural Revolution.

When the leadership liberalized their restrictions on religious activities as part of the reform programme in the late 1970s, they did not anticipate any substantial growth of religion, as may be inferred from the key party document on religious policy (Document # 19).[1] The phenomenal upsurge of religion in the 1980s took party leaders by surprise, and they lacked a legislative framework to curb this development which increased challenges to party rule: ideological, since religious doctrines do not accord with Marxist orthodoxy; and societal, since autonomous religious organizations are by definition a challenge to the monolithic state.

This chapter describes how the CCP, particularly in 1994, attempted to re-assert control over religious affairs. The first section outlines a

---

This writer would like to thank Dr. Alan Hunter, of the East Asian Studies Department, University of Leeds, who read through this manuscript, corrected numerous mistakes, and gave many helpful suggestions.

theoretical and ideological discussion which was conducted over the past few years in party journals and some academic publications. The trend of the debate was to formulate policies that would integrate religious believers more tightly into the communist state, to shepherd them into the socialist fold.

The second section reports a series of high-level meetings held in late 1993 and in 1994. They are interesting in that they illuminate the procedures whereby new policies are announced, discussed, and made known to the leaders of the "patriotic" organizations. The third section provides details of the new decrees and regulations that emerged from this policy shift, and the fourth is a survey of the religious groups and their responses.

(1) Ideological Discussion on Religion and Policy Making

By the mid- to late-1980s, the government was well aware of the phenomenal growth of religious groups, especially within the Protestant community.[2] Scholars generally attribute this growth to the transcendental aspiration of human beings, ideological bankruptcy of communism, and the need for existential certainty in times of rapid social change.[3] Instead of reflecting upon social reality with the intention of revising the possibly outdated Marxist theory on religion, the party theoreticians tried hard to defend Marxism and to force reality into the rigid framework of the Marxist interpretation of religion. They argued that the growth of religion was due to the lack of scientific education and materialistic worldview among the people, the ignorance of the peasant population, the lack of government control on religious activities, the epidemic of religious superstition, and infiltration by politically hostile forces.[4]

There is a tradition of limited discussion among party theoreticians concerning the nature of religion, and the handling of religious affairs. In the early 1980s, a relatively liberal view on religion prevailed. At the same time, as the rural areas became more prosperous all sorts of religions enjoyed rapid growth. Additionally, surveys suggested that increasing numbers of intellectuals and professionals or those who do possess scientific knowledge, also believed in God.[5]

Nevertheless, clinging to their dogmatism, party theoreticians regarded religion as an ideological obstacle to the realization of socialism. Despite the deletion of the phrase "religion is the opium of the people" from the 1982 official party document # 19 on religion,[6] many local party publications in 1994 still openly called religion the "opiate of the people which is backward, conservative, absurd, and prevents the progress of science and social development."[7] Consequently, they advocated both the strengthening of administrative controls to curb the growth of religion, especially in rural areas, and the re-inforcement of atheistic and "scientific" education among the masses to liberate them from the "distorted" worldview of religion. Some even linked the increase of crimes in rural areas to the growth of unregulated religious activities.[8] A national propaganda campaign was also called to denounce religious superstition.[9]

These leftist views on religion were often endorsed by the senior party leadership,[10] gained much popularity especially among the lower ranking cadres,[11] and influenced their attitudes as they implemented government policy towards religious groups. Except for overseas scholars and a few university-based Chinese academicians, there is little sign of open discussion, among the party theoreticians and policy-makers on the interpretation of religious phenomena, other than from a Marxist standpoint. Therefore, the Chinese government constantly interprets religion as ideologically incompatible with socialism and inferior to socialism.

Within this context of incompatibility, the government advocated the policy of "adaptation of religion to socialist society" to situate religion in the current social reality. Actually this concept, in the milder form *xietiao* (to coordinate, to harmonize), had been advocated since 1981, as part of a theoretical framework to accommodate religion in socialist society.[12] This concept basically argued that religion could make a contribution to the building of society. The focus was on what religion could offer to society, rather than that religion should modify itself in order to be allowed to exist in the society.

In 1990, the CCP began to suggest the term *shiying* (to adapt, to suit), through a major UFWD document,[13] to replace the former term. Soon, party-related journals began using this new term,[14] and discussions on religion after 1992 generally followed the trend.[15] However, it was Jiang Zemin who made the term official at the 1993 national UFWD Conference. He also expounded, or rather dictated, the connotation of the term in the context of religion.

Jiang Zemin stated that the party's policy on religion, and the strengthening of legal controls over religion, were meant to guide religion to adapt to socialist society. Since religion was a historical phenomenon, it would have a long-term presence in socialist society. This adaptation would not require believers to abandon their idealism, theisms or religious belief, but it would require them to support the socialist system and the leadership of the CCP. Furthermore, religious bodies should reform those religious institutions and doctrines that were not compatible with socialism. Also, religion should use its doctrines, practices, and certain positive elements in morality to serve socialism. He concluded with the emphasis that the only political basis for religion to survive in socialist society would be the total support of socialism by religious believers.[16] In other words, "adaptation" required religious bodies to reform themselves to conform to the mode designed by the civil authority.

Jiang's view was discussed among religious affairs cadres and religious personnel at various levels. Concerning the policy of "adaptation," government cadres felt that it would be their sacred duty to guide religion into socialist society, under the assumption that religious believers were misled by religious doctrines into an absurd worldview resisting social development. They generally agreed to strengthen their control over religious activities, and to exercise the authority vested in them by various decrees and regulations on religious administration.

At the national meeting of RAB officers held in May 1994, the RAB took steps to improve its ability to gather and exchange data on religious activities. The RAB installed over 2,000 fax machines in all its local offices so that information on local religious activities could be sent immediately to the central office in Beijing for appropiate action to nip any unrest in the bud. The RAB also encouraged horizontal exchange of information as a more effective means to track religious activities, especially those conducted without official sanction such as the ministry of itinerant preachers. The RAB also established an Information Synthesis Department to synthesize all the data pouring into the central office.[17] All these measures reflected the increase of government control on religion.

Regional religious affairs offices varied their requirements on "adaptation," depending on local situations. The Guangdong Provincial Office, being in the most reformist area, stressed economic development. The Provincial Party Deputy Secretary Zhang Guoying told the provincial religious leaders that "adaptation" should be interpreted as the mobilization of believers to develop the province's economy, including attracting foreign investments through the overseas contacts of religious believers.[18] This emphasis in economic development has been echoed by some other provincial leaders, such as those in Liaoning and Hunan,[19] and elaborated by a party-endorsed academician.[20]

Other provincial leaders, with more leftist views, interpreted "adaptation" with different connotations. Some saw "adaptation" as the strengthening of atheistic education and the curbing of illegal religious activities (activities without government sanction).[21] Others stressed the need to limit religious development, for example preventing the re-emergence of feudal religious privilege,[22] prohibiting the influence of religion in civil administration,[23] and increasing vigilance on possible foreign infiltration — a reflection of their paranoia over the "peaceful evolution" conspiracy.[24] Therefore, the interpretation of the policy on "adaptation" was determined by local party leaderships depending on their regional political situation. The religious groups themselves had very little to say. However, no government leaders have, so far, demanded that religious groups should change or reform their doctrines and institutions. Perhaps the government had too few qualified theologians among their ranks to suggest such reform, and the religious groups were silent in this area hoping to avoid any controversy.

(2) Major Meetings

The Religious Affairs Bureau had presented the draft of a "religious code" back in 1988.[25] But drafting such legislation seemed to be a very complicated project and had been suspended for several years. The Bureau then tried to draft regulations on particular religious matters and circulated these drafts to religious leaders during 1993, seeking their feedback. On 15 September 1993, the Committee on Religion of the Chinese People's Political Consultative Conference (CPPCC) agreed on the principle of enacting legislation on religion, and endorsed the proposal to issue individual legal regulations on religious affairs.[26] This meeting set the stage for the promulgation of national decrees on religious affairs.

A month later, the People's Political Consultative Conference News (*Renmin zhengxie bao*) ran a major article insisting on the necessity of guiding religion to adapt to socialist society,[27] thus setting the political tone for the official announcement of this policy by Jiang Zemin at the national UFWD conference held in November 1993. Jiang, at that conference, even pressed for the reformulation of those religious doctrines and practices which are not compatible with socialism.[28] With the political directives established, the administrative apparatus was set in motion to implement these new religious policies.

In mid-January 1994, the provincial and national directors of the Religious Affairs Bureau met in Beijing for five days to discuss the theme of adapting religion to socialist society, as advocated by Jiang Zemin.

During the same meeting, these directors discussed the legislative administration of religious affairs; they stressed that decrees on religious affairs were meant to set a clear parameter for religious activities, to distinguish those which were legally protected and those which would be criminalized.[29]

A few days later, the government summoned the national religious leaders (leaders from the various government-sanctioned "patriotic" religious organizations[30]) to Hainan island for a ten-day conference. At this conference, the national directors from RAB and UFWD expounded the government's new religious policy on adaptation to socialist society, and sought endorsement for the policy from religious leaders. Many of the religious leaders stated that their main concerns were not with adaptation, but mainly with the following areas: the lack of effective official action to protect their rights for example in the recovery of property, the lack of legislation to protect believers, the excessive control of RAB in religious matters, and the conflicts of economic interest between the RAB and religious groups, especially over tourist sites. However, the government's intention at this conference was not to hear complaints, but to impose its policy. Government cadres repeatedly stressed that the aim was to strengthen legal controls over religious affairs, and that the new policy was regarded as appropriate.[31]

On 29 January 1994, Li Ruihuan, member of the Standing Committee of the Political Bureau of the CCP, called the national religious leaders to Zhongnanhai for a New Year tea party. He lectured them on the historical inevitability of the adaptation of religion into socialist society, and defined the current political mandate of religion in Chinese socialist society, namely, to guide believers to support the party's policy on economic reform.[32]

Not all religious leaders echoed Li's aspirations. Bishop K. H. Ting of the Protestant Church, for example, expressed the frustrations felt by religious believers under the government's administrative supervision. He blamed the current religious situation — the uncontrolled growth of religion — on the leftist bias among many religious affairs cadres who often interfered in internal religious matters, provoking resentment among religious believers and driving many religious groups underground.[33]

Two days later Premier Li Peng signed a State Council Order to issue two religious decrees, the first religious law in China since 1949: Decree # 144 *Regulation Governing the Religious Activities of Foreign Nationals Within China*, and Decree # 145 *Regulation Governing Venues for Religious Activities*.[34] These two decrees became the official reference for provincial legislative bodies in drafting local regulations to administer religious affairs, and empowered cadres to exercise their authority in governing religious matters.

(3) National and Regional Religious Regulations

After three years of drafting, on 31 January 1994 the State Council finally issued the two decrees (# 144 and # 145) on religion.[35] The first concerned foreign nationals in China, and the second targeted the usage of religious venues. Decree # 144 set out clear parameters for religious activities in which foreign nationals could participate in China.[36] Foreigners (including overseas Chinese from Hong Kong and Taiwan) could arrange religious activities among themselves with prior approval from the civil authority. They could not participate in any non-sanctioned activity nor at any non-approved venue. If they participated in the religious activities of a Chinese religious organization, they needed to have prior approval by both the religious body and the Religious Affairs Bureau. All activities beyond this parameter were deemed illegal.[37]

The principles behind this decree seemed to be both a demarcation between foreigners and Chinese in religious activities, and the legitimization of religious activity by civil authority. It aimed to curb the increasing amount of interactions between Chinese believers and their overseas counterparts, especially those driven by zealous missionary motives often without government approval. It also empowered the RAB cadres to discipline any foreigner who steps over the religious boundary defined by this decree.[38]

Decree # 145 basically called for the proper registration of all venues for religious activities. This decree seemed to target the numerous unregistered Protestant family churches and those religious communities who autonomously built Catholic churches and Buddhist or Daoist local temples. These groups were usually not on good terms with the government-endorsed religious organizations, or lived in places where there were no branches of government-recognized religious organizations. Local cadres were caught in a dilemma when they tried to control these groups. On the one hand, the constitution grants freedom of religious belief to Chinese citizens, which the cadres have to respect; violation of this right may damage the image of the government. On the other hand, these groups are administratively illegal, for they do not belong to the government-

Bringing Religion into the Socialist Fold 17.9

approved organizations; and they may easily develop into underground political forces jeopardizing social security, for they have well-established organization structures.[39]

The unregistered groups existed in a legal limbo, often subject to the mercy of local cadres. Many were forced to remain clandestine. Consequently, the government found it difficult to keep track of them. With the new decree, these groups faced a hard choice: to exist illegally and subject to penalty, or to join the government-sanctioned religious organization subject to government control. Furthermore, the cadres could even refuse to register a group, forcing it to disband. The legal right to exist as a religious group now resided in the hands of government cadres.

In May 1994, the government inserted an amendment to the "PRC Public Security Administrative Penal Code" which would impose penalties on unregistered groups, groups that had been ordered to disband, and groups that failed to achieve registration. The amendment also penalized activities related to superstition and the outlawed Daoist sect *Yiguandao*.[40] With this amendment, violation of religious regulations now became a matter of social security within the purview of the public security apparatus.

Also in the same month, the national RAB office issued the *Regulation Governing the Registration of Religious Venues* and urged all religious groups, even those which had already received proper registration, to re-register.[41] It also demanded that local governments process such applications within a set time framework, a positive measure to prevent the procrastination of many local cadres in administrative matters. By the end of 1994, the RAB had devised a standardized application form for registration and for the licence of religious venues. It ordered all religious groups to begin this new registration process as the main working agenda in 1995.[42]

Through this exercise, the RAB hoped to gain a better control over religious activities by having properly registered groups under their auspices. However, many religious leaders saw it as another means for the RAB cadres to take money from religious groups, since the applicants would have to pay for the licencing fee. Some even feared that it might give official endorsement specifically to corrupt RAB cadres to extort money from believers through the registration process. Such corruption was commonly seen in 1993, and occasioned numerous complaints from religious believers leading to the issue of a RAB Document # 180 on 15 June 1993, banning such abusive practices by cadres.[43]

After the release of the Decrees # 144 and 145, provincial governments began to draft their regional religious regulations, often with a more restrictive tone than the national decrees: a tradition of current Chinese bureaucratic practice — rather left than right. To cite a few examples, on 22 March 1994, the Guangxi government issued the *Guangxi Autonomous Region Temporary Regulations on Administration of Religious Affairs*.[44] This regulation echoed the spirit of Decrees # 144 and 145, with additional items on the regulation of religious personnel: all religious personnel had to be validated by religious bodies, to be recorded by the RAB, and to operate within designated areas. On 10 April 1994, the Shaanxi government came up with *Regulations Governing the Usage of Religious Venues*.[45] Basically it followed the Decree # 144, with a few refinements such as the number of religious personnel allowed in each venue.

On 7 June 1994, the Ningxia government announced a rather restrictive *Ningxia Hui Autonomous Region Temporary Regulations on Administration of Religious Affairs*.[46] Perhaps due to the constant unrest of the Muslims in this region, often under the guise of religious activities, the Ningxia government declared that all religious personnel must be approved not only by religious bodies but by the civil authority, and that they must carry a proper license when they conduct religious activities. Failure to carry the licence would be illegal. The regulations also prohibited the installation of powerful loud speakers at the religious venue, and the disruption of regular social activity under the pretext of religion. These additions seemed to target particularly the mosques, which publicly call the faithful to pray at regular intervals during the day. Other provinces promulgated various similar regulations.

After the national policies on religion had been announced, they were transmitted down to various provincial RAB/UFWD offices through regional transmission meetings (*chuanda hui*). Parallel to these regional meetings, various religious organizations also held meetings at different levels to study the new policies. Sometimes, local RAB/UFWD and religious organizations would hold joint meetings to save time. It was at these meetings that the policies would be translated into concrete actions.

To give some examples, Heilongjiang held a meeting in March 1994 which prepared to issue the *Heilongjiang Regulations on the Administration of Religious Affairs*, in Summer 1994.[47] Hubei had its meeting in July, emphasizing the prevention of illegal religious activities.[48] Sichuan held a meeting in May, and promoted its own regulation on religious personnel which emphasized the licensing of all religious workers.[49] Guangxi had a meeting in April to promote its newly drafted regulation; the Guangxi government even sent teams of cadres to re-inforce these regulations in different parts of the province during the summer,[50] resulting in the arrest of several itinerant evangelists in Guilin.[51] Similar meetings were held in Ningxia in July,[52] and elsewhere. Through these meetings, the government, in general, hoped to assert its authority on religious affairs through legislative means. To what degree it achieves its objective remains to be seen.

(4) The Major Religious Communities in 1994

The implementation of the government's policy often depends upon many complex factors. In official statements, all religious groups express their gratitude to the party's brilliant policy on religion — a standard rhetorical device.[53] However, these groups may have their own pressing agendas in mind, and their objectives may be far removed from those of government policy.

(a) Protestants

The size of the Protestant community has been a controversial issue among scholars. The official number of believers could be anywhere from 8 to 10 million while the numbers suggested by overseas researchers ranged from 20 million to 100 million. At the end of 1994, a scholar published a rather meticulous head count of Chinese Protestants and argued that there were at least 18.7 million Protestants in China with a possible maximum of 29 million. His calculation was based both on published regional official figures and on private sources from unregistered groups.[54] Whether the correct figure is 10 or 30 million may be an academic argument of limited interest; but even the lowest estimate shows a phenomenal increase of Chinese Protestants, who in 1949 numbered less than 1 million, and in 1982 merely 3 million. On the one hand, the Chinese Protestant Church enjoyed a period of rapid growth, achieving some prominence both in Chinese society and among the international ecclesiastical community. On the other hand, this growth also brought along new sets of problems hitherto not experienced by the Christian community in China. One example was the acute shortage of competent leadership, which compromised the quality of management in local churches, and which often compounded by personality clashes among local leaders.

The national Protestant Three Self Patriotic Movement/Chinese Christian Council (TSPM/CCC) tried hard to address these problems at the national conference held between November and December 1993. This conference called for democratic leadership, transparency of church accounts, and appointments of younger leaders.[55] These appeals seemed to address the numerous complaints expressed by laity and young clergy who had suffered from the authoritarian leadership of some of the older church leaders. Embezzlement of church funds was not uncommon in these churches. Often, local churches asked the national TSPM/CCC to step in, and such requests tested the authority of its national leadership.

The appeals made by the national conference raised new tensions in some churches, since church members interpreted them as an endorsement from the national hierarchy to set up rival organizations to compete for power against the original leadership. As the conflicts mounted, they provided opportunities for the RAB and PSB to exploit the situation: these agencies could step in claiming to restore social order by elevating the nature of the issue from merely internal church conflicts into an issue of social security. A typical example was the arrest of Protestant ministers in the city of Shenyang in April 1994.[56]

Two young pastors of the officially sanctioned Dongguan Church in Shenyang exposed the embezzlement of church money by senior clergy. Taking the appeals voiced by the national conference as their guideline, several thousand church members met and elected a new governing body to check the church account books, contravening an explicit prohibition from the Municipal RAB Director. The RAB and PSB, siding with the senior clergy, raided the church with several hundreds officers, took away all the records of church accounts, and threw the two young pastors into detention. One was released on bail. The other, Rev. Gao Lianyi, has been in jail since April, waiting to be tried on charges of instigating social unrest.[57] With the backing of the RAB, the two senior clergy declared the new governing body illegal and re-affirmed their own leadership. When local church members appealed to the national TSPM/CCC, the latter tried to intervene, but two of their representatives were threatened and expelled by the Shenyang PBS.[58] This case highlighted some of the problems currently faced by the Chinese Protestant community, and illustrated the limitation of the national TSPM/CCC's authority in local affairs.

Another case concerned the forceful removal of the outspoken Rev. Yang Yutong of Gangwashi Church in Beijing, which highlighted the issue of rejuvenation of leadership. This Church has been known for its sheltering of dissidents and its bold messages which often challenged the authorities. Since September, police had constantly harassed its leaders.[59] The Beijing TSPM/CCC officially retired Rev. Yang, since he was over 70 years old, and appointed a young pastor, against the wishes of the congregation, to replace Yang.[60]

The new national CCC Acting General Secretary, Dr. Han Wenzao, who is himself over 70 years old, sided with the Beijing TSMP/CCC and urged Yang to step down. This gesture would both strengthen ties between the national and Beijing TSPM/CCC, and please the government. Although it sounded reasonable to ask Yang to retire and make room for a younger pastor, many septuagenarians and octogenarians still held important national and regional TSPM/CCC posts: for example the national leader Bishop K. H. Ting, and the two allegedly corrupt clergy in Shenyang. The affair revealed an interesting contrast. Although the national TSPM/CCC wished for a younger generation of leadership and had purposely appointed some young leaders at the national TSPM/CCC meeting held in November 1994,[61] other considerations — political loyalty, relationship with the older leaders, security of the older generation, etc. — were often more important than the issue of age. The issue of age could easily become a political means to remove dissenters.

Another major concern among the national Protestant leadership was the increase of contacts between overseas Christian communities with their counterparts in China. Such contacts benefited the Chinese churches, since they enabled the churches to receive overseas financial and material resources. Regional churches, especially those located in the southern and coastal regions, began to deal directly with overseas Christian organizations, bypassing the national TSPM/CCC which should, according to government regulations, serve as a clearing house for all foreign contacts with the Chinese Church. These independent contacts were encouraged by local government authorities for potential benefits to the local economy. Often, these contacts would tempt the local church leaders to openly solicit funds from overseas, an action that could compromise the Three-Self Principle (Self-Support, Self-Administration and Self-Propagation) upheld by the TSPM/CCC. At the same time, this trend — part of the growing increase in regional autonomy and decrease in central authority in China — took away the monopoly of foreign contacts from the national TSPM/CCC and weakened its authority over regional churches. It also undercut many benefits otherwise gained by the national TSPM/CCC.

Lamenting this situation, Bishop K. H. Ting, the head of the national

TSPM/CCC, made a strongly-worded speech at the national meeting in November 1994. He emphasized that no regional church should have foreign contact without endorsement from the national office for, Ting argued, the national office had much better knowledge about international Christian bodies than regional churches. In order not to fall prey to hostile foreign agencies operating under the cloak of religion, regional churches should consult and receive approval from the national office when dealing with foreigners. Further, no one should plead for help from overseas sources, since that would betray national dignity.[62]

Behind these noble ideas lay the fear of regional autonomy leading to a loss of authority by the national TSPM/CCC, as illustrated by the following example. The Hong Kong Christian Publisher's Association planned a four-day Christian book fair at the Guangdong Union Theological Seminary in mid-November 1994. This book fair, the first since 1949, was approved by the provincial TSPM/CCC and the provincial RAB without informing the national TSPM/CCC. After two days, the book fair was ordered to close down immediately on the authority of the central government after a recommendation from the national TSPM/CCC. All the books, originally designated as a gift to the seminary, were confiscated. Apparently, the national TSPM/CCC sent a strong signal to the Guangdong TSPM/CCC, showing its displeasure at Guangdong's independent dealing with overseas Christians.[63]

As for the promotion of the new religious decrees and policies, the executives of the national TSPM/CCC held a meeting in March 1994 to discuss these matters. The "adaptation" theme was rather abstract so it attracted little discussion. What concerned the Protestants most was the regulation on registration of religious venues. The non-TSPM/CCC house churches would worry that registration was a government tactic to force them into the fold of the TSPM/CCC. The national TSPM/CCC immediately pointed out that the registration would be with the government, rather than with the TSPM/CCC, and would enhance the legal protection of the believers. It hoped to encourage the non-TSPM/CCC Christians to register,[64] and later, Bishop K. H. Ting gave a lengthy interview promoting this registration.[65] The official TSPM/CCC echoed this theme by running stories on their positive experience with the new regulations.[66] At the same time, many house churches in Shanghai received the Decree # 145 from the RAB, and pressure mounted to force them to register.[67]

The continuous abuse of the rights of believers and the arrest of Christians repeatedly hit the media headlines throughout the year. In

Hunan, Dongkou County, a Christian was beaten to death by the authorities in January.[68] There were numerous reports of arrests of Christians who propagated their faith without government approval in Fujian, Guangdong, Guangxi, Henan, Anhui, Shanghai, Beijing and Hunan. There were also expulsions of overseas Christians, such as the American charismatic minister Rev. Dennis Balcombe in February. Some were linked with the dissident movement,[69] or operated among the Christian groups not sanctioned by the government,[70] while others were caught up in internal politics such as the arrest of Rev. Gao Lianyi of Shenyang. All of these were local incidents; there was no evidence to suggest any national effort at co-ordinating these events. The incidents reflected the most significant factor determining the fate of Christians in China: not the regulations, nor the TSPM/CCC, but the attitudes of local cadres towards Christianity, as they were the people who interpreted the regulations and implemented the policies.

(b) Roman Catholics

Since the 1950s, the Catholics in China have been divided into the pro-Rome and the pro-government (patriotic) factions. Each has its own hierarchy, clergy, and seminaries. The former is illegal and underground, the latter is less popular yet open. In the universal Catholic communion, some support the underground faction, regarding it as the true Church, and consider the patriotic faction to be schismatic or in a state of apostasy, since it has consecrated bishops without sanction from Rome. Others urge Rome to recognize the patriotic faction as a gesture towards reconciliation with the Chinese Church, and as a positive step towards re-establishing formal relationship with China, broken off since the early 1950s.[71] The attitude of Rome has been ambiguous on this issue, and Sino-Vatican relationship have been at a standstill.

In general, the Catholic Church in China has enjoyed a steady growth, and now numbers from 6 to 10 million followers, depending on whether one accepts figures from the official source or estimates including reports from the underground factions. The Church benefits from the current social trend of "religious fever" as people with no prior religious background, flock to the church seeking some meaning in life (such as the case of the Catholic Church in Urumqi, Xinjiang).[72] Some Dioceses, like the one in Inner Mongolia, actively draw converts through their members's relations with friends.[73] A new seminary has also been opened, the 24th

Catholic seminary in China.[74] Beneath the surface of this seemingly encouraging news, there are strong undercurrents challenging the course of the Chinese Catholic Church.

The two factions of Chinese Catholics were often at odds with each other, for both asserted their orthodoxy among the faithful. At the national level, the underground hierarchy — Chinese Bishops' Conference in the Mainland (CBCM) — in 1993 issued a 12-point statement to the Vatican and a year later an open pastoral letter to all the Chinese Catholics, claiming its legitimacy and urging the Universal Church to recognize it as the only Catholic representative in China.[75] The position of the CBCM was hard-line, leaving no room for independently consecrated bishops unless they repented. The CBCM also applied to join the Federation of Asian Bishops's Conference (FABC).[76] Meanwhile, the officially sanctioned Chinese hierarchy sent delegations representing the Chinese Catholic Church to attend the Manila International Catholic Youth Conference, presided over by the Pope in January 1995.[77] Both groups tried to win support for their own claims of orthodoxy as the legitimate Chinese Catholic Church.

At the local level, they might help each other out, as was the case in Fujian where the government-sanctioned Fuzhou Church helped the underground faction to build a church in the township of Heshang; but these examples were rare.[78] In most cases, the factional differences caused great disharmony, as in Wenzhou,[79] and severely weakened the Church, in some cases even resulting in physical violence.[80] Reconciliation was not yet in sight.

As well as the problem of factionalism, there were several other pressing issues facing the Chinese Catholics: lack of clergy, regional harassment by cadres, registration of venues, and the Sino-Vatican diplomatic impasse. Among the several million Chinese Catholics, there are perhaps slightly more than 1,000 priests in the officially sanctioned church (nearly half of whom are in their 70s and 80s), and about the same number in the underground faction. Unlike Protestantism where an untrained laity can conduct services of worship, Catholic religious activities centre on a priest who should have undergone several years of training. With the economic boom, especially in the coastal provinces, fewer young Catholics find the religious vocation attractive.[81] The lack of priests to provide basic sacramental and pastoral services had been especially pressing in some areas such as Hainan province.[82] Although refresher courses and short-term overseas training[83] were provided to upgrade the quality of the

Chinese priests, the sheer number of Chinese Catholics, compounded with the uneven distribution of those with a religious vocation, greatly overburdened the few young priests currently serving in the Chinese Church.

The Catholics, like the Protestants, faced pressure from the government for the registration of the venues when the Decree # 145 was issued. This regulation targeted the underground Catholics, and several bishops from this faction were summoned by the government to discuss the matter. They were told by the government to register their groups by spring 1995 at the latest, otherwise they would be illegal and the government would disperse them. After the amendment of the Social Security Act in May, some regional authorities raided unregistered Catholic activities in Shanghai, Henan, and Jiangsu. These signals worried many underground bishops. Some began to relocate their underground convents and seminaries while others discussed the possibility of registration, provided that they would not need endorsement from the officially sanctioned Catholics.[84] The impact from this issue of registration is yet to be seen, but it has already generated differences in opinion among the underground Catholics.

During 1994, there had been constant reports concerning arrests of priests, bishops, and laity of the underground faction and raids on religious activities. Particularly hard hit were underground Catholic activities in Xinjiang, Qinghai and Gansu.[85] These areas with large Muslim population, experienced some social unrest, sometimes fanned by religious rivalries. The local governments seemed to be tough on any form of unsanctioned religious activities. Other reports of official harassment usually reflected a local cadres's attitude on national religious policy; sometimes these local policies even ran contrary to the central policy. For example, the burning of chapels in Wuxian, Jiangsu, was in fact a personal vengeance by local RAB cadres against Catholics.[86] On the Feast of the Assumption of Mary, the local PBS in Yujiang, Jiangxi, arrested 3,000 pro-Rome Catholics and beat up many of those who went for the annual pilgrimage. This incident revealed the "leftist" orientation of local cadres, as officially they should adopt moderate and persuasive measures only.[87] The walkout of seminarians from the Sichuan Catholic Seminary in April 1994 was a protest against the appointment of a RAB official, a party member, as the deputy director of the seminary.[88] This appointment ran contrary to the spirit of national policy: cadres should not interfere with the internal administration of religious affairs. The abuse of power by local cadres has been a common occurence, and the Catholics were not immune.

The Chinese Catholic Church broke new diplomatic ground in 1994 when the Jilin Diocese established relations with the Suwon Diocese of South Korea.[89] This relationship implied the official recognition of the government-sanctioned Jilin Diocese by a foreign Catholic hierarchy. Further, Cardinal Wu of Hong Kong paid an official visit to the Chinese Church in November 1994, at the invitation of the RAB. This trip signified a positive development in the Sino-Vatican relationship. The Vatican also delivered many messages expressing its desire to normalize relationships with China. The final obstacle would be the diplomatic ties between Taiwan and the Vatican, which China insisted the Vatican sever as the condition for discussions. As the Pope met with the Catholic delegation from the government-sanctioned Chinese Church in Manila, the Sino-Vatican relationship became closer than ever.

(c) Daoist, Buddhist, and Muslim Communities

The Daoists drew little attention in the media for they did not have an organized structure like the Christian churches, and hence posed little threat to the government, nor were they affiliated with any foreign institution that might cause official unease. The most common religious issues concerned jurisdiction over historical sites where famous temples were built, which were usually popular tourist sites with a lucrative income. Often a temple would not be returned to Daoist groups because of the income generated from tourism; the RAB would then intervene. Usually the profits were divided among the RAB, the temple, and perhaps the local tourism office.[90] Except for their struggles to control these sites, the national Daoist leaders were usually docile, giving unqualified endorsement to the government's new policies and decrees on religion.

The only new issue raised by the Daoists was the regulation and licencing of the *Zhengyi* sect of Daoist priests, taken up at the national Daoist Association in October 1994.[91] Contrary to the *Quanzhen* sect, whose 7,000 members were well-trained celibates living in temples, this sect of around 40,000 priests were married laymen living at home, who usually inherited the role from the family, father to son, and earned their income from performing liturgies for the people. They were in great demand in rural areas, where peasants invite these priests to conduct services for funerals, weddings, and other important occasions. It could often be a profitable profession, and has also attracted charlatans posing as Daoist priests. Also, the government had banned all "feudal superstitious activities," which are often hard to distinguish from Daoist religious activities. Further, a secret Daoist sect, *Yiguandao*, had been regarded by the government as a counter-revolutionary clique, and local cadres might confuse it with ordinary Daoist activities. Therefore the Daoist Association saw the need to regulate and licence their own priests in order to protect themselves. In fact, as early as 1991, the Anhui Provincial Daoist Association had issued temporary regulations on Daoist temples and the *Zhengyi* priests.[92] Recent decisions by the national Daoist Association merely formulated the practices of its provincial chapters.

As the government tried to guide Buddhists into the socialist fold, the trend was on the one hand to commercialize the Han Buddhists, and on the other hand to pacify the Tibetan Buddhists. Buddhist temples, like their Daoist counterparts, were often important tourist sites. As the government urged adaptation of religion to socialist society, one major trend was promoting commercial enterprises. Many local government units urged Buddhist monks into service industries such as opening vegetarian restaurants and hostels, and organizing admission charges.[93] Some minted Buddhist gold coins,[94] others built statues of Buddha to attract tourists.[95] Whether or not this commercialization was in line with Buddhist teaching was not the government's concern, but had already caused some objections in Buddhist circles.[96]

Tibetan Buddhists have long been a major problem for the government as the Tibetan Independence Movement has often been based in Lama Temples and closely related with the exiled spiritual leader the Dalai Lama. Major riots had also broken out in the past and been crushed by force. In 1994, the government adopted a stick and carrot policy: it strengthened security control over the dissidents, and increased support for the sanctioned religious activities. In February, the Tibetan authorities doubled or tripled the jail sentences of dissident Tibetan nuns for their defiant activities in Drapchi prison. One had her jail term increased from 5 to 14 years; another, from 9 to 17 years.[97] At the same time, the government poured in large amounts of funding to restore the Potala Place — one of the most sacred temples of Tibetan Buddhism,[98] renovated the prayer hall of Phagsba,[99] built a senior Tibetan Buddhist College,[100] and initiated the editing of the monumental Tibetan Complete Collection of Buddhist Scriptures.[101] The government also put on a big show to affirm the spiritual authority of the 17th Living Buddha Garmaba, the 10-year-old Karmapa Chilaidoje, by inviting him to attend the National Day Celebration in Beijing.[102] This Living Buddha would be the spiritual leader of the Karma

Kagyu Branch of Tibetan Buddhism and had stirred up controversy concerning his authenticity because a rival faction in Sikkim had claimed to have identified the real Living Buddha.[103] The Chinese authorities vehemently refuted the rival's finding, and affirmed that their preferred Living Buddha had already taken up the holy throne at the Curbo monastery with the approval of the RAB.[104] Apparently, the RAB claimed to have the ultimate authority to authenticate the religious status of the Living Buddha, a clear example of civil control over religious affairs in Tibet.

Since the outbreak of anti-government riots in Autumn 1993 in northwestern China, heavily populated by Muslims, the government had stepped up security measures. There was little news of unrest, but tensions were mounting.[105] Heavy sentences were imposed on Islamic agitators in Qinghai.[106] Recent regional religious regulations, such as the one issued by Ningxia provincial government in June 1994,[107] also reflected a heavy handed policy targeted at the Muslims. The national Islamic Association had little activity other than the echoing of the government's intent.[108]

Conclusion

In 1994, the government tried to define the role of religion in socialist society as a tool to enhance economic prosperity under strict official control. In fact, the most important contribution religion could offer to society today may be its moral values, but this area is totally excluded from consideration by Chinese leaders. Although local cadres might recognize such values, and many openly praised religious believers for their exemplary behaviour, officially Communist morality as symbolized by the spirit of Lei Feng is superior to religious morality. With the rapid change in social values, accelerated by the "get rich" trend and consumerism, China needs to search for a moral basis to sustain such development, and the potential contribution from religion should not be overlooked.

The Chinese leaders still cling to the outdated Marxist interpretation of religion as a distorted world view obstructing social progress. This interpretation influenced policy-makers to curb the natural growth of religion by administrative measures. In fact, what hindered social development might possibly be this archaic social view itself. By emphasizing administrative measures, religion would either lose its vitality and become domesticated by socialism, or go underground and be easily marginalized into religious fanaticism. Both conditions would lead to a self-fulfilling prophecy for the Marxist theory on religion, and be a great loss to society.

From a political perspective, the tightening of religious administration in 1994 could be viewed as part of an overall strategy of strengthening authoritarian rule in order to stabilize society for the post-Deng transition of power. Social unrest would not be tolerated during this critical phase especially among religious groups living in Tibet and northwest China.

By emphasizing administrative measures, despite the noble ideal of improving legal safeguards in China, the authorities actually created more opportunities for cadres to abuse their power. In any event, the main problem did not seem to be a lack of laws. On the contrary, so many regulations were issued that even government cadres themselves had difficulty keeping abreast. More important was the moral and educational quality of basic-level cadres who often ruled like local dictators. The regulations on religious affairs were thus a two-edged sword: protecting believers on the one hand while, on the other, giving cadres more power to oppress believers.

Meanwhile, religion keeps on growing in spite of increasing government restrictions. As regional authorities gain more autonomy, the local climate for religious development varies subject more to local cadres' attitudes than to central government directives. Hence the more China heads towards a more pluralistic social setting, the more variations in religious progression, or regression, can also be anticipated. Religion will therefore develop its unique role in the Chinese society, quite different from the policy of "adaptation" dictated by the CCP leadership.

Notes

1. In 1982, the CCP issued a 30 page Institutional Secret Document entitled: *Basic Policy and Stand Point Our Country Should Have on Religious Questions During This Period of Socialism.* For an English translation, see *Issues and Studies* (August 1983), pp. 72–90.
2. For example, a 1994 survey by the Mishan City (Heilongjiang) Religious Study Group discovered that the Protestant community had enjoyed a 45% growth since 1992. See "The Religious Situation in Mishan City and the Means to Response," *Heilongjiang tongzhan* (Heilongjiang United Front) (August 1994), pp. 23–24. See also Changchun Academy of Social Science Project Team, "Analysis of Religious Fever," *Shehui kexue tansuo* (Social Science Studies), Changchun, No. 2 (April 1992), pp. 39–43.

3. See Jonathan Chao, "The Course and the Prospect of the Christian Fever in China," *Ming Pao Monthly* (December 1994), pp. 44–49; Alan Hunter and Chan Kim-kwong, *Protestantism in Contemporary China* (Cambridge: Cambridge University Press, 1993).
4. Although the phase "Peaceful evolution" disappeared from government documents on religion in 1994, this fear of foreign infiltration is very strong especially among middle and lower ranking religious cadres. Personal communication with many religious cadres in Southern China, June/July 1994.
5. A recent survey in Beijing suggested this trend, see "Beijing Zero Point Survey and Prediction," *Zhongguo qingnian yanjiu* (China Youth Study), No. 33/34 (October 1994), p. 63.
6. This phrase appeared in the original draft and was deleted by the personal order of the reform-minded late party secretary Hu Yaobang. Personal communication from the drafting members at the Chinese Academy of Social Sciences, July 1988.
7. For example, see Wang Haicao, "The Basis for the Implementation of the Policy of Freedom of Religious Belief," *Heilongjiang tongzhan* (September 1994), pp. 28–29.
8. China News Agency, Hong Kong, 5 October 1994.
9. See *Renmin ribao* (People's Daily), 22 January 1994; 7 May 1994; and 20 June 1994.
10. For example, the daughter of Deng Xiaoping, Deng Nan, openly advocated the promotion of scientific knowledge as a means to combat religous influence in Tibet, and suggested that religion is an obstacle to scientific development, see *Keji ribao* (Science and Technology Daily), 2 September 1994.
11. For some typical examples, see Lang Gufeng and Qi Yulin, "Thoughts on the Current Religious Situation in Rural Areas," *Liaoning tongzhan yuekan* (Liaoning United Front Monthly) (April 1994), pp. 22–23; and Chen Suning, "Controversy on the Causes and Characteristics of Religion in Rural Areas in China during the New Era," *Qiusuo* (Seeker), Changsha, No. 3 (June 1994), pp. 46–49.
12. Xiao Ziku, "A Discussion on the Adjustment of Religion in Our Socialist Society," *Shanghai shehui kexue xueyuan xueshu jikan* (Quarterly Journal of the Shanghai Academy of Social Science), No. 1 (March 1981), pp. 137–46.
13. "CCP Central Committee Notification Concerning Strengthening United Front Work," 14 July 1990, reprinted in *Mainland China Studies*, Vol. 36, No. 5 (May 1991), pp. 104–11.
14. For example, Min Gong and Chen Yunglian, "The Problems on the Adaptation of Religion in Socialism," *Xinyang shifan xueyuan xuebao* (Xinyang Teacher's College Journal) (September 1991), pp. 18–25, used this new term with a harsher tone on religion than their previous article published on a

similar topic just one year ago in the same journal; see the same authors, "The Key to Normalized Religious Activities in Rural Areas Is Guidance," *Xinyang shifan xueyuan xuebao* (March 1990), pp. 29–35. Obviously these authors followed closely the changes of the party's attitude on religion.

15. For example, see He Bingji, "Re-examination of the Questions of Adaptation of Religion in Socialism," *Xinjiang shehui jingji* (Xinjiang Society and Economy), No. 1 (January 1992), pp. 30–33; Huang Tao, "Questions of Adaptation of Religion in Socialist Society," *Tongyi zhanxian* (United Front), Wuhan, No. 4 (August 1992), p. 8; and Li Ziren, "On the Relationship Between Socialism and Religion," *Guizhou shehui kexue* (Social Science in Guizhou), No. 5 (October 1993), pp. 58–62.
16. *Renmin ribao*, 8 November 1993.
17. *China News and Church Report*, 7 October 1994.
18. His speech is recorded in the *Guangdong TSPM/CCC Newsletter*, No. 3 (June 1994), pp. 6–7. Internal restricted publication.
19. Li Manchun, "How Can Religion Serve the Economy of Socialism," *Tongzhan yuekan* (United Front Monthly), Liaoning (September 1994), pp. 10–11; He Shuhan, "How Can Religious Work Adapt to the Socialist Market Economy?" *Hunan tongyi zhanxian* (Hunan United Front) (May 1994), pp. 11–12.
20. Lin Xiaoren, "The Search for Direction for Religion in China and the Market Economy," *Studies in World Religion*, No. 2 (June 1994), pp. 100–108.
21. Daqi United Front Office, "Knowledge and Practice of Guiding Religion to Adapt into Socialist Society," *Neimenggu tongzhan lilun yanjiu* (Inner Mongolia Studies on Theory of United Front), No. 2 (April 1994), pp. 25–26.
22. Kan Guangxian "Correctly Implement the Party's Religious Policy," *Heilongjiang tongzhan* (August 1994), pp. 25–26. Kan is the director of Chahar United Front Work Department.
23. See *Ningxia ribao* (Ningxia Daily), 4 July 1994.
24. See Liu Lingui, "Emphasizing the Problem of Religion and Nationality," *Heilongjiang tongzhan* (July 1994), pp. 9–11. Lin stressed that international foreign hostile forces are using religion to sabotage the Chinese socialist regime, and that the government should root out these foreign infiltrations among the religious groups.
25. The Drafting Committee on Religious Ordinances of the Religious Affairs Bureau, "Some Questions Concerning the Drafting of the Religious Ordinances," April 1988, mimeographed, 4 pages.
26. *Renmin zhengxie bao* (People's Political Consultative Conference News) 23 September 1993.
27. Wu An, "Guiding Religion to Adapt into Socialist Society," *Renmin Zhengxie bao*, 28 October 1993.
28. *Renmin ribao*, 8 November 1993.

29. *Renmin ribao*, 17 January 1994.
30. During the 1950s, the government helped to build five national patriotic religious organizations: Catholic, Protestant, Buddhist, Daoist, and Muslim. They are the only religious organizations officially recognized by the Chinese government. Believers have to register with their respective organizations; otherwise they are considered as illegal. These organizations ceased to exist during the Cultural Revolution and resumed their existence after 1980.
31. The national UFWD journal faithfully published the complaints raised by the religious leaders in its report, followed by the official declarations of the government, see *Zhongguo tongyi zhanxian* (China United Front Monthly), No. 3 (March 1994), pp. 17–18.
32. *Renmin ribao*, 30 January 1994.
33. See *Qiao* (Bridge), No. 64 (April), pp. 3–5.
34. *Renmin ribao*, 8 February 1994.
35. One of the Catholic leaders in China told a Hong Kong religious weekly that the government began the drafting of these two decrees three years ago and had received concensus from religious leaders in September 1993, see *Kong Kao Pao* (Hong Kong Catholic Weekly), 18 March 1994.
36. *Amity News Service* has issued an English translation of these two decrees.
37. The RAB published three featured articles officially commenting on the details of this decree, see *Fazhi ribao* (Legal Daily), 29 June 1994; 6 July 1994 and 13 July 1994.
38. Several foreign Christians went to Henan in February to conduct religious activities and were expelled by the local authorities, who cited this decree, see *South China Morning Post* (Hong Kong, *SCMP*), 17 February 1994.
39. For example, a traveler in Wuhan this year saw a local document about Christian peasants banding together to oppose corrupt local officials who arbitrarily imposed heavy taxes on them. *China News and Church Report*, 7 October 1994.
40. PRC Chairman Order # 24 on the Approval of the Amendment on the PRC Public Security Administrative Penal Code, 12 May 1994. See *Release of Executive Committee of PRC NPC*, No. 239 (June 1994), pp. 35–47.
41. See *Tianfeng* (Heavenly Wind) (June 1994), p. 5.
42. Personal communication with religious leaders in China, December 1994.
43. See Chan Kim-kwong, "Religion in China 1993," in *China Review 1994*, edited by Maurice Brosseau and Lo Chi Kin (Hong Kong: Chinese University Press, 1994), p. **19**.16.
44. See *Guangxi zhengbao* (Guangxi Government Administrative Journal) (May 1994), pp. 2–5.
45. *Shaanxi zhengbao* (Shaanxi Government Administrative Journal) (June 1994), pp. 14–15.

46. *Ningxia ribao*, 4 July 1994.
47. Yang Mupeng, "Religious Work Is Important in UFWD," *Heilongjiang tongzhan lilun yanjiu* (Studies on Heilongjiang United Front Theory) (August 1994), pp. 20–21.
48. "Further Improving Work on Nationality and Religion in the New Situation," *Minzu dajiating* (Big Family of Nationality) (August 1994), pp. 10–12.
49. *Fazhi ribao*, 18 May 1994.
50. *Fazhi ribao*, 19 October 1994.
51. *News Network Internation-News Service*, 17 August 1994.
52. *Ningxia ribao*, 9 July 1994.
53. For a typical example, see the speeches by various national religious leaders on the new religious decrees, *Fazhi ribao*, 13 March 1994; and the official publications of these religious organizations, such as Commentator, "The Happy Step," *China Muslim*, No. 3 (June 1994), pp. 3–4.
54. News Network International commissioned Tony Lambert to undertake this study, see *China News and Church Report*, 21 October 1994.
55. See *Tienfeng* (January 1994), p. 3.
56. See Bai Mingguan, "Scandals in the Shenyang Church: Government Arrested Pastors and Suppressed Believers," *Contemporary Monthly* (Hong Kong) (October 1994), pp. 4–6.
57. As this case caught the attention of the international media, see *SCMP*, 7 September 1994, or *Overseas Chinese Daily News* (Hong Kong), 3 October 1994, the Chinese government came up with a very different version of the story and charged Rev. Gao Lingyi with the Criminal Code # 159 (obstruction of official business), see *China News Agency* (Shenyang), 5 October 1994.
58. For the complete story, see *Qiao*, No. 67 (October 1994), pp. 2–9. Rev. Gao was released without charge on 27 January 1995; see *SCMP*, 22 February 1995.
59. *SCMP*, 25 November 1994.
60. Throughout November and December, there were many reports on this issue, see *SCMP*, 25 November 1994.
61. See *Amity News Service* (December 1994), p. 6.1.
62. *Amity News Service* (December 1994), p. 6.10.
63. See editorial comment in *Qiao*, No. 68 (December 1994), p. 2.
64. *Tianfeng* (May 1994), pp. 10–11.
65. *Tianfeng* (June 1994).
66. *Amity News Service* (October 1994), p. 5.2.
67. *News Network International*, 18 October 1994.
68. The wife of the deceased tried to sue the local PSB and was harassed by the local authorities. This author obtained a copy of the appeal letter written by her.

69. *SCMP*, 3 June 1994.
70. The case of Rev. Dennis Balcombe, see *China Talk* (August 1994), pp. 5–6.
71. For the background of Sino-Vatican tension, see Chan Kim-kwong, *Struggling for Survival: The Catholic Church in China from 1949–1970* (Hong Kong: Christian Study Center on Chinese Religion and Culture, 1992).
72. See the case of the Catholic Church in Urumqi in Xinjiang, in *Xinjiang gongren bao* (Xinjiang Worker Daily), 22 March 1994.
73. *Asian Focus*, 4 December 1994.
74. The Tianjian major seminary was opened in September 1994, *Asian Focus*, 30 September 1994.
75. *Asian Focus*, 14 January 1994; *Kung Kao Pao*, 17 February 1995.
76. *Asian Focus*, 17 June 1994.
77. *Ming Pao*, 12 January 1995.
78. *Asian Focus*, 29 January 1994.
79. *Kung Kao Pao*, 22 July 1994.
80. Bishop Jin Luxian, "A Small Boat on the Ocean," *Qiao*, No. 68 (December 1994), pp. 11–14.
81. *Kung Kao Pao*, 20 May 1994.
82. The only active priest, 82 years old Fr. Huang Zhongwen, died in a car accident in May 1994. The 3,000 Catholics in this province had since been without a priest. *Kung Kao Pao*, 15 July 1994.
83. In 1994, two teams of Chinese priests went to Hong Kong and Belgium for short term theological trainings.
84. *Kung Kao Pao*, 11 November 1994.
85. *Kung Kao Pao*, 9 December 1994.
86. *Kung Kao Pao*, 9 September 1994.
87. *Kong Kao Pao*, 4 November 1994.
88. *Kung Kao Pao*, 14 October 1994.
89. *Asian Focus*, 19 August 1994.
90. For example, see the story on the Baiyun Taoist Temple in Beijing, *China Daily*, 1 October 1994.
91. *Renmin zhengxie bao*, 13 October 1994.
92. *Regulations on Control Over the Zhengyi Priests in Anhui Province*, 18 December 1991, by Anhui Daoist Association, in Anhui PBS, *Anhui Religious Chronicles* (Hefei: Anhui RAB, 1992), pp. 122–23. Internal material.
93. *Sing Tao Daily* (Hong Kong), 12 September 1994.
94. *China Daily*, 12 July 1994.
95. *China Daily*, 29 October 1994.
96. *Ming Pao*, 14 January 1994.
97. *SCMP*, 22 February 1994.

98. Gyayang and Wang Mingxing, "Potala Palace Retains Munificence," *Beijing Review* (8–14 August 1994), pp. 7–10.
99. New China News Agency, 27 January 1994.
100. *Zhongguo xinwen she* (Beijing), 23 November 1994.
101. *Renmin ribao*, 21 July 1994.
102. *China Daily*, 27 September 1994.
103. See Lea Terhune, "Divided House," in *Far Eastern Economic Review* (24 March 1994), pp. 36–38.
104. The *Zhongguo Xizang* (China's Tibet) had a long feature article on this Living Buddha in No. 6 (December 1994), pp. 5–14.
105. *Qinghai ribao*, 21 February 1994.
106. There had been some Islamic factional clashes resulting into many deaths. The government stepped in and imposed heavy sentences on some of these factional leaders, *SCMP*, 21 February 1994.
107. *Ningxia ribao*, 7 June 1994.
108. For example, see editorial comment on the National Islamic Association Conference, *China Muslim*, No. 2 (April 1994), pp. 2–3.

18

Regaining the Initiative for Education Reform and Development

Suzanne Pepper

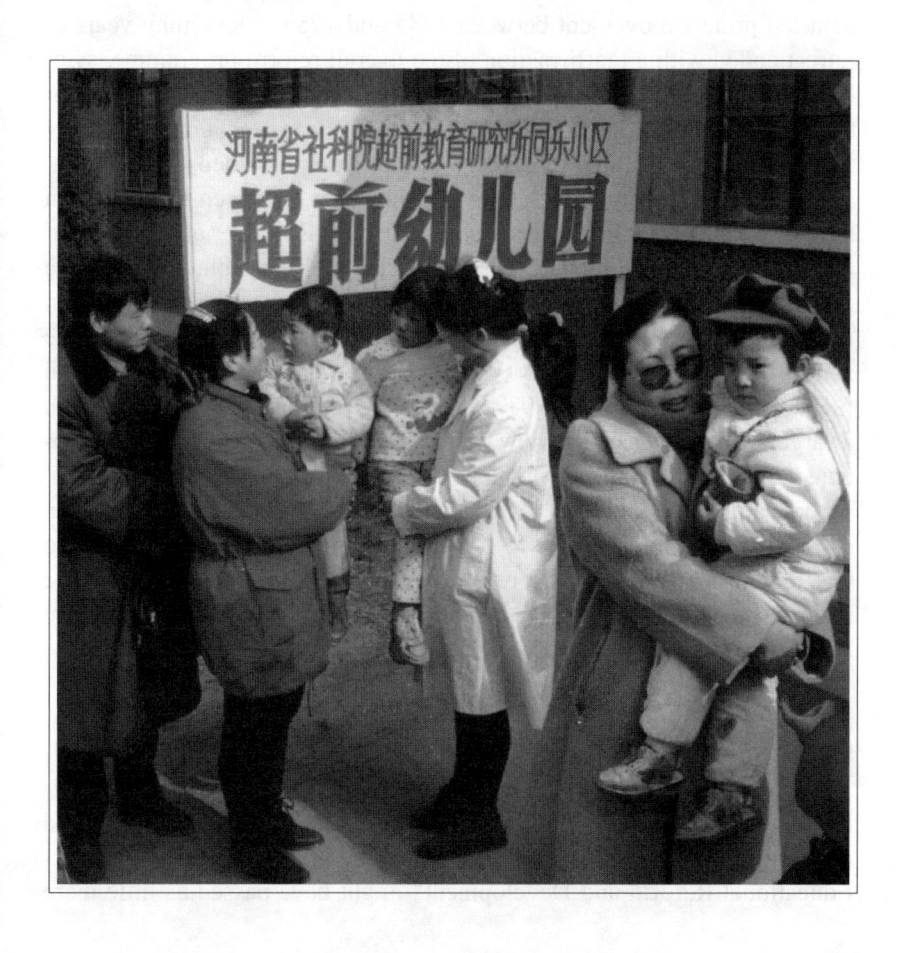

On the surface, 1994 was a year of much activity and progress for China's educational development. Basic reform principles enunciated in the late 1970s were reaffirmed, while adjustments and correctives continued at a brisk pace. The chief reformulations of this course were the "Outline for China's Educational Reform and Development" and the Teachers' Law. Both had been announced the year before and were intended to serve as authoritative guidelines through the end of the century.

Together the two documents also epitomize the reform and adjustment sequence of the post-Cultural Revolution era. More immediately, they signify Beijing's response to the multiple dislocations that had emerged within the education sector after a decade of reform. The seemingly insoluble problems being registered in the mid-1980s had contributed to the general collapse of public confidence which in turn precipitated the student-led protest movement between 1985 and 1989. Intervening years of retreat ended with a reaffirmation of the overall reform programme, symbolized by Deng Xiaoping's "southern tour" in 1992. The "Outline for China's Educational Reform and Development" was proclaimed explicitly as an extenuation of the reform revival Deng's tour heralded.

Another key feature of that revival, however, has been its promotion by the post-1989 political leadership. Accordingly, we are deprived of insights such as those allowed even in official published sources during the 1987–1989 years, when contradictions produced by a decade of reform were maturing along with a relatively open political climate. Despite some zones of candour especially concerning educational economics and finance, the net result since 1989, has been to present for the public record a largely one-dimensional view of education events with little differentiated reflections from the public concerned whether students, teachers, school administrators, or local authorities. Hence the interpretation adopted here which attempts to add some further dimension by assessing that record of the 1993–1994 reform revival from past perspectives. The perspectives are those of the late 1980s, when the consequences of reform for China's educational development were being most clearly articulated.

Reaffirming Reform: The 1993 "Outline"

But for the publicity surrounding its proclamation in February 1993, and continuous references to its authority since, the "Outline for China's Educational Reform and Development" might have passed as little more than a formal reassurance after the period of post-1989 uncertainty. Reform would continue to be promoted in all its manifestations as before; overseas studies and international exchanges would be maintained; intellectuals would be respected at least in their professional capacities — even if not as a source of dissenting political ideas or challenge to Communist Party rule. Motives were clearly drawn: Beijing sought to regain the initiative for reform but not at any political price. Communist Party leadership over education would be "firmly upheld" along with the commitment to train "disciplined socialist individuals."

In terms of basic orientation and content, however, education reform would remain consistent with the earlier benchmark "Decision on the Structural Reform of Education," issued in 1985. Accordingly, development would continue to be based upon: the nine-year compulsory education system; vocationalization at the secondary level; local responsibility for elementary school funding and administration; financial contributions and management by private individuals and public organizations as well as the state; and a promise that whether central or local, all government appropriations for education must increase at a rate faster than the increase in regular state revenues. Centralized government control over the tertiary level would devolve into greater autonomy for individual institutions of higher learning and an end to the unified state-controlled student enrolment and job assignment plans, as well as to state-funded room, board, and tuition for all students.[1]

On closer inspection, however, and in light of subsequent initiatives proclaimed in its name, the 1993 "Outline" not only "expanded and deepened" reform but anticipated the breaking of some new ground as well. In the former category of expanding upon established principle and practice, three points stood out for the emphasis they received: privatization, finance, and tertiary-level reform. The "Outline" thus indicated a renewed effort to encourage "people in all walks of life" to run schools and invited "international cooperation" toward that same end (Article 16). Funding stood out as a major priority with itemized endorsement for all sources tapped to date, including the now standard dedication to increased government appropriations; improved collection of local education surcharges on product, value-added, and business taxes; increases in student tuition and fees; encouragement for profit-making school-run enterprises and services; voluntary donations and charities; and the creation of educational foundations, loans, and insurance funds. Targets were fixed in terms of specific proportions of government budgets to be allocated for education. Pay rises for teachers were mandated with the aim of bringing their salaries up to those of comparable personnel in state enterprises (Articles 42, 47, 48, 49, 50).

At the tertiary level, the venerable enrolment, job assignment, and tuition reforms for students would remain "gradual." But institutions of higher learning were otherwise enjoined to keep pace with the renewed momentum of economic reform by developing more rapidly and rationally. At the same time, 100 leading universities would be further strengthened in an open revival of the much-debated key-point educational concept left discreetly unpublicized in recent years. The new programme aimed to safeguard quality and allow China to achieve advanced world standards (Articles 5, 9, 18, 19).

The line between deepening reform and breaking new ground seemed to be drawn at two interrelated points. Both had remained pillars of structural reform at the secondary level, despite their unpopularity. One concerns a partial lifting of the quantitative constraints imposed in the late 1970s on senior secondary schooling, after a decade of Cultural Revolution mass-oriented growth. Hence the new mandate to "vigorously universalize senior secondary schooling in major cities and economically-developed areas along the coast" (Article 5).

The other point of change was an apparent softening of the unrelenting demand for vocationalization. The 1985 "Decision" had made vocational and technical education the centrepiece of secondary school reform. It reiterated the two-track goal — excoriated during the Cultural Revolution decade and exonerated in the late 1970s — of establishing a one-to-one ratio between the number of students enroled at the senior secondary level in general and vocational/specialized technical schools respectively (Chapter 3). By contrast, the 1993 document made no mention of the two-track ratio and the consequent need to divide young people into two groups from an early age. Instead, vocational and technical education was stressed more as a function of job training and therefore as an adjunct rather than an alternative to regular secondary schooling (Article 8).

Finally, underscoring its peculiar mix of continuity and new beginnings, the "Outline" was accompanied by a change of leadership at the centre. Li Tieying, Minister in charge of the State Education Commission (herafter, SEC), was replaced in March 1993, by vice-minister, Zhu Kaixuan. He Dongchang, senior vice-minister and head of the SEC's Communist Party Committee, lost both posts in mid-1992, during a move against leftist conservatives evidently opposed to Deng Xiaoping's new reform drive. Li and He had remained at the helm throughout the 1989 crisis and its aftermath, but the two leaders seem to have parted ways by 1992. Care was taken otherwise to declare a smooth transition and Li retained his ranking within the party-state hierarchy.[2]

Zhu Kaixuan was introduced to the public as "scholarly" and "affable," a characterization no doubt drawn to allay fears given his unconventional (for a Chinese academic) credentials. These were acquired during a short period in the People's Liberation Army airforce (1950–1952), followed by a long career at the defence-related and politically-correct Beijing Aeronautics Institute (1952–1985).[3] Finally, according to the responsibility divisions within the top party-state leadership, education was among the briefs assigned to Li Lanqing when he became a vice-premier, also in March 1993.

As though reenergized, education leaders have undertaken an impressive workload, claiming authority in each instance from the 1993 "Outline." Besides the usual sequence of annual meetings and announcements, major initiatives taken to further its aims have been: the Teachers' Law promulgated in October 1993, to go into effect on 1 January 1994; a national education conference sponsored by the Party Central Committee and State Council in June 1994, to promote ongoing implementation of the "Outline"; a national rural education work conference in September; and the drafting of a new Education Law. Emphasis throughout has remained as in the 1993 policy document, on educational economics, privatization, and tertiary level reform. Publicity has been discreet concerning the points of anticipated change for secondary schooling, perhaps because of their background in the socially divisive policy struggles of earlier decades and the controversy that seems to surround them still.

Basic Education and the "New" Crisis of 1993

In current Chinese parlance, basic education usually refers to the elementary level (grades one through five or six). The term can also include the three-year junior secondary course as well since together these two levels comprise China's mass education system as defined in the Compulsory Education Law. The crisis of 1993 was in the first instance economic and its dimensions were not confined to this system. But they were drawn most sharply there and Chinese sources focussed most systematically on consequences for these basic education levels.

That the promise of a new beginning paralleled the reality of renewed crisis was not entirely coincidental since the new beginning for education had been designed to regain the initiative not just by deepening reform but also by addressing some of its most persistent problems. Foremost among those acknowledged — in keeping with the overall post-1992 strategy of economic openness combined with varying degrees of political constraint — were a cluster of interconnected issues related to educational finance.

1993: The Crisis Defined

The annual meetings of the National People's Congress (NPC) and the Chinese People's Political Consultative Conference (CPPCC) in March 1993, thus yielded some relatively sharp quotations from deputies representing the education sector. They evoked memories of the late 1980s when representatives set precedents with the candour of their critical commentaries on education issues including those both socially devisive and otherwise. Published accounts in 1993, however, were confined almost exclusively to funding and related problems.

According to the most forthright account, there was talk once more of a "crisis" in education deriving now from inadequate resources. Deputies blamed local leaders who, even in economically developed areas, diverted education funds to other purposes and held that education was less important than economic construction. As a result, teachers were poorly paid and inadequately housed while the practice of issuing paychecks several months in arrears remained widespread. Many were quitting the profession or taking up secondary jobs to make ends meet. Toward that same end, schools were arbitrarily imposing numerous extra fees, causing a rise in drop-out rates among students. Project Hope (*Xiwang gongcheng*), a government-run charitable foundation established (in 1989) to help relieve this last problem, could not keep pace with demand. Contributions from the project had allowed tens of thousands to return to school, while many more continued to leave for economic reasons making a mockery of the Compulsory Education Law. Deputies dubbed it the "bean curd law" or one in name only.[4]

Other opinions were less sharply worded but all reiterated the same points.[5] So too did Minister Zhu Kaixuan who subsequently identified the four main problems in education as: insufficient funding, arrears in teachers' wages, indiscriminate school fees, and rising drop-out rates among students at both the elementary and junior secondary levels.[6] But he blamed local governments for ignoring the centre's demand that they allocate more money to education. By contrast, delegates' submissions, reflecting local grass roots opinions, tended to trace the problems to a common origin in the mid-1980s decentralization of education financing and management.

Education Funding and Reform

The two perspectives are in fact two sides of the same coin, indicating problems rooted in the fundamentals of economic reform rather than education *per se*. Education is among the social services to have suffered negative consequences under the impact of newly emergent market forces and localized financial responsibility. The application of these fundamentals to educational financing has been introduced earlier in these pages and elsewhere by others.[7] To recapitulate, since 1978, state allocated funds for education have increased at an annual average rate of 15%. At the same time, however, control over income and expenditure has changed drastically.

Under the old system, central policy and financial appropriations were mandated at the centre and implemented by provinces and counties accordingly. In this manner, for example, even though rural commune middle schools were funded at different rates of expenditure in rich and poor areas, the state nevertheless undertook responsibility for financing at least one middle school per commune. State-salaried (*gongban*) teachers were paid in the same way, as were locally-hired (*minban*) teachers' monthly cash subsidy payments. Additional state funds were parcelled out in varying amounts by county education bureaus to help construct and maintain elementary and junior middle schools, otherwise supported (in kind and with local labour) by the collectively-run village production brigades, with overall coordination by commune management.

Under the new order, implemented progressively since the mid-1980s, except for major policies and general plans, authority is decentralized to the provinces and below. Among the policies and plans are new arrangements whereby each level must become self-supporting, that is, must assume responsibility for collecting and allocating the funds necessary to support schools run at that level whether village, township, county, prefecture, or province. Villages were expected to finance their own elementary schools and townships (which succeeded the old communes) their own junior middle schools. Senior secondary schooling is the county's responsibility in rural areas. Cities and their constituent districts divide responsibility for the schools serving them. Most tertiary institutions are now run by provinces with a minority funded by the central government and some by sub-provincial entities.

In fact, the decentralization formula has evolved into a complicated division of labour and responsibility known as "separate-level running of schools and separate-level management" (*fenji banxue, fenji guanli*). Running (*ban*) schools includes fund raising and improving conditions, while management (*guanli*) refers to other matters such as personnel appointments, guidance for education and teaching work, etc. By 1990, five models had emerged in urban and rural areas based on various combinations of power sharing and responsibility divisions.[8]

Provinces differed somewhat in their application of this pattern. Some revenue sharing up and down the line continued to varying degree, but not as a reliable source of matching funds or assistance for townships and village schools in economic distress. In this as in other sectors, the gap between actual allocations by local governments and adquate expenditure is supposed to be filled by funds from "multiple channels" (*duoqudao*). The largest component of the latter comes from the above-mentioned tax surcharges that local governments are authorized to collect specifically for education. Other sources include student fees, school-run profit-making ventures, and charitable donations.

Teachers' Salaries

The potential consequences of the new arrangements were recognized from the start and provoked a strong grassroots reaction when they were formally announced in 1984. Those consequences were soon manifested in fact. The four problems acknowledged by Minister Zhu in 1993, were already present and accounted for by the late 1980s, and were well represented in the education "crisis" reporting from 1987 to 1989. Whether these problems were actually ameliorated during the immediate post-1989 years or only disappeared from public view remains unclear. One authoritative explanation claimed that a sudden upsurge occurred during 1992 and 1993, with the phenomenon of unpaid teachers' salaries in particular reaching epidemic proportions nationwide. According to this account in the Beijing weekly, *Liaowang* (Outlook), the SEC calculated, conservatively, that unpaid teachers' salaries totalled 1.43 billion yuan as of May 1993. By Teachers' Day (10 September), Minister Zhu was proclaiming the problem, "unprecedented in amount, duration, and extent" since 1949.[9]

Defaulted or late payment of salaries, in whole or in part and sometimes months in arrears, were reported from virtually every province with some richer localities also among the offenders. But the poorest or weakest school support systems, inevitably rural, naturally suffered the greatest impact. Teachers were leaving their posts in ever greater numbers to seek other jobs and secondary employment, sometimes causing small rural schools to close down altogether or take on lower-paid less qualified substitute teachers as replacements.

According to the *Liaowang* account, this problem had existed throughout the 1980s, but was confined then to locally-hired (*minban*) rural teachers whose remuneration, but for the small monthly state subsidy all received, was tied to annual variations in the local economy.[10] The convergence of three developments in 1991–1992, was offered by way of explanation for the sudden spread of this phenomenon to include state-salaried teachers as well.

First, was the culmination of the reform process for educational financing itself. Prior to "about 1991," the poorer counties or "nearly 1,000" (of China's total 2, 000 counties) were still guaranteeing payment of *gongban* teachers' salaries with back-up assistance from prefectural or provincial finance departments. This protection was then withdrawn leaving each county entirely on its own, in final realization of education finance reform as introduced in the mid-1980s. Hence, the full impact of assigning the sub-county villages and townships responsibility for financing their own schools was also finally registered at this time. In effect, all teachers whether state-salaried or locally-hired were placed on the same footing since all were now wholly dependent upon the economic and financial health of the particular communities in which they served.

Second, after Deng Xiaoping's southern tour in early 1992, all levels of government hastened to increase economic investment in local enterprises, development zones, real estate, etc. Funds budgeted for education, of which teachers' salaries were the largest component, were tapped as one of the few readily available sources of investment capital in rural micro-economies. In this manner, state-salaried teachers began to receive the same treatment as *minban* teachers and all were, in any case, suffering the same fate as agricultural producers themselves since the practice of giving IOU's in lieu of cash payment for crops sold under contract also peaked at this time.

Third, the previously guaranteed "state" supplement for locally-hired teachers had, since 1986, become a township responsibility collected within each township as a special funding item. But after rural economic problems worsened overall and chaotic conditions for rural finance could no longer be ignored, the central government in 1993 undertook a more concerted effort than in previous years to reduce rural burdens with instructions aimed at limiting the new-won power of local authorities to manage their own affairs by collecting the money to pay for them. Some provinces responded to the centre's initiative in this respect by including the *minban* teachers' supplement among the burdens to be eliminated or temporarily suspended, thus eliminating this minimal guarantee for their locally-hired teachers as well.[11]

Initially, as decentralization of educational funding and management progressed, local authorities commonly complained that central leaders in Beijing were still making all the decisions while localities had won only power to pay the bills. By 1992–1993, however, the devolution of responsibility was essentially complete. Beijing then had to contemplate the logical result of its decisions, namely, that it had lost the power to enforce them. Hence, the steady supply of urgent circulars, statements, and instructions in 1993–1994, all aimed at prodding localities to address the consequences of an as yet unreconstructed mechanism for educational finance.

Although arrangements to induce compliance remain unclear, especially given repeated admissions that the SEC and other authorities had been issuing directives for several years to correct associated problems, central leaders called for solving them more forcefully "through legislation." As suggested, the initial effort in this regard, the Compulsory Education Law (*Yiwu jiaoyu fa*) of 1986, is enforced when it can be and honoured in the breach otherwise. Similarly, the new Agriculture Law promises that, "the state shall implement compulsory (*yiwu*) education in the countryside" (Article 49).[12] And the long-awaited Teachers' Law undertakes, among other things, to protect the rights and interests of those in the teaching profession with specific provisions against defaulting on salaries and diverting educational funds to other purposes (Article 38). The law also promises teachers "step-by-step" pay increases until their remuneration is comparable to that of other state employees (Article 25) and similar increases for locally-hired *minban* teachers until their pay is on par with that of regular state-salaried teachers (Article 31).[13]

Nevertheless, publicity surrounding the promulgation of the Teachers' Law was especially intense, as was the threat of "discipline and punishment" for those diverting education funds, and the notice of enforcement as of 1 January 1994. An accompanying State Council circular also offered more details than usual on how local authorities might actually fulfil the law's intent, suggesting that the final go-it-alone phase of the responsibility system for educational finance would be eased at least for the time being. Thus, localities unable to guarantee funds for schools and teachers' salaries, "can for a given period of time" revert to county management of educational financing. The village educational fund surcharge can also follow the system of "township collection and county management," with the aim of guaranteeing funds for *minban* teachers' salaries. Those for state teachers would be raised mainly by the county, but provincial and prefectural governments were to "exert the greatest effort" to help out. Finally, the circular stipulated that localities where the problem of defaulted teachers' salaries remained "serious" should not be permitted to engage in new building construction or purchase new automobiles.[14]

School Fees

Although widely cited as companion symptoms of the educational crisis, arbitrary increases in school fees and consequent rising student drop-out and child labour rates attracted much less attention in 1993. They were therefore less well documented and drew only the standard round of official admonitions. Recalling similar efforts in 1989, 1991, and 1992, the SEC could only try again in 1993, noting that the phenomenon of arbitrary fee collection seemed to ease, but then rose again even stronger than before, "causing an intense reaction throughout society."[15]

Attempts at statistical illustration were also equivocal at best. One of the more systematic accounts on the school fees problem could cite only national averages for 1991, there being no later figures available. Following provisions of the Compulsory Education Law whereby the state undertakes to provide nine years of free education through the junior secondary level, schools may not charge tuition as such through the ninth grade. "Miscellaneous fees" are permitted, however, explaining the apparent contradiction between the claim of "free" schooling and the issue of burdensome fees. Accordingly, in 1991, miscellaneous fees averaged RMB 30.10 per student in ordinary middle schools and RMB 12.89 at the elementary level.

Seeking to explain further how this relatively modest sum could have provoked such controversy, the writer could only point to a list of "blind spots" or fees which schools charged at will, over and above the "state stipulated" items that could be charged and had been aggregated for the national averages just cited. The list comprised four categories of items: (1) those added to the sanctioned fees (e.g., for computer training, repeating a grade, dossier management); (2) unauthorized commission fees added to those for the sale of textbooks and supplies to students which were authorized; (3) local government levies which schools pass on to students (e.g., for public sanitation, rat catching, land management, security); (4) extra fees for students enroled outside the school plan.

Using as an example the charges at a Hunan secondary school for one semester in 1992, the grand total was RMB 109 per student at the junior secondary level. Of that sum, the actual "miscellaneous fee" items added up to only RMB 12, or 11% of the amount paid. Fees or students living in school dormitories were substantially higher at RMB 334 per student per semester, and higher still for those at the senior secondary level.[16]

Student Attendance

Consequent student drop-out rates were even more diffcult to quantify and subject to widely varying presentations. Conventional wisdom, deriving from a host of surveys in the late 1980s, holds that the main cause of student drop-outs is inability to pay ever-rising fees and the finding continues to be reaffirmed. For example, a survey conducted in 42 Henan counties in 1992, showed 9.2% of all children aged seven to 14 years, were not attending school, a rate up by 1.4 percentage points over 1991. The main reason given, accounting for 26% of the drop-outs was inability to pay fees. Additionally, 5% claimed they quit school to help support their families.[17]

It was this discovery, moreover, that led to the creation of Project Hope. The charitable foundation solicits contributions from urban and overseas Chinese to cover school fees specifically for poor rural children who would otherwise be unable to continue their studies. According to figures issued by its leaders, the project had been able to help about half-a-million youngsters nationwide by the end of 1993, or one in 10 of those seeking its assistance.[18] A year later, the number of beneficiaries had risen to 860,000.[19]

Nevertheless, despite many statements both official and otherwise about rising student non-attendance in tandem with rising school fees, official compilations seemed unable to agree on whether drop-out rates were actually rising or falling. Thus, according to the SEC's formal year-end statistical bulletin, the drop-out rates among junior secondary school students was 5.78% for 1992, a slight increase over 1991's 5.46%. The rate rose again to 7.1% for 1993. Drop-out rates at the elementary level were not given.[20] The State Statistical Bureau's year-end bulletin reported 1993 national drop-out rates of 7.1% and 2.3% at the junior secondary and elementary levels respectively.[21]

By contrast, a State Statistical Bureau sample survey conducted to assess changes between 1990 and 1993, showed that 11.88% of children aged between six and 14 (the elementary through junior middle age groups) were out of school in 1993, a rate *down* from 19.07% in 1990. Additionally, 15.33% of all seven-year-olds were out of school in 1993, or 17.5% for rural areas alone, the latter *down* by 9 percentage points from 1990.[22]

Yet the Bureau's year-end bulletin claimed the entrance rate (*ruxuelü*) for elementary-school-age children was 97.7% for 1993. And the rate of elementary school graduates continuing on to the junior secondary level rose from 79.7% in 1992, to 81.8% in 1993.[23]

By further contrast, however, figures announced in early 1993, based on the fourth national census, showed that among 12-year-olds, only 25% were actually attending school, and 39% had already started working. The rate of school attendance among 16-year-olds was also dropping.[24]

As with "miscellaneous fees," one key to the apparent contradictions lies in the standardized formula used to define dropping out. This formula, adopted in the mid-1980s, was designed to measure achievement in the most positive way possible. When official announcements want to emphasize the positive, they therefore need only cite the formal enrolment, consolidation, graduation, and promotion rates. These, however, do not reflect the number of youngsters who enrol but do not attend, or the cumulative number who drop out over time. Thus, the rate of school-aged children entering school (*ruxuelü*) refers only to the percentage of the total number of school-aged children *who have enroled*. The consolidation rate refers only to the number of students *at the end of one school year* who continue on to the next and, conversely, the drop-out rate refers only to those who do not. Similarly, the promotion rate into junior secondary school refers only to the number of students who continue on among those who have *actually graduated* from elementary school, but not the percentage of the total age group, or even the total number who have enroled in the first grade (or even the total number in the graduating class). The percentage of the age group in school or which has completed school, are usually much lower than the enrolment, graduation, and promotion rates, and are also much less frequently used — as in the examples cited above.[25]

1994: The Crisis Resolved?

The speed with which the crisis of 1993 was defused can only be noted while the search for substantiating evidence continues. Provinces were reported rushing to meet the 1 January 1994 deadline for paying teachers' salaries, which was extended to the Chinese New Year-Spring Festival holiday, a month later. But by March, at the 1994 NPC-CPPCC meetings, Li Lanqing and Zhu Kaixuan declared the problem "basically solved," except for some localities which still owed small amounts of supplementay bonuses and subsidies.[26] According to their reports, the crisis was already history and business as usual had resumed. All levels were working to prevent a recurrence and toward that end, provisions of the November 1993 circular would remain in effect. Otherwise, the "Outline" was providing guidance and the Teachers' Law direction, while progress was recorded on all relevant points. State investment was up, so too were all enrolment rates, and reform was continuing on track.

The same crisis-under-control posture was maintained throughout the year, reinforced by a steady current of publicity surrounding the national education work conference in June and its follow-up provincial counterparts, a rural education conference in September, and completion of the draft of a more comprehensive Education Law in November.[27] Also throughout the year, however, more detailed accounts maintained a sober counterpoint. They suggest an ongoing state of "crisis management" while more fundamental solutions for problems symptomatic of the reform era remain elusive. A selection of such negative indicators can be briefly summarized, together with some specific positive initiatives announced during 1994.

Most basic on the negative side is, of course, inflation and Li Lanqing readily acknowledged its impact on educational funding. Allocations for education in the 1994 state budget were up 18.5% over 1993, a rate higher than the overall increase of financial revenue following policy guidelines. But Li admitted that the increase was offset by inflation.[28]

An extended nationwide study by the SEC's Education Development Research Centre traced China's educational difficulties to three endemic defects: (1) Development priorities treated economics and material resources as primary, while education and manpower remained at best secondary. (2) Old ways of management had been broken, but viable new alternatives were still not in place. Hence, "no effective macro-management system can begin to be built, so overall direction and control are not forceful in dealing with new troubles and problems which have arisen in educational practice." In other words, effective mechanisms for overall direction were lacking, and individual schools lacked the means of managing their own affairs properly as well. (3) Funding had grown ever more difficult and unless effective solutions were adopted, the goal of basically achieving nine-year compulsory education for all children by the year 2000 would be difficult to realize.[29]

The SEC's Personnel Office, investigating the new exodus of teachers, found multiple causes of which delayed pay packets was only one. Others were: exclusion of teachers from benefits and subsidies received by other state-salaried employees; collapse of the public health care system and lack of adequate health insurance leading to indebtedness and ill health; poor housing; few opportunities for promotion; heavy workloads; and of course new opportunities for more lucrative employment elsewhere.[30]

China Education News began the 1994–1995 school year with an in-depth retrospective on the school fees problem noting that despite efforts in many localities, "chaotic phenomena" still existed. And despite the data being drawn mainly from the 1993 fall semester in Hunan province, conclusions were presented as generalized contemporary fact. The common denominator underlying all was inadequate budgetary allocations by local governments. Provincial authorities had set clear standards on the number of items for which charges could be collected, by how much they could be raised, and so on. The province could only recommend not enforce, however, and localities typically made up the shortfall by increasing fees. Underfunding existed in town and countryside alike, but in the latter a major aggravating factor for Hunan was decontrol of its grain market in 1993. A rural education surcharge had been included along with the agriculture tax in grain procurement contracts. Without that automatic collection mechanism, only 60% of the revenue that should have come from the rural education surcharge was actually collected in 1993.[31]

A similarly in-depth assessment of student drop-outs, or more specifically its corollary child labour, also dated from 1993 but pointed to the same kind of fundamental reform-induced causes. Repeated injunctions by authorities high and low had failed to deter the practice which contravened the Compulsory Education Law's provision against children under 16 entering the workforce. Reasons were both economic and educational creating both great demand and a ready supply. As for demand, poorer families needed extra income and the fast-growing small enterprise sector profited from lower-cost child labour. Simultaneously, the education system's own failings were encouraging students to drop out. Limited opportunities for tertiary education reduced incentives at the secondary level which was commonly viewed as college preparatory only. Nor was secondary schooling adequately tied to job requirements on the labour market. Finally, the imbalance between available elementary and secondary education was great, with too few middle schools to accommodate all elementary school graduates. And inevitably, such factors had the greatest impact in poorer rural areas where compulsory education was difficult to implement.[32]

The June 1994 party-state work conference carried forward the search for fundamental solutions. Only the second conference with such high-level sponsorship in the post-Mao era, it laid down a "complete plan for organizing and mobilizing efforts to implement the 'Outline for China's Educational Reform and Development'." A subsequent State Council "Opinion" summarized the proceedings. Seemingly upstaged by the intervening 1993 crisis, the "Outline" was now reaffirmed on all points.[33] Specific initiatives pursuant to their implementation, announced during the summer and fall, included the following.

The SEC undertook to increase supervision and control over local governments' use of education funds, and government responsibility for implementing compulsory nine-year schooling was reaffirmed. Except in "a few" well-off regions, managing rural schools would be a county-level responsibility. In poor areas where educational funds could not be guaranteed, power for their overall management should reside in the county government while governments at and above that level should create special support funds.

The rate of surcharge for educational funds both in urban and rural areas was reaffirmed at 3% of the three commercial taxes. Provinces could devise their own methods of collecting education fund surcharges from rural enterprises not subject to the three taxes. The 1993 proscription against collecting more than 5% of farmers' annual net per capita incomes for village and township expenses remained in effect. But of the sum collected, 30–40% should be earmarked for local education expenditure. These educational surcharges, used to pay *minban* teachers and school operating expenses, could not be reduced or diverted to other uses.[34]

The state also pledged to set up educational banks and use other financial methods to secure more funds. Far from being relieved of fundraising responsibilities themselves, however, schools were encouraged to persevere with the state promising more low interest loans and tax breaks to school-run businesses. As a first step in preparing to set up an education bank, the inauguration of China Education and Science Trust and Investment Corporation was announced in September. It was advertised as China's first non-profit financial institution designed solely to raise and manage funds for schools and education-related enterprises.[35]

Provisions of the Teachers' Law were to be honoured in all respects. Additionally, state-salaried teachers should be granted the same medical benefits as other state-salaried or government employees in their localities. As a first step toward meeting the promise to regularize all *minban* teachers by the end of the century, the SEC announced that 150,000 of the nation's 2.3 million *minban* teachers would be transferred to state-salaried status by the end of 1994.[36]

Finally, besides the now-routine injunctions against indiscriminate fees, the SEC was contemplating three more substantive steps to reduce student drop-outs. The measures were cited in an otherwise unconfirmed announcement by SEC Vice-minister Liu Bin at one of the follow-up work conferences being held province-by-province to transmit the letter and spirit of the national June conference proceedings. The three measures are: abolition of the failure or repeater system (*liuji zhidu*); restoration of the student grant-in-aid system (*zhuxuejin zhidu*); and requiring host localities to assume responsibility for educating the children of non-resident or migrant workers living in their communities.[37]

These measures acknowledge some of the education system's own responsibility which is but infrequently cited as a cause of student dropouts. The practice of failing students and making them repeat grades was abandoned during the 1966–1976 years, but restored soon thereafter. When in use, the practice tends to be applied systematically to enforce certain pre-determined standards of achievement. It can also be misused to hold poorer students back deliberately with the aim of pushing up promotion and graduation rates. Much criticized in the past on political grounds (that the system was being used by "bourgeois" educators to discriminate against working class children), teachers nevertheless acknowledge, as did Vice-minister Liu, that students held back are more likely to drop out. Hence, to further the aim of universalizing education through junior middle school, "as of now, in principle" the practice is no longer being followed.

The student stipend system was a standard feature of all school budgets in years past to help cover fees and expenses for students in economic need. The system was abandoned in the 1980s, and Project Hope became a substitute. Children of migrant workers represent a new problem with host localities typically excluding from local schools all who are not permanent local residents, or charging them much higher fees. One report, citing 1992 statistics, estimated a migrant labour population of over 60 million — usually rural residents seeking temporary employment in cities. About one-tenth were under 16 years of age and the great majority (some 70%) were thought to be in the pre-school age-group. But no schooling was available for most of the remaining 30% since most could not afford the higher fees charged non-resident students.[38] The residential registration system is now under review and so too is the practice of excluding non-resident children from schools.

Annual year-end summations offered few details on net 1994 achievements in overcoming the crisis points of 1993. Thus, "a few" localities were again defaulting on teachers' salaries, reported Li Lanqing. Overall, funding, incomes, and housing were still "extremely pressing" problems for schools and personnel. Some localities were also still leaving townships and villages to fend for themselves, acknowledged Zhu Kaixuan.[39] Fortunately, the year-end publication of a speech by Liu Bin suggested the extent of the problems outstanding. As of July 1994, he said, only eight localities were continuing to pay all their teachers on time (Beijing, Shanghai, Tianjin, Tibet, Guangdong, Hainan, Yunnan, and Ningxia). Some provinces were still unwilling even to report their relevant statistics to Beijing.[40]

The number one pressing point in Zhu Kaixuan's 1994 year-end summary, however, was arbitrary and exorbitant school fees. Both he and Li Lanqing also acknowledged the negative social reaction provoked by the new breed of expensive private schools. In fact, Li declared that if these schools did not mend their unspecified excessive ways they would be banned. His attack reflected widespread ambivalence over the whole question of private schooling as one of many officially-encouraged expedients. Initial publicity for the "Outline" seemed to condone even élitist private schools designed specifically to serve China's new rich. But their ostentatious advertising in 1993 as high class schools (*guizu xuexiao*), was ill-timed, ill-received, and soon criticized by SEC leaders.[41] A more socially acceptable style is now encouraged and private schools at all levels from kindergarten through college are usually referred to as being *minban* or "run by the people." Some are funded entirely from private sources including loans and student fees; others are called *minban gongzhu* or "run by the people with public assistance."

The term *minban* has a long populist history but was used most extensively during the late 1950s and 1960s, to distinguish schools run by local communities or collective work units with little or no government help. The *minban/gongban* distinction among teachers today is a holdover from that time. During the Great Leap Forward in 1958 and 1959, however, the term *minban* was also used briefly as it is now to include schools run by private individuals and social groups. The main difference at present is the euphemistic attempt to disguise expensive private schools beneath the humble *minban* umbrella. In fact, although most private school fees are higher than those at public schools, only about 40 of the former are said to be in an élite class of their own catering to China's new super-rich.[42]

Nevertheless, the current generation of *minban* private schools overall may be headed in the same direction as their earlier counterparts which were, ironically, never very popular. Pressures from "society" — parents, educators, and authorities — inevitably led to the absorption of successful schools into the state system and atrophy of all others. The current pressure to regularize *minban* teachers is only the latest example of this phenomenon which has always worked against using *minban* schools as anything other than a temporary expedient. Similarly, these schools at least at the elementary and secondary levels are said to be suffering from all the old familiar defects: unreliable funding, fees even higher than those charged by public counterparts, lack of qualified teachers, poor quality students, erratic management, uncertain standards, etc. Hence, "at present, a great majority of students and parents still prefer public elementary and middle schools."[43]

Yet one variation on the theme does appear to have found a receptive audience. Old timers may not believe their eyes, but the press is reporting a *sishu* revival as part of the new emphasis on private schooling. *Sishu* is the old name for private tutor schools. Along with household teachers, these small one-tutor one-room classes were traditional China's only means of conveying elementary education. They were also viewed by early modern

Chinese reformers as synonymous with the Dark Ages because they continued to use the old Confucian primers and character glossaries, thus perpetuating at the mass level a tradition overthrown along with the imperial examination in 1905 and the imperial system itself in 1911. Nevertheless, *sishu* remained a popular and inexpensive alternative to modern schooling both in town and countryside until 1949.

Today, the traditional form and name have revived (presumably without the Confucian primers) as the only alternative in rural communities for children who cannot afford to attend regular schools. Advantages are the same as those cited before 1949, namely, the *sishu*'s cost-effective format and flexibility. The current version can provide basic literacy and numeracy at half the cost of regular schooling. An account from one county in western Hunan cited the comparative costs for an elementary level student: upwards of RMB 350 per year in regular school fees, by contrast with between RMB 120–180 for one year of *sishu* instruction which can be negotiated in kind for families with cash flow problems. Profits from an average class of 30 students are about RMB 2,400 per year or twice the annual income of an elementary school *minban* teacher in that locality.[44]

Statistical impressions of private school growth vary widely indicating that actual numbers are probably not known. A selection of those published in Chinese sources is shown on Table 1, along with the official figures for the regular system.

Portents of Change: Vocationalization and the Senior Secondary Level

Yet uncertainties surrounding private school development are minor compared with those at the senior secondary level where the 1993 "Outline" seemed to anticipate significant policy changes. These have not been extensively publicized but carry far-reaching implications which are evidently a source of ongoing internal debate. As noted, emphasis on vocationalization in the 1993 "Outline" was markedly reduced by comparison with past pronouncements. The "Outline" also called for universalizing senior secondary schooling in economically developed areas. The latter provision was clear and unequivocal, suggesting a major reversal of post-Cultural Revolution practice.

In the late 1970s, education policy-makers declared themselves

Table 1. Private (*minban*) Schools and the National System, Number of Schools (and of Students in Parentheses)

(Students: millions)

	Private schools				National system
	1991[a]	1992[b]	1993[c]	1994[d]	1993[e]
Kindergartens		13,800 (0.53)		16,990 (0.72)	165,197 (25.5)
Elem./sec. combined	1,199	1,600 (0.20)			
Elementary	655	863 (0.05)	4,000 (0.65)	4,030 (0.65)	696,681 (124.2)
Secondary	544	673 (0.13)		851 (0.13)	96,744 (53.8)
Jr. sec. only			550 (0.08)		
Tertiary combined				800	1,065 (2.5)
SEC approved		10		15	
Others		40			
Province approved		500			
Non-formal training schools, programmes		10,000		30,000	

Sources: Private schools:
  (a) *Zhongguo jiaoyu bao*, 24 November 1992, p. 2;
  (b) *Renmin ribao*, 4 August 1993 (article by Zhu Kaixuan, p. 3); elementary and secondary breakdown only, in *Xinhua* News Agency (Chinese), (Beijing), 18 March 1993 (report by Li Tieying), trans. in FBIS-CHI-93-052 (19 March 1993), p. 19;
  (c) *Zhongguo jiaoyu bao*, 18 January 1995 (speech by Zhu Kaixuan);
  (d) *Xinhua* News Agency (English), (Beijing), 17 June 1994, in FBIS-CHI-94-118 (20 June 1994), p. 36; edited versions of same report also in *Guangming ribao*, 20 June 1994, and *Zhongguo jiaoyu bao*, 1 July 1994.
  National system:
  (e) *Zhongguo tongji nianjian, 1994* (Statistical Yearbook of China, 1994), edited by Guojia tongji ju (Beijing: Zhongguo tongji chubanshe, 1994), pp. 557–61. Private schools are not listed as a separate category in this compilation, nor is there any indication as to whether they are included within the figures shown. Presumably they are not, at least at the tertiary level. Secondary level figures do not include skilled workers schools (for the full complement, see Table 4). State Statistical Bureau preliminary aggregates for 1994 include total student enrolments only. They are, at the elementary, secondary (exclusive of skilled workers schools), and tertiary levels: 130 million, 56.4 million, and 2.8 million, respectively (*Renmin ribao*, 1 March 1995).

liberated from the Maoist norm of universal 10-year (combined elementary and secondary) schooling. Among other things, they reestablished the old definition of senior secondary education as college preparatory and closed two-thirds of the nation's senior middle schools in a massive readjustment most of which occurred between 1978 and 1981 (see Table 2). A lesser degree of downsizing was enforced at the junior secondary level as well.

Table 2. Changing Structure of Secondary Education, Number of Schools (and of Students in Parentheses)

(Students: millions)

	1977[a]	1981[a]	1987[b]	1991[b]	1993[b]
Senior (*gaozhong*)					
General (*putong*)	64,903	24,447	16,930	15,243	14,380
or college prep	(18.00)	(7.15)	(7.74)	(7.23)	(6.57)
Specialized*	2,485	3,132	3,913	3,925	3,964
(*zhuanye*)	(0.69)	(1.07)	(1.87)	(2.28)	(2.82)
Junior (*chuzhong*)			75,927	70,608	68,415
	(49.80)	(41.45)	(41.74)	(39.60)	(40.82)
Vocational (*zhiye*)		2,655	8,381	9,572	9,985
		(0.48)	(2.68)	(3.16)	(3.63)

* The main types of specialized senior secondary schools are: engineering, agriculture, forestry, medicine, economics/finance, politics/law, physical education, and teacher training.

Sources: (a) *Zhongguo jiaoyu nianjian, 1949–1981* (China Education Yearbook, 1949–1981), (Beijing: Zhongguo dabaike quanshu chubanshe, 1984), pp. 981, 982, 1000, 1001, 1017.

(b) *Zhongguo tongji nianjian, 1994* (Statistical Yearbook of China, 1994), (Beijing: Zhongguo tongji chubanshe, 1994), pp. 558, 561.

Former Chinese teachers who were working within the school system when the cutbacks began, recalled general restrictions stipulating that the proportions of elementary school graduates continuing on to junior secondary schools should be reduced to 70%, while no more than 30% of the graduates from this level should be allowed into regular senior middle schools. Written directives specifying such proportional restrictions remain unpublished but by the early 1980s when downsizing was basically completed, national statistics showed promotion rates of approximately 70% and 30% at those two levels, down from 94% and 71% respectively in 1976.[45]

Reductions were imposed in town and countryside alike, but the impact was not so uniformly registered. As a rough rule of thumb, schools targeted for closure were those opened during the Cultural Revolution decade, and since the rural sector had been the chief beneficiary then, it had the most to lose afterward. Abolished were all the junior middle classes attached to elementary schools — which had made possible the high promotion rates into junior middle school. Abolished as well were most of the senior secondary sections of commune middle schools which had been established at the rate of at least one school per commune. City schools also generally reverted to a 12-year curriculum (six years each at the elementary and secondary levels), while rural schools tended to retain the five-year elementary course.

The new norm was one junior middle school per rural township, serving an average area somewhat smaller than that included in a commune. Official statistics recorded 54,000 communes in 1982, and 83,000 townships in 1985. A 1982 commune had an average population of 15,000; a 1985 township had 10,000.[46] The pattern was retained while rearrangements and redesignations continued. By 1991, the number of rural townships (43,660) and rural town administrations (11,882) combined (55,542) essentially matched that of the communes a decade earlier. Meanwhile, by 1992, the number of junior middle schools located within these rural communities had been further reduced to 59,000.[47] A substantial net gain was thus allowed to stand at the junior secondary level in the countryside. But given the general problems of distance, terrain, lack of mechanized transport, and the added costs of boarding at school, a rural system limited to only one school per commune (that is, an area roughly the same size as the old commune) cannot be expected to educate all children living within its boundaries. Hence the shrunken structure of rural junior middle schooling also belies the much-proclaimed national goal of achieving universal nine-year schooling.

Also abandoned in the late 1970s, was the attempt to extend senior secondary education throughout the countryside at the commune/township level. Complete or senior middle schools were reconcentrated in county seats and other comparable size towns where the practice of closing the latest additions to the middle school establishment was nevertheless also followed. According to the most commonly announced standards, at the county level and below, the rule was to retain one full-day senior middle school for every 100,000 people. The results are illustrated in Table 3.

The definitive one-to-one ratio at the senior secondary level, between regular and technical schooling, was then imposed upon the downsized system. Regular senior secondary graduates formed the college candidate

Table 3. General Senior Secondary Education, in Urban and Rural Areas, Number of Schools (and of Students in Parentheses)

(Students: millions)

	1965[a]	1977[a]	1981[a]	1990[b]	1993[c]
Urban (*chengshi*)	1,315 (0.56)	7,610 (3.54)	6,069 (1.96)	5,028 (2.16)	4,793 (2.13)
County seats and towns (*xian zhen*)	2,193 (0.63)	6,377 (2.57)	5,951 (2.17)	5,828 (3.28)	5,983 (3.22)
Rural (*nongcun*)	604 (0.12)	50,916 (11.9)	12,427 (3.02)	4,822 (1.73)	3,604 (1.21)
Administrative divisions: number of counties	—	—	2,136	1,903	2,166

Sources: (a) *Zhongguo jiaoyu nianjian, 1949–1981*, p. 1005; counties, 1981: *Zhongguo tongji nianjian, 1981* (Statistical Yearbook of China, 1981), (Hong Kong: Jingji daobao chubanshe, 1982), p. 1.
(b) *Zhongguo jiaoyu chengjiu, 1986–1990* (Achievement of Education in China, 1986–1990), (n.p.: Renmin jiaoyu chubanshe, 1991), p. 66; counties, p. 2.
(c) *Zhongguo tongji nianjian, 1994*, pp. 580–81; counties, p. 3.

pool; technical and vocational school graduates filled the need for skilled intermediate-level technicians. This two-track system was further refined with those schools designated as élite key-points — within the regular or ordinary (*putong*) track — adjusted and trimmed until they were producing approximately 600,000 senior middle graduates each year. The number more or less matched that for college freshmen enroled annually from 1985 through 1991.

The sudden unexplained provision for universal senior secondary schooling in major cities and developed coastal areas was presumably related to the sudden increase in demand for college students, yet another change traced to resurgent economic growth since 1992. The number of college freshmen increased to 754,000 that year, 924,000 the next, and was 895,000 in 1994.[48]

This sudden increase obviously disrupted the carefully crafted mechanism for producing college candidates. Nevertheless, the "Outline" authorized universal senior secondary schooling in an open-ended way, without reference to any vocational ratios. References to vocational education itself were also couched in unusually permissive terms, or at least terms more internationally acceptable than theretofore. This raised the possibility of a new more flexible approach, and perhaps a redefinition of senior secondary schooling in deference to the acknowledged general dislike of the two-track design or rather the vocational track within it. Even the World Bank had finally gone on record (in an internal 1991 reference work) reminding Beijing leaders of the drawbacks associated with vocationalization. These had enjoyed a long and well-documented history in the international development literature, and were reproducing themselves in China's contemporary experience as well.

The drawbacks of vocational education for school-age youth on a mass scale, as opposed to apprenticeship or specific job training programmes, have been a matter of record throughout most of this century. Practical problems include greater expense and difficulty in equipping and staffing such schools, as well as the difficulty of matching course content with jobs available to graduates. Social drawbacks concern the inferior reputation such schools typically have by comparison with their "real" regular counterparts which inevitably draw the brightest students from the most economically secure families.[49]

As further indication of a possible retreat on vocationalization, NPC delegates in 1993, had reflected the trends of the day on this issue too. Some university presidents among the delegates voiced their concerns about current middle school structure, designed as it was to supply annual demands for college freshmen. Such a "narrow bridge" was not conducive to training a large workforce for modernization. All students, whether or not they went on to college, "should have a command of math, physics and chemistry as well as a good understanding of Chinese culture and history."[50]

If liberal educators were being encouraged to articulate such thoughts in 1993, however, the same could not be said in 1994. Statements by the ranking spokesmen, Li Peng and Li Lanqing, also seemed to differ in emphasis with the latter emerging as a far more energetic promoter of vocational schooling. But no clues were left to explain these uncertainties until the June 1994 work conference and follow-up State Council "Opinion." In fact, such silence was no doubt deliberately imposed to muffle sounds of controversy that must have attended the "Outline's" provisions on secondary schooling. Few issues in the history of China's educational development have had more tumultuous impact than those related to the distinctions between mental and manual labour, and urban/rural disparity. And few have been more carefully avoided in public discourse during the post-1976 reform era when so many policies have enhanced these divisions in the name of overall development.

The "Outline," of course, perpetuated that trend by authorizing universal senior secondary education for urban and coastal areas, at a time when rural schools were being especially hard hit by the cumulative effect of financing reforms. And on this point, too, international development advisors have found cause for concern, pointing to the ever widening urban-rural gap in terms of restricted educational opportunities and facilities for the rural population. But lest anyone conclude otherwise, namely, that the "Outline" might actually be turning education back toward a more uniform kind of school system — with a retreat on vocationalization and universal secondary schooling for localities that could afford it as first steps — the mid-1994 clarification set matters straight. Vocationalization was reaffirmed with renewed vigour, as if to signal that any temptations on that score had been placed firmly aside.

Li Peng delivered the main work report at the June conference. "Vocational education has not yet received enough emphasis in actual work," he said. "It is necessary to overcome the outdated concept of belittling vocational schooling. It must be clearly understood that for a relatively specific period of time (*xiangdang yige shiqi nei*), a very important and pressing task for our nation's education work will be to develop vocational education vigorously on the basis of nine-year compulsory schooling."

The centrepiece of the effort would remain at the senior secondary level where he claimed the one-to-one ratio had already been achieved. Technical and vocational schools together now accounted for half the total number of all senior middle school enrolments. Henceforth, the goal for such training would be raised from 50% to 70% of all junior secondary graduates continuing on to the senior level. Additionally, vocational education should be promoted at the post-elementary level in localities which had not yet universalized a nine-year compulsory system. And even in those areas that had, "vocational courses may be added to school curricula as is necessary."

Li Peng's only deference to critics at home and abroad was the proviso that, "based on individual aspiration, circumstance, and possibility, all graduates from the various levels and kinds of vocational education, should be allowed to continue to higher levels of training." Also, "a rationally proportionate education system should gradually be set up whereby elementary, secondary, and tertiary general and vocational education all develop together and are linked with each other.... The system should be such that all society places the same emphasis on school diplomas and vocational certificates."[51]

The State Council's follow-up "Opinion" on implementing the "Outline" provided further clarification:[52]

> Large cities and coastal areas with a relatively high degree of economic development can, on the basis of nine-year compulsory education, actively universalize senior secondary schooling (including both regular and vocational education at the senior secondary level). Regular senior secondary schooling can develop appropriately on the basis of each locality's needs and capabilities. By the year 2000, students in regular senior secondary schools can reach 8.5 million more or less. Each county can run one or two middle schools to serve as all-county key-points. For the nation as a whole, about 1,000 key-points should be maintained as experimental or model senior middle schools (Article 3).
>
> ... Most localities should vigorously develop secondary vocational education, with the main emphasis on the post-junior middle level. Eventually, 50% to 70% of all junior secondary graduates should enter secondary vocational schools or vocational training centres. By the year 2000, as a national average, the various kinds of vocational schools should account for about 60% of all students admitted annually and studying at the senior secondary level; in cities that have universalized senior secondary schooling, the proportion can reach 70% (Article 4).

Barring some revelation of the internal debates on this issue, however, only future practice will reveal for certain whether the mid-1994 policy statement can be taken at face value. The clarification, in any case, raises as many questions as it answers. It acknowledges that vocational education is still unpopular, but leaves decisions on expanding regular academic senior secondary schooling to the localities which are responsible for paying all the bills. Hence, how Beijing aims to enforce its unpopular dictum remains unclear. Also, the various vocational categories may or may not actually represent what they purport to be (for the full complement, see Table 4). No definitions are available, nor are the standards used in compilation. Schools might, in other words, be misrepresenting themselves in deference to the policy imperative. This was done initially, in the early 1980s, when they often declared themselves vocationalized by simply dividing up students with a classroom or two studying vocational subjects while everyone else carried on using the regular academic curriculum.

Nevertheless, not content to reaffirm their vocational goals at the senior secondary level, SEC policy-makers are further adapting them for use in junior middle schools with particular reference to the countryside. Here, too, terms are not defined and "rural" in contemporary usage

Table 4. Secondary Schooling, 1993[a] **and 1994**[b]

Type	Number of schools	Number of students
General (*putong*)		
Senior	14,380	6,569,100 (6,644,000)
Junior	68,415	40,822,000 (43,170,000)
Specialized (sr. level only)		
Technical	3,046	2,098,300
Teachers training	918	722,000
Skilled workers schools (sr. level)	4,477	1,739,000 (1,822,000)
Vocational		
Senior	8,403	3,063,500
Junior	1,582	562,400

Sources: (a) Guojia jiaoyu weiyuanhui jihua jianshe si (State Education Commission, Planning and Construction Department), *Zhongguo jiaoyu shiye tongji nianjian, 1993* (Educational Statistics Yearbook of China, 1993), (Beijing: Renmin jiaoyu chubanshe, 1994), pp. 2, 12.

(b) State Statistical Bureau preliminary aggregates for 1994 include total student enrolments only (see, *Renmin ribao*, 1 March 1995). These figures are shown (in parentheses) in the "number of students" column.

can mean anything from village and township to county seats and even prefectural towns. But the SEC is currently preparing a new junior secondary curriculum intended for use in rural schools which will reduce the standard 13 required subjects at that level to only eight. A range of practical subjects will be added as electives according to local needs and demands. About 100 schools are scheduled to introduce the new curriculum on a trial basis during the fall semester, 1995.[53]

Continuing Reform at the Tertiary Level

Although no major new departures have been announced for higher education, newly appointed Minister Zhu Kaixuan declared reform at that level the most difficult to accomplish. Reasons were self-evident. Perhaps more than any other sector of Chinese society, institutions of higher learning had borne the full force of post-1976 change. Every major reform goal had already been introduced by the late 1980s, sometimes with careless abandon and ensuing tensions contributed to the upsurge of college student activism from 1985 onwards. Zhu Kaixuan was thus picking up, in 1993, where the reform drive had halted when disaster finally struck in 1989. His job was to carry through during the second decade of reform, initiatives that had provoked some highly ambivalent consequences following first round introductions in the 1980s.[54]

To mark this new beginning, the SEC ended year-long off-campus military training imposed as exemplary punishment in 1989, for all freshmen at Beijing and Fudan Universities. The principle of limited basic military training for college students was nevertheless reaffirmed.[55] As a further gesture in the same direction, politics was removed from the list of required examination subjects for all candidates taking the national college entrance examinations, sciences and engineering section, in 1994. Politics remained a required examination subject for all liberal arts candidates, who accounted for about 40% of the 2.5 million taking the examinations in 1994.[56]

Student Enrolment, Tuition, and Job Assignment

The specific question of political dissent and disloyalty was only one of several issues for college students in the late 1980s, however. Undoubtedly, more urgent during the immediate pre-1989 years was the problem of employment. This impinged in turn on the SEC's interrelated tripartite plans for enrolment, tuition, and job assignment reform. But the problem was also exacerbated by structural reform that had already occurred throughout the education system. And it was this kind of dilemma, created by a reform process that seemed to be stumbling on an accumulation of its own consequences, unable to move either forward or back, that led to the crisis of confidence in 1988 and 1989. The three-part plan had thus produced by 1989, one of the main "tough spots" to which Zhu Kaixuan was referring when he noted the key points of difficulty for education reform. The plan can be summarized briefly as a basis for measuring Zhu's success in untying the knots and carrying forward his mandate.

The "old" system — free college education for all, admission on the basis of a pre-determined national college enrolment plan, and guaranteed state job assignment upon graduation — has not been followed in pure form since the late 1970s. Plans for change were announced at that time and, as testimony to the obstacles encountered, have taken 15 years to reach the present partially reformed state. Student stipends were gradually eliminated, replaced by a student loan scheme in the mid-1980s, while expenditures for room, board, books, etc., began to grow. By 1985, the rising cost of a college education was one of several provocative questions on students' minds as the level of debate and discontent on college campuses also began to rise. Beijing nevertheless persevered with its reform agenda.

According to the timetable announced in 1988, Guangdong province was assigned to go first, with all institutions of higher learning nationwide following in a phased sequence until the reform package had been extended to all students sometime in the mid-1990s. Accordingly, college freshmen would have to pay tuition, beginning with those in Guangdong in 1988. When these tuition-paying students graduated two or four years later, depending on their study programmes, they would be responsible for finding a job on their own.

Freshmen at the 36 institutions administered directly by the SEC were next in line, scheduled to begin paying tuition in 1989, and all other post-secondary schools were expected to follow suit by the early 1990s. Teacher training institutions, schools for national minorities, and the specialized senior secondary schools were all initially exempt. Amounts paid would be low at first but rise thereafter. Guangdong began with a variable tuition charge of RMB 100–150 per semester, depending on the school and specialty. Self-financed (*zifei*) students or those paying upwards of RMB 500 per semester, in return for lower admissions scores, were treated as a separate category "outside the plan." Such students were limited by SEC directive to a small proportion of each school's total intake each year, but their numbers too would be allowed to rise in the future. Individual institutions would retain all tuition and fees collected.

At first, however, many students continued to be enroled much as before. Such students represented two functions served by the old system that could not be performed under the new, namely, allowing students from poorer families to attend college, and guaranteeing enrolments in certain essential specialties and occupations which tended not to attract sufficient applicants (e.g., teacher training, agriculture, forestry, geology, mining, etc.). The solution was to retain for as long as necessary, a dual formula whereby students with sufficient means could enrol in the new way and apply to study in specialties of their choice. Other students would continue to receive a more fully subsidized education but in assigned specialties with job assignments to match. In Guangdong, just over half the 1988 freshman class continued to be enroled in this state-directed category.[57]

Announcement of these reforms provoked a small storm of controversy in 1988, with the loudest outcry directed against the one change thought to have been most eagerly anticipated, namely, freedom of employment.

Reasons for this surprising result varied depending on the perspective. Parents and students decried the reform as premature, demanded safeguards to guarantee a level playing field, and protested that only sons living in big cities with well-connected parents could benefit in the contemporary social climate.

By contrast, school administrators and government authorities tended to explain the phenomenon differently. The problem, they said, was not one of opportunities but expectations, or those too high for the opportunities available. Still, the mismatch was new, suddenly highlighted but not created by the latest reform initiatives. Here again reasons were twofold. They concerned: (1) the changing structure of employment opportunities; and (2) the social origins of students themselves. For approximately a decade after 1976, college students could be secure in their aspirations as work units adjusted personnel, transferred out Cultural Revolution appointees, and replenished rosters with new graduates. But by the late 1980s, demands had been met. Preferred assignments in big cities and prestigious work units were no longer plentiful. Opportunities were shifting instead to small towns and enterprises where intermediate-level personnel were more appropriate than regular four-year college graduates. The situation was such by 1988, that even Beijing University graduates were being obliged to adjust their expectations downward.

As for the students' origins, Cultural Revolution demands for worker-peasant enrolments had been firmly repudiated and it was still a commonplace in the late 1980s to say that college students were all city-bred children of cadres and intellectuals. The key-point college preparatory stream had been rebuilt specifically to train the best and brightest who were inevitably from such families. Only just liberated from the Cultural Revolution requirement that urban cadres and intellectuals should go "down" to the countryside and into manual labour assignments, students from these backgrounds could not be expected to turn downwards once more. Even students who were themselves from county towns, said educators in 1988, aspired to something better after graduation. And as they acquired greater freedom, they were increasingly using it to reject unwanted state job assignments.

SEC measures to overcome this impass after 1988 were overshadowed by the political crisis and subsequent news blackout applied especially to matters concerning China's college students. But the plan to charge tuition was separated from the companion employment reform. Tuition went forward while the modified method of "arranging" job assignments, already in use, was retained. Accordingly, students who can find their own jobs do; students in various contracted and state-directed programmes accept state assignments; others are placed in work units on the basis of mutual agreement between student and employer.

As a means of adjusting aspirations, the SEC had also decided by 1988 that the system was producing more four-year graduates than the economy could absorb. The aim therefore was to restructure higher education until there were at least as many students enroled in two-year post-secondary (*zhuanke*) programmes, as in regular four-year undergraduate courses.

Surveying this reform package five years later, several relevant points of change stand out; an increased demand for college graduates and consequent enormous rise in student admissions since 1992; a similar rise in short-course enrolments; the claim that over half of all college students are now of rural (*nongcun*) origins; and a greatly increased proportion of self-financed students, as well as high uniform tuition rates for all students at leading universities.

On the matter of tuition, Zhu Kaixuan reported in 1993, that the number of self-financed students had continued to rise with about 30% of all college students nationwide paying between RMB 2,000 and RMB 3,000 annually. He claimed that this amount represented only 30–40% of actual costs. Other students were paying at variable rates, from RMB 300 to RMB 700 annually, depending on school and specialty. Figures are not available to show precisely how many students are paying how much tuition, but numbers in the main admissions programmes are shown on Table 5. It should be noted, however, that these programmes are the simplified categories used in official SEC compilations and do not adequately reflect the complicated mix of admissions procedures and terminologies that have evolved. But old and new ways would be followed together, explained Zhu. Charging tuition was correct and would be continued. The problem was to gauge society's ability to absorb the increases and proceed accordingly.[58]

A few months later, he elaborated promising that plans for tuition increases would continue to contain provisions for poor students. This was necessary, he said, since over 50% of China's 2.5 million college students were of rural origins and many would be unable to afford higher fees.[59] With as yet no explanation for this startling new development, the SEC provided statistics on the 2.5 million candidates taking the 1994 national college entrance examinations in July. Only 39% were from cities and towns (*chengzhen*), while 61% were rural.[60]

Nevertheless, the next fee increase applied to the 1994 freshman class, albeit to only about 10% thereof. Called "merging the tracks" (*binggui*), the pilot programme was introduced at leading universities including 29 still under direct SEC administration. The aim is to eliminate distinctions that have evolved since 1988, between richer and poorer college students, and to reestablish the link between tuition payment and freedom of choice in employment. Under the experiment, all 1994 freshmen at the 37 participating universities must pay standard rates for tuition and incidental fees ranging from RMB 500 to RMB 1,100 annually, depending on school and specialty. All students must pay at the same variable rates and the practice of allowing lower admissions scores for students paying the highest self-financed rates is abolished. But abolished as well are the distinctions between what is generally referred to as the state assignment plan (*guojiarenwu jihua*) for students paying less to study in less popular fields, and the more flexible regulated plan (*tiaojiexing jihua*) for students able to pay more. These two categories (which overlap and are not coterminous with those in Table 5) also tend to have differing enrolment standards but with the latter higher than the former. Finally, all freshmen enroled under the 1994 experiment will be responsible for finding their own jobs after graduation.[61]

The experiment was declared a success in all respects after enrolment had been completed for 1994. Standards were maintained while, "parents and students accepted such changes calmly."[62] The experiment also points the way forward since the official aim is to continue reducing distinctions between the state assignment and adjustable categories until the two become one with all students (or as many as possible) enroled in the same manner.[63]

The requirement that all candidates must take the unified national college entrance examinations and be enroled within each school on the basis of uniform passing scores also lays to rest, at least for the time being, perennial questions as to whether the restoration of the examinations in 1977 should be permanent. Their role now appears to have stabilized with the reduction of examination subjects to only five — whether for liberal arts or science/technology candidates. But additionally, a pre-test or preliminary has been introduced in recent years. Each province now requires all graduating seniors to pass provincially unified examinations (*huikao*) on each of the nine main subjects (including politics) in the senior secondary curriculum.[64]

If the 1994 experiment was in fact accepted "calmly," one reason

Table 5. College Students in the 1990s, Some Relevant Indicatiors

	Student origins[a]	
	1994	
	Urban (*chengzhen*)	Rural (*nongcun*)
College candidates 2.5 million	39%	61%

	Admissions programmes (number of students)	
	1989[b]	1993[c]
State plan enrolments (*guojia renwu*)	1,799,977	1,926,451
Enroled under contract with sponsoring work units (*weituo peiyang*)	172,939	372,032
Self-financed (*zifei*)	74,089	231,668
In-service training, cadres and teachers	35,106	5,366

	Course type (number of students)	
	1989[b]	1993[c]
Regular courses (*benke*)	1,321,190	1,417,357
Short courses (*zhuanke*)	760,921	1,118,160

Sources: (a) *Zhongguo jiaoyu bao*, 7 July 1994.
(b) Guojia jiaoyu weiyuanhui jihua jianshe si (State Education Commission, Planning and Construction Department), *Zhongguo jiaoyu tongji nianjian, 1989* (Educational Statistics Yearbook of China, 1989), (Beijing: Renmin jiaoyu chubanshe, 1990), pp. 24–25.
(c) Guojia jiaoyu weiyuanhui jihua jianshe si, *Zhongguo jiaoyu shiye tongji nianjian, 1993* (Educational Statistics Yearbook of China, 1993), (Beijing: Renmin jiaoyu chubanshe, 1994), pp. 20–21.

might be the economy's renewed demand for college graduates. This trend began in 1992 and has led to the surge in college admissions, noted above, as well as expansion at the senior secondary level. Like its authorization of the latter primarily in major cities and coastal regions, however, the SEC also makes no secret of the tertiary sector's faster growth in developed areas. These are expected to invest in higher education by a greater margin than do poorer inland regions and the consequent widening gap is accepted as an inevitable consequence of this development strategy.[65] Hence the rise in college admissions is occurring disproportionately where economic development is also spurring demand.

The impact on college students' employment prospects was first noted in 1992, with hopeful reports of selective improvement. In January 1992, "most" 1991 graduates had found jobs. By contrast, two years later, "more than 95%" of the 1994 seniors had been placed within a month of graduation.[66] Yet questions remained as to whether students' expectations had been adjusted "downward" or were simply being allowed to rise with the new opportunities. Hence, Beijing's education bureau responded in the new way to this old problem by setting up a special fund. Each graduate willing to work in remote or less-developed regions was promised RMB 1,000 to RMB 5,000 as an "encouragement" bonus.[67]

Moreover, as job assignment preparations began for the 1995 graduating class a new problem appeared, reflecting the SEC's success in promoting its 1988 decision to boost short-course college programmes. While the planned 1:1 ratio has not quite been achieved (see Table 5), about one-third of the 1995 graduates are in such programmes for which there is now an indifferent demand. The need for these half-educated young people, especially those with science and liberal arts degrees, is "extremely small." Instead, demand is greatest for regular graduates in fast-developing coastal provinces, evidently leaving inland areas and unpopular professions in much the same difficulty as before.[68]

Perhaps the biggest question mark, however, concerns the students' origins since no follow-up information has been provided to explain their "rural" backgrounds nor anything else about them. The rural claim was no doubt made to counter the 1980s assertion that only urban cadres' and intellectuals' children could qualify for college within the restructured system. One possible explanation is that the students are from county seats and small towns (see Table 3), which are often referred to in categoric fashion as "rural." In this blanket use of the term, it extends to everyone living in such towns and their rural hinterlands, without distinguishing town dwellers from farmers, much less the diffuse category of registered rural residents (*nongye hukou*).[69] But that even the latter, registered rural residents, could account for so large a percentage of college candidates seems unlikely — without major changes in rural school patterns, the keypoint school establishment, and college entrance requirements. For example, the expanded enrolments since 1992 may have been recruited more heavily from county town schools, although this seems at odds with the current emphasis on big city and coastal growth. Related data which might help substantiate the claim are also lacking, such as what kinds of secondary schools are producing the current generation of college students:

whether regular key-point, county town key-point, non-key-point, or vocational-technical.

Adapting to Society's Changing Needs

Most unsettling for tertiary institutions themselves, however, have been the composite of reforms perhaps best summarized as those aimed at adapting higher education to society's changing needs. So comprehensive were these adjustments during the 1980s, that institutions were bombarded with more demands for change than they could possibly absorb, in all aspects of their existence: economic, administrative, and academic. The political crisis of 1989 and its aftermath actually offered a certain kind of respite from the perpetual motion of the years before. At present, the reforms are again proceeding at a pace as fast as the cumbersome workings of Chinese higher education will allow. The SEC's 1992 manifesto for renewed higher education reform provided the fullest account of this revival, while aims are summarized in the 1993 "Outline" and all supporting documents.[70]

Among the interrelated goals reaffirmed in 1992 and most actively pursued since, are: (1) rapid quantitative growth well beyond the targets initially set for the year 2000, plus a parallel project to guarantee a quality key-point core within the burgeoning tertiary system; (2) economic diversification to expand sources of funding beyond government budgets; (3) curricular changes to meet economic demands and local requirements; (4) rationalization or reorganization in pursuit of administrative efficiency.

These goals were reiterated in Zhu Kaixuan's 1994 New Year message. China's institutions of higher learning, he said, should "develop on a larger scale, raise quality, rationalize structures, and be much more efficient."[71] Essentially, the objective is to produce with existing resources, more tertiary-trained personnel at levels and with aspirations appropriate to China's needs. This objective still assumes foreign input, investment, and study abroad. But the aim is to create a more home-based self-sufficient system than that developed during the 1980s.

Fast-paced growth has been the outstanding feature of this reform plan as implemented during the past two years, and the much-publicized "Project 211" should be seen as companion to the renewed drive for quantitative growth. The project — to maintain 100 universities at key-point level for 21st century development — is part of the reform revival package for higher education announced in late 1992. It aims to concentrate resources around a quality core within the fast-expanding system that will allow Chinese higher learning to maintain standards and ultimately achieve advanced world levels.

Meanwhile, quantitative growth and the diverse methods used to achieve it dominated development in 1993 and 1994. Typically, official statistics obscure as much as they reveal about both growth and methods. For example, Zhu Kaixuan has claimed that private or non-governmental *minban* development is most important at the tertiary level and statistics cited in official sources do indicate striking growth. As noted in Table 1, however, the more formal State Statistical Bureau compilation does not contain a separate *minban* category, nor does it indicate that non-government school statistics are included in overall totals.

Nevertheless, the formal compilation does offer one clue as to how growth is being pursued. Overall nationwide enrolments have risen (from 2.04 million in 1991 to 2.54 million in 1993), while the number of institutions has actually fallen (from 1,075 in 1991 to 1,065 in 1993).[72] If successful, the reforms these figures reflect will have an impact on Chinese higher education going well beyond quantitative indicators. Chinese sources refer to these reforms as rationalizing structure and scale or optimizing resource use.

At issue are two features of Chinese higher education so deeply rooted that neither a communist revolution nor 15 years of reform have yet succeeded in eroding them. Most enduring is the faculty-student ratio. Throughout most of this century, foreign advisors and consultants have consistently credited Chinese higher education with the most inefficient ratios — or the fewest students per teacher — in the world. Today the average international faculty-to-student ratio is about 1:15, whereas China's is around 1:6.[73]

The second key feature of China's universities has been their enclosed self-contained community design. This is primarily a creation of the 1950s, when China rebuilt its tertiary system using that of the Soviet Union as model. The narrowly defined specialties and institution-specific disciplines proved resistant to change in the 1980s, for reasons that had less to do with academic conservatism than with other functions Chinese universities also perform as socialist-style work units for the academic communities within them. Now, a decade later, the SEC appears determined to try again. Optimal goals have been set and written into the latest reform documents: 3,500 students for a regular four-year college (up from the current average of 2,500) and, 2,000 students for post-secondary *zhuanke* institutions (up from the present average 1,000). The SEC calculates that in this manner, existing facilities should be able to accommodate 50% more students.[74]

As one means of achieving this goal and other academic benefits of scale as well, the SEC is also promoting once more the merger of China's smaller institutions to form "giant" Western-style comprehensive universities. Several such mergers were announced in 1994, including a new Shanghai University created from the amalgamation of four existing Shanghai institutions. In the same vein, five universities in Beijing reached agreement on opening optional courses to each others' students, cooperating on research projects, and jointly building student dormitories.

The main trend for the time being, however, is in the opposite direction with established universities "rationalizing" their operations by setting up small branches and training centres. These are seen to serve several functions by: employing superfluous staff and giving them a second source of income; earning extra revenue for the parent institutions from fee-paying students; and offering market-oriented training courses not necessarily included in the regular curriculum or offering regular courses to non-regular students. In this manner, Hangzhou University has established five branch schools, one with the cooperation of mass media organizations to train journalists, another for students majoring in economics, and so on. Such offshoots of regular institutions seem to cater to small student bodies of only a few hundred at most and probably account for the large number of new *minban* tertiary-level schools shown in Table 1.

This tertiary level growth has also challenged the overarching reform principles of increasing decentralization and institutional autonomy — much as did the complete decentralization of rural school finance in 1991. Hastening similarly to devise damage-control measures after the fact, Zhu Kaixuan reaffirmed the decision to encourage all kinds of "open-style" school operations to promote growth. But, he said, the pace had outstripped economic development and schools' ability to cope with the rapid rise in student numbers. Lacking adequate funds, regular institutions were taking advantage of the new flexibility to raise revenue without regard to academic discipline or campus facilities, "running classes and issuing diplomas with abandon."[75]

In any event, "overheating" could scarcely have been avoided given the promotion of expanded enrolments and *minban* schools, while simultaneously giving regular institutions a degree of autonomy to enrol fee-paying students and sponsor their own "private" ventures as well.

The inevitable result was a huge increase in regular enrolments and uncontrolled private school growth. According to custom, the SEC had issued a preliminary 1993 enrolment plan for regular tertiary institutions of 789,000. In reality, institutional discretion produced a national freshman class of 925,000.[76]

Among the more forceful of the ensuing admonitions was an SEC circular singling out the Hengyang City Medical Training Centre in Hunan, as an exemplary case for criticism and reprimand. This self-proclaimed college-level medical course was enroling students who had not passed the college entrance examinations, in return for RMB 2,200 annual tuition fees.[77] The strong reaffirmation of the national college entrance examinations in 1994, was also proclaimed as one of the few sure ways of maintaining "macro-regulation" over higher education. The SEC announced that only students who had passed the national unified examinations would be issued graduation certificates and that these were being made forgery-proof.[78]

Conclusions in Retrospect

Given the uncertainties and unanswered questions, conclusions can only be tentative. Some comparative impressions may nevertheless be drawn taking as a benchmark problems being articulated for China's educational development in the late 1980s, after a decade of post-Mao reform. At the elementary level, the main problematic then was rural education weakened by decollectivization of the economic base which had sustained an extensive network of village and commune schools. Reforms for secondary schooling cut across the urban-rural divide with massive reductions at the senior level and unpopular vocationalization prescribed as the alternative for all who could not gain admission to general schools. These latter were redefined as the college-preparatory stream and further differentiated with the reconcentration of resources both human and material in urban-based key-point schools. The tertiary sector was, however, assigned to absorb the fullest measure of reform goals with major changes introduced for virtually every aspect of college life.

The draconian methods used to restore order after June 4, 1989, at least gave Beijing leaders a breathing space to assess their options. But they then emerged from the period of crisis and consolidation to pick up essentially where they had left off. Almost all the main ingredients of the reform agenda for education reemerged intact, including those which had provoked controversy and complaint.

Nevertheless, within the ultimate parameters of political control aimed at suppressing political dissent, various damage control measures have aimed at defusing underlying tensions. These measures include an energetic public relations campaign to which SEC leaders are obviously devoting much time and effort. This is the same exercise which has made it difficult to document and verify policy implementation and public reaction in the foregoing account. But many points in the exercise are aimed at mollifying academic public opinion and do address specific concerns of China's school communities. Most obvious in this respect were the modification of military training for students at Beijing and Fudan Universities, as well as the termination of He Dongchang's tenure at the SEC. Two additional points are noticeable by their absence and reflect the effort to downplay socially divisive issues. Beijing authorities in the late 1980s, evidently alarmed at the brain drain their reforms had set in motion, were exploring measures to force students overseas to return home and those at home to accept socially responsible job assignments in rural locales. These official concerns have not been abandoned but if punitive pressures are being exerted internally, they are at least not reflected in the sources available.

Additionally, Beijing authorities have acknowledged many crisis points directly attributable to the reform agenda. The agenda itself remains essentially unchanged and substantive corrections are not necessarily in evidence. But the authorities seem determined to project the image of a "caring" government searching honestly for viable solutions. Hence the succession of laws, circulars, conferences, speeches, and survey reports, all designed to show that problems are being acknowledged and studied in anticipation of measures to set matters right. This sequence has continued since 1993 over salaries, the status of *minban* teachers, housing, health care, student drop-outs, child labour, migrant workers' children, the household registration system, and rural school reform.

If the SEC's schedule of investigative research is impressive, however, so too are the problems many of which have actually intensified in the early 1990s under the renewed reform drive. For elementary schooling, the final stage of decentralization was pushed through, precipitating a nationwide crisis of unpaid teachers, rising school fees, and student dropouts. So successfully has the system now been decentralized that Beijing cannot even force provinces to report their progress in implementing central laws and directives aimed at coping with the crisis. Hence it is probably safe to conclude that the delivery system for elementary education in the countryside is now even weaker than in the late 1980s.

One major change is the decision to allow universal senior secondary schooling in cities and developed coastal areas. But the cost of reform at the secondary level has from the outset been measured in terms of the inequalities it was designed to enforce. In fact, success is now claimed in this area too with the goal of a 1:1 ratio finally achieved between general and vocational enrolments at the senior secondary level. A new vocational curriculum for rural junior middle schools is also being planned. The aim is to rationalize education by providing two separate forms of schooling — one practical and work-oriented, the other academic and college-preparatory — in anticipation of life's inevitable realities. The many difficulties associated with this unpopular dual approach nevertheless remain among the least publicized of all items on the education reform agenda.

Successes at the tertiary level have come more slowly but also at a cost and with mixed results. Tuition, enrolment and job assignment reforms are continuing their ponderous progression. Of the three, raising tuition has proved the easiest. Job placement by "market allocation" remains an elusive goal for college graduates. So too does the partially reformed socialist alternative of trying to design college courses to meet society's needs and channel student aspirations accordingly.

Most intriguing, however, is the sudden new claim that over half China's college students are now "rural." This contrasts sharply with one dominant impression created by the current state of reform overall, namely, the growing disparities not just between rich and poor but specifically between urban rich and rural poor. For education, this distinction is marked in many ways. Most extreme is the contrast between the new super-rich private schools and their humble *sishu* counterparts. The one charges thousands of yuan in annual tuition, fees, and deposits. The other is reviving after a 40-year hiatus as the only affordable equivalent at RMB 1–200 per year for poor rural families.

The recent decision to permit universal senior secondary education in cities and developed coastal areas also underlines the growing urban/rural inequalities. So too do rural school patterns; comparative enrolments in urban, small town, and rural senior middle schools; the urban-centred key-point school establishment; and college entrance requirements enforced through a rigorous sequence of competitive provincial and national examinations based on the general college-preparatory curricula. Thus, the

SEC may have redefined "rural" to mean anyone not from a major metropolis. But the definition itself may say more about concerns raised by developing disparities than it does about the actual origins of China's college students. It also points to some very old social controversies in the history of China's 20th century educational development, provoked by the gap between town and countryside, that seem to be reviving in the early 1990s as disparities intensify once more.

Notes

1. For these common points shared by two major reform blueprints, see: "Zhonggong zhongyang guanyu jiaoyu tizhi gaige de jueding" (Decision of the Chinese Communist Party Central Committee on the Structural Reform of Education), 27 May 1985, in *Renmin ribao* (People's Daily), (Beijing), 29 May 1985; and, "Zhongguo jiaoyu gaige he fazhan gangyao" (Outline for China's Educational Reform and Development), issued by the CCP Central Committee and the State Council, 13 February 1993, in *Zhongguo jiaoyu bao* (China Education News), (Beijing), 27 February 1993. All *People's Daily* citations herein refer to the national domestic edition. In January 1995, the standard English translation for *Zhongguo jiaoyu bao* was changed to *China Education Daily*.

2. For example, *Renmin ribao*, 30 March 1993; and, *Xinhua* News Service (English), (Beijing), 29 April 1993, in Foreign Broadcast Information Service (hereafter, FBIS), (Washington, DC), FBIS-CHI-93-081 (29 April 1993), p. 21. He Dongchang headed the Education Ministry in 1985, when it was upgraded to commission status and served therein as senior vice-minister from then until his ouster in 1992. He has long been identified as "conservative" and most recently with the cause of leftist Deng Liqun. Deng nevertheless remains an ideological force to be reckoned with at *China Education News* which is a SEC publication (e.g., see, issue of 30 August 1994, p. 1). He Dongchang's reputation as a hardliner derived especially from his association with the effort to impose political discipline and fight "bourgeois liberalism" within the academic community during the post-1989 years. See, for example: *Agence France Presse* (Beijing), 15 January 1992 and 17 June 1992; *Kyodo* News International (Hong Kong), 5 March 1992 and 16 June 1992; Daniel Southerland in *Washington Post* Foreign Service (Washington, DC) 26 August 1989, 18 April 1990, 18 May 1991; and, Lin Musen, "He Dongchang xiatai qianhou" (Before and After He Dongchang's Removal), *Chengming* (Hong Kong), No. 7(1992), pp. 23–25.

3. *Zhongguo jiaoyu bao*, 7 April 1993, Zhou Daping, "Xin ren guojia jiaowei zhuren Zhu Kaixuan tan: Zhongguo jiaoyu gaige de jinpo renwu" (Newly Appointed Head of the Education Commission Zhu Kaixuan Discusses the Pressing Tasks of China's Education Reform), *Liaowang zhoukan* (Outlook Weekly), overseas edition (Hong Kong), No. 16 (19 April 1993), pp. 8–9; *Zhongguo xinwenshe* (China News Agency), (Beijing), 9 April 1993, trans. in FBIS-CHI-93-079 (27 April 1993), p. 24.
4. "Lianghui jujiao: hushi jiaoyu jiang shi Zhonghua minzu de zainan" (Focus on the Two Sessions: Neglecting Education Will Mean Disaster for the Chinese Nation), *Zhongguo xinwenshe* (Beijing), 25 March 1993.
5. See *Zhongguo jiaoyu bao*, 18 through 26 March 1993. Records from the Consultative Congress, a united front advisory body for intellectuals and non-communist personages, showed that delegates introduced a total of 1,799 submissions or opinions during the March 1993 session, of which 209 addressed educational issues. Most of these concerned the need for more investment and better teachers' compensation including especially housing and salaries at the tertiary level and remuneration for rural school teachers (*Zhongguo jiaoyu bao*, 25 March 1993). A total of 2,093 delegates attended the CPPCC March 1993 session.
6. *Xinhua* News Service (English), (Beijing), 24 August 1993, in FBIS-CHI-93-164 (26 August 1993), p. 28.; also, Zhu's report to the NPC Standing Committee, in *Xinhua* (Chinese), (Beijing), 28 October 1993, trans. in FBIS-CHI-93-208 (29 October 1993), p. 14; full text in *Zhongguo jiaoyu bao*, 30 October 1993.
7. Leslie Nai-kwai Lo, "The Changing Educational System," in *China Review 1993*, edited by Joseph Cheng Yu-shek and Maurice Brosseau (Hong Kong: Chinese University Press, 1993), esp. pp. **22**.12–20; Lynn Webster Paine, "Progress and Problems in China's Educational Reform," in *China Briefing, 1994*, edited by William A. Joseph (Boulder, Colorado: Westview Press, 1994), esp. pp. 125–40; Cheng Jieming, *Zhongguo jiaoyu gaige* (China's Education Reform), (Hong Kong: Commercial Press, 1992), esp. chaps. 4 and 7.
8. For a clear summary of these complicated evolving arrangements, see, "Jichu jiaoyu: jichu jiaoyu difang fuze fenji guanli" (Basic Education: Local Responsibility and Separate-level Management for Basic Education), *Zhongguo jiaoyu nianjian, 1990* (Yearbook of Education in China, 1990), (n.p.: Renmin jiaoyu chubanshe, 1991), p. 99.
9. Zhou Daping, "Tuoqian jiaoshi gongzi: yige bixu zhuajin jiejue de wenti" (Defaulted Teachers Wages: A Problem That Must Be Firmly Resolved), *Liaowang zhoukan* (Outlook Weekly), domestic edition (Beijing), No. 42 (18 October 1993), p. 8; also, Zhu Kaixuan's October report to the NPC Standing Committee.

10. China's school teachers have since the 1950s, been distinguished between those with regular credentials receiving state salaries, and those less qualified who are hired by local communities and paid from local earnings. The two are commonly referred to as *gongban* and *minban*, respectively. By the early 1970s, most urban *minban* teachers had been "regularized" or brought within the state-salaried system leaving locally-hired *minban* teachers to serve primarily in rural schools. There they have continued to work side-by-side with *gongban* colleagues, usually for much less pay and no pensions or other benefits. As of 1990, about 40% (or 2.3 million) of China's (5.58 million) full-time elementary school teachers were locally-hired. Of the three million full-time teachers in general secondary schools, 307,408 were locally-hired and virtually all worked at the junior secondary level. See, *Zhongguo jiaoyu chengjiu: tonji ziliao, 1986–1990* (Achievement of Education in China: Statistics, 1986–1990), edited by Guojia jiaoyu weiyuanhui jihua jianshe si (State Commission, Planning and Construction Department) (n.p.: Renmin jiaoyu chubanshe, 1991), pp. 61, 75. In 1994, SEC sources cited 2.3 million as the total number of *minban* teachers (*Zhongguo jiaoyu bao*, 29 June and 14 November 1994).

11. Among the major documents marking the centre's 1993 effort to halt the related practices of defaulting on payments to farmers and excessive local levies were: a party-state "Urgent Circular on Drastic Measures to Reduce Peasants' Burdens" (text, *Nongmin ribao* [Farmers' Daily], Beijing, 23 March 1993); a new Agriculture Law (text, *Renmin ribao*, 4 July 1993); and an elaborate party-state circular itemizing the types of local levies to be abolished or revised (text, *Renmin ribao*, 25 July 1993). The latter was reminiscent of lists drawn up by rural reformers in the 1930s, when the system of local burdens and levies was usually described as "kaleidoscopic" and rural teacher' salaries were often in arrears.

 If the July circular was actually intended as a guide for local action, the main item on education levies was equivocal, allowing much scope for variable interpretation in practice including that cited in the *Liaowang* account. Accordingly: "Raising funds for rural education can be temporarily stopped or abolished, except for the specific amounts approved to reconstruct dangerous school buildings," by the designated authorities (Section I, part 1, item 14). Among the contributions to be categorically abolished were those to be spent on reaching targets for new school buildings and the creation of educationally advanced townships and counties (Section II, items 2, 3, 4). Nor was any education item included among the 29 types of fees permitted to continue (Section I, part 5).

12. *Renmin ribao*, 4 July 1993.
13. Text, *Teachers' Law of the People's Republic of China* (*Zhonghua renmin gongheguo jiaoshifa*), in *Renmin ribao*, 3 November 1993.

14. "Guowuyuan bangongting guanyu caiqu youli cuoshi xunsu jiejue tuoqian jiaoshi gongzi wenti de tongzhi" (State Council Office Circular on Adopting Firm Measures for Quickly Solving the Problem of Defaulted Teachers' Salaries), Gongbanfa (1993) 78 hao, 16 November 1993, in *"Zhonghua renmin gongheguo jiaoshifa" xuexi xuanchuan cailiao* (Study Propaganda Materials for the "Teachers' Law of the People's Republic of China"), (n.p.; n. pub., December 1993), pp. 25–26.
15. Editorial, *Zhongguo jiaoyu bao*, 28 August 1993. Texts of SEC and accompanying State Council circulars aimed at curbing excessive fees are in *Zhongguo jiaoyu bao*, 28 August 1993, and 2 October 1993, respectively.
16. *Zhongguo jiaoyu bao*, 10 March 1993.
17. Henansheng nongcun shehui jingji diaocha dui, "Nongcun xueling ertong shixue de xianzhuang, yuanyin ji duice" (The Current Situation of Rural School-aged Children's Non-attendance, Its Reasons, and Solutions), *Renkou yanjiu* (Population Research), (Beijing), No. 3 (1994), p. 64.
18. *Ming Pao* (Hong Kong), 11 January 1994. The projects' work has been covered extensively by *Ming Pao*. See also, Huang Zhuanhui, *Zhongguo "xiwang gongcheng" jishi* (A Report on China's "Project Hope"), (Hong Kong and Beijing: Wenhui chubanshe and zuojia chubanshe, 1994). Controversy over the integrity of project finances was reflected in a *Next Magazine* article (*Yizhoukan*, Hong Kong, No. 202 [21 January 1994], pp. 48–59). Besides threatening to sue publications which wrote in this vein, however, Beijing set up a National Supervisory Commission for Project Hope in December 1994.
19. *Zhongguo jiaoyu bao*, 21 November 1994.
20. SEC statistical bulletins, texts, in *Zhongguo jiaoyu bao*, 15 March 1993 and 19 March 1994, respectively.
21. Text, *Renmin ribao*, 1 March 1994.
22. *Xinhua* News Agency (English), (Beijing), 14 November 1994, in *Summary of World Broadcasts* (hereafter, *SWB*), BBC Monitoring, Reading, England, FE/2157 G/10 (19 November 1994).
23. *Renmin ribao*, 1 March 1994.
24. *Zhongguo tongxunshe* (China News Service) (Hong Kong), 25 February 1993, trans. in *SWB*, FE/1630 B2/4 (6 March 1993).
25. The definitions have been widely reprinted, e.g.: "Xiaoxue jiaoyu" (Elementary School Education), *Zhongguo jiaoyu nianjian, 1982–1984* (China Education Yearbook, 1982–1984), (Changsha: Hunan jiaoyu chubanshe, 1986), pp. 76–78.
26. *Xinhua* News Service (Chinese), (Beijing), 13 and 15 March 1994, both trans. in *SWB*, FE/1951 S1/4 (21 March 1994). Only Beijing and Tibet had reportedly never defaulted in paying their school teachers; 16 provinces plus Shanghai and Tianjin met or "basically" met the 1 January deadline. Of the 10

provinces which did not, Henan was the worst offender with 120 million yuan still in arrears. Others in this category were: Hubei, Anhui, Hebei, Inner Mongolia, Hunan, Shaanxi, and Fujian (*Renmin ribao*, 12 January 1994).
27. The Education Law draft was approved by the NPC Standing Committee in November (*Zhongguo jiaoyu bao*, 22 November 1994), and was formally adopted at the March 1995 meeting of the NPC (text in, *Renmin ribao*, 22 March 1995).
28. *Xinhua*, 15 March 1994 (see above, Note 26), budget statement, text, *Renmin ribao*, 25 March 1994.
29. Guojia jiaowei guojia jiaoyu fazhan yanjiu zhongxin, "Jiaoyu tizhi gaige de xin silu" (New Thoughts About Education System Reform), *Liaowang* (Beijing), No. 9 (28 February 1994), pp. 4–7.
30. Yang Chunmao (SEC Personnel Office Director), "Jichu jiaoyu de jichu zai dongyao" (The Basis of Basic Education Is Being Undermined), *Liaowang* (Beijing), No. 4 (24 January 1994), pp. 13–14. A national conference was held in October to "exchange experiences" on the teachers' housing problem (*Zhongguo jiaoyu bao*, 23 October 1994). As with salaries and housing, the declining ability of the state-sponsored health insurance system to cover expenses for state-salaried school employees became a serious problem in the early 1990s. For a detailed account, see the three-part series in *Zhongguo jiaoyu bao*, 8, 15, and 22 January 1995.
31. *Zhongguo jiaoyu bao*, 24 August 1994. For another analysis also citing 1993 autumn semester data, and discussing government efforts in 1993 and 1994 to control school fee increases, see, Zhou Daping, "Gui zai you xu, nan zai you xu: guanyu zhongxiaoxue shoufei de guancha yu sikao" (The Important and Difficult Thing Is Order: Observations and Reflections on Collecting School Fees), *Liaowang* (Beijing), No. 46 (14 November 1994), pp. 14–19.
32. *Gongren ribao* (Worker's Daily), (Beijing), 27 August 1993.
33. Texts of conference speeches by Jiang Zemin, Li Peng, and Li Lanqing are in *Zhongguo jiaoyu bao*, 20, 21, and 22 June 1994, respectively. Other conference news in *Zhongguo jiaoyu bao*, 15 through 18 June 1994. The State Council's follow-up "Opinion on Implementing the 'Outline for China's Educational Reform and Development'," 3 July 1994, is in *Zhongguo jiaoyu bao*, 28 August 1994.
34. State Council, "Opinion on Implementing the 'Outline' ..." (Article 23), and Li Peng's June conference speech.
35. "Opinion on Implementing the 'Outline' ..." (Article 24), and *China Daily*, 14 September 1994.
36. "Opinion on Implementing the 'Outline' ..." (Article 26), and *Zhongguo jiaoyu bao*, 14 November 1994.

37. *Xinhua* News Agency (Chinese), (Xian), 20 November 1994, in *Wen Wei Po* (Hong Kong), 21 November 1994.
38. From a three-part series in *Zhongguo jiaoyu bao*, 21, 23, and 24 January 1995. Also on the urban/rural residency division, see Note 69.
39. *Renmin ribao*, 12 and 19 January 1995; *Zhongguo jiaoyu bao*, 12 and 18 January 1995.
40. Liu Bin, "Guanyu shenhua nongcun jiaoyu zonghe gaige de jige wenti" (Some Problems on Deepening the Comprehensive Reform of Rural Education), *Renmin jiaoyu* (People's Education), (Beijing), No. 12 (1994), p. 7.
41. For example, *Renmin ribao*, 4 August 1993 (article by Zhu Kaixuan, p. 3).
42. Xi Ling, "Sili xuexiao duowei toushi" (Multi-dimensional Perspective on Private Schools), *Shehui* (Society), (Shanghai), No. 3 (1994), p. 34.
43. *Zhongguo jiaoyu bao*, 23 June 1994; also *Zhongguo jiaoyu bao*, 2 February, 6 June, 25 and 28 November 1994.
44. *Guangming ribao* (Guangming Daily), 16 October 1994.
45. *Zhongguo tongji nianjian, 1988* (Statistical Yearbook of China, 1988), (Beijing: Zhongguo tongji chubanshe, 1988), p. 889; and *Zhongguo jiaoyu nianjian, 1949–1981* (China Education Yearbook, 1949–1981), (Beijing: Zhongguo dabaike quanshu chubanshe, 1984), pp. 1001, 1021.
46. *Statistical Yearbook of China, 1983* (Hong Kong: Economic Information and Agency, 1983), p. 148; Statistical Yearbook of China, 1986 (Hong Kong: Economic Information and Agency, 1986), p. 109.
47. *Zhongguo tongji nianjian, 1992* (Statistical Yearbook of China, 1992), (Beijing: Zhongguo tongji chubanshe, 1992), pp. 323, 726.
48. *Zhongguo tongji nianjian, 1994*, p. 562; and *Zhongguo jiaoyu bao*, 17 November 1994.
49. For an early account of the practical drawbacks based on Chinese experience, see Lu-Dzai Djung, *A History of Democratic Education in Modern China* (Shanghai: Commercial Press, 1934), chap. 6, esp. pp. 135–38. The classic account in the international literature is, Philip J. Foster, "The Vocational School Fallacy in Development Planning," in *Power and Ideology in Education*, edited by Jerome Karabel and A. H. Halsey (New York: Oxford University Press, 1977), pp. 356–65.
50. *Xinhua* News Agency (English), (Beijing), 30 March 1993, in FBIS-CHI-93-060 (31 March 1993), pp. 36–37.
51. Text, Li Peng's report, in *Zhongguo jiaoyu bao*, 21 June 1994.
52. Text, State Council's "Opinion," in *Zhongguo jiaoyu bao*, 28 August 1994.
53. *Renmin ribao*, 28 January 1995. The new curriculum is part of the comprehensive reform of rural education publicized at a national conference in September 1994. Speeches from the conference are in *Renmin jiaoyu*, Nos. 11 and 12 (1994).

54. A SEC manifesto for renewed tertiary-level reform actually preceded the 1993 "Outline": "SEC Opinion on Hastening Reform ... in Higher Education," 8 December 1992, text, in *Guangming ribao*, (Beijing), 18 February 1993.
55. Over 300 institutions of higher learning require a few weeks of basic training during the four-year undergraduate course (see, Li Tieying's interview, in *Zhongguo jiaoyu bao*, 30 March 1993).
56. *Zhongguo jiaoyu bao*, 21 June 1994 and 7 July 1994.
57. For details of the late 1980s reforms, see Suzanne Pepper, *China's Education Reform in the 1980s*, China Research Monograph No. 36 (Berkeley: University of California, 1990), chap. 7.
58. Zhu's report to the NPC Standing Committee, in *Zhongguo jiaoyu bao*, 30 October 1994. Specialized senior middle schools began charging tuition in the early 1990s.
59. Zhu's comments at an NPC press briefing, in *Zhongguo jiaoyu bao*, 14 March 1994.
60. *Zhongguo jiaoyu bao*, 7 July 1994.
61. See the 1994 enrolment regulations, in *Zhongguo jiaoyu bao*, 21 June 1994. Most other accounts cite a higher figure of RMB 1,000 to RMB 1,500, which may be inclusive of dormitory fees (e.g., *Zhongguo jiaoyu bao*, 5 April 1994 and 9 May 1994). Nor is it clear that the experiment actually aims to abolish the practice of allowing some students to enrol "outside the plan" (assuming their examination scores are equal to others), in return for the highest self-financed rates cited above.
62. *Zhongguo jiaoyu bao*, 17 November 1994, and *China Daily*, 14 November 1994.
63. See the State Council's "Opinion" on implementing the "Outline" (Article 16).
64. For example, *Zhongguo jiaoyu bao*, 21 June 1994 and 13 August 1994.
65. See the SEC's "Opinion" on higher education development (Article 3), in *Guangming ribao*, 18 February 1993; and *Xinhua* News Agency (English), (Beijing), 22 May 1993, in FBIS-CHI-93-099 (25 May 1993), p. 24.
66. *Xinhua* News Agency (English), (Beijing), 9 January 1992, in Joint Publications Research Service (Washington, DC), JPRS-CAR-92-013 (9 March 1992), p. 15; and *China Daily*, 26 July 1994.
67. *Xinhua* News Agency (English), (Beijing), 4 April 1994, in *SWB*, FE/1972 G/6–7 (15 April 1994).
68. Zhou Daping, "Ruhe huanjie gaoxiao biyesheng gongxu maodun" (How to Solve the Contradition between Supply and Demand for College Graduates), *Liaowang*, No. 3 (16 January 1995), pp. 10–11.
69. The household registration system remains formally in effect as a means of population control, but is also in a gradual process of revision to permit more

flexibility. According to official statistics, as of early 1994, 900 million people were regarded as being "peasants" with domiciles in the countryside, that is, registered rural residents. But of that number, only 797 million or 88% resided in the countryside, while the remaining 105 million have moved into urban areas. Of those still residing in the countryside, 523 million were working-age of whom only 420 million were actually engaged in agricultural pursuits, while the remainder worked in "non-agricultural spheres." See, *Zhongguo tongxun she* (Hong Kong), 19 January 1994. trans. in *SWB*, FEW/0319 WG/10 (9 February 1994).

70. For an explanation based on the SEC's 1992 plan, see, Zhou Daping, "Guojia jiaowei fuzeren jiu jiakuai gaige he fazhan gaodeng jiaoyu da benkan jizhe wen" (A Responsible Person from the SEC Answers Questions by Our Reporter About Quickening Reform and Development of Higher Education), *Liaowang*, overseas edition (Hong Kong), No. 51 (21 December 1992), pp. 8–9.
71. *Renmin ribao* and *Zhongguo jiaoyu bao*, 12 January 1994.
72. *Zhongguo tongji nianjian, 1994*, pp. 558, 561.
73. Ibid., p. 570; also, Zhou Chuan, "211 gongcheng — wo guo gaodeng jiaoyu xiandaihua jianshe de dianjixing gongcheng" (Project 211 — A Foundation-laying Project for Our Country's Modernization of Higher Education), *Jiaoyu yanjiu* (Education Research), (Beijing), No. 1 (1994), p. 38. For an early reference, see C. H. Becker et al., *The Reorganisation of Education in China* (Paris: League of Nation's Institute of Intellectual Co-operation, 1932), chap. 9. World Bank studies throughout the 1980s and into the 1990s have also consistently cited this problem.
74. For example, the SEC 1992 "Opinion" on higher education reform (Article 2); also Zhou Daping, "Guojia jiaowei fuzeren ..." (Note 70), p. 8.
75. Zhu's NPC Standing Committee report, in *Zhongguo jiaoyu bao*, 30 October 1993; and his 1993 year-end report, in *Zhongguo jiaoyu bao*, 13 January 1994.
76. *Zhongguo jiaoyu bao*, 7 April 1994.
77. *Zhongguo jiaoyu bao*, 5 February 1994.
78. *Xinhua* News Agency (English), (Beijing), 10 May 1994, in FBIS-CHI-94-091 (11 May 1994), p. 22; and *Zhongguo jiaoyu bao*, 21 May 1994.

19

Economic Development and Institutional Change: Vascillating at the Crossroads

Carsten Herrmann-Pillath

1. After the Boom: The Challenge of 1994

Entering 1995, the outside world's mood regarding China's prospects for rapid growth and further moves toward the market economy has changed. Headline stories involving Lehman Brothers, Venturetech, McDonalds and pirated CDs point to events that remind many observers and business people of the still unpredictable conditions in China: they see the rule of law as the most important ingredient in the market economy.[1] In China, this issue is all the more important because the Chinese as well as the rest of the world know that China's rapid growth will only be possible if large-scale foreign direct investments (FDI) in energy, transport, environment, communications, and education are there to ease the much-discussed "bottlenecks" in the economy. But this sort of FDI is different from producing shoes in China. It is intimately linked to China's legal infrastructure. And this legal infrastructure also affects other major determinants of economic development, such as the role of Hong Kong as a major link between China and the world.[2]

Between 1994 and 1995, however, other major problems in the Chinese economy such as inflation and the apparent inability of the central government to cope with the challenge have again come to the fore.[3] Hence, there is now some danger that changes in the attitude of the outside world toward China might generate negative results with respect to China's development, such as a decline in FDI which might otherwise contribute to easing the bottlenecks. Therefore, the linkage between China and the outside world's perception of it is a key factor of her development.[4] Given the many divergent views and problems of measurement, one of the basic challenges for academic analysis as well as practical action is to sort out the fundamentals that determine medium- and long-run institutional change and growth.

Unfortunately, assessing Chinese economic development in the 1990s

---

Research reported in this chapter received the support of the Volkswagen Foundation within the framework of the "European Project on China's Modernization: Contemporary Patterns of Cultural and Economic Change," headed by this writer and Helmut Martin, University of Bochum. I am especially grateful for the assistance of Dr Song Xueming, Franz Vogg and Thomas Templin. Thanks are also due to Fan Gang who provided valuable material on Chinese views concerning the state of the economy in late 1994.

is an extremely difficult task. Most observers agree that it is no longer meaningful to talk about China's economy in terms of national averages. Nevertheless it is still common to analyze China's inflation, China's infrastructural development or China's foreign economic relations. However, the crucial issue as regards Chinese economic policy today is regional development with large absolute differences between the provinces and larger regions and with divergence or convergence (depending on the yardsticks used).[5] This issue covers many aspects of economic change in China, as for instance, divergent agricultural development or regional differences in the distribution of state-owned enterprises which, however, may be caused by sectors not related to regional development *per se*.[6] Whereas in the 1980s the Chinese leadership tried to rely on a policy of unbalanced regional development in order to foster growth of the economy as a whole, in the 1990s important policy measures are directed at regaining a path of balanced regional growth. This change of emphasis was at least partly a reaction to the perceived failure of the "trickle down" strategy favouring the coastal regions in the 1980s.

Between 1992 and 1994, Chinese policy-making took two different approaches to a solution that we will assess in the following pages. After Deng Xiaoping's southern tour in the spring of 1992, China was drawn into a quasi-Maoist campaign toward a market economy which "removed" many institutional obstacles inhibiting rapid change in the inland provinces. This triggered a remarkable economic boom which made some observers in the West believe that China would become the world's next "economic superpower." However, that approach was followed by considerable problems in maintaining social stability and stability-inducing administrative structures. In 1993 and 1994, the central government tried to remould institutions and organizations as outlined by the Central Committee decision on the socialist market economy in autumn 1993.[7]

The year 1994 may therefore be regarded as a watershed for China's economic development and institutional change as a whole. As we will see, the crucial problem is how to set up an institutional framework for achieving convergent regional development. Once the boom is past, China needs to settle down in a new economic system for the next century. Many important acts of legislation were passed in 1994, but it will require several years for them to be turned into reality. Some measures, like the new Corporate Law, will only be fully realized in the next century.[8] If those efforts prove successful, China will continue her rapid growth. But if China fails to build suitable institutions, the bubble may burst.

Hence it is the main contention of this chapter that 1994 was decisive for China's future in two respects which also form the basic questions addressed in this chapter. First, has China embarked on the road to balanced or convergent regional development? Second, will the central government be able to design institutional as well as infrastructural frameworks for regional development, or will China reshape itself by means of a declining central role in China's political, societal and economic dynamics?[9] Section two of this chapter will assess the Chinese business cycle from a regional perspective through the end of 1993. This will be followed by an examination of China's macroeconomic development in 1994. Finally, important aspects of institutional change in 1994 will be analyzed in an attempt to answer the two questions raised above.

2. The Chinese Business Cycle and Long-term Growth: A Regional Approach

Assessing China's Wealth in 1994: A Choice from the Menu

First of all, we need to broaden our view of China's growth. Table 1 gives an overview of different estimates of China's gross domestic product (GDP) per-capita in RMB and US dollar, using different methods of computing the exchange rate, and by using different indices of purchasing-power parity (PPP). The magnitude of GDP as well as annual growth rate varies greatly depending on the method used. Although it is clear that one cannot use the method based on official exchange rates to assess change and development, using alternate approaches also gives rise to serious methodological problems.

Reasons underlying difference between PPP and the exchange rate are well-known. But the Chinese experience seems to be a puzzle. The large gap between the exchange rate and the PPP is conventionally explained as reflecting the fact that the former is a marginal value with respect to tradeables, whereas the latter is an average value including both tradeables and non-tradeables. If the productivity gap between a country's tradeable sector to that of the world average is larger than the gap in the non-tradeables sector (as in the case of services) then the PPP and the exchange rate will differ systematically. This is normally the case in a developing country. Hence one could argue that as development proceeds, the gap should diminish. However, China experienced a systematic

Table 1. China's Per-capita GDP According to Different Estimates

Jahr	BSPoff	BSPoff	BSPoff	World Bank	WPT5	Taylor	BSPtr	BSPppp
	1993 prices Yuan	Current prices US$	1993 prices US$	Current prices US$	1993 prices US$	1993 prices US$	1993 prices US$	1993 prices US$
1978	1007	222.7	503.4	230.0	2531.8	594.2	409.3	610.6
1979	1088	265.6	539.3	260.0	2673.7	628.7	436.4	651.0
1980	1133	304.3	544.4	290.0	2878.9	657.2	445.9	665.2
1981	1165	281.5	456.2	300.0	—	679.9	456.2	680.6
1982	1226	272.1	415.6	310.0	—	729.3	479.5	715.4
1983	1333	287.5	425.5	300.0	—	791.5	526.2	785.0
1984	1531	288.4	410.3	310.0	—	893.8	604.9	902.5
1985	1697	277.2	379.6	310.0	3347.3	982.6	668.9	997.8
1986	1779	263.3	349.7	300.0	—	1044.1	700.6	1045.2
1987	1900	279.9	356.9	290.0	—	1133.8	747.6	1115.3
1988	1960	343.1	419.8	330.0	3024.5	1231.5	767.3	1144.6
1989	1860	379.7	442.9	350.0	—	1265.2	724.2	1080.4
1990	1967	325.9	361.7	370.0	—	1299.3	766.5	1143.5
1991	2145	330.3	351.4	370.0	—	1385.0	836.3	1247.6
1992	2401	379.5	390.9	470.0	—	1555.8	934.9	1394.6
1993	2663	462.2	462.2	—	—	1743.8	1033.8	1542.3
1994	2907	407.5	399.5	—	—	1935.6	1139.7	1700.3

Quoted or calculated according to the methods used in:
BSPoff: GDP according to the *State Statistical Yearbook* and calculated according to the official exchange rate;
World Bank: *World Development Report*, different issues;
WPT5: R. Summers and A. Heston, "A New Set of International Comparisons of Real Product and Price Levels Estimates for 130 Countries, 1950–1980," *Review of Income and Wealth*, Vol. 34, pp. 1–25, and Summers and Heston, "The Penn World Table (Mark 5): An Expanded Set of International Comparisons, 1950–1988," *Quarterly Journal of Economics*, 1991, p. 352.
Taylor: J. R. Taylor, "Dollar GNP Estimates for China," CIR Staff Paper No. 59, Center for International Research, US Bureau of Census, Washington, DC, 1991.
BSPppp: Author's calculations of PPP, using Taylor's base year value of absolute PPP and calculating US$/RMB relative inflation rates.
BSPtr: Author's calculations of PPP, taking the 1981 US$/RMB exchange rate as PPP.
Calculations by Song Xueming.

widening of the gap between the PPP and the exchange rate, contrary to the textbook predictions. Two explanations come to mind. Both of them presuppose that there is a large gap between China's tradeables sector and that of the world in terms of productivity. In the first explanation, the growth of the tradeables sector increases its weight in determining the exchange rate; and in the second, the productivity of the tradeables sector has been lagging further behind that of the world's productivity. Since the exchange rate is a marginal concept, the first explanation is discarded in favour of the second, which means that the alleged "greater wealth" of China simply mirrors extensive growth at the expense of productivity advances.[10] This seems to be the inevitable conclusion from the comparison between changes in the exchange rate and PPP and can only be rejected if the argument concerning PPP as a yardstick of wealth is rejected.

In the export sector, this fact is reflected in the speed by which the cost of earning one dollar from exports in China catches up with changes in the exchange rate. This was the case since the early 1980s and again in late 1994 when it was reported that those costs reached RMB8.5/US$1. Of course, the other side of the coin is the simple fact that many Chinese industrial enterprises cannot compete with imports, a problem at the heart of the General Agreement on Tariffs and Trade (GATT) issue and the Chinese practice of heavily protectionist tariffs.[11]

Apparently, there has been no discussion of what our choice of the computing method may mean if regional differences in purchasing power are considered, too. If we choose one of the most simple approaches, provincial figures may simply be computed by taking account of regionally divergent inflation measured according to a base year to the present (see Tables 2a, b, for figures computed for the provinces base year 1981 according to Taylor's method). This is done in Figure 1 for 1993 (provincial GDP figures for 1994 were not yet available at the time of writing).

There would be substantial changes in our view in China's economic development if such a simple exercise were to become the basis for standard evaluation. For example, the differences in levels of GDP in terms of provincial PPP-US$ do not show the same magnitude as compared with the deflated figures using the official data. Moreover, the relative positions of provinces also change. As compared with the official data, this means that there are provinces whose GDP in terms of PPP-figures deviates more from the national average (e.g., Hunan in the negative direction or Xinjiang in the positive direction) as well as the other way round (including Guangdong, Shanghai and the rest of the rich regions on the positive side). Or, Fujian is ahead of Shandong according to the official figures, and just the other way round according to the PPP calculation. Hence we could argue that there is no justification for taking Chinese statistical data at face

Figure 1. Deviation of Per Capita GDP from Country Average by Provinces in 1993 (%)

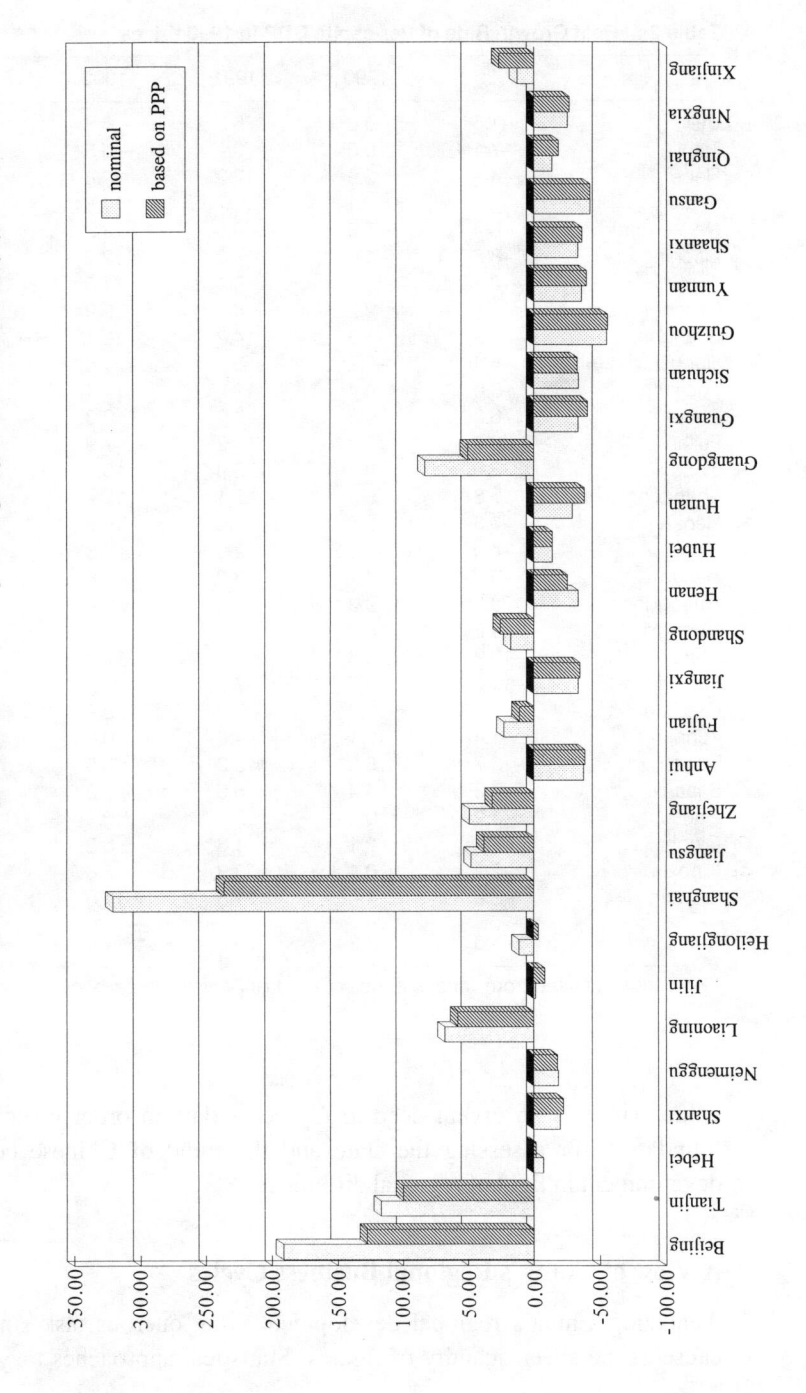

Table 2a. Real Growth Rate of Per-capita GDP in 1990 Prices*

	1989	1990	1991	1992	1993
Beijing	−1.5	−0.6	6.9	6.8	1.2
Tianjin	−7.1	0.6	0.2	6.5	9.9
Hebei	−4.9	3.9	12.2	12.4	18.1
Shanxi	−2.2	7.1	1.7	10.8	7.1
Neimenggu	−6.4	7.0	6.0	8.3	11.6
Liaoning	−8.6	−1.0	4.8	12.5	20.3
Jilin	−12.5	0.6	−0.4	11.5	14.8
Heilongjiang	−2.4	2.2	6.4	5.9	8.7
Shanghai	−11.8	−3.9	4.2	12.1	18.1
Jiangsu	−8.4	−0.2	5.7	24.8	16.9
Zhejiang	−8.0	4.4	12.8	14.4	15.4
Anhui	−6.2	−0.8	−8.0	10.3	16.5
Fujian	−2.7	7.4	14.2	17.9	25.1
Jiangxi	−6.9	9.2	5.9	13.3	8.2
Shandong	−5.8	5.4	13.1	15.7	20.7
Henan	−7.3	2.5	7.0	14.6	17.0
Hubei	−4.9	4.9	2.0	5.3	7.9
Hunan	−9.0	7.1	5.2	4.8	10.2
Guangdong	−3.8	9.3	17.9	18.4	14.3
Guangxi	−5.3	8.3	10.6	17.7	11.4
Hainan	−10.9	3.8	7.7	17.3	26.8
Sichuan	−11.0	9.7	7.8	7.2	11.3
Guizhou	−7.0	2.9	7.3	5.1	4.6
Yunnan	−1.4	18.1	4.6	6.8	5.5
Tibet	−12.7	8.5	15.2	2.6	−3.2
Shaanxi	−7.3	4.4	6.0	3.0	8.8
Gansu	−5.2	0.3	2.7	9.1	1.3
Qinghai	−8.7	2.1	1.8	5.2	9.2
Ningxia	−2.2	0.1	3.3	3.8	8.5
Xinjiang	−2.2	4.6	11.8	11.5	9.8
China	−5.0	4.3	9.2	11.9	10.8

* Percent calculated from various issues of *China's Statistical Yearbook*.

value. There is an urgent need to reprocess data in order to lay a solid foundation for assessing the state and the trend of Chinese economic development in light of regional differences.

A View of China's Regional Business Cycles

Analyzing China's regional development is an onerous task simply because of the sheer quantity of figures. Statistical approaches may help to

Table 2b. Real Growth Rate of National Income Per Capita, in 1990 Prices

	1979	1980	1981	1982	1983	1984	1985	1986	1987	1988	1989	1990	1991	1992
Beijing	7.8	7.1	—	—	—	14.6	13.7	-0.2	-1.1	10.2	6.9	1.0	5.8	13.3
Tianjin	6.0	2.8	1.1	1.8	5.9	10.5	14.7	3.7	5.7	4.0	0.0	-1.6	2.7	8.6
Hebei	15.6	-5.0	-1.2	7.6	10.6	13.9	12.1	3.9	8.4	9.7	2.2	-0.7	7.2	12.0
Shanxi	3.7	-0.6	1.9	16.6	10.4	20.3	7.0	3.0	0.7	6.2	3.0	1.1	1.6	12.0
Neimenggu	4.2	3.6	6.5	17.5	5.9	13.8	12.9	0.4	4.4	10.4	1.1	4.6	7.0	7.2
Liaoning	2.6	3.5	-4.9	2.3	11.5	15.0	11.3	6.7	8.4	9.2	1.6	-3.0	4.0	13.6
Jilin	1.0	12.0	3.7	6.0	23.7	11.4	6.8	5.8	14.8	11.7	-5.8	0.8	2.6	11.7
Heilongjiang	10.0	3.2	-1.7	5.3	9.3	8.9	4.2	7.7	5.0	6.1	2.5	2.7	1.6	3.2
Shanghai	14.0	3.9	2.7	3.0	5.4	12.2	12.1	2.3	5.5	9.7	2.0	-1.9	7.6	14.2
Jiangsu	16.3	14.3	8.0	8.4	13.1	17.8	16.1	9.2	9.0	14.4	-1.1	1.7	6.5	26.5
Zhejiang	12.1	4.7	10.5	10.9	5.7	22.2	24.2	12.4	11.4	10.4	-0.5	3.9	15.4	15.5
Anhui	3.3	14.1	5.8	6.7	6.8	18.6	15.0	9.0	6.5	6.6	2.7	-0.3	-6.0	20.2
Fujian	11.8	0.2	12.0	5.3	2.2	16.2	16.3	4.5	9.8	14.1	7.1	1.5	13.1	19.9
Jiangxi	5.6	—	3.0	6.3	5.0	10.3	13.2	4.7	8.1	9.2	4.3	0.9	5.8	11.7
Shandong	8.1	8.6	6.7	6.7	10.2	17.6	9.4	6.5	14.1	12.2	2.6	0.9	11.6	16.5
Henan	15.4	3.8	6.3	0.3	19.5	10.3	-13.7	4.1	13.1	6.0	2.0	-1.2	5.3	14.3
Hubei	8.3	2.7	7.8	8.8	5.9	19.5	15.3	3.6	5.0	5.0	0.3	-1.9	2.6	5.1
Hunan	4.9	12.3	3.0	8.3	5.3	8.7	10.3	6.4	4.1	9.3	1.0	1.0	5.5	5.5
Guangdong	3.9	6.2	8.3	7.2	3.6	13.9	17.0	7.4	14.3	26.9	4.9	4.6	16.8	19.7
Guangxi	—	—	5.0	12.2	2.0	2.5	8.5	6.2	7.4	2.4	2.3	4.4	9.9	17.8
Hainan										—	3.4	4.2	9.1	14.2
Sichuan	11.0	6.9	1.6	7.3	7.8	13.8	13.3	4.4	7.9	7.0	0.3	2.4	6.1	9.6
Guizhou	5.7	1.2	1.3	13.6	12.2	17.2	6.3	6.3	8.1	4.8	2.3	0.4	8.3	3.4
Yunnan	1.8	6.0	4.6	12.9	7.1	12.0	10.1	2.0	9.0	16.1	4.1	6.9	4.3	6.2
Tibet	—	—	—	—	—	—	10.8	-11.0	9.0	5.8	0.8	1.6	10.1	0.4
Shaanxi	7.7	5.9	0.0	9.0	5.2	15.7	14.1	4.9	7.4	9.7	2.0	0.1	7.5	3.9
Gansu	-1.6	6.1	-11.4	6.7	13.8	11.7	13.7	10.8	3.9	11.3	6.3	1.2	5.2	8.7
Qinghai	—	—	—	8.0	9.9	12.7	24.4	6.4	2.4	9.5	-0.9	0.3	1.8	8.0
Ningxia	2.2	5.5	-3.7	2.3	13.7	13.6	12.6	7.4	3.4	9.7	5.7	-1.1	0.9	5.4
Xinjiang	9.7	5.2	8.8	7.6	11.5	10.7	14.7	7.3	6.0	9.5	3.6	3.1	11.9	4.9
China	5.6	5.1	3.5	6.7	8.8	12.4	11.6	6.5	7.8	9.7	1.6	4.7	6.2	14.6

* Percent calculated according to the *State Statistical Yearbook* and the *Guomin shouru tongji ziliao huibian, 1949-85* (Zhongguo tongji chubanshe, 1987).

distill the crucial aspects. But there are many problems with respect to the coherence of data series and with the length of the period amenable to analysis.[12] Furthermore, one can argue that the specific (may be even unique) features of provinces or larger regions deserve much greater attention than general features of development which can be extracted by means of trends and mean values of statistical analysis.[13] Therefore, in the subsequent analysis, we need to look at the Chinese business cycle in terms of complete sets of data and not in terms of summary statistics. Those data, however, have been manipulated a bit in order to provide a more accurate picture of reality.[14] We will only be able to take stock of developments up to 1993 which will enable us to assess the point of departure in 1994.

After the Tiananmen incident, China experienced a pronounced swing in her notorious stop-and-go business cycle which also altered attitudes toward China in the West. The austerity drive in 1989/90 led many observers to believe that China would enter a path of economic decline similar to the other socialist planned economies. After Deng's effort to mobilize support for reform, however, strong forces of growth were released regaining for China the reputation as being one of the most successful cases of transition from a planned to a market economy.[15] Both of the above assessments may however be wrong because they focus too closely on the short term effect of the business cycle rather than the stable long-term trends of the economy and because they do not pay attention to the considerable differences in regional development.

Unfortunately, we cannot scrutinize the regional business cycles in terms of GDP figures with the exception of the most recent cycle between 1989 and 1993. Therefore one still needs to use the net material product or national income (*guomin shouru*), a concept in the socialist national accounting system. In Table 3 we report data on GNP and National Income data in 1990 prices as well as their per-capita values. The deflator is specific for each province so that the regional differences in the inflation rate are taken into account. The per-capita values seem to be preferable to the aggregate values because they immediately provide insight into the possible welfare effects of the business cycle which feedback into the political economy of institutional change in the provinces as well as political conflicts between the provinces and between the provinces and the centre.

The message of Tables 2a, b may be summarized as follows:

- the last swing of the business cycle was by far the sharpest in the

history of reform, probably including an absolute average decline of per-capita output in 1989 for the majority of the provinces;
- during the downturn, the differences in regional growth rates increased rapidly. Such a phenomenon did not occur in a similar manner during the ups and downs of the mid-1980s;
- recovery until 1993 led to converging, but still very different, provincial growth rates, with a remarkable gains in 1993;[16]
- regionally divergent growth may be linked to the fact that, during the slump, several provinces registered no growth in per-capita output for several years whereas others grew continuously.

To cite an example, in one of the core regions of state industry, the Northeast, the downward swing in the business cycle led to a hefty decrease in real per-capita GDP. One may safely assume that from the late 1980s to 1993 the business cycle in the Northeast revolved around a trend of almost no medium-run growth. The Northeast's recovery has been lagging behind since 1992. This has to be explained by the fact that roughly 60% of the state enterprises in that region face such serious financial problems, as expanding triangular debt amounting to RMB 100 billion in those three northeastern provinces by 1993.[17] This performance is duplicated in other provinces which are heavily dependent on state industries. These provinces include such extreme cases (in terms of the level of income) as Shanghai and Guizhou. Other regions, in particular the coastal provinces of Guangdong, Shandong and Jiangsu, had different experiences. The absolute decline in the level of welfare was not large in 1989, and the expansion of economic activities in 1992 and 1993 led to a virtual leap forward in terms of per-capita GDP.

Many analysts have pointed out that regional differences in growth are caused by regional differences in the distribution of state enterprises as well as the degree of economic dualism between industry and agriculture.[18] The experience of the last business cycle could support a radical version of this view: the business cycle masks the deep cleavage between provinces where change and development take place and those provinces where this is not the case. Pronounced regional differences in the business cycle can be explained by differences in long-term dynamics of growth. As, for example, is revealed in pronounced regional differences of the response to austerity measures. Hence it is meaningless to assess China's long-term prospects or the past record of reforms in terms of national averages.

The Regional Business Cycle as an Indicator of Divergent Structural Change

Such a view may be supported by other observations. For instance, business cycles in market economies normally feature pro-cyclical changes of such indicators as labour productivity and investment.[19] In Tables 3a, b, c, real growth rates of productivity (defined as the growth rate of national income per employee) for the provincial economies and for the industrial

Table 3a. Real Growth Rate of Labour Productivity (in Industry)*

	1986	1987	1988	1989	1990	1991	1992
Beijing	−2.51	3.42	2.53	−3.69	−4.34	5.16	17.05
Tianjin	−1.35	4.43	2.68	−5.12	0.64	−1.44	4.93
Hebei	−0.04	5.98	0.48	1.94	3.58	4.85	12.31
Shanxi	−1.26	−3.71	−5.00	4.48	−0.75	7.89	8.32
Neimenggu	−0.77	6.22	2.24	4.41	−3.02	6.61	6.02
Liaoning	−2.01	4.95	−1.43	−1.39	−7.58	4.68	14.41
Jilin	−3.56	15.91	1.94	−7.81	−3.85	0.12	15.57
Heilongjiang	2.81	7.27	−1.31	−1.14	−5.26	−2.74	1.34
Shanghai	−6.23	−0.88	−1.26	−7.12	−2.22	2.13	14.15
Jiangsu	0.88	2.17	−2.74	2.67	4.43	8.93	28.78
Zhejiang	2.42	3.79	−0.40	2.39	1.76	11.86	26.28
Anhui	11.44	−0.77	0.18	4.13	1.13	2.83	9.29
Fujian	5.01	3.74	4.44	2.79	0.13	6.67	9.89
Jiangxi	2.14	−0.59	−0.81	3.98	−4.62	8.01	12.12
Shandong	−8.36	12.46	−1.73	4.91	4.01	4.37	19.10
Henan	6.63	1.65	−2.37	−0.30	3.06	4.24	22.69
Hubei	−0.23	6.50	−18.98	27.36	−4.86	7.05	8.24
Hunan	−20.36	22.61	−0.62	1.79	1.49	1.45	1.11
Guangdong	−0.99	4.24	4.40	−2.47	8.27	21.00	17.07
Guangxi	3.20	2.85	−2.66	−1.80	6.93	8.78	17.35
Hainan	—	—	—	−5.84	−2.62	8.36	17.77
Sichuan	−3.15	7.55	2.18	−6.15	0.20	4.04	13.25
Guizhou	−28.05	22.67	13.00	−5.16	0.09	−0.86	10.62
Yunnan	10.60	11.99	15.32	6.28	10.97	3.19	3.11
Tibet	−23.62	7.06	4.70	67.11	−27.56	28.28	−3.50
Shaanxi	−2.85	3.64	14.05	1.94	1.69	4.02	5.96
Gansu	−8.20	−3.01	−5.85	1.59	4.40	2.49	2.78
Qinghai	5.79	8.89	9.56	2.51	−4.84	−5.60	4.95
Ningxia	1.85	−3.34	8.96	8.62	−5.40	−1.88	9.23
Xinjiang	1.70	−1.36	3.71	4.87	0.26	10.26	6.54
China	−2.12	14.79	1.96	0.00	2.25	8.09	15.02

* Percent, national income per employee, in 1990 prices calculated according to the figures (%) in the recent issues of the *Chinese Statistical Yearbook*.

Economic Development and Institutional Change

Table 3b. Real Growth Rate of Labour Productivity (GDP per Employee)*

	1989	1990	1991	1992	1993
Beijing	2.91	−0.61	12.52	9.26	12.71
Tianjin	1.16	2.39	7.04	10.72	8.85
Hebei	2.11	1.02	7.83	10.60	11.59
Shanxi	2.30	2.09	0.52	9.55	10.58
Neimenggu	1.54	4.84	2.90	8.48	6.80
Liaoning	1.51	−0.90	2.94	9.50	11.91
Jilin	−6.86	0.82	2.58	8.42	11.75
Heilongjiang	1.91	1.34	4.15	5.93	3.77
Shanghai	4.24	3.02	5.15	14.97	15.36
Jiangsu	0.99	3.18	8.46	24.27	16.43
Zhejiang	−1.08	2.56	13.10	16.65	21.10
Anhui	2.32	0.00	−5.70	13.23	17.17
Fujian	4.15	3.01	7.68	14.95	18.93
Jiangxi	2.18	1.77	5.36	13.05	10.86
Shandong	0.18	2.22	8.98	16.08	17.71
Henan	1.89	0.57	3.61	9.74	11.39
Hubei	0.98	0.45	2.91	11.10	9.37
Hunan	0.42	1.62	5.14	9.80	9.33
Guangdong	4.05	7.84	12.91	18.04	16.01
Guangxi	0.86	3.50	9.09	14.50	15.08
Hainan	2.58	7.27	7.82	19.71	18.60
Sichuan	0.43	1.44	3.90	10.17	11.43
Guizhou	−0.30	−1.02	6.38	6.19	7.03
Yunnan	3.55	5.27	2.79	7.86	6.77
Tibet	8.24	7.56	0.18	5.70	5.14
Shaanxi	0.01	0.72	5.37	6.17	10.81
Gansu	7.25	2.53	3.40	6.87	9.07
Qinghai	−0.40	0.75	1.98	4.63	7.79
Ningxia	4.43	−0.05	1.88	4.47	6.12
Xinjiang	4.68	5.60	9.32	9.92	6.48
China	2.16	1.27	4.73	10.26	9.80

* Percent, in 1990 prices.

sector are given as far as figures are available and can be processed according to the *State Statistical Yearbook*. There are pro-cyclical changes in productivity, but the degree varies across regions. This is particularly true for industry. Whereas provinces like Guangdong and Jiangsu rebounded quickly after the downturn of 1989, the Northeast as well as Shanghai responded slowly. Shanghai shows no relationship between the business cycle and productivity change in industry until 1991. It may be possible that productivity in terms of national income (Table 3c), hovers around a longer-term negative trend which is reflected in the rapid growth

Table 3c. Real Growth Rate of Labour Productivity (National Income per Employee)*

	1986	1987	1988	1989	1990	1991	1992
Beijing	-3.47	4.14	5.23	-5.86	-2.27	-3.37	12.21
Tianjin	2.74	4.15	2.72	-7.88	1.07	2.21	9.69
Hebei	1.43	7.21	2.21	-6.37	5.63	7.52	10.54
Shanxi	-3.46	-5.09	-0.79	-1.52	8.06	-1.71	10.94
Neimenggu	-0.89	3.17	12.18	-5.30	5.33	3.54	6.61
Liaoning	4.23	6.14	1.49	-6.66	-2.74	2.78	13.04
Jilin	-1.08	11.43	-4.52	-14.14	2.88	-2.75	8.99
Heilongjiang	7.88	4.79	-3.13	-3.71	4.69	-3.07	4.15
Shanghai	-2.73	2.71	-0.49	-9.50	-1.36	0.97	16.27
Jiangsu	5.10	6.07	-1.35	-7.62	3.37	3.78	27.14
Zhejiang	6.38	7.96	1.08	-8.30	0.58	11.42	15.10
Anhui	4.21	2.84	-2.05	-5.73	-1.40	-10.09	17.67
Fujian	1.35	8.11	3.95	-3.20	5.06	7.27	16.81
Jiangxi	-0.39	4.41	-2.39	-5.78	9.44	5.06	11.30
Shandong	0.15	10.76	1.40	-2.84	1.89	8.12	14.42
Henan	3.88	9.74	-3.71	-6.08	4.89	5.28	12.47
Hubei	3.57	5.93	-2.41	-7.38	2.34	1.30	5.95
Hunan	4.22	3.44	-4.96	-10.30	6.78	2.73	4.56
Guangdong	4.00	8.41	4.41	-7.20	8.79	16.53	18.54
Guangxi	4.21	5.51	-2.14	-3.16	7.41	7.91	16.57
Hainan	—	—	—	-11.32	2.24	5.31	14.81
Sichuan	-1.07	6.72	3.44	-11.52	5.27	3.66	8.27
Guizhou	2.90	4.46	1.57	-10.58	-1.09	6.10	2.35
Yunnan	-1.38	7.09	5.67	-3.82	19.11	1.68	5.17
Tibet	-18.54	3.01	7.80	-9.59	7.57	31.65	1.20
Shaanxi	0.72	4.91	4.32	-5.46	4.51	1.88	3.37
Gansu	3.79	2.32	1.13	-5.28	5.38	0.72	7.70
Qinghai	7.18	2.48	7.32	-7.05	-0.86	-2.90	6.92
Ningxia	6.32	-1.26	7.58	-1.80	-3.51	-0.51	5.04
Xinjiang	-3.74	8.90	10.04	-0.63	5.87	9.97	4.64
China	2.23	7.30	3.07	-6.58	3.58	5.03	13.69

* Percent, prices of 1990.

of losses not only in the state enterprises but also the township and village enterprises (TVEs).[20]

A similiar lack of strong pro-cyclical response can be observed in Guizhou and the western provinces. However, this impression might change if productivity in terms of GDP is scrutinized (data are available up to 1993). For instance, Shanghai displays the highest continuous growth of productivity among all the provinces. The rapid growth of the service and real estate sector from 1992 to 1994 probably contributed to this phenomenon, assuming all the characteristics of a "bubble economy." At least in 1993, provincial productivity changes moved in different directions, with some achieving stronger growth (Shandong, Zhejiang and Shaanxi) and others (Yunnan, Heilongjiang and Hubei) lower — sometimes significantly lower — growth. Thus the meaning of the difference between GDP and National Income figures is difficult to ascertain.

If we look at Tables 4a, b to assess another important pro-cyclical feature of ordinary business cycles, namely investment (excluding FDI), we may reach a similar conclusion. This is important because the long-term trend of growth is determined by divergent investment activities in

Table 4a. Investment in Fixed Assets as a Percentage Share of GDP*

	1988	1989	1990	1991	1992	1993
Beijing	39.64	32.06	38.11	36.46	37.15	44.05
Tianjin	34.12	30.11	29.46	38.43	42.41	35.50
Hebei	35.73	28.61	22.21	25.68	27.87	27.42
Shanxi	36.92	30.08	30.25	33.80	31.42	35.62
Neimenggu	25.08	21.67	22.67	28.28	36.63	41.45
Liaoning	32.84	27.22	26.98	29.39	33.21	35.24
Jilin	27.74	27.22	23.74	26.88	29.39	34.59
Heilongjiang	31.58	27.05	25.66	25.92	28.54	29.45
Shanghai	43.05	35.06	30.50	30.12	33.44	30.45
Jiangsu	33.62	26.42	27.47	31.01	37.43	34.61
Zhejiang	32.18	26.94	30.82	33.04	36.36	42.56
Anhui	28.96	19.47	20.64	22.51	26.07	28.15
Fujian	26.41	21.10	23.30	23.75	27.61	19.97
Jiangxi	24.88	20.17	16.94	19.75	22.20	26.26
Shandong	48.66	27.96	25.13	28.06	30.18	29.01
Henan	28.64	22.72	23.18	25.82	25.58	28.21
Hubei	25.33	17.56	17.98	18.04	24.43	27.50
Hunan	24.29	17.43	17.13	19.90	25.58	25.11
Guangdong	36.66	29.12	27.63	28.45	40.92	37.27
Guangxi	25.93	19.12	17.46	19.79	24.50	28.08
Hainan	28.27	33.38	41.27	41.02	61.40	55.92
Sichuan	25.60	22.20	19.38	22.69	26.93	27.96
Guizhou	24.08	16.52	17.92	18.11	20.65	24.48
Yunnan	28.21	22.35	20.84	24.71	29.08	38.78
Tibet	38.05	32.02	39.22	48.21	43.84	49.09
Shaanxi	32.41	27.51	26.99	27.54	26.94	81.63
Gansu	28.51	21.31	23.99	25.48	27.79	27.01
Qinghai	46.89	33.63	32.47	32.98	36.30	43.41
Ningxia	39.06	31.03	33.68	37.82	42.75	44.19
Xinjiang	38.47	36.15	34.89	35.20	44.94	52.14
China	32.15	26.21	25.16	27.75	32.83	34.69

* Based on recent issues of the *Chinese Statistical Yearbook* (FDI excluded).

Table 4b. Social Investment in Fixed Assets, Per-capita

(in RMB)

	1983	1984	1985	1986	1987	1988	1989	1990	1991	1992	1993
Beijing	545	724	984	1073	1310	1506	1406	1750	1869	2395	3427
Tianjin	501	609	826	878	937	1055	992	1006	1424	1896	2046
Hebei	118	157	204	238	313	413	364	296	397	513	679
Shanxi	174	258	337	356	385	383	377	416	495	546	764
Neimenggu	147	204	255	228	250	282	263	301	416	627	904
Liaoning	198	263	377	476	579	700	647	656	790	1072	1577
Jilin	133	185	273	282	334	394	335	377	454	598	908
Heilongjiang	209	257	337	370	410	452	449	460	530	677	871
Shanghai	639	764	974	1149	1482	2092	1908	1695	1928	2640	3410
Jiangsu	170	209	242	377	499	586	496	533	658	1071	1368
Zhejiang	111	163	262	320	450	552	505	618	774	1047	1693
Anhui	91	120	156	191	221	253	204	220	235	324	467
Fujian	100	128	203	218	278	322	303	357	430	624	652
Jiangxi	86	104	126	148	165	220	198	186	235	317	464
Shandong	124	182	121	287	374	459	413	394	514	694	908
Henan	80	114	164	200	204	255	228	240	293	350	499
Hubei	117	153	206	205	264	300	234	262	281	439	632
Hunan	88	97	144	166	199	241	186	196	252	374	474
Guangdong	156	222	315	361	430	679	633	640	787	1437	1818
Guangxi	59	74	109	140	160	189	161	161	208	320	498
Hainan	—	—	—	—	—	337	453	594	661	1261	1799
Sichuan	68	90	142	150	185	217	207	206	267	365	493
Guizhou	59	78	111	103	111	158	123	139	158	204	293
Yunnan	69	99	142	169	168	211	193	221	283	287	660
Tibet	105	250	355	230	329	371	318	436	639	635	796
Shaanxi	101	133	190	206	253	284	293	305	353	391	1458
Gansu	88	114	160	181	209	256	213	249	285	363	412
Qinghai	267	320	393	429	500	619	461	478	531	665	977
Ningxia	135	198	305	379	420	404	376	438	531	686	870
Xinjiang	206	251	328	375	390	506	542	575	703	1087	1561
China	134	177	243	286	337	410	372	389	476	670	917

the regions during the business cycle. If investment activities increase in varying degrees in the provinces during the upward phase of the cycle, then initial conditions for the next cycle will move in different directions. Looking at the relationship between investment and GDP during the last cycle, this seems to be the case: there are significant differences among the provinces in terms of the level of investment as well as the responses to the expansion of 1992 and 1993. One needs to distinguish between level and response. For example, Tianjin and Qinghai show a comparatively high level, with only a weak response until 1993, whereas Guangdong shows a similar level but a more pronounced pro-cyclical change in investment. Remarkably, it is only in 1993 that the overall response is strong in those provinces which have a large share of state-owned enterprises. But there are also provinces, like Shandong, which show no clear reaction during the 1992–1993 boom.

In order to assess how such a pattern shapes the initial conditions of the next cycle, it might be fruitful to examine relevant per-capita figures. Since we cannot deflate the figures by means of regionally specific deflators for investment, we have to use nominal figures for gross fixed capital formation. Here we learn that the slump of 1989/90 even led to an absolute decrease of capital formation across provinces, implying an even stronger shrinkage in real terms (although high inflation in 1988 caused a relative decrease of the reference level). The length of time needed to resume pre-slump levels differs across provinces. For instance, many provinces in the Yangtze River Valley (including Shanghai) only surpassed 1988 investment levels in 1992, when there was still a shortfall in real terms. But since 1992 there has been a clear response to the expansion in all the provinces, albeit at very different levels. Since the level is measured in gross and nominal terms, we may therefore assume that there were no substantial net additions to the real capital stock at least in some provinces during the last cycle. A necessary consequence is the fact that those provinces will not be able to raise growth rates enough to achieve convergent regional development.

Convergent Growth but Divergent Potential for Growth: A Revisionist View of Regional Disparities in China

The investment process in China cannot be understood if the underlying ownership structure is not scrutinized. It is a well-established fact that the recent cycle was primarily driven by the rapid expansion of investment demands, and not by consumption. Tables 5 and 6 show two aspects of the ownership structure of investment in Chinese provinces: first, the significant share of domestic fixed-capital investment by state-owned enterprises; second, the inflow of FDI is related to the overall amount of domestic investment. The evidence is clear-cut.[21] In almost all the provinces, the share of domestic investment undertaken by state-owned entreprises for some provinces (e.g., Shanxi, Liaoning and Guizhou) as well as for China as a whole surged to an all-time high in 1993. This accords with the observation that state banks still channel credits to state enterprises as a matter of priority. Hence we can describe the last cycle as a boom without institutional change. This becomes obvious through comparison with the cycle of the mid-1980s when the share of state enterprises receiving investment in many provinces decreased. Given the notorious economic inefficiency and losses in the state sector, the recent intensification of state investment seems to be a serious obstacle to future growth.

The picture is incomplete unless we examine the relative share of FDI which in provinces like Guangdong begin to overshadow the share of state investment in domestic investment without FDI. The issue has grown in importance since the influx of foreign capital surged in 1992. As is shown in Table 6, the main problem in assessing the magnitude of FDI pertains to the exchange rate used to value FDI. One could reasonably argue that an appropriate choice for 1993 might be the new exchange rate set on 1 January 1994 because the same rate prevailed at the swap markets during 1993 and was decisive in linking China to the world economy in that year. But applying the January 1994 rate leads to astonishing changes in the structure of capital formation. Shanghai's share of FDI was above 50% and Fujian received more FDI than the province's own investment.

However, even if we classify as "non-state" investment the sum of FDI, the number of provinces undergoing structural change in capital formation during the last cycle still remains a minority.[22] This could change if FDI continues to flow into China at a rate similar to that between 1992 and 1994, given the above-mentioned effects of the exchange rate for computing relative magnitudes. But endogenous change in the structure of capital formation is slow and weak.

Figures on the ownership structure of investment can serve as an indicator of structural change in institutions. Figures on employment may serve as a litmus test for real structural change. Table 7 reports the share of agricultural employment in overall employment. In most of the provinces, the slump was accompanied by an immediate rise in agricultural

Table 5. Share of State Enterprises in Total Social Investment in Fixed Assets*

	1983	1984	1985	1986	1987	1988	1989	1990	1991	1992	1993
Beijing	78.8	77.5	77.1	83.3	82.6	81.9	79.5	79.7	79.9	86.5	88.8
Tianjin	85.4	79.2	82.3	84.8	80.1	80.2	80.2	81.6	84.6	79.0	82.3
Hebei	66.3	56.4	55.3	55.1	48.4	46.5	47.2	60.9	51.9	62.2	68.0
Shanxi	70.0	70.6	72.9	74.7	75.0	72.2	73.9	73.6	74.6	81.1	79.1
Neimenggu	84.7	74.0	74.0	77.1	73.4	74.4	76.4	78.5	79.0	81.6	83.1
Liaoning	76.7	75.6	77.2	77.3	78.6	78.8	79.2	82.7	82.0	83.6	74.7
Jilin	75.6	63.3	60.6	67.5	70.7	74.2	72.4	71.6	75.1	80.4	83.2
Heilongjiang	90.7	82.9	79.7	82.1	82.4	84.3	81.7	82.7	85.7	88.4	91.7
Shanghai	85.6	81.9	80.7	84.3	83.4	75.4	73.2	84.6	83.5	77.3	89.8
Jiangsu	43.8	40.0	51.4	39.7	39.5	40.1	36.7	35.9	37.9	37.9	41.7
Zhejiang	48.4	42.0	37.4	38.0	32.0	30.3	31.4	30.5	29.8	35.0	35.2
Anhui	51.7	50.9	51.5	52.4	49.1	47.9	53.1	54.3	59.3	64.1	61.0
Fujian	64.3	61.3	67.3	66.7	62.6	58.4	57.2	59.6	62.3	63.7	95.1
Jiangxi	65.4	64.3	57.8	58.3	56.2	51.1	54.3	66.7	64.6	66.4	67.0
Shandong	49.7	47.5	52.0	54.7	52.3	52.0	48.2	55.1	53.2	57.3	60.7
Henan	59.5	55.5	50.8	46.4	52.0	52.3	53.1	52.1	56.2	61.0	62.4
Hubei	65.7	59.8	59.4	62.4	59.7	63.1	61.2	66.1	72.9	72.6	73.4
Hunan	47.7	42.2	50.9	48.2	48.2	48.7	54.0	56.7	58.5	62.5	65.0
Guangdong	64.0	63.2	71.8	68.3	60.8	54.9	51.3	66.3	67.4	64.0	73.5
Guangxi	64.7	58.3	57.1	55.0	63.4	68.4	62.0	60.0	60.5	66.1	76.5
Hainan	—	—	—	—	—	70.7	80.2	78.0	91.7	91.3	96.4
Sichuan	75.0	61.4	64.4	65.7	66.5	64.1	64.8	73.4	70.1	69.9	68.7
Guizhou	69.8	65.1	64.1	74.9	79.2	66.6	81.4	79.3	81.1	84.5	76.7
Yunnan	80.4	72.5	69.3	57.4	63.1	61.7	57.8	61.1	65.5	68.4	67.6
Tibet	96.0	94.4	89.7	94.8	57.1	60.4	63.0	69.9	64.5	81.5	90.1
Shaanxi	79.6	68.1	66.7	71.4	69.3	70.8	67.9	68.9	65.0	70.0	31.0
Gansu	85.9	83.1	75.8	79.0	82.6	80.7	82.2	82.0	81.7	78.9	78.2
Qinghai	95.8	82.8	84.3	89.7	91.5	83.8	90.0	89.2	89.8	89.9	87.2
Ningxia	91.1	81.1	86.2	83.3	79.4	72.0	72.8	78.2	80.2	78.3	75.5
Xinjiang	92.9	88.9	88.5	79.4	80.7	79.6	77.9	84.8	85.6	88.3	84.4
China	69.5	64.7	66.1	65.5	63.1	61.4	61.3	65.6	65.9	67.1	70.4

* Percent, calculated according to recent issues of *Chinese Statistical Yearbook*, without FDI.

Table 6. Share of FDI in Total Investment by Domestic Investors*

	1988	1989	1990	1991	1992	1993	1993[†]
Beijing	11.52	8.25	6.99	6.40	7.33	10.10	15.08
Tianjin	2.57	1.39	2.00	5.45	3.41	18.58	27.73
Hebei	0.30	0.77	1.17	1.22	1.94	5.32	7.94
Shanxi	0.23	0.35	0.14	0.14	1.82	2.17	3.23
Neimenggu	0.40	0.29	0.78	0.10	0.21	2.44	3.63
Liaoning	1.82	1.89	4.73	6.12	6.61	11.57	17.26
Jilin	0.39	0.47	0.90	1.48	2.75	6.82	10.19
Heilongjiang	1.64	1.37	0.83	0.59	1.63	4.22	6.30
Shanghai	3.29	6.51	3.67	2.99	7.64	39.56	59.05
Jiangsu	1.24	1.47	1.77	2.59	10.90	17.19	25.65
Zhejiang	0.71	0.96	0.91	1.54	2.98	8.23	12.28
Anhui	0.76	0.30	0.52	0.42	1.59	5.38	8.04
Fujian	5.89	14.91	14.10	18.93	40.32	80.66	120.39
Jiangxi	0.42	0.47	0.51	1.14	4.44	6.51	9.72
Shandong	0.90	1.83	2.65	2.62	9.26	13.77	20.56
Henan	1.16	0.92	0.26	0.79	0.94	3.93	5.87
Hubei	0.53	0.88	1.07	1.60	4.57	8.72	13.02
Hunan	0.34	0.78	0.56	0.87	3.12	8.42	12.57
Guangdong	11.56	13.04	18.61	20.41	21.75	36.22	54.06
Guangxi	1.00	2.99	2.49	1.89	7.16	23.03	34.38
Hainan	20.62	12.33	12.57	21.25	28.67	32.36	48.29
Sichuan	0.65	0.22	0.52	1.48	1.54	6.01	8.97
Guizhou	0.74	1.24	1.11	1.43	1.59	2.47	3.69
Yunnan	2.08	0.42	0.43	0.17	1.07	2.18	3.25
Tibet	0.01	0.00	0.00	0.00	0.00	0.00	0.00
Shaanxi	4.66	3.91	2.24	1.42	1.89	2.69	4.02
Gansu	0.16	0.09	0.11	0.39	0.02	0.71	1.06
Qinghai	0.38	0.00	0.00	0.00	0.12	0.41	0.61
Ningxia	0.07	0.00	0.06	0.04	0.06	1.58	2.36
Xinjiang	0.26	0.04	0.29	0.01	0.00	1.22	1.81
China	2.64	3.09	3.75	4.22	7.73	14.58	21.76

* Percent, calculated according to recent issues of the *Chinese Statistical Yearbook*.
[†] FDI calculated in RMB; figures for 1993 are calculated according to the official exchange rate and the exchange rate of 1 January 1994.

employment, given the widespread closures of TVEs and return of migrant workers from the cities to the countryside. Since 1992, the boom hastened structural change again. However, if we compare the figures from the mid-1980s with the figures of the 1990s, we see that the speed of structural change is different in the provinces and that the 1992–1993 boom has a strong impact on structural change in the short-term. For instance, in the industrialized regions of the Northeast, while there is a low share of agricultural employment, structural change is almost at a standstill (Jilin

Table 7. Share of Agricultural Employment in Total Social Employment*

	1985	1986	1987	1988	1989	1990	1991	1992	1993
Beijing	15.7	14.6	14.2	13.4	13.7	12.8	12.2	11.2	11.1
Tianjin	20.7	19.9	19.4	18.9	19.4	19.4	19.1	18.6	18.1
Hebei	62.4	60.7	58.3	57.2	58.2	58.8	59.2	58.3	56.9
Shanxi	47.6	47.1	45.8	45.4	46.2	46.7	46.7	45.5	45.1
Neimenggu	55.0	53.6	52.4	51.3	51.5	51.6	52.0	50.6	50.1
Liaoning	33.3	33.0	31.9	31.2	31.8	32.0	32.4	31.3	30.5
Jilin	43.4	43.8	43.4	44.6	45.6	46.6	46.1	46.2	45.2
Heilongjiang	33.1	32.4	31.6	30.6	32.0	32.4	32.8	31.6	31.6
Shanghai	14.5	12.6	11.4	10.3	10.0	9.8	9.0	8.6	8.5
Jiangsu	50.2	47.5	45.6	44.7	46.1	46.5	46.8	45.4	43.4
Zhejiang	54.4	53.3	51.9	50.7	52.2	52.6	52.0	51.0	46.6
Anhui	70.9	70.1	68.3	67.3	67.9	68.0	68.1	66.8	63.8
Fujian	60.1	59.3	58.5	57.7	57.5	57.2	56.7	55.2	53.1
Jiangxi	64.5	63.6	64.2	62.8	64.2	63.9	63.3	60.7	55.7
Shandong	65.0	62.9	61.5	60.2	60.6	60.6	61.4	59.6	58.1
Henan	72.0	70.2	68.3	67.3	67.6	67.9	68.2	67.2	64.8
Hubei	57.9	57.2	56.8	56.5	57.3	57.7	58.1	56.6	54.5
Hunan	72.7	68.7	69.8	69.7	71.0	71.0	70.2	67.8	64.5
Guangdong	57.1	55.0	52.7	51.0	50.9	49.8	48.0	45.4	42.1
Guangxi	78.8	77.9	76.7	75.7	75.7	75.4	74.5	72.3	69.1
Hainan	0.0	0.0	0.0	53.2	53.4	53.4	52.9	52.0	50.9
Sichuan	74.3	73.2	72.0	71.3	72.1	72.1	71.3	69.5	66.4
Guizhou	78.7	75.3	77.2	77.6	77.8	77.8	77.7	77.6	77.4
Yunnan	76.6	76.5	76.4	76.6	76.9	77.0	76.9	76.6	76.3
Tibet	79.2	78.9	78.7	78.6	80.7	79.1	78.4	78.4	76.6
Shaanxi	63.5	61.9	61.0	62.2	62.2	62.6	62.6	62.4	61.4
Gansu	61.7	60.1	62.4	64.1	64.1	64.4	63.2	62.6	60.0
Qinghai	57.9	56.1	56.3	56.6	58.0	58.0	58.2	58.8	58.5
Ningxia	61.2	60.3	59.1	58.6	58.2	58.9	59.0	58.5	58.3
Xinjiang	48.7	45.2	44.9	44.5	44.7	44.4	43.8	42.9	43.1
China	60.9	59.4	58.5	57.9	58.6	58.8	58.6	57.3	55.2

* Percent, based on recent issues of the *Chinese Statistical Yearbook*.

shows a larger share of agricultural employment in 1993 as compared to 1985). A similar observation can be made for poor provinces like Shaanxi, Guizhou, Yunnan and even Hubei and Hunan which, however, show an acceleration of change during the boom that may be linked to migration. This picture is in contrast with rapid structural change in Guangdong, Jiangsu and Zhejiang. We may therefore conclude that the recent business cycle not only leads to slow structural change in the majority of China's provinces, but also to major differences in performance (compare, for example, Guizhou and Sichuan).

Summarizing our statistical analysis, its seems erroneous to assess the business cycle for China as a whole. Economic dynamics differ markedly among the provinces. This observation is not just valid for the past but is also essential for the assessment of future development. Many observers agree that in the past decade, there may have been changes in the relative economic development of the provinces, but no rapid increase in regional inequality.[23] In fact, as mentioned above, this picture might be even more pronounced with respect to PPP figures. But even if one only reviews national income data, a simple regression exercise shows that between 1980 and 1992 the growth rate was higher in the poorer provinces, implying that convergent rather than divergent development took place (Figure 2 for the general relationship between wealth and growth, 1978–1992). Thus, a review of the historical record and use of simple statistical indicators such as national income indicate that the much-quoted view of growing regional disparities between the provinces is wrong.

Our reflections on more complex indicators of growth and business cycles in China lead to the conclusion that although this may be true today, the picture will change in the future because the recent cycle brought exaggeration to the fore regarding structural differences among the provinces, especially in terms of the conditions for further development. This was the most important reason for the sense of crisis within the Chinese leadership which accompanied the last cycle through all its stages and which may not fit the Western view of China as an economic giant of the 21st century.

If we generalize audaciously, China in late 1993 had different macroregions with distinct business cycles and their own particular institutional and real structures, e.g., the industrialized Northeast with its high share of state-owned enterprises; the Upper Yangtze River with its dualistic economy a legacy of the Third line Campaign; the southeastern coastal region with its high degree of integration with the world economy and economies of "Greater China." The structural divergence among the regions was not as pronounced in the 1980s and hence presented no fundamental challenge to policy making. But the question is whether convergence actually resulted from the trickle-down approach favouring the coastal regions.

One could put forward a revisionist position: it is well known that those structural differences together with central economic policies triggered regionalization in terms of policy making and even regional protectionism in the 1980s and grew even more pronounced in the late 1980s and

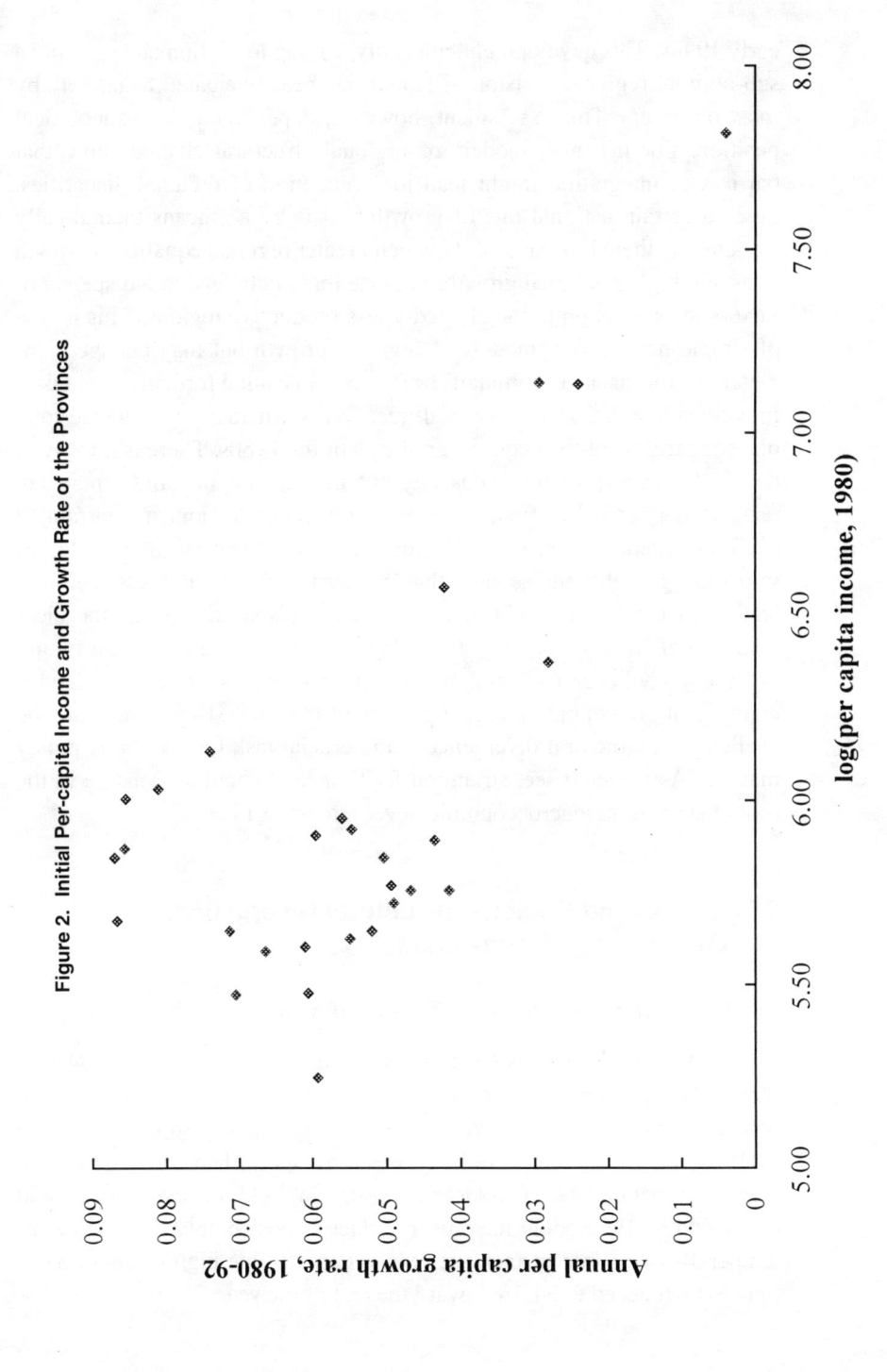

Figure 2. Initial Per-capita Income and Growth Rate of the Provinces

early 1990s. This development, allegedly leading to friction and possibly a sub-optimal regional division of labour has been evaluated negatively by most observers. This assessment, however, depends on one's theoretical position. For instance, models of regional structural change show that barriers to integration might lead to a reduction of regional disparities, given a certain national rate of growth.[24] It is by no means theoretically evident that there is a trade-off between greater regional equality in growth rates and higher national growth, because this might lead to a dispersal of factors of production to the allegedly less productive regions. This is true of simple neoclassical models of regional growth but may change completely if, for instance, cumulative processes in capital formation are taken into consideration. Hence the real question is whether convergence took place regardless of the economic policies of the 1980s. There is no way to decide between possible scenarios, but in the case of China there are reasons to assume that, first, regionalization and protectionism contributed to a convergence of growth (with possible, but not necessarily real, losses in overall growth); and second, that greater integration and less regionalization in the future might lead to growing disparities, given the clear evidence of structural divergence today. Regional disparities are a future, not a past, challenge for China because the country has so far experienced convergent growth but divergent potential for growth. Hence, meeting the challenge of structural divergence is the crucial task for economic policy making. As we shall see, structural frictions and contradictions lie at the root of short-term macroeconomic development in 1994.

3. Inflation and Regional Structural Divergence: "Overheating" Re-revisited

Applying the Naive Quantity Theory of Money

The paramount issue of short-term economic development in 1994 was obviously inflation. This could easily have been predicted in or even before 1992. In fact, the growth rate of the broad money supply decreased in 1989, only to increase quickly the next year when the growth rate surpassed that of 1988 by a large margin.[25] In 1993, the even more rapid expansion of 1992 could have been reduced considerably, but until September 1994 the rate of increase reached an all-time high of about 37%, only to be reduced to 34.4% toward the end of the year.

According to the elementary quantity theory of money, in the long-term, price levels are determined by the growth rate of the money supply relative to real output. Since there are many institutional obstacles to the rapid adjustment of absolute prices to an increase in the money supply in China, we may safely assume that there is a comparatively long lag (3–4 years) between the growth of the money supply and changes in price levels.[26] Hence, inflation in 1994 is the initial response to 1992 monetary expansion. Since then the rapid growth of money supply has further fuelled inflation. This simple causal relationship is often obscured in Chinese policy discussions on "overheating" because emphasis is mostly on credit policy as the direct lever of monetary control. However, changes in the financial sector of the Chinese economy have loosened up the relationship between credit in the narrow sense (at least as defined by published monetary statistics) and the money supply, so that they are not highly correlated. One reason is the growing importance of banks outside the state sector and interbank-lending. Both presumably are now included in the item "others" on the balance sheet of China's financial sector in the *Statistical Yearbook*.[27]

Of course, this assessment depends on the growth of real output as well as on the changes in the velocity of money. Regarding the latter, it is difficult to distinguish between the different motives for holding money in bank accounts and hence between financial deepening as measured by the relation between the quantity of money and GDP and a medium-run disequilibrium with respect to the velocity of money. Because of the still under-developed structure of the Chinese financial system, a certain share of deposits has to be regarded as an accumulation of wealth rather than money for transactions. If the financial system deepens further, we may expect that depositors' portfolios will be reshuffled in favour of stocks and bonds. This is actually the reason behind the very strong demand for stocks and bonds in the Chinese economy, which has led to illegal trading in many places, including rural areas. However, changes in portfolio structure do not alter the amount of money already in circulation.

So, the analysis faces the problem that short-term changes in the velocity of money cannot be fully determined relative to a supposedly long-term stable velocity or even a stable demand for money. Evaluation always depends on the assessment of the maturity of the financial system relative to the level of economic development and to the demand for financial services. A reasonable guess will be that China's economy is still in need of further financial deepening so that the growth of money broadly defined should partly be interpreted as a substitute for the accumulation of wealth and, hence, should not be seen as inflationary. One observation which supports such a view is the fact that only in 1992 did M1 grow faster than M2. In 1994, M2 so far has increased at a higher speed than M1 (34.4% as compared to 26.8%). But we cannot give a full account of the difference in terms of the distinction between "money" and "wealth."

This problem is also related to the assessment of the development of private savings. In 1994, the trend of previous years continued with private savings increasing rapidly (43%, with a current stock of about RMB 2 trillion). This growth has been financed by the rapid expansion of the money supply in previous years.[28] The main problem is not to explain this performance, given negative real interest rates, despite official efforts to index interest rates to inflation for private deposits. Unless there is an attractive alternative, and given a certain compensation for inflationary losses, savings are simply a better choice than private hoarding of money. This seems to be particularly true for the rural population who in 1994 demonstrated a strong inclination to expand their savings deposits.[29] The urban population was especially anxious about the future, with the spectre of rising unemployment looming on the horizon.

One real problem is accounting for the artificial situation where the state banks actually operate at a loss with lower interest rates for credits than deposits, and with the People's Bank of China (PBOC) subsidizing interest on deposits again since March 1994. In February 1995, this subsidy will add 10.38% to regular interest rates. This subsidy, of course, dwarfs the meagre rise of 0.24% in interest on deposits implemented by the PBOC on January 1, 1995.[30]

Any argument concerning a reassessment of private savings in terms of the money-wealth dichotomy depends on an assessment of the stability of the financial sector. But in this regard we may argue that without strong government intervention and administrative regulation, the Chinese banking system would simply crash since private savings actually back a large share of credits without value.[31]

A similar analytical mess occurs when one tries to distinguish between nominal growth and the long-term trend of real output. For assessing the inflationary impact of the growth of the money supply, short-run real effects on growth (as in the last two years) should be filtered out from the analysis. However, the many changes in the economic system as well as the still short time series make it a risky estimate to construct a time series for the growth of potential output.[32]

Again we will propose a reasonable guess based on regional development figures. The recent boom is linked to a strong expansion of fixed investment by state enterprises. The possible effects on potential output depend on the growth of capital stock as well as on productivity. There is now a highly diversified literature on productivity with diverging and even contradictory views.[33] Common sense would seem to win out here, in other words, there was and still is no pronounced growth of Total Factor Productivity in state enterprises, as compared to TVEs. Our figures on regional development fit this hypothesis because the higher the share of state-owned enterprises in a province, the fewer the achievements in labour productivity which would have to be based on more efficiently utilized capital equipment.

If this assessment is accepted, it is likely that the recent boom did not lead to an increase in potential output that matches the short-term rates of nominal growth, or achieve a given decrease in the velocity of money. Hence we assume that a considerable share of the past and present growth in the money supply will feed inflation in the years to come. However, if one juggles the figures, it is also evident that inflation will not surpass say, 30% per year. Given the considerable challenges of structural and institutional changes, this still seems to be a basically stable situation, in particular if there is no loss of overall control of the money supply. The crucial question is not whether the Chinese economy will experience equilibrium macroeconomically but whether there will be institutional stability in the financial sector, avoiding crashes and bursting bubbles.[34] Doubts have already been raised regarding the interest rate structure of deposits and credits.

Regional Development and the Pitfalls of Aggregate Analysis

The large differences in the nature of the business cycle across regions of China make it extremely difficult to analyze and design monetary policies. In theory, a given rate of increase in the money supply might have no inflationary impact in a region with a strong growth of potential output and structural changes in the financial sector lagging behind, whereas in a region with a sluggish growth of potential output and a weaker demand for wealth, the inflationary impact may be strong. In a fully integrated market economy, such regional differences in the business cycle would be equalized through national capital markets in such a way that rising real interest rates in booming regions would attract money from the other regions to support further growth, while reducing the inflationary pressure in the region with sluggish long-term growth. Hence we see that one crucial assumption underlying conventional applications of the quantity theory of money on a national economy is the existence of a national capital market with a high degree of integration.

This condition is not yet fulfilled in China. So far, most observers agree that integration among the different regions of China is now weaker than in the early 1980s. This is also true with respect to capital flows.[35] But if there is no integrated capital market, then there is no direct link between the growth of the national money supply and regional inflation. One would need to assess regional changes in the money supply and other determinants of growth as well. For instance, since there is also comparatively weak trade integration among provinces, growth in potential output and hence supply conditions in the regional markets can differ. If there is a sluggish regional growth of output in a certain region or province, but at the same time a strong growth of the regional supply of credit, than the inflationary impact is stronger there than in other regions. This will be felt sharply in the non-tradeables in the context of China's regional economic structure. The non-tradeables not only include services but also many goods, because of the bottlenecks in the transportation system.[36]

The role of the fiscal system is no longer of importance for redistributing capital and money among the provinces.[37] The relative fiscal decline of the central government during the last decade was one of the main determinants of the growing regionalization of the financial system. That is to say, redistribution of capital between the provinces occurred indirectly through the banking system simply by providing credits to regions where (virtual) long-term real rates of interest were much lower than in other regions, thereby resulting in a *de facto* subsidy to the former which was ultimately financed by the inflation-tax. We cannot assess the magnitude of this subsidy, but an indirect indicator is the strong pressure to redirect credit into high-growth regions which seems to be the main cause of the above mentioned rapid growth of the "others" category in the credit plan. In any event, the realization of a certain regional allocation of credit is only possible by means of the central government's administrative intervention. Concrete mechanisms establishing this link are, for example, direct credits from the PBOC devoted to supporting commercial state banks in their bad debt with state enterprises.[38] It should be stressed that low real interest rates do not depend on the level of GDP in the provinces. On the contrary, higher relative growth could lead to higher real interest rates in the poorer provinces. Again, the share of state enterprises might be a more important determinant. Hence, inflation in China is closely linked to divergent regional development. Disinflating the economy is therefore extremely difficult unless capital flows across regions in response to market forces and interregional redistribution is organized through fiscal transfers.

Our reflections on Chinese inflation cannot conclude without mentioning the most remarkable feature of inflation in 1994, as compared to the previous years, and which has been commented upon by many Chinese observers. In 1994, tight credit controls led to a decrease of demand in the producer goods market. For instance, it was reported that material distribution organizations above the county level experienced a decline in turnover of about 11%, compared with a rise in the demand for consumer goods of about 30%.[39] This change in the structure of demand even led to a decline of prices for material goods in mid-1994, with an immediate impact on policy analysis.[40] Specifically, analysts concluded that in so far as a one-time shock in agricultural prices was the most important single cause of inflation in 1994, inflation would not persist.

The problem with such analysis is that it ignores the quantity theory of money and argues from the sectoral perspective. In China, this can be particularly misleading because there is no direct link between sectoral changes and macroeconomic variables. For instance, government intervention might cap further expansion of demand for investment goods without affecting other macroeconomic aggregates. We have already mentioned that there is no clear-cut relationship between growth of credit and inflation.[41] Hence, the real issue is not whether there is a "cooling down" in the material goods sector, but what is going on in the other sectors. This again raises the question of how to assess the massive piling up of private savings deposits. We will come back to this point in section 5. At this stage in our journey through 1994, understanding inflation in China also requires paying attention to the active role of the policy-makers and advisors and their subsequent decisions in influencing macroeconomic development.[42] Even if the above-mentioned view of inflation in 1994 is correct, its main effect might be a continuing loss of control of monetary aggregates because of the response of policy-makers who may conclude that inflation is no big issue after all.[43] The main fault is short-sightedness, not of the analysis proper but of policy discourse following the presentation of analysis.

Given these observations and considerations, what remains of the idea of "overheating"? In fact, this is simply another of the many "averages" which should be discarded, for it is a political concept without any precise analytical meaning. Moreover, since inflation in China is closely linked to structural problems and in particular to divergent regional development, it cannot be controlled by macroeconomic policies at all except in the short-run. The clear-cut institutional separation of the financial sector from the fiscal sector within the complex context of regional development is much more decisive in curing inflation in the long run. Indeed, this was one of the core issues of economic reform in 1994.

4. Economic Policies in 1994: The Challenge from the Centre

Reasserting the Power of the Centre by Means of Socialist Interventionism

The two most important innovations in economic policy-making of 1994 pertain to the issue of "delinking" problems of regional development from the monetary sector. First, the centre tried to reestablish its role as a pivot for interregional fiscal transfers by means of recentralizing tax revenues; second, within the banking system, "policy banks" were separated from the other special state banks. This attempt at centralization is quite remarkable and can also be observed in many other areas such as trade or industrial policy. Therefore we may conclude that more is at stake than divergent regional development.

In 1994, the centre tried to make the socio-economic system regress to a situation with control in the hands of a unitary central state. Since many observers have described China "changing shape" or undergoing "deconstruction," this observation should not be taken as a mere slogan.

However, the current strategy of the central government is directed at regaining central control and pushing marketization forward at the same time. Hence there is a certain affinity between the economic policies of 1994 and ideas of "neo-authoritarianism" which were fashionable before 1989. From an even broader perspective, the impressive 1994 record of the Chinese government in terms of law-making and formal institution building can also be seen as an attempt to "rationalize" the socio-economic process in line with a strong national state. It should be noted that this may be the underlying reason why the new approach of the centre seems to have enjoyed strong support by many economists in Beijing (especially

Economic Development and Institutional Change 19.31

those in their 40s and 50s). Indeed, the relevant documents show the influence of well-trained economists (with technical terms like "natural monopoly" emerging in State Council documents). There is a widespread discomfort with the "irrationality" of the current state of China's evolutionary journey to the market, and a strong demand for "conscious design" by the state. Hence there is a link between the general intellectual climate regarding, for instance, social change and perceived instability, on the one hand, and the continuous quest for a strong interventionist role by the national state, on the other. This role includes certain interventionist approaches toward the market economy in the guise of "industrial policy."[44]

Such a view may explain why almost every policy measure in 1994 is ambivalent, if the ideals of a liberal market economy and not the simple criterion of marketization are applied as a yardstick. This is not only an academic question but is of great importance when evaluating China's attempts at further institution building according to the rules of GATT. The main internal contradiction in economic policies in 1994 seems to be the clash between China's claim of moving quickly toward a fully-fledged realization of the "socialist market economy" while the formation of a regime of interventionist policies by legal means continues simultaneously. This will lead to sharp conflicts with GATT rules, for instance, regarding legal provisions for export promotion and import restrictions. In fact, most of the new institutions so far not only support marketization but at the same time strengthen the interventionist and even arbitrary power of the centre. The following are only a few examples:

- The new taxation system does not include a systematic method of fiscal redistribution, although there is a first-round assignment of certain taxes to the local and central governments respectively. The centralization of the value added tax (VAT) might boost the centre's capacity for second-round redistribution, but there is no general rule for realizing this, aside from referring to simple stipulations regarding distribution to preserve the *status quo*.
- The new rules for industrial policy are remarkably "modern" and show the influence of Western economics on policy-making in China. But those ideas are applied in a neo-mercantilist fashion, namely, the centre no longer plans the allocation of goods but instead carefully regulates sectoral and regional changes in the economy. The main instrument is the control of local investment

plans, and a clear revival of the role of the State Planning Commission.

- The mercantilist approach is also obvious in the new Foreign Trade Law. The law is not highly specific but contains several flexible clauses which allow the central government to intervene in trade, particularly imports.
- Finally, China's new forex system provides the conditions for further marketization by abolishing the dual exchange rate, and strengthens instruments for central policy intervention through the monopolization of the market by the different state banks.

Compared with the ideas of neo-authoritarianism, the message of 1994 is therefore mixed because there is a clear drive toward "marketization" but no clear trend toward the "market economy." Hence it seems that the qualifier "socialist" is being taken seriously.[45] The main reason seems to be that the centre is trying to stop the devolution of its power by asserting its control over the market process but not the market. If it succeeds, the result may be an outright interventionist market economy in which the centre is one of the key players in both external and internal trade.

Changing Clothes: The Discovery of Industrial Policy

One of the most significant signs of Chinese economic policies taking this direction was the tough policy stance toward futures markets which were highly publicized just one year earlier.[46] The centre still forbids trade in "vital" goods like cotton or steel and (as of September) in rice and oil as well. The number of trading places has also been drastically reduced. The main reason was that the development of futures prices very quickly mirrored the strong distortions in the price system and the expectations of high future inflation by market agents. Hence, the central government also resorted to price controls (price ceilings were imposed in the case of 15 futures markets which were allowed to continue trading).

Regarding external relations, this heavy-handed interventionist approach is already evident, e.g., the policy mix in the automobile sector where a vigorous import-substitution (*guochanhua zhengce*) policy with tightly controlled FDI is going to be implemented.[47] In the next five years, China is expected to become self-sufficient in motorcycle production and to be able to supply over 90% of the national market by domestic production. The state wants to apply a variety of methods to boost China's automobile industries, including tough controls of imports and even prohibiting the import of used cars. Such an approach is fully supported by the new law on foreign trade in which the infant-industry argument plays an important role. Chinese society is to be geared toward the idea of everyone owning a "family car," so the State Council guidelines even include provisions for teaching traffic rules in elementary schools.

Such an approach is also followed in recent State Council regulations on industrial policy which, for instance, explicitly favour the development of TVE's in the central and western regions of China, on the one hand , but which simultaneously assign the competence in regional and structural policies on TVE's to the State Council and the State Planning Commission in particular thereby depriving the local governments of the way to show initiative.[48] The provinces are required to develop detailed regional and local industrial policies and submit them for approval by the State Council. Those plans will then guide, for example, the allocation of credits. In 1994, it became obvious that this approach will also affect foreign trade, China's desire to enter GATT notwithstanding. For instance, in mid-1994 it was decided to grant a monopoly of foreign trade to certain companies if essential commodities were involved, such as wool, cotton, wheat, fertilizer, steel and timber.[49]

The future policy toward TVE's will be of interest because we have already observed a strong drive to transform those enterprises into share companies. Together with a serious enforcement of the new labour law, this could mean tightening government regulations with the hidden aim of creating a more favourable environment for state enterprises. Furthermore, contrary to the view that "collective" ownership is a disguise for the TVE's drive to privatization, it seems that in 1994 the corporatization of TVE's will lead to local governments and other public organizations playing an even stronger role in managing those enterprises.[50]

Is it possible to assess the possible success or failure of the interventionist agenda at this stage? Two or three years are needed to implement the new system. Having laid down the legal framework in 1993 and early 1994, in April the State Commission for Restructuring the Economic System released a list of core issues for reform in 1994 which seemed to work again through the treadmill of slow changes in the institutional setting of China's economy.[51] The sequence of measures may be significant because the first item is the modernization of the state enterprise management system, the second item pertains to ongoing changes in fiscal and financial institutions.

The Roots of the Interventionist Agenda: Redistribution of Power

So far, the new institutions seem to be the object of intensive bargaining between the centre and the other agents in the economy. The main reason is that most of the 1994 policy measures focus on the relation between the centre and the local authorities, from provinces to the grassroots level.

If we examine some of the regulations (especially those on taxation), it is evident that there are many loopholes even before implementation. For instance, the centre failed to centralize revenue from income taxation to achieve redistribution purposes, and there are still legal means for reducing the tax burden for companies. Furthermore, the issue of extra-budgetary funds is not addressed by the new regulations, leaving open the possibility of manipulating and channelling of taxes funds into local coffers. But even with those legal or quasi-legal loopholes, there seems to be strong resistance against the new system at the local level. In the second half of 1994, the provinces far surpassed the centre in the collection of tax revenue (39% growth rate as opposed to 11%).[52]

One of the crucial issues linking fiscal problems, credit and regional development is the question of state enterprises. Many observers see them as the most important cause of the recurrent loss of control over the money supply.[53] Indeed, one worrying phenomenon in 1994 was the simultaneous expansion of the money supply and the growth of triangular debt which in the first half of 1994 was estimated as between RMB 600 and 700 billion roughly equal to the total amount loaned to industrial enterprises in 1993.[54] But analysts do not pay enough attention to the question of the regional distribution of state enterprises, which is at the heart of the fiscal and monetary problems.[55]

Not only is there a macro-regional imbalance in the distribution of loss-making state enterprises, e.g., between the Northeast and the Yangtze delta region, but also the problem of sub-regional imbalances. It is reported that a high percentage of loss-making enterprises is in the smaller cities and at the county level, whereas in larger cities, state enterprises can be very successful, especially in the Yangtze delta region. In Guangdong, for example, there is a marked difference between the state enterprises in the highly developed regions, on the one hand, and those in the more backwards counties and county towns. Here success in meeting growth targets on the average does not reflect the sometimes hopeless situation of state enterprises.[56]

If this subregional distribution is roughly equivalent to the distribution of budgetary responsiblity for the respective enterprises, then the current tax system still means that because of the regional assignment of the income and corporate taxes there are immediate repercussions on local budgets. The strong pressure by local authorities on banks to support state enterprises will therefore persist, either to boost business for the profitable ones and generate more income tax, or to help loss-making enterprises stave off unemployment. This pressure may grow because the budgetary means for support have been reduced.[57]

It is against this background that the reform of the banking system should be evaluated, since the separation between so-called "policy banks" and "commercial banks," and related credit funds, is directed at controlling the influence of local governments on the allocation of credit.[58] In former times, this influence led to the much deplored diversion of credit funds from agriculture to industry, or to the misuse of investment funds for paying wages in loss-making enterprises. But at the end of 1994, there was little to suggest any immediate effect on the behaviour of local governments. The resistance might already have been reflected in the slow progress in implementing the reform. But in December, Zhu Rongji resumed his tough stance toward local bank managers, which at least further boosted his image for willingness to use regulative levers common in commodity economies. This includes the use of tight credit quotas for the newly designed "commercial" credit system which is part of a full-fledged attempt at gaining control of the local use of funds. The newly established State Development Bank will also be relied on to achieve direct control of credits for investment finance.[59] Recent demands on the part of the National People's Congress to place control of the money supply in its hands should be interpreted as a direct counter-attack by regional delegates against the policies of the centre.[60]

Additional market-oriented reforms might be redirected by local authorities, resulting in over-expansion of credit by local branches. For instance, there were reports that speeding up the application of the bankruptcy law is simply another way to force local banks to back the credits of those companies, now only in order to pay off creditors (e.g. in triangular debt chains). It is estimated that at least 20% of oustanding credit are in fact defaults, and an additional 30% are only honoured in terms of interest but not in terms of return of principal. Hence about RMB 1,500 billion of funds present serious problems for the state banks. Other data point to the complete depletion of assets of state enterprises and 50% of them are estimated to have negative net worth were financial claims against them settled. In one large-scale survey, irretrievable "triangular debt" amounted to 24.5% of the capital losses (RMB 59.9 billion). The stock of accumulated debt is so large that interest payments have become a major issue for enterprises, absorbing 40% of the net growth of earnings resulting from price increases.[61] So far, mortgaging and other methods of guaranteeing credits are still primitive, and thus the business of credit in the narrow sense continues to be the core activity of the banks. Hence, the issue of financial stability discussed in section 3 is closely linked to the issue of the relationship between the centre and the local authorities.

Given the fact that one of the weakest links in the Chinese tax system is its decentralized structure, the reaction of local governments in county towns and medium-sized cities will also be crucial for achieving the goals of the tax reform.[62] For instance, just after the introduction of the new system local authorities began to give tax refunds following payment of taxes, not to mention the immense problems of educating a possibly unwilling local administration in the use of the new bookkeeping procedures for implementing VAT.[63] This can be understood if one understands that the majority of medium-scale loss-making state enterprises with excess workers are located at the lower end of the government hierarchy.

Fortunately, the new tax system gives local authorities incentives to develop small and medium-scale enterprises as well as the services sector because those taxes will also be distributed to them.[64] This could eventually lead to the creation of new job opportunities for workers in state enterprises and speed up structural change. But on the other hand, the centre's new industrial policies are evidently geared toward supporting medium and large-scale state enterprises. There is a contradiction between the objectives of tax reform — which should abolish irregular tax allowances and the reduction of interest before tax — and the objective of industrial policies to promote certain enterprises and industries by special tax and credit policies. Of course, it is assumed that from now on industrial policies should be controlled by the central government. But the experience of the last decade raises doubts about the ability of the centre to exert such control.

In that regard, the message conveyed by the new system to local government may be ambivalent because the particular provisions for tax sharing also follow short-term industrial policy objectives. One example is the attempt to centralize consumption taxes on profitable local industries such as cigarettes, cosmetics or cars. It is obvious that the sharing of certain taxes between the centre and the provincial governments aims at crushing resistance to the newly designed national industrial policy growing out of particular fiscal interests at the local level. However, from the viewpoint of the requirements for a long-term stable redistribution pattern, this mix of different objectives in the tax reform will weaken local commitment to the new system.

At the end of 1994, rumours still suggested a heightened tension between the central government and the local government (*difang zhengfu*), with the former personified since 1992 by the role of Zhu Rongji to which the symbolic weight of Jiang Zemin has lately been added with some sharp and open criticisms of local governments.[65] Indeed, the State Council's document on the tax sharing system stipulates that local interests should be looked after. It introduces certain measures which will freeze the final distribution of taxes as of 1993, with the centre's share only growing in the future. This seems to permit room for widespread manipulation of tax figures by the provinces. Proponents of local political resistance against the new system also form alliances with factions in the central leadership, in particular the so-called "conservatives." Hence strong measures seem to have been taken by the centre in late 1994, including the open criticism of "regionalism" and "factionalism."

However, the many positive reports issued in late 1994 on the success of the tax reform, particularly higher tax receipts by the government, still await detailed evaluation. The data show a 25.5% increase to RMB 731.4 billion in 1994, with the different industrial and commercial taxes representing RMB 451.3 billion.[66] Aside from the fact that "tax receipts" might not mean taxes actually transferred among different levels of the tax administration, a larger share of the rising tax income results from the increased taxation of imports. VAT and consumption tax revenue on imports amounted to RMB 62.26 billion in 1994.[67] Since it is unclear to what extent those taxes will be refunded to joint-ventures, and since Chinese importers have to pay the new taxes anyway, much of the so-called success of the tax reform might be explained by the increased taxation of foreign trade and investment, which does not lead to any conclusions regarding the internal tax administration.

In sum, there is still no solution to the problem of how to disentangle the intricate relation between the fiscal and the financial sectors. The clash between local and central interests continues to be the source of China's macro-economic instability. This also means that regional development is of the utmost importance for macro-economic stability, since local interest groups focus on their peculiar regional context. Hence much more is at stake than interest rates or inflation. Constitutional issues of allocating rights and power within the state come to the fore.[68] But in order to assess the challenge of 1994, attention should be paid to another important aspect of China's economic development which is also closely linked to the problem of inflation.

5. Welfare, Growth and the Rural Question: Who Will Be the Winner?

Prices and Redistribution

Aside from the far-reaching policy measures of 1994, the year is also important for assessing growth prospect in China. Many observers praise China for having achieved strong growth in personal material welfare and expect this to continue in the future. However, one should not forget the fragile state of individual living standards in China, if only to understand the worries of the Chinese leadership about social stability. The crucial question in this regard is the interaction between ongoing price reform and inflation. Those analysts who take Chinese figures on inflation for granted are plainly wrong. They forecast 1995 developments based, for instance, on the decline of year-to-year inflation rates at the end of 1994 (which, however, still show large spreads among the provinces with a year-to-year index of 114.0 for Beijing and 130.3 for Hunan).[69] As a rule, the higher the inflation rate, the stronger the administrative interventions and the less reliable the official figures on inflation.

In 1994, price reform was promoted again in the interest of upstream industries (such as steel, energy etc.) and of agriculture. Such reform has also had and will have a strong regional impact. But in the past, measures favouring agriculture only had an effect for a few years due to the impact on farm inputs of rising free market prices which inevitably widened the scissors gap to the detriment of the peasants. This was also the case in 1994 causing the government to raise procurement prices for cotton once again in order to solve the recurrent incentive problem. The reaction of relative prices, though strong on the surface, stayed within certain limits.[70] However, in the case of grain, where the government raised procurement prices in June 1994, it should be noted that (1) the resulting overall price increases were much higher in many inner provinces than along the coast, probably reflecting sluggish agricultural development as well as deficiencies in market infrastructure; (2) there was sometimes an even stronger reaction with downstream products like eggs and pork, and (3) the net result of the price increase for rural incomes can be neligible if the rapidly increasing input costs of grain production are taken into consideration. As in earlier times, the impact of those changes in relative prices will depend heavily on whether the urban sector will have to adapt fully to the new prices or whether an adaptive change of the price level, namely inflation, will serve to shelter the cities indirectly, finally eroding the changes in relative prices through managing the money illusion of peasants.

However, understanding Chinese price regulation in the urban sector is a difficult task because many responsibilities for price surveillance and control have been transferred to the local level since the mid-1980s.[71] This is especially true for the cities where local authorities have to confront the reaction of the urban populace to rising prices. Since 1989, a complex system of indirect price control has been built. It includes the local control of price ceilings and the establishment of public buffer stocks. Furthermore, special measures have been taken to guarantee the supply of cheap vegetables to the cities.[72] This includes designating special sites to grow vegetables for urban consumption (either controlling agricultural output prices directly or crowding out independent peasant producers by means of subsidized prices) and a fully-fledged system of price reporting (*jiage shenbao*) and price auditing (*jiage shenpi*). Hence even in the case of vegetables, the much-quoted view that the free market reigns supreme might be incorrect if viewed more closely. The many problems involved in preserving agricultural land devoted to vegetable production near the cities serves as an indicator of price distortions. In fact, the aim of the preservation of those areas led to the announcement of quotas for agricultural land-use at the beginning of 1995.[73]

In late 1994, the real importance of price controls for stabilizing inflation in the cities became obvious even to the ordinary visitor to China, who observed people once again queuing up in front of state-owned retail stores. Representatives of the central government even argued that the state should control 70–80% of trade in grain and edible oil, although this would not lead to structural changes in the distribution system. Grain coupons had already been reintroduced in many Chinese cities in the autumn of 1994, receiving much publicity at the end of the year.[74] The relevant State Council document clarifies the role of local governments. This, however, simply means that the above mentioned levers of price control have been backed and strengthened.[75] Furthermore, although price policies for cotton have led to a much acclaimed vigorous increase in production, there are still considerable problems in fulfilling procurement quotas, causing the government to cling to tough restrictions on cotton marketing.[76]

It is difficult to assess the degree of economic discrimination against the peasants within this context, but we may conclude that in 1994, too, the long-run devolution of central price controls in 1994 should not be perceived as growth in the share of truly free market prices. Instead, the grey area of locally administered and managed prices has increased considerably. Analysts in China point to the fact that this system continued to be geared toward urban interests and to discriminate against the peasants.[77] In early 1995, there were strong incentives to exploit this system to the disadvantage of farmers since almost all Chinese commentators on inflation agree to the crucial role of agricultural prices in pushing up the inflation rate.[78] The preferred cure for inflation is short-term price control and medium-term "support for agriculture" through fostering investment, supply of inputs or regulation of land use. So far, however, this kind of support has not proven very successful just as the current problems which have been induced by similar policies pursued in the past.

The Fragile State of Urban Wealth

Hence the hidden contradiction between urban and rural interests remains unresolved. The main reason is clear if we examine a survey of urban income in Beijing and Luoyang which has been released by the Taiwan-based *China Times Business Weekly* and which has been taken as evidence by the editorial of the publication as the epitome of the urban "consumer revolution."[79] There is a remarkable increase in living standards, especially in the consumption of durable consumer goods. But there is, as always in China, the problem of whether the glass is half full or half empty: the vast majority of city dwellers are far from well off. Even in Beijing, over 20% of the population have a per-capita income of 600–1000 per month, where the high cost of living results in consumption patterns whereby 85% of the population spend more than 50% of their income on food. The majority of the population visit parks or cinemas less than once a month, and around 40% only go shopping (aside from daily necessities) once a month. Their consumption patterns are understandably sophisticated with the exception of a wealthy sub-group of "yuppies." This is happening against the background of a very pronounced drive to gain status through wealth. People assess their status according to their perceived position on the income ladder, namely in pecuniary terms.

Spending on durable consumer goods is possible only because housing is virtually free of charge. Urban residents accumulate savings because they are preparing for changes in this regard, which are still uncertain because the problems of both city planners and the central leadership regarding housing reform are numerous. The survey demonstrates that the impact of inflation on the well-being of the urban population would be greater if prices for food and clothing were freed completely. Actually some two-thirds of the population already believe that increases in income do not keep up with inflation, and that real income is perceived to have decreased. This is particularly worrisome because one of the most remarkable results of the survey is an asymmetry between the actual position of the respondents on the income scale, and their subjectively perceived position. In particular, members of the so-called emerging middle class systematically downgrade their position. Together with their high expectations for the future, this can be an explosive mix if increasing inflation erodes real incomes further.

As conditions in the cities are getting less and less tolerable to manage politically, a supply of cheap agricultural goods is crucial for social stability. However, together with a speeding up of bankruptcy procedures for state enterprises there is a high risk that the majority of city dwellers in China may face an immediate deterioration in the satisfaction of their basic needs. This is why in recent bankruptcy cases, worker resistance revolved around the problem of food, i.e., families simply fear they will be unable to meet their elementary daily needs. As a matter of fact, the strong growth of urban wage funds in late 1994 mirrored the growing concern of the urban population about the possible decline in real incomes. The new Labour Law, designed to provide a legal framework for a true labour market, now for the first time provides a formal justification for indirectly indexing wages to inflation by means of minimum wage regulations. However, this law only applies to the urban population and not to rural migrants working in the cities.[80]

China's consumer revolution is still closely linked to the rural question. Although the State Statistical Bureau announced larger increases in rural than in urban incomes for 1994, this was the result of a long-delayed and stepwise adjustment of procurement prices which began in 1993 after several years of nearly stagnating real per-capita income in the countryside. However, the problems with respect to the second big ticket item in urban spending, clothing, remain unsolved.[81] In 1994, past conflicts of interest regarding domestic trade in cotton, silk and wool continued, including price wars, local export controls, large-scale attempts to cheat procurement organizations, tough administrative controls on trade and black markets and, most importantly, the continuation of the state cotton monopoly. Unless the cotton trade and cotton prices are tightly controlled, the state textile industries can not survive nor can urban dwellers enjoy a cheap supply of clothing.

One area where urban-rural conflicts of interest will intensify in the future is taxes.[82] Since the 1980s there has been much worry about irregular levies imposed on the peasants by the local authorities. However, there have only been attempts by local authorities to tighten the formal tax administration below the county level. This can be viewed as a failure in carrying out tax administration, which should be remedied by reducing irregular levies and improving regular taxation. However, in 1994, the new tax system did not tackle the question of rural taxation through the establishment of a systematic local tax sharing scheme but instead assigned only agricultural taxes to the local level, with the notorious black box of "local government" (*difang zhengfu*) reaching from the province to the administrative village hence without any regulation on the relations between the different levels of "local governments." The old "contractual system" (*baogan*) still operates between the counties and their villages and townships, on the one hand, and the county seats, on the other. There are already clear indications that county governments will try to shift the burden of higher taxes imposed by the centre onto the villages and townships. Indeed, this is the centre's intention because rural taxes are assigned to the local level and because there is a systematic under-taxation of certain economic activities in the countryside. Hence if the fiscal pressure of upper-level goverments on the county governments increases, this will immediately heighten fiscal tension between the counties and the "village" (*xiang*) and "township" (*zhen*) level governments.

Our considerations above referred to China without paying attention to regional variation. However, the problems mentioned are very different between the regions, implying that the political economy of price policies and inflation is different. In late 1994, it was reported that the magnitudes of changes in real incomes of urban residents varied depending on the city in question. For instance, people in Chengdu and Guangzhou enjoyed an increase of over 20%, whereas people in Chongqing and Xian had to be satisfied with a meagre 3%, and those living in Taiyuan and Nanjing faced a decline in real income.[83] This will, of course, eventually lead to intensive haggling over the redistribution of taxes and credit among the provinces.

6. Outlook

China's immediate future appeared darker in late 1994 than at the beginning of the year. Looking at the figures commonly quoted to describe the situation in 1994, this message seems overly pessimistic (see Table 8). But those figures only give a superficial impression. Confronting reality necessitates dealing with much more detailed and intricate, sometimes elusive, items of information referring to the state of regional economies. In that regard, recent concerns about the quality of Chinese statistical data are only the smallest of the issues at stake.[84]

Table 8. 1994 Economic Indicators

		%
GDP	RMB4380 bill.	11.8
Value added of primary sector	RMB 823.1 bill.	3.5
Value added of secondary sector	RMB2125.9 bill.	17.4
Value added of tertiary sector	RMB1431 bill.	8.7
Total grain output	444.5 mill. tons	−2.5
Value added of industry	RMB1835.9 bill.	18
Value added of light industry	RMB 766.8 bill.	19.6
Value added of heavy industry	RMB1069.1 bill.	16.5
Fixed assets investment	RMB1592.6 bill.	15.8
Value added of traffic and transport sector	RMB 224.7 bill.	6
Value added of post and telecommunication sector	RMB 69.3 bill.	50.2
Value of retail consumption	RMB1605.3 bill.	7.8
Increase of consumption prices		24.1
Export	US$121 bill.	31.9
Import	US$115.7 bill.	11.2
Foreign capital used	US$ 45.8 bill.	17.6
Direct foreign investment	US$ 33.8 bill.	22.8
Bank deposits	RMB2932.8 bill.	37.1
Increase of money supply (M2)		34.4

Source: *Jingji ribao*, 1 March 1995.

For many areas that cannot be covered in these pages, problems have surfaced which seem to accumulate as formidable obstacles blocking the way forward. Thus, China's infrastructure requirements may not be met because of the difficulties faced by foreign investors in China and because of the impending US$100 billion foreign debt.[85] The GATT issue is still unresolved. After cutting the link between trade issues and human rights in 1994 and solving one of the most difficult aspects of US-China relations, trade friction between the US and China nevertheless intensified again. As I have argued elsewhere, GATT also has far-reaching consequences for China's regional development and may have unforeseen influences on the capability of the central government to deal with the political economy of domestic trade and investment.[86] There are already signs that organizations involved in controlling internal trade might direct their attention to foreign trade as well. This was suggested by a campaign-like national drive against "fake" goods allegedly flooding China from the outside.[87]

The Chinese government still has much to learn about the meaning of a market environment for China's external economic relations. For instance, Dai Xianglong, Vice-Chairman of the People's Bank, recently pointed out the "discovery" that the central bank can no longer fully control the growth of the money supply if a certain exchange rate target is pursued under the new forex system.[88] Building foreign exchange reserves now means growth of the monetary base, and maintaining a certain price level can only be achieved if other components of the monetary base are decreased, such as refinancing the special banks. The latter, of course, would put additional pressure on credits to state enterprises. Hence, the Central Bank simply allows money to be injected into the economy, giving much room to further policy-induced business cycles in the future, including, for example, widening the scissors gap between agricultural inputs and output prices. One way out is to revalue the RMB, which would, however, boost imports and dampen exports.

But it seems to be the case that China pursued a monetary policy targetted at the exchange rate, thereby endogenizing the money supply. The short-term result was a very quick shift in the trade balance with a real jump in exports and the switch to a positive trade balance, while the medium run effect was inflationary. It should be added that maintaining the exchange rate imposes heavy costs on state enterprises and on heavy industry, in particular with their very high degree of import dependency. For example, imports make up almost 80% of net output value in the chemical industry. So there is thus added pressure on the profitability of industry in China.[89]

The Chinese government has yet to learn that, in matters of economics, conflicting targets cannot be realized simultaneously.

Trade-offs have to be weighed and prudent choices have to be made. However, so far the reaction has been to resort to even more government intervention as China remains vacillating at the crossroads.

Many of the economic policies discussed in this chapter may have unintended consequences. For instance, even at the institutional level one can imagine that the 1994 tax reform will not achieve its desired result of strengthening the centre's capacities. Instead, tax reform is likely to provide a sort of constitutional and administrative guarantee of the rights of the provinces.[90] However, the most important visible consequence today is the increase in migration within China. There is a direct link between macroeconomic cycles, the change in relative prices of agricultural inputs and outputs, and the incentives for peasants to leave home. It is estimated that 25 million migrant workers joined the mobile labour force in 1994. Furthermore, compared with the "blind flow" (*mangliu*) a few years back, migrants today are well-organized either along informal lines (such as family ties) or through public or semi-public organisations.[91] The main driving force of this large-scale movement is the relative decline in rural income since the mid-1980s, which by 1993 had widened the rural-urban gap making it similar in degree to that as of 1978.[92] Compared to the old system of compulsory procurement, state planning and administered prices, a much more complex system of exploiting the peasantry to support the cities exists today (perhaps unintentionally) and produces much the same results as the old command economy. Compared with earlier times, however, peasants now at least have the choice of migrating to the cities despite the barriers that still deny rural people full access to urban residency.[93]

China's true peasant revolution may be taking place at the end of the 20th century. But the main challenge is not directed at the centre. If we look back we realize that social change and macroeconomic development are closely related to the immense structural diversity of China's regions. This diversity is reflected in economic changes as well as in the political processes. Hence migration affects the interface between the economy and the polity, and theoretical approaches toward both should try to meet that challenge. Then it becomes obvious that the real political push will hit the decentralized power structure of the country, which has been called, amongst others, "cascade authoritarianism" from the political perspective and "local public ownership economy" or "regional corporatism" from the economic point of view.[94] The centre, however, should attempt to resolve possible breakdowns and ruptures. This will not come about through heavy-handed interventionism but by building a new constitutional framework and bolstering the rule of law. We are back to the basics.

Notes

1. Amongst many statements, see *South China Morning Post*, 9 and 22 December, 1994; *Far Eastern Economic Review*, 12 January 1995, pp. 64ff., and *China Trade Report*, No. 1 (1995), p. 3 ("The moneymoon is over"). It should be stressed that following some of the bad news, favourable treatment of "big ticket" investors such as McDonalds by central government intervention exemplifies also a failure of the rule of law. Even Hong Kong billionaire Li Ka-shing asked the Chinese government to establish reliable procedures for resolving conflicts between Chinese companies and foreign investors, see *Zhongshi zhoukan* (China Times Business Weekly), 11 December 1994, p. 48.
2. *Far Eastern Economic Review*, 26 January 1995, pp. 18ff.
3. *Far Eastern Economic Review*, 9 February 1995, pp. 44ff., makes some stinging remarks on the different "scapegoats" of inflation.
4. Kokubun Ryosei, *Nichi-bei-chuu no bimyoo na doraianogaru* (The Delicate Triangle between Japan, the United States and China), *Seikai* (The World), August 1994, pp. 46–49. The author argues that managing perceptions among Japan, the US and China should be a policy objective because it is an important determinant of China's future change.
5. In discussions about divergent development in China, the basic distinction between differences in the rate of change of certain indicators and differences of the absolute values is often forgotten. See Tsui Kai-yuen, *Cesuan Zhongguo shengji diqu chaju de wenti* (The Problem of Measuring the Regional Differences between the Provinces of China), in *Zhongguo diqu jingji fazhan yanjiu*, edited by Liu Shucheng et al. (Studies in the Regional Economic Development of China), (Beijing: Zhongguo tongji chubanshe, 1994), pp. 166–80. This point is important for setting the semantics right: If we speak of "convergent regional development" this cannot mean "convergence of growth rates," because only divergent growth can reduce the absolute distance between the provinces.
6. For instance, Tsui Kai-yuen, "Decomposition of China's Regional Inequalities," *Journal of Comparative Economics*, Vol. 17 (1993), pp. 600–27. Tsui argues that the rural-urban income gap (a nationwide as well as an intra-regional phenomenon) is an important determinant of regional inequalities. This suggests that there are determinants of spatial inequality which are not spatial in essence.

7. *Zhonggong zhongyang guanyu jianli shehuizhuyi shichang jingji tizhi ruogan wenti de jueding* (Resolution of the Central Committee of the CCP on Some Questions of Building the Socialist Market Economy), *Renmin ribao* (People's Daily), overseas edition, 17 November 1993. For a survey of the developments in 1993, see the relevant chapters in *China Review 1994*.
8. *China News Analysis*, 1 October 1994.
9. This expression is Gerald Segal's, "The Muddle Kingdom? — China's Changing Shape," *Foreign Affairs*, Vol. 73, No. 3 (1994), pp. 43–58.
10. This could be related to Paul Krugman's lucid arguments on a general deficit of intensive growth in the so-called "East Asian Miracle," see Paul Krugman, "The Myth of Asia's Miracle," *Foreign Affairs*, November/December 1994, pp. 62–78. At least in the case of China, Krugman appears to be right.
11. The figure was quoted in *Yatai jingji shi bao* (Asia-Pacific Business Times), 8 December 1994. On the second point, note the preference by southern Chinese consumers of steel for imported steel, since the local product is much more expensive. The government hence imposes special tariffs and a consumption tax. See *South China Morning Post*, 23 December 1994. For a general overview of the productivity issue related to the GATT-problem, see Y. Y. Kueh, "Industrial Deregulation and Economic Restructuring in China: A GATT Perspective," in *The East, the West and China's Growth: Challenge and Response*, edited by D. Cassel and C. Herrmann-Pillath (Baden-Baden, Nomos, 1995).
12. For a survey, see Hsueh Tien-tung (Xue Tiandong), *Zhongguo diqu de zonghe fazhan zhibiao tixi* (A Comprehensive System of Indicators of China's Regional Development), in *Zhongguo diqu jingji fazhan yanjiu*, edited by Liu Shucheng et al., pp. 22–56.
13. For instance, in Song Xueming's analysis of the determinants of divergent regional development in terms of New Growth theory, technical progress as a residual plays a very important role. See his "Regionale Wirtschaftsentwicklung in China, 1978–1993," in *Duisburg Working Papers in East Asian Economic Studies, 1995*. However, this is a mere statistical description of development *per se*, not an explanation of why technical progress is different in the provinces.
14. The data will be published soon in Carsten Herrmann-Pillath (ed.), *Wirtschaftliche Entwicklung in China's Provinzen und Regionen, 1978–1992, ein statistisches Handbuch* (Economic Development in China's Provinces and Regions 1978–1992, Statistical Handbook (Baden-Baden, Nomos, 1995).
15. One outspoken protagonist is Justin Linyi Fu, together with Fang Cai and Zhou Li, "Why China's Economic Reforms Have Been Successful: The Implications for Other Reforming Economies," mimeo, January 1994, Beijing.
16. Until the third quarter of 1994, this has remained valid, see *China aktuell*, No. 10 (1994), p. 1047.

17. See Cong Ming, "Dongbei dazhongxing qiye kaocha yinxiang" (Impressions from Research into the Medium and Large Scale Enterprises in the Northeast), *Zhongguo gaige* (China reform), No. 4 (1994), pp. 25–27.
18. For a penetrating analysis of those problems in the Yangzi region see Maruyama Nobuo (ed.), *Changjiang ryuuiki no keizai hatten, Ajia no keizai ken III* (Economic Development at the Yangtze River, Economic Regions of Asia III), (Tokyo: IDE, 1993).
19. For a useful survey of those indicators see Jürgen Kromphardt, "Konjunkturtheorie heute: Ein Überblick" (The Theory of Business Cycles Today: A Survey), *Zeitschrift für Wirtschafts- und Sozialwissenschaften* (Journal of Economics and Social Science), Vol. 109 (1989), pp. 176ff.
20. This is a remarkable observation, since the 1990s saw a strong central as well as local support for modernizing Shanghai's economy, boosting investment since 1992 when the productivity figure jumped upwards. However, the results seem to be mixed. See Zhou Xiaomen, *1994 nian shang ban nian Shanghai gongye yunxing xianzhuang ji wenti* (Performance and Problems of Shanghai's Industry in the First Half of 1994), *Zhongguo gongye jingji yanjiu* (Chinese Industrial Economics Studies), No. 10 (1994), pp. 62–64. The main problem is that a considerable share of Shanghai's state enterprises (in particular those which are "exclusively state owned" (*guoyou duzi qiye*) cannot digest the changes in the financial system, e.g. leading to a rapid increase of interest expenditures which before 1994 were not hurting. Hence the long-term decline of Shanghai's state industry has not ceased and seems to be leading to an increasing loss of competitiveness, even on the domestic market. So far, collective and *san zi* enterprises could change this picture, but the situation is still fragile. A useful survey of Shanghai's problems up to the end of 1993 is Gao Ruxi and Yu Yihong, *Shanghai jingji: tingzhi yu zai qifei* (The Shanghai Economy, 1953–1993: Stagnation and New Take-off), *Ershiyi shiji* (21st Century), No. 24 (1994), pp. 148–57.
21. I have made the following point already in my paper, "China's Transition to the Market: A Paradox of Transformation and Its Institutionalist Solution," in *The Political Economy of Transformation*, edited by Hans-Jürgen Wagener (Heidelberg: Physica, 1994), pp. 209–41. However, most observers until 1994 clung to the view that the overall decline of the share of state industries in Gross Material Production mirrors a shrinkage of the state sector as such. Only in the wake of the boom was it realized that this indicator is seriously misleading. See *Far Eastern Economic Review*, 7 July 1994, p. 60.
22. Hence I feel that the assessment by the IMF is a bit overly optimistic, see Wanda Tseng et al., "Economic Reform in China — A New Phase," IMF Occasional Paper No. 114 (Washington, DC: IMF, 1994), pp. 36ff.
23. For example, Maruyama Nobuo (Note 18), pp. 40ff.

24. On the following, see Paul Krugman, *Geography and Trade* (Cambridge and London: MIT, 1991), pp. 69–100.
25. Quarterly figures on the money supply are now published by the People's Bank. For past figures, see the new *China Financial Outlook* published by the People's Bank of China and quoted in *China aktuell*, No. 10 (1994), pp. 1047ff. For the year-end value see *Far Eastern Economic Review*, 9 February 1995, pp. 58, 63 and *South China Morning Post*, 28 January 1995.
26. In Germany, the Central Bank estimates that up to 50% of the effect of any over-expansion of the money supply is realized after three years and completely only after six years. See Monatsberichte der Deutschen Bundesbank, Januar 1992, "Zum Zusammenhang zwischen Geldmengen- und Preisentwicklung in der Bundesrepublik Deutschland" (Monthly Reports of the German Central Bank on the Relation between Growth of Money Supply and Prices in Germany), pp. 20–29. In Wanda Tseng et al. (Note 22), pp. 54ff. It is attempted to apply the agnostic Granger causality approach between different macro-economic aggregates affecting the inflation rate. The results are mixed and need to be interpreted carefully. The main problem seems to be that the institutional characteristics of China's credit sector lead to close parallel movements between the money supply and industrial production, so that causality may be interpreted in both directions. In the end, inflation is best explained by inflation.
27. See *Zhongguo tongji nianjian 1994*, p. 544. In Shenzhen and Guangdong, the State Special Banks now only account for less than 50% of the financial market, see Xie Ping, "Lun guojia zhuanye yinhang de gaige" (On the Reform of State Special Banks), *Jingji yanjiu* (Economic Research), No. 2 (1994), p. 25. The PBOC announced that it would control this outflow of funds from the state banking system to the different "non-bank financial institutions," *Jingji ribao* (Economic Daily), 27 January 1995.
28. *South China Morning Post*, 5 January 1995.
29. On rural deposits see *China Daily*, 10 and 11 January 1995. The ABC is now the country's largest savings bank, with RMB 837.7 billion in private savings deposits. However, it is well known that Chinese consumers seek out alternatives like gold, which has seen a 200% increase in internal trade volume. See *South China Morning Post*, 9 January 1995. The steep rise in personal foreign currency deposits may also be linked with such behaviour, see *China Daily*, 11 January 1995.
30. *China Daily*, 6 January 1995 and *South China Morning Post*, 23 January 1995. However, at the end of the year, black market interest rates in Guangdong were reported to be 30% (with a higher risk premium), see *South China Morning Post*, 27 December 1994.
31. According to *Xinwen bao* (News Daily), 27 November 1994, the ample supply of deposits relieves state banks from the problem of a negative gap

between deposits and credits which in former years had to be financed by the PBOC. However, the report said that the increase in deposits causes growing problems with current business earnings. The PBOC customarily refinanced the state banking system when the reserve ratio dropped severely, as in autumn 1993, only to issue credit ceilings in December. See Dai Xianglong, "Huobi zhengce jianchi shixing wenjian de" (Monetary Policy Remains Stable), *Zhongguo jinrong* (China Finance), No. 3 (1994), p. 7. On the growing importance of private agents for the capital market and its stability, see also Wang Guogang, "Guomin: Zhongguo ziben shichang de zhongyao juese" (The People: Important Actor on China's Capital Market), *Jingji yanjiu*, No. 12 (1994), pp. 19–27.

32. However, Zuo Dapei, "Kornai-Koeffizient, effiziente Betriebe und Wirtschaftswachstum in China, 1978–1993," (Kornai-Coefficient, Efficient Enterprises, and Economic Growth in China, 1978–1993), Duisburg Working Papers in East Asian Economic Studies, No. 16 (1995), tried to estimate China's "natural growth rate" according to a simple model along new neoclassical lines. The result is a natural growth rate of about 9%, which represents the long term growth of potential output.

33. Two surveys are Gary H. Jefferson and Thomas G. Rawski, "Enterprise Reform in Chinese Industry," *Journal of Economic Perspectives*, Vol. 8, No. 2 (1994), pp. 47–70, and Wing Thy Woo (Hu Yongtai) et al., "Zhongguo qiye gaige jiujing huode le duoda chengjiu "(How Great Was the Actual Success of Enterprise Reforms in China?), *Jingji yanjiu*, No. 6 (1994), pp. 20–32. I follow the second line of thought.

34. This is also the conclusion in Robert McKinnon, "Financial Growth and Macroeconomic Stability in China, 1978–1992: Implications for Russia and Other Transitional Economies," *Journal of Comparative Economics*, Vol. 18 (1994), pp. 438–69.

35. See Anjali Kumar, "China's Reform, Internal Trade and Marketing," *The Pacific Review*, Vol. 7, No. 3 (1994), pp. 331ff. See also Carsten Herrmann-Pillath (ed.) (Note 14), where it is argued that the difference between national income (*goumin shouru*) and national income utilized has declined markedly, relative to the level of national income in almost all the provinces. Since this difference simply mirrors provincial balances of trade, the decline of trade integration goes hand in hand with a decreasing degree of integration in terms of capital flows, including domestic as well as international flows. Compare the results reported by He Juhuang et al. "Zhongguo guomin shouru de diqu jian liudong" (The Inter-regional Flow of National Income in China), in *Zhongguo diqu jingji fazhan yanjiu* (Note 5), pp. 292–302, where the picture is not as clear because only aggregated macro-regional figures are given and not the figures for single provinces. However, since 1993 the picture might have changed, because inter-bank lending served as a vehicle for

inter-regional capital flows of an unprecedented magnitude, which were driven by large inter-regional differences in interest rates. See Geng Xiao and Haiyan Gao, "The Engine of Growth and the Root of Inflation in the Chinese Economy," *China Review 1994*, edited by Maurice Brosseau and Lo Chi Kin (Hong Kong, Chinese University Press, 1994), p. **9**.9. We have mentioned the strong expansion in the "others" category of the state credit plan that already in 1993 featured a RMB 175 billion excess of related credits over related deposits. Those are the outflows which presumably moved to the south.

36. The problems in assessing the Chinese inflation rate in the local context are discussed below. However, the prices of many local non-tradeables are administered, while at the same time the impact of inflation (as distinguished from changes in relative prices) is difficult to estimate, for example, consider the recent price hikes in entrance fees for public gardens. See Tang Ren, "Shui neng guan guan Beijing shi?" (Who Can Govern Beijing?), *The Mirror*, No. 12 (1994), pp. 39–41. See also *China Trade Report*, No. 10 (1994), p. 3. For the considerable interregional differences in prices for many goods, see Nakajima Seiichi, "Price Reform in China," *JETRO China Newsletter*, January–February 1993, pp. 6–15.

37. See Kojima Reeitsu, "The Growing Fiscal Authority of Provincial-Level Governments in China," *The Developing Economies*, Vol. XXX, No. 4 (1992), pp. 315–16.

38. *South China Morning Post*, 21 December 1994, where it is reported that the PBOC has injected an additional RMB 7 billion of reserves into the special bank system in order to support their dealings with state enterprises.

39. See *Jingji cankao bao* (Economic Information Daily), 22 December 1994. Accordingly, prices in the material goods sector were reported to have changed little. In July the prices for industrial inputs were reported to have fallen 8.4%. See *Shenzhen tequ bao* (Shenzhen Special Economic Zone Daily), 20 December 1994. However, this does not concur with many observations of industries complaining about the large gap between market prices and planned prices for their product, as in the case of urea and liquefied petroleum gas. See *South China Morning Post*, 24 January 1995. We cannot assess the extent to which government intervention has influenced prices in the material goods sector. It should be noted that a similar decline in producer's goods prices also took place in mid-1993, without an impact on the acceleration of inflation in 1994. See Hu Shaowei, "1993–1994 nian shengchan ziliao shichang xingshi fenxi yu zhanwang" (Analysis and Prospects of Trends in the 1993–1994 Market for Producers' Goods), *Zhongguo gongye jingji yanjiu* (China Industrial Economics Studies), No. 3 (1994), p. 24. For problems with input price hikes see also *Caizheng* (Finance), No. 8 (1994), p. 42. This argument also seems to contradict the observation that 1994 saw strong growth in fixed-asset investment estimated

at 28.5%. See *South China Morning Post*, 11 January, 1995. For state-owned units, a figure of 49.5% growth was mentioned in *Renmin ribao*, 5 January 1995.

40. For instance, the Chinese Academy of Social Sciences (CASS) argued in October 1994 that inflationary pressure had subsided and that macroeconomic policies should not take the current inflation rate as a guidepost for targeting credit policies. See "Zhongguo jingji zheng zai 'ruan zhuo lu' hongguan zhengce quxiang ying shedang song guimo kongzhi" (China's Economy Is Making a "Soft Landing" and Macroeconomic Policies Should Take a Position of Appropriately Loose Aggregate Control), *Zhongguo shehui kexue yuan yao bao* (Important News of the CASS), No. 1509 (28 October 1994). Compare also the different statements in *Zhongguo gaige* (China Reform), No. 9 (1994), pp. 6–10. However, the data mentioned did not mirror the substantial increases in the price of energy and agricultural staples which took place in 1994, including, for example a price hike for crude oil of 60%.

41. The results reported in Wanda Tseng et al. (Note 22), pp. 54ff., strongly support this view.

42. I have analyzed this at length in *Institutioneller Wandel, Macht und Inflation in China: Ordnungstheoretischen Analysen zur Politischen Ökonomie eines Transformationsprozesses* (Institutional Change, Power, and Inflation in China: On the Political Economy of Transition) (Baden-Baden, Nomos, 1991), pp. 131–210.

43. In 1994 there was a heated discussion about an article by Zuo Dapei, "Guchui pengzhang yu liyi qudong, Zhongguo jingji xuejie ye yao fan fubai" (Propagating Inflation and the Profit Motive, Chinese Economists Also Should Fight against Corruption), *Jingji xue xiaoxi bao* (Economics Information Daily), 2 February 1994. The paper accused economists of talking dishonestly about the dangers of inflation in order to receive material advantages from politicians who could use their arguments to justify, for instance, further expansion of credits at the local level. The reaction was tough. See the same journal on March 10, or in *Jingji yanjiu ziliao* (Economic Research Materials), No. 3 (1994), pp. 55ff. and in *Gaige* (Reform), No. 4 (1994), pp. 5–8. This discussion shows that there are deep-seated problems with independent research and the relationship between policy analysis and political decision-making. The whole story is also reported by the former leading party intellectual, Su Shaozhi, in "Zhonggong zhongyang jingji huiyi biexi" (An Analysis of the National Economic Conference of the CCP), *Cheng Ming*, No. 1 (1995), p. 33.

44. A similar observation has been made by Maurice Brosseau in his discussion of the "traditional reflex" of intellectuals. See *China News Analysis*, 1 January 1995, p. 5. For an example of the rational legitimization of industrial policy see Sun Wenbo and Wu Qiang, "Wo guo jingji feiqi jieduan de tedian ji

chanye zhengce quxiang" (The Special Features of the Take-off Stage of Our Economy and the Direction of Industrial Policy), *Zhongguo gongye jingji yanjiu*, No. 9 (1994), where it is even argued that China is entering the stage of "heavy industrialization." In general, the current concern for the many so-called bottlenecks in Chinese economic development leads many people to link further marketization (development) with a strong interventionist central state. The symbol of this, of course, is the Yangtze Three Gorges dam project. For recent policy statements on more direct state control of the economy, see *South China Morning Post*, 21 January 1995.

45. Hence at the end of 1994, there was widespread confusion about the direction of current economic policies, when, for example, Li Peng called stock markets "experimental." See the comment in *Far Eastern Economic Review*, 29 December 1994/5–January 1995, p. 29. In fact, even Zhu Rongji cannot be called an advocate of a "market economy." He was recently quoted warning against "blindly adoring Western economics textbooks." Zhu offered the view that free market prices will lead to an irrational use of resources, economic inequality and injustice, all well known evils as seen from the Marxist viewpoint of a market economy. See *Shenzhen tequ bao*, 20 December 1994. Su Shaozhi, in "Zhonggong zhongyang jingji huiyi biexi" (An Analysis of the National Economic Conference of the CCP), *Cheng Ming*, No. 1 (1995), p. 34, also points to the fact that Zhu now stresses planning and state ownership more than previously and openly criticizes economists like Li Yining.

46. See the survey in *China aktuell*, No. 10 (1994), p. 1048, and *Far Eastern Economic Review*, 27 October 1994, p. 29. It was announced that the tight-fisted approach toward futures markets would continue in 1995. See *South China Morning Post*, 17 December 1994 and 16 January 1995. However, Guangdong province announced it would not comply. See *South China Morning Post*, 23 January 1995. This paper cannot discuss the role of emerging capital markets in 1994, but suffice it to say that in this "modern" segment of the market system, government interventionism is rampant and continues to be official policy, such as in the case of the massive financial support of the Shanghai stock market in August, 1994. See *South China Morning Post*, 3 January 1995 and *Zhongguo zhengquan bao* (China Exchange Daily), 14 December 1994, even concluded that the movements on the stock markets in 1994 were almost completely "politically motivated."

47. The regulation on the new industrial policy and the automobile industry have been published in *Guowuyuan gongbao* (State Council Bulletin), Nos. 12 and 15 (1994), pp. 496–505 and 630–38. A useful survey of the current state of the industry is Ishiro Katsuji, "China's New Auto Industrial Policy," *JETRO China Newsletter*, November–December 1994, pp. 2–5. For the new law on external trade see *Renmin ribao*, overseas edition, 14 May 1994, p. 2. However, recently the central government announced a similar approach to all

FDI in terms of "production strategies," see *South China Morning Post*, 20 December 1994. Industrial policy objectives are also mentioned in many major laws which have been released in recent years, as for instance in the corporate law where it is asserted that the development of corporate finance should follow industrial policies of the State Council, see *Guowuyuan gongbao* (State Council Bulletin), No. 30 (1994), p. 1440.
48. For a comment on this approach, see Jiang Lin and Gao Xiaosi, "Xiangzhen qiye fazhan de zhanlüe zhuanyi" (Shift of the Strategy regarding TVEs), *Jingji yanjiu*, No. 4 (1994), pp. 23–28.
49. *Liang an jing mao tongxun* (Straits Economic Relations Newsletter), No. 9 (1994), p. 14.
50. This process started already in 1993, when local governments implemented corporatization with the aim of boosting collective enterprises which began to suffer from competition with private enterprises, in particular with managers changing their jobs. See Ma Rong et al. (eds), *Jiu shi niandai Zhongguo xiangzhen qiye diaocha* (Investigations into China's Village and Township Enterprises in the Nineties), (Hong Kong: Oxford University Press, 1994), p. 442f. It is said that now about 10% of TVEs have been converted into so-called stock companies, see Guoji shangbao (International Business Daily), 4 November 1994. And there are cases of a real recollectivization, see *Far Eastern Economic Review*, 17 November 1994, p. 32.
51. See *Guowuyuan gongbao*, No. 14 (1994), pp. 561–66 and comments e.g. in *Zhongguo gaige*, No. 8 (1994), pp. 6–10.
52. A survey can be found in *China aktuell*, No. 9 (1994), p. 929, and No. 12 (1994), p. 1188.
53. Geng Xiao and Haiyan Gao, "The Engine of Growth ..." (Note 35).
54. *China News Analysis*, Nos. 1513–1514 (1–15 July 1994), p. 5.
55. On this see for instance Qian Jiajun and Peng Shaozhong, "Guanyu guoyou qiye jianshao rongyuan wenti de diaocha yanjiu" (An Investigation into the Problem of Decreasing the Number of Superfluous Workers in State Enterprises), *Zhongguo gongye jingji yanjiu*, No. 8 (1994), pp. 20–24.
56. On Jieyang county in Guangdong see Lin Xiongbo, "Qiye kuisun: xianzhuang, chengyin ji duice" (Losses of Enterprises: Current Situation, Causes and Remedies), *Zhongguo tongji* (China Statistics), No. 4, (1994), pp. 20–22. For a more general assessment cf. Lau Pui-king, "Industry and Trade," in *Guangdong, Survey of a Province Undergoing Rapid Change*, edited by Y. M. Yeung and David K. Y. Chu, (Hong Kong: Chinese University Press, 1994), pp. 124ff.
57. In many regions there seems to prevail a sense of crisis after the introduction of the new system which sometimes is explicitly linked to the needs of the enterprises, see e.g. from Heilongjiang Chen Ying, "Dui wo sheng shishi fenshuizhi caizheng tizhi gaige de chubu sikao" (Preliminary Thoughts about

the Implementation of the Reform of the Tax-sharing System in Our Province), *Caizheng*, No. 9 (1994), pp. 19–20.
58. For a general evaluation of the banking system reform in 1994 see Dan Baoqing/Zhu Yunxiang, "Hui mou jiusi ni shui xing chuan, jinrong tigai yi nian jinzhan chihuan jiezheng fenxi" (Looking Back on Sailing against the Current, An Analysis of the Crucial Issues in One Year of Retardation of Progress in the Reform of the Financial System), *Zhongguo shichang jingji bao* (China Market Economic News), 12 December 1994. A similar assessment can be found in *Jingji ribao*, 16 December 1994, where it is also mentioned that now the criteria for "policy loans" are too broad and soft.
59. *South China Morning Post*, 7, 19, 29 December 1994, and 6 January 1995. This was actually called "state planning" by the Vice-Governor of the PBOC, see *South China Morning Post*, 16 January 1995. See also *Jingji ribao*, 16 January 1995.
60. On those demands, see *South China Morning Post*, 28 December 1994.
61. Yang Yumin/Liu Fujiang, "Dui 1994 nian gongye jingji xiaoyi zoushi de panduan" (Assessing the 1994 Trends in Industrial Productivity), *Zhongguo gongye jingji yanjiu*, No. 7 (1994), p. 27, *Zhonghua gongshang shi bao* (China Business Times), 20 December 1994, and *South China Morning Post*, 10 January 1995. In a seminar at Beida in Beijing, Gao Shangquan gave the figure of the outstanding debt of the state enterprises representing 80% of their net wealth.
62. For report from Sichuan, see Liu Fengtong, "Jiceng xin shuizhi yunxing zhengchang" (The Routine of the New Tax System at the Grassroots Level), *Caizheng*, No. 6 (1994), pp. 22–25. Cf. also *Zhongguo shuiwu*, No. 6 (1994), p. 1, and for a general evaluation, *Shi chang bao* (Market Daily), 20 December 1995.
63. Furthermore, when talking about tax reform at least in a note it should be mentioned that society, i.e. the people, also strikes back: Tax authorities regarded the administration of the personal income tax a "failure," see *Hong Kong Standard*, 12 December 1994.
64. For a related analysis see Qi Shouyin, "Shi xi xin fenshui zhi fang'an de zhengce daoxiang" (Trying to Analyze the Policy Implications of the New Approach toward the Tax-sharing System), *Caizheng*, No. 6 (1994), pp. 45–48.
65. See Yan Hua, "Zhu Rongji tuixing fenshuizhi zao weigong" (Zhu Rongji's Push toward the Tax-sharing System Faces Attack from All Sides), *The Nineties*, No. 12 (1994), pp. 44–45, and *Cheng Ming*, No. 1 (1995), pp. 9ff. The problems were already rampant at the introduction of the new tax system when provinces falsified tax figures. There was a sharp statement of the finance minister before the NPC in March 1993, see *Caizheng*, No. 5 (1994), p. 3.

66. *South China Morning Post*, 9 and 15 January 1995.
67. *Jingji ribao*, 10 January 1995. The central government will continue to tap this source of tax receipts by lifting many exemptions for joint ventures, see *South China Morning Post*, 23 January 1995. Of course, this is a sensible approach in order to arrange for just competition. But no immediate conclusion follows regarding the overall success of the tax reform. Anyhow, there seem to be no data on the relative contribution of the foreign trade sector to the alleged success of tax reform, see *South China Morning Post*, 15 January 1995. But there are many signs that the Chinese government is going to focus on China's foreign trade for boosting revenue, see *Far Eastern Economic Review*, 26 January 1995, p. 53.
68. Indeed, there were reports that mainland scholars participated in designing far-reaching proposals on regional democracy and federalism, see *South China Morning Post*, 19 December 1994.
69. This is the common approach, see amongst many others *South China Morning Post*, 17 December 1994, The regional data have been published in *Jingji ribao*, 21 January 1995.
70. Pang Shaolin/Zou Wenhui, "Liang jia tiaozheng zhi hou" (After the Regulation of Grain Prices), *Zhongguo tongji*, No. 9 (1994), pp. 43–44. On the price scissor issue, see, e.g., *South China Morning Post*, 29 December 1994.
71. I have surveyed those changes in Carsten Herrmann-Pillath (Note 42), pp. 371–76. To my mind, most observers do not pay enough attention to local price control and put too much emphasis on the price policies of the central government. But then the real meaning of the recently published guidelines for reform of priced-institution (e.g., see, *Guowuyuan gongbao*, No. 14 [1994], pp. 561–66) cannot be understood. These include amongst other measures, the "building of a system of surveillance and control" for the prices of agricultural products (*jianli nongfu chanpin shichang jian kong tixi*) which, of course, is implemented at the local not the central level. See also, *China News Analysis*, No. 1512 (15 June 1994), p. 3. There were news items on some new instruments of price regulation, like the establishment of a "price regulation fund" (*jiage tiaojie jijin zhidu*) in many cities. See, for example, *Zhongguo jingying bao* (China Management Daily), 2 December 1994.
72. On the "vegetable baskets" in Shanghai see e.g. Li Zishun, "Jiajin jianshe xin yi lun 'Cai lanzi' gongcheng" (Speedily Building the New Round of the "Vegetable Basket" Project), *Zhongguo gaige*, No. 6 (1994), pp. 28–30. This policy is still in focus in 1995, see *Jingji ribao*, 11 January 1995. One should add that there are very strong interventions in the market. For instance, in Taiyuan there was the invention of "non-profit sales" which means that trade in vegetables is controlled by the local government and nobody is allowed to buy more than one kilogram at one time, see *Jingji ribao*, 24 January 1995.

73. *South China Morning Post*, 21 December 1994 and 6 January 1995.
74. *South China Morning Post*, 17, 29 and 30 December 1994, 6 January 1995. News items refer to Hunan, Anhui, Sichuan and the whole Northeast. The figure on 70–80% state control was provided by *Jingji cankao bao*, 22 December 1994, where the idea of state planning also extends to the whole agricultural input distribution system, too. Policies toward strengthening state control on prices were already taken in mid-1994, see *Liangan jingmao tongxun* (Economic Relations Across the Straits Newsletter), No. 9 (1994), p. 12.
75. In effect, local governments released tighter regulations on price control a bit earlier, like in Hanchuan county near Wuhan, where an explicit list of prices of important goods was released on December, see *Hanchuan bao*, 27 December 1994. The policy has been even more pushed in the Chinese New Year preparations, see *Renmin ribao*, overseas edition, 6 January 1995.
76. Compare e.g. *Jingji cankao bao*, 8 November 1994, with *Jingji ribao*, 10 January 1995.
77. The director of the Rural Development Institute, CASS, Chen Jiyuan, takes this attitude toward the "vegetable basket" system, see the interview entitled "Chen Jiyuan tan: dangqian wo guo nongye mianlin de shen cengci wenti" (Chen Jiyuan on Some Deep-structural Problems of Agriculture in Our Country), published in *Zhongguo gaige*, No. 5 (1994), pp. 30–32. Cf. in the *China Review 1994*, the paper by James Kaising Kung, "Peasants in a 'Hot Pot': Pushing the Limits of a Biased Strategy against Agriculture?."
78. See, for example, *South China Morning Post*, 5 January 1995.
79. See Zhongshi zhoukan bianji bu, "Da lu chengshi xiaofei geming — Beijing, Luoyang shimin xiaofei diaocha baogao" (The Consumption Revolution of Mainland China's Cities — Report on the Investigation into Consumption of Beijing and Luoyang City Dwellers), *Zhongshi zhoukan* (China Times Business Weekly), Nos. 154, 155 (1994), pp. 37–45, 44–51. The editorial is in the latter, p. 3. The report mirrors the situation in mid-1994.
80. For instance, the situation in Heilongjiang was very difficult in 1994, leading to hardships for many workers. In April the Governor and the Party Secretary were dismissed, presumably because of their handling of the state enterprise issue which was followed by worker's protests. See Wen You, "Gongyouzhi wei zhu hai ku Heilongjiang" (Heilongjiang's Bitterness with "State Ownership First"), *Cheng Ming*, No. 12 (1994), pp. 28ff., and on 1994 labour disputes in general see *South China Morning Post*, 7 December 1994. At the end of the year there were rumours about similar dismissals in Sichuan and Hubei, see *Far Eastern Economic Review* 29 December 1994–5 January 1995, p. 12. The strong pressure of workers in the cities induced a complete loss of control of the wage fund which grew 31.7% in the first three quarters

of 1994 (with the state enterprises being the main culprits) although there was a national investigation of the development of "consumption funds" since September, *Zhongguo tongji*, No. 11 (1994), p. 7. The expansion has been financed through the banking system from the beginning of 1993, see Han Wenxiu, "1994 nian tonghuopengzhang qushi fenxi" (Analysis of the Trend of Inflation in 1994), *Zhongguo gongye jingji yanjiu*, No. 9 (1994), p. 6. For more details see *China aktuell*, No. 11 (1994), p. 1125, and on regional differences including figures of 46.1% growth for Shanghai, *China Daily*, 7 January 1995. This expansion took place with a growing share of non-wage payments to workers, according to a statement by Gao Shangquan at a seminar which took place at Beida in early January 1995. On minimum wages, see *South China Morning Post*, 5 January 1995. Minimum wages were established at the local level earlier in 1994, for instance, in Xiamen, a year-by-year adjustment to the inflation rate was introduced, see *Liang an jingmao tongxun* (Straits Economic Relations Newsletter) No. 9 (1994), p. 18. Whether discrimination against migrant workers will also include administrative control of their movements is still unclear although there were already attempts at closing the urban labour market, see *South China Morning Post* 14 December 1994. It should be mentioned that in 1994, with the publication of "Looking at China from the Third Eye," urban resentment against migrants found a very sharp expression in the public, see *South China Morning Post*, 10 December 1994.

81. See the survey in *China aktuell*, No. 10 (1994), p. 1049, and for a more detailed analysis of the situation at the beginning of 1994, see *China News Analysis*, No. 1506 (15 March 1994). However, similar controls on the grain markets have been established much earlier in the year, too, see *Guowuyuan gongbao*, No. 15 (1994), p. 639. The issue is also linked with the problems of futures markets which we already discussed in section 4, cf. *Far Eastern Economic Review*, 27 October 1994, p. 29.

82. See views from Jiangsu, Ji Jin, "Jiakuai jianli sheying fenshuizhi yaoqiu de difang caizheng xin geju" (Speeding up the Formation of a New Pattern of Local Finance That Fits the Requirements of the Tax-sharing System), *Caizheng* (Finance), No. 7 (1994), pp. 16–17, and from Hebei, Cheng Fengchao and Gao Zhili, "Shixing fenshuizhi hou difang caiyuan jianshe zhanlüe zai xuanze de jiben silu" (Basic Thoughts on New Options for Building Local Fiscal Resources after the Implementation of the Tax Sharing System), *Caizheng* (Finance), No. 10 (1994), pp. 36–38. In the late eighties and the early nineties such a snowball effect from the provincial to the "*xiang*" and "*zhen*" levels could already be observed within the "*baogan*" system. See the detailed discussion in Shi Chuan and Carsten Herrmann-Pillath, *Die Krise des chinesischen Steuerstaates: Probleme des Fiskus in Kreisen und Dörfern* (The Crisis of the Chinese Fiscal State: Problems of Fiscal Management in

Countries and Villages), Special Report of the Federal Institute for East European and International Studies (Cologne, 1992).
83. The figures were quoted in *Zhongguo yinjin bao* (China Transfer Daily), 20 December 1995.
84. There is a growing need for the central government to implement tight administrative and disciplinary approaches against falsification of statistics at the local level, which is reportedly also related to the general difficulties in maintaining administrative procedures, see Chen Yuanchou et al., "Xiang xujia shuzi xuanzhan" (Declaring War against False Figures), *Zhongguo tongji*, No. 11 (1994), pp. 10–12. One example pertains to statistics of TVE's. In some regions output figures are said to be faked to an extent of 30–40%, see *Ya Tai jingji shibao* (Asian-Pacific Economic Times), 8 December 1994. However, the State Statistical Bureau recently affirmed that China's data are reliable, see *South China Morning Post*, 21 January 1995.
85. *Far Eastern Economic Review*, 10 November 1994, pp. 56–61.
86. Carsten Herrmann-Pillath, "Growth and the Claim to Big-Power Status in China," *Aussenpolitik, German Foreign Affairs Review*, No. 3 (1994).
87. In November, Fujian was reported to have established a special system of "security control" for nine import items including cars, refrigerators and air conditioning units. See, *Liang an jingmao tongxun*, No. 12 (1994), p. 20.
88. *Guoji shangbao* (International Business Daily), 20 November 1994. Scholars noted the problem earlier, citing the trade-off between inflation and the stability of the exchange rate. See Sun Mingchun, "Lun waihui guanli tizhi gaige dui wo guo huobi zhengce de yinxiang" (On the Effects of the Forex-system Reform on Monetary Policy in Our Country), *Jingji yanjiu*, No. 8 (1994), pp. 52–56.
89. *Far Eastern Economic Review*, 20 October 1995. On import dependency of China's industry see Xu Kangning, *Wo guo gongye jinkou yicun de fenxi* (The Import Dependency of the Industry of Our Country), *Zhongguo gongye jingji yanjiu*, No. 7 (1994), pp. 36–40.
90. This point was raised by Maurice Brosseau. See *China New Analysis*, 1 January 1995, p. 8.
91. The figure was quoted in *Jingji ribao*, 21 January 1995. Recent surveys on migration include, Zhonggong zhongyang zhengce yanjiu shi nongcun zu (Rural Study Group of the CCP Central Committee Policy Research Department), *Guanyu nongcun li kuaqu liudong wenti de chubu yanjiu* (Preliminary research into the Inter-regional Movement of Rural Workers), *Zhongguo nongcun jingji* (Chinese Rural Economy), No. 3 (1994), pp. 3–8, and Luo Yousheng/Liu Jianwen, "Nongcun laodongli kuaqu zhuanyi: xianzhuang, chengyin yu duice" (Interregional Migration or Rural Workers: Current Situation, Causes and Policy), *Zhongguo nongcun jingji* (Chinese Rural Economy), No. 8 (1994), pp. 3–10.

92. This is the result of a detailed study by the State Statistical Bureau, see *Guojia tongji ju nong diao cong dui keti zu* (Study Group of the Comprehensive Rural Survey Team of the State Statistical Bureau), "Cheng xiang jumin shouru chaju yanjiu" (A Study of the Income Differential between Urban and Rural Residents), *Jingji yanjiu*, No. 12 (1994), pp. 34–45.
93. There is now a growing concern, for instance, about the practice of cities charging high fees for urban development to people from other places, see *Jingji ribao*, 9 January 1995.
94. The phrase "cascade authoritarianism" was coined by the Japanese political scientist Amako Satoshi'. See his "kasukeedo kata ken'i shugi no kanoosei" (The Possibility of "Cascade Authoritarianism"), *Seikai*, No. 8, 1994, pp. 39–45. The "local public ownership economy" is Fan Gang's expression, see his, "Competition between Brothers: Problems of Divergent and Regional Development in China," (Note 11), edited by D. Cassel and C. Herrmann-Pillath (Baden-Baden, Nomos, 1995). The author has analyzed regional corporatism in Note 42.

20

Fiscal Reform in 1994

Christine Wong

The urgency of fiscal reform to support China's transition to a market economy hardly needs to be argued. Through 1993, the macroeconomic implications of "making do" with the Soviet-type tax system far into the market transition process were well-known. The relaxation of centralized control over the economy quickly eroded the interlocking mechanisms of revenue-generation — fixed prices rigged to favour industry, state ownership of industry and restricted entry, and compulsory procurement and trade. As these mechanisms weakened, the budget shrank from over 35% of GDP on the eve of reform to less than 15% in 1993, reducing government's ability to allocate resources and limiting reform options. As government expenditures have not declined in pace, persistent budgetary deficits have also exerted inflationary pressures on the economy.

The microeconomic implications of the Soviet-type tax system were also clearly adverse, as differential rates of indirect taxes across products and sectors distorted resource allocation, attracting socially wasteful investments in many high-tax sectors such as cigarette and liquor production. In addition, the production-based (rather than income-based) tax system contributed to the duplicative investment pattern across regions and helped to forge a mutually dependent, collusive relationship between government and enterprises that has hindered the progress of reform in Chinese industry.[1] Moreover, the industry-dependent tax structure has helped to perpetuate the pattern of overindustrialization beyond the "Stalinist development strategy" and into the period of market reform. The pattern has been extended even into the countryside, where, to expand their tax base, rural governments are vying with one another to promote township and village enterprises, sometimes beyond what is socially optimal. The high income tax rates (of 55% on state and collective enterprises) and unequal tax treatment of different types of enterprises have reinforced incentives for tax evasion and distorted resource allocation.

Reform in intergovernmental revenue sharing arrangements was also urgently needed because the Soviet-type system had become increasingly unenforceable, contributing to fiscal decline. Under the pre-reform system, revenues were collected by local governments and shared upward with the

---

This paper draws from Christine Wong, with Kam Wing Chan, Christopher Heady and Loraine West, *Financing Local Government in the People's Republic of China*, a report for the Asian Development Bank (ADB), December 1994. Views expressed in this paper are solely those of the authors, and not the ADB.

central government. The system was highly redistributive, requiring rich provinces to turn over large portions of revenues to the central government to finance transfers to poor provinces.[2] The adverse effects of the very poor incentives thus created were held in check by monitoring that was fairly straightforward, since revenue capacity was relatively easy to determine given fixed prices and tight central control over entry into industry. Central control over the budgetary process also limited opportunities for hiding unauthorized expenditures and reduced incentives for cheating at the local level. In the reform period, by contrast, monitoring of tax effort has become far more difficult, as price shifts and unrestricted entry into industry caused changes in tax capacity in every region. At the same time, decentralization of budgetary control means that local governments now have both the motive and opportunity to shield local revenues from sharing with higher levels.[3]

The 1994 Tax Reform

It is against this backdrop that the government announced a comprehensive reform of macroeconomic management at the Third Plenum of the 14th Party Committee in November 1993. Among the provisions of the *Decision on Issues Concerning the Establishment of a Socialist Market Economy* are a fairly comprehensive package of measures aimed at reforming the fiscal system.[4] The programme is designed to address three areas of concern: to provide adequate revenues for government, especially central government; eliminate the distortionary elements of the tax structure and increase its transparency; and revamp central-local revenue sharing arrangements.

Among the key provisions of the package is a major reform in indirect taxes that extends the value-added tax (VAT) to all turnover, eliminating the product tax and replacing the business tax in many services. It has simplified the tax structure by reducing the number of VAT rates from the previous 13 (ranging from 8 to 45%) to primarily a single rate of 17%, although "preferential rates" of 13% and 6% are applied to some basic necessities for which the government wants to limit price increases (such as for urban water supply), and a few low profit industries (e.g. coal mining) to help them through the transitional period. The reform also unifies the turnover tax treatment for domestic and foreign enterprises by eliminating the consolidated industrial and commercial tax previously applied to foreign enterprises, placing them also under the VAT.

The reform in direct taxes has unified the tax rate on profits for state-owned, collective and private enterprises. This eliminates a major source of distortion that had existed under the previous system, by removing the unequal treatment of enterprises under different ownership. The top nominal rate of taxation has been reduced to 33% from 55%. The income adjustment tax has been eliminated, along with contributions to the Energy and Key Transport Fund and the Budget Adjustment Fund, which had absorbed 25% of enterprise after-tax profits. Offsetting these reductions is the elimination of a number of exemptions, most notably the pre-tax repayment of loans from enterprise profits.

A new personal income tax has replaced three former taxes: the personal income tax, the personal income adjustment tax, and the individual enterprise income tax. This places Chinese citizens and foreigners on the same tax schedule, although it does not eliminate the unequal treatment of different incomes by source.

As consistent with preparations for rejoining GATT, the reform also reduced import duties on 1898 products in November 1993, and another 234 products were reduced in 1994.[5] The number of industrial and commercial tax types has been cut from 32 to 18.

At the same time, a number of new taxes have been introduced, such as a consumption tax on luxury goods including alcohol and tobacco products that is levied in addition to the VAT, which is akin to the excise tax that is applied in many countries. There are also new taxes on capital gains on land transfers, on inheritance, and on stock market trades, etc.

Revenue Sharing Reform

The centre-piece of the reform package is introduction of the tax sharing system (*fenshuizhi*), which is fundamentally changing the way revenues are shared between the central and provincial governments. Under the tax sharing system (TSS), new lines are drawn dividing revenues into central fixed, local fixed, and shared incomes. Central fixed incomes include customs duties, the consumption tax, VAT revenues collected by customs, income taxes from central enterprises, banks and non-bank financial intermediaries; the remitted profits, income taxes, business taxes, and urban construction and maintenance taxes of the railroad, bank headquarters and insurance companies; and resource taxes on oceanic oil extraction. Local fixed incomes consist of business taxes (excluding those named above as

Fiscal Reforms in 1994

central fixed incomes), income taxes and profit remittances of local enterprises, urban land use taxes, personal income taxes, the fixed asset investment orientation tax, urban construction and maintenance tax, real estate taxes, vehicle utilization tax, the stamp tax, animal slaughter tax, agricultural taxes, title tax, inheritance and gift taxes, capital gains tax on land, state land sales revenues, and resource taxes derived from land-based resources. Shared incomes consist solely of VAT revenues, which are shared at the fixed rate of 75% for the central government, and 25% for local governments.

To phase in the new revenue divisions, the central government has introduced two modifications to the TSS. First, to guarantee each province's base revenues for 1994 to be no less than those in 1993, the central government committed to making a transfer to each province of:

$$PBR - LT - 0.25 \times VAT$$

where PBR is the province's base retained revenue, LT is the province's local tax revenue in the base year (1993), VAT is the VAT revenue from that province.

In other words, for 1994 the base revenue of each province is taken to be its level of retained revenue in 1993 (which was its total revenue minus the amount remitted to the central government). This transfer is designed to allow the province to maintain the same level of expenditure in 1994, after accounting for its local tax revenue and its share of VAT.

The second modification is over the sharing of increases in revenue. If the central government's revenue from VAT and consumption tax in a particular province increases above the previous year's level, they return 30% of that increase to the province concerned. In other words, there is an extra transfer from the centre to the province of:

$$0.3 \times [0.75 \times (\text{VAT increase}) + (\text{CT increase})]*$$

where CT is the consumption tax revenue from that province.

This means that for any increase in provincial revenue that results from increases in consumption tax and VAT, the province receives 30% of

---

* The original intent was to use the national growth rate of VAT in the formula, but a concession was made to provinces in implementation whereby the provincial rate is used.

the gain to the central government, and the results of the system are as follows:

1. For an increase in consumption tax, the province receives 30% of the increase, and the central government receives 70%;
2. For an increase in VAT, the province receives $0.75 \times 30\% + 25\% = 47.5\%$, and the centre receives 52.5%.

These formulas for sharing additional revenues are of particular significance because of the designation of the base revenue figures in nominal terms. This means that, as inflation proceeds through the 1990s, the role of the 1993 base revenue figures will be gradually eroded, and the revenue shares going to the provinces will be determined increasingly by the formula for the division of revenue increases.

To avoid exacerbating the existing problem of poor local effort in collecting central government taxes, tax administration is to be reformed under the 1994 programme, with the establishment of a national tax system (NTS) to collect central government revenues, and a local tax system to collect local taxes. This is achieved by splitting the existing tax bureaus into central and local tax offices. The main responsibility of the NTS is the collection of VAT and consumption tax — they collect all of both taxes and then transfer 25% of the VAT revenue to the local government.

In the administration of the VAT, the "invoice method" is being introduced nationwide as the basis for calculating tax payments due, replacing the previous chaotic system which allowed taxpayers to choose from among different methods.[6] With these new measures, Chinese tax administration is gradually moving toward the achievement of international standards.

Assessing the Reform Package

The 1994 fiscal reform package receives high marks for its comprehensiveness. Since the inception of reform numerous attempts have been made to alter the tax structure and improve incentives for local tax effort.[7] However, these attempts aimed at marginal changes but left intact two central features of the Soviet system that have proved problematic in a decentralized economy — the differential rates of indirect taxes across products and sectors allowed taxes to play an unintended resource allocation function, and local tax administration conferred joint "ownership" of revenues that required negotiated sharing between the central and local governments and eroded incentives for local tax collection. In contrast, the 1994 package marked the first attempt by the government to fundamentally change the fiscal system by rooting out these troublesome features, including an overhaul of tax administration.

The reform package also gets high marks for greatly simplifying the tax structure and improving transparency, which should in turn aid monitoring and improve revenue collection over time. Unfortunately, implementation has been marred by the inadequate time that the tax bureau had to prepare for the change. International experience suggests substantial periods of time are required. For example, a two year period of planning and taxpayer education is generally advised before the introduction of VAT. The period allowed in this case was much shorter: although many of the proposals had been discussed for a number of years, final approval was only given a few months before the reforms were due to be implemented. This meant that the separation of the tax bureaus could not be achieved before the new rules came into effect. It has also meant that VAT is being applied using the invoice method for the first time with neither the taxpayers nor many of the local tax officials being fully prepared for its use. As a result, there has been a good deal of confusion in implementation, especially since the "invoice method" was introduced along with the switch of the VAT from an "embedded tax" (*jianeishui*) to one levied outside the price (*jiawaishui*). In some localities incorrect calculations and double-taxation have caused price increases and been blamed for contributing to inflationary pressures.[8] However, these are likely to be transitory problems that should not affect the long-term benefits of the reform programme in modernizing the Chinese tax system.

More problematic is that reforms left intact the division of direct tax revenues according to enterprise ownership (or subordination), whereby central enterprises pay income taxes to the central government, a provincial enterprise pays income taxes to the provincial government, etc. This may continue to provide incentives for duplicative investment and biased treatment of enterprises in a given region and will prove a hindrance to the expansion of enterprises beyond their local markets to other regions.

Whether the reform programme will achieve the objective of improving buoyancy of the fiscal system (or increase the share of budgetary revenues in GDP) is more difficult to ascertain. In the design process, the government was centrally concerned that the choice of VAT and income tax rates should ensure revenue stability in the short term. These were estimated in a number of studies to require a rate of 17–18% for the VAT to replace current revenues from the three turnover taxes, and a rate of 33–35% for income tax rates on enterprise profits.[9] Both are close to the rates adopted. In the long run it is expected that revenue growth (in terms of GDP) would come from the reduction of tax exemptions given by local governments, currently estimated at 30–40 billion yuan annually, or 15–20% of total VAT revenues.

Actually tax revenues rose substantially faster in 1993 than both inflation and GDP, for the first time in several years, with indirect tax revenues growing by 49.6%. However, much of the increase may have been the outcome of strategic behaviour by local governments, which scrambled to collect as much as they could to raise their revenue base after the announcement in August 1993 that the TSS would adopt as the base retained revenues the amounts collected in 1993.[10] These produced a large reported increase in tax revenues, partly due to improved enforcement and partly due to the collection of owed back taxes. The Ministry of Finance believes that some of the increase may have even included enterprises being persuaded to pay taxes in advance to boost the figures.

In 1994 the growth in indirect tax revenues and total revenues was somewhat lower — for the first eight months indirect tax revenues were 33% higher than the same period in 1993. Even this was partly boosted by the new requirement that every province achieve revenue growth pegged to their 1993 increases. In order to prevent provinces gaining from artificially inflated revenues in 1993 and to ensure revenue growth in 1994, the Ministry of Finance set targets for revenue growth for each province, called *kaohe zhibiao*, or reference targets, with higher targets for those provinces suspected of having padded their 1993 collections. For those provinces that fail to meet their target, the Ministry threatens to reduce correspondingly their base retained revenue figures.

Whether the reforms will improve revenue buoyancy depends first of all on how they affect incentives for local revenue collection. Even though a key aim of the TSS reform was to put central-local fiscal relations on an objective, non-negotiable basis, there appears to be some uncertainty about how rigorously the TSS will be implemented, with many local governments adopting a wait-and-see attitude through 1994. One problem is that the TSS is not a "pure" tax assignment system — even though many taxes have been assigned, the sharing of the dominant tax source, the VAT, has required contracting to be applied to the second-round of revenue sharing.

There is some danger that the spirit of TSS reform has already been tarnished by the episodes of concession in 1993–1994. Many have criticized as excessive the concessions made in 1993 to rebate to provinces sufficient revenues to make up to the 1993 base levels. These concessions to appease local governments not only deferred the achievement of a rising central share of revenues, they also left sharing formulas that are so complex that even in the Ministry of Finance very few can articulate the specifics of the division.

Moreover, while handing down revenue growth targets to each province in 1994 can be seen as a clever manoeuvre by the central government to deal with the problem of provinces inflating base revenue figures, it has also re-introduced the harmful individual negotiation between province and centre that was characteristic of the contract system.

Building an effective NTS is critical to ensuring improved revenue collection and revenue buoyancy — with the centre claiming 75% of VAT and 100% of consumption tax revenues, local tax agents have weaker than ever incentives for collection under the TSS. The task of building a NTS should not be underestimated. Setting up the new institutions, introducing new management techniques, setting up coordination with the local tax bureaus, and training staff to monitor taxpayers, etc., will all take time. As of the end of 1994, only a few major cities had completed the process of "dividing up family assets" in the split-up of existing tax bureaus. Getting them all set up and working effectively may take years.

Finally, improved buoyancy depends on the government's ability to rigorously apply the new tax laws. There are indications that the 1994 reform has not succeeded in eliminating negotiation over tax liabilities. The State Council is overseeing the granting of tax preferences and has made a number of new concessions, including the introduction of the 6% VAT rate for industries such as urban water supply and brick-making. Also, concessionary income tax rates of 18% and 27% have been introduced for enterprises in financial difficulty. This process of case-by-case examination is worrisome, since it threatens to erode the objectivity of the new tax system and reintroduce "softness" into tax obligations, undermining the whole spirit of reform.

Remaining Issues

One of the immediate effects of the 1994 reform is that in 1994 many local governments appeared to be experiencing severe cash flow problems in the transition to the new tax sharing system. Under the TSS, revenues from the

VAT and consumption tax are collected directly by the NTS and channelled to the central treasury. Even though the central government returns 25% of the VAT and a portion of total revenues to the provinces on a monthly basis, delays in the return of these funds were reportedly causing many local governments to defer all capital expenditures, and even to withhold wage payments to civil servants. The problem of deferring wage payments was worse at lower levels, which have to wait for disbursements from the province, and where wages are a major portion of total expenditures.

Another problem of the hastiness in implementing the reforms is that many provinces had not yet established tax sharing schemes with subordinate levels of government. As a result, through 1994 cities and counties were not sure whether the tax sharing with their provincial government for the year would follow the rules of the previous contract system or follow a formula similar to that between provinces and the central government. This uncertainty is harmful because it prevents local governments from planning their expenditure properly.

While the 1994 reforms have moved the fiscal system significantly toward greater transparency and a sounder basis for revenue sharing, they are very much incomplete. The Ministry has once again juggled the intergovernmental division of revenues but left expenditure assignments intact. Since the tax sharing reform was designed specifically to shift revenues toward the central government, it will lead to a squeeze on local budgets unless new local revenues can be found. However, the reform did not confer autonomy for introducing new taxes, changing tax rates or the tax base on local governments, so that its revenue-mobilizing effect is likely to be limited at the local level.

To further the TSS reform, expenditure assignments must also be realigned, along with a devolution of taxing powers to local governments. In response to the new revenue divisions, in some localities, governments are resorting to selling public assets such as land, urban residency permits, and public housing, as means of raising revenues for financing social expenditure. The wave of privatization of housing stock at highly concessionary prices that swept through many cities in 1993 and 1994 so alarmed the government that the State Council called for a temporary halt to housing sales by early 1994. The government must watch these developments carefully and impose appropriate regulations to ensure efficient and equitable use of funds thus generated.

Introducing a new system of intergovernmental transfers is an urgent task in the wake of the 1994 reforms, as the development of new tax and revenue sources will inevitably favour rich regions that have greater revenue-generating capacity. The government must increase transfers to poor regions, which are at present inadequate. Regional income differences are very large in China, and these differences have led to large disparities in tax capacity and service provisions across provinces. The ratio of highest to lowest per capita income is around 6 to 1 across provinces. At subprovincial levels this ratio is even bigger — for example, in one township in Guizhou, the ratio of highest to lowest per capita income is 10:1 across the dozen villages.

Through the 1980s and early 1990s, intergovernmental transfers have diminished in relative terms. For example, in Guizhou, the poorest province in China, the portion of provincial expenditures financed from central subsidies has declined from nearly 60% in 1980 to less than 20% in 1993. Forcing the province increasingly toward self-financing has meant provisions of basic services that fall far short of central government mandated targets. For example, the central government has called for providing nine years of compulsory free education, a level already met in virtually all large cities. Yet, in Guizhou no city has met this target as of 1994, including the provincial capital of Guiyang. Similarly, national guidelines call for every village to have a medical clinic or station, and every township to have a central hospital. In Guizhou only one-third of the villages have clinics. Given the low degree of population mobility in China (so that few Guizhou residents can seek to escape poverty or better social services elsewhere), insufficient fiscal resources in the poor areas are causing large populations to be exposed to inadequate basic services. This is an issue that deserves urgent attention, especially where clearly enunciated national goals are not being met.

Finally, reform of intergovermental relations must take account of issues of "off budget" finance. Through the reform period, the combination of decentralization, liberalization, and growing fiscal pressures on local budgets have led governments to turn increasingly to users' fees and levies to finance local services. By 1992, extrabudgetary revenues controlled by local governments and administrative agencies amounted reportedly to about 4% of GDP.[11] In addition, rural governments at the county and township levels controlled another 1–2% of GDP in "self raised funds."[12] There is likely to be substantial undercounting of these funds. These are substantial portions of government resources, equal to more than one-third of total revenues.

Even though these fees and levies have been widely criticized as chaotic and excessive, many are actually levied as quasi-taxes with the blessing of and occasional supervision by higher level governments. Their *raison d'être* consists of the following factors: (1) There were insufficient revenues within the budgetary system to finance expenditure responsibilities at the lower levels of government. (2) Opportunities for levying these fees sprang from the lack of legal protection for assets of enterprises and individuals against fiscal predation, and (3) The lack of supervision over the scope of work for local governments opened the door to excessive levies.[13] Until these issues are addressed, fiscal reforms that deal only with the formal budget and its division of resources will not only leave intact a large and problematic sector that needs urgent attention, but may indeed create more pressures for further growth in that sector.

Notes

1. Christine Wong, "Between Plan and Market: The Role of the Local Sector in Post-Mao Reforms," *Journal of Comparative Economics*, September 1987.
2. Nicholas R. Lardy, *Economic Growth and Distribution in China* (New York: Cambridge University Press, 1978).
3. The history of this evolutionary process was discussed in Christine P. W. Wong, "Fiscal Reform and Local Industrialization: The Problematic Sequencing of Reform in Post-Mao China," *Modern China*, April 1992; and Christine Wong, Christopher Heady and Wing T. Woo, *Fiscal Management and Economic Reform in the People's Republic of China* (New York: Oxford University Press, 1995).
4. *China Daily Supplement*, 17 November 1993.
5. Zhou Xiaochuan and Yang Zhigang, "Achievements and Problems in the 1994 Tax Reform," paper presented at the Conference on "The Next Steps for Economic Reform in China," Beijing, August 1994.
6. Wong, Heady and Woo (Note 3).
7. Michel Oksenberg and James Tong, "The Evolution of Central-Provincial Fiscal Relations in China, 1971–1984: The Formal System," *The China Quarterly*, No. 125 (March 1991), pp. 1–32.
8. For example, Zhou and Yang (Note 5) report that some enterprises incorrectly added the taxes paid by suppliers (which should have been rebated) to their own invoice prices, thus raising the level of prices.
9. See, for example, Zhou Xiaochuan, *Zhongguo caishui gaige* (China's Fiscal and Tax Reform) (Beijing: Renmin chubanshe, 1993).

10. See Tsang Shu-ki and Cheng Yuk-shing, "China's Tax Reforms of 1994: Breakthrough or Compromise?" *Asian Survey*, Vol. 34, No. 9 (September 1994), pp. 769–88, for a description of strategic behaviour in Guangdong.
11. See Wong, Heady and Woo (Note 3), Annex II.1.
12. "Financing Local Government in the PRC," *China Daily Supplement*, 17 November 1993.
13. See Christine Wong, "Financing Local Government in China: Feasts, Famines, and Growing Regional Disparities," *Journal of Comparative Economics*, 1994.

21

Financial Restructuring

Tsang Shu-ki

1. 1994: A Year of Macroeconomic Reforms

China launched in 1994 a comprehensive economic reform programme that covered the fiscal system, central and commercial banking, foreign exchange, trade, investment and enterprise management. Important decisions were taken in the Third Plenum of the Fourteenth Central Committee of the Chinese Communist Party (CCP) held in November 1993, which produced a document entitled *Decision of the CCP Central Committee on Issues Concerning the Establishment of a Socialist Market Economic Structure* (hereafter referred to as the *Decision*).[1] Given the overheating situation in the economy, the reform package was a bold step taken by the government in building a more market-oriented economy with effective macroeconomic control mechanisms. Top officials stressed that while the reforms were to be coordinated, there was a need to achieve a breakthrough in some key areas.[2] In the multi-faceted programme, measures on the fiscal, monetary and foreign exchange systems were apparently assigned top priorities. In any case, public attention has so far focussed on these macroeconomic changes.

In conception at least, the macroeconomic reforms of 1994 were radical moves, and their major objectives were to restructure the operation of the economy, particularly its financial aspects, and the way through which authorities could exert influence on it. Such an attempt however came into conflict with three different sets of factors: (1) resistance by parties of vested interests who benefited from the old systems and stood to lose under the new arrangements;[3] (2) the lack of corresponding progress at the microeconomic level, e.g., enterprise reform in the state sector; and (3) cyclical movement in the economy which worked against measures that aggravated the inflationary pressure in general and the worsening illiquidity and insolvency in the state sector.

This chapter looks at two major aspects of the reform programme: (1) central and commercial banking; and (2) foreign exchange. The relative achievements and setbacks on these two fronts are quite revealing, as they throw light on the dynamic interaction between the central government and the local authorities, the conflict between reforms and macroeconomic stability, as well as the uneven developments in the Chinese reform process. Most commentators would agree that the foreign exchange reforms have been much more successful than the banking reforms. In the process of discussion, I shall also look into the new "triangular trade-off" in China's economic policies and the compromises that had to be made in 1994.

2.1 Preludes to the Banking Reforms of 1994

The 1994 banking reforms were related in a rather complex manner to the problems encountered in the preceding two years, and it may be useful to start with a short review.[4] Financial disorder had become rampant by the first half of 1993, although the inflationary situation was not as bad as 1988. As huge amounts of funds were irregularly channelled to long-term projects such as economic development zones (EDZs) and property developments, as well as short-run speculative activities in the stock and futures markets (together constituting the so called "three new fevers" — *xin san re*), the consequences of further uncoordinated expansion could be very serious.

There was also an upsurge of the activities of non-bank financial institutions (NBFIs) in 1992–1993. Unauthorized borrowing and lending, involving many NBFIs, had become widespread since 1992. Moreover, many of the NBFIs were established by local branches of specialized banks as a vehicle to circumvent central scrutiny. Ignoring state restrictions, some local banks diverted massive amounts of funds to these financial institutions. In 1992, the sum total of net lending by the specialized banks to the other financial institutions amounted to more than RMB60 billion yuan. The situation continued to worsen in the first half of 1993.[5]

The frantic scramble for funds reached a climax in the first half of 1993. On the one hand, there was a rapid expansion of direct fund-raising by enterprises. On the other, a massive decline of deposits in the banks was observed. Many financial institutions illegally raised interest rates to attract deposits, and underground banks and funds operators charged exorbitant lending rates, a few even on a daily basis.[6]

Despite the proliferation of direct fund solicitation, there was little doubt in the minds of authorities that the crux of the problem was still with the banking sector, which nurtured the NBFIs. The illiquidity of many local branches of the specialized banks was heading for crisis. The cash reserve ratios of many of them fell below the 5% "warning level" in 1992, and the situation further deteriorated in 1993. By the end of the first quarter, the average cash reserve ratio of the specialized banks was only 3.6%, while the ratio of some branches in Zhejiang province slid even below 1%.[7] Irregular interbank borrowing and lending was also a big problem, where many bank branches used short term funds to extend long term loans.

Hence the central government felt compelled to do something to restore financial order and to cool down the economy. A sixteen-point macroeconomic adjustment package was unveiled in early July 1993,[8] and over half of the measures were administrative in nature. However, the adjustment essentially lasted for only two months, as credit was significantly relaxed again from September onwards.[9]

With hindsight, there can be two possible interpretations of the policy reversal. First, the tightening of credits caused severe hardship for a large number of unexpected victims, including many state enterprises and worthy projects. It again revealed dramatically the dilemma facing the central monetary authority: macro-control might not produce the desirable micro-effects; but any waiving of macro-control would lead to even more serious micro-problems. Second, the government did not really intend to engineer a general clamp-down on the economy. It was practicing the so called "stop-go" (*zou zou ting ting*) approach instead of repeating the past cycles of *laissez faire* on the upswing and "hard braking" on the downswing of the economy. In any case, both arguments can be used to support the view that the government was actually using the 16-point programme as a prelude to the comprehensive reform launched later.

Let us begin by looking at the first interpretation. A key problem in this regard is the fact that the specialized banks, the pillar of the Chinese financial system, have yet to become truly commercialized despite all the reform attempts since 1984. The crux is that of balance-sheet fragility in the specialized banks.[10] Table 1 presenting their aggregate balance sheet provides the key evidence.

As Table 1 shows, the specialized banks were heavily dependent on the central bank, the People's Bank of China (PBOC), for funding. In 1988, net liabilities to the PBOC amounted to RMB 217.61 billion, or 17.95% of their total assets. They formed an important source to bridge the huge loan-deposit gap of RMB 355.96 billion, which represented 29.36% of total liabilities. The situation improved somewhat by the end of 1993. Net liabilities to the PBOC equalled 13.87% of total assets and the loan-deposit gap was 13.0% of total liabilities. In any case, the aggregate balance sheet still looked precarious. Unlike their commercial counterparts outside the country, over 70% of the special banks' funds were loans, rather than diversified into a portfolio of assets with different degrees of liquidity, risk, and returns. An additional problem was that a substantial portion of the loans was "policy loans"[11] with very low liquidity and, low returns, if any. Many of the "commercial" loans, extended to ambitious investment projects and speculative activities, also faced

Financial Restructuring

Table 1. Balance Sheet of the State Specialized Banks Year-end, 1988 and 1993

Unit: RMB billion

	1988	1993		1988	1993
Liabilities			Assets		
Deposits	668.61 (55.14)	2140.01 (62.23)	Loans	1024.57 (84.50)	2586.97 (75.22)
Due to PBOC	336.12 (27.12)	961.26 (27.95)	Required reserve	80.96 (6.68)	270.83 (7.88)
Own capital	91.44 (7.54)	154.33 (4.49)	Due from PBOC	37.55 (3.10)	213.56 (6.21)
Other liabilities	116.30 (9.60)	183.44 (5.33)	Cash	10.36 (0.85)	42.30 (1.23)
			Other assets	59.03 (4.87)	325.38 (9.46)
Total	1212.47 (100.00)	3439.04 (100.00)	Total	1212.47 (100.00)	3439.04 (100.00)

Source: Simplified from People's Bank of China, *China Financial Outlook '94*, July 1994, Table 3–4, pp. 89–90.

Note: Numbers in brackets are percentages. PBOC — People's Bank of China; deposits and loans refer to those denominated in the *Renminbi* only. Foreign currency deposits and loans are lumped into other liabilities and other assets respectively.

repayment difficulties. According to some estimates, as much as 30% of the total outstanding loans of the banking system could be regarded as at risk in 1993.[12]

Facing such a fragile financial structure of the banking system, the PBOC had been caught in a dilemma in its attempt to implement monetary control. The evolution from the initial "gap control" in 1984–1985 to the later system of reserve requirement and relending did not markedly change the situation. Given this kind of lopsided balance sheet, the impact of any tightening by the PBOC would be drastic as there were very little liquid assets out of which the banks could switch. To restore balance, they had few alternatives other than curbing new lending and demanding enterprises to repay outstanding loans. This would generate severe knock-on effects in the economy as a whole. It was one of the key reasons why the PBOC was usually reluctant to reign in unless things were really out of control.[13] To get out of the dilemma, it had become obvious that real reforms in the central and commercial banking systems needed to be implemented.

Two related problems rendered it more difficult to deal with the situation in 1993: (1) the commitment of funds to long-term investments such as infrastructural construction and the EDZs, the rising importance of the non-state sector, as well as the continued monetization of the economy had all raised the demand for money and credit;[14] (2) the problems of the financial deterioration of the state-owned enterprises and triangular debts re-emerged even as the economy was on an upswing. While they were no justifications for indiscriminate loosening of credit, these two factors meant that any "across-the-board" retrenchment could be very inefficient and costly.

As to the second interpretation, i.e., the one related to the "stop-go" approach, one basic motivation is exactly the increasing difficulty associated with a general clamp-down. Moreover, given the structural changes in the economy and the shifts in behavioural patterns among different parties (consumers, public and private enterprises, local governments), there is a need for Beijing to re-think the balance between macro-adjustments and reforms. A case can be made that macroeconomic policy in China should be more reform-oriented in the sense that it should cater more for systemic changes rather than short-run supply-demand balance in the economy. In other words, if bigger institutional progress can be achieved, then greater cost, say in terms of higher inflation, may be acceptable. I have called this a "triangular trade-off" (among growth, inflation and reform), in contrast to the bivariate trade-off (between growth and inflation) along the "Phillips Curve" in a typical market economy.[15]

Under such a view, Beijing deliberately tightened credit two times (last quarter of 1992, July–August 1993) in a stop-go manner before the launching of comprehensive reforms in November 1993. It would then be misleading to call the 16-point package an "austerity programme," as the government did not intend to impose hardship on the economy. The basic objective was rather to pinch the financial bubbles and restore order in the banking sector largely by engineering a change in expectations. This approach was of course very different from the past "make-or-break" cyclical pattern, under which overheating was allowed to get out of control before crude administrative measures were used to brake the upswing.

Both of the above interpretations can no doubt be criticized as rationalizing the actions of the Chinese authorities. Some commentators would say that the "austerity programme" launched by Zhu Rongji in late June 1993 was later simply compromised by factors ranging from Deng Xiaoping's intervention, the seriousness of the "triangular debts," as well as resistance from local authorities. This author does not however think that the comprehensive macroeconomic reform package was devised *impromptu*. Hence when launching the 16-point programme, Chinese leaders should already have had the various reforms in mind. Indeed, a writer has revealed that, at the National Finance Working Conference chaired by Zhu Rongji in July 1993, a consensus was reached among participants that the problems of financial disorder could only be solved by the deepening of institutional reforms. After the conference, other than implementing measures to restore order, the formulation of the proposals on financial reforms also passed from a stage of "nurturing" into one of substantive drafting and revision.[16]

In any case, reform fervour soon dominated the economic scene as the government launched initiatives that aimed at quickly establishing an effective macroeconomic control mechanism. As far as radical fiscal and monetary reforms in China are concerned, there have been no lack of justifications. As we have argued elsewhere, macro-instability in China since 1979 has been the result of, among other factors, the lagged development of a new mode of macroeconomic control under a situation of systemic changes. That in turn could be attributed to the basic philosophy and strategy underlining the Chinese reforms.[17]

Hence, it seems logical that a breakthrough on that front was needed. As to what had to be done, opinions about the short-term and medium-term strategies for the reform of the fiscal and monetary systems had been converging even *before* the comprehensive package. A series of reports by the World Bank on options of fiscal and monetary reforms[18] were well echoed within China.

Regarding the monetary system, a popular view was to rectify the problems of balance-sheet fragility and the lack of autonomy of the specialized banks by shifting the "policy loans" in their portfolio to newly established, non-profit-seeking financial institutions responsible for long-term credit, import and export trade, and agricultural development. Having shed the burden of loans with low viability and returns, the truly "commercialized" banks would behave more rationally, while the "policy banks" could carry on with their strategic functions. An alternative, or more accurately, transitional measure was to have two separate balance sheets for the two types of loans extended by the specialized bank.[19] Competition might be promoted by allowing a larger number of banks to be set up, particularly at regional and local levels, while more financial markets should be developed to widen and deepen the system. Moreover, the effectiveness of the central bank ought to be strengthened through the enhancement of its status and autonomy in the political hierarchy, the introduction of more monetary instruments, and the liberalization of interest rates.

The resolution of the Third Plenum of the Fourteenth Central Committee of the CCP in November 1993 turned out to be relatively cautious in tone.[20] The professed aim was to "initiate a socialist market economic structure by the end of the 20th century." No massive privatization of state assets and enterprises was proposed, nor a rapid floating of the *Renminbi*. Instead, the *Decision* stressed a balance between maintaining gradual progress and order on the one hand and the need to achieve breakthroughs in key areas on the other. The most emphasized "key areas" appeared to be the reforms in the taxation and the monetary systems, and the explicit intention was to increase the ability of the central government to mobilize resources and to influence the economy.

Nevertheless, the so-called breakthroughs looked mild. In paragraph 19, the *Decision* sketched the financial reforms which threw out few surprises and remained vague. No concrete time table for implementation was proposed. It stressed the need to build an effective central banking system which adopted modern measures such as the reserve ratio on deposits, the PBOC's lending rate, and open market operations to replace direct quantitative control of credit. It talked about the establishment of a "monetary policy committee" for the timely adjustment of monetary and credit policies, but gave no clues as to whether its structure and functions would be similar to the Federal Reserve Board of the US or the Council of the German Bundesbank. Contrary to the suggestions of some commentators, the *Decision* did not stipulate that all provincial and district branches of the PBOC should be closed.[21] That was a radical proposal intended to sever the link between the PBOC branches and vested interests at the local level. Instead, the document said that "the branches of the People's Bank of China are clarified as agencies of the head office, and active efforts should be made to create conditions for setting up trans-regional branches."

While policy banks were to be formed, the "specialized banks should gradually change into commercial banks and, when necessary, rural and urban co-operative banks should be set up step by step." No significant liberalization of interest rates was proposed, but the "central bank should make timely readjustments of the benchmark interest rate and allow the deposit and loan interest rates of commercial banks to float freely within a specified range." All in all, despite the desire for breakthrough, the Chinese authority was careful not to become adventurist.[22]

2.2 Difficult Economic Environment for Banking Reforms

As it turned out, the actual banking reforms implemented in 1994 were of even more limited scope than the broad outlines stated in the *Decision*. There was no news about the "monetary policy committee" during the year and the attempt to commercialize the banking system appeared half-hearted as the government had to battle the twin problems of rising inflation and a deteriorating financial situation within the state-owned sector. Decisions on the monetary stance and credit allocation were heavily influenced by political as well as economic considerations, and they were often pushed through by administrative means.

After a slight dip in the second quarter, consumer inflation went up to as high as 27.7% in October 1994, compared with the average rates of 14.7% for 1993 and 18.8% for 1988 (the peak of the last cycle).[23] The major factor was, however, not any acute imbalance between aggregate supply and demand. Nor was there any panic buying or bank runs like the explosive situation in 1988. Moreover, prices of the means of production were very stable and some even fell rather substantially as investment also showed signs of easing. The real growth rate of completed investment in fixed assets declined from 22% in 1993[24] to 17% in 1994.[25]

According to the preliminary estimates of the State Statistical Bureau (SSB), consumer prices and retail prices rose 24.2% and 21.7% respectively in 1994, making it the worst year since 1951. The SSB reckoned that among the 21.7% surge in retail prices, about 14% (or 65% in proportion) was "cost-push" and 7.7% (or 35% in proportion) was "demand-pull" in nature. In terms of commodity composition, the 35% rise in food prices was the culprit, pushing up the general price level by as much as 12.1%.[26]

We can probe beyond the statistical decomposition exercise. Basically, consumer inflation in 1994 was fuelled by large increases in procurement prices for grain and cotton, chaos in the food marketing system, and one-off effects of the reform measures in taxation and foreign exchange, plus the "usual" investment drive and hikes in wages. The contradictory situation of surging retail prices and falling producer prices suggests that the inflation problem in China was a mixed result of: (1) measures to pacify farmers and to a less extent wage earners (particularly employees in state enterprises, civil servants and teachers); (2) imperfection in the marketing network where rent-seeking behaviour prevailed; (3) further price liberalization despite overheating; (4) reform measures in taxes and foreign exchange the effects of which were passed on to end-users in ways both justifiable and otherwise. In a manner of speaking, this was the price that had to be paid for the distributional tug-of-war, the uneven furtherance of liberalization, and market imperfection. The latter two aspects require the "completion" of reforms to cure, and the Chinese government has been courageous in being willing to pay the price to make progress in the reforms. The first one is socio-political in nature, highlighting the unstable nature of the triangular "reform-inflation-unemployment" trade-off.[27]

To put it in another way, while the inflation of 1994 was no simple cyclical overheating in the conventional sense, the Chinese government took the risk of tolerating higher prices in order to push forward macro-economic and microeconomic reforms, but was also forced to increase the incomes of many sectors to keep social discontent under control. Moreover, it adopted a stop-go approach in this new trivariate venture to avoid big mistakes, which in the eyes of unsympathetic commentators looked more like inconsistency, e.g. the "zig-zag" in credit policy.

Nevertheless, administrative measures were increasingly adopted to in 1994 to complement the stop-go approach. Inspection teams on investment and pricing were set up in March and they roamed through different regions in the country to clamp down on "unscrupulous practices" and to search for villains. On the other hand, the government was anxious not to overkill, as triangular debts and unemployment emerged to become a new headache, especially among state enterprises.

Official figures released in the second quarter of 1994 showed that the financial health of state-owned enterprises had drastically deteriorated. In the first quarter of the year, as many as 49.6% of these enterprises reported losses, 15.4 percentage points up from the same period of 1993, while the total amount of losses rose by 79.7% and profits dropped by 42.4%. These announced statistics caused an uproar worldwide. Then Chinese officials warned belatedly that one had to be careful in assessing these figures because they reflected largely the changes in financial and accounting regulations implemented in the second half of 1993, which required the explicit recording of many implicit costs and hidden losses not revealed in the past.

In any case, there was little doubt that the state-owned sector was in trouble. One estimate puts it that if GDP growth slips to 6%, the rate of underemployment and unemployment in the state-owned sector might shoot above 20%.[28] A top official admitted in May that 6% of the state-owned industrial enterprises were facing insufficient production orders and 4% had actually stopped production, although they were mainly in old

Financial Restructuring 21.11

industries such as textiles. Beijing's response to the plight of state enterprises was to relax credit selectively, providing mainly working capital for state enterprises in key sectors. For example, specialized banks were asked in the first half of 1994 to lend RMB4 billion to 70-odd state-owned iron and steel enterprises as working capital, to keep them afloat.

There were however signs that the financial health of the state sector was improving, albeit not very significantly. For the first six months of 1994, the proportion of enterprises reporting losses decreased to 46.3%, while total amount of losses rose only by 22.8%. By the end of November, the proportion of loss-reporting enterprises fell to 41.4%, while "the rate of increase in losses was 52.1% lower than that in the same period of 1993."[29] It is not clear, though, how much of the improvement was a result of the selective credit policies that the government had practiced and how much of it was simply due to the distorting impact of the new financial and accounting regulations being netted out.

As noted above, the Chinese government was careful in ensuring that the incomes of major sectors grew faster than inflation, which in itself was an inflationary practice. In the first half of 1994, real earnings of urban and rural residents rose by 9.4% and 13.3% respectively. Much of these increases were facilitated through bank credit. An indication was that wages and other payments to individuals disbursed by banks amounted to RMB 99.52 billion in November 1994, representing an increase of RMB 30.1 billion or 43.5% over the same month in 1993.[30]

These hikes in incomes were however matched by an impressive rise in bank deposits. In the first quarter of 1994, the total amount of urban and rural savings deposits went up by RMB186.1 billion. The increase grew to RMB314.56 billion by the end of June, swelling total savings deposits by 21.3% in six months' time. Such an expansion was 239% of that observed in the first half of 1993 (RMB131.48 billion). At the end of 1994, the total amount reached RMB2107.9 billion, up RMB631.5 billion or 41.5% from a year ago.[31]

The deposit expansion was a reflection that the overheating of the economy had not generated any severe imbalance in consumer psychology and explained why there was no panic buying or bank runs although the inflation rates were higher than in 1988. It also significantly increased liquidity in the banking system, which the PBOC under Zhu Rongji closely monitored. The degree of flexibility in the hands of the central bank was therefore much higher than in 1993. It could more easily channel funds to keep selective sectors afloat, while keeping an eye on the inflationary consequence. In 1994, total loans by the state banks increased by RMB 514.8 billion, up 30.94 billion or 6.4% from the increase in 1993.[32] That translated into a 19.9% rise in state bank loans in 1994, which compared with 22.7% in 1993 and an average growth rate of 20.4% in 1989–1993. Although the original growth target of RMB 480 billion was exceeded, the aggregate credit stance of the PBOC could still be regarded as slightly tight, particularly measured against the surge in deposits. In any case, all these meant that the initiatives still lay with the government, rather than with banks on purely cost-benefit considerations.

2.3 The 1994 Banking Reforms in Practice

It should therefore cause little surprise that under such a situation marked progress in the reform of the banking system and the establishment of modernized, flexible, but effective monetary control would be difficult. In any case, some steps were taken, including those at the top layer of the hierarchy. The internal control mechanism of the central bank was re-centralized, with the abolition of the credit granting power of its branches[33] as well as the profit-retention system. The link between fiscal deficit and monetary expansion was severed, as the Finance Ministry had to issue bonds to cover its revenue shortfall instead of borrowing from the PBOC.[34] At the same time, several pieces of legislation, including the Central Bank Law, the Commercial Bank Law, the Commercial Bill Law and the Insurance Law were drafted or scrutinized. Attention was focussed on the Central Bank Law and the Standing Committee of the National People's Congress had a rather lively debate about it.[35]

At the same time, three policy banks were established as promised. They were: (1) The China State Development Bank (SDB); (2) The China Import and Export Bank (IEB); and (3) The China Agricultural Development Bank (CADB). They officially started functioning in April, July and November of 1994, respectively. The SDB, with an initial registered capital of RMB 50 billion provided by the government over a four-year period, issued financial bonds of RMB 75.8 billion to domestic banks and financial institutions in 1994.[36] It also raised commercial loans of US$50 million and issued US$100 million worth of bonds overseas. Its task was to take over the policy loans of the People's Construction Bank and the functions of six investment corporations controlled by the State Planning Commission: with priorities assigned to low-interest loans for key infrastructural and industrial projects.[37] A total of RMB 86.2 billion in loans covering over 400 projects (including the mammoth Three Gorges Dam Project on the Yangtze River and the Beijing-Kowloon Railway) was planned by the SDB for 1994.[38] The IEB had an initial registered capital of RMB 3.4 billion and planned to issue RMB 1.7 billion worth of bonds in 1994. It was supposed to extend an amount of RMB 3 billion in loans to finance the import and export of major plants, equipment and products.[39] Finally, the CADB was capitalized at RMB 20 billion. Unlike the SDB and the IEB, the CADB was empowered to set up a branch network to accept deposits from the public.[40] It was to take up the policy lending functions related to agriculture from the PBOC, the Industrial and Commercial Bank of China, as well as the People's Construction Bank of China,[41] and its major task was "to manage state policy loans for grain, cotton and oil procurements for reserves, state purchases of farm produce and agricultural development projects."[42] On top of these three banks, a national policy bank on housing was also contemplated by the Planning Commission and the Construction Ministry although no concrete time table emerged.[43]

Several points may be noted in this regard. First, the planned capital base of the three policy banks was less than half of the combined equity of the specialized banks at the end of 1993, which stood at RMB 154.33 billion.[44] Second, other than the CADB, the SDB and IEB could only top up their capital by issuing bonds and borrowing from domestic and financial institutions, rather than collecting deposits from the public. Their sources of funding were therefore limited. Third, the total lending of the policy banks, at least for the immediate future, looked small compared with the outstanding loan balance of the specialized banks, which amounted to RMB 2586.97 billion at the end of 1993.[45]

Given such operational sizes, it is not difficult to understand that the commercialization of the specialized banks would face some problems. The categorization of "policy loans" and "non-policy" or "commercial" loans encountered few theoretical barriers and, according to a source of the author, this effort was completed by June 1994. But the transfer of *existing* policy loans from the specialized to the policy banks was an entirely different matter. Assuming a 20% overall ratio, they would exceed RMB 520 billion in 1994. Not all of these policy loans were "bad" or "doubtful," but it is foolhardy to deny that a substantial portion of them could be so characterized, at least in the short run. Unless the specialized banks also divert to the policy banks part of their capital and working funds, it might not be viable for the latter to start operation should they have to take over the entire portfolio of policy loans. But if the specialized banks do so, they may be in trouble themselves, given their balance-sheet fragility.

After all, it is a problem of absorbing bad-quality loans in a banking system with low liquidity and problems of solvency. Unless fresh capital funds can be raised on a large scale or massive write-offs are tolerated, the only alternative is to proceed slowly, in the hope that economic growth provides the cushion allowing costs to be apportioned in an acceptable manner among parties of vested interest through a drawn-out bargaining process. Premier Li Peng had said in early 1993 that the separation of policy banks and commercial banks was a task that would "require several years or an even longer period."[46]

A key issue is to ensure an adequate capital base for both types of banks after the re-structuring. According to a report, the combined losses of state enterprises at the local and central levels amounted to RMB 34.6 billion in the first eleven months of 1994,[47] representing 16% of the total capital funds of the state banks at the end of the third quarter of the year.[48] Those were realized losses. If 20% of the loans were at stake, it would be over 270% of their capital funds.[49] The shifting of the policy loans to policy banks may ease the burden of the specialized banks, but not entirely. How much, if any at all, of the existing policy loans the new policy banks would accept is also a question with heavy political overtones. For the policy banks to be financially viable will indeed be difficult, unless they start totally afresh. A gradual programme of separation seems necessary. One possibility is to institute cross-shareholding between the policy and the specialized banks to share the costs and benefits of transition. However, the evaluation of their asset values and share prices presents technical and political problems.[50] Nevertheless, the Chinese authority has not taken that course. One possible reason is that it would have been very troublesome to engage in such a bargaining process in 1994 when so many things were happening.

As for the "commercialization of the state banks," the only major step taken in 1994 was the implementation of an "asset and liability ratio management system," which was regarded as temporary and transitional given "the specific situations" in China.[51]

The incremental loan/deposit ratio (i.e. the increase in loans divided by the increase in deposits) was applied to the four state banks, while the loan-deposit ratio (i.e. the outstanding balance in loans as a percentage of the outstanding balance in deposits) was imposed on the Bank of

Financial Restructuring

Communications and other commercial and joint venture banks. Such a differential treatment was mainly a concession to the problem of financial fragility of the specialist banks. As can be calculated from Table 1, the loan/deposit ratio of the latter, on the basis of outstanding balances, was 120.89% at the end of 1993. It would be almost impossible to bring the ratio down to 75% or below any time soon. The range of the excess reserve ratios (≤ 5–7%) was, on the other hand, supposed to give the PBOC some flexibility to cater for the different situations of various banks.[52]

The ratios on interbank borrowing and lending seem strange to outsiders. However, they were put in place to restrict the practice whereby banks borrow short from the interbank market and lend long to customers, disregarding problems of illiquidity and risks — a practice which plagued the financial system, particularly in 1993. As to the loan quality indicators, they were fixed "after considering the average quality levels of existing

Table 2. Stipulated Asset and Liability Ratios for Commercial Banks in 1994

Loan/deposit ratios	
1. Loan/deposit ratio	≤ 75%
2. Incremental loan/deposit ratio	≤ 75%
3. Long and medium-term loan/deposit ratio (of maturity of one year or more)	≤ 120%
Liquidity ratios	
4. Liquid asset/liability ratio (of maturity of one month or less)	≤ 25%
5. Excess reserve ratio	≤ 5–7%
Concentration ratios	
6. Single customer loan ratio	≤ 15%
7. Ten largest customers loan ratio	≤ 50%
8. Shareholder loan ratio	≤ 100%
Interbank ratios	
9. Interbank borrowing ratio	≤ 4%
10. Interbank lending ratio	≤ 8%
Loan quality indicators	
11. Overdue loan ratio	≤ 8%
12. Non-performing loan ratio	≤ 4%
13. Bad loan ratio	≤ 2%
Capital adequacy ratios	
14. Capital adequacy ratio	≤ 8%
15. Core capital adequacy ratio	≤ 4%

Sources: Adapted from Mao Hungjun, *Zhongguo jinrong tizhi gaige xin jucuo* (New Measures in the Financial System Reform in China), (Beijing University Press, July 1994), pp. 109–25; and Hongkong Bank China Services Limited, *China Monthly Report*, November 1994, pp. 15–16.

loans in the country" and might be tightened with the improvement of the operation of the commercial banks.[53] Finally, it was explicitly recognized that it would be difficult for the banks to fulfil the capital adequacy ratios in the short run. Improvement by stages was allowed, but a deadline by the end of 1996 was stipulated.[54]

Overall, there was a high degree of "softness" in the asset and liability ratio management system, which showed quite a number of "Chinese characteristics." On the other hand, because of the need to control inflation and the general operational state of the specialized banks, the PBOC was wary of giving the banks too much freedom in the name of reform. Administrative instructions on loans (e.g. working capital loans for the ailing state sector) were frequently issued. Moreover, loans for fixed asset investments were put explicitly under mandatory plans in 1994.[55]

In any case, as a result of these measures to control bank behaviour as well as the phenomenon of rapid deposit expansion mentioned above, the financial situation of the banking system apparently improved in 1994. For example, on the basis of the "national banking system credit funds balance sheet," the loan-deposit ratio was 113.9% at the end of 1993.[56] It fell to 106.1% by the end of September, 1994.[57] While total deposits increased by 20% in those nine months, the balance of outstanding loans rose only 11.7%.

Other than the reform of existing banks, new forms of commercial banking have been mooted for some time. The idea of establishing rural and urban cooperative banks, which was floated in 1993 and included in the *Decision*, was not put into practice in 1994. At the end of 1993, there were 50,856 rural credit cooperatives with a combined deposit of RMB 429.73 billion,[58] and over 4,000 urban credit cooperatives with deposits of RMB 134.0 billion.[59] Obviously, regional cooperative banks could only be formed by merging some of these cooperatives, which again involved a great deal of bargaining over the distribution of costs and benefits. Moreover, there are various models of cooperative banks (e.g. German, Japanese and Indian models), and the prototype for a "Chinese" model still requires further thinking.[60] It appears that the establishment of urban cooperative banks was given priority,[61] if only because it was easier or more important. On the other hand, the PBOC approved in July 1994 a proposal by the All-China Federation of Industry and Commerce to set up the first private shareholding commercial bank — the Ming Sheng Bank — in the country. With an initial capital of RMB 2.0 billion, the bank was expected to start operation sometime in 1995.[62]

Some preparatory steps were also taken to allow foreign banks to engage in *Renminbi* businesses. A regulation on foreign financial institutions promulgated on 1 April 1994 laid the legal foundation. In Beijing and Xiamen, foreign banks were allowed to engage to a limited extent in the selling and buying of foreign currencies against the *Renminbi*, while the Liu Chong Hing Bank of Hong Kong opened, through the Bank of China, a savings branch in Shantou.[63] Citibank and the Hongkong and Shanghai bank were, on the other hand, authorized to dispense *Renminbi* through automatic teller machines (ATMs).[64] According to Zhou Zhengqing, vice president of the PBOC, the prerequisites for further expansion included: (1) real progress in the commercialization of the specialized banks to enhance their competitiveness; (2) the establishment of a coherent legal framework for banking; and (3) the creation of a level playing field for all banks with regard to taxation and other financial burdens.[65] Experts in China also emphasized that the process could only be gradual and transitional measures to restrict foreign banks in their *Renminbi* operations (including those of their branch networks, the amount of *Renminbi* deposits to be collected, loans that can be extended, the imposition of special reserves, etc.) might be necessary.[66]

Other reform initiatives included measures to improve the regulation of the financial system which involved further house-cleaning efforts to close illegal financial institutions, the strengthening of the approval, monitoring and supervision procedure for NBFIs, and the severing of unauthorized links between party, government and military units and the NBFIs.[67]

3.1 The Wide-ranging Foreign Exchange Reform of 1994

In comparison, the foreign exchange reforms were more progressive than the banking reforms, in both theory and practice. The pledge to unify the dual (official and swap) rates within five years was made by top officials in early 1993, apparently in a bid to speed up China's re-entry to GATT. During the second half of the year, the proposal to merge the official and the swap market rates in 1994 gained wide currency. Then in late 1993, the government unveiled a relatively radical reform package for its foreign exchange system, major features of which included the unification of exchange rates, the enhancement of the degree of current account convertibility, and the transformation of the foreign currency trading system into a bank-based market.[68]

Although it did not constitute a "shock therapy," this "three-in-one" reform package was more advanced than most had recommended or expected. There were worries as to whether China had sufficient foreign exchange reserves and possessed the necessary macroeconomic instruments to stabilize a unified and liberalized *Renminbi* in a bank-based trading system, particularly as inflation remained unabated. While some "watering-down" did occur during the actual implementation of the reforms, the new regime turned out to be surprisingly stable and the *Renminbi* actually strengthened in the course of 1994, in contrast to pessimistic forecasts.

Other than such relatively minor measures as the termination of the foreign exchange certificates (FECs), major features of the package included the following:[69]

(1) The dual exchange rates were unified by the abolition of the official rate on 1 January 1994.

(2) The convertibility of the *Renminbi* was enhanced through the abolition of the approval procedure for acquiring and using foreign exchange for normal current account transactions, which was a form of rationing exercised by swap centres under the State Administration of Exchange Control (SAEC).

(3) The system of currency trading was transformed from one centred around swap markets into a bank-based one. Designated foreign exchange banks were to carry out foreign exchange trading in place of the swap centres. A national inter-bank market was established on the basis of the national exchange in Shanghai.

(4) The foreign exchange retention quota system for domestic enterprises and units was abandoned, and all their foreign exchange earnings arising from exports had to be sold to designated foreign exchange banks.

(5) To improve the system of "managed float" for the unified rate, the People's Bank was to set a middle rate in the light of market supply and demand in the previous day, around which designated foreign exchange banks could quote buying and selling prices. Foreign banks could apply to become designated foreign exchange banks.

(6) Designated foreign exchange banks could develop forward hedging services for customers.

(7) Foreign currencies would not be allowed to circulate inside the country.

In general, importers of items still covered by various forms of trade restrictions (quotas, licenses, registration etc.) would face under the new system only one hurdle (trade approval) instead of two (trade approval and foreign exchange authorization) as in the pre-1994 situation. They could go to any designated bank to acquire foreign currency by producing the necessary trade approval documents. Officially, the *Renminbi* became "conditionally convertible under the current account." With regard to capital account transactions, no significant changes were announced.

Apparently, the intention of the PBOC was to trade greater freedom for enterprises to buy foreign exchange for more immediate central control over their foreign exchange earnings. The abolition of the retention quotas and the imposition of the foreign exchange settlement system (*jie hui zhi*) were more conservative than the mainstream recommendation of achieving 100% cash retention for domestic enterprises and units and could be regarded as a centralization attempt. It was however sweetened by the enhancement of current account convertibility, which probably reduced resistance from exporters. Other aspects also exceeded the expectations of many.[70] On the whole, although the announced liberalization programme was not a "big bang," like that adopted in Poland, Russia, or Bulgaria, it did combine three separate moves into one single package:

(1) The unification of the dual exchange rates.
(2) The enhancement of the degree of convertibility of the *Renminbi* through the abolition of foreign exchange authorization procedure for domestic enterprises and units, as far as normal current account transactions were concerned.
(3) The transformation of currency trading into a bank-based market system: the swap centres were to be abolished and designated foreign exchange bank branches became mini-trading centres authorized to offer quotes within the limits set by the PBOC.

These three measures were essentially *independent* policy choices. The dual rates could be unified with no impact on the degree of convertibility. After all, China had a unified exchange rate before 1980 and in 1985–86.[71] If convertibility was to be enhanced, there was no need to abolish the swap centres and opt for bank-based currency trading. Indeed, the mainstream recommendations in the past few years focussed around a combination of (1) and various versions of (2), i.e. most advocated the unification of the dual rates plus enhancing convertibility through the liberalization of monitoring procedures in the swap centres as well as the expansion of their scope and functions.[72]

The establishment of a system of bank-based currency trading to replace the 100-odd swap centres was the most important move. It was not widely advocated in 1992–93. In the first quarter of 1994, officials gave the impression that trading in all swap centres would be terminated on 1 April 1994. However, it turned out that they were reserved for foreign-invested enterprises (FIEs) to buy and sell foreign currency, although domestic enterprises and units had to turn to the banks.

The new system was a notable step in the liberalization of the Chinese foreign exchange system. The unification of the dual exchange rates would eliminate the accusation that China was using the rate differential for unfair trade practices — often raised in the negotiation over China's GATT re-entry. On the other hand, a bank-based market is theoretically superior to the swap centres as far as market efficiency is concerned. Competitive quotations by banks offer customers more choices than auctions and matching in a much smaller number of heavily manipulated swap centres. A nationally integrated inter-bank market also facilitates the flow of funds and provides a more effective focal point for the PBOC to implement open market operation to smooth out the exchange rate.

Nevertheless, concern remained whether China was prepared for all these changes in one stroke. A key question was whether the many designated bank branches could properly scrutinize the necessary approvals and authorizations for currency transactions, so as to ensure that convertibility was kept within the limits set by the government and prevent a leakage of capital. A bank-based market obviously requires a sufficient number of experienced banks and brokers as well as a viable framework of control. A worry in China was that designated foreign exchange bank branches might not have enough expertise and resources to handle such a rapid transformation process.

As a control measure, the PBOC applied the principle of self-balance to the trading of foreign exchange by a designated bank. A "proportional control" system was implemented, under which the foreign exchange working funds of a bank should be proportional to the volume of foreign exchange earnings settled through it and its total foreign exchange assets. The ratios were determined by the PBOC. Any surplus or shortfall had to be rectified through the inter-bank market or with the PBOC. In essence, the system was similar to a "retention system," albeit one for banks instead of enterprises. Since a great deal of loopholes existed in the management of the swap centres in 1993, the effective supervision of a bank-based market naturally caused some worry.

3.2 Surprisingly Satisfactory Results after the Reforms

The new system came into full operation on 1 April 1994 after a transitional period of three months. The results so far have been mixed. On the one hand, the exchange rate of the *Renminbi* has been surprisingly stable. On the other, although the degree of currency convertibility has been enhanced, the extent of liberalization has been less than that proclaimed by some officials and their advisors.[73]

Alongside the move toward a bank-based trading system, China also established a nationwide interbank market — the China Foreign Exchange Trade System (CFETS) in Shanghai. By the end of 1994 it had linked up the bank-based markets in nineteen major cities. Its trading prices were therefore the most indicative of the exchange rates of *Renminbi* in the new regime. On 4 April 1994, the first trading day, the Chinese currency was sold at RMB 8.6967/US$ in the CFETS. It later strengthened to RMB 8.6736/US$ on 4 May, and 8.6591 on 3 June 1994. The upward trend continued in the second half of the year, and the currency ended 1994 at 8.4462. The rates quoted by banks and financial companies in Hong Kong were very close to these prices, showing that the CFETS rates were at least regarded as reasonable by the offshore free market, which was legitimized by the decision of the Chinese government in March 1993 to allow Chinese citizens to bring each an amount of RMB 6,000 out of the country.[74]

The post-reform stability of the Chinese currency was probably due to several factors. Firstly, the downside pressure on the *Renminbi* was limited anyway. The average market rate was about RMB5.8/US$ in the second half of 1991, so the price of 8.70 already implied a depreciation to the tune of 35%. Secondly, although monetary policy seemed relatively relaxed in 1994, the major beneficiaries were farmers, civil servants, and selected state enterprises. Most enterprises faced a shortage of *Renminbi* funds. To obtain them, some enterprises were forced to sell foreign currencies.

Thirdly, the average foreign exchange cost of exports (*huanhuai chengben*) for Chinese enterprises by the end of 1993 was still less than

RMB7.0/US$ (i.e., the average *Renminbi* cost of earning one US dollar by exporting goods was below RMB7.0).[75] One of the reasons for this apparently surprising phenomenon was the huge supply of rural migrant labour in the coastal export zones, which kept a lid on wages. In so far as Chinese exporters were still major players in the liberalized foreign exchange market, they might already be quite happy with the present level of the exchange rate. One proviso for this observation is that because of continued inflationary pressure, the average cost had by the second half of 1994 risen above the RMB8.0/US$ level.

Fourthly, and partly as a result of the above factors, the state balance of China's foreign exchange reserves went up from about US$20 billion to US$28 billion in the first quarter of 1994. The foreign exchange settlement system and the narrowing trade deficit certainly also helped. In June 1994, China actually chalked up the first trade surplus in 16 months, and the state balance of foreign exchange went up to US$31.8 billion. By August, the cumulative trade balance for 1994 had swung back to surplus, which turned out to be US$5.4 billion for the whole year. The state balance in foreign exchange reserves rose to US$39.83 billion by the end of September,[76] and climbed to US$43.7 billion a month later.[77] At year-end, the amount reached US$51.6 billion, representing an increase of US$30.4 billion within a short time span of twelve months.[78] Such a dramatic rise was largely a result of the improvement in the trade balance, the increase in foreign investments, and a net inflow in China's foreign debt account. It was estimated by the Deputy Director of the Policy Research Department of the People's Bank, Xie Ping, that in the first ten months of 1994, there was a net inflow of foreign funds to the tune of US$23 billion.[79] These developments strengthened the hands of the PBOC and the SAEC in stabilizing the exchange rate. According to a report, sales of foreign currency exceeded purchase by over US$8 billion in the first half of 1994.[80] For 1994 as a whole, the SAEC Director, Zhu Xiaohua, revealed in a national conference in January 1995 that in the banking system there was a net sale of US$16.6 billion for trade transactions and a net sale of US$10.5 billion for non-trade transactions.[81]

While these developments led to a 2.7% appreciation of the Chinese currency within 1994, they also caused some problems in the monetary system. Sales of foreign exchange by domestic units as well as FIEs inevitably resulted in the creation of base money for banks and *Renminbi* deposits for the sellers, which was regarded by many as a key factor behind the 23.8% rise in enterprise deposits, as well as the increases of 26.8% and

Financial Restructuring 21.23

34.4% in *M1* and *M2* respectively in 1994,[82] and one that contributed to the inflationary pressure. This view is rejected by some, who argue that the deposits so created were backed by "physical goods," and were different from money created through bank credit which might not be so and could therefore be inflationary.[83] Such counter-argument is however dubious as the "physical backing" of any country's balance-of-payments surplus is likely to be available overseas rather than inside the country itself. Larger amounts of imports, say foods or related inputs, would no doubt have alleviated to a certain extent the problem of inflation in 1994, although the costs would have been a trade deficit and a smaller foreign exchange reserve. Nevertheless, the 23.8% rise in enterprise deposits in 1994 was not that much higher than the average growth of 21.7% in 1989–1993. There were also indications that the increase was at least partly due to a change in enterprise behaviour in response to a relatively tight credit situation and a lack of investment outlets (with the cooling down of the *xin san re*), i.e. it was in a way a result of "deposit hoarding." To that extent it would not be inflationary.

Anyway, those who expected "free floating and convertibility" when the new system came into full operation on 1 April 1994 faced an anticlimax.[84] The exchange rate was allowed to float around the "middle rate" by a maximum of 0.25% — a very narrow band indeed. On the other hand, the total number of designated foreign exchange bank branches, which had direct and indirect access to the CFETS, was estimated to be only about 2,000 in 1994, and they were constrained by the proportional control system on their foreign exchange working balance. It appeared that the SAEC and the PBOC were able to monitor their foreign exchange transactions and keep leakages within tolerable limits.

Of course, the stability of the *Renminbi* cannot be taken for granted. SAEC Director Zhu Xiaohua emphasized in early 1995 that there was a need to strengthen the management of the settlement and sales of foreign exchange in the bank-based market, to plug the loopholes in laws and regulations and the actual system of implementation to prevent a mixing up of capital account transactions with current account transactions, and to effectively supervise the designated banks in their scrutiny of authorization documents for foreign exchange payments and receipts to prevent the acquisition of foreign currency through "false contracts and false documents."[85] This emphasis reflected that there were still serious problems in the new regime of enhanced convertibility and the pre-reform worry about gate-keeping was not unjustified. Should the government decide to speed up the process of liberalization, the leakage problem must be effectively addressed.

On the other hand, if the government fails to control macroeconomic overheating properly, expectations-driven selling of the currency might emerge, at least in the black markets inside China and the free market in Hong Kong. Overall, though, I am of the opinion that, with a combination of the stop-go approach, selective credit control, soft price caps and other administrative measures, chances are relatively high that the Chinese government could successfully engineer a soft landing for the economy. The downside risk for the *Renminbi* should therefore be limited in the short run. Indeed, it should not be surprising if the currency continues to strengthen somewhat in the course of 1995, unless something dramatic occurs with regard to the robust inflow of foreign funds into China as a result of jitters about "the post-Deng era" or if political chaos prevails in the transition. A bitter trade war with the United States, which would seriously dampen the investment atmosphere, might also produce significant adverse effects.

3.3 Impact on FIEs and Foreign Banks

Since China promulgated the first set of rules on foreign exchange controls for foreign-invested enterprises in August 1983, effort has been made to give them flexibility. In general, an FIE has to open a foreign currency account with the Bank of China or other approved financial institutions. Permission is required to have more than one bank account or to open one abroad. All foreign exchange receipts are to be deposited into the account. In principle, China has kept to the requirement of self-balance in foreign exchange for foreign-funded enterprises. Over the years, measures to help enterprises achieve such balance have evolved. On the eve of the 1994 reforms, they included:

1. 100% retention in cash for export earnings;
2. permission to settle in *Renminbi* payments regarding domestic labour remunerations, material costs, and taxation;
3. permission to sell products of advanced technology and quality in foreign currency in the domestic market;
4. comprehensive compensation to foreign-funded enterprises under which they could purchase China-made products and re-sell them abroad;

Financial Restructuring **21**.25

5. preferential treatment to reinvest *Renminbi* profit by foreign partners in domestic enterprises which could generate foreign exchange earnings, including partial refund of paid income tax and permission to remit abroad their lawful share of the increased earnings;
6. permission to raise *Renminbi* loans mortgaged with foreign exchange when a foreign-funded enterprise faced a surplus of foreign exchange but a shortage in *Renminbi*, and the funds raised could be used as working capital or for investment in fixed assets;
7. access to the swap markets for foreign-funded enterprises since they were allowed to sell their foreign exchange revenue from trade and non-trade deals, investments and foreign currency loans and buy foreign exchange for production and profit remittance;
8. permission to sell a portion of their processed products in the domestic market and receive *Renminbi* or, when approved, foreign currency.[86]

With the proliferation of swap centres and the privileged access to them by FIEs, it might be fair to say that to fulfil the balancing requirement, these enterprises did not face any intrinsic difficulties. Basically, they could meet any shortfall in foreign exchange by buying from the swap market, provided of course that they were prepared to pay the price, which might fluctuate.

On paper, the foreign exchange arrangements for FIEs remained unchanged with the reforms of 1994.[87] The eight types of measures that had been developed to help FIEs to balance their foreign exchange would continue to operate, with one notable exception: the prohibition of the circulation of foreign currencies and their use as means of payments inside the country. The upshot was that FIEs would in theory no longer be allowed to sell products and services in China and receive foreign exchange (in contrast to measures (3) and (8) discussed above). This could affect not only the problem of foreign exchange balancing but also that of exchange rate risks associated with long-term projects having lengthy payback periods because the risks were shifted back to the FIEs themselves. The Chinese had yet to develop any proper hedging facilities through forward or futures markets for the *Renminbi*, despite an experiment in Shanghai since 1992. The Chinese authorities were apparently quite aware of this problem. A piece of good news in this regard in late 1994 was that the CFETS had submitted a feasibility report to the central government to launch forward contracts (RMB/US$ and HK$/RMB) in 1995, with maturity periods of one to three months.[88]

There were other direct and indirect effects arising from the "three-in-one" reforms. First of all, the unification of the dual rates at the much cheaper "market" rate was good news to potential foreign investors, as the value of their capital investment denominated in the *Renminbi* would increase. With unification, moreover, there would no longer be any foreign exchange loss in fund flows as a result of the rate differential between fund injection and fund repatriation. Foreign investment should therefore be encouraged.

Since the unification was equivalent to a *de facto* devaluation, the net impact for FIEs which had already been operating in China depended on the currency composition of their revenues and payments, and could be positive or negative.[89] The abolition of the FECs might also create some problems for FIEs which received them as revenue.

The move toward a bank-based trading system, on the other hand, should benefit FIEs in so far as market efficiency was enhanced. There was however the worry that individual bank branches lacked the economies of scale that a swap centre had, and the inter-bank market would take time to function properly. So FIEs in need of large amounts of foreign exchange might actually be worse off initially, as informal "rationing" at the bank branch level could be even more parochial and arbitrary. In any case, the Chinese government decided to keep the swap centres for the use of FIEs even after 1 April 1994.

The reasoning was that, unlike domestic parties, FIEs were not required to sell their foreign currency earnings to designated banks, "therefore there is no point for the banks to meet their hard currency needs."[90] In any case, according to an official report, there were little problems for the FIEs even though they were constrained to operate in the swap centres. In April 1994, there were net sales of US$135 million and HK$64 million in 19 major centres.[91] By the end of August 1994, the cumulative balance of transactions in the swap centres was reported to be net sales of US$1.3 billion.[92] An apparent reason might have been the record inflow of foreign capital into China in the preceding two years. Despite the possibly large portion of in-kind investments, the monetary component that was forthcoming provided a comfortable cushion for the balance of recurrent foreign exchange revenue and expenditure of the FIEs. In any case, given the very satisfactory situation in the foreign exchange trading system after the reforms, the government seemed to become increasingly confident.

There were reports that the FIEs would soon be allowed to participate directly in the bank-based market and that the swap centres might be abolished.[93]

The participation of the foreign banks and financial institutions in the CFETS in Shanghai also turned out to be more limited than anticipated and triggered considerable controversy. Foreign banks could only sell, but not buy, foreign exchange in the national centre, and to serve their needs for a working balance in *Renminbi* they were allowed to exchange it from the central bank. The latter amount was however limited to 5% of their equity. Moreover, according to one report, before foreign banks could join the centre they were required to make various deposits to the People's Bank, apparently with no interest returns.[94] While such measures had limiting effects on the convertibility of the Chinese currency, they probably contributed to its initial stability. In any case, the situation was later changed; members of the CFETS in Shanghai no longer had to make deposits for trading, and foreign banks could both buy and sell for their clients, although they themselves might still only sell foreign currency in the system. The reason was that they were not supposed to have *Renminbi* funds since they were not yet allowed to operate borrowing and lending businesses denominated in *Renminbi*.

3.4 Timetable for Full Convertibility

Rumours spread in late 1993 and early 1994 that China had made a pledge to GATT or the US to turn the *Renminbi* into a fully convertible currency by 1997, so much so that a top monetary official in Hong Kong said openly that he expected that such would be the case.[95] If a pledge of this kind had really been made, the "three-in-one" reform package was undoubtedly a natural choice, as full convertibility can only be implemented in a bank-based market system which requires time to gear up. This however came into conflict with the objective stated in early 1993 by Vice Premier Zhu Rongji, who also took over the governorship of the People's Bank in mid-1993. He said that the *Renminbi* could become fully convertible only when China's foreign exchange reserve (the state balance plus the Bank of China balance) reached the US$100 billion level. The chance for this reserve target to be realized by 1997 did not look very promising at the beginning of 1994.

Then in an interview with the *Xinhua* News Agency which was published on 6 March 1994,[96] the Director of the SAEC, Zhu Xiaohua, said that "China will strive to achieve the full convertibility of the *Renminbi* in the current account within six years." This was of course a far cry from the goal of reaching full convertibility for both the current and the capital accounts within three years. If the report carried weight, the decision makers in Beijing might be slipping back to the original schedule of floating the *Renminbi* within 10 years.

In October, Zhu Xiaohua reportedly said in a seminar in Shanghai that "the year 2000 will be the final year to meet the goal" of realizing the "free convertibility of the *Renminbi*," and that "China will press forward to achieve the aim according to the timetable."[97] It was not clear who had set the timetable in response to whose demand, if any, and why the year 2000 would be "the final year." Then a high ranking trade official Yu Xiaosong revealed the "truth" behind the mystery. In a talk to the Marco Polo Club in Hong Kong on 24 November 1994, he said that at the 16th Meeting of the China Working Committee of GATT, the Chinese delegation proposed a series of liberalization and concessionary measures to speed up its re-entry into the world trade body, including "the realization of the free convertibility of the *Renminbi* in the current account within six years after the re-entry to GATT."[98] After so much ado, China seemed to go back to square one: but this was only a promise on the deadline for current account convertibility, conditional on China's GATT re-entry. It would not be binding unless China was re-admitted to GATT. On the other hand, as a GATT member, or more precisely a World Trade Organization (WTO) founding member, China might decide to implement a more rapid process of foreign exchange liberalization. In any case, the timetable for also achieving capital account (and hence full) convertibility for the *Renminbi* remains unspecified. Reports in late 1994 had it that a vice president of the PBOC, Chen Yuan, "optimistically estimated" that the *Renminbi* could be turned into a "convertible" currency by 1998, "two years ahead of the schedule."[99]

4. Concluding Remarks

The financial restructuring in 1994 was of a significantly different kind compared with past attempts. A much greater emphasis was placed on achieving breakthroughs in some key reform areas on top of macroeconomic adjustment. It represented a major shift in government strategy and policy, perhaps as a result of greater confidence after a decade of relatively successful reforms, or alternatively, simply because the problems arising from procrastination had become too pressing. The timing of the reform measures (in the third year of overheating) was somewhat unfortunate, as an earlier launch seemed more rational. Nevertheless, under the stop-go approach the central government had already called "time out" twice since the Deng whirlwind of early 1992 before the comprehensive package of 1994. This should not go without notice by informed commentators.

On the surface, banking reforms have had much less success compared with the foreign exchange reforms. Such a comparison may be unfair, as they dealt with different problems and were affected by dissimilar factors. The reform of the banking sector is inextricably interwoven with that of the whole economy, particularly the state-owned sector. Its financial fragility is almost a mirror image of that of the enterprises that it has been sustaining, often neglecting pure cost-benefit calculation. Both technicality and socio-political considerations dictate that a relatively long process is needed to sort out the mess. This is not to mention the fact that the Chinese government was forced to resort to administrative means to keep inflation from bursting through the seams in its stop-go experiment, the effectiveness of which was of course far from perfect. Against this background, one cannot simply brush aside the banking reform measures actually implemented in 1994 as insignificant.

The achievements of the foreign exchange reforms were much more significant, measured against the mainstream recommendations in the pre-1994 period and pessimistic forecasts about its viability in a year of double-digit inflation. The exchange rate being the price of the home currency against foreign monies, reforming its formation and trading mechanism would meet less resistance in implementation as it is more general in nature and intrudes less into specific interests.[100] As to the stability of the *Renminbi*, favourable external factors have been rather crucial. The major concern is whether they would continue in the future and for how long. In 1993–1994, there were conflicting signs about the direction and pace of the foreign exchange reforms from Beijing. The Chinese government has apparently been under pressure from various external and internal quarters concerning the future of the *Renminbi*. With all the twists and turns in promises, backtracking, and optimistic forecasts, it does not seem to have made up its mind on exactly what to do in the coming years. This kind of institutional uncertainty may persist for some time. Anyway, the framework for a potentially much freer foreign exchange system has been established. Should the macroeconomic atmosphere and the external environment improve in the future, the possibility of another bold attempt cannot be ruled out. The same can actually be said about the banking reforms, albeit to a lesser extent.

Notes

1. For the full text in English, see *China Daily*, 17 November 1993.
2. See for example the speech of He Guanhui, the Deputy Director of the State Commission for Economic System Reform, in the National Work Conference on Economic System Reform, which was reported in *Renmin ribao* (People's Daily), 6 December 1993, p. 1.
3. For a discussion of the political economy of China's macroeconomic reforms and the reasons why they have so far lagged behind, see Tsang Shu-ki and Cheng Yuk-shing, "China's Tax Reforms of 1994: Breakthrough or Compromise?" *Asian Survey*, Vol. XXXIV, No. 9 (September 1994), pp. 769–88.
4. See also Geng Xiao and Haiyan Gao, "The Engine of Growth and the Root of Inflation in the Chinese Economy"; and Lok Sang Ho, "Financial Restructuring in 1993," in *China Review 1994*, edited by Maurice Brosseau and Lo Chi Kin (Hong Kong: Chinese University Press, 1994), chaps. 9 and 10 respectively.
5. State Statistical Bureau of China, "Financial and Monetary Developments in China in the First Half of 1993 and Its Implications for the Second Half of the Year," *Current Chinese Economic and Financial Reports*, No. 6 (1993), CERD Consultants Ltd., Hong Kong.
6. See Tsang Shu-ki, "Recent Developments in China's Financial Sector," paper presented in a seminar organized by CERD Consultants Ltd., Hong Kong, 15 June 1993, and Tsang Shu-ki, "Financial Disorder and Macroeconomic Reforms in China," *Hong Kong Economic Papers* (Hong Kong: Hong Kong Economic Association), No. 23 (1994), pp. 1–14.
7. State Statistical Bureau (see Note 5).
8. See *Sunday Post* (Hong Kong), 4 July 1993.
9. As admitted by the central bank, the amount of new loans extended by the state banks in the last four months of 1994 amounted to RMB 338.35 billion, representing 70% of the total bank credit of the year! See the People's Bank of China, *China Financial Outlook '94*, p. 19.
10. For concise discussions of the theoretical and institutional background to this problem, see Tsang Shu-ki, "Controlling Money during Socialist Economic

Reform: The Chinese Experience," *Economy and Society*, Vol. 19, No. 2 (1990), pp. 217–41; and Gavin Peebles, *A Short History of Socialist Money* (Allen and Unwin, 1991), chap. 3.
11. According to a report, the shares of policy loans in the outstanding loan balances of the four specialized banks were estimated as follows: 20% for the Industrial and Commercial Bank, 30% for the Agricultural Bank, 15% for the Bank of China, and 45% for the Construction Bank. See *United Daily News* (Hong Kong), 13 November 1993.
12. Tsang Shu-ki, "Recent Developments in China's Financial Sector" (Note 6); and Tsang Shu-ki, "Financial Disorder and Macroeconomic Reforms in China" (Note 6).
13. See Tsang Shu-ki, "Controlling Money during Socialist Economic Reform ..." (Note 10); and Tsang Shu-ki, "Financial Disorder and Macroeconomic Reforms in China" (Note 6).
14. See Tsang Shu-ki, "Financial Disorder and Macroeconomic Reforms in China" (Note 6), for an exposition of this point using a modified quantity model.
15. See Tsang Shu-ki, "Why a Soft Landing Is Possible," *Sunday Post* (Hong Kong), 22 May 1994; and Tsang Shu-ki, "So Far So Good for Chinese Economy," *Sunday Post*, 7 August 1994.
16. See Mao Hungjun, *Zhongguo jinrong tizhi gaige xin jucuo* (New Measures in the Financial System Reform in China), (Beijing University Press, 1994), p.8. The author is an economist in the Headquarters of the PBOC.
17. See Tsang Shu-ki and Cheng Yuk-shing, "China's Tax Reforms of 1994 ..." (Note 3) and Tsang Shu-ki, "Financial Disorder and Macroeconomic Reforms in China" (Note 6).
18. See The World Bank, 1990a, *China: Revenue Mobilization and Tax Policy*, 1990; and *China: Financial Sector Policies and Institutional Development*, 1990; and *China: Reform and the Role of the Plan in the 1990s*, 1992.
19. For the latter, less ambitious proposal, see The World Bank, *China: Financial Sector Policies and Institutional Development* (Note 18). However, in early 1993 top leaders already seemed to be in favour of the more radical approach of setting up "policy banks." See *Jinrong shibao* (Financial News), 21 March 1993, p. 1.
20. The document consisted of 10 parts and 50 paragraphs. See *China Daily*, 17 November 1993.
21. See for example the interview of Guo Shuqing, a top economist in the Planning Commission, by Peter Seidlitz of *Handelsblatt* before the Third Plenum. It was reprinted on *Sunday Post*, 14 November 1993, under the title "China bites the bullet on reform." The suggestion was made by Guo, who reportedly said that the reform package would be "the beginning of changes that will alter totally China's system."

22. A related example is the concessions made on the centre-piece of the 1994 fiscal reforms, the tax assignment system, whose professed objective was to increase the revenue share of the central government. See Tsang Shu-ki and Cheng Yuk-shing, "China's Tax Reforms of 1994: Breakthrough or Compromise?" (Note 3).
23. Comparison based on the "overall consumer price index of residents." See CERD Consultants Ltd., Hong Kong, *China's Latest Economic Statistics*, Part Two, November 1994, and *Statistical Yearbook of China 1994*, p. 231.
24. *China Financial Outlook '94* (Note 9), p. 10.
25. CERD Consultants Ltd., *China's Latest Economic Statistics*, January 1995, Part One.
26. Ibid., Part Two.
27. Tsang Shu-ki, "So Far So Good for Chinese Economy" (Note 15).
28. See Tsang Shu-ki, "Sanjiao pinghengzhong tuchu wending" (Emphasizing Stability in a Triangular Balance), *Guangjiaojing* (Wide Angle), Hong Kong, April 1994, pp. 26–28.
29. *Wen Wei Po*, 12 January 1995, p. A3.
30. CERD Consultants Ltd., Hong Kong, *China's Latest Economic Statistics*, Part Two, December 1994.
31. According to the statistical release of the PBOC. See *Wen Wei Po*, 28 January 1995, p. A3.
32. Ibid.
33. *China Financial Outlook '94* (Note 9), pp. 34–35.
34. See Wu Jinglian, "1994 nian gaige shiji pingjia yu 1995 nian gaige zhongdian shexiang" (Assessment of the Results of the 1994 Reforms and Thoughts on the Foci of the 1995 Reforms), *Gaige* (Reform), No. 6 (November 1994), pp. 5–10.
35. *Ta Kung Pao*, 25 August 1994.
36. *Zhongguo zhengjuan bao* (China Securities News), 29 December 1994, p. 1.
37. "The Three Policy Banks Begin Operation," *China Economic News*, 19 December 1994, pp. 3–4.
38. See Note 36.
39. Ibid; and "Policy Banks: China's New Experiment in Banking Reform," *China Briefing*, HongkongBank China Services Limited, December 1994.
40. "Beijing Sets Up Another 'Policy' Bank," *South China Morning Post* (Hong Kong), 21 November 1994.
41. "Policy Banks: China's New Experiment in Banking Reform" (Note 39).
42. "The Three Policy Banks Begin Operation" (Note 37).
43. *Wen Wei Po*, 9 December 1994.
44. *China Financial Outlook '94* (Note 9), p. 90.
45. Ibid.

46. As reported in "Separating Policy and Commercial Functions," *Financial News*, 15 January 1993, p. 1.
47. *Wen Wei Po*, 12 January 1995, p. A3.
48. *China Economic News*, 21 November 1994, p. 25.
49. There are various estimates of the size of bad debts in China's banks. Liu and Qian tentatively put the ratio at 20% to 30%. See Liu Zunyi and Qian Yingyi, "Guanyu Zhongguo de yinhang yu qiye caiwu de chongzu wenti" (On the Recommendations on the Financial Re-organization of Banks and Enterprises in China), *Gaige* (Reform), No. 6 (November 1994), pp. 25–38. More pessimistic speculation was as high as 40%. See *South China Morning Post*, 26 May 1994.
50. See Tsang Shu-ki, "Financial Disorder and Macroeconomic Reforms in China" (Note 6). See also Liu Zunyi and Qian Yingyi, "Guanyu Zhongguo de yinhang yu qiye caiwu de chongzu wenti" (Note 49).
51. See Mao Hungjun, *Zhongguo jinrong tizhi gaige xin jucuo* (Note 16), pp. 109–25.
52. Ibid., p. 115.
53. Ibid., p. 116.
54. Ibid., pp. 120–21.
55. Ibid., p. 114.
56. *Statistical Yearbook of China 1994*, p. 544.
57. *China Economic News*, 21 November 1994, p. 25.
58. *Statistical Yearbook of China 1994*, p. 547.
59. Mao Hungjun, *Zhongguo jinrong tizhi gaige xin jucuo* (Note 16), p. 139.
60. Ibid., pp. 139–54.
61. "Credit Co-ops to Form Banks," *China Daily*, 8 November 1994, p. 2.
62. *China Daily*, 11 September 1994.
63. *Ta Kung Pao*, 27 November 1994.
64. Hongkong Bank China Services Limited, *China Monthly Report*, November 1994, p. 17.
65. *Ta Kung Pao*, 27 November 1994.
66. *Ta Kung Pao*, 7 November 1994.
67. HongkongBank China Services Limited, *China Monthly Report*, November 1994, p. 16.
68. For a detailed discussion of the evolution of the Chinese foreign exchange system up to the reform package of 1994, see Tsang Shu-ki, "Towards Full Convertibility? China's Foreign Exchange Reforms," *China Information* (The Netherlands: Leiden University), Vol. IX, No. 1 (Summer 1994), pp. 1–41.
69. For the full text of the announcement on the foreign exchange reform in Chinese, see *Wen Wei Po*, 30 December 1993. The English version was published in *China Daily Business Week*, 16 January 1994.

70. For a summary of the mainstream proposals before the 1994 reforms, see Tsang Shu-ki, "Towards Full Convertibility ..." (Note 68), pp. 19–21.
71. Ibid., pp. 3–4.
72. Ibid., pp. 19–21.
73. I have described the developments after 1 April 1994 as a case of *lei sheng da, yu dian xiao* (big thunder, small rain drops). See Tsang Shu-ki, "Big Thunder a Storm in the Currency Teapot," China Business Review, *South China Morning Post*, 5 May 1994. However, I was comparing the actual measures after April with the proclamations in the preceding months, rather than with the mainstream recommendations before 1994, which were undoubtedly surpassed.
74. Tsang Shu-ki, "Towards Full Convertibility ..." (Note 68), p. 11.
75. From a source of the author.
76. According to the Deputy Director of the SAEC, Ling Zedi. See *Wen Wei Po*, 30 November 1994, p. A2.
77. *China Daily*, 1 December 1994.
78. According to the statistical release of the PBOC. See *Wen Wei Po*, 28 January 1995, p. A3.
79. *Wen Wei Po*, 2 December 1994, p. A6.
80. *Wen Wei Po*, 13 July 1994, p. A2.
81. *Wen Wei Po*, 20 January 1995, p. A3.
82. See *Wen Wei Po*, 28 January 1995, p. A3.
83. See for example "Waihui chubei wubai yi shihe guoqing" (Foreign Exchange Reserve of 50 billion Suits the Country's Situation), *Wen Wei Po*, 12 January 1995, p. A3.
84. In the first quarter of 1994, many analysts outside China talked about a "shock therapy" in China's macroeconomic reforms. Even after the implementation of the full system in April, a major news service still opined that "China ... on January 1 launched a 'big bang' of financial reforms." See "Beijing to Limit Exchange Rates," *South China Morning Post*, 3 April 1994.
85. *Wen Wei Po*, 20 January 1995, p. A3.
86. See Laurence J. Brahm, *Foreign Exchange Control in China: A Strategic Guide for Corporate Survival* (Longman, 1993), for a detailed description of the practical mechanisms.
87. Indeed, Section 6 of the "announcement" of the reform package began with the sub-heading "The foreign exchange management system of foreign invested enterprises will continue with the present arrangements."
88. "China Forex Move Sounds Death Knell for Swap Markets," *South China Morning Post*, "Business Post," p. 1, 30 November 1994.
89. For existing investments, the tax implications of unification for the depreciation of past capital stocks also remained to be clarified.

90. *China Daily*, 2 April 1994.
91. *Wen Wei Po*, 5 May 1994.
92. *United Daily News* (Hong Kong), 8 September 1994, p. 22.
93. "China Forex Move Sounds Death Knell for Swap Markets" (Note 88).
94. *South China Morning Post*, "Business Post," p. 1, 1 April 1994. According to the report, "foreign bankers were angry and confused about the proposed changes" and that the controversy threatened "to escalate into a diplomatic issue" as some bankers had turned to their embassy to put pressure on the Chinese authorities to clarify the changes.
95. See "Colony's Banker Says Yuan Faces Deadline in '97," *Asian Wall Street Journal*, 28–29 January 1994. Mr Joseph Yam, chief executive of the Hong Kong Monetary Authority, reportedly said that the Chinese currency must become fully convertible in 1997, or market forces in Hong Kong would set its exchange rate.
96. See *Wen Wei Po*, 6 March 1994.
97. See "China Hopes to Turn *Renminbi* Into Free Exchange by 2000," *China Economic News* (Beijing), 10 October 1994, p. 2.
98. *Wen Wei Po*, 25 November 1994, p. A12.
99. See for example *China Economic News*, 26 December 1994, p. 3. Like so many confusing reports on this issue, it did not specify what "convertible" meant.
100. That was why price reforms should and could lead enterprise reforms, a sequence consistent with that observed in China. For a theoretical discussion, see Deepak Lai, "The Fable of the Three Envelopes: The Analytics and Political Economy of Reform of Chinese State Owned Enterprises," *European Economic Review*, Vol. 34 (September 1990). See also Tsang Shu-ki and Cheng Yuk-shing, "China's Tax Reforms of 1994 ..." (Note 3), pp. 772–73.

22

The Rural Economy of China

Yunhua Liu

1. Introduction

After 15 years of economic reform, the rural economy of China has embarked on the road to a market economy. The well-known family responsibility system to some extent has successfully solved the question of property rights and allowed farm households to act as independent economic players, leading to a significant growth in agricultural output and a rapid increase in peasant income in the early 1980s. From 1978 to 1984, the average annual income growth rate in the countryside was 15.1%.[1] By the third quarter of 1993, 95% of counties and cities in China had freed grain prices.[2] In 1994, the major focus of market reform in agriculture was to foster a fair and stable market for agricultural products. Stagnation of agricultural production and high inflation in the late 1980s, however, quickly wiped out the benefits that peasants had gained previously. From 1989 to 1991, the real annual income growth rate was only 0.7% for peasants. Nor did rapid economic growth in 1992 and 1993 confer much wealth upon the peasants.[3] Compared with the rapid development in big cities and in the commercial and industrial sectors of the coastal areas, much of the Chinese countryside is again lagging behind and the future prospects of rural China are gloomy. Recently, much attention has been paid to the slow income growth in this sector.

Although there was an upturn in grain production in 1992 and 1993, there were serious problems on many fronts, including a low income growth rate, a lack of scale economies, sluggish investment in agricultural production, low prices for farm produce, heavy tax burdens on peasants, surplus labour and high input costs. All of these problems place obstacles on the road to rural economic development in China. Deeper reforms are called for to combat the widening income gap between the urban and rural areas. With a rural population of more than 900 million, development of the rural economy exerts a significant influence on the national economy. Monitoring the changes occurring throughout China's rural economy can give us a better understanding of the economy overall. This chapter will provide an overview of the development taking place in rural China over the past few years, with an emphasis on 1994. The issues to be discussed

---

I am grateful to Dr Tsui Kai Yuen and Dr Chen Kang for their comments and suggestions.

include the trends of agricultural production, property rights and the land contract system, agricultural pricing, agricultural investment, the rural labour force, tax burdens on peasants, rural living standards and rural enterprises and industrial firms.

2. Trends in Agricultural Production

One significant phenomenon in agricultural production in China is that the grain sector emerged from five years of stagnation in the late 1980s, and that the rise has continued for the past three years. In 1993, grain output attained a historically high level — 456.4 million tonnes. The grain output in 1994 was 445.0 million tonnes (see Table 1), less than in 1993, because the summer harvest decreased by 2 million tonnes and the total sown area in 1994 decreased by 12 million mu (1 mu = 0.16 acre).[4] Agricultural output of different crops in the past ten years is shown in Table 1. A pattern evident from the table is the unsustainable increase in grain output. Although natural disasters played a part in destabilising agriculture output, another important reason for the cyclical fluctuations is fluctuation in government purchasing prices. At present, peasants are free to sell their products on the market, but there are still certain procurement quotas for grains and other agricultural products. Besides, the government is a large buyer in the free market and can affect market prices significantly. Decline in wheat output in 1994 and an increase in the output of early-season rice are primarily responses to last year's low price of wheat and high price of rice.[5] The same is true for the production of cotton. In Table 1, we also see that the composition of agricultural products is changing toward high-value products. Meat production doubled and oil seed output increased by more than 50% in the past decade. This is caused by an increase in the demand for commercial agricultural products. To produce high-value products with more labour and capital input is a way to increase opportunity for labour use.

Cotton production has been disappointing. In 1993, the output was 3.74 million tonnes, 17% lower than 1992. In 1994, the output of cotton was 4.24 million tonnes, while annual demand was 4.5 million tonnes. In the first half of 1994, the market price for cotton went up from RMB15,000 to RMB18,000 per ton (US$1 = RMB8.5 in 1994), three times higher than the government purchasing price.[6] In early 1993, the market price was about RMB7,200 per ton. The main reason for instability

Table 1. Agricultural Output 1984–1994

(in millions of tonnes)

	Grain	Rice	Wheat	Corn	Oil seeds	Cotton	Meat
1984	407.3	178.3	87.8	73.4	11.9	6.26	—
1985	379.1	168.6	85.8	63.8	15.8	4.15	19.3
1986	391.5	172.2	90.0	70.9	14.7	3.54	21.1
1987	403.0	174.3	85.9	79.2	15.3	4.25	22.2
1988	394.1	169.1	85.4	77.4	13.2	4.15	24.8
1989	407.6	180.1	90.8	78.9	13.0	3.79	26.3
1990	446.2	189.3	98.2	96.8	16.1	4.51	28.6
1991	435.3	183.8	96.0	98.8	16.4	5.68	31.4
1992	442.7	186.2	101.6	95.4	16.4	4.51	34.3
1993	456.4	177.7	106.4	102.7	18.0	3.74	38.4
1994	445.0*	175.7**	—	100.2**	19.0*	4.24*	42.0*

* *Renmin ribao* (People's Daily), 11 January 1995.
** *Zhongguo xinxibao* (China Information), 16 January 1995.
Source: *Statistical Yearbook of China, 1994*.

in cotton output is that cotton is still controlled by the central government. The price of cotton relative to that of grain declined from 1985 to 1989.[7] Low and unstable government purchasing prices discouraged peasants from producing cotton and resulted in shortages of the fibre.

Reviewing the record of grain output, one may ask: does China have a grain problem? In his 1994 paper, D. Gale Johnson wrote that China does not have a grain problem. Instead, he says, it has a number of policy problems associated with the procurement, storage, and marketing of grains.[8] The vastness of China in itself is an insurance mechanism even though regional disasters occur almost every year.

There is a paradox in China's agricultural production — the price paradox. Given the demand and the free market mechanism, an increase in supply can cause a decrease, or no increase in prices. However, an increase in the supply of agricultural products with a limited amount of land can generate higher costs. Further increases in agricultural output are in turn constrained by limited demand. Concerned about social instability in urban areas when there are shortages of agricultural products, the Chinese government encourages peasants to produce more grain. Whenever the price of agricultural products rises sharply, the government always tries to lower them, thus curbing the rise in peasants' income. To narrow the income gap between the rural and urban areas, free market prices for agricultural products should be maintained. Whether China can afford protected agricultural prices for peasants remains uncertain for the time being. Another point is that the composition of agricultural products should be revised from low-value products to high-value products to cope with the limited demand and increase peasants' income.

Despite the many problems, the gross output value of agriculture in China has increased substantially over the past decade, though at a rate lower than that of the whole economy (See Table 2). Whether this trend can be maintained in the future depends on how the existing problems are solved.

Table 2. Rural Population, Labour Force, Sown Area, Agricultural Gross Output Value and Real Growth Rate

Year	Rural population, in million	Rural labour force, in million	Total sown area, million hectare	Agricultural gross output value, billion yuan (current)	Real growth rate of output (%)
1990	896.0	420.1	148.4	766.2	7.6
1991	905.3	430.9	149.6	815.7	3.7
1992	911.5	438.0	149.0	908.4	6.4
1993	913.3	442.6	147.7	1099.6	7.8
1994	—	—	146.8*	1402.0**	4.5**

* *Zhongguo xinxibao*, 16 January 1995.
** Wu Xiaohua, "1994 nian xia bannian nongye xingshi yu nongchanpin jiage zoushi fenxi" (The Second Half Year of Agriculture and Agricultural Pricing of 1994), *Zhongguo nongcun jingji*, December 1994, p. 11.
Source: *Statistical Yearbook of China, 1994.*

3. Property Rights and Land Contracting Systems

Reforms in property rights involve two aspects of rural property — arable land rights and other real property rights. The ownership of arable land is probably the most controversial issue in the realm of property rights in rural China. Critics of the household responsibility system point their fingers at the lack of scale economies. Fleisher and Liu provide empirical evidence that consolidation of multiple-plot farming in a typical household could lead to an 8% increase in productivity.[9] Consolidation of land among households is also expected to improve economies of scale. At present, the household responsibility system is maintained and guaranteed by the government. The government has issued a decree that household land contracts will be extended to 30 years after current contracts expire. Transfer of rental rights has also been legalized.[10]

Due to shortcomings in the household responsibility system, many new proposals concerning land allocation are being discussed by academics and policy-makers. In a few places, experiments have been conducted by the government and by local people. However, given the success of the household responsibility system in the past ten years, drastic changes in land allocation are unlikely to take place in the near future. In fact, pressure to reform the current land allocation system comes mostly from those areas enjoying rapid economic development and from the suburbs of big cities where most of the surplus labour has been absorbed by the commercial and industrial sectors and where specialization in non-agricultural activities can provide farmers a better living. Considering the fact that more than 100 million surplus labourers are still relying on agricultural production for a living, farming beyond the single-household scale in less developed areas may not be an urgent problem. Fleisher and Liu (1992) also showed that current household production by and large exhibits constant returns to scale. Theoretically, when the land-labour ratio and indigenous technology change, the optimal scale changes too. Actually, land-labour ratios and farming technologies in south and north China are different. Heterogeneous resource endowments and unbalanced economic development in China demand diversified land allocation systems; people in different localities are carrying out these experiments by themselves. In fact government policies on land allocation lay down the ground rules; local governments can only implement these rules according to their own local conditions. A summary of the new experiments and hotly-debated proposals follows:

(1) Fixed land contract policy. Land allocation under the household responsibility system was based on egalitarianism with respect to household size. Frequent changes in household size over the years seriously affected stable land contracts and increased transaction costs. Fixed land contracts stipulate the amount of land contracted by a household regardless of the change in family size over time. One county in Guizhou province fixed the length of contracts at 20 years from 1987 onwards. Meanwhile, contracted land rights were permitted to be transferred, released, exchanged, or even mortgaged to banks for loans.[11] In fact, fixed contracts had already been a common practice in the rural areas. The advantage of this method is to give peasants a guarantee of land use rights and to increase their incentive to invest in the land. The disadvantage is unequal land distribution over time.

(2) Two-Field System (*Liang tian zhi*). The two-field system was

introduced on an experimental basis in Pingdu city, Shandong province.[12] Under this system, a small amount of land is assigned to a household to grow food grain. The rest of the land is left for bidding. Able peasants could bid to contract for more land, while those who have got other jobs might give up the unused land right. The problem with scale economies is solved to some extent with the two-field method. But, in the long run, the uncertainty inhibits peasants' incentives to invest in the land.

(3) Land rights sharing system. In an experimental land allocation scheme approved by the central government for Nanhai county, Guangdong province, a certain number of shares of land rights are assigned to peasants. This method is aimed at overcoming the problem of small-scale farming and clarifying land ownership. In the Pearl River Delta, per capita arable land is only 0.5 mu. A family with five members has only 2.5 mu for farming. Because of such factors as the distance of the land from the home and varying land quality, a single household's land may be divided into five or six plots, resulting in problems in machinery use, irrigation and management. Accompanying the rapid economic development in Guangdong province, rural household labour is drawn to the industrial and commercial sectors. The land belonging to these households is thus less carefully cultivated, or even abandoned, and yet remains under contract. To solve this problem, such temporary measures as allocating additional land to able peasants or collectives based on preference were adopted. Nanhai county's experiment with land-rights sharing assigns a certain number of land shares to peasants according to their age, number of family members and other factors. All land is managed by a corporation using large-scale agricultural technology. All other collectively-owned assets are also divided into shares and assigned to peasants. Peasants can leave their shares of the corporation to their children, but cannot claim a refund from the corporation. The corporation is run according to the rules of a modern publicly held company. Diseconomies of scale are therefore avoided; land rights are assigned to peasants, and yet the ownership is not completely privatized.[13]

Land privatization in China is a political issue. It not only challenges communist ideology, but there is also a fear of getting into the vicious cycle of land concentration and revolution, generated by population pressure in the rural areas. While maintaining the household responsibility system in much of the countryside as the main mechanism for land allocation, some government-approved districts or areas with special characteristics are seeking more creative land-rights systems.

In addition to experiments in land allocation, a widespread phenomenon with respect to ownership reform in rural China is the formation of corporations which own assets rather than land. Township and village enterprises are the major target for reform in the area of property rights. Although the general tendency is to form modern corporations, as officially documented in the new corporation law of 1 July 1994, achieving this goal is complicated because of the constantly evolving situation of rural enterprises.

4. Agricultural Pricing

In addition to reform in property rights, agricultural pricing is another battle-field for economic reform in rural China. Once 95% of China's counties and cities had freed grain prices in 1993, market-oriented reform in agricultural pricing was almost complete. However, in 1994 there was some backstepping in agricultural pricing due to a decrease in output and to high inflation. Some cities even re-established the old grain coupon system. The complaint heard for the past four years "it is hard to sell grain" was suddenly reversed. In 1994, government procurement prices for agricultural products in the summer were lower than the market prices, especially so with respect to oil seeds. The cotton market is still under central government control. In December 1994, the Chinese government banned the export of rice and corn to ease upward pressure on grain prices. By October 1994, grain prices in 35 big cities had increased by 61% compared to the year before. A key factor is that the government raised grain prices by 60% in 1994. It was said that grain shortages were due to droughts and floods and that the government did not purchase enough grain the year before. The government resumed the quota procurement policy in order to buy enough grain.[14]

The goal of economic reform in agricultural pricing is to form a national integrated agricultural product market conducive to stable prices and supply. Agricultural price reform can roughly be divided into three stages. From 1979 to 1984, agricultural prices were gradually adjusted upward and a small percentage of agricultural products was purchased by the government at negotiated prices. A two-tier pricing system emerged. Some price incentives were introduced into the market. From 1985 to 1991, market prices and government procurement prices coexisted side by side. Peasants had to fulfil procurement quotas first before selling the rest of their output at market prices. The third stage extends from 1992 to the present. The objective of building a full-fledged market economy in agriculture was actively pursued by the central and local governments and basic market institutions were formed. In the early 1980s, agricultural products with market-determined prices accounted for about 10% of output. In the mid-1980s, they accounted for about 50% and now account for 90%.[15] However, the functioning of an integrated national market is far from mature. Under the name of a free market, some state-owned grain firms sell heavily when grain prices are low in order to maintain a low maintenance cost, and stop selling when grain prices rise in order to earn higher profits in the future. This creates regional conflicts and market segmentation between rich and poor areas. There are also drastic fluctuations in agricultural prices, calling for macro-control. To maintain stable grain prices and to protect peasants, the central government has set up a special grain storage system, and a grain-price insurance fund is in the pipeline.[16] With regard to the grain storage system, the government influences the market price of grain by selling during a shortage and buying when there is excessive supplies. The grain price insurance fund is a financial institution that ensures the grain storage system runs smoothly.

Table 3 shows the government purchasing price index of agricultural products, indicating that prices for rice, wheat, corn, oil seeds, and meat fell for two or three years. Although the government could not force peasants to sell more than their quota of products, purchasing prices did have a strong influence on market prices.

The dilemma is simply that high government purchasing prices stimulate agricultural production, but at the cost of pressures on government spending on guaranteed purchases. This is why peasants had difficulty

Table 3. Government Purchasing Price Index of Agricultural Products

(last year as 100)

	Grain	Rice	Wheat	Corn	Oil seeds	Cotton	Meat
1990	93.2	92.6	92.0	97.6	101.1	129.1	92.9
1991	93.8	95.9	94.2	88.2	97.9	102.1	96.6
1992	105.3	97.4	110.1	108.2	95.8	95.0	106.3
1993	116.7	124.6	105.4	119.2	120.7	111.5	114.5
1994*	140.0	—	—	—	—	160.0	—

* Xinhua News Agency, China Economic Information Service, *China Economic Information*, CEIS1115021, 16 November 1994.
Source: *Statistical Yearbook of China, 1994.*

selling their products from 1990 to early 1993 when output levels were at a historic high and prices kept falling. A clear pattern of drastic ups and downs in government purchasing prices since 1978 can be observed in Table 4. The first upturn of agricultural purchasing prices in 1979, plus dramatic institutional changes in the following years, resulted in a record grain output in 1984. The second upturn of prices took place in 1988 and 1989, leading to another record year for grain output in 1990. But between the peaks, there was either price stagnation or price falls. According to *China Economic Information*, in December 1994, the central government raised grain purchasing prices by 40% and cotton purchasing prices by 60% in 1994.[17] Such a volatile price policy cannot foster a stable environment for agricultural production. In 1994, market prices for agricultural products in urban areas throughout China suddenly soared. To control runaway inflation, to quell rising dissatisfaction in the urban areas and to maintain an appropriate income level for peasants, the central government must handle agricultural policy-making with great care.

Table 4. The Overall Government Purchasing Price Change for Agricultural Products

(in %)

1978	1979	1980	1981	1982	1983	1984	1985	1986
3.9	22.1	7.1	5.9	2.2	4.4	4.0	8.6	6.4

1987	1988	1989	1990	1991	1992	1993	1994*	
12.0	23.0	15.0	−2.6	−2.0	3.4	13.4	30.0	

* Estimated by Agricultural Research Centre of the Ministry of Agriculture, "Shang bannian wo guo nongcun fazhan he gaige shitai fenxi" (The First Half Year Agricultural Development and the Reform), *Zhongguo nongcun jingji*, September 1994, p. 13.
Source: *Statistical Yearbook of China 1994*.

Another dimension of agricultural pricing is the price of inputs. Although there are some fluctuations in the relative prices of agricultural inputs, the prices of chemical fertilisers and pesticides increased either at or above the national inflation rate. Only agricultural machinery prices maintained a slow rate of increase, because prices of industrial products were historically high. Since chemical fertilisers and pesticides are major industrial inputs in agriculture, the cost of agricultural production increased.

Closely related to agricultural price fluctuations is peasants' income. Whenever the government pursues high economic growth and a series of macro policies are implemented to reform industry, international finance, and other sectors, the result is either high inflation or low agricultural prices. Peasants' incomes face very uncertain prospects.

5. Agricultural Investment

Lack of investment in agriculture is commonly believed to be one of the reasons for slow growth in agricultural output and the rate of increase of peasants' income. In late 1994, China's mass media kept sending out strong signals from the central government that agriculture would be the top priority on the national economic agenda. The key indicator of the government's determination was the pledge of more inputs for agricultural production by central and local governments. However, rapidly diminishing returns on inputs due to limited arable land will be a real constraint not only to government investment but also to private farmers' investment in agriculture.

In 1993, government investment expenditure on agriculture amounted to RMB44.1 billion. Table 5 shows government expenditure on agriculture. These expenditures were used for such purposes as agricultural administration expenditure, capital construction, agricultural research, aid for peasants' production and rural social welfare. From Table 5 we can see that the percentage of total government investment in the agricultural sector declined from 1978 to 1988. In 1994, investment in agriculture from different government sources increased by RMB17.5 billion.[18] RMB16 billion was poured into a nation-wide drive to develop irrigation networks and water-control facilities. This programme, which will continue through the spring of 1995, is expected to irrigate more than 1 million hectares of farmland, improve irrigation in 4.2 million hectares of land and increase output on 1.3 million hectares of low-yield farmland.[19] Ever since the household responsibility system was adopted, local governments, communes and collectives were no longer willing to invest in agriculture. Local governments often diverted central government funds earmarked for agricultural to other uses. One investigation on agricultural projects worth RMB1.74 billion in 16 provinces indicated that 46% of the funds were held by local governments in 10 provinces.[20] Local officials pursuing high output value diverted agricultural investment funds to other sectors, primarily industry.

Besides government investment in agriculture for large public

Table 5. The Central Government Investment Expenditure in Agriculture

(Unit: billion yuan)

	Total	Expenditures on agricultural production and administration	Appropriations for capital construction	As percentage of national total expenditure (%)
1978	15.1	7.70	5.10	13.6
1983	13.3	8.70	3.40	10.3
1988	21.4	15.9	4.00	7.9
1990	30.8	22.1	6.67	8.9
1991	34.8	24.4	7.55	9.1
1992	37.6	26.9	8.50	8.7
1993	44.1	32.3	9.50	8.4

Source: *Statistical Yearbook of China 1994*, p. 219.

projects, private peasants are the major investors in their own agricultural production. Astonishingly, in the past decade, peasants' investment in fixed production assets has dropped by almost two-thirds.

There are a few reasons behind this phenomenon. (1) Low returns on agricultural investment due to diseconomies of scale, limited land and low prices of agricultural products: because of limited land and small plot, returns on additional investment in agricultural production assets are constrained. The rate of return was estimated to be about 7.6%.[21] In addition, government purchasing prices also affect the return on agricultural investment. Comparing government purchasing prices for agricultural products with peasants' investment in fixed production assets, it is clear that when agricultural purchasing prices declined in the early 1990s, peasants' fixed assets investment for production dropped to a low of 6.8% of total fixed-asset investment. (2) Investing in housing as an inflation hedge: the second reason behind declining fixed production assets investment is high inflation. Following the 18.5% and 17.8% inflation in 1988 and 1989 respectively, farm household investment in residential housing jumped from 67.1% in 1988 to 74.1% of total investment in 1990. Fleisher et al., estimate that every percentage point increase in inflation caused households savings to flow to housing at a rate of RMB28 per person, while productive capital increased by RMB14.5.[22] (3) Short-term behaviour induced by land contracts: investment in land is obviously discouraged by the uncertainty surrounding land contract system.

It is easy for the central government to vary their share of investment in agricultural production by simply changing policies. But to stimulate private peasants to invest more could involve more difficulties. Without

Table 6. Farm Household Annual Investment in Fixed Assets and Building Construction

(in billion yuan [current price])

	Total	Residential housing investment	Percentage of housing investment in total (%)	Purchase of fixed assets for household production	Percentage of assets purchase for production in total (%)
1984	37.9	23.9	63.1	11.3	29.8
1985	47.8	31.3	65.5	12.8	26.8
1986	57.5	38.8	67.5	7.2	12.5
1987	69.5	48.7	70.1	9.2	13.2
1988	86.5	58.1	67.1	12.4	14.3
1989	89.2	64.2	72.0	9.8	11.0
1990	87.6	64.9	74.1	9.9	11.3
1991	104.3	75.9	72.8	13.0	12.5
1992	100.6	67.9	67.5	6.8	6.8
1993	113.8	76.0	66.8	12.2	10.7

Source: *Statistical Yearbook of China 1994*, p. 182.

appropriate return on investment, peasants will channel their savings either into housing or non-agricultural activities. Theoretically, a higher return on capital may be the result of better technology, which improves productivity, or higher prices. Comparing food quality and the prices of agricultural products in China with those of developed economies, the consumption of high-quality agricultural products in China is extremely low. This means that the demand for high-quality agricultural products may grow in the future, rendering further increases in agricultural prices possible. The government therefore should abandon policies that favour urban areas so that increase in agricultural prices may lead to more investment by private farm households in agricultural production.

Another source of investment in China's agriculture is foreign capital. By the end of 1993, RMB63.5 billion of foreign investment was earmarked for agriculture.[23] Through foreign investment, advanced agricultural technology may be introduced. Improving rural financial institutions can also help peasants to obtain the capital they need.

6. The Rural Labour Force

Currently, China's rural population is 913 million with a labour force of 443 million, of which 123 million work in rural enterprises and industry, and 320 million in agricultural production.[24] According to one survey, the average household labour input for agricultural production per annum is only 158.8 working days.[25] There are about 200 million farm households in China, with an average household size of 4.59 members.[26] Supposing each household has one labourer engaged in farming, the surplus labour force will total 120 million. Other estimates put the surplus labour at 150 million. Fifty to 60 million migrant workers from the countryside have become a particular phenomenon in China since the late 1980s.[27]

How to deal with surplus labour that is increasing at a rate of 10 million per year becomes an urgent and a challenging problem.[28] According to one viewpoint, the slow income growth of the rural areas is due to limited employment opportunities. Increasing prices of agricultural products cannot completely solve the problem because high prices will only discourage demand and encourage imports. Rapidly expanding township and village industry provides a possible solution. But lack of capital, technology and trained labour are all insurmountable impediments to the process of labour transfer from agriculture to industry.

7. Tax Burdens on Peasants

In recent years, heavy tax burdens on peasants in rural China have become a serious problem. Tax burdens vary with the locality. Official taxes levied on peasants consist of two components. One is the 3% agricultural tax imposed by the central government which is paid either in kind, at government procurement prices, or in cash. The other component is local taxes collected by local governments. These taxes are called the "three holdings and five contributions," that is, three holdings for villages and five contributions for towns. Such taxes are to be used by local governments below the county level as promulgated in December 1991, by the State Council. It is stipulated that "local taxes" should equal 5% of the income of a village or town in the previous year. The general tax rate for peasants therefore is roughly 8%. Urban residents are exempt from these taxes. But local governments overstep the tax laws and the actual taxes peasants pay are far higher than the official rate.

In 1992, payments of "local taxes" totalled RMB60.98 per person nation-wide, or 7.8% of peasants' average income. The amount was lower than in 1991 and the same as in 1990.[29] The overall tax rate in 1992 was 10.8%. With an annual average income less than RMB1000 per person, a tax rate of 10.8% is certainly not low. Local governments collect taxes from peasants in various ways. One 1994 survey in Sichuan province shows that the number of fees levied in one county was over 200: 23 from the central government, 56 from the provincial government, 76 from different administrative organisations in agriculture, animal husbandry and fishery, 70 from the bureau of machinery and electricity, 14 from the bureau of transportation and 13 from birth control offices. In the county in question, the tax rate was as high as 14%.[30] In 1993 and 1994, the central government adopted new policies to enforce rural tax laws to reduce the heavy tax burdens on peasants and some progress was achieved.

Heavy tax burdens on peasants threaten social stability in rural China. Conflicts and tensions between peasants and local officials are often reported. Peasants' income is severely affected by various explicit and implicit taxes. In the long run, without strong support for the rural sector, the rapid growth of the urban economy will be affected too. To solve the problem, reform in rural taxation is inevitable.

8. Rural Living Standards

Given the small amount of available land and limited opportunities in the industrial sector, increases in peasants' income are naturally constrained. The government's pro-industry policy from 1949 to the late 1970s kept peasants' income low. Since the introduction of rural reform in 1979, peasants' incomes have risen substantially but during the second half of the 1980s, they were stagnant. Table 7 shows the rural per capita income in different years at current prices. The real income growth rate is calculated based on the rural retail price index. Peasants' net income increased by 6.5% in 1992, and, 4.4% in 1993 after taking into account the effects of inflation. In 1994, when inflation reached 24%,[31] rural per capita income grew by 5.0% in real terms and reached RMB1200 in current value (See Table 7). Table 7 depicts an unstable income growth pattern for peasants over the past decade. Income growth was negative in 1988 and 1989. The situation has improved in the past few years. As mentioned in the section on agricultural pricing, unstable government purchasing prices and inflation are important causes of income fluctuation in the rural areas.

With unstable and low incomes, improvement in peasants' living standards in recent years has been slow. The gap between urban and rural income is widening. In 1987, per capita income in the urban areas was

Table 7. Rural Per-capita Net Income

(Yuan [current price])

Year	Per-capita net income	Growth rate of real income (%)*	Urban per-capita income as times of rural
1985	397.6	4.7	1.7
1986	423.8	1.5	2.0
1987	462.6	2.7	2.0
1988	544.9	–0.6	2.1
1989	602.0	–7.0	2.1
1990	686.3	10.5	2.0
1991	708.6	1.2	2.2
1992	784.0	6.5	2.3
1993	921.6	4.4	2.5
1994	1200.0**	5.0**	—

* Calculation based on rural overall retail price index. *Statistical Yearbook of China, 1994*, p. 238.
** *Renmin ribao*, 11 January 1995.
Source: *Statistical Yearbook of China, 1992* and *1994*.

twice as high as that in the rural areas. In 1993, it grew to 2.5 times that of the rural areas.

Table 8 shows consumption of goods by peasants in the past four years. Consumption of food and clothing in rural China is stable, basic necessities are no longer a problem. The main increases took place in housing and durable goods. Since housing is privately owned in rural China, peasants view housing as their principal asset. Faced with high inflation, it is not surprising that they put most of their savings into housing and durable goods.

Looking beyond national averages, unbalanced development among different regions and different groups paints a very different picture. In general, the rural areas in the eastern coastal provinces and the suburbs of big cities have much higher living standards than the more remote northern and northwestern regions. Out of 1903 counties, 500 are classified by the government as being in poverty, with a total population of 80 million having a per-capita annual income of less than RMB300 in 1993.[32]

9. Rural Enterprises and Industrial Firms

The main characteristic of rural enterprises and rural industrial firms is that their resources are linked to the rural sector. Employees in these

Table 8. Rural Per-capita Major Consumer Goods During 1990 and 1993

	1990	1991	1992	1993
Grain (kg)	262.08	255.58	250.50	266.02
Pork, beef and mutton (kg)	11.34	12.15	11.83	11.68
Edible vegetable oil (kg)	5.17	5.65	5.85	5.66
Sugar (kg)	1.50	1.40	1.54	1.43
Cotton and chemical fibre cloth (m)	2.64	2.73	2.68	2.44
Bicycles, per hundred households	118.33	121.64	125.66	133.39
Sewing machines, per hundred households	55.19	55.84	57.31	61.31
Washing machines, per hundred households	9.12	10.99	12.23	13.82
Refrigerators, per hundred households	1.22	1.64	2.17	3.05
Motorcycles, per hundred households	0.89	1.10	1.42	2.14
Black and white TVs, per hundred households	39.72	47.53	52.44	58.30
Colour TV sets, per hundred households	4.72	6.44	8.08	10.86
Per-capita living space, (m^2)	17.80	18.50	18.90	20.70

Source: *Statistical Yearbook of China 1994*, pp. 285, 288.

enterprises are peasants and still rely directly or indirectly on agriculture for a living. Labour quality in these enterprises is far lower than in urban firms. One special feature of township and village enterprises (TVEs) in China is that a large number of the enterprises are collectively owned. The TVEs use simple technology and the production processes are resource-intensive. Their products include minerals, primary construction materials, small agricultural machinery, food processing and minor consumer goods.

During the last decade, the fast expansion of TVEs provided new hopes for economic development in rural China. In 1993, the total output value of TVEs accounted for 36% of the nation's total[33] and employment reached 123 million, or 27.8% of the total rural labour force.[34] During the first half of 1994, according to the bureau of TVEs in the Ministry of Agriculture, the total output value of TVEs grew by 44%.[35] The bureau also predicted that in 1994, the total output value of rural industry would account for over half of the nation's total industrial output value. Table 9 shows the basic indicators of TVEs over the past decade.

Two aspects of TVEs are crucial to economic development in rural

Table 9. Major TVE Indicators for the Past Ten Years

	Number of enterprises (million)	Employment (million)	Gross output value (100 million yuan, current price)	Per-capita labour income from TVEs (yuan)	Per-capita income from TVEs as % of per-capita total net income
1985	12.2	70.0	2728	22.2	5.6
1986	15.2	79.1	3541	—	—
1987	17.5	88.1	4764	—	—
1988	18.9	95.5	6495	33.4*	6.1
1989	18.7	93.7	7428	38.5*	6.4
1990	18.5	92.6	8462	42.0	6.1
1991	19.1	96.1	11622	43.5	6.1
1992	20.8	105.8	17975	53.1	6.8
1993	24.5	123.5	31541	68.0	7.4
1994	—	—	45419**	—	—

*   *Statistical Yearbook of China, 1993.*
** Estimated according to Bureau of TVEs of Agriculture Ministry, *Lianhe zaobao*, Singapore, 29 October 1994.
Source: *Statistical Yearbook of China, 1994.*

China. One is the job-creating effect for the huge body of surplus rural labour. Another is the income-generating effect for peasants. For the past ten years, a total of 53.5 million rural labourers were absorbed by TVEs. The average annual rate of labour absorption is about 5 million. The rural labour force, however, increased by an average annual rate of more than 8 million during the same period.[36] Obviously, given such absorption rates, the unemployment problem will worsen by the end of the century. On the other hand, in the coastal provinces, with their rapidly developing TVEs, labour employed in TVEs ranged from 31.7% to 50.9% of the rural labour force in 1993 (See Table 10). It can be predicted that the government will pay more attention to the surplus labour problem and encourage further development and the spread of TVEs inland.

In the last column of Table 9, we see that peasant income from TVEs increased steadily, though slowly. But the development of TVEs is very unbalanced in rural China. Coastal provinces received the benefits first. In 1993, peasants' per capita net income in the six coastal provinces (Guangdong, Fujian, Zhejiang, Jiangsu, Shandong and Liaoning) ranged from RMB953 to RMB1675, higher than the national average of rural per capita net income. In addition, only in the municipalities of Beijing, Tianjin and Shanghai, and in Heilongjiang and Hainan provinces did peasants

Table 10. Peasants Per-capita Net Income and TVE Employment Percentage of Coastal Provinces in 1993

	Guang-dong	Fujian	Zhejiang	Jiangsu	Shan-dong	Liaoning
Employment of TVEs as % of rural labour force	37.3	35.9	31.7	34.0	37.9	50.9
Per-capita net income (yuan)	1674.8	1210.5	1745.9	1266.9	952.7	1161.0

Source: *Statistical Yearbook of China, 1994*, pp. 328, 362.

have per capita net incomes above the national average. While in 1980, Jilin, Hunan and Xinjiang had incomes above the national average, all other provinces differed slightly from the national average.

How inland provinces will catch up with the coastal provinces is a major problem. Inland provinces enjoy the advantages of cheap labour, cheap land and abundant resources. Their disadvantages are a lack of capital, technology, infrastructure and knowledge of the market economy. The Chinese government has advocated promoting the development of TVEs in inland provinces. But what policies they will develop and how they will be implemented is still unclear.

10. Conclusion

To maintain the momentum of rapid economic growth in China, strong support for the rural sector is necessary. Without substantially improving living standards of 900 million rural inhabitants, economic development and the stability of China are threatened. During the past decade, low profits from agricultural production led to an unstable supply of agricultural products. In 1994, a shortage of agricultural products was one cause of a high inflation rate that severely affected the Chinese economy. Meanwhile, slow income growth in rural China became a serious social problem. The deeply entrenched pro-industry and pro-urban policy is one of the factors behind the widening income gap between the rural and urban areas. Heavy tax burdens, sluggish investment in agriculture by governments and private peasants, and limited employment opportunities are all factors that constrain income growth in the countryside.

Alarmed by these problems, the Chinese government has revised its development strategy lately and has given agriculture top priority on the economic agenda. Whether the Chinese government has really changed its policy orientation is unclear.

To carry out such a policy is obviously not an easy task. For instance, property rights for land and other assets need to be reformed further to meet diversified needs in different localities; the pricing system needs to be regulated to form a truly integrated national market; the tax system has to be reformed to clearly delineate the rights and duties of peasants; and more than 120 million surplus rural labourers need to be transferred to other industries. In addition, the household registration system that effectively segregates the rural and urban population should be revised to foster a free flow of labour and capital between the two areas.

Prospective policies aimed at increasing peasants income should seek three related objectives: (1) Reforming the price and tax systems to ensure fair and stable prices for agricultural products and fair taxes for peasants. But the effect of policies in this area on peasants' incomes is somewhat limited. Once distortions are removed, policies aimed at increasing peasants' income by removing price restrictions and lowering tax burdens will be less effective. Nevertheless, those policies will produce immediate results in the short run. (2) Raising productivity by reforming institutions, improving technology and providing more investment. Such policies will have a profound influence on the economy. (3) Developing new industries to absorb surplus labour. To achieve this goal, sources of capital, technology and trained labour need to be identified. Township and village enterprises offer one possible solution. The above three objectives are closely inter-related. Only when a majority of the peasants have increased their income will there be a substantial expansion of the market for industrial products and an increase in the farmers' ability for agricultural and non-agricultural investment. Further transfer of labour to the industrial sector is possible with more industrial investment. If China is going to balance its development between the rural and urban areas, there is inevitably a long way to go.

Notes

1. "Jiushi niandai nongcun gaige de zhuti" (The Major Issues of Rural Reform in the 1990s), *Zhongguo nongcun jingji* (Chinese Rural Economy), January 1994, pp. 3–8.

2. The Institute of Rural Development of the Chinese Academy of Social Sciences, "Guanyu dangqian nongcun ruogan zhongda wenti ji duice jianyi" (The Current Problems in Rural Areas and Policy Suggestions), *Zhongguo nongcun jingji*, September 1994, pp. 3–9.
3. See Note 1.
4. Agricultural Research Centre of the Ministry of Agriculture, "Shang bannian wo guo nongcun fazhan he gaige shitai fenxi" (The First Half Year Agricultural Development and Reform), *Zhongguo nongcun jingji*, September 1994, pp. 10–15.
5. See Note 4, p. 13.
6. Liu Jinjiang, "Wo guo ying dui liang mian changqi shixing baoliang baojia" (Grain and Cotton Protection Price Should Be Imposed in the Long Run), *Nongye jingji wenti* (Agricultural Economics Issue), October 1994, p. 43.
7. Li Zhiqiang, "1994 nian mianhua shengchan qushi" (The Trend of Cotton Production in 1994), *Zhongguo nongcun jingji*, June 1994, pp. 25–27.
8. Johnson, D. Gale, "Does China Have a Grain Problem?", *China Economic Review*, Vol. 5, No. 1 (1994), pp. 1–14.
9. Fleisher, Belton and Yunhua Liu, "Economies of Scale, Plot Size, Human Capital, and Productivity in Chinese Agriculture", *Quarterly Review of Economics and Finance*, Vol. 32, No. 3 (Autumn 1992).
10. See Note 4. The new policy was announced in late of 1993. This new policy has been cited in a few places, even in Chinese official speeches, but the title of the government document is unavailable.
11. Li Qin and Ding Yuankang, "Shixing zengjia renkou buzai fendi de fanglue" (The Strategy of Fixed Land Contract), *Zhongguo nongcun jingji* (Chinese Rural Economy), February 1994.
12. Chen Jiyuan, Han Jun, "Deng Xiaoping de nongye liangge feiyue sixiang yu Zhongguo nongcun gaige" (Deng Xiaoping's Thought of Two Jumps in China's Agriculture and Rural Reform), *Zhongguo nongcun jingji*, October 1994, p. 8.
13. Wang Zhuo, "Zhongguo nongcun tudi chanquan zhidu xinlun: Nanhai xian de jingyan" (A New Land Right System in Rural China, the Experiment of Nanhai County), *Zhongguo nongcun jingji*, May 1994.
14. *Lianhe zaobao*, Singapore, 22 December 1994.
15. Li Binkong, "Shenhua nongchanpin jiage gaige de jiben silu" (Some Basic Thinking for Deepening Agricultural Pricing Reform), *Zhongguo nongcun jingji*, January 1994.
16. See Note 15, p. 18.
17. Xinhua News Agency, China Economic Information Service, *China Economic Information*, CEIS1115021, 16 November 1994.
18. Han Jun, "Dangqian nongcun jingji xingshi toushi yu jinqi gaige de silu"

(The Current Situation of Rural Economy and Recent Reforms), *Zhongguo nongcun jingji*, January 1994.
19. Xinhua News Agency, China Economic Information Service, *China Economic Information*, CEIS1206039, 7 December 1994.
20. Zhang Yi, "Nongye touru buzu de yuanyin ji duice" (The Reasons and Policies toward Lack of Agricultural Investment), *Nongye jingji wenti*, May 1994.
21. Fleisher and Liu (Note 9).
22. Fleisher, Belton, Yunhua Liu and Hongyi Li, "Financial Intermediation, Inflation, and Capital Formation in Rural China," *China Economic Review*, Vol. 5, No. 1 (1994).
23. Note 17.
24. *Statistical Yearbook of China, 1994*, p. 85.
25. Yunhua Liu, "Institutional Constraints and Mobility of Labor and Capital in Rural China," unpublished dissertation, 1993, p. 20.
26. *Statistical Yearbook of China, 1994*, p. 276.
27. See Note 18, p. 14.
28. See Note 1, p. 5.
29. *Agricultural Yearbook of China, 1993*, p. 120.
30. Sun Gongli, "Sichuan nongcun shikuang diaocha: kezheng meng ru hu" (Survey of Rural Reality in Sichuan Province: Heavy Taxes More Threatening Than a Tiger), *Dangdai yuekan* (Contemporary), November 1994. pp. 80–81.
31. *Lianhe zaobao* (news from central planning commission of China), Singapore, 22 December 1994.
32. Xiao Zhuoji, "Zhongguo chengxiang jumin shenghuo shuiping tigao" (Rising Living Standards in Urban and Rural China), *Lianhe zaobao*, Singapore, November 1994.
33. *Lianhe zaobao*, Singapore, 15 December 1994.
34. *Statistical Yearbook of China, 1994*, p. 85.
35. *Lianhe zaobao*, Singapore, 29 October 1994.
36. *Statistical Yearbook of China, 1994*, p. 327.

23

Foreign Trade and China's Growing International Presence

Ho Yin-ping

Introduction

The story of the East Asian Newly Industrializing Economies (NIEs), namely Hong Kong, Singapore, South Korea and Taiwan, adopting outward-looking economic policies and thereby achieving rapid economic growth has been well documented.[1] Various studies have put forth a diverse list of explanations for this outcome. While most writers recognize the effect of trade on economic growth, many argue that one key reason trade has been central to these economies has to do with their small size: Hong Kong and Singapore are just cities, Taiwan is no larger than the Hainan Island, and South Korea is also a mere peninsula economy. But do these small-size arguments really cast doubt on Alfred Marshall's dictum that: "The causes which determine the economic progress of nations belong to the study of international trade"?[2] The question is, in effect, whether a large continental country can also successfully adopt a similar outward-oriented development strategy and reap rapid economic growth. Clearly, the case of China in the late decades of the twentieth century suggests an affirmative answer for the Marshallian progressive role of international trade.

Stop-go cycles notwithstanding, over the period 1978–1994 real gross national product (GNP) growth in China has averaged some 9% per annum, about triple the rate recorded by the advanced economies grouped in the Organization for Economic Cooperation and Development (OECD). This growth rate has been accompanied by rapid expansion in China's international trade. Among the world's leading exporting economies, China rose from thirty-second in 1979 to eleventh place in 1992, and is likely soon to move further up that world league table. Without doubt, opening up to the outside world in the context of a relatively liberal trade climate has been crucial to China's phenomenal growth record. None the less, the growing international presence of China's economy and its impact on the world's trading environment warrant the need for more decisive actions on economic reform and trade liberalization in China.

Correspondingly, spurred by a renewed Dengist vision to further expedite modernization and accelerate the structural transformation of the national economy, China's evolving "socialist market economy," as ratified by the Fourteenth National Communist Party Congress in October 1992, greeted 1994 with a new round of economic reforms in the foreign trade and investment, foreign exchange system, fiscal and tax structure, banking and enterprise management. These include the unification of the foreign exchange rates, the promulgation of China's first foreign trade law, a unified income tax law with the value added tax as the main turnover tax, the institution of a tax revenue sharing system between the central and local governments and between the state and enterprises, the separation of policy banks from commercial banks and enhancing of the independence of the central bank for monetary management, among others.

The impetus of these latest reform measures, coupled with their precursors, boosted China's real gross domestic product (GDP) by 11.8% in 1994, compared to 13.4% and 12.8% in 1993 and 1992 respectively, its third consecutive year of double-digit growth. In value terms, China's GDP, as announced by Premier Li Peng in his government work report to the annual session of the National People's Congress on 5 March 1995, crossed the threshold of four trillion yuan to reach 4,380 billion yuan (US$511 billion) in 1994.[3] The blazing growth rate, however, has raised the spectre of overheating and inflation. As measured by retail prices, the rate of inflation accelerated from about 13% in 1993 to 21.7% in 1994, and substantially overshot the planned rate of below 10% for the year. Likewise, the consumer price index also escalated to 24.2% in 1994, the highest rate of price hikes since 1978.

Although an autonomous increase in total nominal expenditure relative to potential output accompanied by an expanded money supply is usually the fundamental cause of inflation, China's soaring inflation these days is, to a considerable extent, a by-product of its continued reforms in domestic prices, foreign trade and investment for a robustly growing economy. Leaving aside those substantial price hikes in farm and sideline products due to natural disasters such as flooding and drought last year, alongside the on-going price reforms and profiteering by unscrupulous agents, increased soft-budget spending to accommodate loss-making enterprises, expansion of fixed asset capital formation and the booming external sector activities were generally believed to be the major factors forcing up aggregate demand and fueling inflation in 1994.

Concerning the good news for a reforming outward-looking economy: in 1994 China's total merchandise exports topped US$121 billion, up from US$91.8 billion in 1993, while its merchandise imports also rose from US$104 billion in 1993 to reach a record US$115.7 billion last year. As such, China's trade balance saw a bounce-back from a deficit of US$12.2 billion in 1993 to a surplus of US$5.3 billion in 1994, which Wu Yi, Minister of Foreign Trade and Economic Cooperation, called a "bumper harvest" for the year.[4] This significant turnaround in the trade balance was, to a large extent, due to the devaluation of *Renminbi* (RMB) at the start of 1994 by 33% against the US dollar, which certainly helped exports. As for foreign capital, in 1994 alone, China has approved a total of 47,490 foreign-funded projects, involving contracted or pledged investment of US$81.4 billion, compared to 83,437 signed projects with pledged investment of US$111.4 billion in 1993. The more gratifying aspect was that, while the number of newly approved foreign-funded projects and the amount of pledged foreign direct investment (FDI) fell in 1994, the disbursed or actual amount of FDI entering China rose from US$27.8 billion in 1993 to US$33.8 billion last year.[5] Indeed, absorbing about 40% of all FDIs going to the developing world in 1993 and 1994,[6] China is now the world's second biggest destination for FDIs, after only the United States.

The massive inflows of foreign capital along with robust export growth in 1994 led to a record surge in foreign reserves. Reportedly, China's official foreign currency reserves net of the Bank of China's holdings, which since 1992 are no longer counted as official reserves, shot up to US$51.6 billion at the end of 1994, an increase of 143% over the previous year's position of US$ 21.2 billion.[7] In view of its thriving export trade so far and its comfortable reserves position, China appears to be well placed to spark further liberalization of trade and investment. All this is good news for open trade and international production, both regional and global.

Entering a New Phase of Foreign Exchange and Trade Reforms

Since China's robust economic growth is a source of concern for the outside world — whether due to overheating or otherwise — foreign exchange rate and foreign trade reforms are crucial to the future development of trade and international production in the global market-place. In particular, a market-based monetary policy cannot work to full effect if exchange rates, which determine the relative price of tradeables to nontradeables, do not reflect underlying demand and supply factors. Hence, in China's efforts to achieve a genuinely market-based economy, there is a great need to liberalize the exchange and trade system.

Foreign Exchange Reform

In the realm of exchange management, by far the most important event that took place last year was the unification of the official and swap exchange rates of *Renminbi* on 1 January 1994. Since then, the former dual track exchange operations have been superseded by a managed float system based largely on direct market purchases and sales. Following this, the long-mooted Foreign Exchange Adjustment Centres (better known as swap centres) are scheduled to be phased out and replaced by a nationwide interbank foreign exchange network for exchange settlements. Today, the Foreign Exchange Trading Centre (FETC), which formally started operation on 1 April 1994 in Shanghai, is the nation's interbank foreign exchange market.[8]

To enhance the new managed float mechanism, a number of supportive measures have been introduced.[9] The major provisions include: (a) abolition of the planned foreign exchange allocations and the stipulated foreign exchange retention scheme whereby domestic enterprises and foreign trade corporations retained a proportion of their foreign exchange earnings and delivered the rest to the state (all enterprises now have to surrender export proceeds to the designated banks, while purchases of foreign exchange can be effected upon presentation of import contracts or other valid documents required for foreign exchange payments); (b) foreign exchange administration for foreign-invested enterprises (FIEs) and foreign banks remains intact;[10] (c) discontinuation of the use of foreign exchange certificates, which had existed since 1980 as a convertible version of the *Renminbi*; and (d) prohibition of the valuation, direct settlement and circulation of foreign currencies within China.

The unified system, which amounts to the cancellation of mandatory planning for the income and expenditure of foreign exchange, represents a significant step toward currency convertibility.[11] Under the present scheme, the stipulated approval of foreign exchange allocation which was previously necessary has been supplanted by the purchase of foreign exchange with *Renminbi* from designated banks upon presentation of the valid papers, thus making *Renminbi* conditionally convertible under the current account. This new setting allows various domestic enterprises dealing in exports to compete on a more equal footing, thereby enhancing their incentive to expand export production rather than indulge in rent-seeking activities. At the same time, imports which used to enjoy preferential policies of "foreign exchange parity," that is, purchasing foreign exchange at the official rate, should now be subject to more market discipline. As for the FIEs, they also stand to benefit from the unified system. Before, the inflows of foreign funds into China were valued at the official rate but profits were repatriated at the swap rate, thus incurring losses in these two-way transactions. Perhaps more important still, the current managed float regime, which has considerably strengthened the link between the monetary and external sectors of the Chinese economy, conforms, albeit partially, to the requirements of both the General Agreement on Tariffs and Trade (GATT) and the International Monetary Fund (IMF) for the foreign exchange rate system of signatory parties and member countries.

Concerning the actual exchange rate movements, when the dual exchange rates were scrapped at the beginning of last year, few had foreseen the subsequent strengthening of the *Renminbi* from about 8.7 yuan to one US dollar at the start of 1994, to 8.44 yuan at the end of the year, an appreciation of over 3% against the US dollar, despite the looming shadow of a 20 percent-plus inflation. Trade surplus aside, it is believed that strong inflows of capital, both in the form of FDI and as speculative hot money from various sources aiming to take advantage of the differential interest return on RMB-denominated deposits, are helping to keep the *Renminbi* stronger against the US dollar than the inflation differential would suggest. The retrenchment measures undertaken by the central government, which have resulted in a domestic credit squeeze, forcing some enterprises to sell their foreign exchange holdings for *Renminbi*, are also believed to be one of the explanatory factors for the appreciation of the *Renminbi* since early 1994. Furthermore, the new exchange system *per se*, which requires all domestic enterprises engaged in foreign trade to submit business receipts and other relevant papers to the designated banks and, accordingly, reduces capital flight by under-invoicing or over-invoicing, has also contributed to the increased supply of foreign exchange to the FETC and hence the surprising stability of the *Renminbi* over the course of the year.[12]

On balance, the decisive unified exchange rate reform has been pushed forward at a pace so steadfastly smooth as to cause surprise and astonishment even within the Chinese government itself. It is important, however, particularly in light of the recent trends in monetary aggregates and price hikes,[13] that the authorities adopt a disciplined monetary policy stance. Otherwise, they could well undermine efforts to keep inflation under control at a time when the economy is moving toward freeing up its currency for current account transactions.

Foreign Trade Reforms

Prior to 1979, China's foreign trade was monopolized by a dozen stated-owned foreign trade corporations (FTCs) and their branches organized along canalized product lines. These FTCs procured and traded the products through a planning system under the Ministry of Foreign Trade (MOFT) — the erstwhile Ministry of Foreign Economic Relations and Trade (MOFERT), presently known as the Ministry of Foreign Trade and Economic Cooperation (MOFTEC), with all their profits and losses absorbed by the state budget. Whereas production enterprises, which did not have any direct access to foreign markets, were given production targets under the central plan for supply to the FTCs. Under this centralized system, China's foreign trade regime was characterized by highly distorted prices and allocative inefficiencies. The process of opening up to the outside world inevitably necessitated the reform of such a monopolized trading system.

Over the past decade or so, the national FTCs have been granted greater autonomy and made more financially accountable for their operations, while progressive decentralization of the system has allowed the provincial authorities to establish their own FTCs and delegated foreign trade rights to many domestic enterprises, both old and new. So far, there were around 9,000 domestic production and trade entities as well as 190,000 FIEs engaged in foreign trade business in China.[14] At the same time, the scope of mandatory planning has been progressively reduced. Guidance planning, export targeting and import control schemes using tariffs, licensing and other economic leverages as major means of regulations have become more important. By early 1994, only 38 export commodities and 11 import items were subject to mandatory plans, compared to over 3,000 plan-controlled merchandise products before 1979.[15]

As a growing number of foreign trade and production enterprises are changing their role from executors of state plans into managers of tradeable goods, decisions concerning foreign trade activities have become increasingly determined by the market rather than administrative decree. However, for purposes of protecting domestic economic activities, regulating the demand for imports, and of ensuring the domestic availability of some key products like rice and maize, direct control over exports and imports have continued through a licensing or quota system for both. Reportedly, there are presently some 138 export commodities and 53 broad categories of import goods still subject to quotas and licensing and, according to Wu Yi, the scope is expected to narrow in the coming years.[16]

Reforms of the post-1978 periods, particularly those of the early 1990s, have transformed the pricing of the tradeable sector at large, in part stimulated by China's efforts to make its trade regime conform to international practices in the context of its negotiations to rejoin the GATT, and in the memorandum of understanding on market access with the US on 10 October 1992.[17] Notably, following the elimination of all direct budgetary export subsidies to the FTCs in January 1991 and the subsequent abolition of the import regulatory duty, which was introduced in 1985 as an import surtax, in April 1992, China has also terminated all import substitution regulations in October 1992 and pledged that it has no intention to reinstitute any lists of import substitutes in the future.[18] Further to these, during the early 1990s the government announced sizeable reductions in tariff levels on a number of occasions. The most substantial of these was in 1992, when custom tariffs were twice reduced by an average of 7.3 percentage points on 3,596 merchandise goods, representing over 50% of dutiable items.[19]

Even with these reductions, however, tariff rates in China, according to a recent World Bank study on China's trade reform, remained relatively high, with an average unweighted tariff rate of 42.8% and a trade-weighted average of 31.9% in 1992.[20] Other than this, China's tariffs, according to the World Bank study, are "more numerous and more dispersed than those of most other large developing countries, with 69 rates and a standard deviation of 30 percent."[21] Yet, the study was also quick to point out that although *de jure* trade restrictions in both tariffs and nontariff barriers (NTBs) were high, by 1992 China's *de facto* import regime had been revealed to be more open than the above description might have suggested. For one, despite its high average nominal tariff rate, China's actual collected duties was only 5.6% of the cost, insurance and freight value of imports, which was more akin to the situation in developed countries (DCs) and was, in fact, only about one-third of the average rate of collection of other less developed or developing countries (LDCs), in large part because of import duty exemptions and rebates.[22] For another, comparative price data appeared to suggest that China's protective measures as high nominal tariffs and NTBs were, in effect, not binding for many tradeables.[23] More pertinently, additional progress was made in lowering tariffs and other import restrictions in 1993 and early 1994. Taken overall, between 1991 and early 1994, China cut import tariffs on 6,537 commodity items.[24]

Having said all this, it is tempting to argue that while China's foreign trade regime remains subject to a complex array of tariffs, NTBs and other distortions, China has become a relatively open trader over the course of the reformist years. In this regard, a recent IMF study also notes that measured in terms of trade intensity, that is, exports and imports as a share of GDP, China's growing integration into the global economy suggests that the actual application of trade policies in China tends to be relatively liberal, albeit selectively so.[25] For all that, however, further unilateral liberalization remains important. To be sure, trade liberalization and greater openness should help China rationalize the structure of incentives for domestic economic activities, harden the market discipline of state-owned enterprises (SOEs), enhance pricing and allocative efficiency and reduce the current inflationary pressures, whereas high tariffs, tariff redundancy and NTBs, be they binding or nonbinding, encourage rent-seeking, under-invoicing, bribing of custom officials as well as smuggling.

Despite occasional reversals and incoherence in strategy, that China has gradually undertaken a market-based reform of its trade regime can hardly be doubted. Nevertheless, in the realm of transparency and legal construction, up until early 1994 much was still unclear about the functioning of China's trade system and rights and obligations of the various parties involved in a given trade transaction. In this regard, too, 1994 was a landmark year. After almost twelve years of drafting, the "Foreign Trade Law of the People's Republic of China," which contains eight chapters, embracing forty-four articles, was officially endorsed by the Standing Committee of the National People's Congress on 12 May 1994 and went into effect on 1 July 1994.

This new foreign trade law, which provides a legal framework for the Chinese government to regulate external sector activities and trade organizations in the national economy, is significant in that it is the first piece of comprehensive trade legislation ever published in China.[26] Until then, the management of foreign trade in China has been subject to complex internal administrative decrees and characterized by obscure policy pronouncements. Apart from abandoning various subsidies schemes practiced in the past, and explicitly stipulating that Chinese foreign trade enterprises should engage in financially independent management, the new law is expected to create an open and transparent environment for foreign entities trading with or investing in China.

While observing by and large the prescribed GATT stipulations, the law retains the existing licensing system and there are provisions relating to the restriction or prohibition of merchandise tradeables. In fact, so far as its conformity with common international practices is concerned, several articles therein appear to be not fully compatible with the GATT system. For instance, there are provisions relating to the restriction of the right to engage in foreign trade (Articles 9 and 14), whereas the GATT system is based on free business activity without official scrutiny and approval. Thus, depending on the injunctions taken in the process of implementing regulations, the law could well serve as a solid footing for China's outward-looking efforts to become more fully integrated into the global economy, or it could be used as a legal basis for the Chinese authority to erect avowedly GATT-complying trade barriers.

After all, the institution of the first foreign trade law, which reflects China's commitment to a nationwide unified foreign trade policy, constitutes an improvement in transparency. Just as well, surely, it lays down a positive foundation for future trade laws and decrees. Seen in this broad perspective, the law still represents a big stride forward in China's intention to deepen trade reforms and abide by international rules, thereby contributing to its application for early re-entry into the GATT. Ultimately, of course, successful implementation of an open and GATT-compatible trade regime in China depends on the very willingness and legal discipline of all levels of government authority in China to uphold such a system.

Opening Up and Growing External Orientation

Eschewing theoretical blueprints or timetables, the Chinese government has adopted a gradual, experimental and pragmatic approach, a strategy of what is called "touching the stones while crossing the river,"[27] to reform and opening up. Yet, in both its rapid economic growth and its orientation toward market economies, China poses a sharp contrast with the former Soviet Union and the economies of Eastern Europe. So far, "China was the only reforming socialist or formerly socialist economy to become a more significant participant in the world economy," as Nicholas Lardy has noted.[28]

While economic reform *cum* trade liberalization is a continuing process, the Chinese experience demonstrates that even gradualism and partial removal of barriers to trade and investment can exert dramatic effects.

Table 1, which outlines the broad trends in merchandise exports, imports, foreign trade proportions (trade intensities), among other external sector indicators, illustrates how far China's external sector and its enhanced role in the world economy has evolved since the open-door policy first came into being. For the past sixteen years since 1978, the money value of China's total exports expanded more than elevenfold and imports grew almost tenfold. Compounded annually, during the period 1978–1994 export value increased by 17% per annum, and import value by 16% a year — more than double the rates for the world's total exports and imports of less than 8% in the same period. As noted, by the early 1990s China's total trade turnover had already surpassed those of all but less than a dozen of the world's largest trading economies. In the process, the Chinese economy, as measured by real GNP, has nearly quadrupled in size.

Declining scope of the foreign trade plan, institutional decentralization as evidenced by the growing number of FTCs as well as the increase in the number of production enterprises with direct trading rights, continuing price reforms,[29] steady depreciation of the real effective exchange rate, the rapid emergence of a vibrant nonstate sector, and the continued surge of the FDIs, all seem to have had a bearing on this record of trade and development growth. In particular, the dynamic nonstate sector that has emerged over the last decade and a half has been one of the most successful aspects of the whole growth process.[30] Today, the share of this leading sector, taking account only of the exports of the township and village enterprises (TVEs) and FIEs, stood at a minimum of 60% of China's total exports, with the bulk of the contribution of these nonstate enterprises originating in special economic zones (SEZs) and other open coastal cities. As a result, the nonstate sector presently accounted for a larger share of the total gross value of industrial output (GVIO) than did the SOEs.

And, from virtually no FDIs in 1979, by 1994 the cumulative total had risen to 221,718 approved projects with a contracted value of US$303.3 billion, US$95.6 billion of which had actually been disbursed.[31] The recorded figures for 1994 alone, as noted, were all the more impressive. In 1994, the export and import value of FIEs totalled US$87.7 billion, up 30.7% over 1993, and its share in China's total two-way external trade rose from 34.3% in 1993 to some 37% last year.[32] Apart from helping to broaden the structure of Chinese output, FDIs have helped China to advance technologically, thereby enhancing its total factor productivity and hence external competitiveness.

For almost three decades after the revolution, until the advent of

Table 1. China's Foreign Trade and Degree of External Orientation, 1978–1994

	1978	1980	1985	1986	1987	1988	1989	1990	1991	1992	1993	1994
Foreign trade (in US$ billion)												
Merchandize exports	9.8	18.1	27.3	30.9	39.4	47.5	52.5	62.1	71.8	84.9	91.8	121.0
Merchandize imports	10.9	20.0	42.3	42.9	43.2	55.3	59.1	53.4	63.8	80.6	104.0	115.7
Total merchandize trade	20.6	38.1	69.6	73.9	82.7	102.8	111.7	115.4	135.6	165.5	195.7	236.7
Merchandize trade balance	−1.1	−1.9	−14.9	−12.0	−3.8	−7.8	−6.6	+8.8	+8.1	+4.4	−12.2	+5.3
Openness and world trade shares (in %)												
Merchandize exports to GNP ratio	4.6	6.1	9.4	11.0	13.0	12.6	12.4	16.8	18.9	19.2	16.9	23.7
Merchandize imports to GNP ratio	5.1	6.7	14.5	15.3	14.2	14.6	13.9	14.4	16.8	18.2	19.1	22.6
Foreign trade proportion to GNP	9.7	12.8	23.9	26.3	27.2	27.2	26.3	31.2	35.7	37.4	36.0	46.3
Share of world exports	0.8	1.0	1.5	1.6	1.7	1.8	1.8	1.9	2.1	2.3	2.5	2.9
Share of world imports	0.9	1.0	2.2	2.1	1.8	2.0	2.0	1.6	1.8	2.1	2.7	2.7
Share of world trade	0.8	1.0	1.9	1.8	1.7	1.9	1.9	1.7	1.9	2.2	2.6	2.9
Memorandum items												
GNP (in billions RMB)	358.8	447.0	855.8	969.6	1,130.1	1,406.8	1,599.3	1,769.5	2,023.6	2,437.9	3,134.2	4,380.0
Official exchange rate (RMB per US$)	1.680	1.498	1.937	1.453	3.722	3.722	3.765	4.783	5.323	5.515	5.762	8.570
GNP (in US$ billion)	213.6	298.4	291.4	280.8	303.6	377.9	424.8	369.9	380.2	442.0	543.9	511.1

Note: China's shares of world trade for 1994 are based on the first annual report of the new WTO, as reported in Sheel Kohli, "Mainland Exports Surge to US$121b," *South China Morning Post*, 4 April 1995.

Sources: Official Chinese statistics are from *Statistical Yearbook of China*, relevant years; and world trade data are from IMF's *International Financial Statistics Yearbook*, relevant years.

open-door economic reform, China maintained a highly overvalued exchange rate in the context of a rigid system of exchange control, thereby militating against expanded trade. Since 1980, however, the official exchange rate *per se* has depreciated more than 470% against the US dollar. Hence some of China's major trading partners and the United States in particular, have begun to argue that China has fuelled its export growth by devaluing its currency. Yet, one noteworthy point in this context is that until the unification of exchange rates in January 1994, the official rate at which foreign trade took place was grossly overvalued, effectively putting a tax on China's own exportables.

In all, continued opening up and liberalization in each of the areas considered above have substantially reduced the bias against expanded trade and international production that was inherent in the institutional settings of the Soviet-style centrally planned economy of the pre-reform era. As a result, China's economy has become increasingly integrated into the global economy, so much so that its merchandise trade turnover accounted for 2.9% of the world's total trade volume in 1994, more than treble the share of some 0.8% in 1978. Likewise, its share of world exports increased from 0.8% in 1978 to 2.9% in 1994, while the import ratio rose from 0.9% to 2.7% in the same period. Concurrently, the ratio of China's merchandise trade volume to its GNP rose from less than 10% in 1978 to 46.3% in 1994, with exports amounting to 23.7%, a dramatic change for a country the size of China. Based on this foreign trade proportion figure, the Chinese economy to date appears to be more than twice as open as that of the United States or Japan.[33] On the import front, the degree of foreign penetration in certain sectors seems to be equally high. For example, in 1993, import penetration was responsible for around one-third of GVIO in China's machinery and transport equipment sector.

At this juncture, however, it must be stressed that the trend in the apparent share of foreign trade in China's GNP is quite deceptive and therefore needs to be treated with caution. For one thing, China's official GNP statistics are likely to be underestimated.[34] For another, these ratios are based on the official exchange rates of the domestic currency. No less significant, Chinese customs data on exports included the full value of exports based on the processing of imported intermediate inputs. All these tend to exaggerate the role of trade and the alleged degree of openness of the Chinese economy.

In large measure, the growing export orientation and concomitant increase in the relative importance of foreign trade in the Chinese economy reflected that over the 1980s and early 1990s trade performance has become increasingly independent of the level of within-plan domestic economic activity. Whereas in the pre-reform era the role of foreign trade in the national economy was to provide a residual balance, the secular expansion of exports in the post-1978 years can no longer be explained merely on the basis of the availability of an exportable surplus, resulting from an excess of planned output over domestic demand, or on the basis of filling the gaps in the material balances, arising from unavailabilities or shortfalls in the domestic economy under the national plans.

That said, over the last reformist decade-and-a-half, a sea change in China's external sector has taken place and, concomitantly, the economy has become more open and integrated with the rest of the world through increased trade and investment. In particular, foreign trade is no more a mere balancing or lagging factor in China's present-day economy but has become that of an important catalyst or a leading sector in its growth process.

China's Changing Trade Patterns

Since the normalization of Sino-US diplomatic and trade relations in January 1979, the year China's market-based reforms and open-door policy actually began, and the subsequent signing of the Sino-US Trade Agreement in February 1980, China has established trade relations with all continents and with most countries in the world. The bulk of its trade turnover is, however, carried on with a small number of major trading partners. A concomitant outcome of China's active trade promotion efforts has been a marked shift in the commodity composition of trade, particularly the changes in the product composition of its merchandise exports.

Direction of Trade

In so far as the direction of trade is concerned, China has traded most intensively with other economies in the Asia Pacific, which has now emerged as the most dynamic and fastest growing region, in terms of both international trade and investment, in the global economy. The rise in trade activity with the Asia-Pacific economies has been most noticeable from the mid-1980s onwards. By early 1990s over 70% of China's export trade and about 80% of its import business were with other Asia-Pacific economies, including Japan, the United States, Hong Kong and the other three Asian NIEs, Canada, Australia and the rest of the Association of Southeast Asian Nations (ASEAN) — Thailand, the Philippines, Malaysia and Indonesia.

On an individual basis, Hong Kong, Japan and the United States dominated throughout the last decade, accounting for around two-thirds of China's total overseas sales and well over 50% of its total imports during the early 1990s. During the same time, the ten top trading partners have accounted for around 80% each of China's exports and imports, as depicted in Tables 2 and 3, respectively. Hong Kong is especially important because of its entrepot intermediary role. According to China's customs statistics, at its height during the early 1990s, Hong Kong was responsible for as much as 45% of China's total exports, one-quarter of China's total imports, making Hong Kong and China the largest trading partners.

However, the gross percentage figures just mentioned should be treated with caution because Hong Kong has served increasingly as a conduit for China's tradeable sector rather than as a final consumer or as an original supplier. Much of the increased export and import volumes during the past decade or so were due to consignment processing of products by Hong Kong companies in the Pearl River Delta region and elsewhere in China and the subsequent re-export of the processed products through Hong Kong to third countries, primarily the United States. As such, information about Hong Kong's re-export to and from China is central to understanding the overall picture of China's genuine trade patterns, whereas the official Chinese trade statistics *per se* are rather misleading.

According to the Hong Kong Census and Statistics Department data,[35] in 1993 Hong Kong's total re-exports, by dint of the booming outward processing activities across the border, reached some US$105.5 billion (HK$823 billion), accounting for 78.7% of Hong Kong's total exports; during the same year the value of re-exports originated from China alone totalled US$60.8 billion (HK$474 billion) — accounting for about 58% of Hong Kong's total re-exports, and some 35.5%, 8.2%, 7.5%, 4.8% and 4.6% of such re-exports from China were destined for the United States, Germany, Japan, the United Kingdom and, intriguingly, China *itself*, respectively. On the other hand, the re-exports destined for China totalled US$35.3 billion (HK$275 billion) — accounting for around one-third of Hong Kong's total re-exports, and some 28.4%, 21.6%, 9.0% and 6.1% of

Table 2. Distribution of China's Merchandize Exports by Major Importing Economies, 1985–1993

	1985	1986	1987	1988	1989	1990	1991	1992	1993
Hong Kong	26.3	31.6	34.9	38.4	41.7	42.9	44.7	44.2	24.0
United States	8.6	8.5	7.7	7.1	8.4	8.3	8.6	10.1	18.5
Japan	22.3	15.4	16.2	16.6	16.0	14.5	14.2	13.7	17.2
Germany	2.7	3.2	3.1	3.1	3.1	3.3	3.3	2.9	4.3
South Korea	—	—	—	—	—	2.0	3.0	2.8	3.1
Russia	3.6	3.9	3.2	3.1	3.5	3.6	2.5	2.8	2.9
Singapore	7.6	3.9	0.6	3.1	3.2	3.2	2.8	2.4	2.4
United Kingdom	1.3	4.6	1.3	1.4	1.2	1.0	1.0	1.1	2.1
Netherlands	1.2	1.5	1.5	1.6	1.4	1.5	1.5	1.4	1.8
Taiwan	—	—	—	—	—	0.5	0.8	0.8	1.6
Rest of the World	26.4	27.4	31.5	25.6	21.5	19.2	17.6	17.8	22.1

Notes: All figures are percentage shares of the corresponding total merchandize exports. The symbol — indicates data not available. As the Federal Republic of Germany (West Germany) and German Democratic Republic (East Germany) were unified on 3 October 1990, entries for Germany prior to 1990 refer to the trade with the former West Germany. Likewise, entries for Russia prior to 1992 refer to the trade with the former Soviet Union.

Source: *Statistical Yearbook of China*, relevant years.

Table 3. Distribution of China's Merchandize Imports by Major Importing Economies, 1985–1993

	1985	1986	1987	1988	1989	1990	1991	1992	1993
Japan	35.6	29.0	23.3	20.0	17.8	14.2	15.7	17.0	22.4
Taiwan	—	—	—	—	—	4.2	5.7	7.3	12.4
United States	12.0	11.0	11.2	12.1	13.3	12.4	12.6	11.0	10.3
Hong Kong	11.4	13.1	19.5	21.7	21.2	26.7	27.4	25.5	10.0
Germany	5.7	1.3	7.2	6.2	5.7	5.5	4.8	5.0	5.8
South Korea	—	—	—	—	—	1.3	1.7	3.3	5.1
Russia	2.3	3.4	2.9	3.2	3.6	4.0	3.3	4.4	4.8
Italy	2.2	2.7	2.9	2.8	3.1	2.0	2.3	2.2	2.6
Singapore	0.6	1.3	1.4	1.8	2.5	1.6	1.7	1.5	2.5
Australia	2.7	3.3	3.1	2.0	2.5	2.5	2.4	2.1	1.9
Rest of the World	27.5	34.9	28.5	30.2	30.3	25.6	22.4	20.7	22.2

Notes: All figures are percentage shares of the corresponding total merchandize imports. Other notes are the same as those appearing in Table 2.

Source: As Table 2.

these re-exports to China were originated from Japan, Taiwan, the United States and South Korea respectively. That seen, the significance of Hong Kong as entrepot centre for China's tradeable sector needs no further elaboration.

Starting from 1993, however, China's customs administration has been exercising more care in the verification of declared destination or origin of imports and exports. This new classification exercise makes China's customs data for the geographical distribution of its merchandise trade turnover in 1993 more realistic than those for earlier years, albeit inevitably complicating the task of tracing changes in the direction of trade over time. The main effect of this more precise origin- and destination-tracing is to downgrade Hong Kong's shares of both exports and imports, thus more clearly recognizing the territory's entrepot role.

Correspondingly, in 1993 China's exports to Hong Kong saw an apparent decline of over 41% and, on the other hand, its exports to the United States, Japan, Germany and the United Kingdom enlarged by 97%, 35%, 62% and 109% respectively. Likewise, Hong Kong's share of imports, as shown in Table 3, also fell from 25.5% in 1992 to only 10% in 1993. None the less, a fair portion of China's diverse exportables passing through Hong Kong to third countries or the procurement of China's imports via Hong Kong from other places of origin is still counted as exports or imports from Hong Kong, for obvious encumbering identification reasons.

After all, according to China's customs data, for most of the individual years during the past decade Japan and the United States have emerged as China's second and third largest markets as well as trading partners. In 1993, China exported US$15.8 billion of merchandise goods to Japan, accounting for 17.2% of China's total exports; some US$23.3 billion of Japanese products, on the other hand, were imported by China from Japan, accounting for 22.4% of China's total imports. Taken together, in 1993 the total Sino-Japanese trade turnover hit US$39 billion, replacing Hong Kong as China's leading trading partner in addition to the largest supplier of China's merchandise imports. This bilateral trade turnover was a hefty 53.9% rise on the 1992 level of US$25.4 billion and represented approximately one-fifth of China's total two-way trade volume in 1993. In a large measure, these upsurges are owing to the new method in the attribution of origin and destination to merchandise goods passing through Hong Kong between China and Japan.

And, according to customs clearance statistics of Japan's Ministry of Finance,[36] the Japan-Sino trade volume topped US$37.8 billion in 1993, up

30.9% from the previous year, while exports from Japan reached US$17.3 billion, up 44.6%, and imports US$20.6 billion, up 21.3%. By Japan's count, in 1993 China pulled ahead of Germany, Taiwan and South Korea to rise from fifth to second place as a country of origin for the first time, stood sixth as Japan's export destinations and second, after the United States, in the league of bilateral trade volumes.

Since 1979, the bilateral merchandise trade flows between China and the United States, driven by many complementary aspects of the two Pacific giants, have grown rapidly. According to China's customs data, China's bilateral trade with the United States grew from some US$2.5 billion in 1979 to US$27.7 billion in 1993, representing a compound growth rate of 18.9% a year, while its exports to and imports from the United States valued at US$17 billion and US$10.7 billion in 1993, having expanded 28.6 and 5.8 times the 1979 levels of less than US$0.6 billion and US$1.9 billion respectively.

However, by the reckoning of the US Department of Commerce, US bilateral trade with China expanded from only US$2.3 billion in 1979 to US$40.3 billion in 1993, representing a compound growth rate of 22.7% annually, while its imports from China soared more than 45-fold, from some US$0.7 billion in 1979 to US$31.5 billion in 1993. Whereas growth of China's exports to the United States was generally strong and steady, US shipments to China, by comparison, experienced considerable year-to-year fluctuations, partly as a result of periodic retrenchment policies in China's rapidly evolving economy, and rose to only US$8.7 billion in 1993, about five times the 1979 level of US$1.7 billion. Thus, according to US statistics, since 1983 the country has had a trade deficit with China.

While the United States has grown accustomed to worrying about its growing trade deficit with Japan, most Americans would be somewhat bewildered to learn that the US deficit with China has grown from less than one billion US dollars in late 1970s, to US$22.8 billion in 1993, the second largest bilateral trade deficit worldwide. The sharp trade deficit with China continued to widen in 1994. With US exports to China amounting to US$9.3 billion, less than one-fourth the value of US imports from China which were worth US$38.8 billion, the US trade deficit with China, its sixth largest trading partner, reached a record US$29.5 billion in 1994, up 29.5% from the 1993 level. The United States trade gap with Japan also widened some 8.6% to an all-time high of US$65.7 billion in 1994, from the 1993 shortfall of US$60.5 billion.[37]

Turning back to the official Chinese statistics, however, some outside observers may be puzzled to note that from the post-1978 period until 1993, China has consistently run a trade deficit with the United States. Closely related to these differing trade deficit or surplus issues is the problem of discrepancies between the official Chinese and US trade statistics. In their calculations of bilateral trade balance or imbalance, both the Chinese customs authority and the US Department of Commerce count their shipments of merchandise goods to each other through Hong Kong as exports to Hong Kong rather than as exports to the United States and, likewise, to China. As a result, official Chinese trade statistics differ widely from the official US figures: both countries overstate their bilateral trade deficits and, conversely, understate the bilateral trade surpluses.[38]

The story is further complicated by the rapid emergence of export-oriented FDI production in China. As a growing number of such FDI firms from Hong Kong, Taiwan and other economies, including the United States, shift their production bases to China, and in addition to its own burgeoning outward-processing activity across the border, Hong Kong has become an increasingly important entrepot for China. In the process, the Sino-US trade imbalance is likely to become even wider. Accordingly, many of the consumer goods that the United States once imported from Hong Kong, Taiwan and elsewhere, are now counted as China's exports, thereby increasing recorded imports from China and lowering the corresponding figures for Hong Kong, Taiwan, among others.[39] It appears, therefore, when factor inputs can cross the border freely, mere bilateral deficits and surpluses are misleading. At present, to be sure, the large and growing trade imbalance between the two, as recorded by the US Department of Commerce, has caused and will continue to engender considerable bilateral tensions. The often contentious trade issues are: the most-favoured-nation (MFN) status between the two, the protection of intellectual property rights in China, the access of US goods and services to the Chinese market, the US export control policy toward China, textiles trade and the application of the US import control laws to products from China, and the business environment in China. Beyond question, in the long run the external commercial relationship will be governed by the degree of success that both countries have in resolving these issues.

Whilst there has always been some amount of indirect trade between Taiwan and the mainland China prior to 1979, the exact amounts of those largely unacknowledged trade flows are difficult to estimate. Following the political and economic reforms on both sides of the Taiwan

Straits, since the mid-1980s the two-way trade volume began to expand, conducted mainly through Hong Kong as in the pre-reforms years. According to official Chinese statistics, China's 1993 two-way indirect trade with Taiwan was valued at US$14.4 billion, up 119.5% over the 1992 level of US$6.6 billion. As a supplier, Taiwan's indirect exports to China went up by 120.5%, to a record US$12.9 billion in 1993, representing 12.4% of China's total imports. The upshot of this huge annual upsurge, albeit due in part to the result of the trade reclassification exercise during the year, is that in 1993, Taiwan overtook the United States as well as Hong Kong to become the second largest supplier of merchandise goods to China for the first time in the post-1949 years. Without question, the trade turnover between Taiwan and China will see further increases in the remainder of the 1990s, as Taiwan removes more restrictions on commercial contacts with China and the economies of Taiwan and Fujian province in south China become increasingly integrated via China-bound investment by Taiwanese enterprises.

While the rapidly growing trilateral trade flows among Taiwan, Hong Kong and the Chinese mainland are turning this Pacific area into a fourth growth pole of the world economy,[40] following the normalization of diplomatic relations between China and the Republic of Korea in August 1992, the development of both direct and indirect trade flows between these two neighbouring economies is no less striking. By China's count, in 1993 the Sino-Korean direct trade volume totalled US$8.2 billion, with the Korean exports valued at US$5.4 billion and Chinese exports at US$2.9 billion, up 63.5%, 104.4% and 18.9% respectively, over their 1992 equivalent levels. By these levels, South Korea, once a minor player in the China trade, is now the fifth largest market for China's exports and ranks sixth as a supplier. More recently, South Korea has also become an important FDI source for Shandong province, just a short boat ride from the Korean peninsula, and elsewhere in China. In this latter respect, Korea's expertise in large-scale industry assures it a growing role in China's outward-oriented economic transformation.

As regards trade with the European Union (EU),[41] as presently known, in 1993 the combined amount of goods exported from China to the EU totalled US$11.7 billion, while its imports from the latter were worth US$14.4 billion, representing 12.7% and 13.9% respectively, of China's total merchandise exports and imports. Germany, followed by Italy, the United Kingdom and France, took the lead among the Sino-EU trade ledger. In 1993, the value of bilateral trade volumes between China and these four leading EU countries aggregated to US$20.6 billion, accounting for 78.9% of the Sino-EU total. In particular, Germany, which accounted for 4.3% of China's total exports and 5.8% of the total imports, ranked fifth highest, only behind Japan, Hong Kong, the United States and Taiwan, in China's trade league table. No less significant, by 1993 the Sino-Russian trade volume had reached US$7.7 billion — up 31% over the 1992 figure of US$5.9 billion, with the Chinese exports valued at US$2.7 billion and Russian exports at US$5 billion. None the less, the bulk of trade turnover between these two largest reforming socialist economies in recent years was still based on barter terms, which embraced about two-thirds of the total bilateral trade business.

To a large extent the pace of growth in China's foreign trade can be attributed to the surge of exported-oriented FDIs. Following the promulgation of the landmark "Chinese-Foreign Joint Venture Law" in July 1979 and the succeeding "Law on Foreign Capital Enterprises" in 1986, a growing number of FDI ventures, to take advantage of China's less expensive labour, are shipping semi-manufactures, parts and components across borders for reprocessing and assembly, thereby further boosting China's overall trade figures. Due to ethnic, cultural and physical proximity factors, Hong Kong is by far the single largest FDI investor in China. It is estimated that as much as two-thirds of the accumulated disbursed FDI in China since 1978 originated from Hong Kong. In 1993 alone, newly disbursed FDI sourced from Hong Kong was valued at US$17.4 billion, accounting for 62.8% of the total. More notably, as high as 80% of the cumulative FDI in Guangdong came from Hong Kong.

More tellingly, it has been estimated that around 80% of Hong Kong business people to date have production bases on the mainland, with more than 30,000 outprocessing enterprises in the Pearl River Delta region of Guangdong alone, while between three and four million mainland workers there are directly or indirectly employed by these Hong Kong-based FDI firms.[42] This FDI outprocessing-based employment figure is larger than the entire economically active population in Hong Kong, or about six to eight times as large as Hong Kong's own manufacturing workforce. Clearly, through expanding trade and investment, a spatial division of labour has been under way for more than a decade. Hong Kong serves as the marketing office and south China as the territory's backyard factory. Of course, Hong Kong's share of FDIs in China is likely to be inflated by the amount of indirect outward investment from other genuine home economies through Hong Kong. In this latter regard, a fair portion of the recorded

FDIs from Hong Kong is believed to be recycled funds or "round-tripping" investment from mainland Chinese entities.

Other major FDI investors in 1993, in ascending percent-order of importance, were Taiwan (11.3%), the United States (7.4%), Japan (4.9%), Macau (2.1%), Singapore (1.8%) and South Korea (1.4%). Apart from the generally open investment climate, preferential policies offered by the Chinese authorities, and the sheer market potential of 1.2-billion consumers, the foremost factor-endowment reason for all these FDI ventures is the surplus low-wage labour prevalent in China. Not surprisingly, by 1994 China had become the world's most favoured destination for FDI investors.

On top of helping to boost China's export earnings and hence its foreign exchange reserve holdings, these inflows of export-oriented FDIs have been an important source of foreign technology and ideas, serving to modernize its reforming economy. Thanks to the continuing FDI flows in the context of an increasingly open-door economic enviromnent, virtually the entire eastern coast of China today appears to display a booming export-oriented economy. Indeed, China is the latest example, as a recent World Bank study has noted,[43] of FDI-led export and technology development in the world. Aside from the likely evolution of China's international presence, all these fast-changing events have important implications for bilateral trade balances with individual countries.

Commodity Structure of Trade

Reflecting the political *dirigisme* of exporting only surplus commodities and the tightly administered export quota restraints, China's merchandise exports were dominated by nonstaple food items and crude petroleum, prior to the late 1970s. Besides the changed market structure, another important outcome of the post-1978 reforms has been a dramatic shift in the commodity composition of China's exports. In the first half of the 1980s, China's exports were still divided about evenly between primary commodities and manufactured products, since the mid-1980s, however, the share of primary goods exports has steadily declined from around 50% down to 18% in 1993, as shown in Table 4. On the other hand, the exports of manufactured goods became dominant and, by 1993, accounted for more than four-fifths of total exports.

Much of this evolving export commodity structure was accounted for by the increased exports of light consumer manufactures, notably textiles,

Table 4. Commodity Structure of China's Merchandize Exports, 1980–1993

	1980	1985	1986	1987	1988	1989	1990	1991	1992	1993
Primary products	50.3	50.5	36.4	33.5	30.3	28.7	25.6	22.5	20.0	18.2
Foodstuffs	16.5	13.9	14.4	12.1	12.4	11.7	10.6	10.1	9.8	9.2
Beverages and tobacco	0.4	0.4	0.4	0.4	0.5	0.6	0.5	0.7	0.8	1.0
Nonfood items	9.4	9.7	9.4	9.3	8.9	8.0	5.7	4.8	3.7	3.3
Mineral fuels	23.6	26.1	11.9	11.5	8.3	8.2	8.4	6.6	5.5	4.5
Animal and vegetable oils and fats	0.3	0.5	0.4	0.2	0.1	0.2	0.3	0.2	0.2	0.2
Manufactured products	49.7	49.5	63.6	66.5	69.7	71.3	74.4	77.5	80.0	81.8
Chemicals	6.2	5.0	5.6	5.7	6.1	6.1	6.0	5.3	5.1	5.0
Products classified by material	22.1	16.4	19.0	21.7	22.1	20.8	20.3	20.1	19.0	17.9
Of which: textiles	—	11.9	13.7	14.7	13.6	13.3	11.3	10.8	9.1	8.4
Machinery and equipment	4.7	2.8	3.5	4.4	5.8	7.4	9.0	10.0	15.6	16.7
Miscellaneous manufactures	15.7	12.8	16.0	15.9	17.4	20.5	20.4	23.1	40.3	42.3
Of which: clothing	—	7.5	9.5	9.5	10.3	11.7	11.0	12.5	19.9	20.0
Products not elsewhere classified	1.1	12.5	19.4	18.7	18.3	16.6	18.7	19.0	**	**

Notes: All figures are percentage shares of the corresponding total merchandize exports. The symbol — indicates data not available, whereas ** means no more applicable. Following a new commodity reclassification exercise in 1992, "products not elsewhere classified" in China's new customs statistics have been subsequently included in different categories of commodities under "primary products" and "manufactured products."

Source: *Statistical Yearbook of China*, relevant years.

apparel, toys, sports goods, footwear and the like. In particular, just within the eight year period 1985–1993, the share of clothing rose by 12.5 percentage points to account for one-fifth of total exports in 1993. Next to clothing, machinery and equipment also saw its share in total exports rise from about 3% in the mid-1980s to 16.7% in 1993.

Leaving aside the steady depreciation of the *Renminbi* and the quantum leap in the utilization of FDI, the fundamental institutional force behind the rapid expansion in China's manufactured exports has, of course, been the successive trade liberalization, domestic price reforms, and opening-up drive to a more market-based economy, ongoing over the past one-and-a-half decades. In contrast to the pre-reform years, China's overall export specialization since the early 1980s, and more fully so by the late 1980s, has been based on its underlying comparative advantage. In this context, revealed comparative advantage estimation in a recent World Bank study suggests that China's export mixes have been moving closely in line with its natural comparative advantage, which lies in labour-intensive manufactures as well as in relatively higher technology exports that can be assembled domestically.[44] The commodities that have emerged as China's most dynamic exports appear to reflect its best comparative-cost advantage in low-wage labour. Textiles and clothing are notably good cases in point. Exports of machinery and equipment, which have been based largely on processing and assembly-type activity, are also essentially labour intensive.

In the realm of labour intensities, perhaps a more telling point that emerges from the same World Bank study is that while the product composition of China's exports has become increasingly labour intensive over the years, within the basket of labour intensive manufactured exports, however, the share of products relying on unskilled labour has been declining since the mid-1980s.[45] To a considerable extent China's export structure appears to be following a path that looks similar to those of the East Asian NIEs. By and large, as real wages and unit labour costs in these more advanced East Asian economies have risen, an important niche has been created for China's exports of traditional labour-intensive goods, as predicted by the Heckscher-Ohlin factor proportions theory and the product-cycle model. To be sure, an abundant supply of low-cost labour has been at the core of China's successful export drive. Not only does that surplus labour enable the country to competitively export labour-intensive consumer manufactures, it also attracts a sizeable number of transnational enterprises to set up manufacturing bases in China.

The implications of China's rapidly changing export commodity structure — which has evolved increasingly in accordance with its intrinsic comparative advantage in the production of labour-intensive manufactures — for the international division of labour and international production of world tradeables are far-reaching. In particular, many of the manufactured goods in which China has a revealed comparative advantage often face major forms of hard core NTBs in the United States and the EU. This raises the possibility that growing new protectionism and trends toward regionalism in most Western countries may constrain further developments in some product lines, especially textiles and clothing.

In fact, according to the World Bank computations, in 1990 the effective NTB coverage ratios of China's manufactured exports were 62% in the United States, 48% in the EU and 27% in Japan.[46] Manufactured exports to the former two markets are subject to higher NTBs because of their concentration on textiles and clothing. Specifically, around 94% each of China's exports of textiles and clothing to the United States, 81% of textiles exports and approximately 70% of clothing exports to the EU were subject to quota restrictions associated with the Multifibre Arrangement (MFA).[47] Apparently, due to their concentration on such sensitive products as textiles and clothing and their heavy focus on the US market, China's exports prospects are more vulnerable to market access problems than most other LDCs. To reduce the risk of these problems, China's export promotion priorities over the latter part of the 1990s should lie in upgrading quality, diversifying into other skilled labour-intensive products that it could pursue without altering the nature of its comparative advantage, and cultivating underexploited markets.

Unlike exports, the pattern of China's imports seem to have remained subject to a conscious import strategy of assuring supply of essential foodstuffs and key raw materials and acquiring embodied technology through the import of capital goods while regarding imports of consumer products as residual. This notwithstanding, in terms of commodity composition, the shift in China's merchandise imports since the early 1980s, as shown in Table 5, appears to be no less dramatic than that in its merchandise exports. Most notably, the share of primary commodities in total imports has declined from some 35% in 1980 to less than 14% in 1993. On the other hand, the share of manufactured goods as a whole has seen a steady increase and, by 1993, accounted for over 86% of total imports. Among these, capital goods (machinery and equipment) accounted for

Table 5. Commodity Structure of China's Merchandize Imports, 1980–1993

	1980	1985	1986	1987	1988	1989	1990	1991	1992	1993
Primary products	34.8	12.5	13.1	16.0	18.2	19.9	18.5	17.0	16.4	13.7
Foodstuffs	14.6	3.7	3.8	5.6	6.3	7.1	6.3	4.4	3.9	2.1
Beverages and tobacco	0.2	0.5	0.4	0.6	0.6	0.3	0.3	0.3	0.3	0.2
Nonfood items	17.8	7.7	7.3	7.7	9.2	8.2	7.7	7.8	7.2	5.2
Mineral fuels	1.0	0.4	1.2	1.2	1.4	2.8	2.4	3.3	4.4	5.6
Animal and vegetable oils and fats	1.2	0.3	0.5	0.8	0.7	1.5	1.8	1.1	0.6	0.5
Manufactured products	65.2	87.5	86.9	84.0	81.8	80.1	81.5	83.0	83.6	86.3
Chemicals	14.5	10.6	8.8	11.6	16.5	12.8	12.5	14.5	13.9	9.3
Products classified by material	20.8	28.2	26.1	22.5	18.8	20.9	16.7	16.4	23.8	27.5
Machinery and equipment	25.6	38.4	39.1	33.8	30.2	30.8	31.6	30.7	38.9	43.3
Miscellaneous manufactures	2.7	4.5	4.4	4.3	3.6	3.5	3.9	3.8	6.9	6.2
Products not elsewhere classified	1.7	5.8	8.5	11.8	12.6	12.2	16.9	17.5	**	**

Notes: All figures are percentage shares of the corresponding total merchandize imports. Other notes are same as those appeared in Table 4.

Source: As Table 4.

over 43% of total imports in 1993, compared to one-fourth of the total in 1980.

The rising share of capital goods reflects, more than anything else, the strategy of using imports as means of acquiring embodied technology for modernization ends. Overall, however, the present share level of capital goods imports in China is not excessive by the standards of other developing economies. In fact, like its export structure, China's import pattern appears to resemble that of its East Asian NIE neighbours. A fair amount of substitution of imports by domestic production in both intermediate and capital goods has also been made over the past decade or so of reform.

When all is said and done, one major point to be drawn from the comparative figures described above is that, whereas the changes in the commodity structure of both exports and imports moved China's pattern of trade to one much more congruent with the country's intrinsic comparative advantage than had been the case in the pre-1978 period, China's evolving economy today presents the picture of a still industrializing economy: labour-intensive products and low-to-medium technology are exported, while high-technology, knowledge-intensive goods are imported.

China and the World Trading System: The Challenge Ahead

There can be little doubt that since the Third Plenary Session of the Eleventh Central Committee of the Chinese Communist Party in December 1978, China has progressively introduced market forces, instituted decentralized economic decision-making, invigorated material incentives and hence profit-seeking competition. Rather than attempting to "cross the river in one leap," China's reforms and opening up to the outside world have often been introduced on an incremental and experimental basis and are sectorally and locally differentiated.[48] Reforms are still far from complete: in redefining property rights, privatization, the role of an independent central bank and of monetary management in the context of hard-budget constraints, as well as liberalizing foreign transactions and factor markets. But by the early 1990s, China has had made an economic "Long March" from the monolithic, centralized and rigidly controlled foreign trade and exchange rate regime of the pre-reform era, toward a multi-layered, multi-faceted, generally market-enhancing system and into the so-called "socialist market economy," thereby promoting China's closer integration into the global economy. The phenomenal upsurge in trade with the outside world and foreign investment in China bears witness to its growing international presence.

Naturally, China's role in the international economy will be enhanced further when it formally joins the GATT, the world's most important international trade system. Yet, the issues surrounding China's official participation are economically as well as politically demanding. Ironically, China was one of the twenty-three original signatories to the GATT, which started operating in 1948. For more than three decades after 1950, when Taiwan withdrew from the GATT, China had no official contacts with this international trading system. Having joined the IMF in April 1980 and the International Bank for Reconstruction and Development (IBRD), more commonly known as the World Bank, in May 1980, China was granted GATT observer status in November 1984. In July 1986, or just four months after China became a member of the Asian Development Bank (ADB) in March 1986, it formally initiated the application process of becoming what is called a contracting party to the GATT. Noting that GATT, together with IMF and IBRD, are regarded by the international economic community as the three major pillars that form the foundation of the global economy, GATT reaccession thus represents the last step marking China's full return to the world development and trading system.

Concerning the GATT, the late 1993 was of historic importance. GATT has been the primary instrument in implementing multilateral tariff concessions and facilitating global trade in merchandise goods through provisional trade arrangements negotiated by the parties. After a period of considerable uncertainty, the long-delayed, crisis-riddled Uruguay Round of multilateral trade negotiations were finally concluded in mid-December 1993, over seven years after the negotiations were launched in Punta del Este, Uruguay in September 1986. In its coverage of issues, the package of the Uruguay Round Agreements, known as the *Final Act Embodying the Results of the Uruguay Round of Multilateral Trade Negotiations*,[49] has been the most ambitious GATT document of the multilateral trade negotiations.

Besides the traditional subjects such as tariff and non-tariff reductions on merchandise goods, the 22,000 page closing documents of the Final Act, as endorsed by trade officials from over 120 countries in Marrakesh, Morocco in April 1994, covers a wide range of new areas such as trade in services, trade-related intellectual property rights, and trade-related investment measures, areas which had never before been regarded as concerns of the GATT system; a review of the GATT principles so as to strengthen and clarify the rules with respect to a number of trade policy instruments — in particular, safeguards, antidumping, subsidies and countervailing measures, thus improving the institutional framework for disputes settlement; the phasing out of the MFA, which for decades governed most of the discriminatory quota restrictions in the area of textiles and clothing, over ten years; likewise, agriculture, which had so far remained largely outside the purview of the GATT, was to be brought under the GATT discipline. Yet by far the most important outcome of the Uruguay Round of the GATT is the creation of a new, albeit long overdue, international trade body, known as the World Trade Organization (WTO), to supersede the existing rules-based GATT system on a more permanent and legally secure footing.

Reportedly, the WTO, which has come into being as scheduled on 1 January 1995, has a more formal structure and much larger mandate for steering international trade policy than its predecessor.[50] Amongst others, it will exercise surveillance over member countries' trade policies and provide a form for continuous multilateral trade negotiations. Perhaps more important still, by administering a strengthened international trade disputes-settlement system, this newly-created, rules-setting body should be in a better position to limit the scope for unilateral and bilateral actions outside the multilateral system and enforce new rules of free and open trade in an increasingly complex and interdependent world. All this notwithstanding, the realization of the benefits of the Uruguay Round and the success of the WTO will depend on the liberalization efforts of individual countries. In particular, whether the WTO meets the world's high expectations both in the remainder of the twentieth century and into the twenty-first will hinge largely on whether the major players — the United States and the enlarged EU particularly, opt to play by the rules or try to bypass the GATT-based multilateralism and pursue their own goals. As a matter of fact, the successful climax of the Uruguay Round notwithstanding, interest in unilateralism, bilateralism and regionalism appears to remain strong. Expectedly, all these themes are likely to be increasingly debated issues in the post-Uruguay Round era.

As to China's economic lot in the successful conclusion of the Uruguay Round, a recent World Bank study suggests that relative to other LDCs China is expected to gain more from tariff reductions and other reforms contained in the Final Act even if it does not become a member of the WTO for three reasons.[51] First, as noted earlier, most of China's exports are manufactured products, whereas most other LDCs have a far higher share of raw materials and other primary goods. These primary products generally face zero or low tariffs in DC markets already and thus do not stand to benefit from Uruguay Round reductions. Second, Uruguay World MFN tariff cuts will tend to erode the margins of special preferences, presently not available to China, such as the Generalized System of Preferences (GSP) in the United States and the Lome Convention and other special regional preferences in the EU given to many LDCs, thereby causing some of their existing trade to be diverted to non-preference receiving countries, notably China. Third, as textiles and clothing products account for a relatively high share of China's total exports, the phasing out of the MFA under the Uruguay Round accord over a ten-year period could be particularly beneficial to China relative to many other LDCs. "These products currently face trade barriers which provide nominal protection of over 100 percent" and, as the World Bank concludes, "a liberalization from these levels offers the potential for maximum trade gains."[52]

There is no cause for euphoria, however. It is important to note that the World Bank's evaluation of the benefits that are likely to accrue to China presumes that the existing GATT contracting parties would grant MFN treatment to China. As is now well known, while most of China's trade partners accord MFN status to its exports, its case with the United States is not a certain story. In fact, for some six odd years now, the survival of the Sino-US MFN trading nexus has been a big annual hurdle in relations. The problem is that the United States is required by its self-imposed domestic legislation to review China's MFN status on a yearly basis. As such, an anticipated Uruguay Round MFN tariff reduction or the phased dismantling of the MFA quotas may not benefit China fully if it loses that status on account of national economic variances or political differences with the United States, its largest trading partner. If the MFN status were withdrawn, US imports from China would be levied at five to ten times the prevailing MFN rates. Such increased spreads between the general and MFN duties would drastically weaken China's competitive position in the US market.

Furthermore, in the case of China, it is also pertinent to point out that even when China joins the GATT as a *new* contracting party, an existing contracting party could, in principle, invoke Article XXXV of the GATT charter, the so-called nonapplication clause, to deny China's automatic access to the GATT-based MFN privileges. It is not improbable that the United States would use this nonapplication clause on China. For all that, however, China is under no illusion that it can afford to stay outside the

GATT-WTO system. Reaping of the long-term benefits from joining GATT-WTO aside, the fact that China has yet to enter this supreme world trade watchdog means it cannot avail itself of the new and more streamlined disputes-settlement mechanism which could be used to resolve contending trade issues, thereby enhancing a sense of security and predictability for both exports and imports. Likewise, as the new WTO has provisions to protect a member country from unilateral trade actions, China would be in a better position to defend itself where it enters the WTO.

Turning to China's GATT reaccession manoeuvres, despite China's unyielding attendance in the Uruguay Round negotiations from the very start as well as its signing in Marrakesh of the Final Act of the Uruguay Round with observer status, after nineteen sessions of strenuous negotiations it failed to meet its self-imposed deadline to rejoining the GATT, thereby becoming a founder member of the successor WTO, by the end of 1994. Indeed, as Nicholas Lardy says: "Perhaps no accession process has been as complex and as time-consuming as China's."[53] In the eyes of MOFTEC trade negotiators, the US trade representatives are seen as the main stumbling block to China's eight-plus years of effort to rejoin the GATT. Many a time, accordingly, China has made plain it holds the United States responsible for most of the hurdles in the path of its reaccession endeavours. From the US perspective, however, China's GATT resumption efforts thus far still fall short of Western world's expectations and it has yet to further demonstrate it could be a free and more open trader as well as to prove it would follow international trade rules. Among the major sticking points holding up the reaccession or accession of China to the GATT-WTO are: wider market access for foreign goods and services, quicker and larger reduction rates in both import tariffs and NTBs, issues in improved intellectual property rights protection, greater transparency and predictability in trade and investment regime, undertakings toward full currency convertibility and national treatment for foreign businesses.

On top of the problem areas above, another key bone of contention in the lengthy negotiation process is in defining China's development status, namely whether as an LDC or a DC, when it is admitted to the GATT-WTO family. The difference in such an "either-or" classified status will materially affect the concessions China must make after joining the GATT-WTO and the time-frame in which they must be carried out. Just now, the US trade officials contend that China was already an "export powerhouse" whose foreign trade volume far exceeded the levels found in other LDCs and, as such, China has to be treated differently and cannot be admitted as an LDC. China, on the other hand, argues that for all intents and purposes it is a developing economy and should be admitted as an LDC, a label which would grant it greater leeway and more time to reform its trading regime in line with the GATT-WTO requirements. To be objective, however, one has to concede that China is a fastidious *dirigiste* economy in historic transition. To safeguard its vastly populous economy from hyper-inflation and socially distressing unemployment, China's open-door reforms and liberalization have been incremental and gradual, which is probably for the best. These facts should be taken into account by those countries in the working party on China's protocol package governing its participation in the GATT-WTO. After all, the debate on China's LDC or DC status is relevant only in the context of the obligations being or not being undertaken.

Closely related to the thorny status issue about China's international trading position in the global economy to date is the soring debate on the inclusion of a special import safeguard clause in China's GATT-accession protocol. The introduction of any safeguard clause on a selective basis, especially one aiming at a single country, constitutes a serious qualification to the letter of multilateral nondiscrimination. Considering, however, that untrammelled growth of China's cheap exports could irreparably damage an importing country's domestic industry once China enters GATT-WTO, some existing GATT signatories and the United States particularly have been insisting that China must agree to a special safeguard clause in the protocol, allowing existing contracting parties to impose either increased tariff duties or NTBs on surges of disruptive exports from China.

To a considerable extent the problem of China's GATT-WTO entry has been closely intertwined with the trading relationship ruling between the United States and China and, as such, progress on the latter front would expectedly smooth the former. In point of fact, of course, China's ultimate accession to the GATT-WTO, which concerns all existing contracting parties, is not merely dependent on a blessing from the United States. Yet, as the world's foremost economic superpower and China's leading export market, the United States is central to China's further integration into the world economy. The economic stakes in relation to the Sino-US trade ties are high. With hindsight, however, since 1989 it has become almost a ritual for the two Pacific economies to threaten each other with a punishing-retaliatory trade war, although a last-minute compromise usually emerges before the actual confrontations begin. A typical case in point is the latest Sino-US Agreement on Intellectual Property Rights, which was concluded on 26 February 1995 just before the United States was to have imposed punitive tariffs on more than one billion US dollars worth of Chinese exports that would have triggered a tit-for-tat measures at the ready.

All this notwithstanding, overall the Sino-US trade climate has been noticeably improved since the US Administration decision on 26 May 1994 to delink human rights concerns from the annual renewal of China's MFN trade status with the United States. In this regard, the aforesaid trade-war averting Intellectual Property Rights Agreement, as officially signed in Beijing by Chinese Minister Wu Yi and US Trade Representative Mickey Kantor on 11 March 1995, was another turning point in Sino-US trade relations. This newly-concluded Agreement, which will provide protection of copyrights, trademarks and patents and the opening of the Chinese market in music, film and computer software, signals a decisive commitment by China to a policy of moving in the direction of a trade regime which will be consistent with the GATT-WTO standard.

To sum up, the growing strength of China's economy and its enhanced impact on the world's trading environment underscores the importance of China being in the GATT-WTO system. In a sense, the acronym(s) — GATT-WTO, as the Chinese trade officials are fond of arguing, appears to be a misnomer for excluding a major trading nation with a fifth of the world's population. Viewed in this broader perspective, the United States along with other OECD countries are urged to work for China's early entry into the GATT-WTO system, so that China will have to comply with international protocols and MFN tariff conventions.[54] Apart from lending a universal outlook to the new WTO, early resumption of China's GATT-WTO participation would help to enhance the smooth operation of the world trading system. For China's part, it should by no means ignore the fact that joining the GATT and being a founder member of the WTO is not just a symbolic act but a demanding reformist commitment, involving the continuing creation and enforcement of a trading regime in the context of a market-based economy that conforms to international trading rules.

In conclusion, there can be little doubt that over the last sixteen years since late 1978 or early 1979, the evolving global economy has become increasingly a source of demand for Chinese production and, concurrently, a source of supply for Chinese productive consumption. The rise of China as a major trading power, which changes much of the whole equation governing the international division of labour and production, may appear to be a mixed blessing for the outside world. As China opens up and adopts decidedly market-oriented reforms, the commodity structure of its exports becomes revealedly more labour intensive, thereby creating considerable competitive pressure for countries resting on low-cost labour for exports. The impact of China's export surges on the global economy, however, should be seen in proper economic perspective.

As David Ricardo has taught us some two centuries ago, the principal gain of international trade is that international division of labour makes countries become more efficient and move into areas where they enjoy a genuine comparative advantage instead of producing merchandise items that can be made much cheaper abroad. The message of this Ricardian tenet is simple: whereas China's export growth has tended to displace a good portion of labour-intensive manufactures elsewhere, many trading nations and the global economy at large, on the other hand, should have stood to benefit from increased income and import demand implied by China's rise. And, while trade is certainly never a one-way street, perhaps the greatest immediate beneficiaries from China's emergence in world markets are likely to be those high-income countries among the OECD grouping. Apparently, those countries are the largest importers of low-wage, labour-intensive manufactured products and the leading exporters of capital- and knowledge-intensive goods that will constitute the bulk of China's needs to build up its infrastructure as well as its increased import demand for high-quality consumer manufactures.

Thus, our foregoing analysis suggests that given its growing presence in the global economy, China needs to be brought as soon as possible into the world trading system. Besides being a win-win solution for world trade tensions to date, China would be expected as an early contracting party in the GATT-WTO system to further expedite and consolidate its open-door economic reform process. This would not only bring China further into the mainstream of global trade and investment reforms, but also help reinvigorate the GATT-based non-discriminatory multilateralism that has served the international trading community so well in the early post-World War II decades.

Notes

1. For informative work explaining the rise of the East Asian NIEs, see, for example, World Bank, *The East Asian Miracle: Economic Growth and Public*

Policy (New York: Oxford University Press, published for the World Bank); and Anis Chowdhury and Iyanatul Islam, *The Newly Industrialising Economies of East Asia* (London: Routledge, 1993).
2. Alfred Marshall, *Principles of Economics*, Eighth Edition (reset) (London: Macmillan, 1949), p. 225.
3. Li Peng, "Report on the Work of the Government" (Delivered at the Third Session of the Eighth National People's Congress on 5 March 1995), reprinted in *Beijing Review*, Vol. 38, No. 13 (27 March–2 April 1995).
4. "Foreign Trade Takes Up New Challenge," *Beijing Review*, Vol. 38, No. 5 (30 January–5 February 1995), p. 7.
5. "Increase of Foreign Capital in China," *Beijing Review*, Vol. 38, No. 10, (6–12 March 1995), p. 29.
6. See Foo Choy Peng, "Investment 'Black Hole' a Boon and Bane to Asian Neighbours," *South China Morning Post*, 8 September 1994; also cf. Robert Cottrell, "A Vacancy Awaits — A Survey of China," *The Economist*, 18 March 1995, p. 12.
7. Li Peng's latest Government Work Report (Note 3).
8. So far, this Shanghai-based Foreign Exchange Trading Centre has linked twenty-three cities through computers. Reportedly, the centre has already accepted 303 financial institutions as its members. Of these, 89 are foreign institutions. For some further description concerning this new nationwide interbank foreign exchange network, see Ren Kan, "Foreign Exchange Reform Advances," *China Daily Business Weekly*, 8–14 January 1995.
9. For details, see Li Ning, "Merger of Dual Exchange Rates Stabilizes Swap Markets," *Beijing Review*, Vol. 37, No. 26 (27 June–3 July 1994), pp. 16–18.
10. Unlike domestic enterprises, FIEs are not compelled to convert foreign exchange revenues into *Renminbi*. Instead, currently FIEs still conduct their foreign transaction business through the local swap centres. Meanwhile, the People's Bank of China is considering a timetable that allows FIEs to buy and sell foreign exchange through the interbank market, thus suggesting an end to the swap centres.
11. As optimistically predicted by Chen Yuan, deputy governor of the People's Bank of China, the goal of making *Renminbi* fully convertible could be realized by 1998, although it remained the State Council's plan to make it fully convertible by 2,000, see Renee Lai, "Yuan Faces Tough Task Converting by 1998," *South China Morning Post*, 10 January 1995. Yet, as concerns the question of moving toward full convertibility on the capital account, the experience of many other countries since the demise of the Bretton Woods System in August 1971 suggests that a measured pace is advisable. Expectedly, generalized opening of the capital account would lead to exchange rate instability unless China's central banking system had established effective

macroeconomic monetary tools such as open market operations and flexible interest rates to influence money supply and other major economic aggregates, notably the general price level.

12. Cf. Zhou Xiaochuan, "Reform of China's Exchange Rate Regime" (Lecture given at the East Asian consultancy, Singapore on 12 October 1994), as noted in John Wong, "Assessing China's Economic Reform Progress in 1994," *JETRO China Newsletter*, No. 114 (January–February 1995), p. 13, note 11.
13. The persistent inflationary pressures and an accommodating central bank have resulted in money-supply (M2) growth averaging some 29% annually over the past five years. More dizzyly, in 1994 the broad money supply rose by 34.4% over the 1993 level, as documented in "Statistical Communique of the State Statistical Bureau of the People's Republic of China on 1994 National Economic and Social Development" (28 February 1995), reprinted in *Beijing Review*, Vol. 38, No. 12 (20–26 March 1995).
14. See Xiao Wang, "Trade Law Meets International Standards," *China Daily Business Weekly*, 14–20 August 1994.
15. See Fan Baoqin, "Internationalizing China's Foreign Trade System," *China's Foreign Trade* (March 1994), pp. 2–4.
16. Wu Yi, "On Sino-US Trade," *Beijing Review*, Vol. 37, No. 14 (4–10 April 1994), pp. 8–10; see also Wu Naitao, "Reform Boosts Foreign Trade," *Beijing Review*, Vol. 36, No. 9 (1–7 March 1993), pp. 20–22.
17. Under this memorandum of understanding on market access, China has agreed to remove two-thirds of import licensing requirement by the end of 1994 and the reduction of other NTB measures. The memorandum also contains a commitment to eliminate all import restrictions, quotas, licensing requirements and other administrative controls on a wide range of products by 1997, with about 75% of such import barriers eliminated within two years. In addition, China has pledged to promote the transparency of the trade system, including the publication of all laws, regulations and decrees that govern trade, in line with the requirements under the GATT.
18. Cf. Wu Naitao (Note 16), p. 20.
19. Ibid. The first reduction covered 225 import items, the second 3,371.
20. See World Bank, *China: Foreign Trade Reform* (Washington, DC: World Bank Publications, 1994), pp. 48 *et sqq.*, especially Table 3.1. In this new World Bank study, trade reforms in China's evolving economy are examined in depth, and much of our discussion *et passim* in this article draws on this well-surveyed report.
21. Ibid., on page xx of Executive Summary.
22. Ibid., pp. 55–57, especially Table 3.3.
23. Whereas the domestic prices for many products, particularly for a range of mature consumer durables such as televisions, sound recorders and washing

machines, in China are still high relative to international prices, they are nevertheless lower than the tariff-inclusive prices of competing imports. It was this characteristic that led the World Bank mission on China's foreign trade reform to conclude that the existing combinations of tariffs and NTBs in China as protective instruments are not fully binding, if not redundant. For further details and arguments, see World Bank (Note 20), pp. 69–78.

24. Wu Yi (Note 16), p. 10.
25. Michael W. Bell, Hoe Ee Khor and Kalpana Kochhar, *China at the Threshold of a Market Economy*, Occasional Paper 107 (Washington, DC: International Monetary Fund Publications, September 1993), pp. 33–35.
26. For some further discussion of this first foreign trade law, see Zhou Ping, "China Adopts Common International Practices," *Beijing Review*, Vol. 37, No. 23 (6–12 June 1994), pp. 4–5; "The Foreign Trade Law of the People's Republic of China," *HKTDC Trade Watch* (June 1994); Morio Matsumoto, "China's Industrial Policy and Participation in the GATT," *JETRO China Newsletter* (September–October 1994), pp. 2–5 and p. 20; and Helen K. Ho, "Foreign Trade Firsts," *The China Business Review*, Vol. 22, No. 1 (January–February 1995), pp. 45–47.
27. In simple words, the expression "touching the stones while crossing the river," as Deng Xiaoping has been fond of saying, means that every decision has to be taken in a down-to-earth approach. In retrospect, China's characteristic gradualist, piecemeal, experimental, incremental, or what is called "two steps forward and one step backward" approach to reforms has by and large followed this pragmatic Dengist idea. In its barest essential, the idea is that: if a reform measure works, it is adopted and generalized; if not, it is discarded or duly modified. On this Dengist conception, see, for example, Zhang Yan, "Deng Xiaoping and Reform in China," *China Today*, Vol. 43, No. 3 (March 1994), pp. 10–15.
28. Nicholas R. Lardy, "The Open-door Strategies: An Outside Perspective," in *Economic Reform and Internationalisation: China and the Pacific Region*, edited by Ross Garnaut and Liu Guoguang (St Leonards, NSW: Allen & Unwin in association with the Pacific Trade and Development Conference Secretariat, Australian National University, 1992), p. 137.
29. In the sphere of price reforms, more than 90% of traded goods in China today, as oft-reported in the press, have their prices determined by market demand and supply instead of administrative decrees.
30. The contours of China's nonstate sector, which has acquired increasing importance in the domestic economy, is not clear-cut at all. In general, enterprises that are under the direct authority of the central government or of provincial governments are considered as state-owned, and all the rest, that is, those under the discretion of prefecture or municipal, county or district, township and village, are regarded as the nonstate sector. In China's official

statistics, there are three main categories of nonstate enterprises: collectives, individual businesses and other enterprises. The latter two categories together comprise what is regarded as the private sector, consisting of FIEs, joint ventures and businesses owned by households or individuals. Collectives can be urban or rural, depending on their affiliation. Rural collectives include TVEs and rural cooperatives. For some fuller details about the sector, see Michael W. Bell et al. (see Note 25), especially p. 13, Box 1; Inderjit Singh, Dilip Ratha and Geng Xiao, "Non-State Enterprises as an Engine of Growth: An Analysis of Provincial Industrial Growth in Post-Reform China," Discussion Paper No. 157 (School of Economics and Finance, University of Hong Kong, April 1994); and the chapter article titled "Economic Reform and the Development of the Non-state Sector: A Case-study of China" in United Nations, *World Economic Survey 1993* (New York: United Nations Publications, 1993).

31. See the unauthored statistical news piece "Increase of Foreign Capital in China," *Beijing Review* (Note 5), p. 29.

32. Ibid. Statistics appeared therein also revealed that in 1994, the export value of FIEs totalled US$34.7 billion, while their imports amounted to US$52.9 billion.

33. According to IMF's *International Financial Statistics Yearbook*, in 1992, for example, the merchandise exports to GNP ratios for the United States and Japan were 7.5% and 9.7% respectively, while the two corresponding import ratios were 9.3% and 6.6%. Accordingly the degree of openness, as measured by this two-way foreign trade proportion, was 16.8% for the United States economy, 16.3% for Japan's, compared to 37.4% for China in 1992.

34. In its widely publicized 1993 *World Economic Outlook*, the IMF has estimated that China's economy, in terms of purchasing-power-parity (PPP) calculations, was the third largest in the world with a GNP of US$1,660 billion and a per capita GNP reaching US$1,450 in 1991. Likewise, according to the World Bank, China has a PPP-based GNP of US$2,350 billion, a per capita GNP as large as US$2,040 in 1991. And, in terms of the purchasing power, the combined GNP of the "Chinese economic sphere," otherwise known as the "Greater China economic community" — encompassing China, Hong Kong and Taiwan, is predicted to surpass that of the United States at the dawn of the twenty-first century, by the year 2002. Here, however, it must be stressed that because of the data problem for estimating the purchasing power of the Chinese currency, all these PPP-based GNP estimates are subject to considerable margin of error and, therefore, need to be treated with great caution. Additional discussion as well as other estimates of China's GNP or GDP based on the purchasing power of the Chinese currency, see Nicholas R. Lardy, *China in the World Economy* (Washington, DC: Institute for International Economics, 1994), pp. 14–18, especially Table 1.3; cf. also Ge Yang,

"China's Rise: Threat or Not?" *Beijing Review*, Vol. 38, No. 5 (30 January–5 February 1995), pp. 23–25.
35. All official Hong Kong trade statistics appearing in this article are adapted or compiled from *Annual Review of Hong Kong External Trade* (Hong Kong: Government Printer, relevant years); whereas, unless otherwise specified, all official Chinese statistics are from *Statistical Yearbook of China* (Beijing: China Statistical Publishing House, relevant years).
36. See China-North Asia Section, JETRO "Two-Way Trade Hits Historical High of US$37.8 Billion," *JETRO China Newsletter*, No. 109 (March–April 1994), pp. 21–22.
37. Cf. United States Information Agency, "Goods Trade Deficit Swells; Services Surplus Stable," *Washington Economic Reports* (15 March 1995), pp. 5–6.
38. Whereas the data problems with official Chinese trade statistics are too well reported, the official US trade statistics pertaining to growing US-Sino trade imbalance are also subject to certain weakness and limitations, thereby understating the importance of China as a market for US goods. In this latter regard, Nicholas Lardy has reckoned that US Department of Commerce's statistics overestimate its bilateral trade deficit with China since 1990 by about one-third. For details, see Lardy (see Note 34), chapter 4; cf. also Yun-wing Sung, "Foreign Trade and Investment," in *China Review*, edited by Kuan Hsi-chi and Maurice Brosseau (Hong Kong: Chinese University Press, 1991), chapter 15.
39. To be sure, the increasing focus by the United States on its growing trade imbalance with China has concealed a considerable offsetting reduction of the deficits with Hong Kong and Taiwan and a strong US export performance onto the Greater China economic sphere, comprising the trio of mainland China, Hong Kong and Taiwan. Factual evidence relating to this US-Greater China trading nexus appeared in Yin-ping Ho, "China's Foreign Trade and the Reform of the Foreign Trade System," in *China Review 1993*, edited by Joseph Cheng Yu-shek and Maurice Brosseau (Hong Kong: Chinese University Press, 1993), chapter 17. In passing, let me take advantage of the space here for pointing out a couple of typesetting errors contained in this earlier chapter article for *China Review 1993*. First, on page **17**.27 therein, the sentence: "For one thing, China's joining GATT will necessitate a revision of the US trade laws." should read: "For one thing, it will necessitate a revision of the US trade laws." As scarcely needs saying, whether China's joining GATT or not has nothing to do with "a revision of the US trade law." The artificial rephrasing of the pronoun "it" in my original typescript by the expression "China's joinging GATT" is misleading. Second, due largely to computer scanning failures the 1992 figures for US exports to Taiwan and Greater China as appeared in Table 6, p. **17**.32 therein should read US$15.2 billion and US$31.9 billion instead of US$13.2 billion and US$29.8 billion,

respectively; correspondingly, the 1992 figures for US trade balance with Taiwan and Greater China should read –US$9.4 billion and –US$28.3 billion instead of –US$11.4 billion and –US$30.3 billion, respectively.
40. A succinct account of the rise of the Greater China circle as a major growth pole of the global economy is to be found in Yun-wing Sung, "The Economic Integration of the China Circle: Implications for the World Trading System" (Paper prepared for China and East Asian Trade Policy Workshop, held at Australian National University, 1–2 September 1994).
41. All Sino-EU trade statistics appeared in this chapter are confined to the EU-twelve, namely Belgium, Britain, Denmark, France, Germany, Greece, Ireland, Italy, Luxembourg, the Netherlands, Portugal and Spain.
42. Cf. Xie Liangjun, "HK Firms Lured to Mainland." *China Daily*, 28 March 1995; and Gao Shangquan, "Economic Changes Know No Boundaries," *China Daily*, 11 April 1995.
43. World Bank, *East Asia's Trade and Investment: Regional and Global Gains from Liberalization* (Washington, DC: World Bank Publications, 1994), p. 49.
44. World Bank (Note 20), pp. 158 *et sqq.* and Annex 7.2 to the report.
45. Ibid., pp. 9 *et sqq.*, especially Table 1.3 therein.
46. Ibid., p. 148 and Table 7.3 therein.
47. In comparison, the low NTB coverage of China's exports in Japan is in large part accounted for by the fact that Japan does not impose MFA quotas on textiles and clothing.
48. For reviews of China's incremental reforms and their impact against the backdrop of the wider debate on "gradualism" versus "big bang" thesis, see Inderjit Singh, Alan Gelb and Gary Jefferson, "Can Communist Economies Transform Incrementally? China's Experience," Discussion Paper No. 169 (School of Economics and Finance, University of Hong Kong, March 1995); Wing Thye Woo, "The Art of Reforming Centrally Planned Economies: Comparing China, Poland, and Russia," *Journal of Comparative Economics*, Vol. 18, No. 3 (June 1994), pp. 276–308; Jingjie Li, "The Characteristics of Chinese and Russian Economic Reform," *Journal of Comparative Economics*, Vol. 18, No. 3 (June 1994), pp. 309–13; Ronald I. Mckinnon, "Financial Growth and Macroeconomic Stability in China, 1978–1992: Implications for Russia and Other Transitional Economies," *Journal of Comparative Economics*, Vol. 18, No. 3 (June 1994), pp. 438–69; Barry Naughton, "What is Distinctive about China's Economic Transition? State Enterprise Reform and Overall System Transformation," *Journal of Comparative Economics*, Vol. 18, No. 3 (June 1994), pp. 470–90; and Chung H. Lee and Helmut Reisen (eds.), *From Reform to Growth: China and Other Countries in Transition in Asia and Central and Eastern Europe* (Proceedings of the conference "From Reform to Growth: China and Other Countries in

Transition" jointly organized by the OECD Development Centre, the OECD Centre for Co-operation with Economics in Transition and the East-West Center, held in Honolulu, Hawaii, 16–17 December 1993) (Paris: OECD Development Centre Documents, 1994).
49. For a press summary on the Final Act of the Uruguay Round, see GATT Secretariat, "The Final Act of the Uruguay Round — Press Summary as of 14 December 1993," reprinted in *The World Economy*, Vol. 17, No. 3 (May 1994), pp. 365–93.
50. Though the WTO was formally inaugurated on January 1995, the GATT structure will contiue to guide the conduct of global trade over the next two years, gradually winding up as the WTO becomes fully operational in January 1997. For reviews of the Uruguay Round agreements and the wider WTO system, see James Walsh, "The World Trade Organisation — Its Characteristics and Challenges, *Global Outlook* (the Economist Intelligence Unit Country Forest, 1st Quarter 1995), pp. 19–23; "The Uruguay Round of Multilateral Trade Negotiations: A Preliminary Assessment of Results," in United Nations, *World Economic and Social Survey 1994* (New York: United Nations Publications, 1994), pp. 79–86; William R. Cline, "Evaluating the Uruguay Round," *The World Economy*, Vol. 18, No. 1 (January 1995), pp. 1–23; Colleen Hamilton and John Whalley, "Evaluating the Impact of the Uruguay Round Results on Developing Countries," *The World Economy*, Vol. 18, No. 1 (January 1995), pp. 31–49; Patrick Low and Alexander Yeats, "Nontariff Measures and Developing Countries: Has the Uruguay Round Leveled the Playing Field?" *The World Economy*, Vol. 18, No. 1 (January 1995), pp. 51–70; Richard Harmsen, "The Uruguay Round: A Boon for the World Economy," *Finance & Development* (March 1995), pp. 24–26; and James V. Feinerman, "A New World Order: Farewell to the GATT and Welcome to the World Trade Organization," *The China Business Review* (March-April 1995), pp. 16–18.
51. World Bank (Note 20), pp. 150–66.
52. Ibid., p. 151.
53. Lardy (Note 34), p. 45. A well-surveyed chronology identifying the key events in relations to China and the GATT since 30 October 1947, the date when the Chinese government authority signs the Final Act of Geneva that creates the GATT, also appeared in the appendix of Lardy's book.
54. A thoughtful argument for supporting the early resumption of China's GATT-WTO contracting party status is given in Lardy's study (Note 34). Besides guiding the reader through the enduring debates over China's accession to the GATT-WTO, in his timely book on China's current heated attempts to accede to the GATT-WTO Lardy also provides subtle policy recommendations to the US Administration regarding the long-term US-China trade relationship to the benefit of the global economy at large.

24

The Evolution of China's Stock Markets

Henry M. K. Mok

Transition to a Share-Holding System

The share-holding reform of Chinese enterprises had its humble beginnings among peasant-run factories in the post-1978 drive for economic reforms, when market-oriented business decisions were first introduced. Township factories and transportation firms sprang up in villages under the contract responsibility system, many of them financed by cooperative share-holdings. Although flawed the contract responsibility system has stabilized revenue flows to the state, improved efficiency in enterprises and contributed to raising a new generation of managers. It serves a useful role in the transition of Chinese state-owned enterprises to share-holding (joint-stock) companies.[1]

Managers of urban enterprises observed with envy the success of the rural and suburban share-holding companies and persuaded local Communist Party officials to approve similar share ownership experiments. Before 1984, state-owned and collective enterprises were under the direct control of the state and were mainly production units. They had to surrender all their operating profits to the Ministry of Finance from which they received budgetary allocations to finance their development. There are about 200,000 state-owned enterprises, including about 8,000 large- and medium-sized enterprises in China.[2] However, the "iron rice bowl" mentality and other production deficiencies cause one-third of these enterprises to operate at a serious loss.[3]

The 1984 enterprise reform relaxed direct state control of state-owned enterprises by introducing market-oriented mechanisms. Greater market orientation called for firms to achieve a balanced budget, autonomous development in business activities and self-discipline. Based on their performances, enterprises were allowed to issue securities and stocks to raise capital. Between 1984 and 1988, thousands of enterprises registered as joint-stock companies and a few floated shares publicly.[4] Starting in 1986, medium- and large-sized state-owned enterprises also jumped onto the bandwagon of share-holding reforms.

The initial issuance of shares was not subject to stringent regulations; they rather resembled bonds. For example, certain "shares" had a guaranteed return and the issuing enterprises promised a buy-back after a

---

The author wishes to acknowledge support from the Center for Financial Research on China (CFRC) and an UPGC earmarked research grant.

specified period. The shares became more standardized after the official openings of the two central exchanges in Shanghai and Shenzhen in late 1990 and 1991. In early 1991, there were only about 60 "limited liability joint-stock companies" in China, which collectively issued RMB500 million worth of shares. By the end of 1991, there were 3,220 share-holding companies with issues amounting to RMB7.5 billion. In that period, 89 companies, 35 of which were located in Shanghai and Shenzhen,[5] and 13 of which were listed on both exchanges, made public stock offers.

Transition to Central Exchanges

Great strides have been made in China's stock market "experiment." Before the formation of the two exchanges, shares of a few share-holding companies approved to go public were traded over-the-counter (OTC) in Shenzhen in 1987. However, the lack of a comprehensive regulatory, accounting and legal framework engendered many problems, including rampant black market activities and price manipulation.

On 27 November 1990, the "Administrative Measures of Shanghai Municipality on the Trading of Securities" were put into effect. The Shanghai Securities Exchange (SHSE) and the Shenzhen Stock Exchange (SZSE) opened officially on 19 December 1990 and 3 July 1991, respectively. The State Council restricted the trading of all shares to these two exchanges.

Behind the scenes, the evolution of this new financial order in China involved a power struggle between proponents advocating different economic and political objectives.[6] However, Deng Xiaoping's inspection tour of the Shenzhen Special Economic Zone around 19–23 January 1992 ended "at one blow" the drawn-out ideological debate. After his visit to the Shenzhen Stock Exchange, Deng pointed out that "some people insist stock is the product of capitalism. We conducted some experiments on stocks in Shanghai and Shenzhen, and the result has proven a success. Therefore, certain aspects of capitalism can be adopted by socialism. We should not be worried about making mistakes. We can close it [the stock exchange] and re-open it later. Nothing is 100% perfect." Deng's Document No. 2 and his economic theories were subsequently written into the party constitution announced at the 14th Communist Party Congress in October 1992, which affirmed "market socialism with Chinese characteristics."

Stock Markets in China

In comparison with New York and Hong Kong, China's fledgling stock markets are small and volatile and are not thoroughly understood by the public. In terms of total market capitalization, the two Chinese stock markets are roughly 10% of Hong Kong. Shanghai and Shenzhen experienced phenomenal growth in the last three or four years. They started, in 1991, with only 13 "A" share listings and a meagre RMB11 billion in total market capitalization. The number of listed "A" and "B" stocks increased to 70 at the end of 1992 and to 169 "A" shares and 34 "B" shares in Shanghai and 118 "A" shares and 24 "B" shares in Shenzhen, respectively, by the end of 1994 (Table 1). In four years, total market capitalization grew by over 40 times with RMB350.5 billion in the two A-share markets and RMB16.2 billion (US$1=RMB8.7) in the two B-share markets. The majority of the shares in Shanghai are in the industrial sector (Figure 1). The Shanghai Stock Exchange is also more than twice the size of its counterpart in Shenzhen.

A Speculative Market

As emerging markets with excessive speculation, market volatility and risk

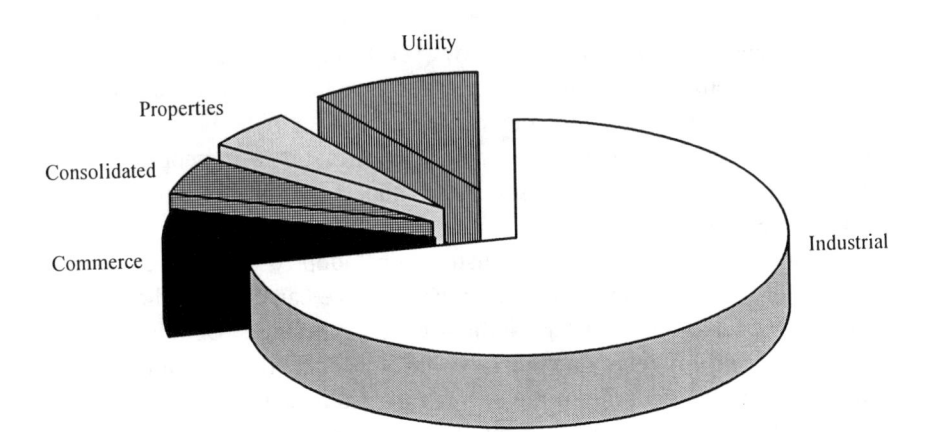

Figure 1. Equity by Industry Sectors (June, 1994)

The Evolution of China's Stock Markets

Table 1. Stock Markets in Shanghai and Shenzhen

	Dec. 1990	Dec. 1991	Dec. 1992	Dec. 1993	Dec. 1994
Shanghai					
Number of listings	(A) 7	(A) 7	(A) 29	(A) 101	(A) 169
			(B) 8	(B) 22	(B) 34
Market capitalization	(A) 1.25	(A) 2.92	(A) 67.9	(A) 206.8	(A) 248.1
(Billion yuan)			(B) 3.6	(B) 12	(B) 11.6
Shenzhen					
Number of stocks		(A) 6	(A) 24	(A) 75	(A) 118
			(B) 9	(B) 19	(B) 24
Market capitalization		(A) 8.08	(A) 44.4	(A) 125.1	(A) 102.4
(Billion yuan)			(B) 3.1	(B) 8.4	(B) 4.6

Source: *Shanghai Securities News, Shanghai Securities Weekly*, 6 January and 6 July, 1992; *Shenzhen Stock Exchange Fact Book 1993*, p. 106.
(A) = "A" shares; (B) = "B" shares.

are high. The Shanghai stock market displayed particular volatility in its four years of trading history (Figure 2). The 300% surge in the A-share market in May 1992 was due to the lifting of price limits. The 70% downturn from mid-1993 to July 1994 was triggered by high inflationary expectations and the financial austerity programme introduced by the central government. The glut caused by the listing of 72 new "A" shares in 1993 and another 68 "A" shares in the first half of 1994 in Shanghai also exerted downward pressure on prices. The 300% price surge in August 1994 was due to the three-measure market rescue plan announced by the China Securities Regulatory Commission (CSRC) in late July 1994.[7] At its peak, daily market turnover was RMB15.6 billion on 6 September 1994 in Shanghai. This is more than twice the average daily turnover in Hong Kong.

Another sign of the speculative nature of China's stock markets is reflected in the high turnover of outstanding shares. In the wake of the announcement of the three-measure market rescue plan by the CSRC, the rate of outstanding shares changing hands was reported to be 3,105% in Shanghai and 1,207% in Shenzhen in August 1994, respectively, the highest in the world.[8] It is generally agreed that the Chinese economy will grow at a rate of 9–10% per year until the end of the century. However, the performance of the China's stock markets appears to be independent of China's economic prospects, while it reacts strongly to policy shifts.

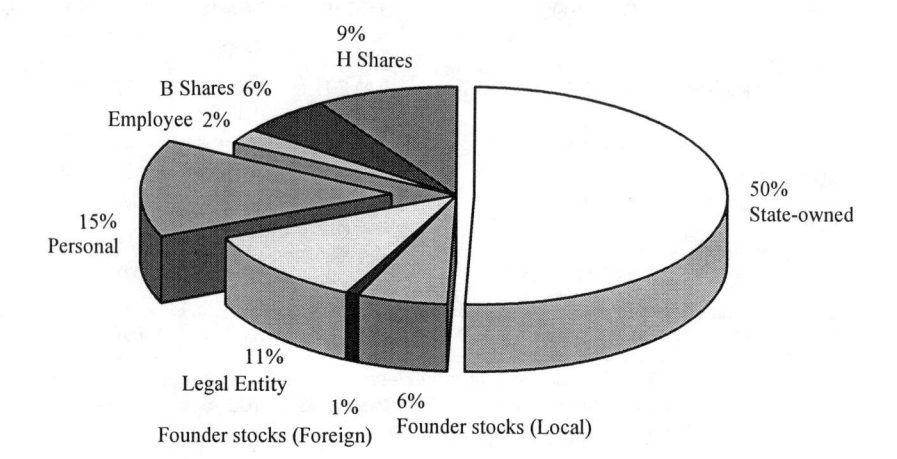

Figure 2. Total Equity by Share-Holdings (June, 1994)

- 9% H Shares
- B Shares 6%
- Employee 2%
- 15% Personal
- 11% Legal Entity
- 1% Founder stocks (Foreign)
- 6% Founder stocks (Local)
- 50% State-owned

Capital Raising

Direct capital raising through new stock issues is generally regarded as the most significant achievement in share-holding reform. The capital-raising effort takes the form of three strategies: (a) floating "A" shares to domestic investors; (b) issuing "B" shares to foreign investors, and (c) overseas listings, such as "H" shares in Hong Kong and "N" shares in New York. A total of 15 "H" shares were listed in Hong Kong and HK$17.9 billion was raised as of December 1994.

However, there have been limited public offers and the state or state agencies still own dominant shares of the listed companies. As is clear from Figure 3 and Table 2, 50.62% (RMB22.61173 billion) of the total equity of all listed companies in Shanghai in June 1994 were state-owned stocks. Only 14.66% of the total equity were individually owned stocks and another 14.87% were "B" and "H" shares. These individually owned shares (mostly "A" shares) and "B" shares are tradeable, while the other types of stocks are not tradeable on the two Chinese exchanges. In fact, the proportion of personal shares was much lower, e.g., only 7% in an early survey.[9] The short supply of tradeable "A" shares has aggravated speculation due to severe demand-supply disequilibrium. At the end of June 1994, total savings in bank deposits in China were RMB1,834.9 billion.[10] There are extremely limited investment alternatives. Even if 10% of these savings is diverted into the stock market, it will swamp the two markets

The Evolution of China's Stock Markets

Table 2. Total Equity by Share-Holders in Shanghai in RMB10,000 (June 1994)

Types	Public offers	Total equity	(%)
State-owned stocks	no	2261173.17	50.62
Founder stocks (Local)	no	262579.53	5.87
Founder stocks (Foreign)	no	33813.54	0.75
Legal entity stocks	no	491103.31	10.99
Employee stocks	no	99179.78	2.22
Individually-owned stocks	yes	654912.43	14.66
B Shares	yes	255777.24	5.73
H Shares	yes	408217.80	9.14
Total		4466756.79	100.00

Source: *Shanghai Securities News 1994*, various issues.

which have a combined market capitalization of RMB340 billion, in the two A-share markets.

Also, because 50% of Shanghai's equity is in state-owned stocks and 10% is in legal entity stocks, little public capital was raised in the market. With the exception of strategic industries, it may be unnecessary for the state and its agents to control as much as 60% or more of the listed enterprises. Ironically, these state-owned and legal entity stocks which are not tradeable are a potential sword of Damocles. If selling of shares transfers risk to other investors, state-owned stocks holding a lion share of the company stops short of this risk transfer and risk is diversified primarily among state agencies. Their unification with common "A" shares is a real issue that is difficult to resolve because it involves the potential loss of state assets to private interests should these shares become tradeable in the two Chinese exchanges.

Toward Internationalization and Enterprise Reform

Beginning in February 1992, share-holding companies turned their attention to tapping international capital. "B" shares — a special form of RMB-denominated stock — were created as a special vehicle to attract foreign capital, avoid foreign debt and partially transfer risk to overseas investors. Because of the high growth rate in China, the flotations were well received. Most "B" shares are in the hands of foreign corporations and institutions. By the end of 1991, twelve limited share-holding companies had issued

Figure 3. Shanghai Securities Exchange "A" Shares Index (19 December 1990 to 30 December 1994)

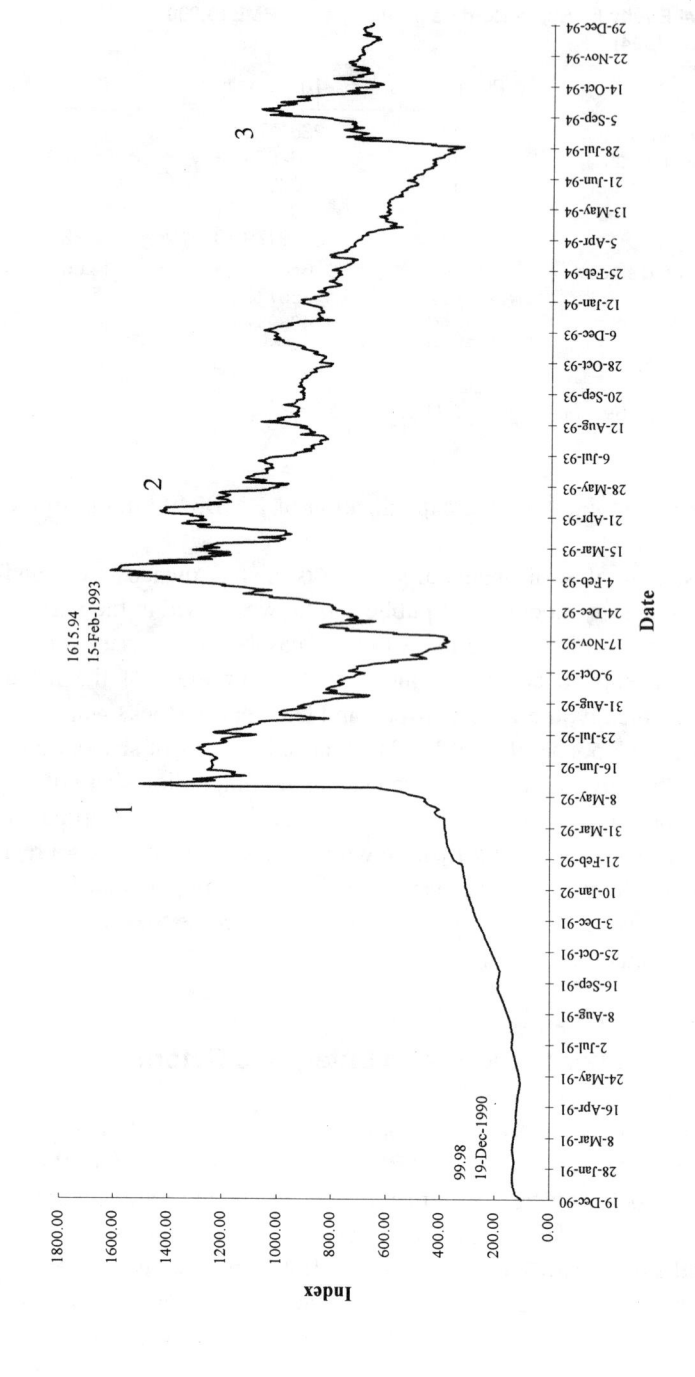

Notes:
1. Lifting of the price-limit restrictions.
2. Introduction of the macro-control policies by the central government.
3. Announcement of the 3-measure market-rescue plan by CSRC.

"B" shares on a premium basis and US$240 million in foreign capital was raised. It was then estimated that US$3 billion of capital from the USA, Japan, Europe, Taiwan and Hong Kong was chasing less than US$0.3 billion of "B" shares.[11] By December 1994, 58 "B" shares were listed on the two exchanges, with a combined market capitalization of RMB16.2 billion.

In the drive for internationalization, Shenyang Jinbei Passenger Vehicle Manufacturing Company, through its holding company Brilliance Automobile Co., listed on the New York Stock Exchange in October 1992 and raised US$70 million. Tsing Tao Brewery Ltd. became the first company to list "H" shares in Hong Kong on 15 July 1993. By December 1994, 15 companies were listed and HK$17.9 billion had been raised.

More than simply a means for raising capital, the stock market is a crucial element in the drive to modernize the teetering state enterprises and thus transform the fabric of Chinese society. By issuing "B" shares, state-owned enterprises become joint-ventures and enjoy a significant tax reduction to a maximum of 15%. This conversion should also bring about enterprise reforms by exposing Chinese managers to international business standards, encouraging market competition, improving management and reducing inefficiencies. Indeed, "B" shares tap foreign capital for the enterprises' future development and raise China's profile in the world's capital markets while transferring risk to foreign investors.

However, two years after its introduction, the "B" share market displayed low liquidity with daily turnovers of about US$5 million both in 1993 and in the first ten months of 1994.[12] The "A" and "B" shares are poor substitutes since the two markets are artificially segmented.[13] Incidentally fluctuations in China's emerging stock markets and those in the Hong Kong market exhibit no *prima facie* causal relation. They remain independent, as they differ greatly in terms of maturity and their regulatory systems.

Despite initial successes, the reform of Chinese enterprises is not without problems. The "separation of state and enterprises," i.e., the separation of the rights of ownership and the management of enterprises, which allows managers more freedom to make market-driven decisions, is but skin-deep. Efficiency of the enterprises remains low.[14] There is thus a pressing need to standardize operations and improve management and efficiency. Although more market-oriented mechanisms are likely to be introduced, the Chinese economy will remain an imperfect market system with a significant component under state ownership. Modernization of the enterprises may cause labour unrest as a result of massive layoffs of inefficient workers. After all, the livelihood of 100 million workers in state-owned enterprises is at stake.

Risk in China's Stock Markets

A 1994 United Nations report disclosed that in 1993, China received US$26 billion of direct overseas investment, second only to the USA (US$32 billion). In other words, China received 13.3% of that year's total world-wide overseas investments of US$195 billion.[15] China's market offers immense opportunities but poses incalculable risk. Higher inflation and an overheated economy loom on the horizon. Both the Shanghai and Shenzhen stock markets are small, and lack depth and breadth. In addition to conventional risk, market players in China are subjected to at least three other forms of risk which also contribute to price volatility: (1) supply/quality risk, (2) systemic risk, and (3) political risk.[16]

(1) Supply/Quality Risk

Before 1993, there was a short supply of tradeable stocks (individually owned stocks) and thus the market was subject to manipulation by big investors. With too much money chasing too few shares, and with domestic investors holding such misconceptions that the listed companies were hand-picked by the government and that the government would not permit any of them to go under, prices became artificially high and ceased to be indicators of performance. The gross underpricing in initial public offers (IPOs) only added fuel to the fire. New A-share issues in Shanghai were 300% to 500% of their offering prices.[17] In a heated scramble for shares, the quality of listed companies became a secondary consideration.

Between 1993 and 1994, there was a glut of new shares. New stocks entered the market in batches at a rapid pace. In Shanghai, for example, 72 new "A" shares were listed in 1993 and a further 68 "A" shares in 1994 before the CSRC announced a halt to the issue of new shares in late July 1994. Inevitably, share prices fell. The quality of listed companies was called into question when it was reported in September 1994 that 70% of all listed companies in Shanghai failed to achieve their forecasted profits in their interim reports.[18]

(2) Systemic Risk

During the formative years of China's stock markets, the regulatory framework was provisional. Information flowed slowly and the system was inefficient. This was exemplified by the "application forms for share lottery" frenzy in Shenzhen in August 1992. Some 750,000 would-be investors queued for days for share lottery forms at RMB100 apiece. The amount of money raised selling these lottery forms was greater than the capital to be raised by the firms. Would-be investors did not even know the names of the new stocks they were applying for, let alone the profit history of the companies.

Information flow is still inefficient. The disclosures of some listed companies are problematic and rumours destabilize the markets.[19] China's Securities Law is still in its drafting stage. It has gone through many revisions but is still pending approval by the National Peoples' Congress. The stock market is such a novelty in China that regulators at times "played it by ear." As a result, market participants are also subject to the risk of frequent changes in regulatory measures. The major problem is that there were no rules during the formative years. Some listed companies chose not to follow the rules, however provisional.[20] There is risk in the system itself.

(3) Political Risk

China's stock market is of more than academic interest. It is a symbol of market socialism and a developing private sector and, as such, a barometer of the economic reform, with obvious social and political ramifications. Fears of a loss of state control, a full-scale invasion of capitalism and "peaceful evolution" all have strong political implications. A true separation of state and enterprises has yet to take place. The emerging stock market in China responds more to policy shifts than market fundamentals. Also, traders' over-reaction to political factors inflict additional volatility on stock prices. The political risk is real, yet incalculable.

Concluding Remarks

Enterprises have evolved from reliance on the state to the separation of state and enterprises, albeit in a superficial manner. China's stock markets have progressed from non-standardized securities to standardized stocks, and from OTC trading to centralized stock exchanges, while capital raising has advanced from domestic to international capital sources.

The two emerging stock markets in China are small, but have huge potential; they are immature yet are developing rapidly. They still lack breadth and depth and appear to be in a constant state of change. Emerging markets are not for the faint-hearted. Overseas regulatory agencies and Chinese officials alike have issued warnings to caution foreign investors about investing in China's stocks.

For China's stock market to develop properly, it is important to maintain "openness," "fairness" and "justice" — the so-called *"sangong"* principles. Broader disclosure of company and market information, and a fair, just, law-based and standardized market will expedite its healthy growth. This is crucial as China internationalizes its stock markets and integrates them with global capital markets.

Notes

1. Li Yining, *Zhongquo jingji hechu qu?* (Where Is the Chinese Economy Heading?) (Hong Kong: Commercial Press, 1989), pp. 1–3. Li identifies four deficiencies under the contract responsibility system for enterprises: (1) the enterprises tend to engage in short-term behaviour; (2) they are hampered by income disparity between the contractors and the workers; (3) they are restricted to the transformation of the enterprises, resource allocation and market development; and (4) separation of ownership and control of property rights is unclear.
2. Xiao Zhouji, "Further Expansion of the Share-Holding Experiment a Must," in *Zhongguo zhengquan shichang* (Chinese Securities Markets), edited by Jin Jiandong, Xiao Zhouji and Xu Shuxin (Beijing: China Finance Publishers, 1991), pp. 212–16.
3. *Hong Kong Economic Journal*, 4 August 1992.
4. As soon as the system of joint-stock companies was introduced in 1984, one trade centre in Guangzhou became the first enterprise to float shares. In September of 1984, the first joint-stock company (Tian Qiao) was established in Beijing. Also, in November of the same year, Feilo Acoustic Co. of Shanghai floated ten thousand shares. They marked the epic beginning of joint-stock system in the PRC. See also Liu Hongru, "Push on Experimenting Joint-stock Systems and Developing Stock Markets," in *Zhongguo zhengquan shichang* (Note 2), pp. 197–201.

5. Jin Jiandong, "China's Stock Market and Its Development," presented at the Fourth Annual PACAP Finance Conference, Convention and Exhibition Center, Hong Kong, 8 July 1992.
6. Bowles, Paul and Gordon White, "The Dilemmas of Market Socialism: Capital Market Reform in China — Part I: Bonds," *The Journal of Development Studies*, Vol. 28, No. 3 (April 1992), pp. 363–85.
7. On 30 July 1994, CSRC outlined a three-measure market rescue plan for the ailing stock market:
   (1) Halt new issues in 1994; and a supervisory period for new issues is to be introduced;
   (2) Experiment with Sino-Foreign fund management companies to gradually attract investments from foreign mutual funds into the A-share market;
   (3) Easier credits or loans to selected brokerage houses to stimulate trading.
8. *Hong Kong Commercial Daily*, 11 November 1994.
9. Cited in Xie Simin, "China's Stock Market — Problems and Future Development," *China Newsletter*, No. 89 (November–December 1990), pp. 18–25.
10. *Hong Kong Commercial Daily*, 1 September 1994.
11. *Hong Kong Economic Journal*, 3 July 1992.
12. *Monthly Market Statistics* (Shanghai Stock Exchange, October 1994), p. 12.
13. See Henry M. K. Mok and Daniel Cheung, "Dynamic Structure and Interdependence of China and Hong Kong's Stock Markets," The Chinese University of Hong Kong, BA Working Paper Series (July 1994), WP-94-11. By vector auto regression and Johansen's cointegration tests, the Shanghai and Shenzhen stock markets are found not to cointegrate, implying no long-run steady state relationship between the two regional markets. There was only very weak short-run Granger causalities from Shanghai to Shenzhen and from the A-share to the B-share market. Typically, the responses to shocks were instantaneous and weak, but with no long-lasting effect.
14. See for example, *Hong Kong Commercial Daily*, 11 November 1994, and also Wang Chunzheng, quoted in "Top Planner Urges State Firm Overhaul," by Louise Lucas, *South China Morning Post*, 17 October 1992.
15. *Shangshi gongsi* (Listing Company), Vol. 13 (1994), p. 3.
16. Henry M. K. Mok and Frank Yao Fang, "Joint Stock Companies and the PRC Stock Market," *Asian Affairs: An American Review*, Vol. 20 (Fall 1993), pp. 123–41.
17. Henry M. K. Mok, "The Aftermarket Performance of IPOs in Shanghai, China," The Chinese University of Hong Kong, BA Working Paper Series (October 1994), WP-94-14.
18. Such poor performance was blamed on the financial austerity programme introduced by the central government. *Hong Kong Commercial Daily*, 1 September 1994.

19. *Hong Kong Commercial Daily*, 19 October 1994.
20. In the maiden issue of *Shangshi gongsi* (1 April 1994), Mr Liu Hongru, Chairman of CSRC, wrote an article entitled *Shangshi gongsi yinggai jinkuai maishang guifanhua de taijie* (The Listed Companies Should Achieve Standardization As Soon As Possible). He pointed out five problems in some listed companies:
    (1) Confusion of rights and responsibility among the shareholders, board of directors and senior executives.
    (2) Some listed companies blindly enlarge their capital base and number of shares, abuse capital use, cover up mismanagement and misuse of raised capital in high-risk speculation.
    (3) Some listed companies do not disclose information as required. Some spend the capital raised on uses other than what was announced in their prospectus.
    (4) Some companies do not follow the rules and regulations on matters related to the conversion and circulation of state-owned stocks or legal entity stocks. Some have converted legal-entity stocks into B shares.
    (5) Some listed companies openly resist the judgement of regulatory agencies and persist in their unlawful behaviour.
    Also see *South China Morning Post*, 28 May 1994.

25

The Individual and Entrepreneurship in the Chinese Economic Reforms

Maurice Brosseau

If one were looking for a date when Chinese managers first displayed a public consciousness of their role as "entrepreneurs," the date would have to be 24 March 1984, when 55 plant managers of the Fujian Factory Managers' Research Society (the forerunner of the Fujian Entrepreneurs' Association) made history by calling on their administrative mentors to "untie (their) hands and decentralize power" (*song bang fang quan*).[1] It mattered little, at the time, whether the declaration was a legitimate plea or, more captiously, an orchestration from on high for national propaganda purposes. Even though the declaration did set the ambience for the promulgation, six months later by the Central Committee plenum, of the urban economic reforms, the call for decentralization of power in March 1994 had made the headlines across the mainland; and for a long time to come, it was to stand as an important symbol. The notion had been superbly crafted, a concise brief of the hopes for and the obstacles to the reforms. Whether these hopes are being realized in 1994, and obstacles to their realization being reduced, is still to be ascertained.

One of the major reasons why the Chinese economy has surged forward since 1978 has to do, no doubt, with the heterogeneous energy displayed at the grassroots levels. This was described, for example, by Ezra Vogel's "entrepreneurial" politicians and businessmen in Guangdong, by Jean Oi's "corporatist" development managed by town leaders and Victor Nee and Frank Young's peasant-cadre power relations and the tension generated by the transformation of the distributive system.[2]

The creative energy of the entrepreneur was also characterized in another way, as the almost marginal or interstitial activity of the private business household (*getihu*) and its potential impact on local politics in Thomas B. Gold's article;[3] on which, David Wank recently commented by indicating rather the built-in dependence of the individual in the private sector,[4] somewhat reminiscent of Jean Oi's rendering elsewhere of patron-client relationship.[5] But, all assume that there is a "certain" order prevailing which permits the activity of the actors to achieve the obvious goal, wealth creation and order conservation. Entrepreneurship, however, is also a challenge to an order and its value system. And however constrained, the Chinese economic reforms have the potential of affecting such order in manners and arenas that may differ from the expected.

The author is grateful to the South China Programme at The Chinese University of Hong Kong for its financial support for this research.

The frequently asked question, "Who is an entrepreneur in the Chinese context?" then takes connotations that are not found in the usual academic treatment of the topic, which rarely ventures into the world of managers toiling in the socialist environment and its economy largely based on publicly owned enterprises. The question is worth investigating in the present Chinese context, in part because the nature of the Chinese economic reforms remains controversial — some even think that they still face a possible reversal — in part because the Chinese themselves have tried forcefully to foster the emergence of such entrepreneurs.

If *entrepreneurs* there are, who are they? Where are they? Where do they come from? And, what is their influence, or, technically, what is their function in the process of the economic reforms? This chapter seeks to investigate the possible effect entrepreneurial behaviour may have on its societal environment, not the rather common investigation of the social-psychological profile which explains the behaviour.

The Chinese Context

For the purpose of this chapter, the unit of observation will be the individuals as they manage their respective units, which can be divided into three rather arbitrary categories: state-owned enterprises (SOE), collective enterprises (often equivalent to the township and village enterprises, TVE) or the private ventures. The individual is an important contributor; even in such bound environment as the state- or collective-owned units of production, the difference between success and stagnation (or plain routine production) is described as the consequence of the manager's performance. This result may explain *why* with such insistence is the manager's role debated — and so much resistance to change exhibited.

Through investment, management contract or leasing arrangement, there are more than ten various forms or categories of ownership or administrative relations; this division represents a kind of commonly used economic stratification accounting for many of the decisions made by the central and local governments. For example, the legislative activity has concentrated on the new definitions of rights and duties of the SOE sector, representing the focused worry of the leadership. Apart from foreign-funded ventures, the other sectors have been, until now, accorded a justification mostly based on administrative regulations, only occasionally on formal laws.* The difficulties faced by the "socialist market" can be explained in part by such discrimination; market relations are still in practice accorded only segmented access and protection.

In the present analysis, only incidental reference will be made to foreign-invested ventures. These have certainly generated an influence on entrepreneurial activity, in the coastal regions in particular. Deng Xiaoping himself even acknowledged that much, when meeting with Shanghai officials on the Pudong Special Economic Zone (SEZ): geography had been one of the major factors behind the choice of previous locations, Shenzhen adjacent to Hong Kong, Zhuhai next to Macau, Shantou's ethnic linkage to Southeast Asian overseas Chinese and Xiamen's proximity to Taiwan. However, the choice made for the sake of simplicity had also meant a loss to the state, as the central leaders had not early enough reckoned with the *talent* (*rencai*) element needed to support reform and development. It was with regret for lost time, Deng said, that Shanghai and its Pudong SEZ had finally been brought to the forefront of reforms in 1990.[6]

The Chinese View of Entrepreneurship

Representing an intimate, and segmented, view, most Chinese mainland's contributors to "entrepreneurship" literature have tried to convince their readers — the usually practiced managers — that they can become initiators. They can do this both by challenging the competitors and by motivating the subordinates to prove themselves at the task, often overtly suggesting taking constructive risks with state assets, a kind of activity which would have been previously quite unthinkable. Behind the descriptions, three areas of concern are present: the relationship between the state machinery and the production unit, between the producer and the market and the managerial practice within the unit.[7] Somewhat less interest has been shown into the ability of the managers of rural collectives (except in its own specialized literature) or the private "enterprisers."

The "normative" entrepreneur takes the characters of the all-round

---

* A change to the 1982 Constitution in April 1988 recognized the legal status of the private (*siying*) sector. Also in 1988, was promulgated *the Provisional Regulations on Privately-managed Enterprises* (*siying qiye zanxing tiaoli*). No draft law is known to have been publicly debated as yet, despite the request by entrepreneurs' associations.

expert in management;[8] his strategic thinking and action is directed both toward the outside and to the internal organizational and motivational questions. On the other hand, the nature of relations with the bureaucracy is interestingly depersonalized and intentionally almost always reduced to the search for suitable definitions of the boundaries between (public) ownership and managerial autonomy. The particular prescriptions and the expectations have varied little over time in the particular publications sponsored by the semi-official managers' associations or the business-oriented bureaux. Indeed, the celebration of the tenth anniversary of the *song bang* plea makes no apology for the need to repeat the call in 1994 despite the relative success realized since then.

That is not to say that the connotations of entrepreneurship have not changed, as Table 1 attests in its forthright forms. The information was gathered by the *Zhongguo qiyejia diaocha xitong* (China's Entrepreneur Survey System), a first in a planned series of national surveys sponsored by a consortium comprising the Industry and Transport Group of the State Council's Research Office, the Enterprise Office of the Ministry of Economy and Trade, the Research Office of the China Entrepreneurs' Association and the office of the journal *Guanli shijie* (Administration World) of the Development Research Centre of the State Council.

The data, as reported, come from the 2,620 respondents of a sample of 5,000 units randomly selected from 550,000 units across the 30 provinces (or equivalent territories) and covering 45 major industrial sectors.

Progress has been made, most magazine articles have been saying; and comparatively to previous surveys of enterprises, in most aspects indicated in Table 1, important demographic advance has been made. Although SOE managers' age remains rather high with an average of 49.5 (4.1 more than the others), their educational achievements are higher than the other categories (a not althogether positive sign as SOEs are well known for their "hoarding" of talents). All the same, the total of 69.2% for all managers with a university degree is 23 percentage points above the results of a 1985 survey. Probably the most remarkable information, in function of the reform effort of the previous 15 years, is the high proportion of SOE managers who are still appointed "according to the method used by the typical planned economic system of old." If progress there has been, on this latter item the autonomy clamoured for is still greatly deficient; little entrepreneurial dynamism can be expected of managers so closely dependent for their career on administrative good will. In other words, in the SOE sector, few can trust the talent market as such, which can be a serious

Table 1. Demographic Data of 2,620 Entrepreneurs in 1993

(in %)

Age	Below 40	41–51	Above 51		
SOE*	11.4	43.3	45.3		
Collective-owned	33.3	44.7	22.0		
Others†	27.5	37.0	35.5		
Average	**14.7**	**44.0**	**41.3**		
Education	9 years	High/tech.	College	Post-graduate	
SOE*	2.9	19.9	37.4	39.8	
Collective-owned	29.9	35.4	25.7	8.9	
Others†	10.3	24.1	35.1	30.7	
Average	**8.0**	**22.9**	**35.3**	**33.9**	
Origins	Technical	Managment	Party/govt.	Worker	Others
SOE*	38.5	35.2	24.0	1.2	1.2
Collective-owned	24.8	46.2	19.0	5.5	4.5
Others†	36.2	41.3	15.9	1.4	4.1
Average	**36.0**	**37.6**	**22.5**	**1.9**	**2.0**
Monthly income	under 300	301–500	501–700	701–1000	above 1000
SOE*	30.8	53.6	11.9	3.1	0.6
Collective-owned	48.8	39.9	5.8	3.4	2.1
Others†	11.7	25.5	19.7	19.0	24.1
Average	**32.3**	**49.0**	**11.5**	**4.4**	**2.7**
Appointment	Govt./ bureau	Workers' congress	Contract bid	Board of directors	Others
SOE*	92.2	4.4	2.7	0.1	0.6
Collective-owned	75.3	16.8	5.2	1.0	1.7
Others†	48.6	2.2	2.2	44.9	2.2
Average	**85.5**	**6.3**	**3.1**	**3.8**	**0.9**

* SOE: State-owned enterprise.
† Private, mixed-ownership, foreign.
Source: "Zhongguo qiyejia diaocha xitong diaocha baogao" (Survey Report of China's Entrepreneur Survey System), *Xiandai qiye daokan* (Contemporary Enterprise Herald), No. 10 (1993), pp. 15–16.

handicap for reforms aiming at creating a fully fledged economic market system.

Relations with the Bureaux

With the intended gradual dissolution of the previous system of planning, by now a more creative autonomy should be exercised. On this question, the intricate nature of change can be measured by another set of data provided by the China's Entrepreneur Survey System's report (see Tables 2 and 3).

Relative to the present inquiry, the standards of entrepreneur-led modernization have been mixed since the role of the Chinese state has also remained prominent. There has been no qualm about the staging of the reforms from the centre downward, or the borrowing from the capitalist West of managerial methods, the latest machinery and foreign trade marketing techniques. The nature of and the spirit behind the future economic system, however, have been said to remain socialist, "with Chinese characteristics." One is, therefore, warranted to ask from which realm the "spirit" of entrepreneurship is expected to stem, as national leaders have been systematically maintaining this mixed set of objectives, even after having formally decided for a market economy in late 1992, at the Fourteenth Party congress.

To help prepare this transformation — and in response to obvious shortcomings of the various experiments with decentralization to plant managers in the early 1980s and the responsibility contracts in 1987 — the State Council had in July 1992 promulgated the *Fourteen Rules for the Managerial Transformation of All-people Owned Industry*[9] as a means to beef up the strength of the Enterprise Law that had come into effect in mid-1988. In contrast to previous declarations and regulatory proclamations, and probably in view of the deteriorating economic conditions in late 1992 and 1993, the government did follow up with the dispatching to the regions of inspection teams empowered to gauge the implementation of the Fourteen Rules (a simplified list makes up Table 3).[10]

Despite these precautions, by about the middle of 1993, only 41% of the surveyed managers could report that nine rules or more had been

Table 2. Implementation According to Size

(in %)

	Large enterprise	Medium enterprise	Small enterprise
Poor (3 rules or less)	6.5	6.2	13.8
Rather poor (4–5 rules)	11.7	16.7	9.8
Average (6–8 rules)	39.8	37.1	35.0
Rather good (9–11)	33.7	32.5	32.5
Good (12 and above)	8.3	7.4*	8.9

* The numbers given do not always add up to 100.
Source: See Table 1, No. 11, p. 14.

Table 3. Managerial Autonomy by Levels of Ownership and Major Types of Enterprises

(in %)

| Autonomy items | mean | Level of administrative ownership ||||| Management forms |||||
		Centre	Province	City	County	None	mean	Contract	Shares	Lease	Delegat.	Others
1 Production decision	88.7	73.1	92.4	92.4	90.3	86.4	86.4	90.4	86.3	50.0	87.7	82.3
2 Pricing	75.9	50.2	73.8	83.4	80.4	72.7	72.7	76.2	75.3	37.5	74.6	76.3
3 Product marketing	88.5	68.4	86.9	94.9	90.9	81.8	81.8	89.4	91.8	37.5	88.5	84.4
4 Input purchase	90.9	84.0	93.9	93.9	89.5	77.3	77.3	91.9	89.0	50.0	90.0	88.2
5 Import-export	15.3	6.9	16.4	18.1	12.9	27.3	27.3	12.1	37.0	25.0	28.5	13.4
6 Investment decision	38.9	34.2	35.0	37.8	47.2	38.6	38.6	39.0	54.0	12.5	36.2	35.5
7 Use of own funds	63.7	68.7	61.7	65.9	56.8	65.9	65.9	65.6	68.5	50.0	55.4	55.4
8 Asset disposal	29.4	22.8	29.9	32.9	27.3	34.1	34.1	29.3	35.6	25.0	31.5	26.3
9 Partnership formation	23.3	22.0	19.2	25.6	22.5	27.3	27.3	23.1	32.9	n.a.	23.1	21.0
10 Hiring of workers	43.5	25.1	33.6	42.9	60.1	68.2	68.2	42.4	61.6	50.0	60.0	33.0
11 Personnel administration	53.7	49.8	46.7	54.9	56.3	63.6	63.6	54.8	58.9	50.0	54.6	43.5
12 Wage decision	70.2	64.0	70.6	71.0	71.0	79.5	79.5	71.5	78.1	37.5	71.5	58.1
13 Internal administration	79.3	76.7	76.2	81.8	78.3	77.3	77.3	80.5	82.2	37.5	80.8	71.5
14 Involuntary donation	7.0	5.1	6.1	5.5	10.5	20.52	20.52	6.1	8.2	37.5	13.8	5.4

Source: See Table 1, No. 11, p. 15.

implemented in their unit by the relevant level of government. As Table 2 indicates, the variation by size was also quite large.

From Table 3, it appears that there had been a common pattern whereby the least controversial aspects of decentralization, i.e., managerial tasks which implied little abrogation of political or financial powers and came closer to routine administration, had been released. But, the decisions, the likes of which impinged on sensitive privileges and were the sources of relative control for — and advantages to — officials, such as import-export, investment, asset allocation, partnership formation, control over personnel appointments, and the right to refuse paying non-budgeted financial contributions (exactions) to the bureaucracy, had been kept largely out of reach of the managers, in other words, the forms of resource allocation which could be kept under some form of patronage. More ominously, the items which had been for so many years the main targets of efficiency, budget constraints and administrative accountability.

It is because of such data that the insistent frequency of the call for entrepreneurs to emerge, since the latter part of the 1980s, also beckons our reflection. The style and content of the articles intimate that the reform successes — for example, in terms of national gross domestic product and income growth rates — have also been relative to factors other than innovative acumen in marketing, managerial techniques, quality products, the absorption of modern technology or the rising productivity of labour. In effect, much of the growth may have been "bought" by sizeable investment and swelling industrial employment.[11] The factor of inputs (*touru*) expansion is the antithesis of, at least a poor substitute for, an economic dynamism moving itself toward "equilibrium" (or to use the expression of Chinese politicians and propagandists: to be self-perfecting, *ziwo wanshan*, the often repeated formulation reminiscent of neo-classical canons!).

The persistent quest for entrepreneurship draws attention to an internal contradiction to reform when much of the "progress" heralded by the news media has been criticized as perilously at the expense of efficiency.[12] The implementation of these rules from the State Council by the different levels of the administration, from the central ministries to the regional bureaux and ultimately to the lower levels of corresponding city, county and township offices, indicates a normative framework which leaves a large autonomy to administrators in the implementation of regulations at various levels. At each level, the party-state organs and their bureaucracies have enjoyed a relatively wide margin of action with regard to the reforms, not to mention a flexible scheduling.

Table 4. Indicators of the Growth Performance of the Chinese Economy, 1978–1993

	1978	1985	1990	1993	Average/year
GNP (billion)	358.8	855.8	1,769.5	3,134.2	9.3%
Nat. income (billion)	301	702	1,438.4	2,488.2	9.3%
Mean wage (RMB)	615	1,148	2,140	3,371	10.6%
Investments in fixed assets					
SOE[†] (billion)	66.872	168.051	291.864	765.797	14.8%
as % of nat. inc.	22.2	23.9	20.3	30.8	
Collective (billion)	4.595*	32.746	52.948	223.134	18.7%
urban		12.823	16.338	60.015	
rural		19.923	36.610	163.119	
Private (billion)		53.522	100.117	147.623	
urban		5.679	12.470	33.850	
rural		47.843	87.647	113.773	

[†] SOE = state-owned enterprise.
* 1980.
Source: *Zhongguo tongji nianjian 1994* (Statistical Yearbook of China 1994), (Beijing: China Statistical Publishing House, 1994), pp. 20–21, 44, 149.

A Non-economic Formulation

The concept of entrepreneurship remains ill-defined to this day — not only in China — largely because so many different scientific disciplines have contested the right to determine its parameters. Within economic theory, the use of the concept challenges the core neo-classical view of the market as an equilibrium-seeking institution; the entrepreneur is portrayed merely as a profit-seeking individual *responding* to the already efficacious appeal of market opportunities. The neatness of the dispensation notwithstanding, many have reckoned that market behaviour may not be all that adaptive and progressive. Joseph A. Schumpeter and his followers thought that entrepreneurs were often needed to overcome routine or unnoticed obsolescence; the entrepreneur in implementing "new combinations" of factors of production engaged in "creative destruction" and opened up new markets, etc., a behaviour crucial to the growth of any given economy.[13]

Other social scientists have laboured in search of a distinct formulation, one which would account for the impact of non-economic values on economic institutions, even the possibility of affecting the latter in ways not predictable by economic theory alone while, at the same time, respecting the latter's internal rationale. Here again, a variety of definitions is current. One formulation which serves well the present purpose, while providing for an exploratory comparison for debates within China, is the schema of "entrepreneurship legitimation" proposed by Amitai Etzioni.[14]

There is a relative affinity between what Etzioni considers the explanation of entrepreneurship as an ethos of economic dynamism (distinct from the frequent successes or failures of individual entrepreneurs too atomized to have a marked effect) and the questions posed by Chinese social scientists studying their country's economic reforms. The point made by Etzioni is that entrepreneurship is an ethos which provides an adaptive test of societal reality that may have become ossified. Because it is new at testing reality, it also needs to be legitimated.

Although an economist, Wang Dingding, for example, has written in a similar vein with an extension into the cultural justification of economic innovation in an environment known for its traditional aversion to individualism and to the pursuit of economic wealth as an objective.[15]

Like other Chinese intellectuals who have pondered over China's modernization, Wang has tried to come to terms with the implications of Weber's view that the traditional Chinese environment, because of its unitary ideological and institutional arrangements, could not have produced an autogenous ethical and social-economic transformation hypothesized to have stemmed from the Puritan effect in *Weber's Protestant Ethic and the Spirit of Capitalism*.[16]

Wang Dingding approaches the question of practice differently from Etzioni's, but both affirm the necessity of considering the process of legitimation, taken in a broad sense, not only in accord with the law, as Etzioni says, but also with the maintenance of order in the process of the division of labour, thus, of cooperation in trust while competing for cost reduction and market share, as Wang insists. Both Wang and Etzioni choose a low-brow demonstration to show how cost accounting can and does determine the possible economic efficacy of entrepreneurship. The possibility of entrepreneurship — the "testing" of economic organization or institution affected by a changing environment — opens the way to what Etzioni calls the possibility of "mega-adaptability," or "the ability of a system to change itself while it is adapting to a changing environment."[17]

Like Etzioni, Wang Dingding sees the potential of economic initiative affecting the societal environment. He is steeped in the painful Chinese history of repeatedly failed modernization since the nineteenth century. He is understandably sensitive to the staging of any entrepreneurial venture; he respects a people sometimes confused by the harrowing complexity of modernization, sometimes reticent at the volatility and fierceness of competition. Though he quotes a few well-known cultural analysts, such as Yu Yingshi, Wang does not see in the relative economic success of post-Confucian societies, like Taiwan or South Korea, an *a posteriori* legitimation of an old Confucian code and of traditional attachment to family; these are not sufficient for the modernization of institutions. The composite may be a useful and necessary catalyst of wealth accumulation, but more is needed in order for the initiative to use wealth accumulation and open new markets (the essence of entrepreneurship), itself built up on the only tool that makes wealth available to the whole of the population, that is a division of labour endowed with trustful cooperation. For this to succeed, an "extended order" is needed which must reach beyond the trust found in the particular "relations circle."[18] Wang, quoting from late Friedrich von Hayek, lists, in addition to a liberal market economy, the new institutions, nowhere to be found in traditional China, to be created: property rights, civil law, a technological civilization, an accounting system, a market, a new definition of government.

Since China has little tradition of civil law, the best way to build trust, and keep costs low, is to start building credibility and proceed with capital accumulation at the usual source, the close circle and the family.[19] While Etzioni's individual entrepreneur is but one soldier among an army assaulting the old to assert the new ethos, Wang's entrepreneur is very much personalized and expected to have a crucial demonstration effect on his circle, both intimate and extended. The entrepreneur is thus defined by three characteristics: innovative spirit, dedication to hard work, spirit of cooperation. The last category maintains the key difference between the personalities involved in the capitalist and the Chinese environments. Ultimately, as competition becomes more compelling, cost accounting is expected soon to make the entrepreneur cut his relation ties (*wei qin*) and seek competence (*wei xian*).[20] "Imbedded" in his environment, Wang Dingding offers a more ambiguous entrepreneurship than Etzioni's. Both are looking for low cost, but Wang keeps alive the ambiguity of personalism; for Etzioni, economic rationality in the Weberian sense is already assumed. Not so for Wang; it still has to grow out of personalism. This ambiguity, pervasive in Chinese economic practice,[21] is frequently as well the inadequate conclusion of other analysts: a familism considered the terminal point of analysis and modernization the combination of such traditional value with some form of western management and technology, such as in Chin Yeoh-chi, Wong Siu-lun, Gordon Redding, etc.[22]

Self-interest, Justice, Competence

The urban reform has been a painstaking journey from planning to gradual decentralization and openness and, after various managerial experiments, it has moved ultimately toward a market-based economy.[23] As the *songbang* quandrary has demonstrated, entrepreneurship could not develop on the basis of an authoritative decision alone.

The state-owned enterprises have been severely circumscribed all through the period at the same time that managers have tried to raise the capacity and meet previous planned obligations. The major criterion of success should have been increased productivity, Deng Xiaoping's own standard. In an other environment, such criterion would have led to a drastic transformation of the publicly owned sector. In the early period of reforms, the SOE sector had already accumulated 87% of the national industrial assets assuring 92% of the national output, but by 1992, their assets still commanding 82% of the total, their share of the market had gone down at a rate of 2% a year to 52%.[24] Despite this dramatic demonstration of inefficiency, the central leaders have kept arguing for the reinvigoration of the SOEs.

There is more to productivity than met the eye behind the prolonged effort at protecting the SOEs' survival. Despite their growing weakness, they are still the main source of tax revenues for the state's coffers and profits for the ministries and bureaux. They also are a major source of secure employment and a model of social and welfare service provision for their huge labour force and dependents. Less visibly, at some levels of administration, especially at the township, party and government have marshalled the SOE sector to act as supplier or guarantor of the local economy. There is even the affirmation that had not these guarantees existed and interference against the private sector, the TVEs would not have achieved their present status and the latter would have already assumed the preponderant role.[25]

Until recently, the propaganda had pressed the managers to be or "become" entrepreneurs (according to that literature). The state as the "owner," here meaning the government at any level, had been taking about 90% of the units' income in taxes and transfers of profits. Out of the remaining 10%, the SOE had to assure all the internal social and welfare services, as well as the numerous new "contributions" (*tanpai*) to official or corrupt causes. In contrast, the collective, foreign-owned and private units never had to pay more than 50 to 55% of their income in taxes; the remaining profits could be plowed back into the improvement and expansion of the unit. In effect, the SOEs' assets were fully utilized, in a true sense mortgaged, to sustain the local economies in the process of developing and enlarging their capital base through the creation of collectives, township and village enterprises etc., assured that their SOEs were protecting the stability of the economy.*

Naturally, the local governments were variously affected by the state of health of the SOEs under their jurisdiction and the latter's ability to maintain a sufficient level of efficiency, productivity and profits. Yang Peixin, of the State Council's Development Research Centre, indicated, for example, that more than 100 counties in Shanxi province had been so burdened by their SOEs' deficits that the local Party and government had had little cash left to pay the salaries of their own officials.[26] An extreme case perhaps, but it was used by the author to typify the reasons behind the urgency of salvaging the economic sector getting close to collapsing.

Entrepreneurship in State-owned Units

Rare are those who, like Wang Xiaojin, the head of Gujing Winery located in Hezhou, Anhui, are able to bring up their enterprise in the course of five

---

* The political-economic question behind this touches on the topic of *tiaotiao kuaikuai* (branch versus local administration of the economy) — a division of jurisdiction under the previous planning system — that the economic reforms started in 1978 may solve by the ultimate recourse to the market. For a study of the topic, see Jonathan Unger, "The Struggle to Dictate China's Administration: The Conflict of Branches vs Areas vs Reform," mimeo, Australian National University, 1987; the fiscal responsibility system instituted in the 1980s certainly aimed at helping local jurisdictions achieve a large measure of self-sufficiency and responsibility toward their own development, cf. Yang Mu, "Taolun: Zhongguo xiangzhen qiye de qiji shi zenyang chuxian de?" (Discussion: How Has the Phenomenon of the Chinese Town-village Enterprise Arisen?) in *Jiushi niandai Zhongguo xiangzhen qiye diaocha* (Survey of Chinese Town-village Enterprises in the 1990s), edited by Ma Rong et al. (Hong Kong: Oxford University Press, 1994), pp. 457–58.

years into the ranking of the nation's top 500 enterprises and leap up 100 places a year to rank 19 in 1994. One of Wang's great achievements took place in 1989 when, only 39 and barely two years as manager, he faced spiralling prices and a shortage of cash. He took the decision to "save the clients first, save oneself last." The feat was to mean his endearment to the state and his clients by the clever recourse to lowering the alcohol content per volume in order to reduce the price to distributors while paying taxes according to the original alcohol rate. He moreover took the responsibility of reimbursing all losses to agents and keeping his prices at the chosen level whether or not the market for such beverages rose again during the year.

As expressed in the report, he has not been averse to taking risk, even having a "yellow card" (a reference to a serious warning to a football player) drawn at him for breach of some regulation; his sacred norm of action is "measure" (*du*) and the ability to "adapt the environment" (*huajing*), a mixture of "caution" and "not being a fool."[27] The philosophy of the leader is based on instilling the spirit of community and exacting a pledge of loyalty (*xiaozhong*). His own acumen at disciplining his employees mixes both severity and high rewards; most revealing is the treatment of a wayward worker who, faced with dismissal, is given a reprieve at the last minute in exchange for grateful dependency (temporary worker status).

Wang Xiaojin's is a story with the ring of reality; his is also an "ideal type" story written up for the effect, but Wang is not the ordinary manager of most SOEs. Of course, he is not alone at being overwhelmingly successful; others like him have seen an opportunity upon appointment to a seemingly hopeless industrial plant to turn it around by bold moves and to "demonstrate," as some are wont to say, the endurable superiority of the state-owned sector. For the great majority of SOE units, however, the story rarely if ever makes the headlines.

As an analyst once said, in the pre-reformed Chinese economic system, the unit of production had not been available to managers as an extension of their managerial prerogative; it had been institutionally designed to *constrain* it. The reforms have tried to change the structure of the role performance, with little success. Chinese factory directors, a Japanese scholar commented to Chinese economists in 1985, had no more authority than work-section leaders in a Japanese factory.[28] After more than 15 years of reform by a gradual decentralization of power, however, the managers have been testing their authority as professionals. They have pursued modernization by the implementation of many new managerial techniques, accounting and marketing methods, generally with low success. They have found it difficult to get recognition.

Chinese managers do not have as full an authority as their foreign counterparts; yet, they are liable for responsibilities (both political or social in nature) that would be considered a waste of precious energy elsewhere. SOE managers are in fact psychologically divided as to the objectives they should be pursuing. Because of the given nature of their position — and despite the incessant publicity about entrepreneurship — the majority thinks in terms of the given and not in terms of greater substantial managerial career prospects for themselves. Rather, they think in terms of the career in the administration. The frequent reference to the creation of an "entrepreneur stratum" (*qiyejia jieceng*), a self-motivating and self-seeking talent market, is still far ahead in the future.

Table 5. Zhejiang Managers' Preferred Form of Ownership

(in %)

System	Rate	Rank order
Share system	53.3	1
Contract reponsibility system	38.3	2
Joint Sino-foreign venture	5	3
Leasing	1.7	4
Other	1.7	4

Source: See Note 30.

The data presented in Table 5 give information on only a tiny portion (61) of Chinese managers of the so called large-and-medium-size enterprises from three major cities of Zhejiang province, namely, Hangzhou, Ningbo and Wenzhou.

Although the contract responsibility system implemented nationally in 1987 seems certain to be phased out and be replaced by the creation of share-holding corporations, the Zhejiang managers still highly value the contract system. They may be reflecting some of the misgivings the corporate ownership has inspired, a good degree of uncertainty over which they will have no or little control. There is no guarantee that the new shareholders and corporate boards will be less inclined to interfere with internal administration. The expert economists' hypotheses based on the common hands-off practice of share-holders in the West is difficult to ascertain, especially in the unpredictable period of transition.[29] However, because of particular personal considerations or the privileged position of units, there is no doubt that a certain number of managers may favour the development of holdings over other forms of ownership transfer because there is a hope that this would create a source of badly needed funding. All in all, however, the corporate boards are going to be, in any event, made up of some trustworthy party and government officials.

As with the simple responses found in Table 5, other information provided by this article makes clear that managers of publicly owned enterprises in Zhejiang are capable of taking the responsibilities that have been handed down to them. However, when there is a choice between conflicting values such as responding to the present requirements and planning for the future (showing some form of creativity), managers generally tend to take care of the present:

> (They) have to a certain extent a general hope of *survival* under the conditions of market competition; they do not have the capacity to seek the long-term development of their enterprise.... The hope that a mere decentralization or restoration of power to the enterprise would do is by far insufficient. There must also exist a motive-link instrument (*liandong cuoshi*)" (between the function of manager and market participation, emphasis added).[30]

When asked a question about their self-identity in the form "What interest does the manager represent?," the great majority responded the manager represented the interest of the unit, the state or the workforce; only 8% (4 out of 61) added to this list the manager's personal interests. "Compared to the leaders of rural township and village or privately owned enterprises, the SOE managers thus have a much smaller scope of action," commented the author. Most often, the manager knows that he can never hope becoming his own man.

The managers are considered by the analysts still to be "learning" from the examples of the rural township and village or the privately owned enterprises competing on the market. Anticipating on a latter part of the chapter, the SOE managers seem to be reacting in the same way as their subordinates, they remain largely passive to the reform dynamics set in motion by superiors. Most are waiting for specific directives to change their routine; until then, they continue to take advantage of all the amenities from the old planned redistributive regime that are still provided.

The Quasi Proprietor

There is another dimension to Table 5 above that has not yet been clarified, that is, the great interest in the share system of ownership that is created by the managers themselves. In Table 5, as many as 53.3% of the respondents were in favour of such form. What was implied there, though not well explained by the authors, was the experience of many other managers who had been able to travel this route with great success but in a way that may not be the vision entertained by the central authorities who are planning and legislating on the transformation of the preponderant administration of ownership. Two summarized examples will suffice.

Both stories have a common feature: the production units in question had been led, previously, by incompetent managers who had made a mess of things. The hero entrepreneurs who emerge are individuals doing a great favour to their respective local leaders by salvaging, one a very important investment, the other an essential source of employment. Interestingly, both managers affirm, as their central argument, that modern industrial organization needs the application of modern management methods.

Du Qingsong, at 45, took over in 1991 the management of a brand new colour television set production unit built only the year before in Xianyang, Shaanxi province, an industrial city on the east-west railway line and on the north shore of Hei river. After investigation of the plant, Du's first "spark" (*huohua*) was to devise a reform model borrowed from the structure of foreign invested ventures: a "special factory" project. With the approval of the Xianyang city government and party committee, Du resolved on transforming the personnel regulations, for both the cadres and workers, and the reward system. Naturally, this meant that from then on all cadres and workers would be hired, given work or fired on merit; the wage system was to reflect work-post profit performance for cadres and a total output piece rate for workers, both guaranteed by a contract system applying to all. Obviously, Du Qingsong did cut through the "gordian knot" of past practices of hiring and posting individuals on the basis of affinity and friendship; former cadres became ordinary workers and capable workers were raised to posts of responsibility. "Some, at first, found it hard to accept but as it became evident with time that effort earned good wages and laziness was punished ... moreover, as the principle of responsibility, power and reward became a unified basis of reward, the personnel gradually understood and agreed."[31]

As explained, this had been only the first step. What followed between 1991 to 1994, was a systematic build-up of a conglomerate in order to stem the dangers of the nascent market forces; to succeed, Pianzhuan (literally, deflection) Factory had to enlarge its base, to seek "economies of scale," diversification and high income. With the help of Japanese and Hong Kong investors, the accumulation of funds from bank borrowing and personnel contributions allowed the original factory to become a corporate holding comprising six different companies specializing in various electronics products from TV sets to satellite dishes, cameras, cordless telephones and then extending into fertilizers (Du's previous work), chemicals, and services. All through, the unique driving force was Du-the-manager, almost alone engaged in all aspects of the development, including travelling abroad to discuss purchases and investments.

If Du Qingsong's success was accomplished over a very short three-year period, without much of a market test, Tao Jianxing of Taizhou, Jiangsu, on the other hand, also ended up creating a large conglomerate, over a period of eight years, starting in 1986, by constantly challenging the market or even creating the market by challenging the "tested" wisdom of his entourage. The rural SOE, located in Taizhou (a population of 250,000 north of the Yangtze river), was also in a relatively backward region, more so at any rate than the towns of heralded southern Jiangsu. Similarly to the previous example, much was made of the fact that the development from a single unit of production into a huge consortium was achieved without any official financial help from the state. This may explain the relative freedom with which the structure of authority and the treatment of the personnel could make such a departure from the rather indulgent discipline reputedly prevalent in the mainstream SOEs elsewhere. Tao, a brilliant mathematics student in college, had taken over, at only 32, from a government office post, after three previous managers had been quickly replaced for incompetence. His reference to modernity was two major Japanese producers, Mitsubishi and Matsushita. The Taizhou municipal bureaux had grown impatient at their previous choices after a major effort had been expanded into combining three small farm implement factories into what had been believed to be a rather modern-looking producer of refrigeration equipment. However, as his counterpart in Shaanxi was also to do, Tao set first on the revamping of the old personnel and reward system: "(It was) the equivalent of getting rid of India's old caste system built on feudal religious principles which had severely segregated the social strata and had paralyzed behaviour,"[32] a gallant way of reformulating Djilas' thesis of the "new class."

Starting with a turnover of RMB10 million from the production of some 40 models of refrigeration equipment, Tao then decided to scrap 30 of them and set on upgrading the process into air-conditioners at the very moment a 100-odd competitors, domestic and foreign, were appearing in China. His choice was the unfamiliar product, outside the known range over which competitors were struggling, the ordinary industrial refrigeration equipment; Tao was promising the small domestic air-conditioner and the very large equipment for the office building, the market for which in these early days of the mid-1980s was still to be created. A Schumpeterian, some would think,[33] Tao Jianxing was foreseeing what his entourage could not. He further raised eyebrows when in 1987, on the basis of the improved 1986 performance (RMB 16 million), he officially set his "351" plan for his employees: that is, in four years raising by stages the output to RMB30 million, 50 million and 100 million. By his set deadline, Chunlan (Spring Orchid) Holdings had achieved RMB 120 million. More confident yet, Tao Jianxing set new "351" turnover targets for up to 1994: RMB 300 million, 500 million and 1 billion; against expectations, the latter was reached in 1992, then RMB 3 billion in 1993, with output reaching 4.3 billion by June 1994, more than doubling last year's output for the same period.[34]

Without financial help from the government, the Chunlan success was achieved by the choice of marketing technique: at first, Tao Jianxing had decided to imitate others' wisdom — not to let anyone else partake of the profit — and to keep it all tightly within the firm by opening its own outlets across the nation. The rising costs of the operation had forced him to reconsider; in 1987, Tao had chosen to forego this costly "profit maximization" and to innovate by turning to the licensing of "independent" trading outlets to the dismay of his own agents. By 1993, again Tao Jianxing foresaw a new change would mean a greater return by changing the terms and inventing "controlled licensing" (*shoukong dailizhi*). Wholesale traders were to invest one share in the corporation equivalent to the amount of their order. Tao was then offsetting the unpredictable financial market, solving for Chunlan its access to capital and avoiding the threat of "triangular debt chains" affecting so many other SOEs in their relations with suppliers, traders and other debtors or creditors.[35]

Without doubt, these examples point at one basic circumstance: the successful "entrepreneur" has been the one able to manage the firm as if it was one's own. The corporate structure has been revolving around one person, a "captain" of industry who could have done well anywhere in the market world. Entrepreneurship has won the day, but there is no indication of the political-administrative debate that goes on behind the scene.

Career Objectives?

The question for the common manager has become one of serving several masters and establishing one's professional credibility. He has had to relearn the tools of the trade, or be taught, in the mind of some Chinese researchers, such as Xun Dazhi, how to create one's own persona, to build oneself as a member of a social stratum (*qunti* or *jieceng*),[36] but in a contrasting way, another author, Jiang Yiwei, pleads for a type of entrepreneur who pursues success and reputation not only by economic performance based on the self-interest of workers but also by creating "the harmony and warmth of the collective" so as to make of the workers under one's command the "great shield" that can protect one's authority.[37] The reality may be very different, especially in the great number of struggling units, as managers know a large portion of the individuals under their command are working virtually half the time, the other half preparing behind the manager's back to take the "plunge" (*xiahai*) into business on their own.

The tension of the reforms has been acutely felt by the workers who are acquainted with the difficulties facing their unit; they are fearful that the reforms are going either to increase the work load or cut down on or eliminate the comprehensive and free welfare protections for oneself and dependents (to get rid of the "tribal mentality"). "We stay only for the health benefits. As soon as they are cut out by the government, we are out of here to pursue the business we have already set up," admitted one interviewee.[38] Others who do not feel they have the ability to go into self-employment wish that those who so linger on would clear the way for them to get on with production and try to assure their job tenure. A threat has grown over time because of the sliding productivity, and, in 1994, the frequent allusions to the possibility of allowing deficit-plagued and unredeemeable units go bankrupt have become more of a certainty. As a saying goes: "Those who should stay (the skilled workers) go away, those who should go, stay."

Expectedly, such behaviour is not the exclusivity of the often underworked labour. "*Zouxue xianxiang*" (literally, "going down the burrow") is widespread among most layers of the personnel, starting with the manager who builds his private factory to produce lucratively the same product under the SOE's brand-name when the same SOE under his official control accumulates inventories that it cannot sell; and then, the highly specialized manager who oversees in his "spare time" ten or more other plants as

Table 6. Rating the Need to Reform for Selected Government Offices

(in %)

Government offices	1 Industrial bureaux	2 Banks	3 Taxation offices	4 Planning/ Economic Comm.	5 Indust. and Commerce Admin.
mean	49.3*	24.4	15.3	8.9	2.0
SOE	47.4	26.5	16.1	8.3	1.8
Collective	53.4	19.7	12.8	11.7	2.4
Share own'ship	52.9	7.8	21.6	13.7	3.9
Others	60.7	20.2	8.3	7.2	3.6

* The reported numbers do not always add up to 100.
Source: "Zhongguo qiyejia diaocha xitong diaocha baogao," *Xiandai qiye daokan*, No. 12 (1993), p. 20.

"honorary manager" or heads a wide-ranging "partnership" arrangement, thus receiving a full manager's salary from each of the sideline outfits![39]

In a sense expressed more forcefully in the course of the year, the business world has been beset with a variety of malaise which reflects the low normative force of morality and the decaying strength of administrative discipline. The incoherent market opportunities have weakened state enterprises, a situation compounded by the behaviour of so many officials in supervisory agencies who either tolerate or are themselves served by the irregular situation. A transitional situation, perharps, which may be corrected with time as reforms are "deepened" and more modern constraints over the personnel are built up. However, until then, the public business sector is bleeding probably as never before.

Collective Sector: Uncertain Characteristics

There has been a second face to reform generating of late numerous headlines: the collective sector, usually taken to mean the township and village enterprises. The older pre-reform collectives, both rural and urban, had been gradually brought under the control of the planning system, especially at the county level. The exception had been the motley rural "five small plants" popularized during the Cultural Revolution and the early 1970s, in part as a measure to counter-balance the strategy of centralizing collective units justified by arguments of upgrading, efficiency and transition to

Table 7. Progress of Township-village Enterprises (1978–1992)

Year	Units (million)	Personnel (million)	GVO* (bill. RMB)
1978	1.524	28.266	49.31
1980	1.425	29.997	65.69
1984	6.065	52.081	170.99
1985	12.225	69.79	272.84
1986	15.153	79.371	354.09
1988	18.882	95.455	649.57
1990	18.504	92.648	846.16
1991	19.089	96.091	1,162.17
1992	20.792	105.811	1,797.54
1993			(2,900.00)

Production by ownership (billion RMB)

	Township	Village	Partnership	Private†
1984	80.86	64.52	12.65	11.75
1988	266.76	206.79	59.14	169.15
1989	309.30	248.93	68.20	213.75
1990	343.16	282.22	72.66	260.07
1991	427.45	344.53	75.55	314.61

* GVO: Gross value of output.
† Private: privately managed (*siying qiye*) and household (*getihu*) enterprises.
Source: Ma Rong, "Daoyan" (Introduction), in *Jiushi niandai Zhongguo xiangzhen qiye diaocha* (Survey of Chinese Township-village Enterprises in the 1990s), edited by Ma Rong et al. (Hong Kong: Oxford University Press, 1994), pp. 6, 9.

communism.[40] As the following suggests, the Ministry of Agriculture which should have administered the collective enterprises would have been the loser to administrative "expropriation" by other more powerful ministries, much in the way the commercial cooperatives (*gongxiao hezuo she*) created in the 1950s on the basis of the peasants' own meager savings — to trade between the village and the city — had ended up fully controlled by the Ministry of Commerce, without compensation.[41]

The direct ancestors of the TVEs seem essentially to have been the "five small plants" in both spirit and reality. Jiangsu leaders, masters in this category, have always dated the beginning of their TVEs to the mid-1960s. Their rapid growth after 1978, especially after the 1983 generalization of the agricultural household responsibility system and the demise of the commune system, could be explained by the nominal administrative conversion. Since then, a great many new ones have been created across the land — approximately 20 million new units — in all spheres of economic activities, from agricultural produce processing to sophisticated high-technology production and professional services.

The great success of the TVE type has excited the journalists but has also grazed a raw nerve in high places. First disdainfully tolerated as a labour-intensive, low technology and low quality form of production due to be quickly eliminated, its explosive growth and gradual improvement have lead to renewed criticism. A debate is going on between two main "schools," one which argues that, because of their very success, the TVEs should be integrated as quickly as possible into the national network and no longer considered a category apart, much less enjoy privileged status. The second argument, endorsed by the Ministry of Agriculture, wants the TVEs to be kept separate, with their own identity, because of their particular contribution to the rural economy. They should not be equated to the other (public) sector as they have a system of internal organization, steering mechanism (*yunxing jizhi*) and a purpose not reducible to the state-owned units. The symbolic stake in this debate — usually argued over the "functions" (productivity, efficiency, adaptability, income and employment opportunities) and the "dysfunctions" (low-caliber products, low-quality technology, the wastage of resources, pollution, ill adaption to the market) — is the long delayed law on TVEs which would define the sector as a *sui generis* and distinct pillar of the national economy. The aim is to assure their status, autonomy and systemic particularities.[42]

Challenging Hypothesis

The argument has been established to a large extent on Deng Xiaoping's own enthusiasm, expressed as early as June 1987 to visiting Yugoslav dignitaries; he had indicated his great satisfaction at the TVEs' expansion and vitality which had not been foreseen nor planned by the central authorities, the result, he had insisted, of the correct choice of a market form of production and services to answer the large local needs.[43]

Probably the most fascinating article on the debate, both as a view on the argument and as a hypothesis on entrepreneurship, appeared in midyear in *Zhongguo xiangzhen qiye bao* (Chinese Town-village Enterprise Journal).[44] The five collaborators on a research project on the nature of the TVEs came to the conclusion that their success indicated the highly adapted nature of their administrative (*guanli*; in the context, the expression links "management" and local politics) methods. The authors believed the local political leaders and managers had created a form of industrial organization that remarkably fitted the Chinese social-cultural context of the rural community, in contrast to the SOEs which could not generate their own improvement in spite of the incentives and privileges granted by the state.

Much of the recent mainland literature on the TVEs brings out the "community" (*shequ*) angle of the success story. Most remarkably, these units have been developed almost exclusively out of the savings of the local communities and in breach of the established ideal of the "large, state-owned, pure" (*yida ergong sanchun*) classic socialist behemoth. There is a pride among certain intellectuals in the countryside having overcome the view heretofore intolerant of the mixing of ownership rights and management arrangements that live in apparent harmony.[45] Much is made of the fact that the Ministry of Agriculture's own definition of the TVE includes both the collective-owned units at the township and village levels and the peasants' own small-group partnerships, cooperative shareholdings, the household self-employed business (*getihu*) and privately managed rural ventures (*siying qiye*). In other words, notwithstanding the political-ideological contrivance, there is an assumed solidarity among these various forms of ownership "against" the definitions of official categories. And, contrary to previous criticisms that many so-called collective units were in fact hiding the true identity of private owners, today much is made of the great complexity of arrangements between private and collective "owners" who seek to maximize the use of assets by cooperative arrangements. In a sense, it is being argued that the "ethos" of economic rationality (its ambiguity?) and close cooperation are more important than the administrative rationality respecting the established conventions.

A Reality Test

The treatment of the private sector is being relegated to the next major section of the chapter, albeit in breach of the offered definition, in order to test separately the two essentially different motive forces at work in these so-called rural TVEs and deal with private urban operators.

The problem with the collective form of ownership (*jiti suoyouzhi*) remains quite intractable as it had been under the pre-reform period. There is little progress on the participation of the households or individuals whose financial assets are being mobilized. Ownership is "in name only" with no or little explicit and legitimate participation of the people in the administration of these assets. The collective-based unit is still a "subsidiary" of the local government or its extension, the local "business corporation" (*gongsi* or *zonggongsi*), and the choice of policies is a function of the administrative interests of the local leaders. If there were a principle of action, it would have to be expediency and ambiguity. Little political or economic uncertainty is needed to influence some local leaders to seek some way to gain some favour or buy protection; there are plenty of reasons that can be adduced to to decree that some units belonging to a lower level ought to be centralized at a higher level (a county secretary seeking to define a collective TVE as a county-level SOE unit, a township government expropriating a village-owned unit in order better to serve the "common good" or to assure better coordination) or, conversely, a collective unit being devolved into private hands or distributed as a "rent." Since the great expansion wave of 1992, strategic consolidation has often emotionally charged relations between the targeted village population and its TVE which have had to bow to the grand plans of an entrepreneur fully endorsed by the township officials. The corporation created in the small Hengdian township, Zhejiang province, has a monopolistic structure hovering over all economic aspects of the town and surrounding villages that would humble any planning system.[46]

But, there are signs that the rural economic development is meeting with a deceleration, and the most important reason given is the "confusion" affecting the definition of ownership. The informality that has been so detrimental to the SOEs is now starting to affect more directly the TVEs as well.[47] The difficulty of determining the real proprietor may be compounded by the effort to extend as quickly as possible an equity share system (*gufenzhi*). The many reasons militating for this development are complex, as much a way to build up the scale (or size) of one's plant, and thus one's economic and administrative ranking (see the next example), into a protective shield against numerous exactions (*tanpai*),[48] as a way to build up economic strength against territory- or sector-based competition.

Business Éite in the Making?

Zhou Yaoting, 52, is a Jiangsu peasant. This background has not kept him from "creating a miracle." He has built up of "his own two hands" Hongdou (Red Bean) Holdings Corporation, the first rural concern in Jiangsu being granted the rank of provincial township and village enterprise (*shengji xiangzhen qiye*). Appointed in June 1983 to a small Wuxi plant on the verge of bankruptcy, the former rural brigade chief has since then remoulded the old plant located in a dilapidated ancestral hall with 90 employees and a few sewing machines (RMB 630,000 of output left in the warehouse to "feed the rats") into a 3,000-worker textile and clothing corporation with RMB 54 million in fixed assets, organized into seven specialized companies overseeing 34 units, some operating overseas.[49]

Zhou Yaoting, the rustic and cunning "peasant," attributes his success to his ability accurately to read business opportunity in the script of politicians. He has been particularly sensitive to the fate of small enterprises renowned in the folklore of the reform for being "small thus capable of quick change" (*chuan xiao hao diao tou*). For him, at ground level, each shift had meant repeated losses in assets, products, technical personnel, etc. To create a large corporate unit to withstand these fluctuations has, from early on, commanded his strategic thinking; his insight into the situation is exemplified by his amalgamation over a few weeks of 50-odd industrial, educational and technical units the very moment he heard in mid-March 1992 of Deng Xiaoping's "southern tour" (*nanxun*) which was to lead the latest national cycle of accelerated growth. Neither had this been the first time the shift in political winds had assisted his acquisition at bargain prices of advanced facilities or production equipments.

The creativity has manifested itself also in devising means to hold the whole together. Here the counter-example has been the ill-fated SOEs, the size and security of which have hampered their progress. At least three stages of reforms have been needed to eradicate, as in examples mentioned earlier, the management habits and patterns of the past. Zhou has called the latter the concealed "exploitation of the 'big-pot'" (*"daguofan" de boxiao*) syndrome whereby the leader had not only been inactive but had moreover punished those who had worked hard. In a first stage, piece-rate wages dramatically raised output and quality. In 1986, strict accountability was brought to bear on every single work post, affecting all administrators, sales, technicians and workers alike, motivated by "wage based on year-end profit" and work group evaluation. In 1988, Zhou created a "firm" in the neo-classical economics' sense: the introduction of the contract system to regulate all aspects of transactions between all sub-groups or units. Zhou Yaoting, in effect, introduced the principle of power delegation and self-interest as means to enforce the strict rules of management and accounting. When, at first, he had 90 workers, he had to care for everyone of them, he said; when the plant grew to 500, he had to manage 20 subordinates; now that there are 3,000 employees, he has to deal with only nine cadres at the corporate centre; the rest is taking care of itself!

Well! Not quite. Zhou Yaoting did invite and hire for one year a Taiwanese textile management expert, Xiao Wenfeng, to investigate the production lines of his best sub-plant and improve both the production flow and the management and training of the personnel. From there, Zhou created, in cooperation with a textile technical institute, his own training programme for all levels of personnel. Thus, a down-to-earth attitude to the political economy of the country has born a "natural" leader, perhaps, but there is only indirect information about what others have considered to be "his luck" of the moment. He, himself, believes that those who are taken by surprise by political decisions — v.g., the macro-economic adjustments of 1993–1994 — have simply failed to "size up the current situation" (*shenshi dushi*).

Another "celebrity," Lu Guanqiu of Zhejiang, has had to follow a more tortuous path. Already the manager of Xiaoshan (Hangzhou) Universal Joint Factory in the late 1970s, he had to face the imminent threat of a worsening national economy and the near impossibility of getting help to upgrade the technology. Though under the "strong" recommendation of superiors to shift to the production of bicycles, Lu by chance came upon news in 1980 that the petroleum industry was to expand oil exploration and that state planning was going to increase motor vehicle production in the next year. Even when pressed by "a gentleman of authority" that the low-quality suppliers to the automative industry faced a severe curtailment, Lu Guanqiu refused to listen. That only the best three of the 56 producers in the nation (his was ranked below 30) were to be allowed to continue produce, did not faze him. In a dramatic gesture, he sent to the scrap heap all the 30,000 universal joints (worth RMB400,000) that had been collected from disgruntled customers to the scandal of the whole personnel. He then embarked on a thorough transformation of the plant equipment and the training of the personnel for a whole year. When finally the suspenseful week-long evaluation was completed, the inspectors gave a resounding score of 99.4, the highest in the nation.[50]

Lu Guanqiu had started in 1969 as one among nine ordinary blacksmiths in what had then been a small repair shop for farm implements. It was in the course of the following decade that the leadership had expanded into more difficult repairs and finally the production of axles and joints for farm machinery. Lu's attachment to the plant explain his own 1983 offer to mortgage his own orchard as risk pledge for his assuming full contractual authority over the plant. Once accepted by the authorities, he proceeded "to restructure the organization of the factory, reform the distribution system, revise the measures for recruiting new workers and formulate rules for quality control and training of personnel." Since then, the factory has established long-term contracts with foreign car makers and has both grown in size and expertise. As factory director, Lu receives a salary equal "to a senior engineer's, treble the average 5,700 yuan of his employees."[51] Like all the other entrepreneurs reviewed here, Lu has steered his factory toward the formation of a factory group with eight affiliated vehicle part factories; he has also diversified into trading, real estate, farm produce, a hotel and a shopping centre, "without any state investments."

Private Ownership?

The complexity of the relationships that have developed between sectors of the economy (SOE, collective and private) is becoming better described by recent research conducted by Chinese scholars. In terms of *songbang*, we cannot avoid the realization, after the reading of one of such studies, that it is the government bureaux which often bind their own "limbs" by trying to save values which conflict with the reform requisites.[52]

There is also ambiguity in the official language which distinguishes the "private" form of enterprise into the *getihu* and the "privately managed" (*siying* and not *siyou*) units. It leads one to wonder what is the implication. At face value, the expression encompasses three types of enterprises: personal investment (*duzi*), cooperative enterprise (*hezuo*) and partnership (*hezi*). The categories imply the common element of private ownership either of funds (as in *duzi* and *hezi*) or funds and materials, equipment, real estate, etc. (as in *hezuo*); the distinguishing feature has to do with the choice of leadership types (single owner or board management) and the corresponding distribution of rights, duties and profits.

Still, there may be more to the choice of expression than a mere reflection of these *bona fide* sources of investment. It may also offer cover to non-family or non-neighbour based investment by anonymous individuals who create a "front" private enterprise, a form of "unpublicised and illegal" investment in China,[53] though not so qualified in Hong Kong and Taiwan; it may be an appellation to bestow transitional legitimacy to a form of ownership believed on the way to a future socialist ownership; it may also provide equivalent ambiguity to private owners seeking a collective registration to facilitate the obtaining of loans or the reduction of taxes, etc.

As with the two forms of public ownership reviewed above, rules and practice of ownership remain in a fluid and conditional state. In a revision of Yang Mu's view quoted above about the true viability or competitiveness of the collective (TVE) in contrast to the private sector,[54] some mainland analysts even offer an optimistic scenario whereby, in the not too distant future, the clarification of the ownership structure and the competition of financial forces will result in the collective economy being gradually integrated into a single public sector appropriated or transformed by the common adoption of shareholdings. Then, the private sector is expected to grow large enough to compete with the public sector and challenge the latter — the "private eating up the public" (*si chi gong*) sector — as was examplified in November 1992 when Chen Jinyi, a Zhejiang entrepreneur, bought in one swoop all seven state- and collective-owned commercial units sold out at a Shanghai public auction. The event so astonished government and academic observers that "they called discussion meetings!"[55]

How, then, to evaluate Wenzhou, in southeast Zhejiang province, which is pressing forward with the building of large corporate bodies combining privately owned ventures. Is the local leadership trying precisely to contain a private sector previously allowed to expand too freely? Or, is it setting the experimental ground rules for a future test of strength with other external forces? In any event, in the last few years the situation has been animated:

> In February 1990, based on the experience in Wenzhou, the Ministry of Agriculture promulgated China's first *Provisional Regulations on Rural Joint Stock Co-operation Enterprises*, defining such enterprises as "the new collective ownership economy of the socialist labouring masses and the major component of rural enterprises...."[56]

Ownership is being separated from management. Due to the expansion of joint stock enterprises and increasingly complex demand on management, the situation whereby people are at once shareholders, producers and managers is no longer considered suitable, explained as a way to improve efficiency. The main stipulations of the Regulations indicate that "a sound accounting system must be established"; it is also specified that 10 to 15% of the after-tax profit is to be put in a collective fund and that "10% of the profits be used for a workers' collective welfare funds and bonuses;"

finally, of the remaining 75% a portion be distributed to shareholders and the remaining portion be reinvested, though it "should be owned by shareholders as new shares" bearing interests and dividends. Therefore, in some of Wenzhou's joint stock co-operative enterprises, "big shareholders are no longer the managers and non-shareholding competent people are being recruited as managers," often from state enterprises. The impression is that former owners are being "phased out" into the anonymous world of equity shareholders, their former enterprise passing to professional managers responsive to local political and administrative offices intent on enlarging the locality's economic strength. Moreover, being revenue "maximizers," the share owners may engage in share swapping — further diluting their proximity to their former enterprise — with the help of an Ownership Transfer Consultation Service Agency, the creation of which was "assisted by the local government."

The Private Phenomenon

Even in 1994, some feel the need to provide the apologetics of the private sector, the major sensitivity to be assuaged naturally being the potential for class conflict between capital and labour. As some of the arguments by Zhang Houyi go, the private entrepreneurs are often considered by their own workers to be in effect of the same social stratum, a condition proven by a worker today becoming himself boss tomorrow, a fluidity reminiscent of Taiwan's situation.[57] Government control through taxation and supervision, moreover, keeps the proto-capitalists from indulging themselves in luxurious life styles and motivates them to reinvest into the expansion of productivity.[58]

As noted by the author, the background of the private entrepreneur has been changing markedly over the years. Recently, the pace of development has increased, after the southern tour of Deng Xiaoping; the years 1992 and 1993 saw extraordinary growth in numbers: at the end of 1993, there were 238,000 units, an increase of 70.4% over 1992 and equal to the total number in 1991(328,000 units in June 1994, almost 38% growth in six months[59]). The personnel totalled 3.726 million, an increase of 60.7% over 1992 and 200% over 1991. The total registered capital was RMB 68.03 billion, an increase of 207.7% over 1992 and 600% over 1991. The industrial production reached RMB 42.17 billion, an increase of 105.6% over 1992 and 300% over 1991. Income was RMB 30.92 billion, 172.2% over 1992 and 500% over 1991. Urban entrepreneurs have been mostly

Table 8. Backgrounds of Private Enterprises' Heads (%)

				Ex-convict,		
Shaanxi, 1983	Village cadre	Technician	Retiree, worker	red guard		
	46.6	20.4	10.7	22.3		

	Village cadre	TVE[a] cadre	School teacher	SOE[b] worker office cadre	Army veteran	
11 provinces, 1988 (97 enterprises)	17.5	18.6	7.2	10.3	11.3	(99.9)[c]

	Cadre	TVE head	TVE worker	Temporary worker	Army veteran
13 provinces, 1991 (1,071 enterprises)	41.5	19.3	12.9	17	9.2

	Resigned	On leave[d]	Retiree	Peasant	Jobless[e]	Getihu[f]	Others
	23.2	1.1	23.3	7.4	42.8	na	2.2
	14.63	15.38	7.66	30.92	12.09	16.08	3.24

	Number of units	Personnel	Registered capital
Eastern region	68.47	65	76.88
Central region	20.17	22	14.63
Western region	11.36	13	8.49

[a] TVE: township and village enterprises;
[b] SOE: state-owned enterprise;
[c] As presented in the original, totals do not always add up to 100;
[d] On leave: cadre or worker on leave of absence without pay but with right to return to original post (*tingxin liuzhi*);
[e] This category combines two original categories of the table: waiting for employment (*daiye*) and unemployed (*wuye*);
[f] *Getihu*: self-employed or household enterprise.

Source: Zhang Houyi, "Siying qiyezhu jieceng zai woguo shehui jiegou de diwei" (The Status of the Privately-led Enterprise Stratum in Chinese Social Structure), *Zhongguo shehui kexue* (Chinese Social Sciences), No. 6 (November 1994), pp. 101–102, 104.

engaged in services (62.5%) while rural entrepreneurs are mostly in industrial production (78.1%). These number are impressive, but they represent a situation still far behind the publicly-owned sectors: private enterprises are in numbers only 3.27% of public units; they have only 1.61% of capital assets and 1.48% of the personnel. These numbers may have to be revised drastically if the estimate of more than 100,000 private units registered as collective enterprises turns out to be truely private; a particular provincial estimate indicates that because of the so-called "six simulations" (fake SOE, fake TVE, fake foreign investment, etc.) the real number of private units would have to be multiplied by factors of 3 to 10; another estimate from a national sample survey considers that 83% of the TVEs would in fact be privately owned. According to Li Xinxin, such problems reflect to a large measure the inadequacy of central and local governments' in implementing proper policies and regulations and in offering a fair treatment.[60] For example, already paying about RMB 95.64 billion in yearly taxes, the private enterprises are estimated to be extorted three times as much in fees, fines or plain poaching.

Market Principle

In the following examples, we can see very ordinary people become successful entrepreneurs. They are the choices of the propaganda machine. In the early 1980s, Zhang Yingtian, of Rugao in Jiangsu, was a temporary worker in a local collective earning RMB 30 a month while his wife tended the fields to feed the family of five. In early 1983, hearing on the radio that the Document Number One of the new year contained a clause encouraging rural folks to engage in self-employment, Zhang decided to bet his life chance on a small foundry, the first *getihu* of his north Jiangsu region. With RMB 140 in his possession he bought scrap iron, charcoal and basic tools to start his business; in one year, he produced RMB 10,000 worth of output. After this success, he decided to go into production of parts for saw-mill equipment. Gradually, improvements to technique and equipment out of every penny earned allowed him in 1990 to seek further expansion by contracting to produce parts for larger machine plants at the very moment the mood in the country, reflected in the comments he got on his project, was very weary of a conservative turn in the national leadership. To which he retorted: "If there is to be a re-socialization (of private property), I will gladly give the enterprise to the Communist Party." His peasant determination allowed him to see his ouput grow to RMB 300,000.

Since then, his venture has reached a multi-million production. As a reward for his dedication, his "detachment" and his success, he has been invited to join party-sponsored Chinese People Political Consultative Congress, Rugao's Association of Industry and Commerce (*Gongshanglian*) and Rugao's Private Entrepreneurs Association.

Zhang Yingtian has remained what he has always been, an ordinary labourer who is ready to work hard, helped by his family, and live without ostentation. His contribution to the village in terms of money and services have only reflected the nature of his attitude which makes the village his larger home with 52 out of 56 able-bodied individuals in the neigbourhood working at his foundry (total labour force of 150). They provide the solid network of discipline which allows him to maintain a simple three-person management team.[61]

Zhang Yingtian is a middle-of-the-road example. Around this kind of locally based and locally oriented venture, there are several different categories of entrepreneurs who work very hard to set up a self-sustaining little venture. From there, background, opportunity or luck draw them to multiply quickly the originally small asset into an extraordinary expansion. The motivation is framed as well by an ability to link up with individuals who are going to offer support and be cooperative. The Xia family of Sheyang in Jiangsu which is producing furniture, or the QS group in Beijing renting store counters selling the latest Guangzhou fashion (an informal but tightly knit group around DS, the leader of a mixed group of relatives and close friends) show a rather similar basic quality of responding to the natural core leader.

The Xia family has developed into a limited liability company worth RMB 10 million in assets and output of RMB 18 million in which the close-knit group work on the principles of a division of labour and accountability. The second is a group of about 20 people who maintain close cooperation while keeping the most important portion of their trading activity and accounting separate from each other: Shi Xianmin calls it "corporation-based leasing," on account of the corporate body that organizes the leasing and also because of the nature of the group-based security arrangement needed to stay physically "healthy" in the competitive environment of the Beijing *getihus*. The QS group exchanges as a loose group only on certain activities such as travelling together to Guangzhou but buying goods separately, gathering to share meal and drink to exchange market information but keeping their accounts separate, banding together to lease floors or counters of market-buildings but adamantly refusing to join such groups as the Association of Industry and Commerce or the Association of the Self-employed (*Getihu xiehui*) which are for those who pursue business with other (opportunistic, political) objectives in mind, a mix that is deleterious to the demonstration of business acumen:

> The principle of business people must be demonstrated by trade.... To engage in business is to make money and not to think over how to earn prestige for someone else.[62]

But, there has been another heavy cost to pay nationwide, the result in Guangdong, for example, being a little bit better known and rather graphically related. Yan Changjiang, young writer of 24 at the time he was invited by Guangzhou's Jinan University Press to draw a picture of recent Guangdong, commented:

> The planning system has already been breached; the market system is already embryonic (*chuxing*); but, true market trust (*xinyu*) has still to be established.... Trust is an "abandoned child" that receives no care. Short-term behaviour is the rule; short-term profit above everything else. (Follows a list of ills: broken contracts, opportunism, broken laws, deficient products, the cheating of friends, the abuse of clients, the pervasive use of "relationships").... The whole economy is not a comprehensive system with effective activity, but a movement forward resulting from a lot of parts bumping (*zhuanglai zhuangqu*) against each other. The parts have no effective supervision; neither does the law have any.
> Initial accumulation (*yuanshi jilei*) — so, in Guangdong, we eat meat while cursing mother![63]

Conclusion

The economic reforms have, by most accounts, become both irreversible and comprehensive, but for whose benefit?

Some analysts have concluded that China has had, on the whole, recourse to a rather remarkable strategy — *a posteriori* — of economic reform and development in comparison with the former Soviet Union, for example.[64] The Chinese's evaluation has been much more ambivalent. Even if the statistics, as rendered by the State Statistical Bureau, have been impressive, the pattern of investment in turn has saddled the central and regional governments with problems of deficient fiscal income and the outlay of scarce resources to subsidize failing productive units. Many patriot intellectuals and economists have expressed their worry at the possible disorder and loss of national integration.

State enterprises, providing the economic services required by the growth of the local economies, to this day, have remained virtually at the margin of the emerging market mechanism, being forced to produce under guidance of planning and supervisory agencies. Excepting a certain number of large enterprises which have been able to diversify into conglomerates or find a *niche* protected by a particular level of government, the great majority of SOEs has not been able to shore up its performance; the common manager has continued to practice his traditional "bounded rationality," and "idyllic manner of life" in Max Weber's terms.[65] But a "shake-out" is certainly on the card, a strategy devised in the course of 1994 at the centre — to judge by the frequent threats emanating from Vice-premier Zhu Rongji and, lately, Wu Bangguo — to let go gradually of the majority of the SOEs in the form of leasing, auction sales, devolution to a lower grade of collective ownership or stage-managed bankruptcy. In a speech delivered on 20 December 1994, the vice-premier-to-be, Wu Bangguo, decried the low productivity and the low efficiency of the state-owned sector: the statistics for January to November 1994 indicated that for all industrial plants from the township to the national levels, for example, the sale of products had gone up by 20.87%, of which 30.88% had been achieved by TVEs, 46.46% by "others" (i.e., private and foreign firms) but only 5.79% by the SOEs. He made very clear to his audience that the objective of the state was becoming less indiscriminate: "deepen the reform of state-owned enterprises, further build up the large and medium scale state enterprises."[66]

Could he have meant either that the burden was going to be passed on to the non-state sectors or the latter were so badly needed that they were being allowed to build themselves up?

After Deng Xiaoping's southern tour of January and February 1992, which set on a new cycle of frenzied activities — especially the "taking the plunge" into business — Guangdong, and most other advanced regions of China, could not have fit more neatly into Amitai Etzioni's schema, producing an ethos of participation which has probably broken for ever the moral bond shackling the pursuit of wealth for its own sake. In line with Wang Dingding's view, the disorder has been conducive to the building-up of new forms of trust (or credibility); the market being so savage and with

The Individual and Entrepreneurship in the Chinese Economic Reforms 25.37

so few rules, that only in the circle of the family or the close-knit small group has it been the way to start for most people. The tally has expectedly been mixed, a broad sense that the pursuit of wealth is having its rewards if one knows how to face the disorder. The traditional tolerance of ambiguity may already be dissolving with the learning of the ability to hold to one's objective.

As indicated in a few places in the preceding pages, the reforms may have been rearranging the distribution of power and wealth beyond the framework that has been employed by analysts such as Vogel, Oi, Nee and Gold, as information filtering through the work of mainland analysts shows interests articulation and distribution on the basis of individual interest already legitimated by society. Individuals and small groups have a relative space within which they may resist being "mobilized." According to the logic of Wang Dingding's view, this is precisely what has to be drawn out of tradition in order to achieve efficiency.

Quite visibly, in contest have been competing two techniques of transformation or reform, a first one as old as the travails of the nineteenth century at bringing forth a modernizing China by investing in imported techniques and tools[67] under the benevolent administration, and a second view of change which starts with an internal tension-generating seizing of opportunities which has been maturing into a realization that the entrepreneur cannot do all on his own. The reforms have challenged the established order; this order itself has to be helped along. In a sense, it may seem surprising that it was under the socialist order of the Chinese Communist regime that the decisive action was taken to instigate on a large scale the very spirit, attitude and motivation necessary to set such a path of development.

Wenzhou, in southeast Zhejiang, had been believed to be an oddly remarkable region for daring to slide into quasi-*laissez-faire*. So it had appeared to many a visiting Chinese journalist or foreign scholar. In effect, the local party leadership had kept inconspicuous during earlier development. Now they have rendered their strategy as the following maxim: at first decentralize later guide (*xian fang, hou dao*); at the second stage, partially decentralize partially guide, (*bian fang, bian dao*); and now return to grasp management and promote development (*xianzai you daoguolai, zhua guanli cu fazhan*), meaning to say that the early innovative activity of Wenzhou had been unobtrusively monitored and allowed to develop. Now that the experiment has proven successful, the numerous small shops are being gradually integrated into collective corporations to gain economies of scale under the managerial control of village or township officials.[68] Is this part of Wang Dingding's ambiguity? That is, is a process of development between the leader and the led reaching to the macro-level, analogous to the relationship between the western state and the bourgeoisie during the creation of political institutions to frame the energy of the new market economy? A further analysis of both the macro- and micro-economic conditions of creativity is needed to understand the nature of the redistribution of power and wealth.

Notes

1. Teng Nengxiang, "'Song bang fang quan' gei qiye zhuru shengji huoli" ("Untie the Hands, Decentralize Power" Gave the Enterprises a Shot of Vital Energy), *Qiye guanli* (Enterprise Administration), No. 151 (March 1994), pp. 6–7.
2. Ezra F. Vogel, *One Step Ahead in China: Guangdong under Reform* (Cambridge, MA: Harvard University Press, 1989); Jean C. Oi, "The Fate of the Collective after the Commune," in *Chinese Society on the Eve of Tiananmen: The Impact of Reform*, edited by Deborah S. Davis and Ezra F. Vogel (Cambridge, MA and London: The Council on East Asian Studies, Harvard University, 1990), pp. 15–36; and, Victor Nee and Frank W. Young, "Peasant Entrepreneurs in China's 'Second Economy': An Institutional Analysis," *Economic Development and Cultural Change*, Vol. 39, No. 2 (January 1991), pp. 293–310.
3. Thomas B. Gold, "Guerilla Interviewing among the Getihu," in *Unofficial China: Popular Culture and Thought in the People's Republic*, edited by Perry Link, Richard Madsen and Paul G. Pickowicz (Boulder, Co, San Francisco and London: Westview Press, 1989), pp. 175–92.
4. David Wank, "Private Business, Bureaucracy, and Political Alliance in a Chinese City," *The Australian Journal of Chinese Affairs*, No. 33 (January 1995), pp. 55–71.
5. Jean C. Oi, "Communism and Clientelism: Rural Politics in China," *World Politics*, No. 2 (January 1985), pp. 238–66.
6. Deng Xiaoping, *Deng Xiaoping wenxuan* (The Selected Works of Deng Xiaoping), Vol. 3 (Beijing: Renmin chubanshe, 1993), p. 366.
7. See Note 1.
8. An irony not lost on Qiu Shan, of the Guangdong Academy of Social Sciences, who speaks of the confusions still found among political leaders and administrators who want to circumscribe the definition to a "standardized entrepreneur" (*zhun qiyejia*) for the managers highly envious of the rural

private enterprises, *Yue-Gang qiyejia bao* (Guangdong-Hong Kong Entrepreneur Journal), 13 May 1989, p. 3.
9. *Renmin ribao* (People's Daily), 27 July 1992.
10. "Liuge diaochazu jiang pu gedi" (Six Investigating Teams Are Going to Spread across the Whole Land), *Renmin ribao*, 6 May 1993, p. 1.
11. Cheng Xiusheng, "Shichang jingji huhuan chuangye qiyejia" (The Market Economy Is Calling on Creative Entrepreneurs), *Zhongguo jingji xinxi* (Chinese Economic Information), No. 15 (1994), p. 3.
12. Chinese and western economists have been debating, through the presentation of increasingly sophisticated analytical techniques, whether the reforms have led to an increased efficiency in production, allocation and scale; for a succinct analysis, see *China: Between Plan and Market* (Washington, DC: The World Bank, 1990).
13. Joseph A. Schumpeter, "Economic Theory and Entrepreneurial History," in *Explorations in Enterprise*, edited by Hugh G. J. Aitken (Cambridge, MA: Harvard University Press, 1967), pp. 45–64; J. A. Schumpeter, "The Fundamental Phenomenon of Economic Development," in *Entrepreneurship and Economic Development*, edited by Peter Kilby (New York: The Free Press, 1971), pp. 43–70.
14. Amitai Etzioni, "Entrepreneurship, Adaptation and Legitimation: A Macrobehavioral Perspective," *Journal of Economic Behavior and Organization*, Vol. 8 (1987), pp. 175–89.
15. Wang Dingding, "Qiyejia suo jubei de qiye jingshen" (The Entreprise Spirit Possessed by Entrepreneurs), *Xinbao* (Hong Kong Economic Journal), 17, 18, 19, 21 and 22 December 1992.
16. Max Weber, *The Religion of China, Confucianism and Taoism* (New York: The Macmillan Company, 1951) and *The Protestant Ethic and the Spirit of Capitalism* (New York: Charles Scribner's Sons, 1958).
17. Ibid., p. 176.
18. Wang Dingding, "Qiyejia suo jubei de qiye jingshen" (see Note 15), 18 December 1992, p. 33.
19. Ibid., 21 December 1992, p. 8.
20. Ibid.
21. Susan Mann, *Local Merchants and the Chinese Bureaucracy, 1750–1950* (Stanford, CA: Stanford University Press, 1987).
22. Chin Yeoh-chi (Ambrose King), "Zhongguo fazhan cheng xiandaixing guojia de kunjing: Weibo xueshuo de yimian" (The Difficulty of China Developing into a Modern Country: One Face of Weber's Theory), *Ershiyi shiji* (Twenty-first Century), No. 3 (February 1991), pp. 56–72; Wong Siu-lun, "Modernization and Chinese Culture in Hong Kong," *The China Quarterly*, No. 106 (June 1986), pp. 306–25; S. Gordon Redding and D. S. Pugh, "The Formal and the Informal: Japanese and Chinese Organization Structures," in *The*

Enterprise and Management in East Asia, edited by Stewart R. Clegg, Dexter C. Dumphy and S. Gordon Redding (Hong Kong: Centre of Asian Sudies, University of Hong Kong, 1986), pp. 1–31.

23. An economic explanation for the choice is the successful growth of the rural enterprises, Yi Chou, *The Practice beyond Property Right Boundaries*, Discussion Paper No. 9302 (Taipei: Chung-Hua Institution for Economic Research, 1993); a political explanation is the adaptive stance taken by the top leadership of the party after the evaluation of the dislocations in Eastern Europe and the Soviet Union in the early 1990s.

24. Du Haiyan, "Cong caichan guanxi ru shou shenhua guoyou qiye gaige" (To Deepen the Reform of State-owned Enterprises Starting with Ownership Relations), *Jingji yanjiu* (Economic Research), No. 5 (May 1992), p. 10.

25. Yang Mu, "Taolun: Zhongguo xiangzhen qiye de qiji shi zenyang chuxian de?" (Discussion: How Has the Phenomenon of the Chinese Town-village Enterprise Arisen?) in *Jiushi niandai Zhongguo xiangzhen qiye diaocha* (Survey of Chinese Town-village Enterprises in the 1990s), edited by Ma Rong et al. (Hong Kong: Oxford University Press, 1994), pp. 459, 461–62.

26. Yang Peixin, "Shenhua gaige de guanjian hezai?" (Where Is the Key to Deepening the Reforms?), *Jingji tizhi gaige neibu cankao* (Internal Reference on the Reform of the Economic System), No. 24 (1993), pp. 16–17.

27. Zhang Zhengxian, "Yiwei qiyejia de 'wenhuaxue'" (The "Culture Science" of an Entrepreneur), *Banyue tan* (Fortnightly Talk), No. 17 (1 September 1994), pp. 32–35.

28. Zhou Shulian, "Lun qiyejia yu shehui zhuyi, qiye zhidu he caichan suoyouzhe de guanxi" (Discussion of the Entrepreneur and Socialism: The Relations between the Industrial System and the Owner), *Qiyejia banyuekan* (Entrepreneur Fortnightly), No. 5 (1989), p. 10.

29. Xun Dazhi, *Lu zai hefang?* (Where Is the Way Out?), (Chengdu: Sichuan renmin chubanshe, 1992), pp. 199–251.

30. Chen Jian Jun, "Guoyou dazhongxing qiye shenhua gaige de shizheng fenxi" (Positive Analysis of the Deepening of Reform amongst State-owned Large and Medium Size Enterprises), *Zhongguo gongye jingji yanjiu* (Economic Research on Chinese Industry), No. 6 (1993), p. 23–24.

31. Li Yong, "Gaige huohua bu xi, Pianzhuan xianquan feizhuan" (The Spark of Reform Does Not Die, Pianzhuan Coils Up to Soar), *Xiandai qiye* (Contemporary Enterprise), No. 4 (1994), pp. 12–13.

32. Zixia, "Ri chu, jiang hua hong sheng huo" (The Sun Rises, Jiangsu's Flower Is Redder than Fire), *Zhongguo qiyejia* (Chinese Entrepreneur), No. 8 (1994), p. 15.

33. Schumpeter suggests that "creative destruction" takes place close to equilibrium to minimize risk; here, Tao Jianxing presses repeatedly for further

disequilibrium and greater risk even though his achievements are not imitated, see Etzioni (Note 14), p. 177.
34. Shi Youlong, Liu Xiaosu and Xin Yu, "Qing zhu zheng ye, xin xi guojia" (His Emotions Are Fixed on Duty, His Heart Is the Nation), *Xiandai gongshang* (Contemporary Industry and Trade), No. 10 (1994), p. 46.
35. Yang Lianmin, Shi Youlong and Liu Xiaosu, "'Chunlan' zai Zhongguo tese de daolu shang tansuo" ("Chunlan" Is Experimenting on the Road with Chinese Characteristics), *Xiandai gongshang*, No. 7 (1994), p. 25.
36. Xun Dazhi, *Lu zai hefang?* (see Note 29), pp. 252f.
37. Jiang Yiwei, "Lun shehui zhuyi de xiandai qiyejia" (On the Contemporary Entrepreneur under Socialism), in *Lun qiyejia jingshen* (On Entrepreneurship), edited by Zhou Shulian, Mun Kin-chuk, et al. (Beijing: Jingji guanli chubanshe, 1989), p. 15.
38. Ji Liping, *Zhongguo "xiahai" chao* (China's Wave of Business "Plunge"), (Shijiazhuang: Hebei renmin chubanshe, 1993), p. 266.
39. An Hua and Xiao Ming, "Qiye neibu 'zouxue' xianxiang yousilu" (Worrying Record of the "Burrowing" Phenomenon within the Enterprise), *Qiye da shijie* (The Wide World of the Enterprise), No. 8 (August 1994), pp. 26–28.
40. Xiao Liang, "Jiti qiye fazhan zhong xuyao jiejue de san da wenti" (Three Big Questions Collective Enterprises in the Process of Development Need to Solve), *Zhongguo gongye jingji yanjiu* (Economic Research on Chinese Industry), No. 3 (1994), p. 46; for a short history of this economic sector, see *Zhongguo xiangzhen qiye guanli baike quanshu* (Encyclopedia of China's Township and Village Enterprise's Management), (Beijing: Nongye chubanshe, 1987), pp. 1–2.
41. A situation apparently that has been progressively corrected in the latter part of the 1980s by partial repayments of dividends but not the capital.
42. Ibid., pp. 46–48; Chen Naixing, Xiao Xu and Wang Yanzhong, "Xiangzhen gongye fazhan zhengce daoxiang yanjiu" (Study of a Policy Orientation for the Development of Town-village Industry), *Zhongguo gongye jingji yanjiu*, No. 5 (1994), pp. 39–44; Fu Xueliao, Wei Xiaobing and Zhao Feng, "Yi xi yi you de Zhongguo xiangzhen qiye" (Chinese Town-village Enterprises are At Once Happy and Worried), *Liaowang* (Outlook), No. 35 (29 August 1994), pp. 12–13.
43. *Deng Xiaoping wenxuan*, Vol. 3 (see Note 6), p. 238.
44. Qi Jingfa, Li Shulin, Zong Jinyao, Lu Yongjun and Zhang Honglin, "Lun xiangzhen qiye guanli chuangxin" (Discussion of the Creativity in Administration of the Town-village Enterprises), *Zhongguo xiangzhen qiye bao* (Chinese Town-village Enterprise Journal), 13 June 1994, p. 3.
45. Song Jinyao and Zou Fanming, "Xiangzhen qiye chanquan zhidu gaige jiben silu" (Basic Thinking on the Reform of the Ownership System of the

Town-village Enterprise), *Zhongguo xiangzhen qiye nianjian* (Chinese Townvillage Enterprise Yearbook), (Beijing: Zhongguo nongye chubanshe, 1994), p. 399.
46. Xu Wenrong, "Yige xiangzhen qiye jituan de zuzhi chuangxin" (The Organizational Novelty of a Township and village Conglomerate), *Zhongguo qiye jingji yanjiu*, No. 10 (1994), pp. 55–59.
47. Ibid., pp. 400–404; Yang Mu, "Taolun: Zhongguo xiangzhen qiye" (see Note 25), pp. 440–43.
48. "Sunan xiangqi fudan jugao bu xia" (Rural Enterprises' Burden in South Jiangsu Keeps Going Up), *Nongmin ribao* (Peasants' Daily), 30 April 1991, p. 2.
49. "'Hongdou' sheng nanguo" (Hongdou Creates a Southern Empire), *Zhongguo qiyejia*, No. 1 (1994), p. 18.
50. "Lu Guanqiu chenggong zhi lu" (Lu Guangqiu's Road to Success), in *Qiye gaige xianxingzhe de zuji* (The Footprints of the Precursors of Enterprise Reform), edited by Gao Shangquan and Ai Feng (Beijing: Gaige chubanshe, 1990), pp. 190–94.
51. Lin Nan and Tang Qingzhong, "From the Farm to the World — Success Story of a Township Enterprise in East China," *New China Quarterly*, No. 30 (December 1993), pp. 76, 78.
52. For a lively description of rules and counter-adaptation in Beijing, see Shi Xianmin, *Tizhi de tupo, Beijing shi Xicheng qu getihu yanjiu* (System Breakthrough: Research on the Self-employed in Beijing City's Xicheng District), (Beijing: Zhongguo shehui kexue chubanshe, 1993).
53. "Woguo siyou qiye de jingying zhuangkuang yu siyou qiyezhu de qunti tezheng" (Management Situation of Chinese Private Enterprises and Common Characteristics of the Owners), *Zhongguo shehui kexue* (Chinese Social Sciences), No. 4 (August 1994), p. 62, note 1.
54. Yang Mu, "Taolun" (see Note 25), p. 440–41.
55. "Zhongguo siyou jingji de da qushi" (The Main Trend of China's Private Economy), in *Siyou jingji zonghenglun* (The Length and Breath of the Private Economy), edited by Ying Kefu and Sun Jianchang (Nanjing: Nanjing University Press, 1993), p. 346.
56. "Wenzhou ren de zhexue tounao" (The Philosophical Brain of Wenzhou People), *Zhongguo qiyejia*, August 1994, p. 37; Xu Jinglong and Hu Hongwei, "Joint Stock Co-operation System Created by Farmers — New Developments in East China's Rural Areas," *New China Quarterly*, No. 27 (February 1993), p. 90.
57. Richard W. Stites, "Industrial Work as an Entrepreneurial Strategy," *Modern China*, Vol. 11, No. 2 (1985), pp. 227–46.
58. Zhang Houyi, "Siying qiyezhu jieceng zai woguo shehui jiegou de diwei" (The Status of the Privately-led Enterprise Stratum in Chinese

Social Structure), *Zhongguo shehui kexue*, No. 6 (November 1994), pp. 100–116.
59. *South China Morning Post*, 14 January 1995, p. 8.
60. "Zhongguo siyou jingji de da qushi" (see Note 55), p. 347; Li Xinxin, "Zhongguo siying jingji fazhan zhong de wenti ji duice" (The Problems of and Solutions to China's Developing Privately-managed Economy), *Jingji yanjiu* (Economic Research), No. 7 (1994), p. 44.
61. Zhang Hu, "Ji siying qiyezhu Zhang Yingtian" (A Record of Private Entrepreneur Zhang Yingtian), *Yanhai jingji* (Coastal Economy), No. 8 (1994), pp. 29–30.
62. Shi Xianmin, *Tizhi de tupo* (see Note 52), p. 303.
63. Yan Changjiang, *Guangdong da liebian* (Guangdong's Great Fission), (Guangzhou: Jinan daxue chubanshe, 1993), p. 246.
64. Keith Griffin and Azizur Rahman Khan, "The Chinese Transition to a Market-guided Economy: The Contrast with Russia and Eastern Europe," *Contention*, Vol. 3, No. 2 (Winter 1994), pp. 95–107.
65. Max Boisot and Liang Xingguo, "The Nature of Managerial Work in the Chinese Enterprise Reforms: A Study of Six Directors," *Organization Studies*, Vol. 13, No. 2 (1992), p. 162.
66. Wu Bangguo, "Tongyi renshi, jin yi bu banhao guoyou qiye" (Let Us Unite Our Understanding, Further Run Well State-owned Enterprises), *Qiushi zazhi* (Seeking Truth Magazine), No. 3 (1 February 1995), pp. 4–5.
67. In the January 1995 issue of *Cheng Ming*, Bao Zunxin was of the opinion that the present reform model, as intuitively framed by the Communist leaders — economic reform with party rule — was but a repetition of the failed late-Qing model of the *yangwu yundong* (westernization movement), or the later *zhongti xiyong* (technical borrowing absorbed by the ambient culture) both characterized as past efforts to secure traditional values and the rule of the incumbents (see Bao Zunxin, "Mantan 'wanqing re'" (Casual Review of the "Late-Qing Fad"), *Cheng Ming*, No. 207 (1 January 1995), pp. 28–31.
68. "Wenzhou ren de zhexue tounao" (see Note 56).

Index

Note: Roman numerals refer to the pages of "Chronology"; the Arabic numerals are composed of two numbers separated by a period; the first in boldface refers to the chapter, the second to the page(s).

Academia Sinica, **4**.5
Africa, **8**.3
Age distribution (table), **11**.10
Agriculture, xxv, xxxiv; **3**.4; **19**.35; **23**.29; government investment (table), **22**.12; household investment (table), **22**.13; investment, **22**.11; output (table), **22**.4; production inputs, **22**.10; products prices (table), **22**.9; purchase price (table), **22**.10
Ai Zhisheng, xxvii
Alaska, **8**.19
All-China Federation of Industry and Commerce, **21**.16
Anhui, **1**.14,16,17; **2**.30; **3**.7,13,42,44; **17**.15; **18**.46; **19**.57; **25**.14
Anti-bourgeois campaign, **1**.28
Arbitration, **6**.15–18; China International and Economic Arbitration Commission, **6**.16–18; International Council on Commercial Arbitration, **6**.16; New York Convention for the Recognition of Enforcement of Arbitral Awards, **6**.16
Art, *The Sun of the New Epoch*, **1**.4
Asia-Pacific Economic Co-operation (APEC), xxxiii; **7**.6,8,11,13; **8**.2,8,10,15,16,20

Asian Games, **1**.34; **4**.9; **5**.12; **7**.13; **8**.8; Hiroshima affair, **1**.30,34; **8**.8, *see also* Olympics
Association of Industry and Commerce, **25**.34,35
Association of Self-employed (*getihu*), **25**.35
Association of Southeast Asian Nations (ASEAN), **8**.13–17,16, 22,27; **23**.15
Au, Sally, **5**.6
Australia, **7**.7; **8**.16; **10**.15; **14**.8,10,16; **23**.15

Ba Zhongtan, **1**.11
Baker, James, **8**.18
Balcombe, Dennis, **17**.15,26
Banking, xxvi; **6**.8,10,13,20; **10**.10; **18**.17; **19**.18,25,26,30,35; **21**.*passim*; asset and liability ratio (table), **21**.15; cooperative banks, **21**.8,16; foreign banks, **21**.17,24–27; **23**.5; joint venture banks, **21**.15; policy banks, **19**.30,35; **23**.3; policy loans, **21**.4,7; specialized banks (table), **21**.5; Banks: Asian Development Bank, **4**.6; **7**.7,8,11,13; **8**.20; **23**.28; Bank of China, **3**.38; **21**.17,24,27,31; Bank of Communication, **21**.14–15;

Bank of Construction, **21**.31;
Bundesbank, **19**.49; **21**.8; China
Agricultural Development Bank,
21.12,31; China Education and
Science Trust and Investment
Corporation, **18**.17; China Import
and Export Bank, **21**.12; China
State Development Bank, xxiv;
19.35; **21**.12; Citibank, **21**.17;
Foreign Exchange Trade System,
21.21; Hongkong and Shanghai
Bank, **21**.17; International
Monetary Fund (IMF), **7**.13; **8**.2;
19.48; **23**.6,9,28,38; Industrial and
Commercial Bank of China,
21.13,31; International Bank for
Reconstruction and Development
(World Bank), **7**.13,14; **8**.3; **18**.25;
21.7; **23**.8,22,24–25,28,29,38;
Lehman Brothers Bank, **1**.30; Liu
Chong Hing Bank, **21**.17; Ming
Sheng Bank, **21**.16; People's Bank
of China, xxiv; **1**.12; **2**.39; **3**.10,24;
5.4; **19**.26,28,44,49,50,51;
21.*passim*; **23**.35,36; People's
Construction Bank, **21**.21
Bankruptcy, xxvi; **6**.24; **13**.4; **19**.41
Bao Ge, **1**.24
Bao Tong, **2**.37,38
Bao Zunxin, **25**.43
Barefoot doctors, **11**.5
Beidaihe, xxx; **1**.12; **3**.19
Beijing (Peking), xxxii; **1**.6,7,22,24;
2.30–31; **3**.6; **5**.4,14; **6**.17;
8.7,17,24; **11**.5,8,22; **12**.2,8,17;
14.9,12; **17**.6,12,15,19,22;
18.18,35,38,45; **19**.30,38,40; **21**.17;
22.18; **25**.34,42
Beijing Association for the Study of
Marriage and the Family, **12**.17
Beijing Jeep, **14**.3
Belgium, **7**.11; **17**.26; **23**.40

Belize, **8**.26
Bo Yibo, **2**.37
Bogor, **7**.7–8; **8**.20
Books, *August 1995: China's Violent
Invasion of Taiwan*, **8**.26; *Deng
Xiaoping wenxuan*, xxxii; *Viewing
China through the Third Eye*, xxv;
1.3; **19**.58; *Xu Jiatun Huiyilu*,
8.27
Bourgeois Liberalism, **18**.42
Bourgeoisie, **16**.4
British Commonwealth, **7**.12
Brittan, Leon, **8**.22
Broadcast media, BBC World Service
TV, **5**.3; Beijing TV, **5**.12; Central
People's Radio, **5**.13; China Central
Television (CCTV), **2**.14;
5.2,4,12,13; China International
Radio, **5**.14; Guangzhou TV, **5**.11;
Star TV, **5**.3
Brunei, **8**.13
Buddhism, **17**.18–20; Curbo
Monastery, **17**.20; Buddhist nuns,
16.2; temples, **17**.8; Tibetan,
17.19–20; Tibetan Buddhist
College, **17**.19
Budget Adjustment Fund, **20**.4
Bulgaria, **21**.19
Burma, **8**.13,16,22,27
Burton, John W., **7**.15

Cambodia, **8**.13,14,15,19,27
Canada, **8**.16; **10**.15; **23**.15
Cao Zhi, **2**.8
Capital Steel (Shougang), **1**.10
Career, bureaucratic, **3**.18
Cassidy, Robert, **7**.14
Catholic Church, **17**.8,15–18;
Federation of Asian Bishop's
Conference, **17**.16; Manila
International Catholic Youth
Conference, **17**.16; Pope, **17**.16,18

Index

Central America, **8**.11
Centre-regions, **1**.20; central-local relations, **20**.6–7; central-provincial relations, **3**.*passim*
Chahar, **17**.23,
Chang, Wilson, xxxiii
Changchun, **3**.22
Chaolian *tongxianghui*, **16**.7f.
Chaozhou, **15**.19
Chen Huanyou, **3**.26
Chen Jiyuan, **19**.57
Chen Kaige, **5**.5
Chen Qi, **5**.12
Chen Qingtai, **1**.33
Chen Shui-bian, xxxiv; **4**.3
Chen Yizi, **2**.8,9,38
Chen Yuan, **21**.28; **23**.35
Chen Yun, xxv; **3**.27,43
Chen Zibao, **16**.16
Chen Ziming, **1**.24
Cheng Andong, **3**.42
Cheng Lianchang, **2**.13,29,40,42
Chengdu, **3**.22; **14**.12; **19**.42
Chiang Ching-kuo, xxxiii; **4**.2; **8**.12
Chien, Frederick, **8**.13
Chin Yeoh-chi (Ambrose King), **25**.13
China Council for the Promotion of International Trade, **1**.28
Chinese Academy of Social Sciences, **1**.17; **17**.22; **19**.52
Chinese Communist Party, Party centre, **2**.28; **19**.3; leadership succession, **1**.8–10;
  Leadership: Politburo, xxv, xxxii; **1**.9,10,11,28; **3**.21,26,43; **17**.7;
  Party Congress: 13th Congress, **1**.7; **2**.2f.,8,12,17,18; **3**.26; 14th Congress, **2**.14; **6**.33; **23**.2; **24**.3; **25**.7; *Plenums*: 3rd plenum of 11th Central Committee (CC), **13**.2; **23**.27; 3rd plenum of 12th CC, **25**.2; 7th plenum of 12th CC, **2**.6,7; 4th plenum of 13th CC, **1**.6; 7th plenum of 13th CC, **2**.13; **3**.7; 3rd plenum of 14th CC, **1**.2,14,19,20,26; **3**.3,5,12,15,21,25; **13**.14; **20**.3; **21**.2,8; 4th plenum of 14th CC, xxxii; **1**.6,10–13,18; **3**.21,26;
  Organization: Central Secretariat, **1**.10; **3**.26; Central Commission for Disciplinary Inspection, xxx; Central Leading Group on Economics and Finance, **2**.39; Central Military Commission, xxviii; **1**.12; **9**.3,8,13; Central Organization and Establishment Commission, **2**.13,32,35; Central Small Study Group, **2**.6; General Office, **1**.11; Leading Group on Foreign Affairs, **2**.39; Leading Group for Ideology and Propaganda, xxviii;
  Departments: Organization Department, **2**.4,7,10,18,19,31; Propaganda Department, **1**.11,18,28; **5**.3–4,6,10,13; United Front Work Department, **1**.13; **17**.2,4,6,10,24;
  Regulations: Outline for the Implementation of Patriotism, xxxi; Overall Conceptual Scheme on Political Structure Reform, **2**.6; Regulations on Disciplinary and Inspection Work in the Party, xxx; Regulations on Supervision within the Party, xxx
Chinese People's Political Consultative Conference (CPPCC), **1**.7,13,26; **5**.4; **17**.6; **18**.6,43; **25**.34
Chongqing, **3**.7,22,23; **13**.7; **19**.42
Christianity, xxv; **17**.*passim*; *see also* Religion
Christopher, Warren, **8**.24

City, economic (*jihua danlie*), (table), **3**.22
Civil Service, **2**.*passim*; career, **2**.17; Provisional Regulations on State Civil Servants, **2**.2; **6**.26; recruitment, **2**.19–20; reform **6**.21,25–29; reform proposal, (table), **2**.15; relations of grade and position (table), **2**.25; salary by position and grade (table), **2**.24; salary standards (table), **2**.23; wage system, **2**.20–27
Civil society, **1**.28; **4**.2; **15**.23–24
Clan, **3**.32
Class, **11**.18; **15**.14; middle class, **19**.41
Clinton, Bill, xxvii, xxviii, xxxi, xxxiii; **1**.25; **8**.3,10,18
Cold war, **7**.2; **8**.15
Commune system, **11**.4,13; **18**.7; **25**.23
Community festivals, **16**.*passim*,
Confucian ethic, **1**.5; **13**.10; **18**.20; **25**.12
Constitution, **6**.22,23,28; **9**.3; **25**.4
Coordinating Committee for Multilateral Export Controls (COCOM), **8**.6
Corruption, xxx; **1**.3,6,16,18,25–27; **3**.2; **5**.4; **6**.2,3,25,27,28,29,32; **9**.18,19
Costa Rica, **4**.8; **8**.11,26
Court: People's, xxvi, xxxiv; role of the courts, **6**.29–31; People's Intermediate Court, **6**.17; People's Supreme court, **1**.25; **6**.16,30; **12**.19
Cradock, Sir Percy, **10**.11
Cultural Revolution, **7**.4; **8**.21; **9**.5,6; **11**.9,14,15,18; **14**.17; **16**.4; **17**.2,24; **18**.2,4,20,23,31; **25**.22
Culture, **16**.3
Currency, **6**.20; **10**.10; convertibility, **21**.27–28; **23**.31; currency reform,

xxiv; exchange rate, **19**.4,6; **23**.11,13; foreign currency, **3**.24; **21**.17; foreign exchange, **3**.4; **6**.18; **21**.*passim*; **23**.2; exchange reform, **23**.5; Foreign Exchange Trading Centre, **23**.5,35; *Renminbi*, **21**.17–21; **23**.6; swap exchange, **3**.24

Dai Xianglong, **19**.44
Dalai Lama, xxvii; **8**.19; **17**.19
Dalian, **1**.22; **3**.7,22; **9**.16; **12**.19; **14**.12
Dansui, **1**.16
Daoism, **17**.18–19; Daoist priests, **16**.2; temples, **17**.8
Daya Bay Nuclear Plant, **10**.6
Defence Budget, **9**.*passim*; (table), **9**.20; revised salaries (tables), **9**.30; salary scales (table), **9**.29; spending, **3**.8; (graphs), **9**.22–23,25–28; (table), **9**.21; spending since 1979 (table), **9**.24; *see also* People's Liberation Army
Democracy, **1**.6–8; democracy movement, **2**.6; **6**.27; Democracy Wall, **7**.5, *see also* Tiananmen incident
Democratic centralism, **1**.11,17,19
Democratic Progressive Party (Taiwan), xxxiv; **4**.3,7; **8**.11; **9**.22
Deng Liqun, **18**.42
Deng Nan, **17**.22
Deng Rong, **1**.9
Deng Xiaoping, xxv, xxviii, xxix, xxxii; **1**.*passim*; **2**.6,12; **3**.26,32,42; **4**.10; **5**.7,8; **6**.10; **8**.3,12,13,20,21, 23; **9**.3–4,9,12,18,19,32; **10**.2,4,8; **13**.2,9; **17**.21,22; **18**.2,4,9; **19**.3,10; **21**.6,29; **23**.2,37; **24**.3; **25**.4,13,24, 27,31,36
Deng Zhenglai, **1**.7
Deng Zhifang, **1**.10

Index I.5

Denmark, **7**.11; **23**.40
Diaoyu island, **8**.6,21,
Ding Guan'gen, **1**.18,27; **5**.3
Dissidence, **1**.24–25
Divorce, **12**.19–20
Dongkou, **17**.15
Drapchi Prison, **17**.19
Drug smuggling, **8**.16
Du Qingsong, **25**.18–19
"Duke economies," **3**.2

Economic Development, **19**.*passim*; deviation GDP per capita (figure), **19**.7; economic indicators (table), **19**.43; growth rate per capita (table), **19**.8; interventionism, **19**.34–38; macro-economic controls, **1**.12,20; per capita GDP (table), **19**.5; performance (table), **25**.10; policies in 1994, **19**.30–38; provincial income and growth (table), **19**.23
Education, xxvi; **18**.*passim*; *China Education News*, **18**.15; commune middle schools, **18**.23; compulsory education, **20**.11; drop-out rate, **18**.6,12,15,17,40; Education Development Research Centre, **18**.15; funding, **18**.6–12; *minban* schools, **18**.19; private schools (table), **18**.21; private tutor school, **18**.19; school fees, **18**.11–12; secondary school, **18**.41; secondary education, general (table), **18**.24; secondary schooling (table), **18**.28; structure of secondary education (table), **18**.22; student attendance, **18**.12–14; teacher's salaries, **18**.8–11; teachers' welfare, **18**.17; tertiary level, **18**.28–36, *see also* Universities; vocational education, **18**.4,20–28,39

El Salvador, **8**.26
Employment, agriculture (table), **19**.21
Energy Fund, **20**.4
Enterprise, **20**.7; collective-owned, **13**.6; **20**.4; **24**.2; enterprise rules implementation (table), **25**.7; foreign invested, **14**.9; **21**.24; **23**.5; **25**.3–4; managers and ownership (table), **25**.16; private, **13**.4,6; **20**.4; rural, **11**.2; **18**.16; self-employed, **13**.6; state-owned (SOE), xxxiv; **1**.15,20; **6**.10,22,23; **13**.2,4,5,8,11; **14**.2,7,9; **19**.*passim*; **20**.4; **21**.10–11; **23**.9,11; **24**.2; **25**.*passim*; town and village (TVE), **19**.14,20, 27,33,54,59; **22**.8,14,16–19; **23**.11, 38; **25**.23–29,36; TVE indicators (table), **22**.18; (table), **25**.23; village enterprise, **20**.2
Entrepreneurs, **1**.17; **6**.11; **16**.3,13; entrepreneurship, **25**.*passim*; China Entrepreneurs' Association, **25**.5; managers' autonomy (table), **25**.8; managers' demographics (table), **25**.6
Environmental protection, **6**.30
Etzioni, Amitai, **25**.11–12,36
Europe, xxxi; **5**.7; **7**.14; **8**.3,4,6; **24**.9; Europe, Eastern, **1**.7; **8**.8,15,28; **23**.10; **25**.40; European Union, **6**.18; **8**.18,22; **23**.20,24,29,30,40

Factions, **1**.8
Family: **12**.*passim*; domestic violence, **12**.16–17; Fertility, **12**.6; food privileges in the family (table), **12**.7; husband-wife activities (table), **12**.8; inheritance, **12**.14; inheritance rights (table), **12**.16; kinship network, **12**.14–15; lineages, **16**.8; man-woman status (table), **12**.4; respect from bearing a

son (table), **12**.13; violence against spouse (table), **12**.16; wife and request for sex (table), **12**.18; woman's status, **12**.10–15

Feng Bing, **3**.16

Film industry, **5**.13; Cannes Film Festival, **5**.5; Tokyo International Film Festival, **5**.5; films: *Blue Kite*, **5**.5; *Farewell to My Concubine*, **5**.5

Financial restructuring, **21**.*passim*

Fiscality, **3**.3; reform, **1**.21; **20**.*passim*; system, **19**.28, *see also* Taxation

Foreign economic relations, **3**.24–25

Foreign investment, **15**.5; **23**.11,19,21

Foreign relations, **8**.*passim*

Foreign trade, **3**.4; **19**.37; **23**.*passim*; trade (figure), **8**.5; trade (table), **23**.12; exports (table), **23**.16; exports structure (table), **23**.23; Generalized System of Preferences, **23**.30; imports (table), **23**.16; imports structure (table), **23**.26; Lome Convention, **23**.30; trading partners (table), **8**.4

Foshan, **16**.17

Four Cardinal Principles, **1**.7; **5**.8; **6**.26

France, xxxi; **1**.9; **4**.15; **7**.11; **8**.14,19; **23**.20,40

Fujian, **1**.22; **3**.14,34,42; **12**.2,10,12; **16**.15; **17**.15,16; **18**.46; **19**.6,18,59; **22**.18; **23**.20; **25**.2

Fuxin, xxxiv

Gang of Four, **7**.4; **8**.20; **9**.12

Gansu, **3**.13,29,42,44; **17**.17

Gao Fang, **1**.7

Gao Lianyi, **17**.12,15,25

Gao Shangquan, **19**.55,58

Gao Yu, xxvi; **1**.27; **5**.4

Garmaba, Living Buddha, **17**.19

Gender, **12**.*passim*; disparities, **11**.9; equality, **12**.9; equality by sexes (table), **12**.4; important thing in life (table), **12**.9; promotion opportunities (table), **12**.5; sex and status, **12**.17–18; spouse opinion (table), **12**.6

General Agreement on Tariffs and Trade (GATT), xxxiii, xxxiv; **6**.2,21; **7**.12–14; **8**.2; **20**.4; **19**.6,31,44,47; **21**.17,20,27; **23**.6,8,10,26,28–34,41, *see also* World Trade Organization

Generational disparities, **11**.9–10

Geneva, xxxiv

Germany, **4**.8; **7**.11; **8**.17; **19**.49; **23**.15,17,18,20,40

Getihu, see Entrepreneur, self-employed

Gilman, Benjamin, **8**.19

Gold, Thomas B., **25**.2,37

Goodlad, Alastair, **10**.6

Gorbachev, Mikhail, **4**.15; **8**.17,

Gore, Al, **4**.9

Government, *see* State Council

Grain, xxiv, xxxi; **3**.21; **19**.38–39; **21**.9,13; **22**.3–4

Great Britain (United Kingdom), (England), **1**.29; **4**.13; **7**.11; **8**.6; **10**.6,9,10,12–15; **23**.15,17,20,40

Great Leap Forward, **3**.19; **9**.6; **18**.19

Greater China, **8**.3,22,24; **19**.22; **23**.38,39

Greece, **23**.40

Guan Guangfu, **3**.13,42

Guangdong, xxvi, xxix, xxxii; **1**.4,12, 13,16,20,22,28; **3**.7,12,14,17,25, 30,34, 43,44**5**.4,5,11,12,14; **6**.8,10,11; **10**.5–6; **11**.11; **12**.12; **13**.6; **15**.*passim*; **16**.16; **17**.5,15; **18**.18,30; **19**.*passim*; **22**.7,18; **23**.21; **25**.2,36

Guangdong Academy of Social Sciences, **25**.38

Index

Guangxi, **3**.13,42; **12**.3; **15**.12,17,22; **17**.10,15
Guangxu, emperor, **16**.8
Guangzhou, **3**.22,30; **4**.18; **9**.17; **10**.6; **13**.8,11; **16**.8,11,17; **25**.34
Guatemala, **8**.26
Guilin, **17**.11
Guiyang, **20**.11
Guizhou, **1**.20,21; **3**.14; **5**.12; **12**.2; **19**.11,18,21; **20**.11; **22**.6
Gulf War, **9**.13
Guo Shuqing, **21**.31

Hainan, **1**.17; **3**.34; **14**.3,7; **17**.16; **18**.18; **22**.18; **23**.2
Han Dongfang, **1**.23
Han Sung Joo, **8**.10
Han Suyun, **1**.5
Han Wenzao, **17**.13
Hangzhou, **3**.23; **25**.16,28
Harbin, xxvii; **1**.22; **3**.21,22,26,30
Hawke, Bob, **7**.7
He Dongchang, **18**.4,42
He Guanghui, **1**.14; **21**.30
Health, public, **18**.15; health care, **14**.8; hospital services, **11**.4
Hebei, **1**.22; **3**.6,16,42; **5**.12; **18**.46; **19**.58
Heilongjiang, **1**.21,22; **3**.3,6,16,21,25, 26,29; **17**.10,21; **19**.15,54,57; **22**.18
Helms, Jesse, **8**.18
Henan, **1**.19; **3**.6,16,42; **17**.15,17,24; **18**.12,46
Hengdian, **25**.26
Heshang, **17**.16
Honduras, **8**.26
Hong Kong, xxvi, xxviii, xxix, xxxiii; **1**.6,10,27,28,29; **4**.12–14,18,20–21, 22; **5**.3,4,7,9,13; **6**.9,16,18,20; **7**.2,6, 8–12; **8**.3,4,11,16,22; **11**.12,19; **14**.3,12; **15**.4,5,6,8,9,15,16,10,22; **16**.*passim*; **17**.8,26; **19**.2,46; **21**.17,21,24,27,28; **23**.2,15,17, 21–22,38,39; **24**.4,5,9; **25**.4,19,29; Hong Kong Monetary Authority, **21**.35; Hong Kong Trade and Development Office, **16**.2
Hong Kong-PRC relations: Basic Law, **4**.12; **7**.3,11; **10**.9,12, *see also* Law; Court of Final Appeal, **10**.13; Hong Kong/mainland cross-holding of assets (table), **10**.5; Hong Kong Stock Exchange, **10**.5; Joint Liaison Group, **10**.9,13; Legislative Council, **4**.13; One country two systems, **10**.8,14; Preliminary Working Committee (PWC), **4**.13; **10**.6,8,11; relations with the PRC, **10**.*passim*; Sino-British Joint Declaration, **10**.4,9,11–12; two-way trade Hong Kong/mainland (table), **10**.3; two-way travel (table), **10**.3

Political parties: Association for Democracy and People's Livelihood, **10**.11; Democratic Alliance for the Betterment of Hong Kong, **10**.11; Hong Kong Alliance in Support of the Patriotic Democratic Movement in China, **10**.9; Meeting Point, **10**.11; United Democrats (Democratic Party), **10**.11,15
Hong Kong Christian Publishers' Association, **17**.14
Hong Kong Red Cross Society, **7**.12
Household consumption (table), **11**.8
Household registration, **18**.48
Housing, **1**.16; **6**.9; **9**.16; **11**.4,5,18,22; **12**.15,19–20; **13**.4,14; **14**.8; **18**.15, 18,40,43,46; **19**.41; **20**.10; **22**.12,16
Hsu Li-teh, **8**.8
Hu Angang, **1**.21
Hu Qili, **2**.37
Hu Shigen, xxxiv

Hu Yaobang, **1**.7,8,13; **2**.8,9; **17**.22
Hua Guofeng, **1**.2,4; **8**.23
Huang Ju, **1**.10–11; **3**.17,26,42
Huang Kung-huei, **8**.26
Huang Ta-chou, **4**.4
Huang Zhongwen, **17**.26
Hubei, **1**.22; **2**.30; **3**.13,23,40,42,44; **5**.12,14; **15**.12,15,16,17,20,21; **17**.10; **18**.46; **19**.15,21,57
Hui Liangyu, **3**.42
Human rights, **1**.29; **14**.10–11; **23**.33
Hunan, **3**.7,42; **15**.9,10,12,18,22; **17**.5,15; **18**.12,15,20,39,46; **19**.6,21,38,57; **22**.19

Ideology, **1**.3,4; **5**.8,10; **8**.17; **11**.3; **12**.2; **16**.2; **17**.3–6
Income, urban **1**.17
India, **7**.11
Indonesia, xxv, xxxiii; **4**.8; **7**.7; **8**.11,13,14,15; **23**.15; Indonesian Communist Party, **8**.13
Industry, **3**.4; **25**.*passim*; rural industry, **22**.16–19
Inequality, **11**.*passim*
Inflation, xxx, xxxi, xxxiii; **1**.12,14,15,18,19; **2**.21; **3**.8,21; **5**.4; **11**.3,12; **13**.7; **15**.21; **18**.14; **19**.*passim*; **20**.2; **21**.2,6,9,10,18, 23,29; **22**.12,15,16,19; **23**.3,6,32, 36; **24**.5,10
Inheritance, **11**.24
Inner Mogolia, **3**.42,44; **17**.15; **18**.46
Intellectual property, **5**.13; **6**.5,18–19; **8**.19; **23**.19,28,31,32
International Atomic Energy Agency, **8**.10
International Organizations, **7**.*passim*; international communist mass organizations, **7**.4; International Labour Organization, **14**.14; International organization with China and Taiwan as members (table), **7**.9; *Yearbook of International Organizations 1993–1994*, **7**.11
Interpol, **7**.12
Investment, **3**.3; **20**.2; **23**.2; **25**.9–10; foreign direct investment, **3**.29; **19**.2,15,18,32,37,44; **22**.13; **23**.4; share of FDI (table), **19**.20; investment in fixed assets (table a), **19**.15; (table b), **19**.16; state enterprises (table), **19**.19
Iraq, **9**.13
Ireland, **23**.40
Islam, **17**.27
Italy, **7**.11; **23**.20,40

Jakarta, **8**.8,10
Japan, xxxiii; **1**.34; **3**.38; **4**.4,8,9; **7**.11,14; **8**.2,5–8,9,16,18,21,22,23; **10**.4; **15**.15; **16**.8; **19**.46; **23**.13,15,17,18,21,25,40; **24**.9; **25**.15,19
Jia Zhijie, **3**.42
Jiang Chunyun, xxxii; **1**.11; **3**.26,42
Jiang Qing, **1**.31
Jiang Yiwei, **25**.21
Jiang Zemin, xxiv, xxvi, xxviii, xxix, xxxi, xxxii, xxxiii, xxxiv; **1**.*passim*; **2**.12,14,34; **3**.26; **4**.10,21–22; **5**.3,8; **6**.33; **7**.7; **8**.7,10,12,15,17,20,23; **9**.4; **17**.4,6; **19**.37
Jiang Zhuping, **3**.42
Jiangmen, **16**.7,8,10,17
Jiangsu, **1**.20; **3**.3,6,12,16,25–26,44; **17**.17; **19**.11,13,21,58; **22**.18; **25**.19,23,26,33,34
Jiangxi, **3**.44; **15**.21,22; **17**.17
Jilin, **2**.30,32; **12**.3; **17**.18; **19**.20; **22**.19,
Jin Guantao, **1**.28
Jin Xin, **3**.16

Index I.9

Jinan, **3**.23,30
Jinmen, **4**.19
Journalists, **1**.27
Jumei, **16**.15
June 4 incident, *see* Tiananmen incident

Kaiping, **15**.19
Kan Guangxian, **17**.23
Kang Youwei, **16**.16
Kantor, Mickey, **23**.33
Kaohsiung, xxxiv; **4**.3,21; **8**.26
Karamay, xxxiv
Karmapa Chilaidoje, **17**.19
Kazakhstan, **8**.22
Kim Il-sung, xxxiii; **8**.10
Kim Jong Il, **8**.10
Kim Young-sam, xxxiii; **8**.10
Kim, Samuel, **7**.4
Kin Si Joong, **8**.9
Kirgyzstan, **8**.22
Koo Chen-fu, **4**.20
Korea, **4**.8; **8**.2; peninsula, **8**.8–10; unification, **8**.19; Korean War, **9**.7,8; North Korea, xxxiii; **8**.9,16,22; South Korea, xxxiii; **8**.8,10,16,22; **15**.5; **17**.18; **23**.2,17,18,20,22; **25**.12
Kuo, Shirley, **4**.6
Kuomintang, **4**.*passim*
Kuwait, **10**.10

Labour, **13**.2; **14**.*passim*; child labour, **18**.15,40; collective action, **15**.11–15,21; collective bargaining, **14**.8,12,13,16; labour arbitration, **14**.5; labour law, **1**.23; labour market, **14**.7; **15**.10; **18**.16; labour productivity (table), **19**.12; labour productivity and national income (table), **19**.14; labour productivity per employee (table), **19**.13; labour relations, **6**.22; labour strikes, **1**.22; surplus labour, **15**.4, *see also* Migrant workers, Trade Unions
Land contracting, **22**.5–8
Laos, **8**.13,27
Latin America, **4**.8; **8**.3
Law: Legal system, **6**.*passim*; public law, development, **6**.21–31
Laws: Budgetary Law, **3**.6,15; Administrative Litigation Law, **6**.6,30; Advertising Law, **5**.6; Agricultural Law, **18**.10,44; Anti-improper Competition Law, **6**.3–7,19; Arbitration Law, **6**.15–18; Auditing Law, **6**.28; Bankruptcy Law, **19**.35; Central Bank Law, **21**.12; Chinese Enterprise Income Tax Law, **6**.20; Chinese-Foreign Joint Venture Law, **23**.21; Civil Law, **6**.15; **12**.15; **25**.12; Commercial Bank Law, **21**.12; Commercial Bill Law, **21**.12; Company Law, **6**.10–13; Compulsory Education Law, **18**.5,6,10,11,16; Consumer Protection Law, **6**.3–7; Corporation Law, **19**.3,54; **22**.8; Criminal Law, **12**.15; Economic Contract Law, **6**.14–15,19; Education Law, **18**.5,14,46; Enterprise Law, **25**.7; Equity Joint Venture Law, **6**.12; Foreign Capital Enterprises Law, **23**.21; Foreign Economic Contracts Law, **6**.14; Foreign Trade Law, **6**.18–19; **19**.32; **23**.3,9–10; Income Tax law, **23**.3; Individual Income Tax Law, **6**.20; Inheritance Law, **12**.15; Insurance Law, **21**.12; Joint Stock Company Law, **6**.11; Labour Law, xxix; **6**.21,22–25,32; **13**.9,10,14; **14**.*passim*; **19**.33,41; Law on the Protection of Rights and

Interests of Women, **12**.19;
Marriage Law, **12**.15,19; Product
Quality Law, **6**.3–7; Public
Security Act, **17**.17; Public
Security Administrative Penal
Code, **17**.9; Securities Law, **6**.13;
24.11; State Compensation Law,
6.21,31; Statistics Law, **3**.20;
Teachers' Law, **18**.2,5,10,14,17;
Technology Contracts Law, **6**.14;
Trade Union Law, **14**.10; Town
and Village Enterprise Law, **25**.24;
Urban Real Property
Administration Law, **6**.8
League for the Protection of
Workers' Rights, **1**.23
Lee Kuan Yew, **1**.5
Lee Teng-hui, xxv, xxxiii; **1**.6,34;
4.*passim*; **7**.8; **8**.8,11,12,19
Lehman Brothers, **19**.2
Lei Feng, **1**.6,17; **17**.20
Li Chunting, **3**.42
Li Guixian, **2**.39,43
Li Ka-shing, **19**.46
Li Laizhu, xxiv
Li Lanqing, **18**.5,14,18,25
Li Peng, xxvi, xxxi, xxxiii;
1.11,12,13,14,19; **2**.*passim*; **5**.3;
8.10,15,16,22; **17**.7; **18**.25,26;
19.53; **21**.14; **23**.3
Li Ruihuan, **1**.13; **3**.26; **5**.3; **17**.7
Li Shizhong, **2**.13
Li Tieying, **18**.4
"Li Yi Zhe," **16**.11
Li Yining, **19**.53
Li Zhengtian, **16**.11,17
Liaoning, xxxiv; **1**.21; **3**.6,7,42; **5**.14;
9.16; **17**.5; **19**.18; **22**.18
Lien Chan, **4**.8,21; **8**.11,26
Lin Biao, **1**.4; **9**.8
Lin Xinxin, **25**.33
Liu Bin, **18**.17,18

Liu Hongru, xxx; **24**.14
Liu Huaqing, **1**.3
Liu Jingsheng, **1**.23
Liu Mingzu, **3**.42
Liu Ronghui, **1**.14
Liu Xilin, **2**.33
Liu Zhongli, **1**.14; **3**.9,13,15
Lo Chi-lap, **16**.17
London, **10**.4
Longgang, **15**.12
Lop Nor, xxxii
Lu Guanqiu, **25**.28
Lu Shangfu, **16**.16
Luo Gan, **2**.13,40
Luoyang, **19**.40
Luxembourg, **23**.40

Ma Zhongchen, **3**.42
Macau, **8**.3,4,22; **10**.8; **23**.22; **25**.4
MacLeod, Hamish, **7**.8
Malacca strait, **8**.16
Malaysia, **7**.7; **8**.13,15; **23**.2,7,15,
27,37
Management, horizontal (*kuaikuai*)
management, **3**.12,20; **25**.14;
vertical (*tiaotiao*) management,
3.12; **25**.14
Mandela, Nelson, **4**.9
Manila, **17**.16,18
Mao Zedong, **1**.2; **3**.31; **8**.6,23; **9**.11;
11.2; **12**.2,20; **16**.11,14,17;
Maoism, **1**.5; **8**.20; **16**.3; **18**.22;
19.3
Market, **5**.10; **13**.9,11,12,14; **16**.3;
22.9; **24**.3,11; market economy,
6.18,22,30,31,32; **19**.10,29,31,39,
44; **25**.4,7,24; marketization, **11**.15
Marriage, **11**.24
Marx, Karl, **15**.3,7; Marxism, **17**.2,3,
20; Marxism-Leninism, **1**.3,19
McDonalds, **19**.2,46
Media, **5**.*passim*

Print media: *Beijing Qingnian Bao* (Beijing Youth Daily), **1**.3; **5**.4,12; *Chaolian Village Gazetteer*, **16**.8; *Cheng Ming*, **1**.7; *China Education News*, **18**.15; *China Times Business Weekly*, **19**.40; *Dangxiao luntan* (Party School Forum), **1**.7; *Der Spiegel*, **1**.9; *Dongfang* (The East), **1**.7,27; *Dushu* (Readings), **1**.7,27; *Economic Daily*, **5**.13; *Far Eastern Economic Review*, **8**.2; *Fazhi ribao* (Legal System Daily), **15**.6; *Guangming Daily*, **2**.14; **3**.16; **5**.13; *Guangzhou Daily*, **5**.11; *Guanli shijie* (Administration World), **25**.5; *Hong Kong Economic Journal*, **1**.6; *Hongkong Standard*, **5**.6; *Jiefang ribao* (Liberation Daily), **1**.11; **5**.11; *Jingbao* (The Mirror), **1**.27; *Liaowang* (Outlook), **18**.8–9; *Ming Pao*, xxvi; **1**.27,28; **5**.4,6; *New York Times*, **1**.9; **8**.2; *People's Daily*, xxvii, xxviii; **1**.11,18; **2**.13,14; **5**.4,11,13; **8**.11; *Qiushi* (Seeking Truth) magazine, **5**.13; *Shenzhen/ Hong Kong Economic Times*, **5**.6; *The Economist*, **1**.30; *Wen Wei Po*, **1**.8,14; **5**.11; *Workers' Daily*, **5**.4; *Xiandai ren bao* (Modern Mankind Daily), **1**.27; **5**.5; *Xiandai yu chuantong* (Modernity vs Tradition), **1**.7,27; *Xinmin Evening News*, **5**.11; *Zhongguo shehui kexue jikan* (China's Social Science Quarterly), **1**.7,27

Mekong river, **8**.16

Mercantilism, neo-, **19**.31

Mesquita, Bruce de, **8**.14

Mexico, **8**.11

Middle class, **11**.19

Migrant workers, **11**.2,13; **15**.*passim*; **18**.18,40; **19**.41,45; **22**.14

Military, *see* People's Liberation Army (PLA)

Militia, **9**.10,16

Mischief (Meiji) Reef, **8**.14

Mishan, **17**.21

Mongolia, **8**.22

Morocco, **23**.28

Moscow, xxxi; **8**.17

Most-favoured-nation status (MFN), xxviii; **1**.24,30; **8**.3,18; **23**.19,30

Murayama, Tomiichi, **8**.7,8

Murdoch, Rupert, **5**.3

Murkowski, Frank, **8**.19

Muslims, xxix; **17**.10,18

Nanhai, **22**.7

Nanjing, **3**.22,29; **4**.18; **10**.43

National income (table), **19**.9

National People's Congress (NPC): xxvi; **1**. 9,23,25,26; **2**.15; **3**.20,42; **5**.4; **6**.21,25; **7**.3; **9**.9; **10**.9,12; **13**.14; **18**.6; **19**.35; **21**.12; **23**.3,9; **24**.11; provincial People's Congress, **1**.21; Guangdong People's Congress, **1**.29; district PC, **1**.17; Standing Committee, **14**.4,15; voting (table), **3**.15; Sessions: 1st session of 7th NPC, **2**.10; 2nd session of 7th NPC, **2**.10; 8th NPC, **1**.13; 2nd session of 8th NPC, xxv; **1**.19; **3**.6,13,15

Nationalism, **1**.4–6

Nee, Victor, **25**.2,37

Neo-authoritarianism, xxv; **1**.5; **15**.2; **19**.30

Netherlands, the, **7**.11; **23**.40

New China News Agency (NCNA), see Xinhua

New Party (Taiwan), xxxiv

New York, xxvii; **1**.30; **10**.4; **16**.2; **24**.4

New York Stock Exchange, **24**.9

New Zealand, **8**.16
Nian rebellion, **3**.32
Nicaragua, **4**.8; **8**.11,26
Ningbo, **3**.22; **25**.16
Ningxia, xxix; **3**.29; **12**.3; **17**.10,11; **18**.18
Nomenklatura, **2**.3,7,15,18–19,20; **3**.19
Northeast China, **19**.11,13,20,22,34
Nunn, Sam, **8**.3

Occupational cleavages, **11**.12–13
Occupational safety, **14**.6
Oceania, **8**.3
Oi, Jean, **25**.2,37
Olympics: International Olympic Committee, **7**.2,13; Olympic committee, **1**.34; Olympic Council of Asia, **4**.9; Olympic formula, **7**.8,11; Olympic games, **1**.23
One country, two systems, **4**.12–14,22
Opium war, **3**.32
Organization for Economic Cooperation and Development (OECD), **23**.2,33,34,
Overseas Chinese, **16**.7,14; **17**.8; **18**.12; **25**.4
Ownership, **3**.45; **14**.3; **19**.17; **24**.9; **25**.16,26

Pan Xincheng, **3**.14
Pan Yue, **1**.3
Panama, **8**.26
Panyu, **16**.15
Paracel (Xisha) islands, **8**.14; **9**.9
Paris, **6**.16
Patriotic organizations, **17**.3
Patten, Christopher, **4**.13; **10**.6,8,10,12
Pearl River Delta, **10**.5; **15**.4,5,7,19; **16**.2,4,5,7–13,14,16; **23**.15,21
Peasants, **1**.17; **3**.32; Peasants' protest, **5**.4
Peng Chong, **2**.37

Peng Dehuai, **9**.8
Penghu, **4**.18
People's Armed Police, **1**.11; **9**.15
People's Liberation Army (PLA): xxiv, xxvi; **3**.3,43; **5**.4; **8**.18; **10**.7; demobilization, **9**.12–14; demobilized cadres (table), **9**.11; regionalism, **3**.27–28; Xinxing Corporation, **9**.17
Colleges: Beijing Aeronautics Institute, **18**.5; Guangzhou First Military Medical University, **9**.17; Military Economic Institute, **9**.4; National Defence University, **9**.9; Navy Service Academy, **9**.6
Departments: Air force, **18**.5; Army, **6**.27; General Logistics Department, **9**.17; General Staff Department, **9**.17
Military regions (MR), xxviii; Beijing MR, xxiv; Chengdu MR, xxiv; Nanjing MR, **9**.16; Xinjiang Military District, **9**.18
People's Procuratorate, **1**.26
Perry, William, xxxii; **8**.7
Persian Gulf, **8**.7
Personnel, **3**.5
Phagsba, **17**.19
Philippines, the, xxv; **4**.8; **7**.11; **8**.11,13; **23**.15
Pingdu, **22**.7
Planning: economic plan, **3**.3,15; **6**.14–15,19; **9**.3–4; **23**.7; **25**.36; central planning (table), **3**.5; five year cycle, **3**.23; 8th FYP, **3**.7,16
Poland, **21**.19
Population, fourth national census, **18**.13; Institute of Population Studies, **12**.3
Pornography, **5**.7
Portugal, **23**.40
Potala Palace, **17**.19

Index I.13

Poverty, **13**.3,6
Prague, **1**.24
Price reform, **3**.8; **19**.25,38,40; **22**.4,8–11,20; **23**.3,7,11,24,37; price control, **1**.25
Private entrepreneurs' background (table), **25**.32; Private Entrepreneurs Association, **25**.34; private ownership, **25**.3,25,29–35
Procuratorate, xxvi; **6**.31
Project Hope, **18**.6,12,18,45, *see also* Education
Property rights, **22**.2,5–8,20; **25**.12; real property, **6**.7–10
Protectionism, **19**.24,
Protectionism, **6**.7,16,
Protestant Churches, **17**.3,11–15,16; family churches, **17**.8; Guangdong Union Theological Seminary, **17**.14; population, **17**.11; Three-self Patriotic Movement, **17**.12–15
Pu Xishou, **3**.13
Public opinion, **1**.27–29
Public Security, **1**.16,18; **15**.13; **17**.2; Public Security Bureau, **6**.27,31; **17**.2,12,25
Publishers, **1**.27
Pudong, **3**.34; **25**.4
Purchasing power parity (PPP), **19**.4–6,22; **23**.38
Putian, **16**.15

Qian Qichen, **8**.15; **10**.8
Qiandao Lake incident, xxvi; **1**.30,34; **4**.11
Qianlong, emperor, **16**.8
Qianmei, **16**.4–7,15
Qiao Shi, xxvi; **1**.13; **5**.3
Qing dynasty, **3**.32; **6**.2; **16**.8; **25**.43
Qingdao, **1**.8; **3**.7,22,30,41; **14**.12
Qinghai, **3**.13,29,44; **17**.17,20; **19**.17
Qiu Shan, **25**.38

Railway, Beijing-Kowloon, **21**.13
Ramos, Fidel, xxv; **8**.14
Redding, Gordon, **25**.13
Regionalism, **3**.*passim*; **19**.24,37; disparities, **19**.17–24; inter-relations, **3**.28-31; regional development, **19**.3,27–30
Regulations: Administration of the Pre-sale of Urban Commodity Housing, **6**.9; Auditing regulations, **6**.28; Examination and Management of Collective Contracts, **14**.10; Fourteen Rules for All-people Owned Industry, **25**.7; Implementation of the State Security Law, xxix; Privately-managed Enterprises, **25**.4; Registration of Religious Venues, **17**.9; Religious Activities of Foreign Nationals Within China, **17**.7; Rural Joint Stock Cooperation Enterprises, **25**.30; Settlement of Collective Disputes and the Setting of Minimum Wages, **14**.10; Settlement of Disputes on Collective Contracts, **14**.10; Temporary Rules for Reward and Punishment (1957), **6**.27; Tentative Measures for Investigating and Hearing Administrative Discipline Cases by the Supervisory Organs (1988), **6**.27; Venues for Religious Activities, **17**.7
Religion, xxv, xxix; **1**.19; **3**.45; **16**.2,4; **17**.*passim*; popular religion, **16**.*passim*; regulations, **17**.8–11; religious policy (Document #19), **17**.2,3
Ren Jianxin, **1**.25; **6**.30
Ren Zhongping, xxviii
Rent-seeking, **23**.5,9; **25**.26
Republican period, **6**.2

Rituals, community, **16**.6
Rural economy, **22**.*passim*; rural labour, **22**.13–14; living standards, **22**.15–16; major consumer goods (table), **22**.17; net income per capita (table), **22**.16; rural question, **19**.38–40; rural-urban inequality, **11**.3–8; statistics (table), **22**.5; tax burden, **22**.14–15; TVE employment and income (table), **22**.19
Russia, xxxi; **8**.2,9,16,17–20,22,23; **21**.19; **23**.16,21

Schools, **11**.4
Schumpeter, Joseph A., **25**.10,40
Seattle, **7**.8; **8**.20
Sects, Quanzhen, **17**.18; Shengyi, **17**.18; Yiguandao, **17**.19
Seoul, **8**.10
Shaanxi, **1**.14,27; **2**.30; **3**.13,16,29,42; **5**.14; **17**.10; **18**.46; **19**.15,21; **25**.18,32
Shandong, xxxii; **1**.8,20,22; **2**.30; **3**.*passim*; **5**.12; **8**.9; **12**.2,3,5,12; **13**.6; **19**.6,11,15,17; **22**.7,18; **23**.20
Shanghai, xxix, xxv, xxx, xxxii; **1**.10–11,12,21,24; **3**.*passim*; **4**.10; **5**.4,11,12,13,14; **6**.8; **8**.7,24; **10**.2,4,10,15; **11**.8; **12**.3,17; **13**.5,7,8; **15**.4,17; **17**.14,15,17; **18**.18,45; **19**.6,11,13,14,17,18,48,53,56; **21**.18,21,25,27,28; **22**.18; **23**.5,35; **24**.3; **25**.4
Shantou, **15**.9,14,18,19; **16**.2,4–7,15,16; **21**.17; **25**.4
Shanxi, xxiv; **1**.5,16; **3**.7,29; **12**.3; **19**.18; **25**.14
Shao Qihui, **3**.26
Shatoukok, **16**.15
Shen Daren, **3**.25–26

Shenyang, xxvii; **3**.7,22,30; **9**.16; **17**.12,13,15
Shenzhen, xxix; **1**.22; **3**.22,30; **10**.4; **13**.10,14; **14**.3,12; **15**.*passim*; **19**.49; **24**.3; **25**.4
Shih Ming-teh, **4**.22
Shougang International, **1**.10,26
Sichuan, **1**.22; **3**.16,29,32,43,44; **5**.14; **12**.9; **15**.4,12,19; **17**.10,17; **19**.21, 57; **22**.15
Siew, Vincent, **7**.8; **8**.26
Sikkim, **17**.20
Singapore, **1**.5; **4**.8,20; **7**.7; **8**.13,15; **10**.15; **13**.10,14; **15**.5; **23**.2,22
Sino-British Joint Declaration, **4**.12
Sino-Indian War, **9**.8
Sino-Vatican relations, **17**.15,18
Social Insurance, **13**.*passim*
Social order, **3**.2; social unrest, **1**.22–24
Social Security, **13**.*passim*; social welfare, **11**.4,
Society for Human Rights, **1**.24
Song Defu, **2**.32,33,36,40
Song Ping, **2**.10,12; **3**.43
Soong, James, xxxiv
South Africa, **4**.8; **8**.11
South China Sea, xxxiii; **1**.29; **8**.14,21
Southeast Asia, xxv; **1**.29; **4**.17; **8**.2,3,7,13–17,19; **15**.5; **25**.4
Soviet Union (USSR), **1**.7,19; **3**.31; **4**.15; **7**.4; **8**.6,8,15,17,18,23,28; **9**.8,12; **23**.10,16; **25**.35,40; Soviet coup (1991), **8**.28
Spain, **23**.40
Special Economic Zones, xxix; **3**.11,29,30,34; **6**.11; **14**.3,9; **15**.2; **23**.11; **24**.3; Technological Development Zone, **3**.11
Spratly (Nansha) islands, xxxiii; **8**.14,15
Stalinist type, **20**.2

Index

Standard of living, **1**.15
State aid (table), **11**.7
State Budget allocation (table), **11**.11
State Council, xxv, xxxi; **1**.18,20; **2**.4,9,10,11,19,28; **3**.11,41,30,44; **5**.5; **9**.13; **6**.13,23,24,25,26,28; **12**.2; **13**.2,10; **14**.2,5,6; **17**.7; **18**.5,11,16,25,27; **19**.31,33,37, 39,54; **20**.9,10; **22**.14; **23**.35; **25**.5,9,14
 Commissions: Economic, **9**.3; Education, **18**.*passim*; Planning, xxiv; **3**.19; **9**.3; **19**.32,33; **21**.21,31; Restructuring the Economic System, **1**.14; **3**.16; **19**.33; **21**.30; Science and Technology, **9**.3; Science and Technology and Industry of National Defence (COSTIND), **9**.3; Securities Regulatory, xxx; **24**.5
 Ministry: Agriculture, **3**.19; **22**.17; **25**.23,24,30; Civil Affairs, **2**.30; Commerce, **25**.23; Construction, **2**.30; **21**.13; Economy and Trade, **25**.5; Education, **18**.42; Finance, **2**.41; **3**. 8,17,36; **20**.8,10; **21**.12; **24**.2; Foreign Affairs, xxvii, xxxii; **1**.8; **2**.11; Foreign Economic Relations and Trade, **23**.7; Foreign Trade, **23**.7; Foreign Trade and Economic Cooperation, **23**.3,7,31; Labour, xxx; **2**.4; **13**.2,9,12; **14**.12–13,14; Labour and Personnel, **2**.4; National Defence, **9**.3; Personnel, **2**.*passim*; Public Security, **5**.3; **15**.4; Radio, Film and Television, xxvii; **5**.3,5,12; Railway, **2**.31; Supervision, **2**.11; Reform of offices (table), **25**.22
 Offices: Administrative Management, **2**.41; Association for Relations Across the Taiwan Straits (ARATS), **4**.19; Auditing, **2**.38; Civil Affairs, **11**.6; Development Research, **25**.14; Environment Protection, **2**.38; Exchange Control (SAEC), **21**.18,22–23; Hong Kong and Macau, **10**.15; Industry and Commerce, **6**.6,25; Marine, **2**.31; Press and Publication, **1**.28; **5**.6; Religious Affairs, **17**.*passim*; Research, **25**.5; Secrecy, **5**.3; Statistics, **1**.15,16; **3**.19–21; **12**.3,23; **18**.13,37; **19**.41,59,60; **21**.9; **25**.35; Tax Administration, **3**.16
Stockholm International Peace Research Institute, **9**.15
Stock market, **24**.*passim*; equity sectors (figure), **24**.4; equity Shanghai (table), **24**.7; Futures market, **19**.32,58; Shanghai and Shenzhen markets (table), **24**.5; Share-holding (chart), **24**.6; Stocks and bonds, **19**.25; Stocks and futures markets, **21**.3,25
Stratification, **11**.*passim*
Succession, political, **3**.31–33
Suharto, xxv
Sun Jiazhen, xxviii
Sun Weiben, **1**.21; **3**.26
Superstitions, **16**.3; **17**.4
Sutter, Robert, **8**.21
Suwon, **17**.18
Swaziland, **4**.8; **8**.11
Sweden, **7**.11
Switzerland, **7**.11

Taichung, **8**.26
Taipei, xxxiii, xxxiv; **4**.3,21
Taiping rebellion, **3**.32
Taiwan, xxv, xxvi, xxxi, xxxiv; **1**.6,30,34; **4**.*passim*; **5**.3,8,13; **7**.2,6,8–12,15; **8**.*passim*; **10**.8,15;

11.12,19; **12**.14; **14**.12; **15**.5,10,13; **17**.8,18; **23**.2,8,17–19,22,38,39; **24**.9; **25**.4,12,28,29,31; Co-ordination Council for North American Affairs, xxxi; xxxiv; **4**.16; Democratic Progressive Party (DPP), **4**.3,7, 9,22; Hiroshima affair, **1**.30,34; **8**.8; Mainland Affairs Council, **4**.6; **8**.26; National Unification Council, **4**.6; New Party, **4**.20; Strait Exchange Foundation, **4**.6,11,19; Taipei Economic and Cultural Representative Office, **4**.16; Taipei Economic and Cultural Representative Office, xxxi; White Paper on Relations with the Mainland, **4**.18
Taiwan Public Opinion Research Foundation, **4**.4
Taiyuan, **19**.43,56
Tamazawa, Tokuichiro, **8**.7
Tanaka, Kakuei, **8**.6
Tang Shubei, **8**.12
Tao Jianxing, **25**.19–20,40
Taxation, **6**.18,30; **9**.16; **13**.8, 11,12;**18**.3,8,15,16; **19**.30,31, 34,42,45; **21**.8,9,24; **22**.20; **25**.30,31; fiscal contract (responsibility system), **3**.6; local tax system, **20**.6; National Tax System, **20**.6; reform, **19**.36; **21**.32; separation of system, **3**.7–9; Soviet system, **20**.2,6; tax categories (table), **3**.10; tax-sharing, **3**.5–18, 24,32; **20**.4–6; **23**.3
Taxes: Business, **3**.10; **6**.20; capital gains, **6**.20; commercial, **19**.37; consolidated industrial and commercial, **6**.20; consumption, **6**.20; income adjustment, **20**.4; personal income, **20**.4; property gains, **3**.17; value-added, **3**.10,25; **6**.20; **19**.31,36,37; **20**.3,4,5,7,8
Technology import, **23**.27
Terzani, Tiziano, **10**.14
Thailand, xxv; **4**.8; **8**.11,13,14; **23**.15
Third World, **7**.3; **8**.23
Three Gorges Dam project, **19**.53; **21**.13
Tian Fengshan, **3**.26
Tian Jiyun, **1**.13,14; **2**.37
Tian Mingjian, xxxii
Tian Ye, **5**.4
Tian Zhuangzhuang, **5**.5
Tiananmen square incident (June 4, 1989), xxviii, xxxiii; **1**.6,9,28; **2**.2,11,12,14,16; **3**.5; **4**.10,15; **6**.10; **7**.5; **8**.13,15,18,20,22; **10**.2,4,7,9; **15**.14; **16**.3; **18**.39; **19**.10
Tianjin, **3**.7,12,16; **11**.8; **15**.4; **18**.18,45; **19**.17; **22**.18
tiaotiao kuaikuai (branch, local), **25**.14
Tibet (Xizang), xxvii; **3**.30,31; **5**.12; **8**.18–19; **17**.21,22; **18**.18,45
Ting, Bishop K.H. (Ding Guangxun), **17**.7,13–14
Trade union, All-China Federation of Trade Unions, xxix; **1**.22; **6**.24; **12**.19; **13**.6; **14**.8,9,14; **15**.3,10,12; free trade unions, **1**.23; Shenzhen Federation of Trade Unions, **15**.11; Trade Union Law, **14**.10
Transport, Key, Fund, **20**.4
Triangular debts, **19**.34–35,36; **21**.6,10; **25**.20
Turkmenistan, **8**.22

Unemployment, xxx; **1**.15; **5**.4; **6**.22,23; **13**.3,6,9,12; **14**.3,7; **19**.35; **21**.10; **22**.18; **23**.32; Unemployment benefits, **13**.11
Union of International Associations, **7**.9

Index

United Nations, **4**.6–8,16–17; **7**.4,12–14; **8**.9,11,12,23; **24**.10; Population Fund, **12**.3
United States, xxxii, xxxiii, xxxiv; **1**.9; **3**.2; **4**.15–16,17; **5**.13; **6**.18; **7**.4,8,11,13; **8**.2,9,13,14,16,17–20, 22,23; **9**.8,12; **10**.4,15; **12**.8; **16**.15; **19**.44,46; **21**.27; **23**.*passim*; **24**.9,10
Universities, **18**.4; Beijing Languages Institute, xxxiv; Beijing (Peking) U., **1**.23; **2**.39; **7**.3; **18**.29,31,40; **19**.55,58; Columbia U., xxvii; Fudan U., **18**.29,40; Guangzhou First Military Medical U., **9**.17; Hangzhou U., **18**.38; Hengyang City Medical Training Centre, **18**.39; Hong Kong U. of Science and Technology, **3**.38; **16**.16; Jinan U., **25**.35; National Chengchi U., **4**.11; National Defence U., **9**.9; Qinghua U., **1**.11,21; Shanghai U., **18**.38; Soochow U. (Taiwan), xxxiii; The Chinese U. of Hong Kong, **4**.13; Zhongshan U., **16**.16; College students indicators (table), **18**.34; graduates' job assignment, **18**.29,33–36,41; private schools, **18**.37,38,41; Soviet model, **18**.37; tertiary education, **18**.28–36; tuition, **18**.29–33,41
Uruguay, **23**.28
Urumqi, **17**.15
Uzbekistan, **8**.22

Vatican, **17**.15,16,18
Venturetech, **19**.2
Vietnam, xxxiii; **1**.29; **8**.13,14,15,22; **9**.6,8,10
Village elders, **16**.6
Vogel, Ezra, **25**.2,37

Wage, **14**.5–6; wage (table), **11**.23

Wang Chengbin, xxiv
Wang Dan, **1**.24; **8**.24
Wang Daohan, **4**.20; **10**.15
Wang Dingding, **25**.11–12,36–38
Wang Hongwen, **1**.31
Wang Jie, **7**.3
Wang Juntao, xxvii; **1**.24
Wang Meng, **1**.30
Wang Qikun, **9**.4–5
Wang Qun, **3**.42
Wang Ruilin, xxviii
Wang Ruoshui, **1**.28
Wang Ruowang, **1**.24,28
Wang Shan, xxv; **1**.3
Wang Xiaojin, **25**.14
Wang Yang, **1**.14
Wang Zhaoguo, **1**.13
Weber, Max, **25**.11,36
Wei Jingsheng, **1**.23; **8**.24
Welfare, **14**.2
Wen Shizhen, **3**.42
Wenzhou, **17**.16; **25**.16,30–31,37–38
Wilson, Lord David, **10**.10,12
Women, **12**.*passim*; **15**.16; access to welfare (table), **12**.11; 4th World Conference, **12**.2,3; legal protection (see also Law), **12**.15–20; National Women's Federation, **12**.3,21; Social norms, **12**.12–13; white paper, *The Situation of Chinese Women*, **12**.2
Wong Kam-cheung, **16**.17
Wong Siu-lun, **25**.13
Workers, **1**.17
World Trade Organization (WTO), xxxiv; **1**.30; **6**.2,18–21; **8**.19,23; **21**.28; **23**.29–34,41; *see also* GATT
World War II, **8**.6; **23**.34
Wu Bangguo, xxxii; **1**.11; **3**.26,42; **25**.36
Wu Chan-chung, Cardinal, **17**.18
Wu Dacheng, **1**.7

Wu Jieping, **1**.9
Wu Yi, **6**.19; **23**.3,8,33
Wu, Samuel, **8**.14
Wuhan, xxvii; **1**.20; **3**.7,22,23,34,40; **13**.7; **15**.16; **17**.24; **19**.57
Wuxi, **25**.26
Wuxian, **17**.17

Xi Yang, xxvi; **1**.27,28; **5**.4,6
Xiamen, **3**.22,30; **4**.19; **19**.58; **21**.17; **25**.4
Xian, xxvii, xxviii; **3**.22,42; **14**.12; **19**.42
Xiao Wenfeng, **25**.28
Xiao Yang, **3**.43
Xie Ping, **21**.22
Xinhua News Agency (NCNA), **1**.16; **2**.13; **4**.18; **5**.13; **10**.11,15; **21**.27
Xinjiang, xxxii, xxxiv; **1**.27; **3**.7,13, 29,31; **5**.12; **9**.17; **17**.15,17; **19**.6; **22**.19
Xu Guangdi, **3**.42
Xu Jiatun, **8**.27
Xu Liangying, xxvii
Xu Songtao, **2**.33
Xue Jingwen, **14**.16
Xun Dazhi, **25**.21

Yam, Joseph, **21**.35
Yan Changjiang, **25**.35
Yan Jiaqi, **1**.28
Yang Baibing, xxiv; **8**.21
Yang Peixin, **25**.14
Yang Rudai, **3**.43
Yang Shangkun, **1**.12; **8**.21; **9**.12
Yang Yutong, **17**.12
Yang Zhengwu, **3**.42
Yang Zhou, **1**.24
Yangtze river, **15**.9,12; **19**.17,22,34, 53; **21**.13
Ye Liangsong, **3**.42
Ye Xuanping, **1**.13

Yeltsin, Boris, xxxi; **8**.17
Young, Frank, **25**.2
Yu Haocheng, xxvii
Yu Pun-hoi, **1**.28; **5**.6
Yu Xiaosong, **21**.28
Yuan Hongbing, **1**.23
Yue Qifeng, **1**.21; **3**.26
Yugoslavia, **1**.21; **25**.24
Yujiang, **17**.17
Yunnan, **3**.13,14,29,30; **5**.12; **8**.16; **18**.18; **19**.15,21

Zagoria, Donald, **8**.21
Zeng Qinghong, **1**.11
Zhang Chunqiao, **1**.31
Zhang Gong, xxiv
Zhang Guoying, **17**.5
Zhang Wule, **3**.42
Zhang Yingtian, **25**.33
Zhang Zhen, **1**.12
Zhang Zhijian, xxiv; **2**.32
Zhang Zhixin, **1**.5
Zhao Dongwan, **2**.11,14,16,17, 20
Zhao Zhihao, **3**.42
Zhao Ziyang, **1**.6–8,9,13; **2**.5,6,8–12, 16,37,38; **3**.22,43; **4**.10; **9**.4
Zhejiang, xxvi; **1**.20,34; **3**.6,7,12, 23,44; **5**.12; **19**.15,21; **21**.3; **22**.18; **25**.16–17,26,28,30,37
Zheng Jiaxiang, **3**.20
Zhengzhou, **1**.20
Zhou Beifang, **1**.10,26
Zhou Guangwu, **1**.10
Zhou Guoqiang, **1**.23
Zhou Jie, **2**.38
Zhou Ruijin, **1**.11
Zhou Shengying, **1**.28
Zhou Xiaochuan, **3**.38
Zhou Xueguang, **11**.25
Zhou Yaoting, **25**.26–28
Zhou Zhengqing, **21**.17
Zhu Kaixuan, **18**.*passim*

Zhu Rongji, xxiv, xxx; **1**.11,13,20, 21,25,30; **3**.12,26; **19**.35,37,53; **21**.6,11,27; **25**.36

Zhu Xiaohua, **21**.22–23,28
Zhuhai, xxix; **1**.22; **15**.6,13
Zou Jiahua, **1**.20